Applying
2011/2012

Applying GAAP 2011/2012

A Practical Guide
to Financial Reporting

David Chopping
Moore Stephens

a Wolters Kluwer business

Wolters Kluwer
145 London Road
Kingston upon Thames
KT2 6SR
Telephone: (0) 844 561 8166
Facsimile: (0) 208 547 2638
E-mail: cch@wolterskluwer.co.uk
Website: www.cch.co.uk

© 2011 Wolters Kluwer (UK) Ltd

ISBN 978-1-84798-369-5

Accounting Standards Board material

Extracts from FRSs, FREDs and Discussion Papers reproduced with the permission of the Accounting Standards Board Limited.

Extracts from SSAPs reproduced with the permission of CCAB Limited.

Crown copyright is reproduced with the permission of the Controller of Her Majesty's Stationery Office.

British Library Cataloguing-in-Publication Data

A catalogue record for this book is available from the British Library.

Typeset in-house at Wolters Kluwer (UK) Ltd

Printed and bound in the UK by Hobbs the Printers Ltd

CONTENTS

Contents

Preface

The endgame seems to be taking longer than originally expected.

The ASB continues to issue amendments to accounting standards; yet, over the last year, although one standard came into force, no entirely new standards have been issued.

However, the proposals for fundamental changes to UK GAAP, and the abolition of it, in its current form, have moved on significantly. During the year, the ASB has issued three exposure drafts that address the issue of the future of UK GAAP. One deals with the proposed structure and framework of the proposed regime, one with the specific proposed requirements for companies that are neither small nor publicly accountable and one with the issues faced by entities that work for the public benefit rather than for profit.

The proposed date of change has moved back a little; strictly six months, but in practice, for most companies, a year. The proposed date of transition is July 2013, but with most companies having accounting periods that end in December or March, this would actually mean 2014. The proposals themselves have moved on from the previous consultations, but the thrust remains the same. The proposals retain a hierarchy of accounting requirements ultimately based on International Financial Reporting Standards (IFRS). Entities with public accountability will be required to comply with IFRS as adopted by the European Union. Other entities will be allowed to use the Financial Reporting Standard for Medium-Sized Entities (FRSME), a UK version of the IFRS for Small and Medium-sized Entities. Small entities will continue to be able to use the FRSSE, although there are significant questions about how long that approach would be sustainable. The ASB is also proposing various exemptions and simplifications for subsidiaries.

The proposed abolition of UK GAAP will simply complete a process that has been in progress for some years. Listed companies (or strictly groups) have fallen outside the remit of UK GAAP since 2005, being joined by those on AIM more recently. Nearly all UK companies have been able to use IFRS rather than UK GAAP since 2005, although this is a choice that has not often been taken, probably largely due to the previous absence of international standards geared towards the requirements of entities which do not have publicly traded securities. For the last few years, the majority of the ASB's pronouncements have been directed towards aligning UK GAAP with international standards. The proposed move to IFRS simply replaces the previous gradualist approach by making a one-off change.

Nonetheless, UK GAAP has not been abolished yet.

This book, like all previous editions, is intended to provide a concise and practical guide to current requirements under UK GAAP. There are comments on historical development and possible future changes, but these are intended only to provide a flavour of how we have got where we are and where we might be going. The majority of the text deals with the requirements currently in force.

Specialist sectors are omitted. Similarly, FRS 26 (and the standards associated with it) has been dealt with only at a very summary level, since very few UK companies are required to comply with it, and few have adopted it voluntarily.

This volume is intended to deal with accounting principles, policies and procedures. It does not contain a comprehensive list of disclosure requirements, even though a disclosure section has been included in the majority of chapters.

David Chopping

London

May 2011

1 ACCOUNTING PRINCIPLES

1.1 INTRODUCTION

1.1.1 The international context

Financial statements are the accountant's summary of the performance of a company over a particular period and of its position at the end of that period. The factors that the accountant uses in preparing those financial statements derive from a number of basic principles.

The definitive statement of basic accounting principles for companies that prepare financial statements in accordance with UK Generally Accepted Accounting Practice (UK GAAP) is currently the *Statement of Principles for Financial Reporting* produced by the Accounting Standards Board (ASB).

However, despite its theoretical status, the *Statement* is, in practice, becoming less relevant as UK practice moves ever closer to international practice. International Financial Reporting Standards (IFRS) are already mandatory for the group accounts of listed UK companies and companies on AIM, whilst all UK companies (other than charitable ones) already have the option of adopting IFRS. Since most UK standards that have been introduced in the last few years are based on international standards, which have not been drafted on the basis of the ASB's *Statement*, it is the international principles that are arguably now far more relevant. The move away from the ASB's *Statement* is certain to continue. The ASB has now issued its detailed proposals on the abolition of UK GAAP in its current form. In its place, it proposes IFRS for entities that are publicly accountable, and the Financial Reporting Standard for Medium-sized Entities (FRSME), based on the IFRS for Small and Medium-sized Entities (IFRS for SMEs), for entities that are not. The UK's existing Financial Reporting Standard for Smaller Entities (FRSSE) would be retained for the time being, but with a high likelihood that it would either be abolished after a time, or at least replaced with a version more consistent with the bases for IFRS and the FRSME (not that these are always the same). The ASB is also proposing the introduction of a Financial Reporting Standard for Public Benefit Entities (FRSPBE). This proposed standard would modify the requirements of the FRSME for entities intended to promote the public benefit rather than generate a profit. The proposals are covered in greater detail in Chapter 24, but most chapters also include comments on the possible impact of the FRSME on accounting practice.

International principles are currently set out in the *Framework for the Preparation and Presentation of Financial Statements*. However, this document was produced by the old International Accounting Standards Committee (IASC) back in 1989. As such, it is long overdue for revision. The International Accounting Standards Board (IASB), which adopted the framework in 2001, has been working jointly with the US standard setter on a revised conceptual framework since 2004. The process still remains at a fairly early stage and is unlikely to be finished for some time. The project would appear to have been delayed by the time that both the IASB and US standard setters have spent dealing with responses to the various issues coming out of international financial problems in the last few years. As a result, to date, out of the eight separate phases of the project, only one has been completed; that dealing with the objective and characteristics of accounting information, two have given rise to exposure drafts and one to a discussion paper, whilst four are officially currently inactive.

There is no prospect of the ASB's *Statement* being updated. As UK GAAP converges with international GAAP, having a separate statement of principles becomes increasingly unnecessary and potentially confusing.

The role of the ASB's *Statement* differs slightly from that of the IASB's *Framework*. Neither is an accounting standard, and, in both cases, the main intention is to guide and underpin the setting of standards. The introductory note to the ASB's *Statement* mentions that:

> Its primary purpose is to provide a frame of reference to help the ASB itself in developing new accounting standards and reviewing existing ones. Its main impact on accounting practice will therefore be through its influence on the standard-setting process. (Question 3, Part 2, Statement of Principles.)

The main difference is that even though the IASB framework is not an accounting standard, it can still have a direct application. This is because, in some circumstances, IAS 8 *Accounting Policies, Changes in Accounting Estimates and Errors* requires that the framework be considered in determining an accounting policy where the matter is not dealt with in any IFRS, and no IFRS deals with a similar or related issue. In such a situation, IAS 8 makes specific reference to the requirement to consider the definitions, recognition criteria and measurement concepts in the *Framework* as they relate to assets, liabilities, income and expenses. The UK's statement does not have any such direct application, although it is, of course, always open to those preparing financial statements to consider its contents if doing so might shed light on a requirement in an actual standard which would otherwise be unclear, or where there is no clear guidance in any accounting standard.

This volume deals solely with UK accounting practice for those entities which are not required, and have not decided, to adopt IFRS. While reference is made to various international standards, often to contrast their requirements with those currently in force under UK practice, this is not intended to constitute a comprehensive summary of international practice. Therefore, and notwithstanding the limitations in its current application as set out above, this chapter deals primarily with the ASB's *Statement of Principles for Financial Reporting*. As noted earlier, comments have been included in most chapters dealing with the potential changes coming out of the introduction of the FRSME.

1.1.2 The Statement of Principles for Financial Reporting

The *Statement of Principles for Financial Reporting* was published in 1999, although its genesis goes back to the *Dearing Report* of 1988. Up until this time, UK accounting had somehow survived without any formal statement of its conceptual underpinning.

Despite the absence of any conceptual framework, it would be fair to say that the basic principles followed by accountants had not changed for many years, and were well understood and accepted by practising accountants. The basic accounting principles were set out in the Companies Act 1985 and in SSAP 2 *Disclosure of Accounting Policies*. Neither of these documents provided, nor attempted to provide, a general theory of accounting.

In summary, the major principles applied by accountants historically had been:

- prudence;
- accruals;
- going concern;
- consistency;
- substance over form, and
- separate determination.

This situation changed when the final version of the ASB's *Statement of Principles for Financial Reporting*, which introduced significant changes to the intellectual basis for accounting practice in the UK, was published. FRS 18 *Accounting Policies* was also published as a replacement for SSAP 2. (FRS 18 is covered in Chapter 2.)

The *Statement of Principles* sets out the principles that the ASB believes (or perhaps believed) should underlie the preparation and presentation of general purpose financial statements in the UK.

More specifically, it is intended to:

- provide a coherent frame of reference for the ASB and others to use in the development and review of accounting standards;
- clarify the concepts which lie behind specific standards, and
- enable standards to be prepared on a consistent basis.

It is not an accounting standard and as such does not directly lead to any particular accounting practice. However, its indirect impact has historically been considerable, although as covered in **1.1.1**, its impact has declined more recently as UK practice converges with international.

There was considerable controversy concerning the production of the statement, of which its gestation period is one indication. It was initially produced in individual chapters which were released for comment in the early 1990s. An initial exposure draft of the complete document was published in 1995 and a second version in March 1999. The final statement was not issued until December 1999.

The ASB initially looked at the principles underlying accounting standards and practice in the UK. The principles that lay behind the standards and practice were, in the ASB's opinion, found wanting. The particular problems the ASB identified were as follow.

(1) The principles, and in particular the standards and guidance reflecting those principles, had been developed in response to particular problems, meaning that they were not necessarily consistent with one another and lacked an overall rationale.

(2) Many of the standards, and the principles and practices that both underpinned and were reflected in them, were showing their age. In the ASB's opinion, many of the accounting principles and solutions had been developed to deal with a manufacturing environment. They did not cope adequately with many modern companies where the treatment of intangible assets and complex financial instruments may be of greater relevance.

(3) They were out of line with international developments.

The conclusion that the ASB drew from its work was that, although many of the principles continued to be of relevance, some would need updating and new ones would need to be added.

This chapter is intended to provide the practitioner with an overview of the contents of the *Statement of Principles* and comments on the way in which this has impacted upon accounting practice in the UK. It will not deal with any potential future impact since, for the reasons set out above, the statement is unlikely to have any direct influence on future UK accounting standards, as these continue to be based more and more on international requirements and therefore ultimately on the IASB's *Framework*. If the ASB's proposals for the future of UK GAAP are accepted, the *Statement of Principles* will be abolished along with all of the specific UK accounting standards.

1.1.3 Application of the Statement of Principles

The *Statement of Principles* was drafted in order to apply to what it describes as general-purpose financial statements, such as the financial statements that UK companies are required to prepare on an annual basis. Mention is made of special-purpose financial reports, that is, financial reports which are prepared in order to meet a very specific need, but these are not the focus of the statement.

The principles are also intended to be broadly applicable to all types of entity required to prepare true and fair financial statements. However, it is noted that the principles are drafted primarily in the context of profit-oriented entities. There is now a separate statement dealing with not-for-profit organisations, with the ASB having issued a *Statement of Principles for Financial Reporting – Interpretation for Public Benefit Entities*. This deals with public sector bodies, as well as other not-for-profit organisations such as charities. It sets out some of the areas where the *Statement of Principles* must be modified for application to public benefit entities. For example, the idea of an asset for a profit-making body includes a requirement that it be capable of generating cash, whether directly or indirectly. This does not apply to public benefit entities which may often have 'assets' which will not, and are not intended to, generate cash. As a result, the definition of assets needs to be widened to encompass items which have the potential to be used to provide a service for which there is a need or want. Similarly, most public benefit entities have incoming resources, rather than income, as would arise in a commercial entity. As a result, the principles of recognition of normal commercial revenues are not appropriate and different principles are required.

It may be that the *Statement of Principles for Financial Reporting – Interpretation for Public Benefit Entities* will be of greater long term relevance than the statement on which it is based. The ASB's proposals for the future of UK GAAP are based on IFRS. One of the problems with this is that IFRS have been designed for profit-making entities and are not appropriate for entities which are not profit oriented and are instead intended to promote the public benefit. As a result, the ASB has issued FRED 45, a proposed *Financial Reporting Standard for Public Benefit Entities* (FRSPBE). This proposed standard is not intended to replace the proposed *Financial Reporting Standard for Medium-Sized Entities* but to supplement it. Public benefit entities will be expected to apply the same accounting rules as all other types of entity, except where the FRSPBE requires or allows a different treatment. The ASB has taken the *Statement of Principles for Financial Reporting – Interpretation for Public Benefit Entities* into account in drafting the FRSPBE.

1.1.4   Legal constraints

The *Statement of Principles* was drafted without taking into account the legislation surrounding the preparation of financial statements which was in force at the time. There were three main reasons for this as follow.

(1)   There were different legal frameworks affecting different types of organisations that were required to prepare financial statements. Attempting to deal with this would either have made the statement overly complicated or virtually impossible to produce.

(2)   The legal framework is not a given, and itself develops over time. One of the subsidiary functions of the *Statement of Principles* was intended to be

to guide the ASB in its responses to proposed developments in company law as it affects the preparation of financial statements.

(3) Even if the legal framework had not been expected to change, there was a value in producing a document which ignored those limitations, even if its implementation must be undertaken within the constraints imposed.

An appendix to the *Statement of Principles* identifies some of the major inconsistencies between the current law, or rather the law at the date the statement was produced, and the principles.

The law on accounting has changed in many ways since the *Statement* was produced, with the most obvious single change being the introduction of the Companies Act 2006, which came into force primarily for accounting periods beginning on or after 6 April 2008. Some of the legal changes have been driven by the availability of the option for UK companies to use IFRS, but also affect those companies which continue to apply UK GAAP. For example, the treatment of dividends has altered fundamentally since 1999, whilst (subject to various conditions) investment properties may now be stated at market value under the Companies Act 2006, whereas this was long prohibited by statute (whilst required by accounting standards). There is, therefore, some logic behind the ASB's approach of ignoring what were then the current legal requirements, since those requirements are not a given and themselves change over time.

1.2 THE OBJECTIVE OF FINANCIAL STATEMENTS

1.2.1 Basic principles

The first section of the *Statement of Principles* deals with the objective of financial statements. As mentioned earlier, the financial statements referred to are general purpose. The purposes of other financial statements and reports may be different. (In practice, their objectives will normally be more obvious than those for general purpose financial statements, since they are often prepared specifically to meet the needs of particular users or categories of user.)

The basic principles are set out as follows.

- The objective of financial statements is to provide information about the reporting entity's financial performance and financial position that is useful to a wide range of users for assessing the stewardship of the entity's management and for making economic decisions.
- That objective can usually be met by focusing exclusively on the information needs of present and potential investors, the defining class of user.
- Present and potential investors need information about the reporting entity's financial performance and financial position that is useful to them in evaluating the entity's ability to generate cash (including the timing and

certainty of its generation) and in assessing the entity's financial adaptability. (Principles from Chapter One, *Statement of Principles*.)

The statement notes that financial statements may be used by a wide range of interested parties, but that it cannot, therefore, be assumed that they are, or even should be, prepared specifically for those parties. The statement runs through a list of possible users of financial statements, including investors, potential investors, lenders, suppliers, employees, customers and government agencies. The statement notes that their interests may differ, but that there are certain common interests. In summary, these amount to the points made in the principles about the need for information on financial position and performance.

The defining group of users is considered to be investors and, to some extent, potential investors. Their major interests are likely to be in the company's financial adaptability and its ability to generate cash. As the statement points out, most other users of financial statements also have the same basic interest, even though the reasons for that need may differ. For example, a customer may have no direct interest in a company's profitability and return, but may be very interested in its ability to continue to supply, which ultimately must depend on the company's ability to generate a return. The longer the other party intends (or wishes) to have a relationship with the company the more their interests are likely to align with those of investors or potential investors.

The statement also points out some inherent limitations in financial statements. They are, for example:

- a conventionalised representation of transactions, which necessarily involves classification and aggregation and the allocation of the effects of continuous operations to particular accounting periods;
- based almost exclusively on financial data and cannot really deal effectively with other types of information, however relevant that may be to an assessment of the position of the company, and
- historical, and cannot take account of future events or transactions, or of future changes in the environment in which the company operates.

It is noted that some of this information can be given in general-purpose financial reports, which may accompany financial statements, such as the information that many listed companies provide in addition to their statutory accounts. With the increase, since the statement was issued, in the amount of detail that has to be provided in directors' reports for all companies other than small ones (see Chapter 3), there has also been an increase in the extent to which such non-financial information must be provided by companies of many sizes.

1.2.2   Information provided

The *Statement of Principles* looks at the various types of information that users might need, and be able to obtain, from financial statements.

This is broken down into information required on:

- financial performance;
- financial position;
- generation and use of cash, and
- financial adaptability.

These aspects are not completely separate and information may overlap between categories.

1.2.3   The impact of the Statement of Principles

This section of the *Statement of Principles* has had a substantial impact on reporting practice. While it does not deal with measurement issues directly, it does implicitly cover the disclosure of items in financial statements. By starting with the user of financial statements, the ASB was attempting to provide a perspective from which it could determine the information that needs to be provided in the financial statements. As a result, it provided a template against which any proposed changes to disclosure requirements could be judged.

There are a number of items covered in the section which, traditionally, would probably not have been seen as being appropriate areas to be covered in financial statements. While the ASB accepts that there is an important role for other information which may be published with financial statements, it is also worth noting that standards such as FRS 29 (*Financial Instruments: Disclosures*) indicate that the ASB is quite willing to envisage requiring companies to provide discursive disclosures and policy statements as part of the basic accounting information. These disclosures go beyond a description or analysis of what is included in the financial statements, and start dealing with some of the financial policies that may have given rise to the transactions. Such documents also indicate the ASB's view of the importance of providing information about items that may not be directly included in the primary financial statements. (Of course, it is worth noting that FRS 29 may be a UK standard, but is actually a UK version of an international standard, IFRS 7 in this case. As a result, it was not drafted by reference to the statement. Nonetheless, the ASB's willingness to embrace the international standard must have been affected by its consistency with the board's own stated principles.)

1.3   THE REPORTING ENTITY

1.3.1   Basic definition

Despite the apparent simplicity of the idea of the reporting entity, it is clear from the history of the development of the *Statement of Principles* that this is one of the areas with which the ASB struggled. It took a very long time to agree the nature of the reporting entity.

While in the case of a clearly discrete entity, such as an individual company without shareholdings in other companies, it may be simple to decide on the boundaries of the reporting entity, not all situations are so clear-cut. The existence of subsidiaries, associates and joint ventures, for example, makes the situation more complex.

The definition that was decided upon by the ASB is that the:

> ... boundary of the reporting entity is determined by the scope of its control. For this purpose, first direct control and, secondly, direct plus indirect control are taken into account. (Principles from Chapter Two, *Statement of Principles*.)

The issue of other parties in which an entity may have influence, but over which it does not have control, is dealt with separately in the *Statement of Principles*.

1.3.2 Direct and indirect control

Control is addressed within this section of the *Statement of Principles* solely in terms of assets. Liabilities are not mentioned, presumably since the idea of control over liabilities makes very little sense. However, it is very clear from the ASB's comments that the *Statement of Principles* is often referring to the net resources that are available to an entity, rather than individual assets or liabilities.

Direct control is described in terms that, not surprisingly, echo the FRS 5 definition of assets, and of control over assets.

> An entity has direct control of an asset if it has the ability in its own right to obtain the future economic benefits embodied in that asset and to restrict others' access to those benefits. An entity has direct control of its own activities and resources but does not have direct control of any other activities and resources. (Para. 2.4(a), *Statement of Principles*.)

Indirect control is stated to exist where an entity has control of another entity that has direct control of the relevant asset. The example given is that of a subsidiary. A parent, therefore, has indirect control of the assets of its subsidiaries. It is also made clear that the relationship between the party which ultimately exercises control and the party with direct control need not be immediate. For example, a company may have sub-subsidiaries. In such cases there are intermediate parties between the ultimate and direct controlling parties, yet control still exists.

Control is described as having two aspects:

> ... the ability to deploy the economic resources involved and the ability to benefit (or to suffer) from their deployment. To have control, an entity must have both these abilities. (Para. 2.8, *Statement of Principles*.)

This is then contrasted with situations where only one of these may be present, such as a trusteeship where the trustee is not a beneficiary. This is consistent with both FRS 5 and FRS 8. It is important to note that control refers to ultimate control and does not imply that there has to be day-to-day involvement. UITF 32, to take just one example, makes it very clear that control can exist even where day-to-day involvement is not only absent, but even not directly allowed.

1.3.3 Control of an entity

The *Statement of Principles* defines control of an entity in the following terms.

> An entity will have control of a second entity if it has the ability to direct that entity's operating and financial policies with a view to gaining economic benefit from its activities. (Para. 2.11, *Statement of Principles*.)

There are various ways in which such control might be demonstrated. The ASB mentions that control may be shown in an interventionist or non-interventionist way and that its basis may also differ. For example, some rights of control may come from legal ownership rights. Others may not involve legal ownership, such as contractual rights of control. The *Statement of Principles* even acknowledges that there may be cases, however rare, where control of another entity may exist without there being any kind of investment.

Rather than attempting to come up with a single basis on which the existence of control can be identified, the *Statement of Principles* notes that it must be determined by taking into account at least three factors which are:

- the respective rights;
- inflows and outflows of benefits, and
- exposure to risk.

While such factors are normally interconnected, there are cases where they may appear to be out of line.

The *Statement of Principles* gives guidance on some of the factors that may need to be considered when determining whether one entity has control of another.

Power of veto and reserve powers

Control implies the ability to prevent others from directing the financial and operating policies of another entity, the controlled entity. Powers of veto and reserve powers may, therefore, form part of the rights by which one entity controls another.

However, it is unlikely that such powers are sufficient on their own to indicate control. The *Statement of Principles* states that such powers do not provide the rights that are also normally associated with control, that is, the rights to deploy the resources of the entity or to ensure the corresponding flows of benefit.

The simplest example of such a situation may be that of a venture capital relationship. A company may require external finance and obtain this from venture capitalists who are provided with certain reserve powers or powers of veto. This does not mean that the company is controlled by the venture capitalists. Instead, the rights are provided as a form of protection. If the company makes progress in the way that was envisaged at its creation, or when the venture capitalists became involved, then there should never be a need to use the rights. Like *Romalpa* (retention of title) clauses in sales contracts, reserve rights should be ignored where there is no intention or expectation that they will be used. They should only be taken into account if and when they are either exercised or become exercisable.

Predetermined operating and financial policies

Where an entity must operate according to predetermined policies, it makes sense to state that no party has control in the sense of direction. Instead, control must be taken from the flow of benefits and risks.

Of course, in practice, in such situations, there is little chance that any party other than the party with the risks and benefits would have been able to predetermine the policies.

Latent control

Where a party has the right to control another, it should be presumed to have control, even if it does not actually appear to exercise that right. The only exception given in the *Statement of Principles* is where it is clear that, in practice, another party is benefiting from the other entity's resources and is involved in their deployment.

Such situations are not unusual. For example, a parent company may provide very high levels of autonomy to its subsidiaries, without in any way detracting from the fact that it retains control. As the *Statement of Principles* mentions, control is not dependent upon whether it is exercised in an interventionist or non-interventionist way. The parent company may be happy to allow the subsidiary to operate largely independently, but whenever it feels that it would benefit more from taking over direct control it has the right and ability to do so. Therefore, it has control.

This differs from the situation with reserve powers and powers of veto, in that latent control is expected to continue and may be exercised at any time. Reserve powers and powers of veto are not intended to be exercised at any point, and usually crystallise only when the original intentions have not been met.

Management but not control

The *Statement of Principles* distinguishes between control and management, as does FRS 8. If one party manages another for its own benefit then it has control; if it manages for another's benefit then it does not.

The existence of an interest in the performance of the managed entity, such as where there is a fee dependent on performance, does not normally alter this relationship. This does not apply in extreme cases, where, for example, the level of the fee is such that it effectively amounts to an interest in the benefits to be created by the entity. For example, if an entity were to pay all of its profits over to a third party, that party having no investment in the original entity, then that party would have control irrespective of who notionally possessed the ownership rights over the controlled entity.

1.3.4   Reporting boundaries

The *Statement of Principles* acknowledges that the boundaries of both direct and indirect control may be relevant to financial reporting. The simplest example of this is that subsidiary companies are required to prepare their own financial statements (showing items under their direct control) while the same resources may also appear in group accounts which show the same items because of the existence of indirect control. The group accounts show all of the resources under the control, both direct and indirect, of the parent undertaking.

1.3.5   Requirement for financial statements

The *Statement of Principles* briefly addresses the issue of which entities should prepare financial statements. However, it says little beyond the fact that entities should prepare and publish financial statements if there is a legitimate demand for them to do so. In terms of what constitutes a legitimate demand, it simply states that the information would have to be useful, and the benefits of providing financial statements should exceed the costs.

1.3.6   The impact of the Statement of Principles

The issues addressed in this section of the *Statement of Principles* have largely been covered by the ASB in FRS 2 and FRS 5. The definition of subsidiaries in FRS 2 is very clearly derived from the idea of control, and that, in the Companies Act 2006, is largely so. The concentration on control has become even more marked than when FRS 2 was first issued. Previously, where one entity controlled another, yet that other entity did not meet the definition of a subsidiary, it may have been caught within the quasi-subsidiary requirements of FRS 5. The preface to the revisions to FRS 2 that were made in 2005 noted that some entities, previously accounted for as quasi-subsidiaries under FRS 5, would in future be treated as subsidiaries under FRS 2.

While FRS 8 is not directly concerned with such matters, its definition of controlling parties is also consistent with the *Statement of Principles*.

1.4 THE QUALITATIVE CHARACTERISTICS OF ACCOUNTING INFORMATION

1.4.1 Principles

The *Statement of Principles* states that accounting information needs to be:

- relevant;
- reliable;
- comparable, and
- understandable.

Materiality cuts across these divisions, since the provision of immaterial information can impair the general usefulness of information. Equally, there is a need for all material information to be provided.

Each of these characteristics is then explained and justified in greater detail.

1.4.2 Relevance

According to the *Statement of Principles:*

> information is relevant if it has the ability to influence the economic decisions of users and is provided in time to influence those decisions. (Principles from Chapter Three, *Statement of Principles.*)

Two characteristics of relevance are identified:

- predictive value, and
- confirmatory value.

Information is considered to have predictive value if it helps users to evaluate or assess past, present or future events. (It is unusual to see 'predictive' value associated with past events.) The *Statement of Principles* makes it clear that it does not assume that information has to be in the form of forecasts to have predictive value.

Information has confirmatory value if it helps users to correct or confirm their previous evaluations and assessments.

These are not seen as being entirely independent characteristics, and the same information may have both predictive and confirmatory value. The example given is that of information on the level and structure of asset holdings of an entity. The provision of such information allows users to make assessments of how the entity may be able to react in the future, but also enables them to reconsider their previous assessments.

The manner of presentation is also seen as being important to the extent to which that information may be relevant. For example, this is used to justify the requirement to disclose exceptional items under FRS 3. If non-recurring events, or extreme examples of events of a recurring nature, are not highlighted in financial statements, then it becomes much more difficult to make any predictions of future performance.

Relevance is also used as the justification for the adoption of the going concern concept. For most companies this is the most likely assumption, and provides information that is most likely to be relevant. This can be made clear by contrasting this with a situation where another concept was adopted. If financial statements were routinely drawn up on the basis of the immediately realisable values of all assets, for example, this would make it much harder to determine the value that those assets can provide to an ongoing business.

1.4.3 Reliability

The principle of reliability is broken down in the *Statement of Principles* between:

- faithful representation;
- neutral;
- free from material error;
- complete, and
- prudence.

Faithful representation

Faithful representation can be glossed as the requirement that transactions or events are portrayed in financial statements in a way that reflects the commercial effect of those transactions or events.

This approach, which underpins the concept of substance over form which itself forms the basic rationale behind FRS 5, accepts that the analysis of transactions and events may be complex. In discussing the way in which a transaction or event is portrayed in financial statements, the *Statement of Principles* recognises that the portrayal will depend on a balance of:

(a) the rights and obligations arising and the weight attached to each;
(b) how the rights and obligations to which the most weight has been attached are characterised;
(c) which measurement basis (or bases) and presentation techniques are used to depict the rights and obligations, and
(d) the way in which the elements arising from the transaction or other event are presented in the financial statements. (Para. 3.9, *Statement of Principles*.)

The problems that can arise in attempting to portray events faithfully are recognised. However hard someone tries to provide a faithful representation, it has to be accepted that it is not always straightforward to:

- identify all relevant transactions and events;
- identify all of the consequences of transactions and events, and
- devise and apply measurement and presentation techniques that make clear the impact of transactions and events.

The *Statement of Principles* mirrors FRS 5 when dealing with the requirement for the substance of transactions to be accounted for (as far as is possible) rather than their form. It even goes on to point out that a group or series of transactions that achieves an overall commercial effect needs to be accounted for as a whole, rather than treated as a series of separate transactions.

If nothing else, the very length of FRS 5 (including the various Application Notes which now supplement it) is an indication of the problems that can be encountered when attempting to determine what actually is the substance of transactions.

Neutrality

The *Statement of Principles* also discusses, albeit briefly, the requirement for neutrality. Information is neutral only if it is free from deliberate or systematic bias. Such bias is most likely to arise where a party involved in the preparation of financial statements is trying to present information in a particular way. For example, the directors of a company might attempt to prepare financial statements in such a way as to make the reported profitability of the company appear as high (or low) as possible. Such information has not been prepared from a neutral perspective and as such cannot be considered to be reliable. However, in practice, the dividing line between deliberate bias and excessive optimism (or pessimism) is not as clear as the *Statement of Principles* might suggest.

Complete and free from material error

The statement also covers the need for information to be complete and free from material error. These sections of the statement are not very helpful. While it cannot be denied that information must be complete to be useful, the idea of completeness as applied to financial statements is fraught with problems. Even the statement acknowledges that in practice completeness is more difficult to apply than it might sound.

> This reference to being complete within the bounds of materiality is important because completeness is relative: financial statements are a highly aggregated portrayal of an entity's financial performance and financial position and therefore cannot show everything. (Para. 3.17, *Statement of Principles*.)

This addresses only one aspect of the problem. It is true that whether or not the information explicitly presented is complete depends on materiality. Financial statements do not include details of immaterial items, since such information would be of little relevance and potentially confusing. However, completeness also refers to the information that might be presented and whether it is encompassed in the existing accounting framework. For example, when FRS 12 was introduced it limited the cases where companies were able to make provisions. In some cases, there is no requirement to disclose the circumstances that were previously seen as justifying the creation of a provision. As a result, information disappeared from financial statements when FRS 12 came into force. Does this mean that those financial statements were less complete after FRS 12 had come into force than they were before? In a sense this has to be true, but obviously not in a way that the ASB would consider to be important. Completeness can only be taken to mean completeness within the framework.

At the other end, FRS 26 (a standard based on IFRS, so not developed by the ASB) requires that companies falling within its remit account for many financial instruments from the date that they become a party to a contract. Such instruments are, therefore, considered to be assets and liabilities, which must be included in financial statements in order for those statements to be complete. Yet most companies in the UK are not required to apply, and do not, in practice, apply FRS 26. Therefore, the same items are often not included as assets or liabilities and are dealt with, if at all, only through disclosure. Does this mean that financial statements prepared by such entities are to be considered incomplete? Presumably not, as the ASB has not chosen to make FRS 26 mandatory for all entities.

Material error is an even more complicated idea. The definition of what is an error is totally dependent upon what is considered to be 'right'. To take the examples of provisions again, the making of some provisions would now be seen as an error. A few years ago it was not, and was seen as at least best practice and often a requirement. To deal with material errors in the *Statement of Principles* is highly self-referential since the definition of an error depends on what the *Statement of Principles* says.

Prudence

Prudence has always been one of the touchstones of accounting. Under SSAP 2, where there were conflicts between the principles of prudence and accruals, it was nearly always prudence that took precedence. The attitude of the ASB to prudence differs significantly. While the *Statement of Principles* continues to state the relevance of prudence, its primary status has been removed.

Prudence is defined as:

> ... the inclusion of a degree of caution in the exercise of the judgements needed in making the estimates required under conditions of uncertainty, such that gains and assets are not overstated and losses and liabilities are not understated. In particular, under such conditions it requires more confirmatory evidence about the existence of, and a greater reliability of measurement for, assets and gains than is required for liabilities and losses. (Para. 3.19, *Statement of Principles*.)

The statement then goes on to list some of the dangers of the overuse of prudence, indicating that the ASB believes prudence has been misused in the past to paint an unnecessarily gloomy picture of many companies' situations.

However, it is not necessary to exercise prudence where there is no uncertainty. Nor is it appropriate to use prudence as a reason for, for example, creating hidden reserves or excessive provisions, deliberately understating assets or gains, or deliberately overstating liabilities or losses, because that would mean that the financial statements are not neutral and, therefore, are not reliable. (Para. 3.20, *Statement of Principles*.)

It is this logic that underpins some of the ASB's changes, such as the introduction of FRS 12. Provisions had, in the ASB's opinion, been made in circumstances where there was no, or a very uncertain, liability. FRS 12 limited the circumstances in which provisions could be made, to ensure that excessive amounts were not being put aside to enable companies to flatter their results in later years and to even out inherently uneven trends. This logic has also been taken into FRS 18, which directly quotes the *Statement of Principles* when dealing with the need to ignore prudence where there is no uncertainty.

1.4.4   Relevance and reliability

If relevance and reliability were always to arrive at the same results, application of the *Statement of Principles* would be straightforward. This is not the case.

The simplest case is where there are two or more bases which are of equal reliability, but where one may be more relevant than the others. In this case, the *Statement of Principles* says that it is the most relevant that should be adopted. For example, there are areas where two or more accounting policies or bases of measurement might be used, with equally reliable results, but one provides more useful information than the other. In that case it is the most useful policy or basis which should be adopted.

The much more complicated situation is where there is direct conflict between relevance and reliability. The *Statement of Principles* deals with this problem very badly, dealing with only one aspect. It does mention this conflict in terms of the timeliness of the provision of accounting information. To take an extreme example, financial information produced one day after the end of a company's accounting period would be highly relevant, but probably not that reliable. Information made available two years after the end of the period would probably be highly reliable, but virtually irrelevant.

The *Statement of Principles* does not even attempt to deal with the much more complicated question of what should be done where there is a direct conflict between relevance and reliability, and the ASB's views on this matter can only be guessed from the standards it has produced.

It appears that the ASB prefers relevance to reliability. For example, the approach of FRS 5 is based on the concept of substance over form. The application of the concept of substance is likely to lead to information that is far more relevant than one based on form. However, it also tends to lead to information that can easily be seen as less reliable. The form of a transaction is usually much more straightforward than its substance. If we were to account for all transactions in accordance with their legal form, we would have financial statements which were highly reliable, as the characterisation of transactions would present little problem. The fact that we are required to account for substance, a much more difficult idea, significantly increases the relevance of information, but is likely to lead to far more disagreements about what actually is the substance of a transaction. The potential for misinterpreting the impact of transactions is much higher, reducing the reliability of the information presented.

Similarly, FRS 12 allows provisions in some cases where there is a constructive obligation, that is, a legitimate expectation has been created in the mind of a third party that a company will do something, but where there is no legal obligation underpinning this. For example, a company's previous practice may indicate that staff bonuses are payable even though there is no contractual entitlement to such bonuses. Provisions for bonuses may, therefore, be made. Whatever merits this approach may have, it leads to a reduced chance of consistency in financial statements as the concept of constructive obligation is inherently vaguer than that of legal obligation. In a particular set of circumstances there is always a possibility that two accountants, both working from the same principles and attempting assiduously to be neutral, may reach a different judgement as to whether a constructive obligation exists or not.

Finally, the issue of relevance and reliability is also at the heart of the ongoing debates concerning the use of fair value information in financial statements. FRS 26 requires fair values to be used for many financial assets. Where market values are used, this is arguably reliable information in so far as a market value is often factual. At the same time, many would argue that this makes financial statements more volatile than they need to be, which might be considered to make financial statements less reliable and relevant, even if the individual amounts within them meet such criteria. However, where an asset is held for a purpose unconnected with its market value at any point in time, some would argue that its fair value is not relevant. For example, if a company owns an investment solely for its generation of income in the form of dividends, then its market value at the balance sheet date is arguably of no relevance. Where values based on market prices are not used, and estimation techniques need to be applied, the problem is even more acute. Even if it is accepted that fair value is relevant to such items, such values may not always be determined on a reliable basis. Is it better that less reliable information be included in the financial statements because it may be more relevant than other information (such as cost) which is more reliable?

It is a great pity that the ASB dodged the issue of the conflict of relevance and reliability, as it undermines the value of much of the *Statement of Principles*. To fail to address the potential conflicts between two of its own core principles is to provide a misleading picture, as it seems to indicate that the conflicts are minor. They are not, and they lie at the core of accounting practice.

A preference for relevance or reliability depends on one's own views about the fundamentals of accounting. The fact that there are areas of conflict needs to be addressed whatever one's basic preference.

1.4.5   Neutrality and prudence

The *Statement of Principles* also glosses over the conflict between neutrality and prudence. It does point out that prudence is a biased concept, whereas the whole point of neutrality is to remove bias. It also makes the point that prudence only applies in situations of uncertainty; where there is no uncertainty there is no place for prudence.

However, when it gets on to dealing with situations where there is genuine conflict, its comments are not very useful:

> when there is uncertainty, the competing demands of neutrality and prudence are reconciled by finding a balance that ensures that the deliberate and systematic understatement of gains and assets and overstatement of losses and liabilities do not occur. (Para. 3.36, *Statement of Principles*.)

That is not terribly helpful when faced with a real situation. Nonetheless, this basis has been taken into FRS 18 and now has to be applied by companies in the preparation of their financial statements.

1.4.6   Comparability

Comparability is broken down between consistency and disclosure.

Comparability is the requirement that, in order to be useful, it should be possible to compare present financial information with that for previous periods or points in time, and that it should be possible to compare information produced by one enterprise with that produced by another.

Consistency

All other things being equal, consistency requires that companies adopt the same accounting policies from one accounting period to the next.

However, the *Statement of Principles* then goes on to stress that this should not been seen as an impediment to the improvement of accounting practices. This matter is dealt with in FRS 3, which requires that where a change in accounting policy is made, the comparative amounts shown should, wherever possible, be adjusted so that they are shown in a way that is consistent with the methods adopted in respect of the current accounting period. Particular accounting standards may override this general requirement, usually where it would not be practicable to obtain the information necessary to make such adjustments for prior periods.

Consistency is also said to be useful in being able to make comparisons between different companies. This comment is, again, limited as the *Statement of Principles* goes on to state that the need for consistency should not be interpreted as a requirement for absolute uniformity. The question of uniformity is covered when dealing with disclosure of accounting policies.

Disclosure of accounting policies

As noted above, the *Statement of Principles* states that consistency of accounting policies between different enterprises is beneficial, but that this does not mean that all accounting policies should be uniform. Accounting standards tend to impose greater uniformity of accounting policies, but such standards do not cover all situations. Equally, some standards allow a certain latitude in the determination of the precise accounting policies that a company may apply, setting out the general principles that must underlie such a policy rather than dictating it.

As a result, in order for financial information to be interpreted properly, the accounting policies on which that information has been based must be disclosed. According to the *Statement of Principles*, this allows users to identify any differences between:

- the accounting policies adopted by a company to account for similar transactions or events;
- the accounting policies adopted by a company from one period to the next, and
- the accounting policies adopted by different companies.

1.4.7   Understandability

This is the requirement that the information provided by financial statements must be understandable, that is, users must be able to perceive its significance.

The degree to which information can be understood depends on the way in which it is presented, the way it has been characterised, aggregated and classified and, equally crucial, the capabilities of the users.

These are not independent. The abilities of users can determine the best way in which information should be presented.

The *Statement of Principles* does make the point that the fact that information may be complicated is no excuse for excluding it from financial statements, if it is also relevant and reliable.

1.4.8   Materiality

Materiality operates largely independently of the other characteristics of useful accounting information.

It is described by the *Statement of Principles* as being a threshold quality. Irrespective of the other characteristics, immaterial information need not be given. Equally, material information must comply with the other characteristics. To take a very simple example, if a company has an accounting policy which affects only very immaterial items, then this policy need not be disclosed. This applies even if, on other bases, the policy is not appropriate.

The fact that immaterial information can be ignored is justified on the grounds that the inclusion of irrelevant material will make it more difficult, not easier, to understand the financial statements. In colloquial terms, it would not be possible to see the wood for the trees.

The *Statement of Principles* gives the following guidance on determining the materiality of items.

(a)   The item's size is judged in the context both of the financial statements as a whole and of the other information available to users that would affect their evaluation of the financial statements. This includes, for example, considering how the item affects the evaluation of trends and similar considerations.

(b)   Consideration is given to the item's nature in relation to:

   (i)   the transactions or other events giving rise to it;

   (ii)   the legality, sensitivity, normality and potential consequences of the event or transaction;

   (iii)   the identity of the parties involved, and

   (iv)   the particular headings and disclosures that are affected. (Para. 3.31, *Statement of Principles.*)

As ever, it is made clear that materiality cannot be looked at solely as an amount. An item may be material in one context when it would not be in another. To take the most common example, in the disclosure of directors' emoluments or related party transactions, it would be inappropriate to use the same level of materiality as might be applied in other areas of financial statements, as a result of the sensitivity of the area. Similarly, in the case of a breach of law and regulations, disclosure might be required of items which would not be considered material in other contexts, due to the unlawfulness of the events.

1.5 THE ELEMENTS OF FINANCIAL STATEMENTS

1.5.1 Principles

The *Statement of Principles* lists the elements of financial statements as:

- assets;
- liabilities;
- ownership interest;
- gains;
- losses;
- contributions from owners, and
- distributions to owners.

Cash flows are ignored, as the cash flow statement deals with only one type of financial effect.

Contributions from and distributions to owners have been distinguished from other items, as, although they are not identified with a particular financial statement, they are different in kind from other changes in the ownership interest.

It is noted in the *Statement of Principles* that the fact that a transaction or event has given rise to one of the elements of financial statements does not always imply that the element will be recognised. The example given is that of an asset, which can only be recognised if it also meets the recognition criteria for assets.

1.5.2 Assets

Assets are defined as:

> ... rights or access to future economic benefits controlled by an entity as a result of past transactions or events. (Principles from Chapter Four and para. 4.6, *Statement of Principles.*)

Other characteristics are commonly associated with assets, but none of these is taken to be a defining characteristic.

Rights or access

The emphasis is on the rights or access and not on the underlying item which may be associated with those rights or that access. While this is, perhaps, a very different way of looking at some assets than has been applied in the past, it is not entirely novel. Prepayments, for example, have long formed part of accounting, and clearly refer neither to a physical asset nor to a debt as such. They refer to the right to do, use or avoid something in a future period without the need to make further payment. No accountant would query this treatment.

The rights and access can be obtained in different ways. Legal ownership is the most common, and will apply in the majority of cases where assets are accounted for. Legal ownership, however, is not a condition for the existence of an asset. A company may have rights over an asset without owning that asset, of which the most common example is a leased asset. This is clearest in the case of an asset held under a finance lease, where the asset appears on a balance sheet notwithstanding the absence of legal title. The finance lease still provides sufficient legal rights to warrant recognition of the asset.

There may also be cases, albeit rare, where there is no legal ownership or legal rights over an asset yet an asset still exists. In this case, the access is limited without there being legal protection for this limitation. For example, a company may have know-how or unpatented inventions. (The question of whether or not such assets should actually be recognised in financial statements is a separate question.)

Future economic benefits

Assets must also give rise to future economic benefits. An item need not be capable of generating future benefits on its own, and may need to be used in conjunction with other items in order to meet the definition of an asset. There may be cases where the future economic benefit is not certain. However, the possibility of future economic benefit is sufficient to warrant treating an item as an asset. Again, this question is separate from the issue of whether that asset can be recognised. For example, a claim with a slim chance of succeeding, made by a company, could be considered an asset. It should not, however, be recognised as an asset in financial statements. The *Statement of Principles* also points out that certain items may be potentially either assets or liabilities. A forward contract, for example, may prove to be either an asset or liability in the fullness of time. It still falls within the definition of an asset, although again the question of its recognition and measurement needs to be dealt with separately.

Future economic benefits must, eventually, mean cash. However, they need not do so directly. In simple terms an item is an asset if:

- it is cash;
- it embodies a right to cash in the future, such as a debtor;
- it embodies a right to services that may be used to generate cash, such as a prepayment, or
- it contains the ability to be used to generate cash or meet liabilities, such as a tangible or intangible fixed asset.

The absence of the ability to generate cash means that an item is not an asset. The example of a prepayment has already been used. If a company has prepaid rent on a factory that is in use, then that represents an asset since the factory will be used over the period covered by the prepayment to generate cash for the business. If a company has prepaid rent on surplus premises that it cannot sublet, then that is not an asset since the premises are not going to be used to generate cash. No prepayment should be included in a balance sheet.

Control by the entity

In order for an item to be an asset the company must also have control over the economic benefit it embodies. This means the ability to obtain those benefits for itself, and to limit the access of others to those benefits.

The *Statement of Principles* mentions that there may be cases where this control does not need to be legally enforceable. It is possible that a company may, in practice, be able to exercise control even where it does not have the legal rights to do so. Social and practical sanctions for non-compliance can be taken into account when determining if there is an asset. This is fraught with difficulties but means, for example, that an unenforceable commitment from a parent company to a subsidiary to provide funds to enable it to meet its liabilities could be considered an asset, on this criterion. (Note that it could not be accounted for as an asset, however, until the support had actually been provided, as it would not meet all of the other criteria necessary to the definition of an asset.)

Since control is an exclusive concept, only one party can account for an asset directly. (More than one party may account for an asset indirectly, as where a company has an asset which is also included in the group accounts of its parent.)

However, the *Statement of Principles* also refers to the 'item of property' which underlies the accounting asset. For example, a building may be an item of property. Financial statements do not include buildings, they include rights over buildings. The item of property may give rise to two, or even more, assets. For example, where one company leases a piece of equipment to another both companies will include an asset in their financial statements which, ultimately, leads back to the item of equipment. However, what each company is accounting for differs, and represents the rights, access and control that each has in relation to the underlying item of property.

A company is considered to control an asset even if it could no longer continue in (or in its) business were it to dispose of that asset. One of the examples given of such an asset is a hotel company which has a single hotel. It cannot sell the hotel and continue in its business. Yet it still has the option of disposing of the hotel, and therefore still has control. This situation is contrasted with other items that might be considered as providing value to a business, such as market share, good management or good labour relations. These items are not directly under the control of the company. While they may be important factors in assessing the value of the company, and assets in that sense of the term, they are not assets in accounting terms.

Past transactions or events

The final element of the definition of an asset is the requirement for past transactions or events.

This requirement exists because of the need to prepare financial statements in respect of discrete accounting periods and at particular points in time. If a company did not have the ability to restrict the access of others to the future economic benefits associated with an item at a particular balance sheet date, then it did not have an asset at that date. Assets which may arise in the future should not be accounted for now.

1.5.3   Liabilities

Liabilities are defined as:

> ... obligations of an entity to transfer economic benefits as a result of past transactions or events. (Principles from Chapter Four and para. 4.23, *Statement of Principles*.)

Obligations

A liability must include an obligation. This means that the company must not be able to avoid the transfer.

This is slightly separate from the point of whether or not there is a certainty of obligation. If a claim is made against the company, then it may not be certain whether there is an obligation. However, if the claim is successful, then the company will not be able to avoid the obligation. As such, consideration needs to be given to accounting for this obligation. (Whether or not the amount is actually included in financial statements is a separate question.)

Most obligations are legally enforceable, but this is not a necessary part of the definition. An obligation may be a constructive one, that is, one which the company must meet because it has created valid expectations on the part of the persons to whom the obligation is owed. For example, if a company is always willing to exchange goods or make refunds, even where there is no legal obligation to do so, this creates a valid expectation on the part of its customers. The company would be allowed to account for any liability existing at its balance sheet date in respect of such obligations.

A decision, however, does not create an obligation, since the decision can be reversed. In order to create an obligation the decision must be irreversible. This matter is primarily dealt with in FRS 12. Taking the example of a decision to close a factory, the fact that a decision has been made creates no obligation. The company (or rather the company's board) may change its mind. The obligation may become constructive once it is notified to the parties, presumably primarily the staff, whom it will affect. At this point an obligation exists and it would be acceptable to account for the liability. (It will become a legal obligation at a later stage, but this is not relevant in determining the accounting treatment.)

More controversially, the *Statement of Principles* maintains that no obligation exists where a company is committed to an activity if it wishes to continue in business, but not otherwise. For example, an airline company cannot continue to operate as an airline if it does not undertake periodic overhauls of its aircraft. However, this is not considered to be a relevant obligation; the company does not have to continue to operate the aircraft.

Transfer of economic benefits

In order for an item to be a liability there has to be a requirement to transfer economic benefits. Anything a company must do but which will truly involve no costs does not give rise to a liability.

As with assets, certainty is not required. A guarantee is a liability, even though there may be no expectation that any transfer of economic benefits will actually take place. The *Statement of Principles* glosses over the question of whether in this case the liability is not recognised, or is recognised but at a value of nil. This is presumably on the basis that the distinction is of no practical import. (For some companies, those complying with FRS 26, financial guarantees may now give rise to reported obligations. However, FRS 26 is the UK version of an international standard, and is therefore not based on the ASB's statement.)

Equally, a liability may need to be recorded at a value other than zero, even where the amount is not known. Again, a claim might be a good example. Depending on the likelihood of a claim against a company being successful, the company may need to account for an amount from zero to the full amount of the claim, or somewhere in between the two. Once it is clear that there is a potential for the transfer of economic resources there is a liability. It is a separate matter to deal with the quantification of the amount that will actually appear in financial statements.

While many liabilities will be met in cash, this is also not a requirement. When dealing with assets, prepayments were given as an example of an asset that will normally not be realised in cash. Looking at the same transaction from the perspective of the other party, there is an obligation that need not be met in cash. If a company receives prepaid rent, then it is obliged to provide the use of premises for a specified period without the right to obtain future payment. This is deferred income and represents a non-cash liability.

Past transactions or events

In order for there to be a liability, the event or transaction giving rise to that liability must already have occurred. The same example can be used as above, in respect of the proposed closure of the factory. The decision to close is not a relevant event. The communication of this decision to affected parties is.

Where a series of events or transactions is required in order to crystallise an obligation, then this is deemed to give rise to the obligation only when any future events or transactions are not under the control of the company. If they are, then no obligation has arisen. For example, agreement to acquire an asset subject to contract creates no obligation, since the party can still avoid the acquisition if it wishes. The granting of an option to a third party does create an obligation, since that party now has the choice as to whether to use the option and the company no longer has control. (Again, this is separate from the issue of whether or not the obligation needs to be recorded.)

1.5.4   Offsetting

Assets and liabilities cannot always be considered in isolation. Sometimes a transaction or event may give rise to both rights and obligations, and consideration needs to be given to whether these items need to be considered separately or in aggregate. Equally, there may be cases where the rights or obligations arising from one transaction or event need to be considered in conjunction with the rights or obligations arising from other transactions or events.

The *Statement of Principles* splits these questions into three, stating that the problem can be broken down into the following questions.

(1)   Definition – when do rights and obligations represent separate obligations and rights, and when do they represent an aggregate item?

(2)   Recognition – when should rights that create an asset and obligations that create a liability be combined into a single asset or liability? This is not considered to be relevant, as there are no cases where the *Statement of Principles* believes that such items should be offset.

(3)   Presentation – when should assets be offset against liabilities in the balance sheet?

The reason that the issue of recognition is not considered to be relevant is that the ASB believes the issue can be resolved into one of definition. If there truly is a situation where there is a separate asset and liability then they cannot be recognised as a single item. If they can be recognised as a single item, then, by definition, they do not constitute a separate asset and liability.

Where a company has the assured right to offset balances and insist on a net settlement, this is considered to be a single item, whether asset or liability. This is irrespective of what is expected to happen in practice.

An unperformed executory contract, which arises whenever a company enters a contract for the future, represents both a right and an obligation, but does not represent an asset and liability. For example, a company enters into a contract under which a third party will construct an asset for it. There will be no obligation until performance (in whole or in part) and no current rights or access to future economic benefits. The company is dependent on the other party also performing their obligations under the contract before the company either has an asset or must meet a liability.

The same analysis applies where a contract is partially complete. In this case there will be an asset and liability (unless discharged) in respect of the work completed, but no asset and liability in respect of the uncompleted element.

The *Statement of Principles* indicates that the incomplete element should be considered as an asset or liability in its own right, although its value is almost certain to be nil, at least at the inception of the contract. This is because in most cases the rights obtained will be equal to the obligations taken on. Whether or not such an item is really an asset or liability is, again, a trivial question since it will have no effect on accounting practice.

It is reasonable to accept the assumption that in most cases the incomplete portion of the contract has a value of nil, but this will not always apply after inception. Accounting for onerous contracts, for example, reflects the fact that the obligations under a contract may exceed the expected benefits. It is implausible that such a contract would have been entered into on this basis, but extremely plausible that as a result of later changes this position may be reached.

1.5.5   Ownership interest

Ownership interest is defined as:

> . . . the residual amount found by deducting all of the entity's liabilities from all of the entity's assets. (Principles from Chapter Four and para. 4.37, *Statement of Principles*.)

The ASB has quite deliberately avoided all questions of valuation. There is no attempt to equate the owners' interest in accounting terms with the value of that interest. It really is seen as a balancing figure.

The *Statement of Principles* points out that there is an important distinction between liabilities and owners' interests, in that creditors have the ability to insist that a transfer of economic resources is made to them regardless of the circumstances, whereas owners do not. This distinction is now far clearer in accounting practice than in the past. Under the original version of FRS 4, certain items were shown as ownership interest, when in fact they were always more akin to liabilities. This changed with FRS 25, which requires a substance over form approach to be adopted, an approach also recognised in the Companies Act 2006. Where shares are, in effect, liabilities, FRS 25 requires them to be accounted for as such.

1.5.6   Gains and losses

Gains and losses are defined as follows.

Gains are increases in ownership interest not resulting from contributions from owners.

Losses are decreases in ownership interest not resulting from distributions to owners. (Principles from Chapter Four and para. 4.39, *Statement of Principles*.)

The terms are intended to be broad, so that they cover gains and losses that currently appear in the profit and loss account and elsewhere.

The *Statement of Principles* treats items as separate gains and losses, even though they may be intimately connected in practice. The example given is that of the sale of an item and the cost of the sale. These are considered to be two separate items, a gain from the sale and a loss from the cost. While such transactions are usually not thought of in these terms, this does reflect the current form of disclosure.

1.5.7   Contributions from owners and distributions to owners

These are defined, respectively as:

... increases in ownership interest resulting from transfers from owners in their capacity as owners.

and

... decreases in ownership interest resulting from transfers to owners in their capacity as owners. (Principles from Chapter Four and para. 4.42, *Statement of Principles*.)

The inclusion of references to owners in their capacity as owners is important to distinguish such changes from those that might result from other transactions with owners, such as sales of assets to owners, which would give rise to gains or losses in just the same way as they would if they were undertaken with an unconnected party.

Most contributions from and distributions to owners are very straightforward, in principle, and give rise to few conceptual problems.

1.5.8   The impact of the Statement of Principles

The definitions used within the *Statement of Principles* had a major impact on UK accounting practice. FRS 5 introduced the definitions of assets and liabilities, and the implications of these were then worked through for a number of years. FRS 12, for example, was an attempt to apply the definition of a liability to provisions. These had previously been seen by many accountants as slightly different from other types of liability. Under FRS 12, they are clearly no more than a sub-class, one which is similar in kind if not in level of certainty. FRS 18 has also brought many of the principles into use, and reflects substantial differences between the approach to accounting principles adopted by the Accounting Standards Committee in SSAP 2 and that of the ASB. FRS 25, whilst based on the international standard IAS 32, and therefore not directly derived from the *Statement of Principles*, is also consistent with the *Statement of Principles* in terms of the definition of a liability.

The whole approach of the ASB to most accounting issues is defined by their approach to assets and liabilities. While it might not be considered fair to characterise their approach as based on the balance sheet, as they recognise many issues with presentation in other financial statements, they clearly see the recognition of assets and liabilities as the fundamental driver of accounting. Performance statements must take their lead from whether or not, on the ASB's definitions, there are consequent assets and liabilities to be included in financial statements. This is made even clearer in the chapter of the *Statement of Principles* dealing with the recognition of items in financial statements. It should be noted that this assets and liabilities approach to the measurement of performance is not supported by any detailed review of the information needs of investors.

1.6 RECOGNITION IN FINANCIAL STATEMENTS

1.6.1 Principles

In the chapter of the *Statement of Principles* dealing with the elements of financial statements, the ASB stresses that this question needs to be dealt with separately from the question of recognition. While it is not possible to recognise an asset, for example, where there is no asset, it is quite compatible with the ASB's approach to accept that there is an asset and then not recognise it.

There are principles covering both the recognition and derecognition of items.

1.6.2 Initial recognition

The basic principles are that:

If a transaction or other event has created a new asset or liability or added to an existing asset or liability, that effect will be recognised if:

(a) sufficient evidence exists that the new asset or liability has been created or that there has been an addition to an existing asset or liability; and

(b) the new asset or liability or the addition to the existing asset or liability can be measured at a monetary amount with sufficient reliability. (Principles from Chapter Five, *Statement of Principles*.)

In most cases it is a transaction that will give rise to the need to recognise an item. However, other events may also give rise to the recognition of an asset or liability. One of the examples given in the *Statement of Principles* is the imposition of a penalty by a court, which will create a liability even though there has been no transaction.

Uncertainty

Uncertainty may affect all stages of recognition, remeasurement and derecognition. The *Statement of Principles* states that ideally all assets, liabilities, gains, losses and other elements would be recognised immediately they arise, but that in practice uncertainty means that this cannot be the case. There may be cases where, for example, a liability exists but cannot be recognised as the amount of that liability is not known. This matter has already been mentioned when dealing with the definitions of assets and liabilities.

In terms of recognition, the *Statement of Principles* identifies two major types of uncertainty.

1   Element uncertainty – uncertainty concerning whether an item exists and meets the definition of an element of financial statements.

2   Measurement uncertainty – uncertainty concerning the monetary amount that should be attributed to an item.

The first question to be addressed is that of element uncertainty. For example, in order for there to be an asset there have to be rights or access, control and future economic benefit. There are cases where one or more of these items may be uncertain, an example of element uncertainty. This justifies the first criterion for the recognition of an asset, being that there is sufficient evidence of its existence. This will never be straightforward since the definition of 'sufficient' can never be precise, and always needs to take account of the circumstances. The *Statement of Principles* stresses that sufficient does not mean conclusive, or many assets would never be recognised.

Exactly the same problems can arise with regard to liabilities.

In determining whether there is sufficient evidence for recognition, account should be taken of:

- the evidence provided by the event that has given rise to the potential asset or liability;
- past experience with similar items, from within the company;
- current information directly relating to the potential asset or liability, and
- evidence provided by transactions of other entities in respect of similar assets or liabilities.

While of some use, this is hardly precise. Given the nature of the question, the precision one would like is probably not attainable.

The second problem to be addressed is that of measurement uncertainty. Having determined that there is an asset or liability, it is still not possible to account for it (as opposed to note it) if it is not possible to attribute to it, with sufficient reliability, a monetary amount. The *Statement of Principles* says relatively little about this problem, which is also addressed in FRS 5, other than to return to its comments on prudence. It points out again that prudence means that there must be:

...

- more confirmatory evidence about the existence of an asset or gain than about the existence of a liability or loss; and
- a greater reliability of measurement for assets and gains than for liabilities and losses. (Para. 5.18, *Statement of Principles*.)

However, it then simply returns to its previous comments about the fact that this does not justify the systematic understatement of assets and gains and overstatement of liabilities and losses.

1.6.3   Derecognition

The principle is that:

An asset or liability will be wholly or partly derecognised if:

- sufficient evidence exists that a transaction or other past event has eliminated all or part of a previously recognised asset or liability; or
- although the item continues to be an asset or a liability, the criteria for recognition are no longer met. (Principles from Chapter Five, *Statement of Principles*.)

The most common situation is also the simplest: where an item is clearly eliminated and should be derecognised. For example, if a company sells an item which was previously in stock, it can no longer treat the stock as an asset. Similarly, when a creditor balance is paid the amount is no longer treated as a liability.

It is also possible that a transaction or event may take place which alters an asset or liability, but which does not completely eliminate it. In this case there may be partial derecognition, or complete derecognition with replacement by another asset or liability.

For example, a company may have ceased to use an item of equipment for its own purposes and have started to lease the equipment out on a finance lease. It no longer accounts for the original asset, as it no longer has the rights associated with the equipment. However, it still has an asset, being its right to the payments under the lease, and will account for this instead. Similarly, a company with a licence may grant a sub-licence with reversion after a set number of years. In this case, the asset has not been sold, but must be partially derecognised to take account of the element of its original stated value that has been sold.

There may also be cases where there is uncertainty as to whether an asset or liability has been eliminated. Prudence is of relevance in these circumstances, in determining whether the asset or liability should be derecognised. In simple terms, more evidence will be required to justify the removal of a liability than an asset. For example, if a company had a claim against another which had previously looked certain but had now become questionable, then it should be derecognised. In the same situation, but in respect of a claim against the company, the liability should probably continue to be recognised.

The other situation is where there has been no change in the underlying nature of the asset or liability, but it no longer meets the recognition criteria. Such situations are likely to be extremely rare and are most likely to arise where any previous quantification, which appeared justified at the time, has now become impossible.

1.6.4   Revenue recognition

The *Statement of Principles* makes clear that revenue recognition does not have relevance separately from the issue of the recognition of assets and liabilities. Put simply, and ignoring transactions with owners as owners:

- if a transaction or event has increased the net assets of a company, then it must recognise a gain, or
- if a transaction or event has decreased the net assets of a company, then it must recognise a loss.

Despite this, the *Statement of Principles* deals with the issue of revenue recognition since it can sometimes be simpler to deal with the problem in these terms than by moving directly to assets or liabilities.

Matching

The statement describes the idea of matching, and recognises that there are two aspects to it.

(1) Time matching – receipts and payments are recognised as gains and losses directly on a time basis, according to the periods which they are intended to cover.

(2) Revenue/expenditure matching – expenditure associated with gains is recognised as a loss at the time that the gains are made, rather than during the period in which the expenditure is made.

The statement attributes a low importance to matching since, as it points out, most expenditure by businesses is made with the hope of producing future gains. If matching were to be applied without restriction this would involve carrying forward expenditure which does not meet the ASB's definition of an asset. For example, advertising expenditure is undertaken with the hope that it will lead to higher profits. This does not mean that previous advertising expenditure can be carried forward as an asset simply because the benefits it is hoped will arise have yet to crystallise. The matching concept might indicate that this amount should be allocated to the future periods expected to benefit, yet there is no asset (as defined), and therefore it must be treated as a current period loss. This is included explicitly in the statement, and is fully recognised in FRS 18, where matching has been removed from the definition of accruals.

Critical events

As noted before, although the area of revenue recognition is determined by the creation or elimination of assets and liabilities, it may be easier and more practical to concentrate on the operating cycle.

The critical event in an operating cycle is the point at which there is sufficient evidence that a gain exists, and it can be measured with sufficient reliability. For most transactions this is probably exactly the same point as the point of performance. For example, on the sale of goods the critical event is usually when the sale is made.

Not all situations are quite so simple. In determining the critical event, in a more complex scenario, account needs to be taken of the following.

(1) When the company has performed all of its material obligations under the contract. (For example, if a company were contracted to provide a piece of equipment it would usually recognise income and costs when the equipment was delivered, if this was subject only to routine installation.)

(2) The existence of any significant contingencies. (For example, a sale subject to a *Romalpa* clause is not usually subject to significant contingencies, as the clause is intended to be a form of debt protection, not a question mark over whether a sale has taken place. Some sale or return agreements may have significant contingencies if it is still relatively likely that a return may take place.)

(3) The stages into which a contract may be broken. (For example, a property development may be broken into a number of separate stages, and income and costs should be recognised as each stage is completed, not deferred until completion of the project as a whole.)

The impact of critical events is also addressed more specifically in FRS 5, and in particular in Application Note G to that standard, as well as in UITF 40 which deals with revenue recognition in the context of the provision of services.

1.6.5 *The impact of the Statement of Principles*

The recognition criteria for assets and liabilities are set out in FRS 5. FRS 18 also carries through the logic of FRS 5 more consistently than had perhaps been seen in company accounting practice in the past. The application note to FRS 5, dealing with revenue recognition, is based on the same logic as the *Statement of Principles*.

1.7 MEASUREMENT IN FINANCIAL STATEMENTS

1.7.1 Principles

The *Statement of Principles* does not attempt to choose between the historical cost and current value bases of accounting. Instead, both are presented as options. In addition, it is also stated that each may be appropriate for separate categories of asset and liability, and therefore that it is not necessary that all the elements of financial statements be measured on the same basis.

Initial recognition is stated to be at transaction cost if the historical cost basis is being used, and value at acquisition or assumption if the current value basis is being used.

Remeasurement is stated to be required when necessary to ensure that:

- assets accounted for on the historical cost basis continue to be stated at the lower of their costs and net realisable value;
- monetary items held in foreign currencies continue to be stated at current exchange rates, and
- assets and liabilities accounted for on the current value basis continue to be stated at their current values.

As with recognition and derecognition, such remeasurement should only take place where:

- there is sufficient evidence that the monetary amount of an asset or liability has changed, and
- the new amount of the asset or liability can be measured with sufficient reliability.

The *Statement of Principles* makes no attempt to make financial statements reflect the value of a company, and explicitly states that this is not the function of financial statements. They may provide information which is relevant to that assessment, when combined with other information, but that is a separate matter.

1.7.2 Alternative bases of measurement

The *Statement of Principles* states that there are various bases on which assets and liabilities could be measured. However, the most important distinction is between systems based on historic cost and systems based on current value.

Three primary bases are identified.

(1)   Historic cost.

(2)   Current value.

(3)   Mixed, being one of a number of combinations of historic costs and current values.

Given the different natures of various categories of assets and liability, the *Statement of Principles* prefers the mixed measurement system and concentrates on the rationale that should underlie the adoption of a measurement basis for different classes of assets and liability.

It strongly rejects the basis (common for tangible fixed assets before the introduction of FRS 15) of remeasuring assets or liabilities at current value, and then retaining those values for a long, or even indefinite, period of time. This basis is considered to undermine comparability of accounting information.

1.7.3   Deciding on measurement bases

The *Statement of Principles* states that in determining the most appropriate measurement bases that should be used for each category of assets and liability appearing in financial statements, account needs to be taken of:

● the objective of financial statements, including the need for information to be both relevant and reliable;
● the nature of the assets or liabilities involved, and
● the particular circumstances.

It is noted that this may change over time. Measurement bases may develop so that items can be stated at current value with sufficient reliability where this was not previously possible. Similarly, access to markets may develop such that the relevance of a measure may increase.

The statement acknowledges that it can be difficult to make general statements about valuation bases, but then goes on to make a few. In particular, it attempts to counter the common view that historic cost accounts are always more reliable than current cost accounts. It points out that pure historic cost is never used and that historic cost accounts also use judgement, such as determining the amount of potential bad debts. Even where it really is cost that is being used, this is not always as objective a fact as might be assumed. The determination of the costs of stock or self-constructed assets may involve considerable judgement and the allocation of total costs in a way that, however acceptable it may be, is not the only method available. In such cases it would be possible to argue that the current value of such items is more objective and therefore arguably a more reliable measure than historic cost. The ASB clearly has a point, but nonetheless historic cost remains, as a general rule, more reliable than current values.

The statement also points out that future intentions may affect which is the most appropriate basis for valuation. Investments, for example, may be held for many different reasons. They may be held for the short term to use resources that are available to the company and to generate a return on disposal. In this case, current value is the most relevant measure. They may also be held for the long term to provide access to benefits through income. In this case, historic cost may be the most relevant measure.

1.7.4 Determination of current value

There is no single measure of current value. The *Statement of Principles* identifies three bases that could be used for determining the current value of an asset.

(1) Entry value, or replacement cost – how much it would cost to obtain an equivalent asset.

(2) Exit value, or net realisable value – how much the company could obtain from the disposal of the asset.

(3) Value in use – the present value of the cash flows to be obtained from the continued use of the asset, either alone or in combination with others.

There are assets where the values may all be similar. In theory, the value of a quoted share should be similar on all three bases since the difference between buying and selling prices is relatively small, and the price should be the market's best estimate of the value it will generate in the future.

For many assets, however, the three bases may come up with widely divergent answers. An item of highly specialised equipment, for example, might have:

- a very high entry value, as it needs to be made to order using specialised skills;
- an even higher value in use, as the company can use it profitably, but
- a very low exit value, as it has no alternative use and could only be sold for its scrap value.

Because of this problem, the ASB's preferred view of current value is that it should take account of all the possibilities in a rational way.

The current value basis selected is that of value to the business or deprival value. This means that the current value is taken as being the lower of:

- replacement cost, and
- recoverable amount.

While recoverable amount is itself taken to be the higher of:

- value in use, and
- net realisable value.

The aim behind this approach is to determine what a business would suffer if it were deprived of the asset.

EXAMPLES

An asset has a replacement cost of £1 million, a value in use of £1.5 million and a net realisable value of £500,000. If the company were to be deprived of the asset the sensible thing for it to do would be to replace the asset, which would cost £1 million. It would do this because it is able to generate a return with a present value of £1.5 million.

The asset, therefore, has a current value of £1 million.

An asset has a replacement cost of £3 million, a value in use of £2 million and a net realisable value of £1 million. If the company were deprived of the asset it would not replace it, but would no longer be able to use it. It would, therefore, have lost its ability to generate returns with a present value of £2 million.

The asset, therefore, has a current value of £2 million.

An asset has a replacement cost of £5 million, a value in use of £3 million and a net realisable value of £4 million. If the company were deprived of the asset it would not replace it. It would also not be able to sell the asset for a net amount of £4 million, which would have been a more sensible course of action than continuing to use it to generate a return with a present value of only £3 million.

The asset, therefore, has a current value of £4 million.

Recoverable amount is used in FRS 11 when dealing with impairment. As in the *Statement of Principles*, the underlying assumption is that companies will sell, or use, assets according to which is most beneficial in present terms. The lower amount is not, therefore, relevant.

The same approach can be adopted for liabilities, although this is less intuitively appropriate. In this case, the concept can be described as relief value rather than deprival value. The relief value of a liability is the lowest amount at which it could be eliminated.

For example, a company may have an onerous contract which involves making payments over the next three years. The amount of that liability at current value can be taken as the lower of the amount which the other party would accept in settlement of the future obligations and the amounts payable under the contract expressed at their present value. These amounts may differ because of the different circumstances of the two parties to the contract.

1.7.5 Measurement on recognition

Where the historical cost basis is being used, assets and liabilities should normally initially be recognised at the fair value of the consideration given or received in exchange for the asset or liability. There may be an exception where an asset or liability arises as the result of an event other than a transaction, when it should be recognised at its fair value at the time it arose.

Where the current value is being used, assets or liabilities should be recognised at their value at the time at which they arise.

In practice, this means, that in nearly all cases, assets and liabilities will be recognised initially at their transaction cost regardless of the measurement basis that is being used. Where a transaction takes place at arm's length, the current value of any assets or liabilities acquired or assumed should be precisely equal to the fair value of the consideration given or received in exchange for that asset or liability.

Unless there is evidence to the contrary, which might arise in relation to a transaction with a related party, for example, it should be assumed that all transactions take place at fair value. This makes accounting easier, since the determination of the amount at which an item will be recorded should then be determined according to whichever element of the transaction is easiest to value.

1.7.6   Remeasurement

In theory, it would be possible to use a pure historical cost basis for preparing financial statements. Items would be stated at their historic costs and the amounts would never be altered for any changes in value. In practice, such a basis is never used. The historical cost basis is usually taken to mean that items are stated at their historic cost, except that:

- assets are written down to take account of a decrease in their recoverable amount, and
- monetary assets and liabilities denominated in a foreign currency are retranslated to take account of movements in exchange rates.

In the second case, the items are still stated at their historic costs in terms of the underlying currency.

The current value basis involves taking account of other changes in value, on the condition that there is evidence of a change in value and that change in value can be reliably quantified. As stated at various points in the *Statement of Principles*, the question of reliability is dependent on having sufficient evidence: and what is sufficient can be a matter of judgement.

What constitutes sufficient evidence will be affected by:

- current information directly relating to the item, such as the condition and current selling price of stock items;
- other entities' transactions in similar assets and liabilities, such as recent transactions in unquoted company shares, and

- past experience with similar items, such as the level of previous warranty claims.

1.7.7 Measurement issues

The *Statement of Principles* identifies a number of issues connected with the measurement of the value of assets and liabilities.

The simplest of these issues is that of going concern. In most cases, it should be assumed that a company is going to continue in existence for the foreseeable future. This has a major impact on valuation bases. For example, recoverable amount is relevant whether historic costs or current value measurement bases are being used, and is defined as the higher of value in use and net realisable value. If a company is not a going concern then the value in use of an asset is no longer relevant, or put another way, is necessarily equal to the item's net realisable value. This could have a major effect on the amounts shown in financial statements.

A more complicated issue is that of discounting. This matter is discussed in far more detail in the ASB Working Paper *Discounting in Financial Reporting*, but the ASB's basic approach to the issue is set out in the *Statement of Principles*. In principle, the ASB supports the use of discounting in virtually all areas of financial reporting. The argument for this approach is that all fair value transactions with effects spread over time already implicitly take account of the time value of money. If this is the case, then all relevant amounts shown in financial statements should similarly take account of that value. For example, if a company takes out a loan to meet a liability and the loan is to be repaid in ten years' time the amount of the principal does not reflect the amount that it will actually pay over the ten years, since it will also have to pay interest over this period. If, alternatively, a company were to enter an agreement to pay the liability in ten years' time, the amount payable would be much higher to reflect the deferred payment. In substance, there is no difference between the two situations and they should be accounted for in the same way. (Of course, there is a difference between the transactions, but this relates to the timing of cash flows, and will be shown in the cash flow statement of each of the ten years.)

The third issue addressed is that of uncertainty. There is often some uncertainty in determining the value of an asset or liability. As with initial recognition, items should only be remeasured if the basis of remeasurement is sufficiently reliable. Prudence is relevant in determining the meaning of sufficiency.

So long as there is both a generally accepted estimation technique and confirmatory evidence it is possible to value an asset or liability.

The approaches mentioned are as follows.

(1)   Market-based measures, so long as there is a reasonably efficient market

for the items. For example, a small stake in a quoted company can be measured with sufficient reliability. It may be more complicated where there is no obvious market based measure. For example, a large stake in a quoted company may be much more difficult to measure since the price would be affected by the fact of disposal.

(2) Expected values, where the population of similar items is large enough to make this approach feasible. For example, a company may be unable to determine which of its debts will not be recoverable, but may be able to use previous experience to determine the total expected level of bad debts.

Other bases are not likely to be as effective, and another best estimate needs to be used. In some cases this may involve recognition of the minimum value.

In cases where there is uncertainty, this should be dealt with through the use of disclosure, to avoid giving the impression that a valuation is more reliable than it really is.

The final issue addressed is that of price changes, or inflation. The *Statement of Principles* stresses the importance of the difference between returns on capital and returns of capital. It then goes on to state that the distinctions drawn in the *Statement of Principles* are satisfactory where prices are stable, but become much less useful where there are significant changes in the general level of prices.

If inflation were high, then adjustments would be needed to distinguish between the maintenance of a company's capital and the return it has generated after maintaining its capital.

If specific types of price change significantly, then an approach would be needed that provides information that distinguishes between the effect of those price changes and all other changes.

1.7.8   The impact of the Statement of Principles

The basis of valuation which the *Statement of Principles* finds unacceptable (the use of values that were current at some time in the past) was largely eliminated by FRS 15, subject to its transitional provisions.

Some of the principles on valuation, preferred by the ASB, are reflected in FRS 11.

1.8 PRESENTATION OF FINANCIAL INFORMATION

1.8.1 *Principles*

The *Statement of Principles* identifies financial statements as the primary financial statements taken together with the notes to these statements, which are intended to amplify and explain those primary statements.

The primary financial statements are taken to be:

- the statement of financial performance (however described, and whether one statement or more);
- the statement of financial position (or balance sheet), and
- the cash flow statement.

The presentation of information on financial performance is intended to focus on the components of that performance, and on the characteristics of those components.

The presentation of information on financial position is intended to focus on the types and function of assets and liabilities, and on the relationships between them.

The presentation of cash flow information is intended to show the extent to which the company's various activities generate and use cash, and, in particular, to distinguish between the cash flows attributable to the company's operations and its other cash flows.

Disclosure of information in the notes to the financial statements is stated to be no substitute for recognition in the primary statements, and does not correct or justify any misrepresentation or omission in those statements.

1.8.2 *Manner of presentation*

The *Statement of Principles* includes the statement that:

> ... the objective of the presentation adopted is to communicate clearly and effectively and in as simple and straightforward a manner as is possible without loss of relevance or reliability and without unnecessarily increasing the length of the financial statements. (Para. 7.1, *Statement of Principles.*)

This statement is hardly objectionable, and could almost warrant being stated as a basic principle in its own right.

The statement goes on to note that it is not practical or appropriate for financial statements to attempt to show every aspect of every transaction or event. Financial statements would be virtually impossible to interpret sensibly if the mass of detail were to be included. The information included in financial statements is highly aggregated, simplified and abstracted and, to a greater or lesser extent, interpreted. This is not seen to be a major problem, as if this process is undertaken properly, the information will be of greater value than the detail since it will:

- convey information that might otherwise be obscured;
- highlight items, and relationships between items, that are of the greatest significance;
- facilitate comparison with the financial statements of other enterprises, and
- be more understandable to users.

The intention of the primary statements is to provide a high level overview of the performance, position and cash flows of the company. The notes are then intended to achieve the following.

(1) They should provide more detailed information on items that have been included in the primary financial statements, such as breakdowns of figures.

(2) They should provide context for, or in some cases an alternative view of, items which have been recognised in the primary statements. For example, where a balance is subject to uncertainty, the primary financial statements will include one amount, but the notes would mention the uncertainties, and might provide a range of possible values, or a maximum, or other relevant information. Similarly, where items are stated at historic costs the notes might cover fair value.

(3) They should provide information that is not included in the primary statements.

For example, a company may have a contingent asset which it does not recognise, in accordance with FRS 12, yet it may disclose the existence of this item in the notes.

1.8.3 Statement of financial performance

The *Statement of Principles* states that it is not important whether there is one statement of financial performance or more, not surprisingly given the ASB's earlier introduction of the statement of total recognised gains and losses. It does, however, state that the headings used, and the items allocated to those headings, are of fundamental importance. Headings are seen as crucial as the items included in statements of performance vary in their characteristics, and this needs to be properly reflected in the way in which they are presented.

The *Statement of Principles* describes good presentation of financial performance as involving:

- recognising only gains and losses in the statement of financial performance (which would imply the removal of dividends, as these are distributions to owners, not losses);

- classifying components by reference to a combination of functions (such as production, selling and administration) and nature (such as employment costs and interest);
- distinguishing amounts that are affected in different ways by changes in economic conditions or business activity (for example, by the provision of segmental information);
- identifying items that are unusual in amount or incidence, judged by reference to the past or expectations of the future (for example, through requirements for the disclosure of exceptional items);
- identifying items that have special characteristics, such as financing costs and tax, and
- identifying items that are related primarily to profits of future periods, rather than the current period, such as research and development.

There should also be a minimum of netting off of items in the performance statement or statements. Gains and losses should only be offset where:

- they relate to the same event or circumstances, and
- disclosing the gross amounts would neither be useful for assessing future results nor for assessing the results of past transactions or events.

The example given is that of the disposal of a fixed asset, where both of the conditions are considered to be satisfied.

1.8.4   Statement of financial position (balance sheet)

The *Statement of Principles* describes good presentation of a company's financial position as involving the following.

(1)   Recognising only assets, liabilities and ownership interest in the balance sheet.

(2)   Delineating the company's resource structure (major classes of asset) and finance structure (major classes of liability and ownership interest). The form of presentation adopted should reflect the nature and liquidity of resources, and the timing of obligations.

(3)   Distinguishing assets by function.

1.8.5   Accompanying information

Financial statements are often accompanied by other information. Such other information may be as a result of statutory requirements, such as a directors' report for a company, or required by listing rules for certain companies, or simply best practice.

The sort of information that may be provided includes trend information, operating and financial reviews, Chairmen's statements, etc.

The aim behind such information is the same as that for the financial statements themselves. It should aim to provide relevant information on the financial performance and position of the company. However, the way in which it does this is very different.

(1)   For example, such information is often in the form of narrative, rather than numbers. While financial statements also include narrative information, inevitably they concentrate most on those areas that can be quantified.

(2)   The information may include historical trends and summaries. Financial statements, in the UK, normally only cover the current and one previous period.

(3)   The information may not be financial in nature, or even have any direct financial effect.

(4)   The information may be in areas that are not yet normally encompassed in accounting and financial reports, such as environmental reports.

The information needs to be consistent with that included in the financial statements, whether or not it relates directly to items that are addressed in those statements or otherwise.

The *Statement of Principles* specifically mentions the need for an Operating and Financial Review, where a company's situation is complex, as is likely to be the case for a company with listed securities. It mentions that such an analysis of the financial performance and position should discuss the following.

(1)   The main factors affecting the company's performance, including the main risks, uncertainties and trends involved in each main business area, and how the company is responding to them.

(2)   The effect of the company's financial position, including the approach it adopts to capital structure and treasury matters.

(3)   The activities and expenditure of the period that can be regarded as an investment of the future. This will cover items that might be considered 'assets' in the colloquial sense of the term, but do not meet the accounting definition or the recognition criteria.

1.8.6   Highlights and summary indicators

Some companies produce highlights and summary indicators, which may be included in or with financial statements. While these cannot present a full picture, they do still have a role in providing information to users whose needs are limited and in providing an introduction to the company's performance and position, which may then be fleshed out by proceeding to the detailed financial statements.

1.9 ACCOUNTING FOR INTERESTS IN OTHER ENTITIES

1.9.1 Principles

The question of group accounting is dealt with in the *Statement of Principles* primarily in the section covering the reporting entity. The final section of the statement also makes some additional comments on group accounting, but focuses primarily on other types of investment which a company may have.

It points out that individual company and group accounts present the interests that a company may have from different perspectives.

When individual company accounts deal with interests in other entities they do so from the perspective of the income and, depending on the measurement basis adopted, the capital growth arising from those interests.

In group accounts, the situation is slightly more complicated, as interests in other entities may be accounted for in one of three ways:

- where there is control, this is dealt with by including the other entity's performance and position in full within the group accounts, then adjusting for the element, if any, that is not attributable to the group;
- where there is joint control or significant influence, the group accounts include the group's share of the results and position, but do not show the whole of the items, to reflect the fact that there is no control, or
- where there is no control, joint control or significant influence, the interests are shown in the same way as with any other asset, and therefore in the same way as they would be treated in individual company accounts.

Group accounts show the interests of all the companies under the control of the parent, but they still do so from the perspective of the shareholders of the parent. As a result, they need to include any items associated with holdings by other shareholders separately, hence the inclusion of minority interests. (The position taken in the statement differs from that under international requirements. IFRS dealing with groups now take far more account of the interests of others, not just the shareholders in the parent, when determining how group accounts should be put together and what disclosure should be provided.)

In terms of business combinations, transactions should be classified according to their nature. Where one company takes control of another it treats this as an acquisition by accounting for each of the assets and liabilities it has acquired, including any goodwill. Where two companies come together to form a new entity where neither party has taken control of the other, this is a merger, and the amounts are treated as though the new entity had always existed. (This is another area where differences remain between UK GAAP and IFRS. IFRS does not recognise the existence of mergers in the way that UK GAAP does, albeit in fairly rare cases. IFRS does allow treatments that are akin to merger accounting, but these are in situations where entities that were already under common control are brought together.)

1.9.2 The role of influence

Investments in other entities can take a number of forms, but the driver of the accounting treatment to be adopted is the degree of influence over the operating and financial policies which the investing company has in respect of the other party.

The comments on degrees of influence included in the *Statement of Principles* are consistent with the rules included in FRS 2 and FRS 9. As it points out, influence normally comes from shareholding, but this is not the only way in which influence can arise, or be demonstrated.

In individual company accounts, little account is taken of the degree of influence. Since such statements only deal with assets and liabilities that are directly controlled by the company, there is no place for assets which are only indirectly controlled, or are merely influenced.

In group accounts, account is taken of assets which are indirectly controlled or influenced. The aim of all of the rules is to equate the accounting treatment with the degree of influence exercised. In the case of control, the reporting company is able to determine the uses to which the assets and liabilities should be put. As a result, it should include the whole of those assets and liabilities. At the same time, it does not always have an exclusive interest in the assets and liabilities and must therefore show the amounts that are attributable to other persons. Hence the inclusion of minority interests. Where there is joint control or significant influence, the company is able to affect the use of assets and liabilities, but not to determine that use. As a result, the appropriate accounting treatment is to account for its share of those assets and liabilities. In other cases, the company cannot directly affect the uses to which assets and liabilities are put, and it is therefore appropriate that they are not reflected.

1.9.3 The impact of the Statement of Principles

The areas which this section of the *Statement of Principles* deals with are covered by FRS 2, FRS 6, FRS 7 and FRS 9.

2   GENERAL REQUIREMENTS

2.1   INTRODUCTION

2.1.1   Sources of requirements

There are a number of requirements that apply to all items included in financial statements, rather than any particular areas. The matters with which they deal have an impact on the basic manner in which financial statements are put together, and in some cases on the information included in the underlying accounting records.

The main such requirements are:

- the statutory requirement for financial statements to give a true and fair view;
- the requirements of FRS 18, *Accounting Policies*, to comply with some basic principles in preparing financial statements and to disclose accounting policies, and
- the requirement of FRS 5 to report the substance of a company's transactions rather than the form of those transactions.

This chapter provides an introduction to these areas. Inevitably, there is some overlap with the areas that have been covered in Chapter 1, which covered the *Statement of Principles* produced by the ASB. The main difference is that this chapter deals only with items that have actually been brought into practice in the UK, either through legislation or through accounting standards. Chapter 1 also deals with areas which are covered by the ASB in their *Statement of Principles*, but which have not had any direct impact on required practice.

2.2   TRUE AND FAIR

2.2.1   The development of true and fair

The idea that financial statements must give a 'true and fair view' has been present in UK legislation since 1947, although similar phrases had been used in earlier statutes. (While the manner in which the requirement to give a true and fair view is covered in statute has changed somewhat with the introduction of the Companies Act 2006, the basic requirement remains.) Nonetheless, earlier legislation had used terms which indicated a degree of objectivity in financial reporting that is probably not attainable. 'Fairness' introduces an element of subjectivity into the assessment of accounting practices that is not present in the term which had previously been used – 'correct'. In this sense the term can be contrasted with 'true', which also seems to be an objective phrase.

It is perhaps useful to attempt to draw some distinction between truth and fairness. The easiest way of doing this is to use a simple example, that of window dressing. Window dressing takes place where a company undertakes a transaction with the primary intention of altering the appearance of its balance sheet. Since the transaction has actually taken place, and has been recorded, the view presented by the balance sheet could be considered to be true; that is, in accordance with the facts. However, it could not be said to be fair; that is, presenting a reasonable picture of the state of affairs of the company. For this reason, full disclosure of the nature of the transaction needs to be provided. For many years this was a specific requirement of SSAP 17 *Accounting for Post Balance Sheet Events* and the FRSSE. When SSAP 17 was replaced with FRS 21, *Events After the Balance Sheet Date*, back in 2005, the specific reference to window dressing in UK GAAP was removed. However, this did not and does not cause any change in practice, since the conflict between truth and fairness will remain and disclosure, therefore, continues to be required.

2.2.2   The meaning of GAAP

One way of defining true and fair might be to state that accounts have been drawn up in accordance with GAAP. However, we could then define GAAP in at least three ways.

Generally accepted accounting principles

Have the financial statements been drawn up in accordance with the basic principles such as going concern, accruals and consistency? On this definition, truth and fairness would be a very broad concept indeed, able to accommodate a wide range of alternative accounting treatments for like items. In effect, this would mean that companies would have little but the basic principles set out in FRS 18 and the statutory instruments supporting the Companies Act 2006 in order to determine their accounting treatments and practices.

Generally accepted accounting policies

For this purpose, policies are those reporting rules which have been codified through, for example, Statements of Standard Accounting Practice, Financial Reporting Standards, Urgent Issues Task Force Consensus Pronouncements and the statutory instruments supporting the Companies Act 2006.

If this definition were to be used, then a company would have a free choice of any methods that are contained in accounting guidance, regardless of how appropriate or inappropriate they might be to the circumstances of the company. In areas without guidance, companies would need to refer to the fundamental accounting principles.

Generally accepted accounting practice

This would include all of the items that fall under policies, as defined above, but would also include elements derived from accumulated professional judgement. This would limit still further the range of accounting practices deemed to be acceptable. An example might be the choice of the method of defining a segment for segmental reporting purposes. This matter is not unambiguously covered in either the statutory instruments supporting the Companies Act 2006 or in SSAP 25, but a range of accepted practices has grown up.

Similarly, this might serve to limit the accounting treatments which a company could adopt even though those methods were specifically mentioned in guidance. The use of an accounting treatment allowed by guidance, but not generally seen as acceptable in the circumstances the company faces, would not be allowed.

This requirement is effectively itself now codified, as FRS 18 contains the following.

> Where it is necessary to choose between accounting policies . . . an entity should select whichever of those accounting policies is judged by the entity to be most appropriate to its particular circumstances for the purpose of giving a true and fair view. (Para. 17, FRS 18.)

This means that, even where there is a choice of accounting policies set out in either statute or an accounting standard, companies are not supposed to make their choice freely. They should choose the most appropriate of the nominally available policies.

It is this meaning of GAAP that is the one normally applied.

2.3   MEANINGS OF TRUE AND FAIR

2.3.1   *Consistent with generally accepted accounting policies and practice*

A good starting point for defining true and fair is to say that the accounting practices that are followed are derived from those that are included in the available set of practices. This would mean that accounting practices are, for example, included in standards, legislation or supported by the judgement of the accounting profession. If this were an acceptable definition of true and fair, then a company would make a choice between the practices that are generally accepted. This definition would view accounting principles as fundamental concepts which have been translated into reporting rules by regulatory bodies such as the Accounting Standards Board or by general professional agreement. Financial statements would be seen as being true and fair if the accounting policies that have been adopted in their preparation fall within the generally accepted reporting rules.

Part of the generally accepted rules is that the format of accounts should comply with that set out in Sch. 1 to The Large and Medium-sized Companies and Groups (Accounts and Reports) Regulations 2008 (SI 2008/410). Two balance sheet formats and four profit and loss formats are allowed. Below, format 1 is shown for the consolidated balance sheet and consolidated profit and loss account. (These differ from the balance sheet and profit and loss account format for an individual company in having certain other headings, such as minority interests, which apply only where group accounts are being prepared.)

Consolidated balance sheet – format 1

(A) Called up share capital not paid

(B) Fixed assets

    (I) Intangible assets

        (1) Development costs

        (2) Concessions, patents, licences, trade marks and similar rights and assets

        (3) Goodwill

        (4) Payments on account

    (II) Tangible assets

        (1) Land and buildings

        (2) Plant and machinery

        (3) Fixtures, fittings, tools and equipment

        (4) Payments on account and assets in course of construction

    (III) Investments

        (1) Shares in group undertakings

        (2) Loans to group undertakings

        (3) Interests in associated undertakings

        (4) Other participating interests

        (5) Loans to undertakings in which the company has a participating interest

        (6) Other investments other than loans

        (7) Other loans

        (8) Own shares

(C) Current assets

    (I)   Stocks

        (1) Raw materials and consumables

        (2) Work in progress

        (3) Finished goods and goods for resale

        (4) Payments on account

    (II)   Debtors

        (1) Trade debtors

        (2) Amounts owed by group undertakings

        (3) Amounts owed by undertakings in which the company has a participating interest

        (4) Other debtors

        (5) Called up share capital not paid

        (6) Prepayments and accrued income

    (III) Investments

        (1) Shares in group undertakings

        (2) Own shares

        (3) Other investments

    (IV) Cash at bank and in hand

(D) Prepayments and accrued income

(E) Creditors: amounts falling due within one year

    (1) Debenture loans

    (2) Bank loans and overdrafts

    (3) Payments received on account

    (4) Trade creditors

    (5) Bills of exchange payable

    (6) Amounts owed to group undertakings

    (7) Amounts owed to undertakings in which the company has a participating interest

    (8) Other creditors, including taxation and social security

    (9) Accruals and deferred income

(F) Net current assets (liabilities)

(G) Total assets less current liabilities

(H)   Creditors: amounts falling due after more than one year

    (1)   Debenture loans

    (2)   Bank loans and overdrafts

    (3)   Payments received on account

    (4)   Trade creditors

    (5)   Bills of exchange payable

    (6)   Amounts owed to group undertakings

    (7)   Amounts owed to undertakings in which the company has a participating interest

    (8)   Other creditors, including taxation and social security

    (9)   Accruals and deferred income

(I)   Provisions for liabilities

    (1)   Pensions and similar obligations

    (2)   Taxation, including deferred taxation

    (3)   Other provisions

(J)   Accruals and deferred income

(K)   Capital and reserves

    (I)   Called up share capital
    (II)   Share premium account
    (III) Revaluation reserve
    (IV)   Other reserves

        (1)   Capital redemption reserve

        (2)   Reserve for own shares

        (3)   Reserves provided for by the articles of association

        (4)   Other reserves

    (V)   Profit and loss account

(L)   Minority interests

Consolidated profit and loss account – format 1

(1)   Turnover

(2)   Cost of sales

(3)   Gross profit or loss

(4)   Distribution costs

(5)   Administrative expenses

(6)   Other operating income

(7)   Income from shares in group undertakings

(8)   Income from interests in associated undertakings

(9)   Income from other participating interests

(10)   Income from other fixed asset investments

(11)   Other interest receivable and similar income

(12)   Amounts written off investments

(13)   Interest payable and similar charges

(14)   Tax on profit or loss on ordinary activities

(15)   Profit or loss on ordinary activities after taxation

(16)   Minority interests

(17)   Extraordinary income

(18)   Extraordinary charges

(19)   Extraordinary profit or loss

(20)   Tax on extraordinary profit or loss

(21)   Minority interests (in extraordinary items)

(22)   Other taxes not shown under the above items

(23)   Profit or loss for the financial year

2.3.2 Consistent with appropriate generally accepted accounting policies and practice

This second definition is an enhancement of the first, because it introduces another vital criterion. Not only must the accounting practices adopted be taken from the set of treatments available, but they must also be the most appropriate of these treatments for the individual business. Effectively, each business no longer has a free choice of accounting practices within the limits set by standards and legislation. The choice of a practice must be dictated by the business's circumstances. The additional criterion is effectively a 'catch-all' clause, intended to ensure that practices are adopted that are consistent not just with the letter of standards and legislation, but also with the spirit.

Of course, this approach to true and fair has little to say about the criteria that should be used to distinguish appropriate from non-appropriate currently acceptable accounting treatments. Accounting treatments that have developed within a particular industry sector may provide some guidance as to what is appropriate, but considerable help is given by the notion that the accounting treatment should reflect the economic substance of the situation. This is discussed in the next section.

As noted earlier, FRS 18 states that it is this approach that companies must use in the preparation of their financial statements, as it refers specifically to the requirement for companies to choose the most appropriate treatment in the circumstances that apply to them. As dealt with below, FRS 18 also sets out some of the criteria that should be applied in determining whether an accounting policy is the most appropriate in a particular case.

2.3.3 Reflecting the substance of transactions

This approach to true and fair implies that the financial statements should be a reflection of the economic position of the company. The key question in deciding the accounting treatment is then, 'will the treatment in the financial statements show the position and progress of a business to a prospective or current shareholder with no inside knowledge of the company?' This is another example of a 'catch-all' clause, but a more restrictive one than before. Although the criterion may be used to identify an appropriate accounting treatment from currently accepted practices, it may also go beyond what is currently acceptable in order to provide investors with adequate information.

For the vast majority of transactions, choosing an appropriate treatment from those which are generally accepted will also reflect the substance of the transaction. The two criteria will suggest the same type of treatment. Accounting standards and statutes provide methods by which the requirement to provide a true and fair view normally can be met. However, when the principle of true and fair is defined explicitly so as to reflect the substance of transactions, this may assist in determining the appropriate accounting treatment.

Whilst it is likely that consideration of the substance of transactions may enrich the implementation and interpretation of accounting standards, there is a danger that financial reporting may become too subjective. If companies were simply to pass directly to the basic principles and entirely ignore the current accounting practices adopted by other companies, investors may well consider the information too unreliable for their purposes. Making comparisons between companies would be difficult for investors.

To a certain extent, the expectations of users of accounts are determined by the nature and extent of information normally disclosed in financial statements. Any company that sought to radically alter its accounting practices, on the basis that the proposed treatments and disclosures would give a true and fair view, would not be meeting the expectations of the users of the accounts. This would itself mean that the accounts would not give a true and fair view, since users would be liable to misinterpret the information provided, and not gain an accurate assessment of the position and progress of the business.

This economic substance definition of true and fair is also, in fact, incorporated in the Companies Act. Presumably, it is this logic that justifies what is commonly called 'the true and fair override'. Companies are required by the Act to breach specific statutory rules, and specific rules contained in accounting standards, where this is necessary in order that a true and fair view be given. Such cases are rare, but the Companies Act still allows for such situations.

Where a company departs from the specific provisions of the Act in order to ensure that its accounts give a true and fair view, an explanation for the departure, together with a statement of its effect, must be provided. This is required by s. 396 of the Companies Act 2006 in the case of individual accounts, and s. 404 of the Companies Act 2006 in the case of group accounts. This statutory requirement is then expanded upon in FRS 18, for companies which are not complying with the FRSSE.

The disclosures required by FRS 18 are:

- a clear and unambiguous statement that there has been a departure from the requirements of an accounting standard, a UITF abstract or companies legislation, and that the departure is necessary in order for the financial statements to give a true and fair view;
- a statement of the treatment which the standard, abstract or Act would normally require, together with a description of the treatment that has actually been adopted;
- a statement as to why the prescribed treatment would not give a true and fair view, and
- a description of how the position shown in the financial statements differs as a result of the departure, including quantification unless this is already evident from the accounts, or if it is not possible to quantify, in which case a statement of the reason should be provided.

Identical disclosure is required by the FRSSE (other than that it refers to non-compliance with the FRSSE itself, rather than accounting standards and UITF abstracts).

These disclosures should be given immediately after the statement that the financial statements have been prepared in accordance with applicable accounting standards, if the company is required to provide this. (Only companies which are neither small nor medium-sized are required to provide this statement. In practice, many small and medium-sized companies provide the statement anyway.) Where the situation continues, the explanatory disclosures should be given in the financial statements of each year which is affected, even if the impact is only on the comparative period.

Another, somewhat less drastic, route for the accounts to reflect economic substance is to make additional disclosures about the company's position. This is also required by the Companies Act when necessary for the accounts to give a true and fair view. In effect, taken together, this means that for larger entities:

- The Large and Medium-sized Companies and Groups (Accounts and Reports) Regulations 2008 (SI 2008/410) and other parts of the Companies Act 2006 represent the minimum requirement, and
- the true and fair override should be invoked only when additional disclosure would be insufficient for a true and fair view.

There are similar provisions internationally. IAS 1 also allows companies to breach specific requirements of International Financial Reporting Standards (IFRS) where this is necessary in order to give a true and fair view. (Strictly, it refers to where it is necessary to depart where compliance would conflict with the objective of financial statements as set out in the IASB's Framework, rather than where the treatment would not give a true and fair view, but the import is virtually identical.) A similar provision has been included in the IFRS for SMEs. As with UK standards, such circumstances are expected to be extremely rare.

Potential impact of the FRSME

The draft of the FRSME, itself based on the IFRS for SMEs, contains the same requirement that where compliance with other provisions of the standard would conflict with the objective of financial statements as set out in the FRSME, then the entity must depart from the specific requirement. Details of such departures are required.

2.3.4 True and fair and small companies

The concept of truth and fairness causes particular problems when applied to the financial statement of small companies. Small companies are allowed to prepare their financial statements in accordance with:

- The Small Companies and Groups (Accounts and Directors' Report) Regulations 2008 (SI 2008/409), and
- the Financial Reporting Standard for Smaller Entities (FRSSE), in whichever version is currently in force. (This is currently the version effective April 2008.)

While neither includes fundamental differences in terms of quantification from the requirements applicable to larger entities, both of these contain a wide range of exemptions from disclosure. Their accounts are still, however, considered to be capable of giving a true and fair view.

The FRSSE specifically addresses the issue of the truth and fairness of small company accounts, and requires that:

> The balance sheet must give a true and fair view of the state of affairs of the company as at the end of the financial year; and the profit and loss account must give a true and fair view of the profit or loss of the company for the financial year. The directors of the company must, in determining how amounts are presented within items in the profit and loss account and balance sheet, have regard to the substance of the reported transaction or arrangement, in accordance with

generally accepted accounting principles or practice. To determine the substance of a transaction it is necessary to identify whether the transaction has given rise to new assets or liabilities for the reporting entity and whether it has changed the entity's existing assets or liabilities. (Para. 2.2, FRSSE 2008.)

This seems to equate truth and fairness with the principle of substance over form. It is an unstated assumption of the FRSSE that, in general, compliance with the disclosure requirements contained within it (including those of statute which are quoted as part of the FRSSE) is sufficient to give a true and fair view. However, there are some borderline cases:

Where there is doubt whether applying provisions of the FRSSE would be sufficient to give a true and fair view, adequate explanation should be given in the notes to the accounts of the transaction or arrangement concerned and the treatment adopted. (Para. 2.5, FRSSE 2008.)

There are dangers with the approach adopted by the FRSSE and by all other accounting standards. If the same phrase is used to refer to very different requirements then problems may arise. The directors of an expanding company may find it difficult to grasp why their financial statements, which have always been deemed and even explicitly stated to give a true and fair view in the past, suddenly fail to do so. They may argue that if they have made no changes in their accounting policies or procedures, if their business has not altered other than through expansion, and they provide precisely the same level of disclosure as before, then how can their accounts be considered not to give a true and fair view any more? This is one of the problems that stem from having different disclosure requirements based on measures of size rather than other criteria. For example, few would object to the fact that companies which do not have listed securities are not required to disclose earnings per share. This difference is based on an underlying difference in status, not on size as such.

The question of small company accounting raises a number of very serious questions about the meaning of the term true and fair. It has long been the case that alternative treatments have been allowed for many items in accounts and that different disclosures have been required. Current small company rules, however, greatly extend the areas of difference. This problem would not go away with the proposed changes to UK GAAP, since it is intended that the FRSSE remain in place. It is relevant, however, that the proposals for larger companies draw a distinction between medium-sized entities and public interest entities. Despite the terminology that is applied, the distinction is connected more with the nature of reporting entities than their size.

2.3.5   True and fair and the Fourth Directive

True and fair is no longer a principle that exists only in the law of the UK (and certain other countries which have been influenced by UK accounting). It is now contained in the accounting rules of the European Union.

2. General Requirements

Early drafts of the European Union Fourth Company Law Directive (the Fourth Directive) simply referred to the principles of regular and proper accounting, making no reference to the requirement that financial statements provide a true and fair view. The true and fair phrase was used in drafts for a revised Directive by 1974, and it is now a requirement of Art. 2 of the Directive that company financial statements give 'a true and fair view of the company's assets, liabilities, financial position and profit or loss'.

In the final version of the Directive, true and fair has two implications.

(1) If following the provisions of the Directive would not lead the financial statements to give a true and fair view, then additional disclosure should be given.

(2) In certain cases, true and fair may mean that departures will need to be made from the individual provisions of the Directive.

In the case of the second implication, Member States have been given the right to draw up definitions of when a case is so exceptional that the need to give a true and fair view should override the detailed treatment rules of the Directive. This case is important in the UK since the implementation of true and fair is usually discussed in terms of measurement rather than in terms of disclosure.

Certainly, in the view of the European Union, disclosure can be a major contributor to giving a true and fair view. Therefore, the additional disclosure route, implication 1, is likely to be the more common response on the Continent.

One danger with the use of a subjective criterion such as true and fair is that there is some potential for abuse. Companies may evade the express requirements of legislation by stating that compliance would not lead to the financial statements giving a true and fair view. Where such a practice becomes widespread, it may be, or at least be seen as, an abuse of the principle. (In Australia, for example, the equivalent of the true and fair override was abolished many years ago as a result of perceived abuses.)

Much modern accounting research supports the idea that disclosure may be more important than accounting measurement. This is based on two ideas.

(1) It is impossible to provide financial statements which will meet the needs of all possible users of those financial statements, so it may be better to provide them with sufficient information to make their own assessments.

(2) Users should be able to process accounting information to construct performance measures for their own purposes.

However, using disclosure as a substitute for adequate accounting measurement should be approached with caution. There is some evidence to indicate that users are not sophisticated in their use of financial statements, and therefore may not look beyond the basic numbers on the face of the accounts.

2.4   THE ACCOUNTING 'PRINCIPLES' OF FRS 18

2.4.1   Introduction

FRS 18 *Accounting Policies* has been mandatory since 2001. The FRSSE reflects the requirements of FRS 18. As a result, comments on the application of the FRSSE are made in the following sections only where there is a significant difference between the requirements of FRS 18 and the FRSSE.

FRS 18 continues to differ from the *Statement of Principles*. It makes no attempt to provide anything approaching a theory of accounting and is solely intended to provide guidance on some basic ideas that should be used in the preparation of financial statements. The standard itself makes little attempt to justify the use of these concepts.

2.4.2   Going concern

FRS 18 does not strictly define going concern, nor does it address this issue in term of concepts or principles. However, with regard to going concern this is of limited practical relevance as it states that information provided by financial statements is usually most relevant if it is prepared on the hypothesis that the company is to continue in operational existence for the foreseeable future. It then goes on to note that this hypothesis is commonly referred to as the 'going concern assumption'. FRS 18 explains that the going concern basis is used because measures based on break-up values are not usually relevant to users seeking to assess a company's ability to generate cash or its financial adaptability. The assumption of going concern status is more important than might at first appear. For example, it underpins the recording of items as fixed assets, and justifies valuation bases which do not take account of the value of items in their current state. Stock, for example, is usually stated at the lower of cost and net realisable value. For items that will not be sold on in their current form, net realisable value takes account of events and actions that are expected and have yet to occur. If the going concern assumption were not applied, then stock would have to be stated at the lower of its cost and its sales value in its current condition. For most raw materials and, especially, work in progress, the value in current condition is likely to be significantly lower than cost.

FRS 18 requires that:

An entity should prepare its financial statements on a going concern basis, unless:

(a)   the entity is being liquidated or has ceased trading, or

(b)   the directors either intend to liquidate the entity or to cease trading, or have no realistic alternative but to do so, in which circumstances the entity should prepare its financial statements on a basis other than that of a going concern. (Para. 21, FRS 18, as amended by FRS 21.)

This differs from the version of FRS 18 prior to FRS 21, since at that time even an intention to liquidate or cease trading was not considered sufficient to warrant moving away from the use of the going concern basis.

If the directors are aware of material uncertainties relating to conditions or events which might cast significant doubt on the appropriateness of the going concern assumption, FRS 18 requires these to be disclosed. This requirement has been of increasing relevance in the last few years. It has also been supplemented by guidance issued by the Financial Reporting Council and addressed to company directors. The latest such guidance was issued in October 2009, and applies to accounting periods ending on or after 31 December 2009. Such guidance is not an accounting standard, nor does it override any of the requirements of FRS 18. Instead, it is intended to provide company directors with assistance in the approach they should adopt to determine the going concern status of the companies of which they are directors, and in making any necessary disclosure required as a result of such consideration.

FRS 18 also notes that the degree of consideration necessary to make an assessment of a company's ability to continue as a going concern depends on the facts of each case.

The FRS points out that a history of profitable operations, which are expected to continue, and ready access to financial resources, indicates that detailed analysis may not be necessary. However, there may also be cases where the directors will need to assess a wide range of factors surrounding current and expected profitability, debt repayment schedules and potential sources of replacement financing. FRS 18 indicates that these considerations also govern the length of time in respect of which the assessment should be made.

FRS 18 contains disclosure requirements where the going concern assumption is not adopted. These are dealt with below.

Potential impact of the FRSME

There is a potentially significant change proposed in the FRSME. This would continue to require directors to make an assessment of a company's ability to continue as a going concern and the de facto definition of 'going concern' would remain the same. However, the period which the directors are required to consider is a minimum of twelve months from the reporting date, not twelve months from the date of approval of the financial statements. This could be important in some cases.

2.4.3 Accruals

As with going concern, accruals has been included in FRS 18. The notes on the development of the standard refer to these two concepts as being 'part of the bedrock of accounting and hence critical to the selection of accounting policies'. Specifically, FRS 18 requires that:

> An entity should prepare its financial statements, except for cash flow information, on the accrual basis of accounting. (Para. 26, FRS 18.)

FRS 18 explains that the accrual basis of accounting requires the non-cash effects of transactions and other events to be reflected, as far as is possible, in the financial statements for the accounting period in which they occur, and not, for example, in the period in which any cash involved is received or paid. The FRS points out that, in rare cases, it will not be possible to reflect the effect of transactions and other events in the financial statements for the accounting period in which they occur, if they are not yet capable of reliable measurement. In such circumstances, recognition will be deferred until reliable measurement is possible. This does not constitute an exception to the basic idea of accruals, but a limiting case.

The key to accruals under FRS 18 is the recognition of assets and liabilities under FRS 5 *Reporting the Substance of Transactions*. FRS 18 notes that the accruals concept lies at the heart of the definitions of assets and liabilities set out in FRS 5 and hence the use of FRS 5's definitions to determine the items to be recognised in the balance sheet is consistent with the accruals concept. An appendix to FRS 18 states that the accruals concept, as defined in FRS 18 and implicit in FRS 5's asset and liability definitions,

> . . . provides a discipline within which the matching process can operate, while still resulting in the simultaneous recognition of revenues and costs that result from the same transactions or events. (Para. 9, Appendix IV, FRS 18.)

FRS 5's definitions of assets and liabilities rely on the idea of 'rights or other access to future economic benefits' or 'obligations to transfer economic benefits', both as a result of past transactions and events. Some simple examples of the FRS 18 principle are as follow.

(1) The recognition of credit sales and trade debtors, and the derecognition of stock as an asset through its inclusion in cost of sales, at the time a sale is made, eg when rights to the benefits and risks inherent in the goods are transferred, rather than at the point at which cash is subsequently received. This is because the transfer of stock to the buyer creates a right to receive economic benefit, ie cash payment, at a later date.

(2) The prepayment of rent on a building, as an asset, ie cash, is transferred in return for rights to economic benefit through the use of the building to generate revenue either directly or indirectly for the period covered by the rental payment. Hence a prepayment can be recognised as an asset by

applying FRS 5's principles rather than those of matching, even though the practical effect is the same.

The application of the accruals concept may have been modified, in specific cases, by the issue of Application Note G to FRS 5, dealing with revenue recognition. This is dealt with separately in Chapter 4.

Accruals are also fundamental to accounting under IFRS. At the level of principle, there are no differences between UK accounting practice and IFRS, whether in their full versions or the IFRS for SMEs, although there are many cases where specific triggers for the recognition of items may differ. The IFRS for SMEs is very clearly based on the accrual concept being limited by the requirements in relation to assets and liabilities:

> This IFRS does not allow the recognition of items in the statement of financial positions that do not meet the definition of assets or of liabilities regardless of whether they result from applying the notion commonly referred to as the "matching concept" for measuring profit or loss. (Para. 2.45, IFRS for SMEs.)

Potential impact of the FRSME

There would be no significant changes coming out of the introduction of the FRSME. The text taken from the IFRS for SMEs quoted above is reproduced in the FRSME, with the only difference being the replacement of 'IFRS' with 'FRS'.

2.4.4 Realisation

Realisation is not really a principle of FRS 18. As a result, the standard does not include any requirements relating to realisation. But it does include some explanatory material. This includes the following point.

> It is generally accepted that profits shall be treated as realised, for these purposes, only when realised in the form either of cash or of other assets the ultimate cash realisation of which can be assessed with reasonable certainty. (Para. 28, FRS 18.)

This is then watered down somewhat as FRS 18 goes on to note that 'realised' may also cover profits relating to assets that are readily realisable.

The FRS notes the requirement in company law that only realised profits should be included in the profit and loss account and that realisation should be determined by reference to generally accepted principles at the time the financial statements are prepared. The FRS also notes that there might be special reasons for departing from these statutory requirements, but that such reasons will not exist unless, as a minimum, the company is satisfied that although a gain is unrealised, it nevertheless exists and can be measured with sufficient reliability. The FRS also points out that it might be necessary to invoke the statutory true and fair override in such cases.

Realisation is not really dealt with in international standards, except in some very specific areas. Realisation is often relevant for legal purposes, such as determining the lawfulness of a company dividend. Such matters are outside the scope of IFRS, even though IFRS can affect the lawfulness of transactions.

The ICAEW and ICAS jointly produce technical releases dealing with the issue of realisation of profits, under both UK GAAP and IFRS, the latest of which is Tech 02/10 *Guidance on the Determination of Realised Profits and Losses in the Context of Distributions Under the Companies Act 2006.*

2.4.5   Objectives and constraints in selecting policies

As noted above, FRS 18 requires that companies do not just choose their accounting policies from those that are generally available, or even those that are simply not prohibited, but that the policies adopted must be those that are most appropriate to the company's circumstances.

FRS 18 sets out specific objectives and constraints against which the appropriateness of accounting policies to the particular circumstances of an entity should be judged:

> The objectives against which an entity should judge the appropriateness of accounting policies to its particular circumstances are:
>
> (a)   relevance;
> (b)   reliability;
> (c)   comparability; and
> (d)   understandability. (Para. 30, FRS 18.)
>
> The constraints that an entity should take into account in judging the appropriateness of accounting policies to its particular circumstances are:
>
> (a)   the need to balance the different objectives set out in paragraph 30; and
> (b)   the need to balance the cost of providing information with the likely benefit of such information to users of the entity's financial statements. (Para. 31, FRS 18.)

The explanation of these objectives and constraints draws heavily on the ASB's *Statement of Principles for Financial Reporting*, which was dealt with in Chapter 1.

Relevance

FRS 18 explains that financial information is relevant if it has the ability to influence the economic decisions of users and is provided in time to influence those decisions. Relevant information possesses either predictive or confirmatory value or both.

FRS 18 also states that appropriate accounting policies will lead to the presentation of financial information that is relevant. Where more than one reliable accounting policy would achieve this result, the FRS notes that the most relevant accounting policy will be that which results in the financial information presented, as a whole, being as relevant as possible. In identifying that accounting policy, FRS 18 states that an entity must consider which measurement basis is most relevant and how to present information in the most relevant way.

Reliability

FRS 18 states that financial information is reliable if:

(a)   it can be depended upon by users to represent faithfully what it either purports to represent or could reasonably be expected to represent, and therefore reflects the substance of the transactions and other events that have taken place;

(b)   it is free from deliberate or systematic bias (ie it is neutral);

(c)   it is free from material error;

(d)   it is complete within the bounds of materiality; and

(e)   under conditions of uncertainty, it has been prudently prepared (ie a degree of caution has been applied in exercising judgement and making the necessary estimates). (Para. 35, FRS 18.)

This contains one of the few mentions of prudence in FRS 18. The FRS also provides the following explanation.

> Often there is uncertainty, either about the existence of assets, liabilities, gains, losses and changes to shareholders' funds, or about the amount at which they should be measured. Prudence requires that accounting policies take account of such uncertainty in recognising and measuring those assets, liabilities, gains, losses and changes to shareholders' funds. In conditions of uncertainty, appropriate accounting policies will require more confirmatory evidence about the existence of an asset or gain than about the existence of a liability or loss, and a greater reliability of measurement for assets and gains than for liabilities and losses. (Para. 37, FRS 18.)

Historically, prudence has always been seen as the most important of the accounting concepts. FRS 18, however, is very clear that there must be limits to the application of prudence. In an attempt to ensure that prudence is not used to understate the profits or financial position of a company, an additional paragraph has been added to FRS 18, which is taken from the ASB *Statement of Principles*, but which was not included in FRED 21 (the exposure draft that preceded FRS 18).

> However, it is not necessary to exercise prudence where there is no uncertainty. Nor is it appropriate to use prudence as a reason for, for example, creating hidden reserves or excessive provisions, deliberately understating assets or gains, or deliberately overstating liabilities or losses, because that would mean that the financial statements are not neutral and therefore not reliable. (Para. 38, FRS 18.)

The prudence concept is also weakened by the following statement regarding balancing the different objectives.

There can also be tension between two aspects of reliability – neutrality and prudence. Whilst neutrality involves freedom from deliberate or systematic bias, prudence is a potentially biased concept that seeks to ensure that, under conditions of uncertainty, gains and assets are not overstated and losses and liabilities are not understated. This tension exists only where there is uncertainty, because it is only then that prudence needs to be exercised. In the selection of accounting policies, the competing demands of neutrality and prudence are reconciled by finding a balance that ensures that the deliberate and systematic understatement of assets and gains and overstatement of liabilities and losses do not occur. (Para. 43, FRS 18.)

It is clear that the ASB have significant concerns about the use, and potential abuse, of prudence. While prudence remains, the ASB have set clear limits to its application. It no longer plays the pivotal role it once did.

Comparability

FRS 18 states that information in financial statements gains greatly in usefulness, if it can be compared with similar information about the entity for some other period or point in time, and with similar information about other entities. The FRS notes that comparability can usually be achieved through a combination of consistency and disclosure.

FRS 18 notes that, in selecting accounting policies, a company should assess whether accepted industry practices are appropriate to its particular circumstances.

FRS 18 points out that such practices will be particularly persuasive if set out in a SORP that has been generally accepted by an industry or sector.

Understandability

FRS 18 notes that information provided by financial statements needs to be capable of being understood by users with a reasonable knowledge of business and economic activities and accounting and a willingness to study with reasonable diligence the information provided. Appropriate accounting policies will result in financial information being presented in a way that enables its significance to be perceived by such users.

2.4.6 Balancing the objectives

FRS 18 notes that there may be tensions between the different objectives, in particular relevance and reliability. The FRS states that where the most relevant accounting policy may not be the most reliable, the most appropriate accounting policy will usually be that which is the most relevant of those that are reliable.

It further points out that it requires accounting policies to be consistent with the requirements of accounting standards, UITF Abstracts and companies legislation. The FRS, therefore, states that cost and benefit considerations will not justify the adoption of an accounting policy that is not consistent with those requirements.

Potential impact of the FRSME

Many of the matters currently dealt with in FRS 18 are also covered in the draft FRSME. This contains a section dealing with the qualitative characteristics of accounting information, which has many similarities with the discussion in FRS 18, but the specific emphases differ. In terms of selection of accounting policies, the FRSME sets out the following considerations to be applied where an accounting policy is not specified by the FRSME. The policy must result in information that is:

(a) relevant to the economic decision-making needs of users, and
(b) reliable, broken down into:

    (i) faithful representation of financial position, financial performance and cash flows of the entity;
    (ii) substance over form;
    (iii) neutrality (freedom from bias);
    (iv) prudence, and
    (v) completeness in all material respects.

2.5 REVIEWING AND CHANGING ACCOUNTING POLICIES

FRS 18 sets out the following requirement regarding review of accounting policies.

> An entity's accounting policies should be reviewed regularly to ensure that they remain the most appropriate to its particular circumstances for the purpose of giving a true and fair view. However, in judging whether a new policy is more appropriate than the existing policy, an entity will give due weight to the impact on comparability, as explained in paragraph 49. (Para. 45, FRS 18.)

FRS 18 points out that companies may take account of recently issued FRSs (ie those that are in issue, but which are not mandatory for the company's current accounting period) in judging whether their accounting policies are still the most appropriate for its particular circumstances. The FRS stresses that the above requirement does not mean that a new standard must be adopted early, but does mean that where it has become necessary to change an accounting policy or implement a new policy, that policy should be aligned with recently issued FRSs wherever possible. The FRS also notes that a company may take account of FREDs in judging whether its present accounting policies are still the most appropriate to its particular circumstances, but also points out an entity must not adopt an accounting policy based on a FRED unless it is consistent with the requirements of existing accounting standards. This is because FRS 18 requires accounting policies to be consistent with accounting standards applicable to the period in question. In practice, there have also been some very major changes from certain FREDs to the FRSs that followed them. Companies which adopt policies on the expectation of a change in requirements run the risk of finding that those changes never take place.

FRS 18 goes on to point out that frequent changes to accounting policies will not enhance comparability over the longer term. Consequently, the impact of past and expected future changes should also be considered when determining whether a potential change is desirable.

Regarding consistency, FRS 18 includes the following statement:

> ... consistency is not an end in itself and therefore does not impede the introduction of improved accounting practices that result in an overall benefit to users. (Para. 49, FRS 18.)

IAS 8 *Accounting Policies, Changes in Accounting Estimates and Errors* provides slightly more detail than FRS 18 on the factors that need to be considered by companies in adopting accounting policies. It splits the choice between those matters that are covered by an IFRS, or an interpretation, and those that are not. Interpretations, the equivalent of UITFs in the UK, are now in the form of IFRICs (International Financial Reporting Interpretations Committee) and were previously SICs (Standing Interpretations Committee).

Where there is a relevant standard, IFRIC or SIC in issue then:

> ... the accounting policy or policies applied to that item shall be determined by applying the IFRS. (Para. 7, IAS 8.)

When IAS 8, and other standards, refer to IFRS generically, this means both standards (whether called IFRS or IAS) and interpretations (whether IFRICs or SICs). This inclusive definition of IFRS is itself included in paragraph 7 of IAS 1. It is, perhaps, unhelpful of the IASB to use the term IFRS both generically and to refer to those specific standards which have been issued since it evolved out of its predecessor body, the IASC.

Paragraph 9 of IAS 8 then makes clear that the reference to IFRS includes any guidance that is stated to be integral to the standard and interpretation, and is therefore mandatory.

Where there is no standard or interpretation dealing with an issue, then IAS 8 requires companies to consider the relevance and reliability of possible policies. In deciding on the policy to be applied:

> ... management shall refer to, and consider the applicability of, the following sources in descending order:
>
> (a) the requirements and guidance in IFRSs dealing with similar and related issues; and
> (b) the definitions, recognition criteria and measurement concepts for assets, liabilities, income and expenses in the *Framework*.

. . . management may also consider the most recent pronouncements of other standard-setting bodies that use a similar conceptual framework to develop accounting standards, other accounting literature and accepted industry practices, to the extent that these do not conflict with the sources [above]. (Paras. 11 and 12, IAS 8.)

There is no UK equivalent of this, although, in practice, reference is sometimes made to other GAAPs (including IFRS) where the guidance in the UK is unclear or does not exist.

The IFRS for SMEs also has a hierarchy, although it differs substantially from that which exists under the IFRS. Where the IFRS for SMEs does not deal with an issue specifically, policies should be determined by reference to their relevance and reliability; firstly by analogy with any matters that are considered in the IFRS for SMEs and, in the absence of such matters, by reference to the definitions, recognition criteria and measurement concepts in that standard. In the absence of a clear answer from such sources, reference may also be made to full IFRS, but this is not mandatory.

Potential impact of the FRSME

The FRSME, being based on the IFRS for SMEs, adopts the same approach. Like that standard, it requires the use of analogy first, and then reference to some of the basic requirements set out in the draft standard.

2.6   ESTIMATION TECHNIQUES

2.6.1   Definitions

Under FRS 18, estimation techniques are defined as:

> The methods adopted by an entity to arrive at estimated monetary amounts, corresponding to the measurement bases selected, for assets, liabilities, gains, losses and changes to shareholders' funds. (Para. 4, FRS 18.)

Examples given of estimation techniques include methods of depreciation (eg straight-line and reducing balance) and estimates of the proportion of trade debts that will not be recovered, in particular where estimates are made by considering a population as a whole.

FRS 18 distinguishes between accounting policies and estimation techniques as follows.

> Accounting policies define the process whereby transactions and other events are reflected in financial statements. . . .

> Estimation techniques implement the measurement aspects of accounting policies. An accounting policy will specify the basis on which an item is to be measured; where there is uncertainty over the monetary amount corresponding to that basis, the amount will be arrived at by using an estimation technique. (Para. 4, FRS 18.)

Measurement bases are:

> Those monetary attributes of the elements of financial statements – assets, liabilities, gains, losses and changes to shareholders' funds – that are reflected in financial statements. (Para. 4, FRS 18.)

FRS 18 notes that measurement bases fall into two broad categories: those that reflect current values and those that reflect historical values. Measurement bases also include methods of measuring fungible assets, such as FIFO and weighted average cost.

The FRS points out that, whether they are prescribed or selected, measurement bases are a matter of accounting policy. Therefore, if certain assets have been stated previously at their historical cost and are now restated to their current replacement cost, this would be a change of accounting policy. Similarly, whether interest eligible for capitalisation under FRS 15 *Tangible Fixed Assets* is actually capitalised or is written off is an accounting policy matter regarding the recognition of an item, ie interest, in the financial statements. The same also applies to development costs under SSAP 13.

By contrast, FRS 18 identifies methods by which the disposal value of a fixed asset may be quantified, such as by reference to recent disposal of similar assets or to publicly quoted prices for similar assets, as examples of different estimation techniques to arrive at the same unknown amount, ie the disposal value.

2.6.2 *Application*

FRS 18 sets out the following requirements regarding selection of estimation techniques.

> Where estimation techniques are required to enable the accounting policies adopted to be applied, an entity should select estimation techniques that enable its financial statements to give a true and fair view and are consistent with the requirements of accounting standards, UITF Abstracts and companies legislation.

> Where it is necessary to choose between estimation techniques that satisfy the conditions [above], an entity should select whichever of those estimation techniques is judged by the entity to be most appropriate to its particular circumstances for the purpose of giving a true and fair view. (Paras. 50 and 51, FRS 18.)

The FRS explains that the purpose of an estimation technique is to arrive at a monetary amount corresponding to a particular measurement basis. Therefore, estimation techniques need to be reliable so a company should, where possible, select whichever estimation technique best approximates to the monetary amount in question. However, FRS 18 notes that it may not be possible to identify that estimation technique with certainty when the financial statements are prepared, because estimation techniques are used only in circumstances where an amount is unknown.

Cost/benefit and materiality considerations are important as estimates are often more costly the more accurate they are. Hence, FRS 18 states that the incremental cost of greater accuracy of estimation may not be justified once improvements in accuracy cease to be material.

When choosing between estimation techniques in circumstances where the FRS requires disclosure of a description of the technique used, FRS 18 notes that a company should consider the extent to which each technique may be understood by users, and the extent to which each will facilitate comparisons with other entities.

FRS 18 includes the following requirement regarding changing estimation techniques.

> A change to an estimation technique should not be accounted for as a prior period adjustment, unless:
>
> (a) it represents the correction of a fundamental error, or
> (b) another accounting standard, a UITF Abstract or companies legislation requires the change to be accounted for as a prior period adjustment. (Para. 54, FRS 18.)

Potential impact of the FRSME

The draft FRSME does not deal with the distinction between accounting policies and estimation techniques in quite the same way as FRS 18. On the face of it, the term accounting policy is used rather more widely than under current UK GAAP. However, it does require the disclosure of details of the key assumptions and other sources of estimation uncertainty that may cause a material adjustment to the carrying amount of assets and liabilities over the year from the balance sheet date. It also requires disclosure of the details of changes in estimates. Such disclosure should be given for the current period, and, if practicable, the likely effect in future periods.

2.7 DISCLOSURE UNDER FRS 18

2.7.1 General

FRS 18 requires the following general disclosures.

(1) A description of each material accounting policy.

(2) A description of significant estimation techniques (see below).

(3) Details of any changes to the accounting policies followed in financial statements for the preceding period, including:

   (a) a brief explanation of why each new policy is thought more appropriate;

    (b)   where practicable, the effect of a prior period adjustment on the results for the preceding period, in accordance with FRS 3 *Reporting Financial Performance*, and

    (c)   where practicable, an indication of the effect of a change in accounting policy on the results for the current period.

(4)   Where it is not practicable to make the disclosures described in (b) or (c) above, that fact, together with the reasons.

(5)   Where the effect of a change to an estimation technique is material, a description of the change and, where practicable, the effect on the results for the current period.

In practice, the level of detail required in describing accounting policies depends on whether they are taken from, and fully described in, accounting standards or companies legislation. In simple terms, the more description in the guidance on the policy the less each particular company has to say in its accounts.

'Significant estimation techniques' need to be disclosed. The FRS notes that most estimation techniques do not require disclosure because the monetary amounts that might reasonably be ascribed to an item will usually fall within a relatively narrow range. FRS 18 states that an estimation technique is 'significant' only if the range of reasonable monetary amounts is so large that the use of a different amount from within that range could materially affect the view shown by the entity's financial statements. To judge whether disclosures are required, FRS 18 states that a company should consider the impact of varying the assumptions underlying that technique. The FRS notes that the description of a significant estimation technique will include details of those underlying assumptions to which the monetary amount is particularly sensitive.

The FRSSE contains rather less disclosure.

(1)   A description of each material accounting policy.

(2)   Details of any changes to the accounting policies previously followed including, as well as the information required for all prior period adjustments, a brief explanation of why each new accounting policy is thought more appropriate and, where practicable, an indication of the effect of the change on the results of the current period.

(3)   Where the effect of a change to an estimation technique is material, a description of the change and, where practicable, the effect on the results for the current period.

Potential impact of the FRSME

The disclosure requirements of the FRSME are very similar to those of FRS 18, possibly slightly wider in that they require disclosure of the impact on each line item affected, although, in practice, this is nearly always how the requirements of FRS 18 are applied already.

2.7.2   SORPs

In some sectors, for example, when dealing with a limited liability partnership, SORPs play a significant role in the determination of accounting policies. As noted above, FRS 18 states that industry practices will be particularly persuasive if set out in a SORP that has been generally accepted by an industry or sector. FRS 18, therefore, includes the following disclosure requirement in relation to SORPs.

> Where an entity's financial statements fall within the scope of a SORP, the entity should state the title of the SORP and whether its financial statements have been prepared in accordance with those of the SORP's provisions currently in effect [see below]. In the event of a departure, the entity should give a brief description of how the financial statements depart from the recommended practice set out in the SORP, which should include:
>
> (a)   for any treatment that is not in accordance with the SORP, the reasons why the treatment adopted is judged more appropriate to the entity's particular circumstances, and
> (b)   details of any disclosures recommended by the SORP that have not been provided, and the reasons why they have not been provided. (Para. 58, FRS 18.)

FRS 18 notes that the provisions of a SORP will cease to have effect, for example, to the extent that they are in conflict with a more recent accounting standard or UITF Abstract. The FRS also notes that the effect of a departure from a SORP need not be quantified, except in those rare cases where such quantification is necessary for the entity's financial statements to give a true and fair view.

Potential impact of the FRSME

The requirements of FRS 18 are carried forward, without change, into the FRSME.

2.7.3   Going concern

FRS 18 sets out the following disclosure requirements in relation to going concern.

> The following information should be disclosed in the financial statements in relation to the going concern assessment required by paragraph 23:
>
> (a)   any material uncertainties, of which the directors are aware in making their assessment, related to events or conditions that may cast significant doubt upon the entity's ability to continue as a going concern.
> (b)   where the foreseeable future considered by the directors has been limited to a period of less than one year from the date of approval of the financial statements, that fact.
> (c)   when the financial statements are not prepared on a going concern basis, that fact, together with the basis on which the financial statements are prepared

and the reason why the entity is not regarded as a going concern. (Para. 61, FRS 18.)

In practice, this has long meant that most companies have not had to disclose any details about their going concern status. Silence is taken to mean that the directors consider the company is a going concern and there is not sufficient uncertainty to warrant disclosure. While this still applies, there has, for obvious reasons, been an increase in the extent of such disclosure recently. There are currently many more companies where such disclosure is necessary than was the case only a few years ago.

The FRSSE contains a simplified version of these disclosures, requiring that directors state any material uncertainties of which they are aware in their assessment of the going concern status of the company, and, where relevant, the fact that the period they have considered is less than one year from the date of approval of the financial statements.

Potential impact of the FRSME

The FRSME contains the same requirement to disclose material uncertainties in relation to going concern, and the same requirement to disclose, where relevant, that the financial statements have not been prepared on a going concern basis. It does not contain a requirement to disclose, where relevant, that the period considered by the directors in making their assessment is less than twelve months from the date of approval of the financial statements. As noted at **2.4.2**, the period required to be considered by the directors is itself stated to be a minimum of twelve months from the reporting date, not the date of approval.

2.8   THE SUBSTANCE OF TRANSACTIONS

2.8.1   Introduction

There is one other general requirement that is the subject of an accounting standard in its own right: substance over form. This is covered by FRS 5 *Reporting the Substance of Transactions*. The issues addressed by FRS 5 largely arose due to problems which were identified during the 1980s. The ways in which companies financed their operations increased in complexity during this period. Often, this complexity led to a separation of the legal title to an asset from access to its economic benefits and risks. The consequence of this was that conventional techniques of accounting often excluded the transactions from the balance sheet. The result of this trend became known as 'off balance sheet finance'. As this name implies, while the issues often arose directly in relation to assets, it was not the omission of assets from company balance sheets that usually concerned people; it was the omission of the liabilities associated with those assets.

As well as excluding transactions from the balance sheet, there could also be important effects on the profit and loss account; for example, a profit could be recorded on the 'sale' of an asset when in fact the transaction was in substance a secured loan.

The objective of FRS 5 is to tackle the fundamental questions relating to the nature of assets and liabilities, and therefore when transactions should be recognised in the financial statements. However, despite addressing these fundamental questions, the standard is quite explicit that the vast majority of items will be unaffected: in most cases the legal form of a transaction and its commercial substance are identical.

The principles of FRS 5 are included in the FRSSE, both in its original and revised versions, but not the details. Notes have been included in the FRSSE on factoring and consignment stocks, which are consistent with the primary standard.

Potential impact of the FRSME

The principle of substance over form is explicitly reflected in the FRSME, but, as with the FRSSE, it contains far less in terms of detailed guidance on how the principle might be put into effect. (There are numerous references, throughout the text of the draft, to the requirement that the accounting for a transaction reflect the substance of that transaction.)

Comments have been made in the sections following, dealing with the potential impact of the FRSME, only where the matter is specifically addressed in that draft.

2.8.2   Disclosure of off balance sheet arrangements

The Companies Act 2006 introduced a new general disclosure requirement covering off balance sheet arrangements. Companies that are not small are affected by the requirements if, during the financial year:

(a)   the company is or has been party to arrangements that are not reflected in its balance sheet, and

(b)   at the balance sheet date the risks or benefits arising from those arrangements are material, (CA 2006, s. 410A(1)).

Where this applies, larger companies must provide details of:

(a)   the nature and business purpose of the arrangements, and

(b)   the financial impact of the arrangements of the company (CA 2006, s. 410A (2)).

In all cases, this information is necessary only to the extent that is necessary for enabling the financial position of the company to be assessed.

Medium-sized companies are required to provide the first of the disclosures included above, but not the second.

While the motivation behind this requirement may be clear, its import is not. As a result, the UITF was asked to address the new requirement, given that the section deals with off-balance sheet arrangements but does so without defining them. The UITF was sympathetic to the request, but in the absence of a definition did not feel that it could provide a formal abstract.

Nonetheless, the UITF pointed out that the requirement ultimately derived from European Union directives, and drew attention to the guidance issued by the Department for Business, Enterprise and Regulatory Reform (now the Department for Business, Innovation and Skills) on accounting and reporting provisions of the Companies Act 2006. This recited the text of the EU Directive dealing with the types of transaction that the EC envisaged for disclosure.

> Such off balance sheet arrangements could be any transactions or agreements which companies may have with entities, even unincorporated ones, which are not included in the balance sheet. Such off-balance-sheet arrangements may be associated with the creation or use of one or more Special Purpose Entities (SPEs) and offshore activities designed to address, inter alia, economic, legal, tax or accounting objectives. Examples of such off balance sheet arrangements include risk and benefit-sharing arrangements or obligations arising from a contract such as debt factoring, combined sale and repurchase agreements, consignment stock arrangements, take or pay arrangements, securitisation arranged through separate companies and unincorporated entities, pledged assets, operating leasing arrangements, outsourcing and the like. Appropriate disclosure of the material risks and benefits of such arrangements that are not included in the balance sheet should be set out in the notes to the accounts or the consolidated accounts.

The UITF also points out that various accounting standards already contain disclosures that may be relevant to off balance sheet arrangements, such as FRS 5 and SSAP 21.

2.8.3 *Principle of substance over form*

The general principle behind FRS 5 is that:

> A reporting entity's financial statements should report the substance of the transactions into which it has entered. In determining the substance of a transaction, all its aspects and implications should be identified and greater weight given to those more likely to have a commercial effect in practice. (Para. 14, FRS 5.)

In essence, most of FRS 5 is concerned with translating this principle into accounting rules. It does not cover all items, and the rules to be applied in accounting for a particular transaction may be contained in other accounting standards. FRS 5 mentions this specifically:

Where the substance of a transaction or the treatment of any resulting asset or liability falls not only within the scope of this FRS but also directly within the scope of another FRS, a Statement of Standard Accounting Practice ("SSAP"), or a specific statutory requirement governing the recognition of assets or liabilities, the standard or statute that contains the more specific provision(s) should be applied. (Para. 13, FRS 5.)

However, the provisions of the other standard have to be applied to the substance of the transaction, and therefore FRS 5 has an important role to play in regulating the interpretation of other standards; in particular, it affects the determination of the recognition of a transaction and when an asset or liability is recognised as arising from that transaction.

For example, SSAP 21 *Accounting for Lease and Hire Purchase Contracts* contains detailed rules for the measurement and disclosure of leases; nevertheless, the requirements of FRS 5 are intended to ensure that leases are classified as either finance leases or operating leases according to their substance, and not simply according to the mechanical application of the '90 per cent rule' referred to in SSAP 21.

In addition to the establishment of the general conditions for recognising assets and liabilities, the standard contains substantial application notes which spell out how the general principles should be applied in a number of important commercial areas. The areas covered by the application notes are:

- consignment stock;
- sale and repurchase agreements;
- factoring of debts;
- securitised assets;
- loan transfers;
- private finance initiative (PFI) contracts and similar, and
- revenue recognition.

For companies which are complying with FRS 26 *Financial Instruments: Recognition and Measurement*, the application notes dealing with factoring of debts, securitised assets and loan transfers ceased to apply from 1 January 2007. The application note dealing with sale and repurchase agreements continues to apply to such companies, but only in respect of items which are not financial instruments falling within the scope of FRS 26.

2.8.4 *Scope of FRS 5*

Some classes of transaction are excluded from the scope of FRS 5. They are:

- forward contracts and futures;
- foreign exchange and interest rate swaps;
- contracts for differences (that is, contracts where a net amount will be paid or received, based on the movement in a price or an index);

- expenditure commitments and orders placed, until the earlier of delivery or payment, and
- employment contracts.

2.8.5 Recognition of assets and liabilities

A necessary part of determining the substance of a transaction is to identify whether or not an asset or a liability is created. Assets are defined as:

> Rights or other access to future economic benefits controlled by an entity as a result of past transactions or events. (Para. 2, FRS 5.)

An asset may also be identified where there is exposure to the risk inherent in the benefits.

Liabilities are defined as:

> An entity's obligations to transfer economic benefits as a result of past transactions or events. (Para. 4, FRS 5.)

Whether or not a transaction results in the recognition of an asset or liability will depend upon an analysis of the transaction's commercial features, rather than just the legal position. Specifically, the analysis should address whether the company has access to the benefits and risks that are normally associated with ownership. Three aspects of a transaction are identified by FRS 5 as being particularly relevant to this analysis.

(1) The commercial rights of access to benefits and risks rather than the legal form of such rights.

(2) How the transaction is connected with other transactions which the company might be entering into.

(3) The options which may be available to the parties involved.

The application notes give advice about which commercial features are likely to be important in specific types of transactions (such as consignment stock and securitised assets), but can be usefully generalised to cover many of the cases where there is a potential distinction between the legal owner of an asset and the party that has all of the effective risks and benefits of ownership.

Examples of potentially relevant benefits and risks include the following.

Benefits

(1) The benefit of any expected increase in the value of the asset.

(2) Benefits arising from any income stream directly associated with the asset.

(3) Benefits arising from any use to which the asset might be put.

(4) Benefits that would arise if the asset were to be developed or improved.

Risks

(1)   The risk of an unexpected variation (adverse or favourable) in the value of the asset.

(2)   The risk of obsolescence.

(3)   The risk associated with destruction or loss of the asset.

These might be some of the factors that should be considered when looking at any situation that is not specifically covered by any of the application notes included with the standard.

One of the key assumptions is that each transaction must have a commercial logic. (This assumption may not always apply where a transaction takes place between related parties, in which case FRS 8 *Related Party Disclosures* may require disclosure, although FRS 5 may not affect the reporting of the transaction.)

It may be possible to understand the impact of a transaction by looking at other transactions to which it is linked, commercially if not legally. One of the aims of FRS 5 is to stop companies being able to achieve the accounting results they require by breaking down a series of connected transactions and then accounting for them separately when, in fact, all of the transactions form part of a whole. It is the combined impact of the various stages that must be accounted for.

In other cases, it may be possible to understand the logic by evaluating the position of the other party to the transaction. For example, where the other party to a transaction receives a lender's return but no more, this indicates that the substance of the transaction is one of financing.

However, in some cases this method of understanding the motives and intentions of the parties assumes that they either have the same beliefs about the future or that we know what their beliefs are. This may not be realistic; indeed, much of the trading on financial and commodity markets would suggest that the opposite assumption (of different or unknown expectations) is more justifiable as a working assumption. Therefore, in practice, it may be wrong to infer the motives of the parties by assuming that they all have the same information and make the same assessments of the likelihood of future events.

When a transaction gives rise to an asset using the above analysis, FRS 5 requires that two additional criteria be satisfied before this asset is recognised in the balance sheet. The purpose of these conditions is to ensure that transactions are recognised on a prudent basis. The two conditions are that:

● there is sufficient evidence that economic benefits will exist, and
● the monetary amount of the item can be measured with sufficient reliability.

The first condition will prohibit the recognition of assets where the rights clearly accrue to the reporting company, but it is not clear that there will actually be a benefit stream associated with the asset. Although the treatment of research and development costs is governed by SSAP 13 and not FRS 5, this is still an example where the application of this test is clear. Where a company undertakes research, it may be clear that the benefits, if any, would accrue to the company, but such costs are not treated as an asset since the 'if any' is crucial, and it is not clear at this stage that there will actually be any benefits.

The second condition is intended to prohibit the recognition of assets which, while they may be identifiable in theory, cannot be quantified in practice, such as many internally generated intangible assets. The recognition of assets in such circumstances would be subjective, potentially misleading and likely to distort comparative rates of return.

Potential impact of the FRSME

The draft FRSME defines assets and liabilities in broadly similar terms to those used in FRS 5. It also includes an extended discussion of the recognition criteria that should also be met in order for items to be recognised as assets and liabilities in financial statements. The specific changes in this area are unlikely to affect accounting practices, although the FRSME may change practice in relation to assets and liabilities which are covered by more specific guidance.

2.8.6   General presentation requirements

FRS 5 is, basically, a standard that deals with recognition rules rather than disclosure and presentation. The only general disclosure requirements contained in the standard are that companies should:

- ensure that the disclosure of transactions in financial statements is sufficient to enable a user to understand their commercial effect, a requirement that will normally be met by compliance with other specific disclosure requirements in statute and accounting standards, and
- disclose the existence and nature of any assets and liabilities which have been recognised, but whose nature differs from that normally associated with items included under the same balance sheet heading.

However, FRS 5 does have an impact on the presentation of financial statements when it comes to offsetting assets and liabilities. There is a general presumption that assets and liabilities should not be set off against each other, and this is recognised in the statutory instruments supporting the Companies Act 2006. However, there have been certain items which have been offset against each other in the past, and FRS 5 introduced specific rules for when this is allowed. Debit and credit balances can be offset against each other only if all of the following conditions are met:

(a)   the reporting entity and another party owe each other determinable monetary amounts, denominated either in the same currency, or in different but freely convertible currencies. For this purpose a freely convertible currency is one for which quoted exchange rates are available in an active market that can rapidly absorb the amount to be offset without significantly affecting the exchange rate;

(b) the reporting entity has the ability to insist on a net settlement. In determining this, any right to insist on a net settlement that is contingent should be taken into account only if the reporting entity is able to enforce net settlement in all situations of default by the other party; and

(c) the reporting entity's ability to insist on a net settlement is assured beyond doubt. It is essential that there is no possibility that the entity could be required to transfer economic benefits to another party whilst being unable to enforce its own access to economic benefits. For this to be the case it is necessary that the debit balance matures no later than the credit balance. It is also necessary that the reporting entity's ability to insist on a net settlement would survive the insolvency of the other party. (Para. 29, FRS 5.)

This limits the extent to which, for example, companies may undertake contras between their debtors and creditors ledgers. Companies are required to take account of the worst case in determining whether or not they can offset balances. While there is some justification for this treatment, it sits rather oddly with much of FRS 5, which requires companies to consider what it likely to happen in practice, rather than what could happen in extremis.

Potential impact of the FRSME

The draft FRSME contains a general prohibition on offsetting, although this is allowed by specific provisions.

2.8.7   Linked presentation

A linked presentation is one in which assets and liabilities are shown gross on the face of the balance sheet, but where both items are allocated to a single statutory heading. In effect, this indicates that while the gross amounts may be relevant, the company's interest is in the residual. This does not amount to netting off, and is entirely unconnected with the rules on offset. Under FRS 5, it can be applied to non-recourse financing arrangements, which show the finance deducted from the gross amount of the item which it finances.

The conditions under which this presentation can be used are strict. The key characteristic of the transaction (or part of the transaction) is that the financing arrangement is ring-fenced so that the maximum loss the entity can suffer is limited to a fixed monetary amount.

The conditions that must be met are as follows.

(1) The finance must relate solely to a specific asset (or group of assets).

(2) If the finance is in the form of a loan then that loan must be secured only on that asset.

(3) The finance must be repayable only from the proceeds generated by the asset or by the transfer of that asset to that financier.

(4) The company must not be able to acquire the asset by paying off the finance or in any other way.

(5) Where losses are made on the asset then the financier must have no recourse against any of the other assets of the company, whether such recourse is legally binding or merely commercially binding.

(6) Inability to repay the finance from the proceeds of the asset must not constitute a default on the contract on the part of the company.

(7) The financier must confirm in writing that it will only seek funds generated from the asset and will not seek recourse in any other form.

(8) The financial statements must disclose that the company need not make good any losses that are suffered as a result of a deficiency of income generated by the asset, and that the financier has provided written confirmation that it has no recourse against the other assets of the company.

EXAMPLE

A company transfers the title of high quality debts of £240 in exchange for non-returnable proceeds of £200; in addition, the company has the right to receive the further £40 under specified circumstances. If the company cannot be required to repay the £200, and the conditions in FRS 5 are satisfied, then a linked presentation on the face of the balance sheet would be required as follows:

	£
Debts subject to financing arrangement:	240
Less non-returnable amounts received	(200)
	40

Given the number of conditions that must be met, it is hardly surprising that such a treatment is comparatively rare.

2.8.8 Quasi-subsidiaries

Ever since the Companies Act 1989 was introduced, the basic tests applied in determining whether or not a company is a subsidiary have not been primarily based on ownership but control. Despite this, in FRS 5, the ASB still envisages circumstances where a company might control another entity, yet that other entity may not fall within the definition of a subsidiary. Under FRS 5, such entities are referred to as quasi-subsidiaries.

The number of quasi-subsidiaries (which was never particularly high) fell for accounting periods beginning on or after 1 January 2005. This is because FRS 2 *Accounting for Subsidiary Undertakings* was amended at the same time as statutory changes were made to the definition of a subsidiary. In particular, the definition of a subsidiary was widened. As the ASB noted in the Preface to the amendments to FRS 2:

> These changes extend the definition of a subsidiary undertaking. As a result some entities previously accounted for as 'quasi-subsidiaries' in accordance with FRS 5 'Reporting the Substance of Transactions' may now meet the definition of a subsidiary undertaking within the meaning of the Companies Act and this Standard. (Para. 4, Preface to Amendment to FRS 2.)

Accounting for subsidiary undertakings is dealt with in Chapter 21.

A quasi-subsidiary, where one can still be identified, is defined as:

> . . . a company, trust, partnership or other vehicle that, though not fulfilling the definition of a subsidiary, is directly or indirectly controlled by the reporting entity and gives rise to benefits for that entity that are in substance no different from those that would arise were the vehicle a subsidiary. (Para. 7, FRS 5.)

The main exception is that pension funds, which in certain circumstances might fall within this definition of a quasi-subsidiary, are specifically excluded by the standard.

In principle, quasi-subsidiaries are treated as though they were subsidiaries and consolidated in the normal way. If a company has no subsidiaries, but does have a quasi-subsidiary, then FRS 5 requires that companies produce pro forma consolidated accounts which incorporate that quasi-subsidiary. The disclosure requirements in relation to quasi-subsidiaries are actually more onerous than those which apply to subsidiaries. The notes to the group financial statements should contain a summary of the financial statements of each quasi-subsidiary, although where there are two or more similar quasi-subsidiaries then the disclosure may be provided on a combined basis.

There is an exception to the normal treatment required by the standard in that a quasi-subsidiary which holds a single asset, or group of connected assets, all of which are financed without recourse to any assets outside that quasi-subsidiary, may be dealt with in the group accounts by the method of linked presentation which was introduced by FRS 5.

However, there are problems due to the interaction between certain exemptions with respect to group accounts and the contents of FRS 5.

The Companies Act 2006 and FRS 2 allow certain subsidiaries to be excluded from consolidation, even though this would normally be required if they fall within certain defined categories. The Companies Act 2006 also allows certain parents not to prepare group accounts either because the group is small, or because the group is a sub-group and meets various detailed conditions. (Under the Companies Act 1985, medium-sized groups were also exempt.)

FRS 5 addresses the first issue, but does not even mention the second.

Quasi-subsidiaries may be excluded from consolidation if:

- they are immaterial, as accounting standards do not apply to immaterial items, or
- they are held exclusively with a view to resale and have not previously been consolidated.

This is slightly more restrictive than the rules which apply to subsidiaries.

The problem area, however, is where companies are not required to prepare group accounts at all. FRS 5 states that:

> Paragraph 35 [dealing with the accounting treatment for quasi-subsidiaries] should be applied by following the requirements regarding the preparation of consolidated financial statements set out in companies legislation and in FRS 2 ... (Para. 36, FRS 5.)

Where a group is small or a sub-group, and complies with all the necessary conditions, both companies legislation and FRS 2 do not require group accounts to be prepared. FRS 5 also states that:

> ... the assets, liabilities, profits, losses and cash flows of a quasi-subsidiary should be included in the group financial statements of the group that controls it in the same way as if they were those of a subsidiary. (Para. 35, FRS 5.)

If a group is entitled to the exemptions from consolidation, then such assets, liabilities, profits, losses and cash flows would not be included in the group accounts, and group accounts would not even be prepared.

If we rely on the fact that quasi-subsidiaries should be treated virtually as if they were subsidiaries, then the same exemptions from consolidation will apply. The most reasonable interpretation of FRS 5 is as follows.

(1) Where a company heads a sub-group, and is entitled to the exemption from consolidation, the existence of a quasi-subsidiary will not give rise to any requirement to prepare consolidated accounts. It should be noted in these circumstances that the quasi-subsidiary will need to be consolidated in the accounts of the ultimate parent.

(2) Where a company is not required to prepare group accounts on the basis that the group of which it is the parent is small, the existence of a quasi-subsidiary will not give rise to a requirement to prepare consolidated accounts, unless the addition of the quasi-subsidiary to the group leads to a breach of the relevant size limits.

Where group accounts are not required, in accordance with the above interpretation, then a summary of the financial statement of each quasi-subsidiary is not required, since the FRS 5 rules specifically refer to this information being needed only if the quasi-subsidiary is included in consolidated financial statements. However, the logic of FRS 5 should be followed through, and all of the information that is normally required to be given in respect of subsidiaries under Sch. 4 to The Large and Medium-sized Companies and

Groups (Accounts and Reports) Regulations 2008 (SI 2008/410) where group accounts are not prepared should also be given about quasi-subsidiaries.

The ASB's failure to address this issue in FRS 5 means that different interpretations are possible. It is thought that the above interpretation is the most reasonable, and that it should be applied unless the ASB, or UITF, issues further guidance.

Potential impact of the FRSME

The draft FRSME does not deal with quasi-subsidiaries in the same way as FRS 5. It does, however, deal with the possibility that special purpose entities (SPEs) may be subsidiaries, where the substance of the relationship indicates that the SPE is controlled by the entity.

2.8.9   Sale and repurchase agreements

The FRS 5 requirements in respect of sale and repurchase agreements apply in all cases, except in relation to transactions involving financial instruments for companies which are complying with FRS 26. Where a company, and a transaction, falls into this category, then the transaction needs to be dealt with in accordance with the rules on the derecognition of items in FRS 26.

Sale and repurchase agreements are arrangements under which the assets are sold by one party to another on terms that provide for the seller to repurchase the asset in certain circumstances. The repurchase price will include a premium which effectively acts as interest for the capital which has been advanced. This premium will often not be recorded as interest, even when finally paid, but will be absorbed into the cost of the purchase. The advantage of such a scheme is that it can both eliminate the finance and the asset from the balance sheet and, in some cases, even record a profit on the sale.

The objective of the accounting analysis is to determine whether the seller has an asset and whether the seller has a liability to repay the buyer some or all of the amounts received from the latter.

Depending on the particular circumstances, the substance (and the accounting treatment) of a sale and repurchase transaction falls into one of three categories.

(1)   The asset is no longer recognised because the transaction is a sale.

(2)   The transaction has changed the asset owned by the seller, in which case the new asset should be recognised at its fair value with any new liability.

(3)   Separate presentation is required because the transaction is a secured loan, and the asset and the liability are shown on the balance sheet. In this case, the effective interest should also be accrued, and no profit should be recognised.

Some features which will indicate that the original asset has been sold are as follows.

(1) There is no commitment for the seller to repurchase the asset (for example, the seller has a call option for which there is a real possibility that exercise will not take place).

(2) The risk of changes in the asset's value is borne by the buyer, such that the buyer does not receive solely a lender's return.

(3) The seller has no rights to determine the use of the asset.

If any of these conditions are not satisfied, then a linked or separate presentation is likely to be required.

2.8.10 The factoring of debts

The rules in the Application Note to FRS 5, dealing with the factoring of debt, do not apply to companies adopting FRS 26, which must instead use the rules on the derecognition of financial instruments included in that standard.

Factoring of debts is a well-established method of obtaining finance, sales ledger administration services and protection from bad debts. The principal features of the factoring arrangement are:

- specified debts are transferred to the factor;
- the factor offers a credit facility whereby the seller may draw up to a fixed percentage of the book value of the debts, and
- the factor may limit (or even eliminate) the recourse to the seller for the debtors that default.

Three presentations of the debts and the finance provided are possible as follows.

(1) Derecognition of the factored debts and no liability shown for the amount received from the factor.

(2) A linked presentation.

(3) Separate presentation.

In order to determine the accounting treatment, the transaction must be analysed to identify whether the seller has any access to the benefits and risks of the factored debts and whether the seller has a liability to repay amounts received from the factor.

The features which may indicate that derecognition is appropriate are:

- the transfer is for a single, non-returnable fixed sum;
- there is no recourse to the seller for the losses, and
- the factor is paid all the amounts received from the debts (and no more) and the seller has no rights to further sums from the factor.

If any of these conditions are not satisfied, then a linked or separate presentation is likely to be required. The features which indicate that a linked presentation is appropriate are that:

- the seller has received some non-returnable proceeds, but has rights to further sums depending on whether the debtors pay;
- there is no recourse for losses, or such recourse has a fixed monetary ceiling, and
- the factor is paid out of amounts collected from the factored debts and the seller has no right or obligation to repurchase the debts.

In all other cases, a separate presentation should be used.

Of particular interest is the treatment of bills of exchange under FRS 5. Upon receipt of a bill of exchange from a debtor, a company might discount it with a bank. Prior to the standard, the company would probably have transferred the amount from debtors to cash, and at the same time noted a contingent liability for the situation in which the customer did not pay the bank, and consequently the bank claimed against the company. Under FRS 5, because the risks have not been transferred from the company, the debtor should remain on the balance sheet, the cash received from the bank will be shown as an asset, and the potential recourse by the bank will be treated as a liability.

2.8.11 Securitised assets

The rules in the Application Note to FRS 5 dealing with securitised assets do not apply to companies adopting FRS 26, which must instead use the rules on the derecognition of financial instruments included in that standard.

Securitisation is a means by which providers of finance fund a specific block of assets, rather than the general business of a company. The main features of the arrangement are that:

- the assets to be securitised are transferred by the company (often called the originator) to a special purpose vehicle (often called the issuer) in return for an immediate cash payment;
- the issuer finances the transfer by issue of debt (often called loan notes), and
- the originator is granted rights to surplus income (and sometimes capital profits) from the assets, after the payment of the amounts due to the loan note holders.

In order to determine the accounting treatment, the transaction will need to be analysed to identify whether the originator has any access to the benefits and risks of the securitised assets and whether the originator has a liability to repay the proceeds of the note issue.

The features which will indicate that the derecognition is appropriate in the financial statements of the originator are:

- the transaction is conducted at an arm's length price and is an outright sale;
- the transfer is for a single non-returnable fixed sum, and
- there is no recourse to the originator for losses.

If any of these conditions are not satisfied, then a linked or separate presentation is likely to be required. The features which indicate that a linked presentation is appropriate are:

- the transaction is not at an arm's length price for an outright sale;
- some non-returnable proceeds have been received by the originator, but further sums are available from the issuer depending on the performance of the securitised assets, and
- there is either no recourse for losses or such recourse has a fixed monetary ceiling.

In all other cases, a separate presentation should be used.

2.8.12   Loan transfers

The rules in the Application Note to FRS 5 dealing with loan transfers do not apply to companies adopting FRS 26, which must instead use the rules on the derecognition of financial instruments included in that standard.

A loan transfer is a means whereby the party (the lender), having the rights to receive the principal and interest payments on a loan from the borrower, transfers these rights to another party (the new lender or transferee). Loans cannot be sold in the same way as tangible assets, but there are three ways by which the benefits and risks of a loan can be transferred.

(1)   Novation – the original agreement is cancelled and replaced with a new one which identifies the transferee as the new lender.

(2)   Assignment – the rights of the lender are assigned by statutory or equitable assignment.

(3)   Sub-participation – the rights and obligations are not transferred, but the lender enters into a back-to-back agreement with the new lender.

In order to determine the accounting treatment, the transaction will need to be analysed to identify whether the lender still has access to any of the benefits and risks of the loan, and whether the lender has a liability to repay the transferee.

The features which will indicate that the derecognition is appropriate are:

- the transfer is for a single, non-returnable fixed sum;
- there is no recourse to the lender for any losses which may arise, and
- the transferee is paid all the amounts received from the loan (and no more) and the lender has no rights to further sums from the transferee or from the borrower.

If any of these conditions are not satisfied, then a linked or separate presentation is likely to be required. The features which indicate that a linked presentation is appropriate are:

- some non-returnable amounts are received by the lender, but there are rights to further amounts depending on whether and/or when the borrowers pay;
- there is either no recourse for losses or such recourse has a fixed monetary ceiling, and
- the transferee is paid only out of amounts received from the loans, and the lender has no right or obligation to repurchase them.

In all other cases, a separate presentation should be used.

2.8.13   ESOP trusts

UITF 38 provides guidance on the accounting treatment and disclosures required for employee share ownership trusts.

Under UITF 38, where a company has effective control of an ESOP trust which holds shares in the company:

- the company should deduct the consideration paid for the shares from shareholders' funds;
- consideration paid or received for the purchase or sale of the company's own shares in an ESOP trust are shown as separate amounts in the reconciliation of movements in shareholders' funds;
- no gain or loss is recognised on the purchase, sale, issue or cancellation of the company's own shares;
- any dividend income arising on own shares is excluded in arriving at profit before tax and deducted from the aggregate of dividends paid and proposed;
- if the company is required to disclose earnings per share, then the shares should be treated as cancelled when calculating earnings per share;
- the company should record as its own liability any borrowings of the ESOP trust that are guaranteed, whether formally or informally, by it;
- finance costs and administrative expenses should be charged as they accrue, not as funding payments are made to the trust, and
- other assets and liabilities of the ESOP trust are recognised as assets and liabilities of the sponsoring company.

There are various disclosure requirements:

- a description of the main features of the ESOP trust including the arrangements for distributing shares to employees;
- the amounts of reduction to shareholders' funds and (for companies with traded securities) the market value of shares held by the ESOP trusts which have not yet vested unconditionally in employees;
- the amount of the deduction from dividend income and dividends paid and payable in respect of shares held in the trust, if material, and

- the extent to which shares are under option to employees or have been conditionally gifted to them.

2.8.14   Employee benefit trusts and similar

UITF 32 *Employee benefit trusts and other intermediate payment arrangements* extends the basic principle of FRS 5 and UITF 38 to deal with certain types of intermediate payment arrangements, primarily, but not exclusively employee benefit trusts. The UITF does not apply to companies that are adopting the FRSSE.

The UITF deals with intermediate payment arrangements, other than ESOPs or pension funds, both of which are covered by other guidance.

The main type of arrangement covered by the UITF is the employee benefit trust. Typically, under such a scheme the company makes payments to a trust, the beneficiaries of which are the employees, and the trust then uses assets accumulated from those payments to pay the employees for some or all of the employees' services. However, the UITF applies to other similar arrangements:

- whether or not there is a trust, and
- where such arrangements are used to compensate parties other than staff (such as suppliers, past employees or charities).

The precise identity of the persons or entities that will receive payments from the intermediary, and the amounts that they will receive, need not be agreed at the outset.

The UITF may also apply regardless of the legal relationship between the company and the intermediary. For example, where the intermediary is a trust, then trust law means that the sponsoring company does not have an unfettered right to direct the actions of the intermediary. However, it will still be considered to have control where it provides the information needed by the intermediary, where the intermediary has been set up in such a way that, in practice, it has little discretion in undertaking its activities, or where it has the right to appoint or veto the appointment of the intermediary's trustees or equivalent.

The UITF addresses two issues.

(1)   Whether the sponsoring entity's payments to the intermediary represent an immediate expense of the entity.

(2)   If the payments do not represent an immediate expense, what is the nature and extent of the sponsoring entity's assets and liabilities after making the payment to the intermediary?

In terms of timing of expenses, the general rule under FRS 18 is that expenses are incurred when a liability arises, not when amounts are paid.

When applied to goods and services, such as employee services, this implies the following.

(1) The expense will be incurred when a liability for the employee costs arises. This will only coincidentally be when payment is made to the intermediary.

(2) The payment made by the intermediary will either settle an existing liability or will be made in advance of the liability arising (ie will be a prepayment).

(3) The payment made to the intermediary will involve the exchange of one asset for another.

As a result, a payment made to an intermediary will represent an immediate expense of the sponsoring entity only if the payment neither results in the acquisition of another asset nor settles a liability. The UITF does not deal with situations which involve the settlement of an existing liability, but instead deals with whether the payment involves the acquisition of another asset.

An asset is defined in FRS 5 as a right or other access to future economic benefits that is controlled by the entity as a result of a past transaction or event. There are two implications of this.

(1) Future economic benefit can be obtained in a variety of forms. In the context of intermediate payment arrangements, probably the most common form is meeting some or all of the cost of services provided to the sponsoring entity. That benefit can be the basis for an asset even though it cannot be turned into cash or distributed in a liquidation.

(2) Control comprises the ability to direct and the ability to benefit from that direction. This need not involve day-to-day intervention and action. Where there is a trust, for example, a company will not have the right to dictate how the trustees discharge their responsibilities, but may still have de facto control. Under FRS 5, when determining whether an entity has an asset, one should look to the substance of the transaction. Given that companies do not generally pay significant amounts to a third party without receiving something in return, the UITF takes the view that when a company transfers funds to an intermediary there is a rebuttable presumption the company will obtain future economic benefit from the amounts transferred and that it, therefore, has control of the rights or other access to those future economic benefits.

To rebut this presumption at the time the payment is made to the intermediary, it will be necessary to demonstrate that either the company:

- will not obtain future economic benefit from the amounts transferred (for example, where the only beneficiaries of the intermediary are charities), or
- does not have control of the rights or other access to the future economic benefits it is expected to receive; this will involve evidence that the

payments made by the intermediary are not habitually made in accordance with the company's wishes.

The presumption of future economic benefit is not rebutted where payments by the intermediary relieve the company from paying for such items as retirement benefit increases or benefits in kind (for example, medical insurance cover). The presumption of control would be rebutted at the time the payment is made to the intermediary if at that time the asset(s) transferred to the intermediary vest unconditionally in identified beneficiaries.

If there is still an asset, no expense has yet been incurred.

If a payment involves an exchange of one asset for another, that will be because the company continues to have the benefit of that money and control of that benefit. This applies even where the intermediary exchanges some or all of that amount for other assets, such as shares in the company. The UITF takes the view that the company has de facto control of the intermediary's assets and should, as a result, account for the intermediary as an extension of its own business. The intermediary's assets, and any liabilities that it has, should therefore be recognised as assets and liabilities of the sponsoring entity. The subsequent accounting for those assets and liabilities and for expense recognition should follow the normal accounting rules. As a result, an asset held by the intermediary would cease to be recognised as an asset of the sponsoring entity when, for example, it vests unconditionally in identified beneficiaries.

When an entity recognises the assets and liabilities held by an intermediary on its balance sheet, it should disclose sufficient information in the notes to its financial statements to enable readers to understand any restrictions relating to those assets and liabilities.

2.8.15   Private finance initiative contracts

An application note to FRS 5 deals with private finance initiative (PFI) and similar contracts. PFI contracts arise when services traditionally provided by the public sector are purchased from a private sector operator. They typically involve the operator in constructing, financing and using a property in order to provide the agreed services. Examples include roads, bridges, prisons and hospitals. One issue which arises in these situations is the ownership of the property. Does the purchaser own the property, and have a corresponding liability to the operator; or is the property owned by the operator? FRS 5 answers this by considering which party has the benefits and risks of ownership. It became apparent to the ASB during the exposure period of the application note that some purely private sector contracts mirror PFI arrangements. As a result, the scope on the application note was widened to cover these situations.

The application note states that the payments to the operator should be split in two.

(1) Those relating to services that are independent of the property, such as maintenance, and catering. These payments are excluded from the assessment of ownership.

(2) Those relating to services for which the property was constructed; for example, in a prison, the provision of secure accommodation for prisoners. The payment for these services determines the ownership of the property.

If these latter payments are exclusively payments for the property, then the contract is, in effect, a lease and is covered by SSAP 21. The operator is the lessor and the purchaser is the lessee.

If, however, these payments include some compensation for the services provided, then FRS 5 should be applied to determine ownership. The application note states that the property belongs to the purchaser (with a corresponding liability to the operator) to the extent that:

- payments vary with the demand for the service;
- the operator does not use the property for third-party activities;
- cost increases are passed on to the purchaser, and
- the purchaser bears the residual value risk at the end of the contract.

2.9   CORRESPONDING AMOUNTS

It has long been a requirement for company law that comparatives be provided for the primary financial statements and most notes, and that they be comparable with the amounts presented in respect of the current year.

As a result of legal changes, it is now for accounting standards to deal with requirements for corresponding amounts in relation to notes and whether those amounts must be comparable with those for the current period. As a result, FRS 28 *Corresponding Amounts* was issued.

FRS 28 is an unusual standard, in that it was intended to retain the status quo ante, and make few changes to the requirements that had previously existed.

FRS 28 requires corresponding amounts for all items in the primary financial statements and in the notes, with limited exceptions. Where amounts for previous periods are not comparable, they are to be adjusted and particulars of the adjustments, including the reasons for it, need to be disclosed. This is the default rule, but it can always be overridden by a specific standard or UITF.

The only significant change that was introduced by FRS 28 was that it removed the previous exemption for corresponding amounts for loans and other dealings in favour of directors and others.

3 THE DIRECTORS' REPORT

3.1 INTRODUCTION

3.1.1 The requirement for a directors' report

This chapter differs from most, since it deals exclusively with disclosure requirements, and does not cover either accounting principles or treatments.

The duty to prepare an annual directors' report is contained in Companies Act 2006, s. 415. The sections that follow s. 415 provide details of some of the information that the report must contain, although most of the items that need to be included in the directors' report are included in Sch. 7 to The Large and Medium-sized Companies and Groups (Accounts and Reports) Regulations 2008 (SI 2008/410) or, for small companies, Sch. 5 to The Small Companies and Groups (Accounts and Directors' Report) Regulations 2008 (SI 2008/409).

The directors of a company at the time the financial statements are approved are required to produce the report, even if they were not directors throughout, or even at any time during, the period that it covers.

The directors' report is sent to the members of a company and, with the exception set out below, to the Registrar of Companies together with the financial statements. However, it does not fall within the statutory definition of annual accounts. If the company is subject to audit, then the directors' report is subject to the report of the auditors only to the extent that auditors are required to provide confirmation that, in their opinion, the directors' report is consistent with the financial statements. It differs substantially from the financial statements or accounts since much of the information it contains is in the form of narrative, rather than amounts.

As dealt with in greater depth overleaf, small companies are required to prepare a directors' report, and this must be provided to the members along with the annual financial statements. However, they are not required to file the directors' report at Companies House. Where a small company takes the option of filing abbreviated accounts those accounts need not be accompanied by a directors' report. Even if a small company chooses not to file abbreviated accounts it can still omit the directors' report from its filing so long as there is a statement in a prominent position at the foot of the balance sheet which states that the company's accounts and reports have been delivered in accordance with the provisions applicable to companies subject to the small companies regime.

The exemption from filing the directors' report also applies to companies which are entitled to the small companies exemptions in relation to the content of directors' reports, although they fall outside the definition of a small company.

This extended exemption applies to companies which meet all of the normal criteria for identifying a small company, except that they are (or were during the year) a member of an ineligible group. (The criteria for qualifying as a small company, with the various exceptions and limitations, are dealt with in Chapter 22.)

3.1.2 Small companies

Small companies must produce an annual directors' report, even if they take advantage of the exemption from filing it. However, it need not contain all of the information that is normally required. For this purpose, a company is entitled to the exemptions if it meets all of the normal conditions for a small company, but also if it meets those criteria other than that it is (or was during the year) a member of an ineligible group.

If the directors have taken advantage of the exemptions available to small companies in the preparation of the directors' report, which is sent to the members, then they must provide a statement of this fact at the foot of their report.

The directors of small companies are exempt from providing the following information in their report:

- a business review;
- an indication of likely future developments in the business of the company;
- details of financial risks;
- a statement of the recommended dividend;
- particulars of post balance sheet events;
- an indication of research and development activities;
- a statement of the fact (where relevant) that the market value of land differs substantially from its balance sheet value;
- disclosures in respect of the employment of disabled persons, and
- disclosures in respect of employee involvement.

Many small companies will also not be required to provide the confirmation in respect of the provision of information to auditors, but this is actually dependent on whether or not they are required to have, or have in fact had, an audit and not directly related to the fact that they are small. Small companies that have in fact been subject to audit are required to provide the statement.

3.1.3 The requirement for a directors' remuneration report

The requirement for a separate report on directors' remuneration was introduced back in 2002 for quoted companies. (For this purpose, quoted companies, in the UK, are only companies with a full listing. Companies on AIM, for example, are not covered by the directors' remuneration report rules since AIM is not a regulated exchange for this purpose. AIM does, however, have its own rules on the disclosure of individual directors' remuneration which go beyond the requirements of UK statute.)

The details of the directors' remuneration report and the additional disclosures required for AIM listed companies will not be covered in this chapter since quoted and AIM group accounts are now prepared in accordance with IFRS and therefore fall outside the scope of this volume. (Although the parent company is still entitled to prepare its own financial statements in accordance with UK GAAP if it wishes, and listed and AIM entities without subsidiaries, which are not therefore required to produce group accounts, may also use UK GAAP, if they wish.)

3.2 DISCLOSURE REQUIREMENTS

3.2.1 *Names of the directors*

The directors' report must state the names of all persons who were directors of the company at any time during the year, whether or not they are still directors at the date at which the report is produced. When group accounts are prepared, this information need only be given in respect of the people who were directors of the parent company. The information need not be given in a single place. For example, although not strictly required, it is common for a list of the directors who hold the post when the report is produced to be placed at the head of the directors' report. The body of the report then contains a section which gives details of those directors who resigned or were appointed (i) during the year, and (ii) between the end of the year and the date of the directors' report. This satisfies the legal requirement.

3.2.2 *Principal activities*

The report should include a description of the principal activities of the company and, if applicable, its subsidiary undertakings during the year. Any significant changes in those activities should also be disclosed.

For substantial companies or groups, the principal activities are often provided in the form of a list, with any changes that have taken place in the period highlighted. Since for companies and groups of this size the financial statements should contain information on different classes of business, subject to certain exemptions from disclosure, there will often be a very close connection between the principal activities noted in the directors' report and any segmental information provided in the notes to the financial statements.

3.2.3 Business review

Companies, other than small companies, are required to provide a business review.

The business review must contain:

- a fair review of the business of the company, and
- a description of the principal risks and uncertainties facing the company.

This is then slightly fleshed out by the specific requirements that the review be a balanced and comprehensive analysis of:

- the development and performance of the business of the company during the year, and
- the position of the company at the end of the year.

There is also the comment that such a review should be consistent with the size and complexity of the business. While such a comment is clearly intended to be helpful, it is difficult to know exactly what sort of depth is envisaged by the legislation, and therefore it can be difficult to judge whether a particular directors' report complies with the requirements. The requirements that the review be fair, balanced and comprehensive can be quite onerous, and directors may find it difficult to determine just how comprehensive, for example, the review needs to be to meet the statutory requirement.

Where necessary, there is also a requirement to include key performance indicators. In the case of large companies these need to cover both financial and non-financial matters, if relevant, but in the case of companies classed as medium-sized they need only cover financial matters. Key performance indicators are defined as factors by reference to which the development, or performance of the position of the business of the company can be measured effectively. Financial indicators may include ratios, but may also include matters not directly derived from the financial statements. Non-financial indicators might include matters related to volumes, employees or environmental matters. The key performance indicators should be those measures which are, in fact, used by the senior management of the company or group in monitoring the performance of the business.

These requirements are not intended to be as wide ranging as those that were originally proposed for the mandatory Operating and Financial Review (OFR), although the legislation requiring such a statement never came into force. The reporting statement on the OFR probably remains best practice, even for private companies. (There is now also the IASB's statement on Management Commentary which was issued in December 2010; this could also be considered. Perhaps not surprisingly, there is considerable overlap between the contents of the IASB's statement and the ASB's statement.)

The mandatory requirements under the legislation focus more on the financial statements, and are intended to highlight any matters of particular importance.

Examples of matters that might need to be covered are:

- comments on individual items of income or expenditure, or on key profitability ratios;
- comments on individual categories of asset or liability, including significant changes, or on any key ratios related to the balance sheet. Assets to be discussed might, for certain types of company, include those that are not recognised in the balance sheet, such as internally generated intangibles;
- details of any major events that have occurred in the year which have affected the business, whether or not their impact has yet been reflected fully in the financial statements;
- details of major changes in the services or products provided by the business, and
- major changes in market conditions which have affected the business.

Where information is provided outside of the directors' report, for example, in a Chairman's statement or OFR, then a cross-reference to where the commentary can be found should be sufficient.

Companies' disclosure of principal risks and uncertainties has been the subject of a lot of criticism, with the Financial Reporting Review Panel (FRRP) issuing a general press notice in February 2011 pointing out problems that they had identified in a number of the reports that they had reviewed. The overarching criticism is that too many such statements are nothing more than boilerplate text. The comments made by the FRRP were that they had dealt with a number of companies where:

- the directors' report did not clearly identify which risks and uncertainties the directors believed to be the principal ones facing the business;
- the report included a long list of principal risks and uncertainties, but this raised a question as to whether all the risks and uncertainties on the list were actually principal ones;
- the description given of a risk or uncertainty was in generic terms and it was not clear how that risk or uncertainty applied to the company's circumstances;
- the disclosure was of a risk framework rather than of the risks or uncertainties themselves, and
- the principal risks and uncertainties disclosed were not consistent with other information given in the report and accounts.

The FRRP also noted that companies should state how they manage the principal risk and uncertainties. While this appears to go slightly beyond the precise wording of the requirements, the FRRP believes this is necessary since the purpose of the business review, as stated in the Companies Act 2006, is to inform members and help them assess how the directors have performed their statutory duty to promote the success of the company. The FRRP considers that this aim can be met in relation to principal risks and uncertainties only if the directors disclose how they are being managed.

For the business reviews of listed companies there are additional requirements, sometimes referred to as an enhanced business review. (Listed companies also have to provide various details of their capital structure and associated matters, in requirements deriving from the EU takeovers directive.)

3.2.4 Future developments

Except for small companies, the directors' report must contain an indication of any likely future developments in the business of the company or any of its subsidiary undertakings. This need not always be a long or complicated discussion, although account also needs to be taken of the requirements, set out above, for a fair, balanced and comprehensive analysis of the position of the company at the end of the year, which may interact with the requirement for comments on likely future developments.

3.2.5 Financial risks

There is a requirement for directors' reports to provide details of the financial risks faced by the company or group. The directors' report must contain an indication of:

- the financial risk management objectives and policies of the company or group, including the policy for hedging each major type of forecasted transaction for which hedge accounting is used, and
- the exposure of the company or group to price risk, credit risk, liquidity risk and cash flow risk.

There is an exemption if such information is not material for the assessment of the assets, liabilities, financial position, and profit or loss of the company or group. This exemption is highly relevant to some smaller simpler businesses where their financial risks may be low, although it will still be difficult to argue that none of the risks are relevant. In particular, liquidity risk probably continues to be of greater relevance to many companies than it was a few years ago.

Companies may also need to consider the requirements of FRS 29, if they have adopted fair value accounting and it is therefore applicable to them, in determining the level and type of disclosure to be provided. At the same time, care should be taken to ensure that the disclosure in the directors' report is not restricted to those risks which are also within the scope of FRS 29. (In October 2009, the ASB published a review of narrative reporting by UK listed companies, which included the criticism that some companies were simply dealing with risks under IFRS 7, the international equivalent of FRS 29, or even simply including a cross-reference to the note including the IFRS 7 disclosures.

Whilst the review was of listed companies alone, this particular directors' report requirement is the same for unlisted.)

3.2.6 Dividends

The report of any company other than a small company must state the amount, if any, which the directors recommend should be paid as a dividend.

3.2.7 Events after the balance sheet date

The Companies Act requires that the directors' report of any company other than a small company contain particulars of any important events that have affected the company or any of its subsidiary undertakings and which have taken place since the end of the financial year.

This could lead to the duplication of material, since FRS 21 requires that material events occurring after the balance sheet date be disclosed in the notes to the financial statements. The normal method of eliminating this problem is to provide the full information in only one place, and to provide a cross-reference to where it may be found in the other. Chapter 18 deals with the identification and disclosure of non-adjusting events after the balance sheet date.

3.2.8 Research and development

The report of any company other than a small company should include an indication of the activities of the company, and its subsidiary undertakings, in the field of research and development. The statement need not deal with complex technical matters, but should provide some details of the company's or group's approach to research and development, and mention any significant individual activities that have been undertaken.

3.2.9 Market value of land

Where, in the opinion of the directors, the market value of land (including buildings) differs substantially from its recorded value in the balance sheet, this fact should be stated. The report should also contain the amount of the difference, with such degree of precision as is practicable.

This disclosure is required only if the difference is such that it should be drawn to the attention of the members and debenture holders of the company, and if the company is not small. This means that it must be material. A statement identifying that there is no such material difference is not required. Nonetheless, it is sometimes provided where otherwise there might be doubt.

Some companies appear to have taken the view that differences need not be disclosed if the market value is equal to or greater than the net book value. The rationale behind this is, presumably, that any difference is then not of such significance as to require it to be drawn to the attention of members or debenture holders, since it does not adversely affect the security of their investment. It is unlikely that this was the intention behind the legislation.

3.2.10 Political and charitable donations

The rules on political donations cover any political organisation in the European Union (EU) and cover expenditure for political purposes, in addition to direct political donations and subscriptions. Political organisations are not limited to political parties, and also cover other organisations that provide support to candidates in elections or attempt to influence the outcome of elections or referenda. Limited disclosures are also required for contributions to non-EU political parties. The rules also apply to independent election candidates; those who are not affiliated to any political party.

Under the rules, if a company:

(a)   makes donations to a registered party, independent election candidate, or any other EU political organisation, or

(b)   incurs any EU political expenditure, and

the aggregate of (a) and (b) exceeds £2,000 during the company's financial year, the following information must be disclosed in the directors' report:

● the name of each party, individual, or organisation to whom a donation has been made, and the total amount of donations to that party, person or organisation during the year, and

● the total amount of political expenditure during the year.

The limits increased substantially, at least in percentage terms, when the Companies Act 2006 came into force, since previously the disclosure threshold had been set at £200.

Additionally, if a company has made any contribution, during the year, to a non-EU political party, the aggregate of those contributions must be disclosed. Contributions to non-EU political parties do not count towards the £2,000 threshold mentioned above. There is also no minimum amount below which this disclosure is not required.

Where a company is a wholly owned subsidiary of a company incorporated in Great Britain, the above disclosures do not apply. However, in such a case, the parent company's directors' report must include information covering the parent and its subsidiaries (whether wholly owned or not) and provide the information for each company individually. The £2,000 threshold then applies to the parent and its subsidiaries in aggregate.

'Donations' are defined widely and include gifts of money or other property, sponsorship, subscription or affiliation fees, payment of expenses incurred by a political party and loans or provision of property, services or facilities on non-commercial terms. Donations do not include subscriptions to an EU trade association, that is, an association whose purpose is to further the trade interests of its members or persons that they represent.

Where a company gives in excess of £2,000 in aggregate for charitable purposes in its financial year, the directors' report must state each purpose for which money has been given and the amount given for each purpose. Money given to persons ordinarily resident outside the UK is outside the scope of this disclosure requirement and does not count towards the £2,000 threshold. This requirement also changed under the Companies Act 2006, since for accounting periods beginning prior to 6 April 2008, the threshold had stood at £200, as for political donations.

Charitable and political donations are not combined for the purpose of assessing whether the disclosure threshold is exceeded.

While not relevant for disclosure purposes, there are also very strict rules on the approval of political donations and expenditure by companies.

3.2.11 Purchase of own shares

The disclosures in respect of the acquisition by a company of its own shares apply if the company acquires them by any of the following methods:

- by purchase;
- by forfeiture or surrender in lieu of forfeiture;
- by purchase in pursuance of a court order;
- by redemption;
- in a reduction of capital;
- indirectly, through purchase by a nominee or any other person, where the company is to have the beneficial interest, or
- by their being made subject to a lien or other charge.

Where a company acquires its own shares, the following information must be disclosed in the directors' report.

(1) The number and nominal value of the shares that have been purchased, together with the aggregate amount of the consideration given and the reasons for their purchase.

(2) The number and nominal value of any shares that have been otherwise acquired or charged during the year, whether directly or through a nominee.

(3) The maximum number and nominal value of such shares that were held at any time during the year.

(4) The number and nominal value of such shares that were disposed of by the company (or any other person holding them on behalf of the company) during the year, or that were cancelled by the company during the year.

(5) For each of the items above, the percentage of the called-up share capital that the shares involved represent.

(6) Where any of the shares have been charged, the amount of the charge in each case.

(7) The consideration received for any of the shares that were disposed of during the year.

3.2.12 Disabled persons

The disclosures in respect of the employment of disabled persons apply only to companies which employ more than 250 persons on average throughout the year, calculated on a weekly basis. This means that the disclosures are not actually required by the majority of UK companies. (It also means that the basis for determining the number of employees for this purpose is not consistent with the basis to be used for determining employee numbers for disclosure, since this is calculated on a monthly basis.)

Where applicable, the disclosures that are required are statements of policy concerning:

- procedures for giving full and fair consideration to applications for employment made by disabled persons, having regard to their particular aptitudes and abilities;
- the continued employment and training of staff who become disabled whilst they are employees of the company, and
- the general training, career development and promotion of disabled persons employed by the company.

No disclosure need be given in respect of disabled persons employed wholly or mainly outside the UK.

3.2.13 Employee involvement

The disclosures in respect of employee involvement apply only to companies which are not small and employ more than 250 persons on average throughout the year, and, as with the disclosure in respect of disabled persons, this is calculated on a weekly basis rather than the monthly basis that is used for calculating the number of employees that needs to be disclosed.

Where this limit is met, the company must include a statement which describes the action that has been taken during the year to introduce, maintain or develop arrangements, the objectives of which are to:

- provide information systematically to employees on areas that concern them as employees;
- consult employees or their representatives regularly so that their views can be taken into account when making decisions that are expected to affect their interests;
- encourage employees to become involved in the company's performance through an employee share scheme, or other means, and
- achieve a common awareness throughout the company of the financial and economic factors that affect the performance of the company.

This disclosure is not required in respect of persons wholly or mainly employed outside the UK.

3.2.14   Reappointment of auditors

There is no requirement for the directors' report to contain a statement dealing with the reappointment (or otherwise) of the auditors. However, it is common practice for this to be included for companies which are still required, or have chosen, to reappoint auditors annually. Such companies are now much rarer. The Companies Act 2006 has basically abolished the requirements for private companies to have annual general meetings and to reappoint auditors annually. This could be achieved before, but elective resolutions needed to be passed. In effect, the 2006 Act has therefore reversed the default position so that a positive decision has to be made to hold meetings and to appoint auditors annually. Where a private company has an auditor already in situ, and with certain exceptions such as where the directors appointed the auditor during the year to fill a casual vacancy, that auditor will be reappointed automatically.

3.2.15   Approval

The directors' report must be approved by the board of directors. It must be signed, on behalf of the board, by either a director or (if the company has one) the company secretary. Every copy of the report that is published by or on behalf of a company must contain the name of the person who signed the directors' report on behalf of the board. The normal practice is for the company secretary, if there is one, to sign the directors' report and for the report to be dated.

If a directors' report has been prepared taking advantage of the small companies exemptions, then it must contain a prominent statement to this effect above the signature.

3.2.16   Branches

The directors' report must, unless the company is unlimited or small, contain an indication of the existence of branches outside the UK.

3.2.17   Payment policy

Some companies are required to provide details of their policy on the payment of creditors in their directors' reports.

The companies which have to state their payment policy in their directors' reports are:

- companies which were at any time during the year public companies, and
- other companies which do not satisfy the size limits for being medium-sized, and which were also a subsidiary of a public company at any time during their financial year.

Where a company is subject to these rules, it must provide the following information in its directors' report:

(a)   whether in respect of some or all of its suppliers it is the company's policy to follow any code or standard on payment practice and, if so, the name of the code or standard and the place where information about, and copies of, the code or standard can be obtained,

(b)   whether in respect of some or all of its suppliers it is the company's policy –

  (i)   to settle the terms of payment with those suppliers when agreeing the terms of each transaction,

  (ii)   to ensure that those suppliers are made aware of the terms of payment, and

  (iii)   to abide by the terms of payment,

(c)   where the company's policy is not as mentioned in paragraph (a) or (b) in respect of some or all of its suppliers, what its policy is with respect to the payment of those suppliers;

and if the company's policy is different for different suppliers or classes of suppliers, the report shall identify the suppliers to which the different policies apply. (para. 12(2) Sch. 7 of The Large and Medium-sized Companies and Groups (Accounts and Reports) Regulations 2008 (SI 2008/410).)

For this purpose, a supplier is defined as any party whose claim on a company would be included within 'trade creditors' if there were any amounts outstanding at the balance sheet date.

There are a number of codes of practice on the payment of creditors, for example, the Prompt Payment Code recommended by (amongst others) the CBI and the Institute of Directors.

Although the above requirements may appear to be straightforward, the legislation is not clear as to whether negative statements are required. For example, when disclosure (c), quoted earlier, is made because the company does not follow a code or standard, few companies actually make a statement to the effect that they do not follow such a code or standard. Although, strictly, the word 'whether' in disclosure (a), quoted earlier, could be interpreted as requiring such a negative statement.

Given the bland nature of many companies' statements of payment policy, the practical value of this disclosure requirement appears highly questionable.

3.2.18 *Payment practice*

Those companies which are required to state their payment policy are also required to state their payment practice.

Payment practice is not based on the directors' interpretation of what they have done, but a specific statutory formula.

Companies must state their payment period based on:

$$\frac{\text{Trade creditors}}{\text{Amounts invoiced by suppliers}} \times \text{Number of days in the accounting period}$$

'Suppliers' are defined in the same terms as for the statement of payment policy. The amounts invoiced should be inclusive of VAT, as VAT amounts will be contained in the balances of trade creditors.

While an interesting idea, this disclosure will not always lead to a fair statement of the company's normal payment period. The figure will be directly affected by how typical the balance sheet trade creditors' figure is of the average during the year. In highly seasonal businesses, for example, the figure may be very misleading.

This disclosure requirement also raises practical issues. As with the disclosure of payment policy, the legislation refers to 'company' rather than to group figures. This means that a parent company's annual report need give no indication of the payment practice of its subsidiaries. Instead, to obtain this information, the reader will need to obtain copies of subsidiaries' annual reports, which are usually much less easily available than the annual report published by the parent. In the extreme case of a parent company which is purely a holding company, strict compliance with this disclosure requirement may amount to a statement such as 'the company has no trade creditors, so the number of creditor days outstanding at the year end was nil'. For all practical purposes, such a statement achieves nothing.

As many major groups are multinational, a group-wide figure for the creditors' payment period may be difficult to calculate and have little meaning, as payment practices around the world vary widely. Instead, it might have been more sensible if the legislation had required parent companies to include information regarding the payment practice of their principal UK subsidiaries, or to include information on a UK group basis. This latter approach has in fact already been adopted by some major groups, which have gone beyond the strict letter of the law to provide information which is likely to be more useful by providing group figures as well as the company ones required by the legislation.

3.2.19   Qualifying indemnity provisions

Companies may, subject to a number of limitations and exclusions, provide indemnity provisions for the benefit of directors. Such provisions are known as qualifying indemnity provisions.

These are of two types. A third party indemnity provision means a provision for indemnity, against liability incurred by a director, to a person other than the company or an associated company. A pension scheme indemnity provision is similar, except that it applies in respect of a director of a company that is a trustee of an occupational pension scheme, against liability incurred in connection with the company's activities as trustee of the scheme.

The existence of such provisions must be disclosed in directors' reports, if they were in place during the financial year to which a report relates, or at the date that the report is approved, and whether they are or were in place in respect of any director of the company or director of an associated company. This applies whether the provision was made by the company or otherwise.

3.2.20   Statement of directors' responsibilities

Many companies provide a statement of directors' responsibilities in their reports and accounts. This is not a requirement of company law or accounting standards. Indeed, it is now quite hard to determine what is the basis for the inclusion of such a statement, although it is expected that such statements will remain common practice.

Until recently, the need for such a statement arose from the responsibilities that were placed on the company's auditors by International Standard on Auditing (UK and Ireland) 700 (ISA 700) *The Auditor's Report on Financial Statements*. This standard required that auditors include a description of directors' responsibilities in their audit report, if such a statement had not been included in the annual accounts. Whilst auditing standards cannot place any direct responsibilities on company directors, this meant that in practice such statements became the norm, if only to avoid the lengthening of the text of the auditors' report that would otherwise occur.

The latest version of ISA 700, effective for accounting periods ending on or after 15 December 2010, places no requirement on the auditor to include a description of directors' responsibilities in the audit report if there is no such statement elsewhere in the report and accounts.

Despite this, there is a clear expectation on the part of the Auditing Practices Board (the body which sets auditing standards in the UK) that such statements will continue. Their Bulletin 2010/2 *Compendium of Illustrative Auditor's Reports on United Kingdom Private Sector Financial Statements for Periods Ended on or after 15 December 2010*, continues to include references to such statements in the illustrative reports. It also provides an example of a suitable statement of directors' responsibilities for a company using UK GAAP which is not publicly traded, although companies are free to amend this to make it more appropriate to their particular position.

> The directors are responsible for preparing the Directors' Report and the financial statements in accordance with applicable laws and regulations.
>
> Company law requires the directors to prepare financial statements for each financial year. Under that law the directors have elected to prepare the financial statements in accordance with United Kingdom Generally Accepted Accounting Practice (United Kingdom Accounting Standards and applicable law). Under company law the directors must not approve the financial statements unless they are satisfied that they give a true and fair view of the state of affairs of the company and of the profit or loss of the company for that period.
>
> In preparing these financial statements, the directors are required to:
>
> - select suitable accounting policies and then apply them consistently;
> - make judgements and accounting estimates that are reasonable and prudent;
> - state whether applicable UK accounting standards have been followed, subject to any material departures disclosed and explained in the financial statements [not required for small and medium-sized companies], and
> - prepare the financial statements on the going concern basis unless it is inappropriate to presume that the company will continue in business.
>
> The directors are responsible for keeping adequate accounting records that are sufficient to show and explain the company's transactions and disclose, with reasonable accuracy at any time, the financial position of the company and enable them to ensure that the financial statements comply with the Companies Act 2006. They are also responsible for safeguarding the assets of the company and hence for taking reasonable steps for the prevention and detection of fraud and other irregularities.

3.2.21   Information provided to auditors

Where a company is subject to audit, the directors' report must contain a statement in respect of each director (individually) that, so far as the director is aware, there is no relevant audit information of which the company's auditors are unaware, and that he or she has taken all the steps that he or she ought to have taken as a director in order to make himself or herself aware of any relevant information and to establish that the company's auditors are aware of that information. The previous legal requirement, which simply made it an offence for a director to make false statements to an auditor, has therefore been extended, so that there is now a positive duty placed on directors to provide information to auditors, even where not prompted by enquiries.

As a disclosure requirement, this is fairly straightforward. What is rather more complicated is the process that directors should adopt to satisfy themselves that they have in fact complied with the requirement to provide such information.

4 REVENUE RECOGNITION

4.1 INTRODUCTION

4.1.1 Application Note G to FRS 5

It was not that many years ago that neither company law nor any UK accounting standard dealt with the general problem of revenue recognition. This changed with the issuing of Application Note G to FRS 5 *Reporting the Substance of Transactions*, which now deals with this area. The Application Note has been effective since 2003. The Application Note has also been taken into account in the drafting of the FRSSE.

Soon after it was published, various issues were raised in relation to the practical changes required by the Application Note, which was perhaps a little unclear. As a result, UITF 40 *Revenue Recognition and Service Contracts* was issued, dealing with the implications for companies providing services (although much of the commentary, when UITF 40 was issued, was in relation to entities that are not companies, but which are nonetheless required to apply UK GAAP in the preparation of their financial statements).

The ASB decided not to issue a full new standard on the issue of revenue recognition, given that it is no longer issuing standards on matters of general import unless they have been developed in conjunction with the IASB or are UK versions of international standards. Hence the creation of an Application Note to an extant standard. As the international standard dealing with revenue recognition, IAS 18, has not been substantially updated for some years (and is now the subject of an exposure draft), the ASB did not wish to adopt the international standard.

The Application Note sets out some basic principles that apply to revenue recognition in all cases, as well as dealing with a number of specific problem areas.

Some other existing standards deal with the methods by which specific forms of income should be recognised. For example:

(1) FRS 9 deals with income from associates and joint ventures (covered in Chapter 21).

(2) SSAP 4 deals with the way in which companies should recognise amounts in respect of government, and similar, grants received (covered in Chapter 12).

(3) SSAP 9 deals with the recognition of income on long-term contract work in progress (covered in Chapter 15). However, SSAP 9 was affected, but

not strictly amended, by the issue of Application Note G. One section of the Application Note deals specifically with the issue of the recognition of revenue on long-term contracts.

(4) SSAP 20 (where a company is not adopting FRS 26 and therefore FRS 23) deals with the recognition of certain profits arising as a result of changes in foreign exchange rates, including unrealised profits (covered in Chapter 10).

(5) SSAP 21 deals with the recognition of income on leases (covered in Chapter 16).

(6) FRS 26 deals with the recognition of certain types of income in relation to financial instruments for companies falling within its scope (covered in Chapter 13).

These specific cases are not considered in this chapter, but are covered in the sections indicated above when dealing with the areas to which they relate.

4.1.2   International financial reporting standards

Revenue recognition is the subject of an international financial reporting standard, IAS 18 *Revenue*. The international standard has often been used as guidance within the UK, due to the previous absence of a UK standard or any detailed guidance, although it needs to be treated with considerable care. International standards are not directly applicable in the UK (for companies following UK GAAP), and there is, therefore, no requirement to comply with their provisions.

IAS 18 makes it clear that it is intended to apply only to the recognition of revenue from normal trading activities such as:

● the sale of goods;
● the rendering of services, or
● the use by others of resources owned by the company that give rise to income, such as dividends on investments, interest on cash balances and similar, and royalties.

It does not deal with items covered in other international accounting standards, or where, for various reasons, normal accounting principles may not be appropriate such as:

● income related to long-term contract work in progress;
● lease income, whether on finance or operating leases;
● government grants received, or
● income of insurance companies on insurance contracts.

However, such limitations do not detract from the value of the standard. In all of the cases that are excluded, there is specific UK guidance available, either from standard-setters in the UK or from the Association of British Insurers.

The standard also contains an appendix, which provides a list of types of items for which a policy for revenue recognition may be required, together with suggestions for such a policy.

IAS 18 provides the following rules for determining when revenue should be recognised on the sale of goods:

> Revenue from the sale of goods shall be recognised when all the following conditions have been satisfied:
>
> (a) the entity has transferred to the buyer the significant risks and rewards of ownership of the goods;
> (b) the entity retains neither continuing managerial involvement to the degree usually associated with ownership nor effective control over the goods sold;
> (c) the amount of revenue can be measured reliably;
> (d) it is probable that the economic benefits associated with the transaction will flow to the entity; and
> (e) the costs incurred or to be incurred in respect of the transaction can be measured reliably. (Para. 14, IAS 18)

While framed in slightly different terms, this is basically consistent with the principles of FRS 5 and, in particular, Application Note G. The reference to the transfer of the 'significant risks and rewards of ownership' is very similar to the 'risks and benefits' referred to in FRS 5.

The IAS also takes a percentage of completion approach to services. This means that where significant services are provided, income should be recognised pro rata, and not on completion.

The current requirements of IAS 18 are largely reflected in the IFRS for SMEs.

The IAS has not been substantially revised for quite a long time, and there is an overall IASB and FASB project looking at updating the standard

The first fruits of this project were seen in December 2008 when the IASB, jointly with FASB, issued a discussion paper giving its preliminary views on revenue recognition in contracts with customers. This was then followed up with an exposure draft issued in June 2010. The core principle behind the draft differs quite considerably from that of the current standards. The basic idea is that entities would recognise revenue as they transfer control of goods and services to customers in an amount that reflects the consideration it receives in respect of those goods and services. The current version of IAS 18 (like Application Note G to FRS 5) takes an approach that is based more on the effort that has been expended by the entity in the earning of revenues, for example, by requiring a percentage of completion approach for any service contracts.

The change in approach would not affect all transactions; for many simple transactions there is no difference in effect between looking at the transaction from the perspective of what is ultimately being supplied and what is ultimately being received. However, in some cases, the difference is substantial. Under the proposals, and depending on the terms of the contract, such revenues may be substantially deferred from those under current practice if the work undertaken has not yet resulted in any transfer to the customer. The draft also deals with the separate performance obligations in a contract, so it does not mean that all contracts would give rise to a later recognition of revenue, and certainly not that all revenues would be deferred until completion of a contract as a whole.

The draft also deals with many other matters related to revenue recognition, including:

- the identification of the separate performance obligations in a contract;
- the allocation of a total transaction price to the separate performance obligations in a contract, including situations where there is no separate market price that can be determined for one or more parts of the contract, and
- the valuation of the total consideration receivable under a contract.

The draft is still under discussion by IASB and FASB, and there may be many changes to the originally issued proposals, with a revised standard expected to be issued by the end of 2011.

Potential impact of the FRSME

The FRSME, like the IFRS for SMEs on which it is based, broadly reflects the requirements set out in the current version of IAS 18. The basic principles are the same as those included in Application Note G to FRS 5, although there may be differences in the precise way that they affect particular situations.

The potential impact of the IASB proposals is hard to gauge. If the IASB makes the significant changes to the revenue recognition standard currently proposed, it is likely that those changes will, at some point, be reflected in the IFRS for SMEs. If this were to happen, there would naturally be some simplification of the requirements in the full IFRS. If the IFRS for SMEs were to change, it would be reasonable to expect that the FRSME would also be changed. The uncertainties involved in this chain make it difficult to predict what the changes might be, and impossible to predict when they might happen.

4.2 GENERAL PRINCIPLES OF RECOGNITION

4.2.1 Exclusions

Application Note G now sets out the basic principles that should be applied for revenue recognition. The Note does not apply to:

- revenues resulting from transactions in financial instruments;
- revenues arising from insurance contracts, and

- all types of revenue which are covered by a more specific standard.

4.2.2 Basic principles

Application Note G to FRS 5 deals primarily with turnover. This is defined as:

> ... the revenue resulting from exchange transactions under which a seller supplies to customers the goods or services that it is in business to provide. (Para. G11, Application Note G to FRS 5.)

The Note then goes on to make it clear that there are other exchange transactions, such as disposals of fixed assets, which do not give rise to turnover.

The fundamental principle for revenue recognition is set out in Application Note G to FRS 5:

> A seller recognises revenue under an exchange transaction with a customer, when, and to the extent that, it obtains the right to consideration in exchange for its performance. At the same time, it typically recognises a new asset, usually a debtor. (Para. G4, Application Note G to FRS 5.)

This fundamental requirement is then broken down into various parts, which can be summarised as follows.

(1) Where payment is received in advance of performance, a liability should be created, and revenue recognised only as the seller obtains the right to consideration through performance.

(2) Where a seller meets its contractual obligations, in part, it should recognise revenue in respect of that part, even where the amount cannot yet be invoiced.

(3) Revenue should be recognised at the fair value of the right to consideration; where the time value of money is material, the amount should therefore be discounted.

(4) Where, at the time revenue is recognised, there is a material risk of default, the recorded revenue should be reduced accordingly.

(5) Subsequent adjustments to a debtor as a result of changes in the time value of money and the credit risk should not be reported as revenue.

One thing that is not mentioned in any of the guidance is billing or invoicing. It does not matter when invoices are raised and, apart from the requirement to take account of the time value of money and the risk of default, it certainly does not matter when amounts are actually received.

It should be noted that the Application Note forms part of FRS 5. While this might sound like a trivial point, the Note is intended to show how to apply the basic principles of FRS 5 in a particular situation. Those basic principles continue to take precedence. This means that the overriding requirement is that the reporting of revenue transactions should be governed by the substance of those transactions, and not the legal form that they take.

The FRSSE has been updated to reflect the basic principles of the Application Note.

Dealing with the sale of goods, there are various events which might (in the absence of the Application Note) be considered as giving rise to revenue:

- when production has been completed;
- when the order is received;
- when a legally binding contract of sale has been entered into by the parties to the transaction;
- when the goods are physically delivered to, or taken by, the buyer;
- when payment is made for the goods;
- when legal title passes to the buyer, or
- when the period during which goods can be returned has expired.

Some of these are more likely to be important than others, but each case needs to be considered on its own merits, and different types of transaction may be properly treated in different ways.

For example, the completion of production for goods which are not subject to a contract is unlikely to be critical, as no contractual obligations have been met. The profit potential that is tied up in the goods would not normally be treated as realised for accounting purposes.

Under the Application Note, the key factor is seen as being the performance of contractual obligations. Subject to the bill and hold requirements, the normal point at which the contractual obligations will have been met is when the goods are physically delivered to, or taken by, the buyer. It is at this point that the contractual obligation to supply goods has been performed, and as such a right to consideration has been earned.

Each of the revenue recognition principles of the Application Note is dealt with in turn.

Payment in advance

The principle that where amounts are received in advance of work being undertaken or goods provided then they should not give rise to revenue, but instead be treated as deferred income, that is, as a liability of the company, is relatively uncontroversial.

In such cases the revenue is recognised as the contractual obligations are met. In effect, the receipt of money in advance affects the balance sheet of the company, but it has no immediate impact on the reported turnover and profit. An asset (cash) and a liability (deferred income) is recorded leading to no change in net assets.

What is likely to be slightly more controversial is the exact application of the principle. However, this problem is actually identical to the problem that arises with all companies complying with the new Application Note: *When have contractual obligations been met?*

Partial recognition

By far the most controversial aspect of the Application Note is the guidance dealing with recognition of revenue as contractual obligations are met.

Under the Application Note, where an entity has partially completed its obligations under a contract it is required to account for the appropriate proportion of revenue. This raises the question of whether obligations are partially fulfilled, or whether there is a key event, yet to occur, which means that the obligations have not been fulfilled at all. When obligations are fulfilled the company has earned the right to consideration, defined and then expanded upon as:

> A seller's right to the amount received or receivable in exchange for its performance. This right does not necessarily correspond to amounts falling due in accordance with a schedule of stage payments which may be specified in a contractual arrangement. Whilst stage payments will often be timed to coincide with performance, they may not correspond exactly. Stage payments reflect only the agreed timing of payment, whereas a right to consideration arises through the seller's performance. (Para. G3, Application Note G to FRS 5.)

With regard to goods, the basic rules are also to be read in the context of the requirements concerning bundling and unbundling of contracts, as dealt with further on. With services, the situation is often far from clear. (It could be argued that this is also an unbundling problem.) There will be services where the situation raises no complex accounting issues, for example:

- very short-term services, such as those provided within one day, where the point for the recognition of revenue is clear, and
- very long-term services, which were already within the long-term contract provisions of SSAP 9.

The latter may be affected by the specific long-term contract requirements included in the Application Note, but are not affected by the general principles.

This leaves a wide range of services that need to be considered in the light of the Application Note.

The crucial question is the extent to which contractual obligations have been met.

This issue is dealt with in UITF 40 *Revenue recognition and service contracts.* UITF 40 has been reflected in the FRSSE since the 2007 version.

While the UITF deals with a number of matters that may arise when dealing with service contracts, such as whether such contracts may fall to be treated as long-term contracts, its most important sections deal with the issue of partial completion of contractual obligations.

The consensus states that:

> Where the substance of a contract is that the seller's contractual obligations are performed gradually over time, revenue should be recognised as contract activity progresses to reflect the seller's partial performance of its contractual obligations. The amount of revenue should reflect the accrual of the right to consideration as contract activity progresses by reference to value of the work performed. (Para. 26, UITF 40.)

This is supplemented in the discussion by a more thorough analysis of the situation:

> Where the substance of a transaction is that the seller's contractual obligations are performed gradually over time, revenue is recognised as contract activity progresses to reflect the seller's partial performance of its contractual obligations. This is the case where the substance of the obligation is either (i) to provide the services of staff, ie where the seller earns the right to consideration as each unit of time is worked or (ii) to require the seller to use its skills and expertise in carrying out acts that will take some time to perform, even when the output is encapsulated in a document, such as a report. In such cases, revenue is recognised to reflect the accrual of the right to consideration as contract activity progresses, by reference to valuation of the work performed as described . . . in relation to long-term contracts. Thus, subject to the considerations . . . [concerning any uncertainties as to the amount the customer will accept and be able to pay], in case (i) the amount of revenue may be derived from the time spent; in case (ii) the amount of revenue will reflect the fair value of the services provided as a proportion of the total fair value of the contract, which will reflect the time spent and the skills and expertise that have been provided. (Para. 18, UITF 40.)

This means that in most cases where there is a service contract, revenue will need to be recognised as services are provided, irrespective of whether obligations have been met in full. Even where, for example, a report needs to be provided in order to fulfil a contractual obligation this will not prevent the recognition of a proportion of the income prior to the preparation of that report.

The amount to be recognised will still raise issues, as it is not necessarily the case that profits accrue evenly over the life of a service contract. This is dealt with below.

However, the principle does not affect work where there is a critical event which must occur in order for the contractual obligations to be fulfilled. Some services do not create any right to consideration unless and until a critical event occurs. In such cases, revenue should be recognised only once that critical event is past.

For example, a fee may be receivable only if a transaction goes ahead. No income should be recognised until the transaction giving rise to that income has itself occurred. In all such cases the contractual obligations have not been met until that final result has been provided. Where work does involve such a critical event, then to the extent that the work is not complete at the year end, it should be treated as work in progress. Such work in progress is governed by SSAP 9, and should be stated under the normal rules of that standard, that is, at the lower of cost and net realisable value.

UITF 40 makes clear that a critical event, for this purpose, cannot be one which is within the control of the party considering whether or not revenue should be recognised:

> . . . this only applies where the right to consideration is conditional or contingent on a specified future event or outcome, the occurrence of which is outside the control of the seller. (Para. 19, UITF 40.)

Fair value of consideration

Most revenues will be received in cash, or other assets, within a relatively short period after the date for the recognition of revenue.

In the fairly rare situations, where this does not apply, then the consideration should be stated at its fair value. This is normally the amount that is ultimately receivable, after discounting. In general, this is only likely to be relevant (or perhaps material) when the amount is receivable more than one year after revenue is to be recognised.

Strictly, fair value is defined as:

> The amount at which goods or services could be exchanged in an arm's length transaction between informed and willing parties, other than in a forced or liquidation sale. (Para. G3, Application Note G to FRS 5.)

Where contractual obligations have been met in full, it will normally be the case that determining the fair value of the consideration will be straightforward. However, a particular problem arises with service contracts where, under UITF 40, revenue is recognised at a point where the service has been only partially provided.

UITF 40 states:

> The amount of revenue recognised should reflect any uncertainties as to the amount which the customer will accept and be able to pay. It may be the case, for example, that even where the contract states that fees are to be calculated on a time basis, the customer will not accept that the time spent is reasonable. (Para. 20, UITF 40.)

This deals with one aspect of the issue, although one that will often be covered by adjusting events occurring after the balance sheet date.

There is still another issue. Application Note G to FRS 5, and UITF 40, strictly deal only with revenue and not profits. In some contexts, this is a slightly misleading comment as, given that costs will not directly change, any change in revenue recognition must automatically have a profit impact. However, it is relevant in the sense that determining the fair value of consideration may depend upon profit estimation, and the Note does not deal with the basis on which profits can be estimated.

It cannot be assumed that profits always accrue evenly over a service contract. Paragraph 18 of UITF 40, quoted above, makes it clear that where a contract is for skills and expertise, and not just for time, then the fair value will reflect both the time spent and the skills and expertise provided. While undoubtedly correct, this will not always be straightforward to apply in practice. Companies may be required to make estimates concerning the relative profitability of different stages and levels of work. Such estimates may take some account of factors such as notional charge out rates, but need not always agree directly to them.

Risk of default

Most companies are unlikely to enter into a transaction where, at that time, they consider there is a significant risk of default.

Nonetheless, where this does occur, the requirement that the consideration be stated at its fair value implies that the revenue recognised should be reduced to the extent that default is expected.

Subsequent adjustments

Where account has been taken of the time value of money and the risk of default, then as time elapses, and as the default risk changes, the Application Note states that such adjustments should not be made to revenue. For example, bad debt charges that arise after the initial recognition of revenue do not give rise to any adjustment to the amount of reported turnover, but are normally treated as expenses of the company. If sufficiently large, such charges might warrant disclosure as an exceptional item. Similarly, adjustments that arise simply as a discount unwinds are interest income, not revenues.

4.2.3 Separation and linking of contracts

The Application Note deals with the separation and linking of contracts. This is also referred to as unbundling and bundling.

The accounting question is whether there is one overall transaction, or a number of separate transactions.

Under the Note, a contractual arrangement should be accounted for as two or more separate transactions only where the commercial substance is that the individual components operate independently of each other. This means that each component represents a separable good or service that the seller can provide to customers, either on a stand alone basis or as an optional extra, or, where one or more components may be capable of being provided by another supplier.

Where contracts are to be treated separately, this is simplest where it is possible to determine the fair value for each component; for example, where the items are also sold separately. In this case, it is fairly straightforward to recognise revenue on each component. For example, a company may sell A and B at £100 each, but is selling A and B together for £190. If it is clear that A, but not B, has been sold at the year end, then revenue of £95 should be recognised. The discount available through buying components together is applied pro rata to those components.

Where this cannot be done, the elements may still be separable where reliable fair values can be obtained for either the completed or the uncompleted components. However, where a reliable fair value cannot be obtained for the uncompleted components, care must be taken to ensure that turnover is not overstated for the completed components. That is because the contract price may be set at a discount from the total amount at which the components would be sold individually. For example, taking the previous figures, if we know that A sells for £100, and A with B for £190, but B is never sold alone, then we might be tempted to assume that B sells for £90. This is not necessarily right. The situation may be the same as in the previous example, with a discount provided because items are sold together.

The Application Note provides various examples.

(1) Sale of software and maintenance – for off-the-shelf packages with support, the support may be separable and there are therefore two transactions. Revenue should be recognised on the sale of software and on the sale of support. This will often mean that all of the revenue is recognised on the sale of the software, but the revenue on the support contract is initially only recognised in part. Where bespoke software is provided, with support which could not be provided by a third party, then this is normally a single service, and should be treated as a long-term contract.

(2) Inception fees – where a fee is charged at the start of a contract, the accounting treatment depends on whether this is integral to the contract. If, for example, this provides a right to lower prices, then it should be spread over the period during which the lower prices apply. If a commercial rate is charged thereafter, then the fee should be recognised immediately.

(3) Vouchers – where a voucher is provided with a purchase then, if the amount is material, provision should be made for redemption, with a corresponding reduction in the initial recording of income. This should be

based on factors such as the period of validity and the likelihood of redemption. Income should then be recognised when redemption takes place. Vouchers provided free can be ignored unless they are likely to give rise to an actual loss, in which case they should be accounted for as an onerous contract in accordance with FRS 12.

The issue dealt with in the third of these points is also covered in the international interpretation, IFRIC 13 *Customer Loyalty Programmes*, which arrives at a broadly similar conclusion and accounting treatment. The UITF information sheet dealing with the adoption of IFRICs into UK GAAP notes that IFRIC 13 is not to be brought in, since Application Note G to FRS 5 already addresses the same issues.

4.2.4 Bill and hold

Bill and hold arrangements are where legal title passes to the customer, but physical delivery is deferred.

The Application Note deals with whether or not a sale should be recognised. The basic principle relates, not surprisingly, to whether the risks and benefits associated with ownership have passed.

The key benefits are considered to be the right to obtain the goods when required, the sole right to the goods and any future cash flows associated with them, and insulation from price changes.

The key risks are slow movement and being compelled to take goods even where they have fallen in value or utility.

In order to account for a sale, the contract for a bill and hold sale should have the following characteristics.

(1) The goods should be complete and ready for delivery.

(2) The seller should not have retained any significant performance obligations other than safekeeping and shipment.

(3) Subject to rights of return, the seller should have obtained the right to consideration regardless of whether the goods are shipped, at the customer's request, to its delivery address.

(4) The goods should be identified separately from other stock and must not be capable of being used to fill other orders.

(5) The bill and hold terms should meet the commercial objectives of the customer, not the seller; for example, the delay in the delivery of the goods is to meet the customer's need.

4.2.5   Sales with right of return

The Application Note also deals with rights of return. It takes a very pragmatic view of such rights, and requires companies to make reasonable estimates of returns, and not just to follow the legal position. It is vital to distinguish between a significant commercial uncertainty concerning returns and a legal right of return. FRS 5, in general, requires that commercially significant risks be considered when determining appropriate accounting treatments, but that commercially insignificant risks should not have a major effect on such treatments. For nearly all sales of goods a legal right of return will exist if the product is defective or not fit for the purpose for which it was intended. This does not usually mean that there is significant commercial uncertainty.

Therefore, as a general rule, where the likelihood of returns is low then it may be possible to ignore the possibility of returns on the grounds that the effect of future returns on the business will be immaterial. In order to be able to adopt this approach it would be necessary to assess the likelihood of returns on a prudent basis. Where the level of returns is predictable and not excessive, then income may be recorded on each individual transaction, but the company should then make a provision at each balance sheet date for the likely level of returns in respect of sales made during the period.

Any subsequent adjustments to expected returns should be made through turnover.

In the rare case where a reasonable estimate cannot be made, then the treatment must follow the contract rights. This will normally lead to fairly significant deferral of revenue. In the most extreme, and even rarer, case, this could preclude the recognition of turnover until all of the rights have expired, or it becomes possible to make a reasonable estimate.

IAS 18 adopts a similar approach to that included in the Application Note:

> . . . Another example of an entity retaining only an insignificant risk of ownership may be a retail sale when a refund is offered if the customer is not satisfied. Revenue in such cases is recognised at the time of sale provided the seller can reliably estimate future returns and recognises a liability for returns based on previous experience and other relevant factors. (Para. 17, IAS 18.)

4.2.6   Principal and agent

Aside from the legal issue of whether a company is acting as agent or principal is the accounting issue. While this does not usually affect profit, it can substantially affect the appearance of the profit and loss account. Where a company acts as agent, it normally just shows commission. Where it acts as principal, it will usually show a much higher turnover since it includes the gross value of the transaction and record cost of sales.

In order to account as principal, a company should normally bear all of the risks normally associated with either selling price or stock.

In addition, there is a presumption that a company is acting as principal where:

- it does not disclose that it is acting as agent;
- it actually performs part of the service, or modifies any goods that are supplied;
- it assumes the credit risk, or
- it has discretion in the selection of the ultimate supplier.

Conversely, there is a presumption that a company is acting as agent where:

- this has been disclosed;
- once the order has been confirmed the company has no further involvement in meeting the contractual obligations;
- the amount of income is predetermined, being either a fixed fee per transaction or a percentage of the contract value, or
- it takes no credit or stock risk, except to the extent that it receives additional consideration from the ultimate supplier.

Some examples given in the Note include the following.

(1) A building contractor who negotiates the price, takes the credit risk, takes primary responsibility for construction and quality and can choose whether to do the work or employ a sub-contractor. In this case the contractor is acting as principal.

(2) An online travel agent who takes prices from the holiday provider, is not responsible for any problems with the holiday, receives a fee per holiday booked and is not involved after the initial stages. The travel agent is an agent.

(3) A department store provides space for concessionaires and receives rental income from the concessionaires. The department store is acting as agent.

Where a company acts as agent, the Note suggests that the gross value of throughput is provided as additional non-statutory information. Where this information is provided then there should be a brief explanation of the relationship of turnover to gross throughput. This is not a mandatory disclosure.

In the last few years, there has been a change to IAS 18 dealing with the treatment of a party as principal or agent in a revenue transaction. The guidance that is now included with IAS 18 is broadly similar to that included in Application Note G to FRS 5, except that it does not take into account whether the party is acting as a disclosed or undisclosed agent.

5 REPORTING FINANCIAL PERFORMANCE

5.1 INTRODUCTION

The main idea behind FRS 3 *Reporting Financial Performance* is that the performance of complex organisations cannot be summarised in a single figure, and that single figures can be used too simplistically by investors. Therefore, the standard requires companies to highlight a number of components of performance, so that readers of accounts may undertake (indeed in some ways are forced to undertake) their own analysis and interpretation of the company's progress and achievements.

This can be described as the 'information set' approach to financial reporting. Rather than attempting to boil down financial performance into one or two simplistic measures, a wide range of information is provided. The reader is, therefore, required to consider a variety of dimensions of performance and to establish the interrelationships between them.

The ASB clearly feels that many of the problems that can be solved by the information set approach are of far less relevance to smaller companies. This is presumably on the basis that they do not tend to have the external investors who must rely upon the information included in the annual financial statements. As a result, the FRSSE, in all of its various versions, including the 2008 version, omits most of the disclosure requirements included in FRS 3.

The main practical effects of the approach of FRS 3 are as follows.

(1) The profit and loss account should analyse all items down to operating profit between continuing and discontinued activities, including acquisitions as a separate sub-category of continuing activities. Part of such analysis must be provided on the face of the profit and loss account, whilst other elements may either be presented on the face of the profit and loss account or dealt with in the notes.

(2) Ordinary activities have been defined very widely, so that it is difficult, in fact impossible, to think of a transaction that might be classed as extraordinary. As a result, there are no longer extraordinary items in UK company accounts.

(3) A statement of total recognised gains and losses is included as a primary financial statement. This includes the profit for the financial year together with any other gains and losses that have been taken directly to reserves. Where a company has no gains and losses other than the result for the year shown in the profit and loss account, it has to make a specific statement

noting that as a result no statement of total recognised gains and losses has been provided.

(4) A note on historical cost profits and losses is included, which reconciles the reported profit with the figure which would have been reported under the historical cost system, where that the company has not adopted such a system.

(5) A reconciliation between opening and closing shareholders' funds is included.

For small companies complying with the FRSSE there is far less disclosure. There is no requirement for an analysis in the profit and loss account between acquisitions, other continuing and discontinued activities, no requirement for a note on historical cost profits and losses, and no requirement for a reconciliation of shareholders' funds. There is a requirement for a statement of total recognised gains and losses, but where the company has no such items other than those included in the profit and loss account, there is no requirement for a 'negative' statement to this effect.

There have been some minor changes to FRS 3 in recent years. The standard was amended in 2007 to resolve prima facie inconsistencies with FRS 26 *Financial Instruments: Recognition and Measurement* and FRS 23 *The Effects of Changes in Foreign Exchange Rates*. In both cases, the change affected only companies which fall within the scope of, or have chosen to adopt FRS 26. However, at the same time, the previous exemption from having to include, in the note of historical costs, profits and losses, any adjustments arising from the practice of market makers and other dealers in investments of marking to market, where this was an established industry practice, was also removed, and replaced with specific reference to adjustments required by FRS 26. This affected a fairly small number of companies, being those which had previously marked investments to market and taken this exemption, but which were not required to adopt, and had not voluntarily adopted, FRS 26. Such companies are now required to provide a note of historical cost profits and losses.

Potential impact of the FRSME

The approach taken in the FRSME differs substantially from that adopted in FRS 3, and some financial statements could look quite different if the FRSME is adopted.

Among the main differences are that the FRSME contains no requirements equivalent to that which is included in FRS 3 for the analysis of acquired, discontinued and continuing operations on the face of the primary performance statements.

The primary statements themselves differ substantially. The FRSME basically requires a company to choose between giving an income statement and a statement of comprehensive income, or to have a single statement of comprehensive income which is then in two parts. A statement of comprehensive income (or the other comprehensive income section of a combined statement) is similar to a statement of total recognised gains and losses, although it is not quite the same. It deals with those gains and losses which are not recorded within profit, but there are differences between the items allowed or required to be treated in this way between current UK GAAP and the FRSME.

The FRSME also requires a statement of changes in equity, which is broadly similar to a note of movements in shareholders' funds.

For the simplest entities, those which have no income or expense items which are not recognised in profit, there is also the option of having a combined statement of income and retained earnings. This then replaces the statement of comprehensive income and statement of changes in equity.

There is no FRSME equivalent of the note of historical cost profits and losses.

One thing that would not change is that there would not, in practice, be extraordinary items. (Although the FRSME differs from the IFRS for SMEs on which it based in this respect, since it replaces the absolute prohibition with a definition such that no items would actually fall within it.)

5.2 THE PROFIT AND LOSS ACCOUNT

5.2.1 *Continuing and discontinued operations*

FRS 3 (but not the FRSSE) requires all profit and loss account headings from turnover to operating profit to be analysed between amounts attributable to continuing and discontinued operations, with acquired activities being shown as a sub-category of continuing operations. This analysis must be given for both the current and the comparative period. The turnover and operating profit must be analysed on the face of the profit and loss account, while the other analyses can be provided either on the face of the profit and loss account or in the notes.

An illustration of the FRS 3 format showing the performance of continuing, acquired and discontinued activities (but omitting the comparative figures) is given in the following example.

EXAMPLE

	£m	£m
Turnover		
from continuing operations	4,194	
from acquisitions	721	
	4,915	
from discontinued operations	930	
		5,845
Cost of sales		(2,132)
Gross profit		3,713
Net operating expenses		(1,042)
Operating profit		
from continuing operations	2,210	
from acquisitions	312	
	2,522	
from discontinued operations	149	
Total operating profit		2,671
Profit on disposal of discontinued operations		75
Profit on ordinary activities before interest		2,746
Interest		(210)
Profit on ordinary activities before taxation		2,536
Tax on profit on ordinary activities		(830)
Profit on ordinary activities after taxation		1,706

In this case, the minimum disclosure has been provided on the face of the profit and loss account and there would need to be additional information provided by way of note to the accounts.

Providing comparative figures is more complicated than it might at first appear. The complication arises because the classification of an activity (between continuing, acquired or discontinued) depends on the status of the activity in the current reporting period, irrespective of its status in the comparative period. This means that activities treated as discontinued in the current year must also be shown as discontinued in the comparatives. This is despite the fact that in the previous period's financial statements they would have been shown as acquired or as normal continuing operations. Acquisitions are much simpler, since acquisitions in the previous year are shown as continuing (or discontinued if appropriate) in the comparatives for the current year. This means that the comparative figures will not necessarily agree, category by category, with those shown in the previous year's financial statements. The aggregate amounts will, of course, be unchanged. These treatments are illustrated in the following example.

EXAMPLE

In 2011, a company has three activities, A, B and C. During 2010 activity C was acquired and during 2011 activity A was discontinued; activity B continued throughout 2009, 2010 and 2011.

The sales figures for each activity are as follows:

	2011 £	2010 £	2009 £
Activity A (discontinued)	400	600	800
Activity B	1,500	1,200	1,500
Activity C	750	700	–

The classification of sales of the three activities into (i) continuing, (ii) acquired and (iii) discontinued in the 2010 and 2011 accounts is shown below. Note that:

- activity C is shown as acquired in the 2010 accounts, but as continuing in the 2011 accounts, and
- activity A is shown as continuing in the 2010 accounts, but as discontinued in the 2011 accounts.

Accounts for the year ended	2011			2010			2009
	Continuing £	Acquired £	Discontinued £	Continuing £	Acquired £	Discontinued £	Continuing £
				1,800	700	–	2,300
	2,250	–	400	1,900	–	600	

As noted above, the analysis of turnover and operating profit for the current year must be provided on the face of the profit and loss account. The analysis of all other items, including all comparatives, may be provided either on the face of the profit and loss account or in the notes to the financial statements.

Operating profit is not a term that derives from the formats included in The Large and Medium-sized Companies and Groups (Accounts and Reports) Regulations 2008 (SI 2008/410). The term is also used in FRS 1 *Cash Flow Statements*, but is not defined there. FRS 3 states that for companies other than those in the financial sector, operating profit means profit before income from shares in group undertakings. It does not define operating profit for those companies that do operate in the financial sector.

Like SSAP 25 *Segmental Reporting*, FRS 3 assumes that no similar analysis of items further down the profit and loss account, such as interest and taxation, will be provided in the financial statements. The main reason for this is that such an analysis may involve a considerable element of judgement and subjectivity. Despite this, an analysis of interest and taxation is allowed, but only if the method and underlying assumptions that have been used in making the allocation are disclosed. (This can be contrasted with the position under the international standard IFRS 5 *Non-current Assets Held for Sale and Discontinued Operations*, which does require such analysis to be provided in the notes. However, IFRS 5 is a very different standard, which requires far less disclosure on the face of the profit and loss account, or rather the income statement or statement of comprehensive income.)

In certain cases, it may not be possible to determine the effect of an acquisition on the results for the period. This might occur, for example, where a business is acquired but its activities are immediately integrated with those of the acquirer, are not kept within a separate subsidiary, and where separate accounting records are not maintained. In this case any figures which were allocated to the acquisition section of the profit and loss account might be somewhat arbitrary, and more likely to be misleading than useful.

In such a case, FRS 3 requires that an indication should be given of the acquisition's contribution to turnover and operating profit. If even such an indication cannot be given then the accounts should state this fact, and explain the reason why the information cannot be provided.

The dividing line between discontinued and continuing operations under the standard may not always be as clear as one might like. Discontinued operations are defined in the following terms:

> Operations of the reporting entity that are sold or terminated and that satisfy all of the following conditions.
>
> (a) The sale or termination is completed either in the period or before the earlier of three months after the commencement of the subsequent period and the date on which the financial statements are approved.
> (b) If a termination, the former activities have ceased permanently.
> (c) The sale or termination has a material effect on the nature and focus of the reporting entity's operations and represents a material reduction in its operating facilities resulting either from its withdrawal from a particular market (whether class of business or geographical) or from a material reduction in turnover in the reporting entity's continuing markets.
> (d) The assets, liabilities, results of operations and activities are clearly distinguishable, physically, operationally, and for financial reporting purposes.
>
> Operations not satisfying all these conditions are classified as continuing. (Para. 4, FRS 3.)

It is not necessary that an activity should actually cease during the period for it to be treated as discontinued. As is made clear from the above, it should also be treated as discontinued if it ceases within the earlier of three months after the end of the year and the date of approval of the financial statements.

In effect, a discontinuance which occurs shortly after the year end will lead to a re-analysis of the profit and loss account for the previous year and the comparatives. It will not normally lead to a different profit being reported for the year, as it is not normally an adjusting event after the balance sheet date under FRS 21 *Events After the Balance Sheet Date*, but it will mean that the profit needs to be broken down into its separate components. This strongly indicates that one of the aims of FRS 3 is to enable the reader of the accounts to make judgements about the expected future of the company, as well as about the events that have taken place during the year.

A discontinuance after the end of the year may affect the reported result if the transaction results in a loss, since the proceeds will usually provide an indication of the value of the business at the balance sheet date.

The effect of losses on discontinuances which occur after the balance sheet date is affected by both FRS 3 and FRS 12 *Provisions, Contingent Liabilities and Contingent Assets*. FRS 12 applies to all provisions for restructuring and similar, potentially including those in respect of discontinued operations. When FRS 12 was introduced it made some changes to the text of FRS 3 itself, although these were minimal, and did not deal with the general problem of discontinuances at a loss. The text of FRS 3 was broadly unaltered, although some references to the disposal of assets were removed.

FRS 12 allows provisions to be made for restructuring costs, including those associated with a discontinuance, subject to a number of detailed conditions. The requirements are set out in detail in Chapter 17, but in summary:

- there must be a formal plan setting out full details of the restructuring, and
- there must be a valid expectation on the part of those affected by the restructuring that it will be carried out, either because it has already started or because the plan has been announced to those affected.

In addition, no obligation arises for the sale of an operation until the entity is committed to the sale, meaning that there is a binding sale agreement in place, and provisions may not be made for future operating losses.

FRS 12 prohibits the recognition of a provision until an event has occurred giving rise to the obligation. This means that it is not possible to provide for a loss as a result of a discontinuance which has taken place after the end of the accounting year, even if it is treated as a discontinuance for the purposes of disclosure.

While FRS 12 is not entirely clear on this matter, it would appear that discontinuances must be treated in exactly the same way as any other restructurings.

Despite this, the effect in practice may be minimal. While FRS 12 may prohibit the recognition of losses associated with discontinuances taking place after the end of the accounting year, these would still be taken into account in any impairment review of the part of the business to be sold. FRS 11 *Impairment of Fixed Assets and Goodwill* requires impairment reviews to be undertaken where there is an indication that the value of assets may be overstated in the balance sheet. Where a business is sold at a loss after the end of the year, this would be a very clear indication of likely impairment. While no provision could be made for future losses, there may be a need to write down the value of the assets associated with the business that is being sold. This may be a different way of arriving at what is effectively the same answer.

Where an activity ceases only temporarily, it should not be counted as discontinued. The standard does not deal with the situation where a company later decides that it will not recommence an activity which it had originally intended to cease only temporarily. While the activity would fall within the definition of discontinued at this later date, there would presumably be no operations to be disclosed under this heading.

The biggest practical problem in determining when an activity should be treated as discontinued is in determining whether or not it has had a material effect on the nature and focus of the company's operations. Unfortunately, the examples given in the explanatory notes do not clarify this point particularly well.

EXAMPLE

The explanatory notes to FRS 3 give an example of a company which has previously served the lower end of the hotel market, and then sells all its existing hotels and buys luxury hotels.

In this case there has been such a clear change in the 'nature and focus' of the company's activities that it is equally clear that it could reasonably be treated as the discontinuance of one form of activity and the commencement of another. Another example is given of a hotel chain, which has previously operated solely in the USA, and then sells its hotels and starts activities in Europe. In practice, it is very unlikely that quite such a situation would be encountered.

Extending the ASB's same basic example, of the hotel business, the situation might be less clear if, for example:

- a company started a gradual process of selling off hotels in one sector of the market and purchasing hotels in another sector, the process taking, say, four years before the change was completed;
- a company sold its hotels in one category and bought hotels in an only slightly higher or in a lower category, or
- a company sold its hotels in central London and opened hotels in towns around London.

It is clear that a key part of the definition relates to the identification of the markets in which the company operates. As the standard implies, one of the considerations will be the segmental disclosure that is provided by the company (or that would have been disclosed if the company had not taken advantage of the exemptions that are available to it under the Companies Act 2006 and SSAP 25). The nature of the production process used by the company is not a relevant consideration. In effect, FRS 3 looks at the external environment within which the company operates, rather than the internal environment.

This is made even clearer when the standard discusses changes which the company might make in its production methods. The standard makes it clear that where a change is undertaken simply to save costs, for example, where a company ceases to manufacture some components internally and sub-contracts this part of the work, then this remains part of the company's continuing activities. This means that a company might, for example, undertake a significant re-engineering of its business without being able to treat any area of its business as discontinued. (There would, however, have to be disclosure of the costs involved in the reorganisation together with an explanation in the notes to the accounts.)

Where an activity is treated as discontinued, only those income and costs that are directly related to the discontinued activities should be reported under that heading in the profit and loss account. This can still leave the problem of any impact that a discontinuance can have on the remainder of the company's business. The standard does address the problem of reorganisation and restructuring costs which arise within the continuing activities but directly as the result of a discontinuance. The standard, perhaps somewhat unfairly, requires that these costs be treated as costs of continuing activities and not as part of the costs of the discontinued activities.

Although it is easy to sympathise with the ASB on this matter, as any other treatment could lead to abuse, it seems equally unfair that continuing activities may include costs which would never have been incurred if the decision to discontinue other activities had not been reached. The approach here seems similar to that taken in FRS 7 *Fair Values in Acquisition Accounting*, where reorganisation costs may not be included in the calculation of the fair value of the acquired assets. The logic underlying both decisions is somewhat stretched, and the main concern seems to be the minimisation of the possibility of abuse. It is a pity that the ASB did not feel able to frame rules in such a way that the potential for abuse could be eliminated, or at least minimised, without requiring companies to show costs in one category which arose directly because of another.

In addition to all of the other disclosure requirements concerning operations, where an acquisition, sale or termination has a material impact on a major business segment, this must be disclosed and explained.

Potential impact of the FRSME

The FRSME does not contain equivalent requirements to FRS 3 in relation to acquired operations. Given that the FRSME is based on the IFRS for SMEs, this is hardly surprising since neither the IFRS for SMEs nor full IFRS contain extensive disclosures in respect of acquired operations. (There are disclosure requirements in relation to business combinations which may provide some of the information that would be required under FRS 3.)

It does contain requirements in relation to discontinued operations, but these bear little relationship to those in FRS 3 and are closer to those in full IFRS (although with substantially less disclosure). In place of the detailed analysis required by FRS 3, a company would have to disclose only:

(a)   a single amount in the statement of comprehensive income comprising the total of:

    (i)   the post-tax profit or loss of a discontinued operation, and

    (ii) the post-tax gain or loss recognised on the measurement to fair value less costs to sell or on the disposal of the net assets constituting the discontinued operation.

5.2.2 Provisions for discontinuance

As noted above, FRS 12 has a major impact on the ability of companies to make provisions for costs which are associated with a termination or sale of operations. The somewhat vague rules that were previously included in FRS 3 were replaced by those in FRS 12 with far more detailed, and onerous, conditions.

Companies may not make provisions for any termination which does not qualify as a discontinued operation unless they can demonstrate the following.

(1)   There is a formal plan dealing with the termination which identifies:

    (a)   the business or parts of a business involved;

    (b)   the main locations affected;

    (c)   the location, function and approximate number of employees who will be compensated for the termination of their services;

    (d)   the expenditures that will be undertaken, and

    (e)   when the plan will be implemented.

(2)   There is a valid expectation on the part of those affected by the plan that it will be carried out, either because the plan has already started to be implemented or because it has been announced to those affected.

Companies may not make provision for costs associated with a sale unless a binding sale agreement is in place by the balance sheet date.

As noted above, companies may still be required to take account of losses arising from terminations or sales in the next accounting period, but this will be through the medium of an impairment review rather than by making provision for the loss directly.

Where a provision can be made under FRS 12, companies must treat this as part of their continuing activities. However, when the operation subsequently qualifies as discontinued then the provision should be shown in the relevant accounting period as utilised against the operating loss and loss on sale or termination of the operation, and included on the face of the profit and loss account.

Potential impact of the FRSME

This is not an area that is likely to change very much as a result of the FRSME. The FRSME contains a section dealing with provisions for restructuring which is very similar to the requirements currently set out in FRS 12.

5.2.3 Profits and losses on the disposal of fixed assets

Profits and losses on the disposal of fixed assets must be calculated by comparing the net sale proceeds with the net carrying amount, whether they were carried at historical cost or at a valuation. This means that revaluation gains which have previously been recognised will not appear in the profit and loss account when they are realised, as shown in the following example.

EXAMPLE

A company purchases an asset, with an expected life of ten years, for £100. After four years, its written-down value is £60 and it has a fair value of £90. Consider two possible treatments, prior to the sale of the asset at the end of the fifth year, for £85.

(1)   No revaluation

By the end of the fifth year the asset will have been depreciated to half of its original value. The profit on the sale is therefore £35 = £85 − £50.

(2)   Revaluation

Ignoring any previous movements, if the company revalues the asset at the end of the fourth year to £90, the revaluation of £30 will be recognised in the statement of total recognised gains and losses. At the end of the fifth year the asset will be depreciated by £15, and the profit recognised on the sale will be £10 = £85 − £75.

The total amount of cumulative gains recognised in respect of the asset will be £40 (£30 on revaluation and £10 on the sale), £5 larger than under no revaluation. This is due to the extra depreciation charged, which is £15 rather than £10.

This example also illustrates the importance which the ASB attaches to the information currently in the statement of total recognised gains and losses, which is itself covered later. The same treatment applies under the FRSSE.

Potential impact of the FRSME

The FRSME does not allow the revaluation of most tangible fixed assets (described as property, plant and equipment) so the question of how to determine the profit on disposal of such an asset does not really arise, since the only possibility is by reference to the carrying value. There is no possibility of there being a revaluation reserve in place that might complicate the issue.

The FRSME does allow the revaluation of some assets, such as investment properties.

5.2.4 *Profits and losses on financial instruments and foreign operations*

As noted earlier, a profit or loss on the disposal of a fixed asset is determined by comparing the proceeds with the carrying amount. Therefore, if there has been a previous revaluation this is not taken into account in determining the profit or loss that is recorded on the disposal. Instead, the previously unrealised gain is transferred to accumulated profits at the point of disposal. This is undertaken as a reserve transfer.

FRS 3 contains a general principle that if a gain or loss has been recognised in the statement of total recognised gains and losses, then it is not recognised again on disposal.

However, there is a problem with this principle when it is applied to some companies which are also adopting other standards which contain requirements which contradict this basic principle. For companies which are required to adopt, or have in fact adopted, FRS 26 *Financial Instruments: Recognition and Measurement*, gains and losses on certain financial instruments may be taken directly to equity. When such an item is sold, or otherwise removed from a balance sheet, any gain or loss included in the profit and loss account must take account of the amounts previously recognised in equity. This is sometimes referred to as 'recycling'. This is contrary to the basic principle of FRS 3, and arises because of a conflict between the basic approaches of the two standards. As a result, FRS 3 allows gains and losses which have previously been included in equity to be included within profit or loss when realised, where this is specifically required by FRS 26.

A similar issue can arise on foreign operations. Where the inclusion of a foreign operation gives rise to exchange differences, and the reporting entity is subject to FRS 26 and therefore also complying with FRS 23 *The Effects of Changes in Foreign Exchange Rates*, then those exchange differences are taken directly to reserves via the statement of total recognised gains and losses. On disposal of the foreign operation the cumulative exchange differences must be included in the calculation of the profit or loss arising on disposal. Again, this differs from the basis principle of FRS 3, which prohibits such recycling. As a result, another exception from the general principle is allowed by FRS 3, and it is the FRS 23 requirement that must be followed.

Neither of these changes affects companies which are not complying with FRS 26. The majority of companies are not required to, and do not, comply with FRS 26. Therefore, these exceptions to the basic principle of FRS 3 are quite limited in their effect.

Potential impact of the FRSME

The FRSME could reduce the problems associated with the exceptions, since there are fewer items which would be stated at fair value with value changes being treated as part of a movement in equity.

5.2.5   Extraordinary items

FRS 3 defines extraordinary items as:

> Material items possessing a high degree of abnormality which arise from events or transactions that fall outside the ordinary activities of the reporting entity and which are not expected to recur. They do not include exceptional items nor do they include prior period items merely because they relate to a prior period. (Para. 6, FRS 3.)

While this, on its own, would appear to allow scope for such items to appear in financial statements, this possibility is unrealistic due to the manner in which ordinary activities are defined under FRS 3. They include:

> . . . the effects on the reporting entity of any event in the various environments in which [the company] operates, including the political, regulatory, economic and geographical environments, irrespective of the frequency or unusual nature of the events. (Para. 2, FRS 3.)

But what other events are there? Given the effective definition of extraordinary items it is not surprising that the standard notes that they are likely to be so rare that no examples can be provided. The standard's guidance on the treatment and disclosure of extraordinary items seems superfluous, given that they will never be encountered in practice. The relevance of much of the distinction between extraordinary and exceptional items has also been eliminated since earnings per share are calculated after extraordinary items. It would have been easier had FRS 3 simply stated that it abolished the concept of extraordinary items, as in practice this is what it has done.

In the theoretically possible event that an extraordinary profit or loss arises, it is to be shown on the face of the profit and loss account. Individual extraordinary items may be shown either on the face of the profit and loss account or in a note.

Potential impact of the FRSME

The FRSME would have virtually no impact, since the definition of extraordinary items remains so narrow that they will not be encountered in practice. The FRSME is based on the IFRS for SMEs, which itself simply prohibits the recognition of extraordinary items. The FRSME instead defines extraordinary items in such a way that they will never be encountered.

5.2.6 *Exceptional items*

Exceptional items are defined as:

> Material items which derive from events or transactions that fall within the ordinary activities of the reporting entity and which individually or, if of a similar type, in aggregate, need to be disclosed by virtue of their size or incidence if the financial statements are to give a true and fair view. (Para. 5, FRS 3.)

Both FRS 3 and the FRSSE, in effect, divide exceptional items into two groups: specifically identified items and all others.

These identified items, which include provisions for such items, are:

- profits or losses on the sale or termination of an operation;
- costs of a fundamental reorganisation or restructuring having a material effect on the nature and focus of the reporting entity's operation, and
- profits or losses on the disposal of fixed assets.

FRS 3 also makes the point that in determining the profit or loss in respect of each of these items, only those revenues and costs that are related to them directly may be taken into account.

FRS 3 and the FRSSE require that these items be shown separately on the face of the profit and loss account, after operating profit and before interest. In the case of companies which are not small, they must be analysed between continuing, acquired and discontinued activities. The location of these exceptional items is shown (in italic) in the following example.

EXAMPLE	
	£m
Turnover	
from continuing operations	4,194
Cost of sales	(2,125)
Gross profit	2,069
Net operating expenses	(1,042)
Operating profit	
from continuing operations	1,027
Profit on the sale of investments	*217*
Profit on ordinary activities before interest	1,244
Interest	(210)
Profit on ordinary activities before taxation	1,034
Tax on profit on ordinary activities	(317)
Profit on ordinary activities after taxation	717

Information on the effect of these items on both taxation and minority interests should also be provided in the notes to the accounts. This may be in aggregate, that is, for all of the categories combined, but should be given individually if the effect of each item is not similar. This might occur, for example, where a subsidiary is restructured and the parent owns 75 per cent of the subsidiary's shares, whereas all restructuring costs derive from the parent's own activities, or those of a wholly owned subsidiary. This disclosure is not required for a small company.

The tax on such items should be calculated by determining the tax that would be payable if the items had not occurred, and then determining the difference from the amount of tax that is actually payable. This procedure may not be necessary where a company pays corporation tax at the full or small companies rate, but may be vital where the company falls into the marginal band. Given that there is no such disclosure requirement for small companies, the FRSSE does not provide a basis for calculating the tax on exceptional items.

In some cases, the net amount of one of these categories may be immaterial, yet it may contain material items. This is most likely to occur with profits and losses on disposal of fixed assets, where the overall profit or loss may be quite small, if there are both profits and losses of similar amounts in the period. Where this occurs, FRS 3 and the FRSSE require that the net amount be shown on the face of the profit and loss account and that the gross profits and losses be disclosed in a note.

All other exceptional items should be included within one of the statutory headings in the profit and loss account (such as cost of sales) and, in the case of companies not applying the FRSSE, allocated, as appropriate, to discontinued, acquired and other continuing activities. The amount of each of these items should then be disclosed by way of a note, or on the face of the profit and loss account if this is necessary to give a true and fair view. Sufficient description should be given in the notes to the accounts to enable the user to understand the effect of the item.

Potential impact of the FRSME

The FRSME does not contain equivalent requirements in respect of exceptional items.

5.2.7   Taxation

A note to the accounts should disclose any special circumstances that affect the overall tax charge or credit for the period, or for future periods. This should include specific comments on any exceptional items that are required to be shown on the face of the profit and loss account.

The effects of a fundamental change in the basis of taxation should be included in the tax charge or credit for the period and separately disclosed on the face of the profit and loss account.

5.3 STATEMENT OF TOTAL RECOGNISED GAINS AND LOSSES

Although the profit and loss account is intended to be inclusive, and therefore includes most of a company's gains and losses, FRS 3 also recognises that the number of exceptions to this general principle is quite high. Such exemptions are provided both by other accounting standards and by the statutory instruments supporting the Companies Act 2006. As a result, there is a danger that users of financial statements may be misled if it is not made clear that there have been movements on reserves giving rise to gains and losses, other than amounts that have been included in the profit and loss account.

For this reason, the standard also requires a statement of total recognised gains and losses as a primary financial statement. This requirement is also included in the FRSSE.

Where there are no gains and losses other than those in the profit and loss account, the standard requires that this be stated immediately below the profit and loss account. This is not required for small companies which are taking advantage of the FRSSE, where the absence of such a statement is taken to be sufficient indication that it is not required.

Items that would appear in the statement of total recognised gains and losses, and not the profit and loss account, include:

- revaluation surpluses, and deficiencies where these have not been charged to the profit and loss account, including amounts in respect of investment properties accounted for under SSAP 19 *Accounting for Investment Properties*;
- currency translation differences on foreign equity net investments, which are not required to pass through the profit and loss account as a result of the exemptions under SSAP 20 *Foreign Currency Translation*, as amended by UITF 19 *Tax on Gains and Losses on Foreign Currency Borrowings that Hedge an Investment in a Foreign Enterprise*, or by FRS 23. *The Effects of Changes in Foreign Exchange Rates, and*
- certain movements, such as actuarial gains and losses, in respect of defined benefit pension schemes under FRS 17 *Retirement Benefits*.

An example of a statement of total recognised gains and losses follows.

> **EXAMPLE**
>
> *Statement of total recognised gains and losses*
>
> | | £m |
> |---|---|
> | *Profit for the financial year* | 3,178 |
> | Unrealised gains on revaluation of fixed assets | 257 |
> | | 3,435 |
> | Currency translation losses on foreign equity net investments | (102) |
> | *Total recognised gains and losses relating to the year* | 3,333 |

Potential impact of the FRSME

The FRSME does not require a statement of total recognised gains and losses, but the statement of comprehensive income (or other comprehensive income section of a combined statement) is broadly similar. It deals with those gains and losses that are recognised by companies, but which are not recognised within profit or loss. The individual items that might fall within such a statement are fairly limited under the FRSME, which is more restricted than current UK GAAP in terms of being able to revalue assets.

5.4   PRIOR PERIOD ADJUSTMENTS

5.4.1   Definition

FRS 3 defines prior period adjustments as:

> Material adjustments applicable to prior periods arising from changes in accounting policies or from the correction of fundamental errors. They do not include normal recurring adjustments or corrections of accounting estimates made in prior periods. (Para. 7, FRS 3.)

This definition is also followed in the FRSSE.

This will exclude the majority of changes to amounts that had already been recorded in prior periods. For example, it does not cover:

- adjustments to provisions for bad debts;
- adjustments to the provisions made for taxation;
- minor omissions of accruals and prepayments;
- revenue recognised in the year which relates to a prior year, but which was not recorded in that prior year as it did not meet the recognition criteria set out in Application Note G to FRS 5, *Reporting the Substance of Transactions*, at the time;
- bad debts recovered which had been written off in previous periods;
- adjustments to the estimated useful lives of depreciable fixed assets, and
- changes to the estimated profit arising over the life of a long-term contract.

All of these items will be considered "... normal recurring adjustments or corrections of accounting estimates made in prior periods". Where the amounts of such items are material they should be separately disclosed, if necessary, in order to ensure that users of the financial statements are not misled, but should not be included as prior period adjustments. But no adjustment to the amounts shown for prior periods is required, and such items are treated as adjustments in the current year, or in some cases such as a change in useful lives, the current year and future years.

Potential impact of the FRSME

The FRSME draws similar distinctions, and allows retrospective adjustment only for the correction of errors and for changes in accounting policy. It does not, however, require an error to be fundamental in order to require correction, although it would still need to be material.

5.4.2 *Changes in accounting policies*

Consistency requires that companies should apply the same accounting policies from year to year to ensure that the amounts shown in their financial statements are comparable. This principle can only be broken where it is necessary in order to ensure that the financial statements provide a true and fair view.

A change in accounting policy may be made only if:

> ... it can be justified on the grounds that the new policy is preferable to the one it replaces because it will give a fairer presentation of the result and of the financial position of the reporting entity. (Para. 62, FRS 3.)

The most common case is where a new accounting policy is required as a result of the introduction of a new accounting standard, or perhaps a new consensus pronouncement from the UITF, although it is not limited to these cases. The same principle applies under the FRSSE. The area of changing accounting policies is also covered in FRS 18 *Accounting Policies*, although this does not affect the treatment that must be adopted in respect of the changes, as set out in FRS 3.

It should be noted that, while most changes in accounting policy as a result of new accounting standards or UITFs are governed by FRS 3, there may be specific transitional provisions included in the new standard which will then override the normal treatment. Some accounting changes, for example, may be stated by the standard bringing them in to be on a prospective basis only, which means that they affect the treatment in the current and future years, but no adjustment is made in respect of items reported in previous accounting periods.

Changes in accounting policies must be distinguished from changes in accounting estimates, or changes in estimation techniques in terms of FRS 18. For example, where there is a change in the estimated useful life of a fixed asset, this is considered to be a change in an accounting estimate. It is not considered to be a change in an accounting policy and, therefore, gives rise to no adjustment to prior periods.

A change in an accounting policy must also be distinguished from a refinement of an accounting policy. As a business develops it may find that it is undertaking transactions which differ in important respects from those that it has undertaken in the past. The existing accounting policies of the company may no longer be appropriate and additional policies may be introduced, or new conditions applied within the framework of the existing policy. Such changes would not be sufficient to fall within the definition of a change in accounting policy for the purposes of FRS 3.

Following an actual change in accounting policy, the cumulative effect of the adjustments to the retained profits at the beginning of the current period should not be treated as a profit or loss in the current year. Instead, the amounts of assets and liabilities in the comparative balance sheet and the opening balance of retained reserves should be adjusted. This should be done by stating the figure that appeared originally, and then showing the adjustment that must be made to this figure as a result of the change in accounting policy. The effect of the adjustment on the result of the previous year should also be stated, where practical, together with the effect on the results of the current year. Where the effect on the current year cannot be calculated then this fact should be stated. Where the effect on the result of the current year is immaterial or similar to that for the previous year, then a statement of this fact will suffice.

In addition, the cumulative adjustments should also be noted at the foot of the statement of total recognised gains and losses, and, in the case of larger companies, included in the reconciliation of movements in shareholders' funds. The following example illustrates the required disclosures.

EXAMPLE

As a result of a change in accounting policy during the year beginning 1 January 2011, a company increases its provision for a liability made in the previous financial year. The provisions note would recognise the increase; the reserves note and the statement of total recognised gains and losses and the reconciliation of movements in shareholders' funds would recognise the loss as follows (in italic).

1. Provisions for liabilities

	£m
At 1 January 2010 (as previously stated)	1,349
Prior year adjustment	*168*
At 1 January 2010 as restated	1,517
Provisions made during the year	218
At 31 December 2010	1,735

---

2. *Profit and loss reserve*

	£m
At 1 January 2010 (as previously stated)	28,667
Prior year adjustment	*(168)*
At 1 January 2010 as restated	28,499
Retained profit for the year	2,586
At 31 December 2010	31,085

3. *Statement of total recognised gains and losses*

	£m
Profit for the financial year	7,267
Currency translation differences on net investments	317
Total recognised gains and losses relating to the year	7,584
Prior year adjustment	*(168)*
Total recognised gains and losses since last annual report	7,416

4. *Reconciliation of movement in shareholder's funds*

	£m
Profit for the financial year	7,267
Dividends	(4,681)
	2,586
Currency translation differences on net investments	317
Net addition to shareholders' funds	2,903
Opening shareholders' funds (originally £35,692 *before deducting prior year adjustment of £168*)	35,524
Closing shareholders' funds	38,427

Where a company publishes a historical summary, this should also be adjusted to take account of the effect of all prior period adjustments on the basis that there has been a change in accounting policy. If this is not possible, then the historical summary should disclose the years that have been changed and those that have not.

Potential impact of the FRSME

Obviously, the accounting policies allowed by the FRSME are not the same as those required or allowed under current UK GAAP. Nonetheless, the procedure for dealing with the accounting effect of changing accounting policies is broadly the same.

5.4.3 Fundamental errors

Occasionally, financial statements may be issued which include errors that are so fundamental that those financial statements do not present a true and fair view. It would not be reasonable to include these figures as comparatives in the next accounting period. Similarly, it would be highly misleading to include the necessary adjustments in the profit and loss account of the current year. Instead, they should be treated in the same way as changes in accounting policies.

Prior period adjustments will not be required where companies have used, or been forced to use, the statutory provisions in respect of defective accounts. Where defective accounts (accounts which do not give a true and fair view or otherwise have not been properly prepared in accordance with the Companies Act 2006) are issued it is possible to withdraw those accounts and provide revised accounts. This will normally be a decision reached by the directors of the company, but it can also be imposed upon them by the courts, possibly at the request of the Financial Reporting Review Panel. Where revised accounts have been issued, there will be no need to make a prior period adjustment on the grounds of fundamental error in the financial statements issued for the next accounting period.

Potential impact of the FRSME

The main difference under the FRSME is that there is no requirement that an error be fundamental in order for a retrospective correction to be made, to the extent that this is practicable. This is likely to mean that the correction of errors in subsequent financial statements would become rather more common under the FRSME than it is under current UK GAAP.

5.4.4   Balance sheet misclassifications

It is also possible that the comparative figures may contain errors in the comparative amounts in the balance sheet, but that those errors have no effect on the retained reserves, for example, where an asset or liability is stated at an appropriate amount but has been misclassified. This matter is not covered in FRS 3. It is suggested that such comparatives should be restated, to ensure that the amounts disclosed are comparable. Where the amounts involved are material, the notes to the accounts should state the nature of the changes, and the reason for them.

There may also be some reclassification, not as a result of any error, but simply to reflect changing circumstances. For example, a company may have a category of asset, such as a sub-category of debtors, which is immaterial in a particular year. In the following year, the amount is sufficiently material to warrant separate disclosure. It would be better to alter the comparatives to agree with the analysis used in the current year. If this is not done then the financial statements could be seen as a little misleading as there will be an apparent comparative of nil when this is not actually the case. Mention should be made of this change, without going into great detail, although the net impact will of course be nil.

5.5 RECONCILIATION OF MOVEMENTS IN SHAREHOLDERS' FUNDS

The profit and loss account and the statement of total recognised gains and losses are intended to measure the performance of the company during the period. However, there might be other changes in the shareholders' funds (for example, movements on share capital) which are important for understanding the changes in the company's financial position.

FRS 3, therefore, requires that a reconciliation of the movement in shareholders' funds be given. Where there have been no changes other than those included in the statement of total recognised gains and losses then, in our opinion, there is no requirement to provide such a reconciliation. Where the reconciliation is included as a primary statement, it should be shown separately from the statement of total recognised gains and losses.

Items that would appear in such a reconciliation include:

- issue of shares, including any issue costs that have been taken directly to the share premium account, and
- redemption of shares, including any premiums paid on redemption that have been deducted from the share premium account.

Dividends would also normally be included in such a reconciliation. Dividends may still be shown in a profit and loss account, although the requirement to do this was abolished in 2005. It is now normal practice to exclude dividends from a profit and loss account, probably on the basis that such treatment has, for many years, been rare under IFRS (and has been prohibited under IFRS with effect for accounting periods beginning on or after 1 January 2009).

EXAMPLE

Reconciliation of movements in shareholders' funds

	£m
Total recognised gains and losses for the year	3,333
Dividends	(1,548)
	1,785
Issue of equity shares	5,060
Net addition to shareholders' funds	6,845
Opening shareholders' funds	20,548
Closing shareholders' funds	27,393

In the example, the reconciliation starts with the total recognised gains and losses for the year. This format is used by a number of companies and contrasts with the example in FRS 3 which starts with the figure of profit for the year.

No such reconciliation is required for small companies taking advantage of the FRSSE.

Potential impact of the FRSME

The statement of changes in equity usually required by the FRSME is, very broadly, similar to the reconciliation of movements in shareholders' funds.

5.6 NOTE OF HISTORICAL COST PROFITS AND LOSSES

Where a company produces financial statements on any basis other than historical cost, then FRS 3 requires that those financial statements include a note showing the historical cost profit, reconciling this amount to the actual profit, if the difference is material. This should immediately follow the profit and loss account or the statement of total recognised gains and losses. This is another note that is not required for small companies which are taking advantage of the FRSSE.

The note must reconcile the two measures of profit on ordinary activities before taxation, and also state the historical cost retained profit for the financial year.

Adjustments would be made for items such as:

- gains recognised in prior periods and realised in the current period; for example, the difference between the profit on the disposal of an asset calculated on depreciated historical cost and that calculated on a revalued amount, and
- the difference between historical cost depreciation and the depreciation charge calculated on any revalued amounts.

Few companies which do not use historical cost accounting are required to provide such a statement. Many of the fixed assets that are commonly revalued are those with long useful economic lives, and therefore the effect of the cost convention is often immaterial with regard to reported profit (even though it may be material with regard to the balance sheet).

The number of companies required to produce such a statement increased, very slightly, in 2007. Previously, in determining whether such a statement was required companies were allowed to ignore adjustments necessary to cope with hyper-inflation on foreign operations and the practice of market makers and other dealers in investments of marking to market where this was an established industry practice. Since accounting periods beginning on or after 1 January 2007:

- the hyperinflation exemption has been specifically restricted to adjustments made under FRS 24 *Financial Reporting in Hyperinflationary Economies* or

UITF 9 *Accounting for Operations in Hyper-Inflationary Economies*. (In practice, this change will make absolutely no difference), and

- the mark to market exemption has been replaced with specific reference to fair value adjustments under FRS 26.

The first change affected a tiny number of companies. The second change also affected a fairly small number of companies; those which are not required to, and do not, comply with FRS 26, but which still have a practice of stating investments at market value and deal in investments as a significant part of their business.

Potential impact of the FRSME

There is no equivalent of this note under the FRSME.

6 SEGMENTAL REPORTING

6.1 INTRODUCTION

6.1.1 The need for segmental information

If a company operates in a single industry sector or trades in only one part of the world, then the interpretation of its financial statements should be relatively straightforward. The reader of the financial statements should be able to make informed assessments of the prospects of the company by looking at the nature of its operations and the changes that are expected to take place in its market. However, where a company operates in a number of sectors, or trades in various parts of the world, then the interpretation of its financial statements is likely to be much more difficult. Since the company is likely to be affected by changes that have taken place in each of its markets, the reader would need to know the balance between its various operations in order to make an informed assessment of the prospects of the company.

Unless the user of the financial statements is made aware of this balance between the different operations, it may be hard to assess, for example:

- the quality of the company's reported earnings;
- the specific risks to which the company or group is subject, relating to its operations rather than other matters such as the way in which it is financed, and
- the areas where long-term growth may be expected.

In order to provide the information needed by the user to make such an assessment, company law requires companies, other than small companies, to provide information in their financial statements about the different activities of the company or group and the markets in which they operate. Such information is normally referred to as segmental information or segmental reporting. Additional requirements are also set out in SSAP 25 *Segmental Reporting*.

There are also the various disclosure requirements relating to a review of the business required in the directors' reports of companies other than small companies, and covered in Chapter 3. These are outside of the financial statements, and primarily involve discussion rather than analysis of the amounts in the financial statements, but they may complement the segmental reporting requirements of both statute and SSAP 25.

Small companies are exempt from most of the requirements, and are required only to give the percentage of their turnover which is attributable to markets outside the UK. Consequently, segmental reporting is not covered in the FRSSE, other than through a cross reference to the statutory requirement.

6. Segmental Reporting

SSAP 25 suggests that the basic reasons for requiring reporting enterprises to provide segmental information are to assist the users of financial statements:

(a) to appreciate more thoroughly the results and financial position of the entity by permitting a better understanding of the entity's past performance and thus a better assessment of its future prospects; and

(b) to be aware of the impact that changes in significant components of a business may have on the business as a whole. (Para. 1, SSAP 25.)

The standard notes that one of its objectives is to ensure that the segmental information provided by businesses is shown on a consistent basis, and so will be comparable from one period to the next. The standard is intended to achieve consistency over time. It is relatively straightforward to ensure that companies provide information in a consistent manner relating to the various accounting periods for which they are presenting information.

However, it may still be very difficult, if not impossible, to draw valid comparisons between different enterprises. Consistency between different companies is much harder to achieve. Apart from any differences there might be in underlying accounting policies, there may also be valid differences in the accounting treatment of common costs and sales between segments. The way in which an enterprise structures its own affairs can have a major impact on the way in which it presents segmental information, independent of the markets or businesses in which it is operating. For example, if there are two businesses which operate in very similar types of industry, and produce and sell in similar markets, they may still present very different segmental information. If one of the enterprises allocates interest-bearing assets to each segment, but the other does not and instead treats them as affecting all segments, then the first enterprise will include interest in its calculation of the segment result, but the second will not. Similarly, the net assets of each segment in the first enterprise will include assets that earn interest, but the second will exclude such assets in its segmental analysis. As a result, even where we know that the segments that are reported are the same between different businesses, it may still be impossible to read very much into the information with which we are presented. Taking the example above, it will almost certainly not be possible to make any informed assessment of the allocation of central interest-bearing assets to the segment for the entity that provides no such disclosure. Direct comparison may therefore be possible, but only on the basis of ignoring interest and interest-bearing assets for both entities, which may not be our preferred method.

In practice, there are also likely to be significant differences in the way in which the segments have been determined. Since there is no single criterion by which a segment can be identified, small differences in the factors used in determining whether a segment is sufficiently different to warrant separate disclosure can have a major effect on the amounts that the enterprise reports. SSAP 25 and The Large and Medium-sized Companies and Groups (Accounts and Reports) Regulations 2008 (SI 2008/410) make it clear that the disclosure of segmental information involves a considerable amount of discretion on the part of the directors. In an area that is so intrinsically subjective, there are almost certain to be considerable differences of interpretation.

As a result of these problems, the use of similar phrases in separate financial statements cannot be taken to imply the use of identical criteria for inclusion in each segment. Each set of financial statements needs to be read carefully, and assessed independently.

The requirements of SSAP 25 and The Large and Medium-sized Companies and Groups (Accounts and Reports) Regulations 2008 (SI 2008/410) mean that segmental information is often provided to the user of accounts, but the user still has to take a great deal of responsibility for the interpretation of that information.

This issue does not just affect those entities which apply UK GAAP. IFRS 8, the international standard which deals with segmental reporting, basically requires the information that is presented in respect of segments in financial statements to be of the same nature, although of course not level of detail, as that which is used for the purposes of running the business. While this approach clearly has many merits, it does mean that it can be very hard to make comparisons between businesses which may have many similarities, but which structure their internal reporting in different ways. Such differences are now also reflected in their external reporting.

Potential impact of the FRSME

Looking forward, the number of companies required to provide segmental information in the UK is likely to fall. The FRSME does not address the presentation of segment information, other than stating that if a company voluntarily provides such information it must describe the basis for preparing and presenting such information.

This would mean that companies falling within the scope of the FRSME would be required to comply with only the statutory requirements. These are considerably less demanding than the requirements of SSAP 25, for the largest companies at least.

6.2   STATUTORY REQUIREMENTS

6.2.1   Basic requirements

The basic requirements for segmental reporting are contained in Sch. 1 to The Large and Medium-sized Companies and Groups (Accounts and Reports) Regulations 2008 (SI 2008/410). Small companies which prepare their financial statements in accordance with Sch. 1 to The Small Companies and Groups (Accounts and Directors' Report) Regulations 2008 (SI 2008/409) are required only to state the percentage of their turnover attributable to markets outside of the UK. There is no statutory requirement for any further analysis, and the FRSSE does not require them to provide any segmental analysis.

The statutory requirements for disclosure of segmental information by other companies are contained in para. 68 of Sch. 1 to The Large and Medium-sized Companies and Groups (Accounts and Reports) Regulations 2008 (SI 2008/410) and can be summarised as follows.

Classes of business

The directors of the enterprise must decide if there are two or more classes of business which differ substantially from each other. If they decide that there are, then each class of business must be described in the financial statements and the amount of turnover attributable to each class must be stated.

Geographical markets

The directors must also decide if there are two or more geographical markets which differ substantially from each other. If so, then the turnover attributable to each market must be stated.

In order to ensure that the amount of information given is not excessive, the Act also contains some details concerning those situations in which information is not required.

> For the purposes of this paragraph –
>
> (a) classes of business which, in the opinion of the directors, do not differ substantially from each other must be treated as one class; and
> (b) markets which, in the opinion of the directors, do not differ substantially from each other must be treated as one market;
>
> and any amounts properly attributable to one class of business or (as the case may be) one market which are not material may be included in the amount stated in respect of another. (Para. 68(4), Sch. 1 to The Large and Medium-sized Companies and Groups (Accounts and Reports) Regulations 2008 (SI 2008/410).)

The wording of this requirement differs, very marginally, from that previously included in Sch. 4 to the Companies Act 1985. Where the requirements now state that items 'must' be treated as one market, the 1985 Act referred to 'shall'.

Exemptions from disclosure

Since copies of company financial statements can be obtained from the Registrar by all third parties, including competitors, enterprises may not wish to provide all of the information normally required if they believe that doing so might harm their business. There may also be other commercial reasons for not wishing to provide the information.

In order to ensure that companies are not required to provide information that would damage their own business interests, the statute contains a clause under which a company can omit the information.

Where in the opinion of the directors the disclosure of any information required by this paragraph would be seriously prejudicial to the interests of the company, that information need not be disclosed, but the fact that any such information has not been disclosed must be stated. (Para. 68(5) Sch. 1 to The Large and Medium-sized Companies and Groups (Accounts and Reports) Regulations 2008 (SI 2008/410).)

The exemption can be used in order to omit the segmental information normally required. Whilst this exemption from providing information on the grounds of commercial sensitivity is unusual, it is not the only instance under the Companies Act 2006 and the statutory instruments that supports it.

The same justification can also be used to omit just a part of that information. In this situation, however, the directors need to exercise considerable care. The presentation of part, but not all, of the segmental information could potentially be seen as even more misleading than its complete omission. A user of the financial statements may be tempted to draw conclusions on the basis of the limited information that has been provided, and such conclusions may be incorrect. The directors of the company must ensure that any segmental information that is provided does not detract from the truth and fairness of the view given by the financial statements as a whole. If there is a danger that incomplete disclosure may lead to erroneous interpretations, then it may be better to omit the segmental analysis entirely.

6.2.2   Problems in the legislation

The rules contained in the relevant Statutory Instrument set down the basic requirements for information by segment. As with many areas covered in accounting legislation, very little detail is provided on how the requirements are to be met. It is left to the directors to determine how best to present this information.

One of the main reasons for the introduction of SSAP 25 was to provide guidance on the interpretation of the highly generalised requirements that were then included in company law. The statutory requirements have become no more precise since SSAP 25 was introduced. SSAP 25 tries to introduce an element of consistency into interpretation, and to deal with a number of problems that arise as a direct result of the lack of detail in the legislation.

(1)   What criteria should be used when trying to determine whether there are different markets or classes of business? While in many cases this might seem straightforward, there are difficulties. Can a company treat 'Europe' as a single market if it is dealing with both western and eastern Europe, or

should they be shown as separate markets? Would operations within the euro zone need to be separated from those that are not?

(2)   Where there are clearly different business sectors or markets, how significant does a segment need to be to warrant disclosure? The statutory instrument refers to materiality in relation to the disclosure of segmental information, but provides no guidance on what should be deemed to be material for this purpose.

(3)   When disclosing the results of each segment, how should costs that are common to all segments be treated? Should they be treated as an entirely separate section, or should they be allocated across all the segments? If they are to be allocated, then on what basis should such an allocation be performed?

(4)   How should associated undertakings be treated for the purposes of segmental reporting? Can they simply be ignored, even if they are material to the company's or group's results? Should they be shown as a separate category, or integrated with the other segments? Does the company need to provide a segmental analysis of the turnover of associated undertakings, even though this turnover is not included as part of the group turnover shown in the profit and loss account?

In the absence of guidance in an accounting standard, it is virtually certain that a number of different practices would arise, which would not be very helpful to the user of financial statements.

6.3   SCOPE OF SSAP 25

6.3.1   All companies

There are two distinct parts to SSAP 25.

The first part deals with the interpretation of the rules contained in statute. This part of the standard applies to all companies except small companies which are complying with the FRSSE. Part of the standard is no longer useful for this purpose, since it has not yet been revised in the light of the abolition of the requirement for companies to show the profit or loss before taxation attributable to each class of business.

SSAP 25 reinforces the statutory exemption from providing segmental information if, in the opinion of the directors, such disclosure would be seriously prejudicial to the interests of the company or group. The wording for the paragraph in the standard dealing with the exemption has clearly – as one would expect – been modelled on that contained in the legislation:

> Where, in the opinion of the directors, the disclosure of any information required
> by this accounting standard would be seriously prejudicial to the interests of the

reporting entity, that information need not be disclosed. The fact that any such information has not been disclosed must be stated. (Para. 43, SSAP 25.)

6.3.2 Additional requirements

The second part of the standard extends the provisions of the statutory instrument made under the Companies Act, and covers such items as inter-segment turnover, segmental profits and segmental net assets. These extensions apply only to companies in which there is likely to be a wide public interest, although other companies are also encouraged to comply. (However, it is worth noting that some of the justification for SSAP 25 is of far less importance now than in the past. The companies in which there is likely to be the greatest public interest are those in which the public can buy shares. Where such a company is listed or traded on one of the major markets, it will now normally be producing financial statements under IFRS.)

Unless the directors voluntarily choose to provide such information, the additional disclosure requirements only apply to a company which:

- is a public limited company, or is the parent undertaking of a public limited company;
- is a banking or insurance company or group, or
- exceeds the criteria, multiplied by ten in each case, for defining a medium-sized company under the Companies Act.

This section of SSAP 25 has now been updated to reflect the changes made by the Companies Act 2006. Banking and insurance companies are now defined in sections 1164 and 1165 of the Companies Act 2006, and have separate Schedules covering their accounting requirements in The Large and Medium-sized Companies and Groups (Accounts and Reports) Regulations 2008 (SI 2008/410).

For a private company, other than a bank or insurance company, it will need to provide the information only if it exceeds two out of the following three limits.

(1)   A turnover of £259 million.

(2)   A balance sheet total of £129 million.

(3)   Number of employees equal to 2,500.

A subsidiary that is not a public limited company, banking company or insurance company will still not need to provide this information, even if it exceeds the limits given above, if its parent undertaking provides segmental information in compliance with the standard on a group basis.

Where a parent undertaking prepares group accounts under UK GAAP, the segmental analysis should be on the basis of the consolidated accounts, and information in respect of the parent need not be given separately.

The exemption available to subsidiaries has been widened as part of the ASB's 2010 improvements project. Strictly, the change in the scope of the standard applies to accounting periods beginning on or after 1 January 2011, but the changes may be adopted early so long as the company discloses the early adoption. The exemption now applies not just to subsidiaries whose parent provides consolidated information under SSAP 25, but also subsidiaries whose parent provides segment information in accordance with IFRS, and in particular IFRS 8. This applies whether the parent applies IFRS as adopted by the European Union or as issued by the IASB. The exemption is not available to subsidiaries whose parent prepares group accounts in accordance with IFRS, but where the parent falls outside the scope of IFRS 8 and has not decided to provide segmental information in the group accounts voluntarily.

6.4   DETERMINING THE SEGMENTS

6.4.1   General principles

SSAP 25 reinforces, and builds upon, the assumption in statute that the determination of the segments to be reported is a responsibility of the directors of the company.

The Large and Medium-sized Companies and Groups (Accounts and Reports) Regulations 2008 (SI 2008/410) state that the directors should consider the way in which the company's or group's activities are organised, without providing a definitive method by which this might be applied. SSAP 25 states that the directors should consider the main purpose of segmental disclosure in arriving at their classification.

On this basis, the segments should be determined by considering the information that is likely to be of value to the user of the financial statements. The standard mentions four factors that may be used in determining where there are separate segments.

(1)   Where the return on the investment differs from that for the company or group as a whole. (Where the activities of the group or company are very diverse, such that there is no standard level of return on investment, then the different returns earned in each geographical area or part of the business may be used in determining whether separate disclosure by segment is required).

(2)   Where there are different levels of risk.

(3)   Where there are different rates of growth.

(4)   Where there are different levels of potential for future development and growth.

In some cases, the use of each of these criteria will result in the same allocation of activities to segments. Where the criteria conflict, it is suggested that they should be used as, effectively, separate tests.

Although areas may appear to fall within the same segment on one of the criteria, if they differ on another then they should be treated as separate segments and disclosed as such in the financial statements. (Naturally, when this is done, consideration still needs to be given to the materiality of each potential segment.) For example, if two possible segments are both achieving similar rates of return, but one has a considerably higher potential for growth, then they should be disclosed as separate segments.

The directors need to reconsider the constituents of each segment annually, and should redefine each segment when necessary. This may lead to a conflict between the requirement for consistency and the underlying objectives of the presentation of segmental information. For example, where there have been changes in the enterprise's business over a period, some segments may need to be split further than in the past due to divergence in one or more of the key factors. An area may have always been considered as a separate segment, but may have been too immaterial for disclosure. When it becomes material then it will need to be separately disclosed. Areas may also converge, in terms of risk and return, so that disclosure as separate segments no longer serves a useful purpose. In order to ensure both that the segments are appropriate to the activities in the period, and that the financial statements are consistent from year to year, the following procedures should be adopted when there is a change in the contents of the segments disclosed.

- The nature of the change in the segments should be stated in the notes to the accounts.
- The reason for the change should be stated.
- The effect of the change on the amounts reported should be given.
- The comparative figures should be restated on the basis of the segments used for the current year.

6.4.2   Classes of business

In addition to the general principles on the contents of each segment, SSAP 25 also provides specific guidance on the factors to be considered when determining the classes of business. SSAP 25 defines a separate class of business as a distinguishable part of an entity that provides a separate product or service or a separate group of related products or services.

In determining the segments, the directors should take into account:

- (a)   the nature of the products or services;
- (b)   the nature of the production processes;
- (c)   the markets in which the products or services are sold;
- (d)   the distribution channels for the products;

(e)   the manner in which the entity's activities are organised;

(f)   any separate legislative framework relating to part of the business, for example, a bank or an insurance company. (Para. 12, SSAP 25.)

The standard then goes on to stress that these factors are intended to be a guide only and that they do not eliminate the need for judgement.

> Although it is possible to identify certain characteristics that differentiate between classes of business, no single set of characteristics is universally applicable nor is any single characteristic determinative in all cases. Consequently, determination of an entity's classes of business must depend on the judgement of the directors. (Para. 13, SSAP 25.)

No individual factor can be seen as the most important in all cases, but the company or group's own internal organisation may provide one of the best indicators of whether or not there are different segments. However, this will only be true if the company or group's own organisation reflects substantial differences in the products or services, or of major differences between the markets being served. In addition, the differences which give rise to these different segments in the organisational structure would need to be those which are of interest to users of accounts; for example, if the divisions in the organisation were based purely on technical similarities in production, these segments may not be the best way of breaking down performance for the purpose of predicting future profits.

Where the reporting entity is a group, the individual group companies may have been set up precisely because of the different nature of their activities. Where it is an individual company, it may be split into divisions which similarly undertake different types of business. In such cases the legal or operating structure can be used as the basis for segmental disclosure.

Whatever factors have led to the segmentation adopted, all of the reported classes of business should be defined in the financial statements.

6.4.3   Geographical segments

SSAP 25 defines a geographical segment as:

> . . . a geographical area comprising an individual country or a group of countries in which an entity operates, or to which it supplies products or services. (Para. 14, SSAP 25.)

The objective of providing a geographical analysis of activities is to allow the user of the financial statements to determine how changes in the political or economic climate may affect the prospects of the company or group. More specifically, the inclusion of such information will assist the user to arrive at a view on a number of factors.

(1)   How changes in the economic climate in particular areas might affect the entity as a whole. It will assist in answering questions such as:

(a) is the enterprise operating in economies that are expanding or contracting, and

(b) is it entering new markets, or is it relying on continued sales in developed markets?

(2) How the enterprise might be affected by political change.

(3) Is it operating in, or selling to, countries that have stable or unstable regimes?

(4) How the enterprise could be affected by exchange control regulations. Is it currently so affected, or is it likely or possible that it will be in the future?

(5) How it might be affected by fluctuations in exchange rates. Is it subject to a high level of exchange risk? If there are changes in the value of one of the enterprise's main trading currencies, what effect will this have on the reported results and position?

As with classes of business, SSAP 25 stresses that the determination of geographical segments must be a matter of judgement, and that there is no single factor that will provide a simple but sufficient division into segments. The standard suggests that physical proximity is certainly not the most important criterion for the identification of separate geographical segments; what matters is that the countries in each of the segments disclosed should have similar levels of profitability, growth, development potential and risk. Markets should be identified on the basis of criteria which affect these, not on the basis of their position alone. For example, for a company that currently deals with both western and eastern Europe, uniting these into one market may agree with physical location, but could be argued to give the user of the accounts very little useful information.

As with classes of business, each reported geographical segment should be defined in the financial statements.

6.4.4 Materiality

The standard requires that information in respect of each class of business or geographical segment be given, if it is significant to the entity as a whole. Under the standard, a segment is significant in the following circumstances.

(1) If its turnover with third parties is ten per cent or more of the total turnover reported in the profit and loss account.

(2) If its segment result, either a profit or a loss, is ten per cent or more of:

(a) the combined results of all profitable segments, or

(b) the combined results of all loss-making segments, whichever figure is the greater.

(3) If its net assets are ten per cent or more of the total net assets of the reporting entity.

In practice, many companies disclose separate segments that are below the significance limits set in the standard. This may be because they are of particular importance, despite their relatively small size, because they have historically accounted for more of the company's operations, or because they are expected to do so in future.

Different considerations apply to associated undertakings, and these are discussed in **6.5.4**.

6.5   DISCLOSURE REQUIRED

6.5.1   Turnover

For companies other than small companies, turnover should be disclosed by class of business and by geographical segment.

Geographical segments can be determined in two ways: either by the location of the enterprise's operations or by the markets in which the products or services are sold. The standard describes these separate analyses by 'origin' and by 'destination'. These are defined in the following terms:

> For the purposes of this accounting standard, origin of turnover is the geographical area from which products or services are supplied to a third party or another segment. Destination of turnover is the geographical area to which goods or services are supplied. (Para. 18, SSAP 25.)

Under the standard, the basic disclosure of turnover of geographical segments should be by their origin. This is because the other items that may need to be disclosed, operating result and operating net assets, will almost certainly have been calculated on this basis, so the disclosure of turnover should be consistent with these measures.

However, if a company is involved in international trade, then the destination of its products may differ significantly from their origin. This information is also needed by the user of the accounts if he or she is to be able to assess the risks to which the enterprise is subject, since the position in the countries to which the company or group is selling is at least as important to the company or group's prospects as the position in their own country or countries. As a result, companies or groups must also state the geographical analysis of turnover by destination, if this differs materially from the analysis by origin. Where there is no material difference, then that fact should be stated.

The statutory requirement for geographical analysis of turnover is by destination, not origin, since it refers to markets. Compliance with SSAP 25 will ensure compliance with the statutory requirement, as turnover must be analysed in both ways if there is a material difference between the two; if there is not, then the turnover by origin will be a close approximation to the turnover by destination.

Sales and transfers between segments can sometimes form a material part of the total turnover of some of the segments of a business. Where this is the case, then inter-segment transactions should be analysed by segment and shown separately. This analysis should only be provided by origin, since the Accounting Standards Committee (ASC) considered that an analysis by destination would be of negligible value to the user of the financial statements.

6.5.2 Segment result

The operating result should be disclosed by class of business and by geographical segment. The disclosure of the result by geographical segment should normally be based on origin (the location of operations), rather than on the destination of sales.

The segment result should be stated before:

- taxation, and
- minority interests.

A more difficult problem is that of interest.

For most businesses, the interest income or expense is likely to be determined by the position of the company or group as a whole, rather than by the position of each segment. For example, the balance between interest-bearing debt and equity used to finance a segment may be determined by factors which are not directly relevant to that segment's activities. In such circumstances, the inclusion of interest in the segment result is likely to be misleading. Profits or losses may be overstated or understated when this is not a reflection of the trading activities of each segment.

There are exceptions to this general rule. Where the earning of interest is a part of the normal operations of the business, then the effect of each segment on the interest paid or earned by the enterprise as a whole becomes an important factor in assessing the segment's results. For this reason:

> . . . it will normally be appropriate for segment results to be disclosed before taking account of interest. However, where all or part of the entity's business is to earn and/or incur interest (as in the financial sector, for example), or where interest income or expense is central to the business (as in the contracting or travel businesses, for example), interest should normally be included in arriving at the segment result. (Para. 22, SSAP 25.)

A similar problem also arises with common costs: costs that are incurred by the enterprise as a whole and which cannot fairly be attributed to one particular segment. Where such costs have been incurred they should be disclosed separately from the segment results, and included in a reconciliation of the segment results to the total result.

It is important to note that the fact that a cost is not directly incurred by a segment does not mean that this necessarily constitutes a common cost, since the cost may be fairly attributable to a segment. For example, if a company's head office incurs a cost on behalf of a segment, then that cost should be allocated to that segment, even though it did not directly incur it. Where costs are allocated to segments for internal reporting purposes; for example, in management accounts, then the basis for such an allocation may also be used for the allocation of such costs for the purposes of preparing the financial statements. However, consideration still needs to be given as to whether or not the allocation provides a fair reflection of the results of each operation. When considering common costs, it is important to go back to the fundamental objectives of segmental reporting. Segmental reporting is intended to provide the user of the financial statements with useful information about the various activities, operations and markets of the reporting enterprise. If a cost is allocated to a segment on an arbitrary basis, simply to reduce the pool of common costs, then this reduces the quality of the information provided, and can make the segmental analysis misleading and open to misinterpretation. Therefore, no such allocation should be made. Where costs can reasonably be identified with a segment, then they should be allocated to that segment, since this information is useful in determining how the segment has fared.

6.5.3 Net assets

The enterprise should disclose the net assets of each class of business and geographical segment.

The treatment of the net assets of each segment must be consistent with the treatment of the segment result. This means that, in most cases, it is only the non-interest-bearing operating assets that should be included, less the non-interest-bearing operating liabilities.

Where the result has been stated after interest, as the earning of interest is an important element of that segment's business, then interest-bearing assets and liabilities should also be included in the net assets.

Assets that are used by more than one segment should be allocated to the net assets of each segment on a reasonable basis. Where assets are not used for operating purposes, they should not be allocated to segments. The argument for this is basically the same as the argument for the omission of common costs from segment results: that their inclusion on an arbitrary basis would be more likely to mislead than inform the user of the financial statements. Loans, advances and investments between segments should not be included in operating assets, unless interest has been charged and this interest has been included in calculating the segment result.

One way in which turnover, result and net assets may be disclosed is given in the following example.

EXAMPLE

	Turnover	Operating profit	Net assets
By class of business			
General industrial	100	25	400
Electrical	350	125	250
Services	150	50	150
	600	200	800
By geographical origin			
UK	100	20	120
Europe	200	60	250
N America	300	120	430
	600	200	800

	Turnover
By geographical destination	
UK	80
Europe	175
N America	250
S America	60
Asia	35
	600

Here, turnover, operating profit and net assets are classified according to the class of business and also by the location of the assets. Note that turnover is also given by geographical destination to comply with SSAP 25.

An alternative presentation of turnover, in matrix format, is shown in the next example using the same data.

EXAMPLE
Turnover

	Total	General industrial	Electrical	Services
UK	100	70	10	20
Europe	200	20	170	10
N America	300	10	170	120
	600	100	350	150

6.5.4 Associated undertakings

Segmental information should be provided in respect of associated undertakings if, in total, they account for 20 per cent or more of the result for the period, or 20 per cent or more of the net assets of the reporting enterprise.

The information given should be:

(a) the entity's share of the results of associated undertakings before accounting for taxation, minority interests and extraordinary items; and

(b) the entity's share of the net assets of associated undertakings (including goodwill to the extent it has not been written off) stated, where possible, after attributing fair values to the net assets at the date of acquisition of the interest in each undertaking. (Para. 36, SSAP 25.)

The information should be given for the associated undertakings taken as a whole, and should be shown separately from the amounts in respect of the group in the segmental report.

This disclosure has, to some extent, been superseded by the disclosures required by FRS 9 *Associates and Joint Ventures* (see Chapter 21).

No information need be given if:

- the information cannot be obtained, or
- the publication of the information would be prejudicial to the business interests of the associate.

If either of these conditions applies, then the reason for the omission of the information should be given, together with a brief description of the business or businesses omitted.

6.6 IFRS COMPARISON

6.6.1 Operating segments

The international standard that deals with segmental reporting is IFRS 8 *Operating Segments*. This standard has been mandatory since accounting periods beginning on or after 1 January 2009, although there have been a few minor changes to the standard since this date. Like its predecessor, IAS 14, this standard is based on the US Standard SFAS 131 *Disclosures about Segments of an Enterprise and Related Information*, but the US standard has itself changed considerably since 1997. As a result, the international standard that is now in force is very different from the standard that it replaced.

It had originally been intended that the standard would apply to listed entities, entities in the process of obtaining a listing, and other entities where assets are held in a fiduciary capacity. In effect, covering most entities in which there is a public interest. However, the IASB's project on small and medium-sized entities (which ultimately resulted in the IFRS for SMEs) overlapped with the development of IFRS 8. The IFRS for SMEs is effectively intended to deal with entities in which there is not a public interest. IFRS 8 is effectively intended to deal with entities in which there is such an interest. As a result, IFRS 8 initially applies only to listed entities and those obtaining a listing and not to other public interest entities, to prevent pre-empting the definition of entities in which there is a public interest, and therefore logically those in which there is not. Despite this, the scope of IFRS 8 has yet to be amended even though the IFRS for SMEs has now been in issue for some time.

The key difference between IFRS 8 and both IAS 14 and SSAP 25 is that IFRS 8 is based primarily on the information provided to management, and in particular the key operating decision maker. IAS 14 and SSAP 25 take little direct account of internal reporting procedures, and are more prescriptive in terms of the segmental information that needs to be provided. IFRS 8 is based on the logic that the same type of information should be provided to external users of accounting information (such as shareholders) as is provided internally, albeit that such information clearly cannot be expected to be in such depth. The definition of an operating segment is therefore dependent largely on internal reporting factors, rather than more objective criteria.

IFRS 8 requires an entity to report financial and descriptive information about its reportable segments. Operating segments are components of an entity about which separate financial information is available that is evaluated regularly in deciding how to allocate resources and in assessing performance. Reportable segments may be individual operating segments, or combinations of operating segments where there are sufficient similarities between such segments to make aggregation acceptable. There are detailed qualitative and quantitative rules on when operating segments may be amalgamated for the purposes of financial statements.

Because of the move towards greater emphasis on internal classification, there is correspondingly greater emphasis on descriptive information about the way that the reportable segments have been determined, the products and services provided by the segments, differences between the measurements used in reporting segment information and those used in the entity's financial statements, and changes in the measurement of segment amounts from period to period. If the segments reported have lost some of their objectivity, it becomes even more important that a full description of all of the implications of the classification that has in fact been used be provided.

The IFRS also requires reconciliations of total reportable segment revenues, total profit or loss, total assets, and other amounts disclosed for reportable segments to corresponding amounts in the entity's financial statements.

IFRS 8 also requires an explanation of how segment profit or loss and segment assets are measured for each reportable segment.

Despite the move towards reporting based on internal information, there are still some requirements concerning more objective classifications. IFRS 8 still requires an entity to report some information about the revenues derived from its products or services (or groups of similar products and services), about the countries in which it earns revenues and holds assets, and about major customers, regardless of whether that information is used by management in making operating decisions.

The IFRS for SMEs does not contain any segmental reporting requirements, on the basis that the need is greatest for those entities in which there is a public interest. As noted earlier, this is also reflected in the UK's draft FRSME which contains no requirements for reporting of segmental information, other than the requirement that if companies provide such information voluntarily they describe the basis for preparing and presenting this information.

7 STAFF COSTS

7.1 INTRODUCTION

7.1.1 The importance of staff costs

The cost of employing staff is often one of the highest costs to appear in a company's profit and loss account. The Companies Act 2006 includes a number of disclosure requirements in respect of staff costs. These disclosures are in addition to those related directly to the remuneration of directors. (Disclosures regarding directors' remuneration are considered separately in Chapter 20 and are not covered in this chapter.) However, the materiality of an area is not always a good guide to its complexity. The largest part of the staff costs to be disclosed will almost always consist of the salaries and wages paid to employees, yet this area normally raises very few accounting problems. The pension cost, while often substantial, is almost inevitably considerably smaller. Yet the calculation and disclosure of the pension charge often causes far more problems to those involved in preparing financial statements. The same applies to share-based payment schemes such as share option schemes, which are comparatively rare, but where they are in place they can introduce considerable complexity into financial reporting even though the amounts involved are not always large.

The amounts included in financial statements in respect of employing staff will usually consist of the following.

(1) Amounts paid directly to employees, for example, their basic salaries or wages, and additional payments for overtime and bonuses.

(2) Amounts:

    (a) either paid to the state on behalf of the employees, such as income tax under the PAYE scheme or employees' National Insurance, or

    (b) deemed to be paid on their behalf, even though the liability does not lie with the individual, such as employers' National Insurance.

(3) Amounts paid, or treated as paid, to other third parties on behalf of the employees. The most typical example would be pension contributions, but there are also other examples such as private medical insurance.

Charges that may need to be made in respect of share-based payments fall outside of this basic situation. Very basically, share-based payment schemes can be divided into those which are cash-settled and those which are equity-settled. As the name implies, with a cash-settled shared-based payment scheme there will usually ultimately be an outflow of cash from the company. While this will often be in different periods to those that suffer the accounting charges, over time the charges will equal the outflows. With equity-settled share-based payment schemes, there is usually no outflow of cash or other assets. The charges against profits will normally lead to corresponding entries within equity.

As noted, pension costs are usually one of the smaller elements of the overall charge for staff yet give rise to a very high proportion of the accounting problems that may be faced when dealing with staff costs. It should also be noted that while ultimately all amounts appearing in company financial statements in respect of pensions will give rise to payments, there may be significant differences in any particular period between the amounts charged and the amounts paid, particularly when dealing with defined benefit pension schemes.

For some years, the treatment of pension costs in company accounts was governed by SSAP 24 *Accounting for Pension Costs*, and the statutory disclosure was supplemented by wide-ranging disclosure in respect of pensions. UITF 6 *Accounting for Post-Retirement Benefits other than Pensions* required that similar principles to those of SSAP 24 be applied for other benefits. The UITF pronouncement, however, affected only a limited number of companies as the provision of such benefits is still relatively unusual in the UK except for companies with strong connections with the USA.

However, accounting for pensions changed fundamentally a few years ago, at least for larger companies which continue to use UK accounting standards. Originally, it was intended that SSAP 24 would be replaced with FRS 17 *Retirement Benefits* with effect from 30 June 2003. However, this was then deferred pending the revision of the equivalent international standard. Finally, the ASB agreed that due to delays in changing the international standard, FRS 17 would need to be implemented in full in the UK for periods beginning on or after 1 January 2005. It was already relevant, since its disclosure requirements had been in force from various dates. For companies adopting the FRSSE, the implementation dates were even later. Under the FRSSE the accounting requirements of FRS 17 were, broadly, deferred until accounting periods ending on or after 22 June 2006.

Retirement benefits are defined by FRS 17 as:

> All forms of consideration given by an employer in exchange for services rendered by employees that are payable after the completion of employment. (Para. 2, FRS 17.)

In addition to pensions, this also covers other post-retirement benefits such as medical care. There is therefore no requirement for a UITF or similar regulation, as all benefits are dealt with in the single standard.

This chapter will deal only with the rules that need to be followed under FRS 17 and the FRSSE.

7.1.2   International standards

IAS 19 *Employee Benefits* covers pension costs and long-term benefits and also addresses other aspects of staff costs not dealt with by FRS 17. As with revenue recognition (Chapter 4) the international standard can be used as guidance within the UK, where there is no specific UK guidance, although care is needed as international standards are not directly applicable and there is no requirement for compliance in the UK.

In relation to aspects of employee costs other than retirement benefits, IAS 19 currently includes the following requirements.

(1)   Short-term benefits, ie those payable wholly within 12 months of the end of the period, such as salaries and most bonuses, raise few problems. The IAS states that provision should be made for accumulating those entitlements and bonuses with a constructive obligation, even where there is no legal obligation. While not covered in any guidance in the UK dealing directly with staff costs, this would be consistent with the general approach to provisions required by FRS 12.

(2)   Long-term benefits (other than retirement benefits), such as long-term profit shares, should be recorded at their present value, less the value of any assets put aside. The period cost should be the total of amounts for the year, adjustments in respect of previous years or scheme changes, and imputed interest. Actuarial gains and losses should be recognised immediately. Again, this would appear to be consistent with general UK practice in related areas.

(3)   Termination benefits, ie those payable on redundancy or a similar event, should be accounted for only when the company has a demonstrable commitment. They should be discounted when payable after 12 months and, for provisions for voluntary redundancy, based on expected acceptance rates. In the UK, provisions for termination benefits fall within the scope of FRS 12 *Provisions, Contingent Liabilities and Contingent Assets*, which is dealt with in Chapter 17.

In relation to pensions, the basic approach set out in IAS 19 has some similarities with both FRS 17 and SSAP 24. Not surprisingly, there is no material difference between any of the standards when dealing with defined contribution schemes. In very broad terms, accounting for defined benefit schemes under IAS 19 is, or rather can be, a mixture of the SSAP 24 and FRS 17 approaches. The approach to scheme valuation is similar to that in FRS 17. However, like SSAP 24, currently, the IAS does not always require immediate recognition of surpluses and assets. Unlike either UK standard, it also allows some deficits to remain unrecognised. While both UK and international practice contain limitations on the recognition of scheme surpluses, the rules in this area also differ.

However, IAS 19 was revised at the end of 2004 and now allows (but still does not require) companies to bring actuarial gains and losses into account immediately in their financial statements. This is similar to the treatment required by FRS 17. Such actuarial gains and losses may either be taken as a charge against profit or dealt with, in the statement of comprehensive income, as part of other comprehensive income. In 2010, the IASB issued an exposure draft which will, among other things, require companies to reflect actuarial movements as they arise. If this change takes place, the international accounting treatment will move closer to that which is required in the UK. The IASB is expected to finalise the standard by May 2011.

7.1.3 Small companies

The requirements of FRS 17 have, basically, been implemented in the FRSSE, but, as noted above, the effective date of the implementation of the requirements was later. In principle, the requirements of the FRSSE are the same as those which apply to larger companies under FRS 17 although, as ever with the FRSSE, there are some reductions in the disclosure required in respect of pension costs.

7.2 COMPANIES ACT REQUIREMENTS

The Companies Act 2006 does not provide very much detail on the accounting practices that need to be applied for staff costs. Instead, it deals almost exclusively with disclosure. There are also a number of exemptions available for small companies – see Chapter 22.

7.2.1 Staff numbers

Companies must state the number of persons they employed during the year, and then categorise these into relevant sections. Small companies are exempt from this requirement (although due to an apparent oversight, this involved legislation requiring disclosure being introduced, and then the exemption for small companies being reintroduced).

The Companies Act 2006 contains the following requirement:

> The categories by reference to which the number required to be disclosed . . . is to be determined must be such as the directors may select having regard to the manner in which the company's activities are organised. (CA 2006, s. 411 (2).)

The implication of this requirement being in the Companies Act 2006 itself, rather than in a statutory instrument, is that it applies equally to companies that prepare financial statements under IFRS as UK GAAP.

As a result of the lack of clarity in the requirement, a number of different practices have arisen, for example:

- categorisation by function, such as marketing, production, administration (often used by smaller companies and groups);
- categorisation by type of business (common for larger companies or groups where there are two or more distinct business segments), or
- categorisation by location, showing the countries in which employees work.

However, some companies do not provide this disclosure at all, presumably because they believe that all their employees work in a single core business. In order to improve disclosure in this area, it would be helpful to categorise employees by business segment on the same basis as used for the purposes of segmental reporting, wherever that is relevant to the company. However, this is not required by statute.

The number of employees should be calculated on a monthly basis. As noted in Chapter 3, this contrasts with the basis of calculation of staff numbers that must be used to determine whether additional staff related disclosures must be provided in the directors' report, which must be calculated on a weekly basis.

7.2.2   Staff costs

The aggregate staff costs for the year must be stated, other than by companies which are small, and broken down into three categories:

(a)   wages and salaries paid or payable in respect of that year to those persons;

(b)   social security costs incurred by the company on their behalf; and

(c)   other pension costs so incurred. (CA 2006, s. 411.)

(Again, this requirement is included in the body of the Act so that it applies to companies producing financial statements under IFRS, as well as those applying UK GAAP.)

The wages and salaries to be disclosed include all amounts in respect of the period under consideration, irrespective of when they were actually paid. This means, for example, that where bonuses are paid to staff in respect of a period, they should be shown as part of the cost of that period, even if they are not actually paid until the next. Some care needs to be taken with this, as FRS 12 may place limits on the accrual of bonuses in financial statements. Bonuses may be accrued so long as there is a legal or constructive obligation for their payment. Legal obligation normally means that it is a term of the employee's contract of employment. This does not generally give rise to many accounting problems as a contractual entitlement is normally clear. The more complicated question is where there is no contractual entitlement and the issue of whether there is a constructive obligation arises. A constructive obligation may arise through, say, a specific statement. So, for example, a company might make a statement that it expects to pay bonuses, in respect of a year, before the end of that year. Even though the actual amounts to be paid will probably be determined after the end of the year; in such a case an accrual may still be made. Similarly, where a company has a previous practice of paying bonuses, then this might give rise to a constructive obligation, that is, staff are expecting to receive them, even if there is no contractual entitlement and the company has made no specific statement that bonuses will be paid for the year. The most complex problems often arise where bonuses were paid, say, in the previous year for the first time. Is there an expectation that bonuses will be paid in the current year? This will always depend on the specific circumstances.

Potential impact of the FRSME

The FRSME could create some changes in the treatment of short term employee costs. UK GAAP currently lacks a standard that deals comprehensively with short term employee benefits. While these normally raise few questions, there are some areas that can be more complex (such as bonuses linked to performance over a fairly short period, but more than one year) where different practices may result. Like the IFRS for SMEs, the FRSME contains a section dealing with all types of employee benefit.

7.2.3   Benefits in kind

A slightly more difficult problem can arise with benefits in kind. A note on the interpretation of Sch. 4 to the Companies Act 1985 made it clear that wages and salaries need not be amounts paid directly to an employee, but can also be an amount paid on their behalf.

> Any amount stated in respect of . . . "wages and salaries" in the company's profit and loss account shall be determined by reference to payments made or costs incurred in respect of all persons employed by the company during the financial year . . . (CA 1985, para. 94(3), Sch. 4.)

For these purposes a distinction needs to be drawn between two types of benefit.

(1)   Amounts paid for the benefit of the employee, where the only benefit to the company is through the continued employment of the staff member, for example, life insurance payments or medical cover.

(2)   Amounts paid primarily for the benefit of the company, but from which the employee also derives some benefit, for example, some entertaining and training costs.

In our opinion the first category should be included as part of the staff costs for the year, as part of the wages and salaries cost disclosed. The second category should be included under another expenditure heading, and not as part of the staff costs. No attempt should be made to allocate the expenditure between the staff costs and the other category of cost.

This distinction may differ from that which is used for tax purposes, but the tax treatment should not necessarily drive the accounting treatment.

The comment quoted earlier has not been included in the Companies Act 2006 (or rather the statutory instrument arising from that Act, which deals with the format for company accounts). This would not appear to represent a deliberate substantive change, and therefore it seems reasonable to assume that the old guidance is still helpful in attempting to apply the current requirements.

7.2.4 Temporary labour

Where temporary labour is employed directly by the company, then the costs incurred should be treated as part of the staff costs for the period. Where a company uses staff employed by another company, and makes payment directly to the other company, then the staff involved are not employees of the first company. Since the required disclosure relates only to employees, it would be inappropriate for these costs to be included in labour costs of the first company. The amount should be included in another expenditure category.

However, this can still leave an area where the treatment is uncertain. For example, with certain sub-contractors, tax and National Insurance contributions must be deducted before payments are made to them.

In these cases, the principle underlying the disclosure is the same; the amounts should relate only to employees of the company. In the absence of other information, whether or not an individual is an employee of the company or not may be provided by the tax treatment of the individual. However, as emphasised in the previous section, there is no reason why the tax treatment should override other information available to the company.

7.2.5 Social security costs

Social security costs only include payments that have been made:

> ... to any state social security or pension scheme, fund or arrangement. (CA 2006 s. 411(6).)

In practice, this means employers' National Insurance contributions for a UK company and the equivalent for an overseas company or branch.

7.2.6 Pension costs

Under the Companies Act 2006, the charge for pension costs need not be the actual amounts paid in the year, but can also include provisions for this purpose:

> 'pension costs' includes any costs incurred by the company in respect of –
>
> - any pension scheme established for the purpose of providing pensions for persons currently or formerly employed by the company,

- any sums set aside for the future payment of pensions directly by the company to current or former employees, and
- any pensions paid directly to such persons without having first been set aside. (CA 2006, s. 411 (6).)

This is important, because the fact that there may be such a difference allows the accounting treatments required by FRS 17 and the FRSSE.

7.3   PENSION COSTS

7.3.1   *The background to SSAP 24 and FRS 17*

The original need for an accounting standard dealing with pension costs arose for two main reasons:

- there were doubts about the appropriateness of the accounting treatment that was previously adopted to deal with pension charges, and
- the level of disclosure of pensions costs was not thought sufficient to provide the user of financial statements with an adequate understanding of the effect that pension costs might have on the position of the business.

With respect to the first reason (the accounting treatment), prior to the introduction of SSAP 24, most companies were simply charging their funding payments to the profit and loss account. Many people considered this to be contrary to the fundamental accounting principle of accruals, now described as the accrual basis of accounting.

There is no necessary correlation, at least not over the short to medium term, between the overall benefits of employing staff and the funding payments that are made to pension schemes in respect of their employment. Funding payments can be altered by companies, within prescribed limits, for reasons unconnected with the performance of the pension scheme. For example, a company can choose to make smaller payments now, and larger payments later, in order to fund a pension scheme. Similarly, the company may decide to make higher payments earlier. The position of the company can affect this as much as that of the pension scheme. It was not considered appropriate that companies should be able to alter the pension charge in company accounts, to some extent at will. Companies' freedom of action is far from absolute: minimum funding rules and the rules on tax deductions on contributions to pension schemes mean that companies can neither excessively underfund nor overfund a scheme. However, there is still some flexibility given to companies, and most people agree that using cash payments alone would not be an appropriate basis for company accounting.

Despite this, some respondents to the FRED that preceded FRS 17 argued that a return to cash accounting was appropriate, given the impact of the Pensions Act 1995 and the tax rules. The ASB rejected this argument, stating that the flexibility this would provide would still be excessive, and pointing out that a return to cash-based accounting would be wholly inappropriate for unfunded and overseas schemes.

With respect to the second reason (the inadequate disclosure), the previous requirements concerning pensions were also considered to be inadequate to help the user of the financial statements in realistically assessing the position of the fund and, more importantly, the effect that this might have upon the company in the future.

The ASC originally intended to deal only with the disclosure problems. However, they subsequently realised that full disclosure, without establishing some valid common accounting practices, can also be misleading. SSAP 24 included a statement of the basic accounting objective, which stressed the accruals concept:

> The accounting objective is that the employer should recognise the expected cost of providing pensions on a systematic and rational basis over the period during which he derives benefit from the employees' services. (Para. 77, SSAP 24.)

While FRS 17 takes a quite different approach to the determination of charges, in respect of pensions, to that of SSAP 24, it is probably fair to say that this objective is still seen as valid, at least to some extent.

SSAP 24 itself was subject to criticism, and even when published was seen by some as a temporary standard which would eventually need to be replaced.

Two specific concerns about SSAP 24 are mentioned by the ASB in the notes on the development of FRS 17. They are:

- that the standard provided too many options to the preparers of accounts, leading to inconsistencies in accounting practice and allowing a great deal of flexibility to adjust results on a short-term basis, and
- that the disclosure requirements did not necessarily ensure the pension costs and the amounts reflected in the balance sheet were adequately explained.

The ASB also mentions that, both in the UK and internationally, there has been a move away from valuations of assets based purely on actuarial figures and towards market values. The amounts calculated and disclosed under SSAP 24 were clearly based on actuarial amounts and took little account of market values.

As a result of these factors, in June 1995, the ASB published a discussion paper on pension costs, followed, in November 1999, with an exposure draft. In November 2000, this became, with some changes, FRS 17. As noted above, there was then further considerable delay before companies actually had to comply with the revised requirements, including a deferral from the originally proposed effective date.

7.4 DEFINED CONTRIBUTION SCHEMES

7.4.1 *Definition*

FRS 17 describes a defined contribution scheme as:

> A pension or other retirement benefit scheme into which an employer pays regular contributions fixed as an amount or as a percentage of pay and will have no legal or constructive obligation to pay further contributions if the scheme does not have sufficient assets to pay all employee benefits relating to employee service in the current and prior periods. (Para. 2, FRS 17.)

Such schemes are often referred to as 'money purchase' schemes. The key elements of a defined contribution scheme are that:

- the cost to the employer for any period is known with certainty, since it is equal to the actual amounts paid or payable in respect of the scheme for the period in question, and
- the risk lies with the individual and not the company; the final pension to be gained will depend upon the performance of the pension scheme and is not guaranteed by the employer.

7.4.2 *Accounting treatment*

Since the cost to the company is clearly known, the accounting treatment for defined contribution schemes is extremely straightforward.

The charge for the year is the amount of the contributions payable by the company. There may be accruals or prepayments at the balance sheet date, since the amounts payable in a period will not always agree with the amounts actually paid in that period. These will simply be treated in accordance with the normal accruals concept and allocated to the period to which they relate.

7.4.3 *Disclosure*

The disclosure requirements for defined contribution schemes are equally straightforward and under FRS 17 are simply:

- the nature of the scheme, ie that it is a defined contribution scheme;
- the pension cost for the period, and
- any outstanding or prepaid contributions at the balance sheet date.

This information need not all be given in one place in the financial statements. Equivalent disclosure is required by the FRSSE.

Potential impact of the FRSME

Unsurprisingly, the FRSME is likely to have little impact on defined contribution schemes. The amount charged will continue to be the contributions payable in respect of the accounting period.

7.5 DEFINED BENEFIT SCHEMES

7.5.1 Definition

Having already provided a description of a defined contribution scheme, FRS 17 states that a defined benefit scheme is:

> A pension or other retirement benefit scheme other than a defined contribution scheme. (Para. 2, FRS 17.)

A similar definition is now used in the FRSSE.

With a defined benefit scheme the employer is required to ensure that the pension fund is able to meet the final pensions, and the risk, therefore, lies with the employer rather than the employee. The final pension may be calculated in a number of ways, but the most common is a percentage of final salary, based on some formula. The employer needs to fund the scheme to ensure that the resources are available to meet the pension obligations, and cannot be certain that the amounts paid in each period will be enough to meet this objective. In most cases, there will be adjustments to the amounts that need to be paid as the actuarial assumptions on which contributions are based prove not to have been entirely borne out by events.

Since the risk is borne by the employer, defined benefit schemes can give rise to significant uncertainty in assessing the financial position of the company. How to account for this uncertainty lies at the heart of FRS 17.

7.5.2 Basic accounting treatment

The basic accounting objective for a defined benefit scheme is the same as that for a defined contribution scheme; the costs of employing staff must be matched with the benefits of their employment. FRS 17 contains a statement of its objectives. This includes:

> The objective of this FRS is to ensure that:
>
> . . .
>
> (b) the operating costs of providing retirement benefits to employees are recognised in the accounting period(s) in which the benefits are earned by the employees, and the related finance costs and any other changes in value

177

> of the assets and liabilities are recognised in the accounting periods in which they arise; ... (Para. 1, FRS 17.)

However, the very different nature of a defined benefit scheme means that even though the objective is the same as for a defined contribution scheme, it is much more complicated to determine exactly how it might be met. One way to reach this objective is to apply actuarial methods to establish the appropriate charge for the period.

FRS 17 uses actuarial methods in determining part of the charge, insofar as this is used to establish the liabilities of the scheme, but the scheme assets are measured at market value.

7.5.3   Schemes covered by FRS 17

As mentioned previously, FRS 17 applies to all types of benefit that may be obtained after retirement. While pensions are, of course, the most common of these benefits, it also applies to other types of benefit such as medical care.

FRS 17 is also intended to be comprehensive in that it covers all forms of the defined benefit pension scheme, whatever their precise nature and wherever they may be situated. FRS 17 makes it clear that it applies to benefits overseas, as well as those that arise in the UK and Republic of Ireland. FRS 17 allows no exceptions to this requirement, even though it may be complex to apply the provisions of the standard to overseas schemes, arguing that it would not be appropriate to have amounts appearing in financial statements, which may have been determined on the basis of two or more methods of calculation. Some people who responded to the FRED that preceded FRS 17 argued that where foreign pension schemes were accounted for in accordance with an accepted accounting standard for pensions, such as FAS 87 in the USA, this should be considered acceptable for the purposes of FRS 17. This argument received short shrift from the ASB:

> ... the Board does not accept this suggestion. While it may sometimes be possible, using options in standards, to achieve a high degree of convergence between the effect of each, where there are differences the Board's standard must be followed. (Para. 63, Appendix IV, FRS 17.)

While implicit in the definition of retirement benefits, the FRS also makes clear that it applies to all forms of schemes set up to deal with benefits after retirement. It specifically mentions that schemes that are operated on a pay-as-you-go basis are covered, and companies must still make provision for the expected future costs (Such schemes are referred to as unfunded pension schemes). In this case, the valuation issues apply only to the liabilities of the scheme, as there are no assets of the scheme held separately from the assets of the employing company.

Similarly, even though an employer may be funded by central government, this does not mean that the employer does not have to apply the rules of FRS 17 in determining the accounting treatment for retirement benefits.

In terms of liabilities, the standard applies only where there is an obligation to provide pensions. However, the FRS points out that liabilities may arise through statute, contract or where it is implicit in the employer's actions. Like FRS 12, this standard can therefore take account of constructive obligations as well as legal obligations.

7.5.4 *Measurement of defined benefit schemes*

While the accountant will have to deal with the results of the valuation of the assets and liabilities of a pension scheme, much of this section of the standard is aimed at actuaries, as they are the ones who will need to take account of the requirements in performing their valuations.

FRS 17 deals with this matter somewhat obliquely:

> The assumptions are ultimately the responsibility of the directors (or equivalent) but should be set upon advice given by an actuary . . . (Para. 23, FRS 17.)

In practice, many of the assumptions that may affect the valuation (such as mortality rates) are outside of the usual area of competence of most directors, and will need to be assessed primarily by the actuary. However, directors will have more input into some of the other assumptions, such as employee turnover and, probably to a lesser extent given the time scales that may be relevant, the rate of salary growth.

FRS 17 changed the frequency of actuarial work for the purposes of determining the amounts that should appear in financial statements. It does not alter the standard triennial full valuation, but does require some work to be undertaken each year:

> Full actuarial valuations by a professionally qualified actuary should be obtained for a defined benefit scheme at intervals not exceeding three years. The actuary should review the most recent actuarial valuation at the balance sheet date and update it to reflect current conditions. (Para. 35, FRS 17.)

The standard points out that the assumptions required for the purposes of accounting may differ from those that are used for the funding valuation. This means that the actuary will have to undertake more than one valuation. The valuation upon which the actuary's funding advice is based may be of little relevance to the amounts that are used for the valuation for accounting purposes.

The annual update should take account of, at least, changes in:

- the market value of scheme assets, and
- changes in financial assumptions, such as the discount rate to be used.

It is not necessary to alter other assumptions unless there is good reason to believe that they have changed substantially.

7.5.5 *Measurement of defined benefit scheme assets*

Under FRS 17 the basic rule for the measurement of assets held within a pension scheme is:

> Assets in a defined benefit scheme should be measured at their fair value at the balance sheet date. (Para. 14, FRS 17.)

While this refers to 'assets', it actually means the net assets of the scheme, that is, the assets less the liabilities other than the liability to pay pensions in the future. Therefore, in deciding on the assets of the scheme for valuation purposes, such liabilities as accrued expenses will need to be taken into account. Assets do not include any amounts that might be attributed to notional funding, particularly as the purposes of this form of valuation is to arrive at amounts that are arguably more relevant for the employer than the scheme itself.

Some guidance is provided on the valuation bases that should be used for the most common categories of assets that pension schemes are likely to hold. The guidance that has been in place since accounting periods beginning on or after 1 January 2009 is that:

- quoted and unitised securities should be stated at their bid price;
- property should normally be stated at its open market value, or another basis which has been determined in accordance with the *Appraisal and Valuation Manual* of the Royal Institution of Chartered Surveyors and related practice statements, and
- insurance policies which exactly match the amount and timing of some or all of the benefits payable under the scheme should be measured at the same amount as the related obligations.

(Prior to 1 January 2009, there was an anomaly in that quoted securities had to be stated at bid price, but unitised securities were still stated at their mid-market price.)

As with FRS 7, when dealing with acquisitions, FRS 17 is not very helpful when it comes to unquoted securities, which should be stated at an estimate of their fair value. There is no further guidance as to how this might be determined.

Similarly, when dealing with insurance policies which do not precisely match some of the obligations of the scheme, the standard states that there are a number of valuation methods that can be used. All it says is that a method should be chosen which gives the best approximation of fair value given the circumstances of the scheme.

Despite a lack of clarity on some specifics, it is unlikely that there will be major problems with determining the asset values of most pension schemes in practice. The types of assets generally held by pension schemes are limited and fall into only a few categories, most of which have fairly readily determinable market values. A fairly high proportion of pension schemes will have no assets other than quoted securities.

7.5.6 Measurement of defined benefit scheme liabilities

FRS 17 states the actuarial method that should be used in determining the amount of the liabilities of the scheme:

> Defined benefit scheme liabilities should be measured on an actuarial basis using the projected unit method . . . (Para. 20, FRS 17.)

While not required by SSAP 24 this was already the most commonly-used basis in practice.

Under the projected unit method the surplus or deficiency is calculated by comparing the present value of the benefits accrued at the date of valuation, taking into account the projected final earnings of the scheme's members, with the value of the assets of the scheme. The terms in which FRS 17 defines the liabilities of a scheme are similar in many respects to FRS 12:

> . . . The scheme liabilities comprise:
>
> (a) any benefits promised under the formal terms of the scheme; and
> (b) any constructive obligations for further benefits where a public statement or past practice by the employer has created a valid expectation in the employees that such benefits will be granted. (Para. 20, FRS 17.)

A similar requirement is provided when dealing with the actuarial assumptions that must be used in the calculation of the liabilities of the scheme:

> The actuarial assumptions should reflect expected future events that will affect the cost of the benefits to which the employer is committed (either legally or through a constructive obligation) at the balance sheet date. (Para. 27, FRS 17.)

The liabilities are therefore both the formal liabilities of the scheme and the amounts that the company has effectively committed itself to pay. As with other standards, the mere decision to alter the nature of future benefits will not give rise to a liability of the scheme. It has to be communicated before an obligation can be recognised.

In some cases, the scheme rules may require that surpluses are shared between the members of the scheme and the sponsoring employer. In other cases, this may not be a requirement of the scheme, but this may have become the established practice such that it has created an expectation on the part of employees that they will stand to gain from any scheme surplus. In such cases, the liabilities of the scheme should be taken to include any amounts that will be passed on to scheme members.

The standard provides examples of some of the expected future events that should be taken into account when determining the amount of the liabilities of the scheme:

- expected cost of living increases that are either provided for in the rules of the scheme, have been announced publicly, or which are awarded under an established practice creating a valid expectation amongst the employees;
- expected future salary increases, and
- expected early retirement, where employees have this right under the scheme rules.

It is not acceptable to take account of any future redundancies, since there is no commitment to make such redundancies. When a company becomes committed to redundancies (and would, therefore, be able to account for the direct redundancy costs in accordance with FRS 12), this is treated as a curtailment or settlement of the scheme. This is dealt with separately under FRS 17.

For similar reasons, it is not acceptable to assume any reduction in benefits on the basis that the company might, at some point in the future, curtail the scheme. The impacts of such a curtailment should only be accounted for as and when they occur.

The standard contains a presumption that the benefits that should be taken into account in calculating the amount of the liability should be established according to the benefits formula that is used to determine the amounts payable. However, an exception is made where the benefits formula is disproportionately weighted towards the later years of service. Unfortunately, FRS 17 does not attempt to define what is meant by 'disproportionately'. Nonetheless, where such a situation exists the benefits should be attributed on a straight-line basis over the period during which the total benefit is being earned.

Since the measurement of the liabilities of the scheme will be affected by a number of assumptions, FRS 17 requires that these be mutually compatible:

> The assumptions underlying the valuation should be mutually compatible and lead to the best estimate of the future cash flows that will arise under the scheme liabilities . . . Any assumptions that are affected by economic conditions (financial assumptions) should reflect market expectations at the balance sheet date. (Para. 23, FRS 17.)

The FRS points out that some of the assumptions will be affected by the same economic factors, and therefore should be compatible with each other. For example, there would normally be some correlation between the expected rate of increases in salaries and the discount rate to be used, since they will both be affected by expectations of future inflation.

The standard requires market expectations to be used at the balance sheet date to ensure that the basis is consistent with that used for the valuation of assets, which, as noted above, must be stated at their market values. The FRS gives one example of how market expectations can be reliably measured. Where the scheme is in a country with long-dated inflation-linked bonds, the yields on such bonds can be compared with the yields on fixed interest bonds of similar standing to provide the market's expectation of future general inflation.

The requirement to consider market expectations at the balance sheet date has, to some extent, led to the issue of UITF 48 *Accounting Implications of the Replacement of the Retail Prices Index with the Consumer Prices Index for Retirement Benefits*.

The need for UITF 48 arises due to the ministerial announcement, made in July 2010, that the Government intends to move to using the Consumer Prices Index (CPI) as the inflation measure for determining the minimum pension increases to be applied to the statutory index-linked features of retirement benefits, rather than the Retail Prices Index (RPI), as in the past. Due to both the constituents of the index and the manner in which it is calculated, CPI tends to be lower than RPI. The potential implication of this is, therefore, that the change may reduce the cost of future pensions, and hence the liability associated with company pension schemes.

However, the situation is more complicated than this.

A scheme may include an obligation for pensions to be linked to RPI, either because this is stated in the terms of the scheme or because this has been implied through previous statements made by the employer, for example, when providing staff with summaries of the scheme. In the latter case, this could have created a constructive obligation. Where the obligation is to provide benefits linked to RPI, then the ministerial announcement will have no immediate effect. It will affect the liabilities of the scheme if and only if the terms of the scheme are altered. If this occurs, then the change will only take place at that point. Whatever mechanism the scheme has for approving changes will need to be followed before there is any impact.

Where a scheme has no intrinsic obligation for pensions to be linked to RPI, but instead such a link arose only because of the legal position, the ministerial announcement had an immediate impact on assumptions about future pensions. Under FRS 17, the change should be reflected in actuarial assumptions since these should be based on expectations at the balance sheet date.

The UITF acknowledges that, in some cases, judgement may be required in deciding into which category a pension scheme falls. Experience since the announcement strongly confirms this, with many schemes (or rather their actuaries, accountants and other advisers) struggling to determine the impact. The problem arises largely because many scheme rules are not entirely clear on the issue of whether any link to RPI was an essential part of the scheme or simply a statement reflecting the legal position at the time. Given that when most scheme rules were drafted the question was of no real relevance, such lack of clarity is forgivable. It remains, however, deeply unhelpful. In some cases, legal advice may be needed to determine the status of the inflation assumption that should be applied to the scheme.

Once the impact of the change has been determined, the accounting impact depends on the category into which the scheme falls.

As noted earlier, if the scheme was required to use the link to RPI, then there will be no accounting impact unless and until the scheme rules are amended. If such a change is made, then the change:

- will be reflected in the accounting period in which the scheme rules are altered, and
- will be treated as a past service cost (or rather a negative past service cost as the impact will nearly always be to reduce liabilities) and therefore reflected in profit.

If the scheme liabilities are not linked to at least RPI, then the change to CPI implied by the ministerial announcement is treated as a change in assumption and, like all other changes in actuarial assumption, treated as an actuarial gain or loss and therefore reflected in the statement of total recognised gains and losses.

UITF 48 was issued in December 2010 and contains no effective date. Instead it states that it should be adopted with immediate effect. In principle, its requirements, therefore, apply to all accounting periods ending on or after the date of the ministerial announcement, being 8 July 2010.

7.5.7   Discounting

The actuary's task does not end with determining the nominal amounts of the future benefits that will be payable as a result of previous service. It is also necessary to discount those liabilities to arrive at their present value. Given the long time periods that are involved in dealing with pensions, this will have a very major effect upon the amounts that are required.

Discounting of obligations has always been a normal part of the actuary's role in determining the position of the scheme. FRS 17 provides details of the discount rate that needs to be used:

> Defined benefit scheme liabilities should be discounted at a rate that reflects the time value of money and the characteristics of the liability. Such a rate should be assumed to be the current rate of return on a high quality corporate bond of equivalent currency and term to the scheme liabilities. (Para. 32, FRS 17.)

This is the rate on an AA status bond or equivalent. In the absence of such a rate, as may arise when dealing with some overseas schemes, the best estimate may be the rate on government bonds, plus a small margin for the assumed credit risk. Such a rate will reflect only a relatively low premium over the risk free rate, reflecting the limited options that are available to an employer in relation to pension liabilities.

FRS 17 rejects the approach of using index linked bond rates for the purposes of discounting, on the basis that the market for such bonds is often relatively small.

7.5.8 Recognition of defined benefit schemes

Once the valuation of a pension or other post-retirement benefit scheme has been undertaken by the actuary, the next question is how to account for any difference between scheme assets and scheme liabilities. FRS 17 requires that:

> The surplus/deficit in a defined benefit scheme is the excess/shortfall of the value of the assets in the scheme over/below the present value of the scheme liabilities. The employer should recognise an asset to the extent that it is able to recover a surplus either through reduced contributions in the future or through refunds from the scheme. The employer should recognise a liability to the extent that it reflects its legal or constructive obligation. (Para. 37, FRS 17.)

The FRS attempts to demonstrate that a surplus in a scheme is an asset, as defined by FRS 5, since it provides rights or access to future economic benefits arising as a result of past transactions or events. An employer has rights to the future economic benefits inherent in a pension scheme surplus since it is normally able to reduce its future contributions to the scheme as a result of the existence of the surplus, or in some cases to receive refunds. The past transactions or events are the original contributions that have already been made by the company and the investment growth and other events that have given rise to the surplus.

Equally, a pension deficit is considered to be a liability on the basis that there is an obligation upon the company to transfer economic resources arising as a result of past transactions or events. The obligation to meet the financial requirements of the scheme will usually come through the terms of the scheme deed, but may also arise as the result of a constructive obligation to make good any shortfall. The past events are the services provided by employees and the pension liability which is already building up as a result of these services.

When the liability a company may have in respect of its pension scheme is being calculated, consideration may also need to be given to any obligations on the employees. In general, where there is a deficit on the scheme it will be the employer that will be required to make good the shortfall. As such, the whole of the deficit falls to be accounted for by the employing company. However, where a scheme provides for part of the deficit to be made good by additional contributions from members, the amount of the deficit to be recognised by the company should be net, that is, reduced by the amount that is to be met by the employees.

Despite the general principle that surpluses in pension schemes are to be considered as assets of the employing company, the FRS limits the amount of any asset that can be recognised in respect of a pension surplus:

> In determining the asset to be recognised . . . the amount that can be recovered through reduced contributions in the future is the present value of the liability expected to arise from future service by current and future scheme members less the present value of future employee contributions. No growth in the number of active scheme members should be assumed but a declining membership should be reflected if appropriate. The amount that can be recovered should be based on the assumptions used under the FRS, not the funding assumptions. The present value of the reduction in future contributions is determined using the discount rate applied to measure the defined benefit liability. (Para. 41, FRS 17.)

This amount is the maximum benefit that the employer could obtain from the current position of the scheme if the scheme did not grow, and if refunds could not be obtained. There is no specified maximum period that needs to be used for these calculations. But, as the FRS points out, the use of discounting means that, in practice, the effect of projecting for long periods will be considerably reduced, limiting the amount that can be treated as an asset.

When determining the amount to be recorded as an asset of the company, no account should be taken of any part of the surplus that may be used to improve the benefits that are available to members. Instead, these are treated as past service costs as and when they occur. Care may be needed when dealing with constructive obligations. The FRS states that it is not just the legal liabilities of a pension scheme that need to be considered, there may also be constructive obligations arising as a result of previous practice. While the FRS precludes companies from taking account of benefit enhancements until they occur, on the basis that there is no obligation until the change takes place, it still requires constructive obligations to be treated in the same way as legal obligations. There may, therefore, be cases where the employer's statements or actions have raised a valid expectation among scheme members that all or part of a surplus will be used to enhance benefits, rather than recovered by the company. In this case, the surplus should be reduced.

When it comes to dealing with refunds or potential refunds, the FRS is clear. Refunds must not be anticipated, and only amounts that have been agreed by the pension scheme trustees at the balance sheet date can be taken into account. This, of course, means that there may be cases where at one balance sheet date a company is unable to recognise a pension scheme surplus, at least in full, as a result of the limitation rules set out above. By the next balance sheet date it may have received a refund which will then be accounted for as income in the period in which it takes place.

7.5.9   Balance sheet presentation

The FRS provides fairly precise rules in terms of the presentation that companies should adopt in their balance sheets.

If a company has two or more schemes, then any assets and liabilities associated with those schemes must not be netted off, but must be grossed up on the face of the balance sheet.

Amounts must also be shown net of any attributable deferred tax, which should, therefore, not be shown together with any other forms of deferred taxation.

7.5.10   Performance statements

Rather than having a single charge for pension costs in company accounts, under FRS 17 it will be possible to have six separate amounts, shown as notes to two separate statements.

The change in the defined benefit asset or liability (other than that arising from contributions to the scheme) should be analysed into the following components:

PERIODIC COSTS

(a)   the current service cost;
(b)   the interest cost;
(c)   the expected return on assets;
(d)   actuarial gains and losses;

NON-PERIODIC COSTS

(e)   past service costs; and
(f)   gains and losses on settlements and curtailments. (Para. 50, FRS 17.)

Current service cost

The current service cost is based on the most recent actuarial valuation with the financial assumptions updated (if necessary) to the beginning of the period. This should be based on the discount rate at the beginning of the accounting period. The current service cost ignores both the current surplus or deficit position of the scheme, and the return on scheme assets, net of the liabilities that are increasing as a result of the unwinding of the discount. The amount of the cost will be provided by the actuary, probably as a rate applicable to pensionable salaries.

The current service cost should be included within operating profit in the profit and loss account, except to the extent that any such costs can be capitalised and included in the cost of an asset in accordance with another accounting standard. The amount will be net of any contributions from employees. It should be shown as pension costs in the sub-analysis required in the notes to the accounts.

Interest cost and expected return on assets

The interest cost for the period arises because the scheme liabilities become one period closer to settlement. The cost is based on the discount rate and the present value of the scheme liabilities at the beginning of the accounting period. It should also take account of any changes in the amount of the scheme liabilities which have taken place in the period.

The expected return on assets is based on long-term expectations at the beginning of the period.

The FRS gives guidance on how the simplest element of the expected return on assets is to be calculated. For quoted government or corporate bonds, the return should be calculated by applying the current redemption yield at the beginning of the period to the market value of the bonds held by the scheme at the beginning of the period.

For the more complicated situation of all other assets, in this case, including quoted equities, the standard states that the expected return should be calculated by applying the long-term rate of return expected at the beginning of the period to the fair value of the assets held by the scheme at the beginning of the period. It should also take account of the changes in the assets of the scheme that have arisen as a result of contributions paid into, and benefits paid out of, the scheme in the year. While the FRS gives precious little guidance, it is worth pointing out that actuaries have always had to estimate the expected return on assets, so this is hardly a new area for them.

According to FRS 17, the expected rate of return should be set by the directors, or equivalent, after obtaining advice from an actuary. It is debatable how realistic this is.

The interest costs and expected return on assets should be netted off and included as other finance costs (or other income) in the profit and loss account adjacent to interest.

For a scheme which, in FRS 17 terms, has neither a material surplus nor deficit at the start of the year the net amount of these two figures should be relatively small, simply reflecting the difference between the discount rate and return rate on the opening net position, plus any adjustments. However, it is important to bear in mind that the actuary's advice, in terms of action to be taken on the scheme, may be based on figures that differ from those used for FRS 17 purposes. As a result, significant differences may build up.

Actuarial gains and losses

Actuarial gains and losses, arising either from a new valuation at the balance sheet date (or from updating the financial assumptions to those at the balance sheet date), should be taken to the statement of total recognised gains and losses.

It would, perhaps, be slightly unfair to describe this amount as the balancing figure, but that will often be the simplest way in which to calculate it. Since the accounts will already include the amount of the expected return on assets and the effect of discounting, it will not be equal to the difference between the current valuation and the previous valuation.

As noted at **7.5.6**, for those UK pension schemes which had no requirement to link pension directly to RPI, and have, therefore, been affected by UITF 48, dealing with the implications of the ministerial announcement in July 2010, the financial statements for the first accounting period ending on or after July 2010 should reflect the change in actuarial assumptions caused by changing the statutory link from RPI to CPI. In practice, some financial statements will reflect this change only in the year after this, as the UITF itself was not issued until December 2010 (although a draft had been issued in October 2010).

The ASB was a little disingenuous in selling, as a virtue of FRS 17, that the actuarial gains and losses will pass through the statement of total recognised gains and losses and not the profit and loss account. Two weeks after FRS 17 was published the ASB issued an exposure draft (FRED 22), which suggested integrating the profit and loss account and statement of total recognised gains and losses into a new all-embracing performance statement. The main elements of the gain or loss with such a statement would be:

- differences between the actual and expected return on assets;
- differences between the actual and expected change in liabilities in the period;
- the result of any changes in actuarial assumptions concerning liabilities, and
- any adjustment necessary as a result of the rules that dictate that it may not always be possible to record all of a pension surplus as an asset in a balance sheet, for example, where a previous limitation no longer applies.

While FRED 22 is now unlikely to lead to a UK standard, it was still a little misleading to issue two documents at virtually the same time, the second of which would negate a stated virtue of the first.

An actuarial gain or loss which has been recorded in the statement of total recognised gains and losses cannot later be recycled through the profit and loss account. This is consistent with the general principle of FRS 3, *Reporting Financial Performance*, which does not allow the same amounts to be recognised in the two performance statements.

(Although there is an exception to this general principle in relation to certain gains and losses recognised in respect of financial instruments under FRS 26 *Financial Instruments: Recognition and Measurement and exchange differences under FRS 23 The Effects of Changes in Foreign Exchange Rates*.)

Past service costs

Past service costs are defined as:

> The increase in the present value of the scheme liabilities related to employee service in prior periods arising in the current period as a result of the introduction of, or improvement to, retirement benefits. (Para. 2, FRS 17.)

Past service costs should be recognised in the profit and loss account on a straight-line basis over the period during which the increases in benefit vest. In many cases, such costs will be granted retrospectively, in which case the whole amount will need to be recognised immediately.

Past service costs exclude all increases which are required by statute, contract or as a result of a pre-existing constructive obligation. These are within the scope of the actuarial assumptions, and any changes will therefore be treated as part of the actuarial gain or loss. As has already been noted, past service costs include those which have been granted out of a surplus within the scheme. These are accounted for only when granted, and are not assumed in advance.

Where a pension scheme has changed its rules to allow CPI to be used in place of RPI for the purposes of increasing future pensions, as allowed by the ministerial announcement in July 2010 and covered by UITF 48, the effect of the change will be dealt with as a past service cost. This will actually be a negative past service cost, as linkage to CPI is likely to reduce and not increase liabilities. Such a change will be reflected in the financial statements of the period in which the scheme rules are actually changed, having gone through whatever approval process is required.

Settlements and curtailments

Where a settlement or curtailment gives rise to losses which were not covered in the actuarial assumptions, then they should be measured at the date at which the employer became demonstrably committed to the transaction, and then immediately recognised in the profit and loss account. Again, as with past service costs, they should not be anticipated. An intention to close a scheme, without action being taken, is not a relevant event for accounting purposes.

Where a settlement or curtailment gives rise to a gain which is not covered by the actuarial assumptions, this should be accounted for only when all parties whose consent is required are irrevocably committed to the transaction, and then recognised in the profit and loss account.

Both gains and losses should be shown as part of operating profit, unless they are specifically identified with an item allowed by para. 20 of FRS 3 to be shown below operating profit.

The reference to items which are not covered by the actuarial assumptions is designed to avoid taking account of items such as early retirement, where this is a normal constituent of the scheme. Such an element of the scheme should be covered by the normal ongoing actuarial assumptions.

Restriction of surpluses

There are some other items that may appear in, or affect, the performance statements, where there is a surplus which, in accordance with the restrictions set out above, the company is not able to recognise.

If a refund is received from a surplus (or part of a surplus) which had not previously been recognised, then the refund should be treated as other finance income adjacent to interest, and separately disclosed in the notes. Similarly, where past service costs, or a settlement or curtailment, give rise to a loss, then that loss can be taken first, out of any unrecognised surplus, which may mean that no amount falls to be accounted for. Only any excess cost over and above the amount of the previously unrecognised surplus will need to be charged to the profit and loss account.

The expected return on assets may also need to be restricted. It must not exceed the total of the current service cost, interest costs, and past service costs, curtailments and settlements, and increase in recoverable surplus. In simple terms, this means that in such a situation (and assuming the recoverable surplus does not increase) the minimum total pension cost in such a company's accounts would be nil. If the assumption were not valid, then the minimum net gain is the amount of the increase in the recoverable surplus. Any other adjustments should be treated as part of the actuarial gain or loss.

Where a recoverable surplus increases as a result of an increase in the active membership it should be treated as an operating gain. It should be remembered that, in determining the initial amount of the recoverable surplus, there is a prohibition on assuming any increase in active membership. The FRS points out that this might arise as a result of an acquisition, but stresses that it is to be treated as a post-acquisition gain and should not be taken into account in the determination of the goodwill arising on the acquisition.

However, a decrease in a recoverable surplus arising from a fall in active members should be treated as an actuarial loss. This is consistent with the above logic as, in contrast to increasing membership, the actuary is allowed to assume declining membership in determining the amount of the recoverable surplus.

7.5.11   Tax

Current tax relief on contributions made to a defined benefit scheme should be taken to cover the items included in the profit and loss account first, and then to cover the actuarial gain or loss included in the statement of total recognised gains and losses. If the contribution exceeds the total of all these items, then the balance should be taken to the profit and loss account, unless it is clear, for whatever reason, that it should be taken to the statement of total recognised gains and losses.

An example of where it would be clear that the balance should be taken to the statement of total recognised gains and losses would be where a company made a special contribution to cover a large actuarial loss.

7.5.12   *Death-in-service and incapacity benefits*

Companies should charge the expected cost of providing death-in-service benefits and incapacity benefits to the profit and loss account as part of the operating profit. Any difference between that expected cost and amounts actually incurred should be treated as an actuarial gain or loss. UITF 35 deals with death-in-service and incapacity benefits. The UITF effectively covers three possibilities. The first, and probably most common, is that the company obtains insurance for the potential benefits. In this case, the charge will simply be the insurance premiums payable in respect of the period. The second is that no insurance is obtained. In this case, the charge will be the estimated cost of paying benefits in respect of employees who have actually died or become incapacitated in the period. The third, and the reason the UITF considered the issue, is where the benefits are provided through a defined benefit pension scheme. In this case, the UITF states that the costs should be measured using the projected unit method, in the same way as for the primary pension liability. The rationale for this is that the actuary valuing the pension scheme will have made an allowance for employees dying or becoming incapacitated before they leave service; as a result it is appropriate that the benefits that would then become payable should also be included in the valuation.

7.5.13   *Multi-employer schemes*

Companies may not always have their own pension schemes. Some companies will be members of a multi-employer scheme. Often, but not always, such schemes are used for companies which form part of the same accounting group. If this is the case, then it is worth bearing in mind that the scheme is only a multi-employer scheme from the perspective of each group company: it is a single employer scheme from the perspective of the group.

If a company is part of a multi-employer defined contribution scheme, then this has no implications for the accounting, since the charge for the year will be equal to the amounts payable in respect of the year, whether the scheme is solely for the employees of the company or otherwise.

In principle, where a company is a member of a multi-employer defined benefit scheme it should account for the scheme exactly as it would if it were a single employer scheme. What this means is that each company should account on an appropriate pro rata basis for the net costs and net position of the scheme. Most such schemes will take account of the potential differences between the workforces of the various companies involved. Wherever this is done, the basis on which this is determined will provide a fair and reasonable basis on which each company can determine its share of the scheme.

FRS 17 allows an exception to the general rule if the employing company is liable only for amounts in respect of the current period, and is unaffected by the previous experience of the scheme:

> Where more than one employer participates in a defined benefit scheme the employer should account for the scheme as a defined benefit scheme unless:
>
> (a) the employer's contributions are set in relation to the current service period only (ie are not affected by any surplus or deficit in the scheme relating to past service of its own employees or any other members of the scheme). If this is the case, the employer should account for the contributions to the scheme as if it were a defined contribution scheme . . . (Para. 9, FRS 17.)

This is likely to be an unusual situation. In most multi-employer defined benefit schemes each participating employer will have to meet their share of any accumulated deficit on the scheme, and will be able to benefit from any reduced contributions that may arise as a result of any surplus. In such circumstances, each company will account for its own proportion of the net costs and net position of the total scheme. However, where a company does not have to take account of the existing position of the scheme in this way, it is, as far as that company is concerned, a defined contribution scheme. In order for this accounting treatment to be applied, there must be clear evidence that the company cannot be required to make any additional contributions to the scheme relating to previous service. This must include the existence of a specified third party that is responsible for making such additional payments to the scheme, should they be required.

There is a further exemption from the general rule where it is not possible to determine the amounts which the company should account for, even though in principle the company is liable for any shortfall:

> Where more than one employer participates in a defined benefit scheme the employer should account for the scheme as a defined benefit scheme unless:
>
> . . .
>
> (b) the employer's contributions are affected by a surplus or deficit in the scheme but the employer is unable to identify its share of the underlying assets and liabilities in the scheme on a consistent and reasonable basis. If this is the case, the employer should account for the contributions to the scheme as if it were a defined contribution scheme . . . (Para. 9, FRS 17.)

In this case, there are additional disclosures that have to be provided, as follows.

(1) The fact that the scheme is a defined benefit scheme.

(2) The reason why sufficient information is not available to enable the employer to account for the scheme as a defined benefit scheme.

(3) Any available information about that surplus or deficit.

(4) The basis used to determine that surplus or deficit.

(5) The implications, if any, for the employer.

As noted earlier, many multi-employer schemes are run for groups of companies. Where such schemes are run in such a way as to preclude each company from determining its own share of the scheme then each company will, in its individual accounts, provide the disclosure required above. In the group accounts the scheme should be treated as a normal defined benefit scheme, as the problem of allocation cannot apply to the scheme as a whole.

7.5.14   Valuation of future healthcare costs

Since FRS 17 deals with all forms of benefit post-retirement, the same principle applies to future healthcare costs as to pensions. The actuary is required to estimate the expected future liability and to apportion this to service in the same way as for all other post-retirement costs. The amount involved must also be discounted in the same way as for other types of benefit.

However, FRS 17 acknowledges that this is more complicated than for pensions. Among the complicating factors are:

- the fact that health care costs tend to increase by more than the general level of inflation;
- the tendency for advances in medical skills and technologies to lead to more expensive treatments, in excess of the increase in cost referred to above;
- the general increase in patient expectations, and
- the effect that cost increases tend to have on companies, governments and insurance schemes in cutting back on the costs they are willing to pay for.

7.5.15   Disclosure

For defined benefit schemes, the FRS 17 disclosure requirements are the following:

- a general description of the type of scheme;
- a reconciliation of opening and closing balances of the present value of the scheme liabilities showing separately if applicable, the effect during the period of:
  - current service cost;
  - interest cost;
  - contributions by scheme participants;
  - actuarial gains and losses;
  - exchange differences, where the scheme is measured in a currency other than the presentation currency (or local currency if the company is applying SSAP 20 rather than FRS 23;

- benefits paid;
- past service cost;
- business combinations;
- curtailments and settlements;

- an analysis of scheme liabilities into amounts arising from schemes that are wholly unfunded and schemes that are partly or wholly funded;
- a reconciliation of the opening and closing balances of the fair value of scheme asses showing separately, if applicable, the effect during the period of:

  - expected rate of return on scheme assets;
  - actuarial gains and losses;
  - exchange differences, where the scheme is measured in a currency other than the presentation currency (or local currency if the company is applying SSAP 20 rather than FRS 23);
  - contributions paid by the employer;
  - contributions by scheme participants;
  - benefits paid;
  - business combinations, and
  - settlements;

- a reconciliation of the present value of scheme liabilities and assets (as above) to the fair value of assets and liabilities in the balance sheet, showing at least:

  - any past service cost not recognised in the balance sheet (on the basis that it has not yet vested);
  - any amount not recognised as an asset due to the limit s on asset recognition, and
  - any other amounts not recognised in the balance sheet;

- the total expense recognised in profit or loss for each of the following, stating the line item in which they have been included:

  - current service cost;
  - interest cost;
  - expected return on scheme assets;
  - past service cost;
  - the effect of any curtailment or settlement;
  - the effect of the limit on the recognition of assets;

- the total amounts recognised in the statement of total recognised gains and losses for:

  - actuarial gains and loses, and
  - the effect of the limit on the recognition of assets;

- the cumulative amount of actuarial gains and losses recognised in the statement of total recognised gains and losses;
- for each major category of scheme assets (including equity instruments, debt

instruments, property and other assets, but which may be further sub-analysed) the percentage or amount that each category constitutes of the fair value of the total scheme assets;

- the amounts included in the fair value of scheme assets for:

  - each category of the entity's own financial instruments, and
  - any property occupied by, or other assets used by, the entity;

- a narrative description of the basis used to determine the overall expected rate of return on assets, including the effect of the major categories of scheme assets;
- the actual return on scheme assets;
- the principal actuarial assumptions used as at the balance sheet date, all in absolute terms and not as a difference in percentages including:

  - the discount rates;
  - the expected rates of return on any assets of the scheme for the periods presented in the financial statements (ie as at the beginning of the periods presented);
  - the expected rates of salary increases (and of changes in an index or variable specified in the formal or constructive terms of a scheme as the basis for future benefit increases);
  - retirement healthcare cost trend rates, and
  - any other material actuarial assumptions used;

- the effect of an increase in one percentage point and the effect of a decrease of one percentage point (in both cases holding all other assumptions constant) in the assumed retirement healthcare cost trend rates on:

  - the aggregate of the current service cost and interest cost components of net periodic healthcare costs, and
  - the accumulated retirement healthcare obligation;

- the amounts for the current and previous four accounting periods for:

  - the present value of the scheme liabilities;
  - the fair value of the scheme assets;
  - the surplus or deficit in the scheme;
  - the experience adjustments arising on:

    - the scheme liabilities, expressed as an amount or percentage of the scheme liabilities at the balance sheet date;
    - the assets of the scheme expressed as an amount or percentage of the assets of the scheme at the balance sheet date;

- the employer's best estimate, as soon as it can reasonably be determined, of contributions expected to be paid to the scheme during the accounting period beginning after the balance sheet date.

UITF 48 notes that companies should provide disclosure that explains the effect of changes on their pension scheme liabilities, arising out of the replacement of the RPI with CPI, for the purpose of determining the statutory index-linked features of pensions. The disclosure will differ between those companies for which the change has involved a change in actuarial assumptions and those companies which have had to change their scheme rules in order to reflect the change. Companies with schemes which are linked to RPI, and where no change has been made to this, may not have to provide any disclosure, as they are unaffected. However, if a change is expected (ie negotiations to change the scheme are at an advanced stage), then it would probably be best practice to mention this, with an estimate of the effect.

7.5.16   Best practice disclosures

The ASB has also issued a reporting statement dealing with retirement benefit disclosures. This is not mandatory, and therefore has no effective date. This does not contain specific disclosures, but instead sets six general principles of disclosure on which best practice can be based. Such disclosure should provide:

- information that enables the users of the financial statements to understand the relationship between the reporting entity and the trustees or managers of defined benefit schemes;
- sufficient information about the principal assumptions that have been used to measure scheme liabilities to allow users to understand the inherent uncertainties affecting the measurement of scheme liabilities, including mortality rates;
- a sensitivity analysis for the principal assumptions used to measure the scheme liabilities, showing how the measurement of scheme liabilities would change with changes in the relevant assumptions that were reasonably possible at the balance sheet date. In each case, all assumptions bar the one being changed should be held constant;
- information that enables users to understand the method of measurement used to measure scheme liabilities arising from defined benefit schemes;
- information that enables users of financial statements to understand the funding obligations the entity has in relation to the scheme, even where this involves estimation, and
- information that enables users to evaluate the nature and extent of the risks and rewards arising from the financial instruments held by defined benefit scheme at the balance sheet date.

The reporting statement was aimed primarily at the largest companies, but is still best practice for others.

Potential impact of the FRSME

The FRSME could have a significant impact on the treatment of pension costs in respect of defined benefit schemes.

The basic treatment, and the rationale behind it, is the same in the IFRS for SMEs. Whilst there are differences in the detail, many companies may see little material effect because the actuarial valuations would be the same as at present, as would the overall movements and balances. There would be some changes in the way movements are presented, but this relates more to the changes to the primary statements generally than specifically to pensions.

The changes would arise where companies used the exemptions proposed in paragraphs 28.19 and 28.20 to the standard. Paragraph 28.18 states that an entity should use the projected unit credit method to measure its defined benefit obligation, where it is able to do without undue cost or effort. If an entity cannot use this method without undue cost or effort, then it may make various simplifications in measuring its defined benefit liabilities in respect to current employees, being:

- ignoring estimated future salary increases;
- ignoring future service of current employees, and
- ignoring the potential impact of in-service mortality.

Paragraph 28.19 goes on to note that the proposed FRS does not require the use of an independent actuary, nor does it require a comprehensive actuarial valuation on an annual basis. Where comprehensive valuations are not undertaken annually, then between full valuations, if the assumptions have not changed significantly, only the assumptions related to employee demographics such as number of employees and salary levels, need to be updated.

If full advantage is taken of the proposed exemptions within the FRSME, then complying with the standard will be far less complex (and costly) than complying with the requirements of FRS 17. The impact on charges for any accounting period is unpredictable, but the simplified actuarial assumptions are likely overall to reduce the reported liability.

Oddly, the requirements in the proposals are even less onerous than the current requirements of the FRSSE.

There are also some specific differences, for example, removing the detail on group plans and requiring a reasonable allocation of total cost.

7.6 PROPOSALS FOR CHANGE

7.6.1 *Proposals for changes to pension accounting*

Both the IASB and the ASB (together with various other standard setters) have issued proposals for changes to pension accounting.

The IASB proposals will not be covered as these relate to IAS 19. (Although, as has already been mentioned, the IASB has now moved to the stage of issuing an exposure draft. If this draft leads to a standard, then one key current difference between IFRS and UK GAAP, the ability, under IFRS, to defer accounting for some actuarial gains and losses, will be removed.)

The ASB proposals were issued in January 2008, and an update, as a result of comments received, was issued in November 2009. The proposals are a very long way from leading to any actual changes in required practice on pension accounting, are extremely high level and go back to the very first principles on which pension accounting should be based. Given the nature of the proposals, there is little point in dealing with them in great depth, but the following provides a summary of some of the issues the ASB has raised.

The ASB notes that a liability for pensions arises in exchange for an employee's services as those services are provided. The amount of the liability will be subject to a number of uncertainties, and specific mention is made of the mortality of scheme members, but these do not affect the existence of the liability. Reflecting first principles, the liability should include all benefits to which there is a present commitment, whether this arises through a legal or a constructive obligation, but should not take account of benefits that are genuinely discretionary. This raises the question of the treatment of future salary increases. At the moment, future salary increases are estimated when accounting for defined benefit pension costs, on the basis that most such schemes pay benefits which derive from final salary, or at least salaries towards the end of a person's working life. However, it is questionable whether this is appropriate given that future salary increases have not been granted, and there is some discretion concerning them. If this view is taken, then pension costs should take account only of current salary levels. If such a change were made then the impact would be to reduce reported pension liabilities, but to increase the accounting effect of salary increases. (The ASB reaffirmed this view in its update of November 2009, but only by a majority.)

The ASB also addresses the issue of which entity should record the liability for pensions. In some countries the liability for pension is directly retained by the employer; in some cases the liability may be passed to another party such as an insurance company, and in some cases (as is typical in the UK) the liability resides with a pension plan which is sponsored by the employer. Where there is a separate pension plan sponsored by the employer then the employer should report a liability only in respect of any guarantee it has given, which the ASB notes is typically the amount by which the liability to pay benefits exceeds the amount of assets in the plan. The ASB then goes on to note that the inclusion of a liability representing only a net deficit assumes that the plan is genuinely independent of the employer, for example where it is governed by trustees that are bound to act in the interests of members rather than in the interest of the employer. If, however, the employer controls the plan, it should be consolidated in the employer's financial statements. This differs from the requirements of current accounting standards which provide an exemption from the usual principles of consolidation for pension plans. However, the ASB also notes that if such a change were made this would be unlikely to affect many UK companies (or rather UK pension plans) since the nature of UK pension schemes is normally such that they could not qualify for consolidation.

The ASB notes that the amount of pension deficits and surpluses can change significantly in a single accounting period, but that some accounting standards (such as IAS 19) permit or require some of these changes not to be reported in the primary financial statements, or to be spread over a number of accounting periods. The ASB rejects this approach, arguing that there is no consistent principle which could justify such a treatment, that it is inconsistent with many other areas of financial reporting, and that it reduces transparency. The ASB, therefore, proposes that all changes in the amounts of pension deficits and surpluses should be reported in the period in which they arise. This is consistent with the approach in FRS 17.

In terms of measuring the liability, the ASB notes that most measures for quantifying pension liabilities are used to enable an assessment of the appropriate level of funding. Such measures rely on a number of assumptions, including the return that is expected to be made on assets in the time before the benefits will be paid. The ASB concludes that this does not provide an appropriate basis for financial reporting since it does not attempt to assess the present burden of the financial liability. The ASB believes the liability should be quantified at an assessment of the cost of settling the benefit, which will typically reflect all future cash flows and therefore the cash flows should be discounted at a risk-free rate. This would be a change from current practice, under which cash flows are typically discounted at a high quality corporate bond rate, and would increase the liabilities reported. The ASB, in principle, also considers that the estimates of future cash flows should include the future expenses of administering the liability. However, in its November 2009 update, the ASB notes that, as a matter of practicality, it has formed the view that it would be more appropriate to expense the costs as incurred.

The ASB notes that, consistent with current standards, assets held in order to fund pension benefits should be reported at a current value. However, current standards including FRS 17 then report the expected return on assets, rather than the return actually made in the period. Where standards require the financial statements to reflect the position of the scheme (as with FRS 17) the difference between the actual and expected return is then dealt with as an actuarial adjustment which does not normally affect reported profits. But the actual return reflects the economic events of the period, whilst the expected return does not. The ASB, therefore, originally proposed that the actual return (including both dividends and changes in the value of the assets held) should be reported in the financial statements, and that information on the expected return should be provided by disclosure only. This view changed by November 2009. At that stage, the ASB accepted that whilst the approach might be conceptually pure, it would not necessarily meet the information needs of users.

The ASB also puts forward proposals for disclosure, based on the principle that the financial statements should give adequate information on pension costs, risks and rewards, and funding obligations. Some of the disclosures are based on the ASB's *Reporting Statement: Retirement Benefits – Disclosures* (January 2007).

The paper also makes some proposals for changes in financial reporting by pension plans.

7.7 SHARE-BASED PAYMENT

7.7.1 *FRS 20 and share-based payment*

Until fairly recently, there was no general UK standard or legal requirement dealing with share-based payment, although the matter was dealt with in some UITF pronouncements.

This situation changed with the issue of FRS 20. FRS 20 is the UK version of the equivalent international standard IFRS 2. It provides guidance on all forms of payment that are made either in shares or that are directly related to shares. While the standard is wide ranging, its greatest impact is likely to be on share option schemes.

FRS 20 is reflected in the 2008 version of the FRSSE. However, there are very basic differences between FRS 20 and the FRSSE.

The treatment of cash-settled share-based payment transactions is identical between FRS 20 and the FRSSE. The difference arises when dealing with equity-settled items. As set out below, FRS 20 basically requires the rights granted in respect of items to be settled in equity to be valued. The FRSSE, in its 2008 version and since its 2007 version, does not require this, and instead requires only disclosure of the situation. This means that larger companies will often have a charge if they enter into, for example, share option schemes, which would not arise within a small company. There is a problem here for a company which is entitled to the FRSSE, but grows and ceases to be so entitled in future years. Such companies may elect to adopt the FRS 20 requirements, notwithstanding the FRSSE exemption, since otherwise they would be required to make a prior year adjustment at the point at which they ceased to be entitled to use the FRSSE. Companies which do not expect such growth are more likely to take advantage of the simplified treatment allowed by the FRSSE. Equally, given that the definition of a small company itself changes over time, and that the idea of extending the FRSSE to larger companies has been mentioned, some companies may decide not to incur the costs of valuations as they consider it possible that they will not fall within the remit of FRS 20 in the future, notwithstanding any potential growth.

For companies not entitled to the FRSSE, the effective date of FRS 20 depended upon their status. Companies which have shares or debt admitted to trading on a regulated market in the EU have had to comply with the new standard for accounting periods beginning on or after 1 January 2005. Of course, many such companies adopted IFRS at this time so FRS 20 did not directly affect them (although as noted above it is virtually identical to IFRS 2 so in practice there were no differences in the accounting treatments adopted). Unlisted companies were given another year before they needed to comply with the new requirements, as they have only had to follow the standard for accounting periods beginning on or after 1 January 2006.

The effective date is not the only relevant date. The FRS applies only to grants of shares, share options or other equity instruments that were granted after 7 November 2002 and which had not vested by the relevant effective date. In respect of such items, comparative figures will need to be restated. For items excluded under the transitional provisions, but still relevant to the company, disclosure of the general terms of the instruments will need to be provided.

FRS 20 is fairly contentious. While few would argue with its requirements where it deals with payments that will ultimately be made in cash, it will often either increase or introduce a charge to the profit and loss account where companies make transfers based on equity instruments, such as on the issue of share options.

FRS 20 is also amended with effect for accounting periods beginning on or after 1 January 2009. The changes affect vesting conditions and cancellations and are dealt with at the end of this chapter. There are further changes, affecting group cash-settled share based payment transactions, which apply to accounting periods beginning on or after 1 January 2010. (Technically, there are also changes to FRS 20 in relation to business combinations. However, these arise only as a result of changes to the international standard dealing with business combinations, which is not part of UK GAAP. Therefore, the ASB has made the changes to FRS 20, only for the purposes of consistency of wording, and there are no changes of accounting treatment arising.)

7.7.2 Scope

FRS 20 applies to nearly all share-based payment transactions.

The simplest example is where a company receives goods or services, for example work undertaken by directors or employees, and all or part of the consideration is in the form of the issue of shares. However, the standard also applies where consideration is:

- in the form of another type of equity instrument, such as a share option, or
- in the form of cash (or other assets), but where the value of that

consideration is based on the price of the company's shares or the price of other equity instruments of the company.

It is the second of these situations which really justifies the title of 'share-based' payment, since the standard covers any transactions which are based on shares, even if that consideration will be paid in another form. Such arrangements are referred to as cash-settled share-based payment transactions. A simple example would be a bonus paid to staff dependent on the increase in the company's share price (share appreciation rights). While it is cash that the company will actually pay, the amount of cash will depend on the change in the share price of the company and such an arrangement would, therefore, fall within the scope of FRS 20.

The standard also deals with cases where the consideration may either be in the form of equity instruments or in cash.

Shares or other equity instruments issued directly as part of a business combination are outside the scope of FRS 20. Such instruments should be dealt with under the requirements of FRS 6.

However, arrangements which are affected by a business combination, but where the issue does not form part of the consideration for the acquisition or merger, are within the scope of FRS 20. For example, where shares are issued to employees on a business combination, or where the terms of an existing arrangement are altered as a result of a business combination, such as where rights crystallise when a company is taken over.

FRS 20 also does not apply to contracts to buy or sell a non-financial item that can be settled net in cash or another financial instrument, or by exchange of financial instruments, as if they were financial instruments. However, FRS 20 does apply where the contract is for non-financial items that will be used in the company's business, and therefore are not a financial instrument.

FRS 20 also applies where a company does not itself issue equity instruments, but where equity instruments are transferred by its shareholders, by its parent or by another group company to parties that have provided goods or services to the company itself.

For the avoidance of doubt, the FRS also makes clear that it does not apply to transactions with employees who are also holders of equity instruments, where the transaction is in that latter capacity. For example, a company might make a rights issue at below fair value. FRS 20 does not apply where an employee, who is also a shareholder, takes up the rights issue in his or her capacity as shareholder. This would be the case even if the employee's share interest had originally arisen as a result of a transaction that was affected by FRS 20.

UITF 41 deals with the scope of FRS 20. The UITF arose as a result of questions about the application of FRS 20 where the value of goods or services received appears to be less than the fair value of the rights issued, or even where there appears to be no clear value received (for example, where a company might issue shares or rights to shares to charities).

Where such a situation arises, UITF 41 requires that the identifiable goods and services received be valued at their fair vale, in accordance with the normal rules of FRS 20, and that the unidentifiable goods or services received be valued at the difference between the fair value of the share-based payment and the fair value of the identifiable goods and services received. Such items are measured at the grant date, but, in the case of cash-settled share-based payment arrangements, are then remeasured at each balance sheet date.

UITF 41 is withdrawn with effect for accounting periods beginning on or after 1 January 2010. This is not on the basis that there has been any change in the requirements, but that those requirements are reflected in the updated version of FRS 20 that applies from that date.

7.7.3 Basic principles

The basic principles of the standard are:

> An entity shall recognise the goods or services received or acquired in a share-based payment transaction when it obtains the goods or as the services are received. The entity shall recognise a corresponding increase in equity if the goods or services were received in an equity-settled share-based payment transaction, or a liability if the goods or services were acquired in a cash-settled share-based payment transaction.

> When the goods or services received or acquired in a share-based payment transaction do not qualify for recognition as assets, they shall be recognised as expenses. (Paras. 7 and 8, FRS 20.)

Put simply, this usually means that the recognition of the asset or expense will take place at the same time for a share-based payment transaction as if it were a normal cash-based transaction, unconnected with shares. Similarly, the rules on whether an item is an asset or an expense are not affected by the fact that a share-based payment transaction was involved. As a general rule, goods will be treated as assets and services as expenses, but there are exceptions in both cases.

What FRS 20 is potentially changing is the amount at which items are recognised, whether asset or expense, rather than their timing. (However, it is worth noting that in some cases companies would have treated transactions at nil value, so the question of the timing of their recognition prior to FRS 20 would have been of no more than theoretical interest.)

7.7.4 Cash-settled share-based payment transactions

Cash-settled share-based payment transactions are those where the company pays in cash (or other assets), but where the amount of cash is determined by reference to the price or value of the company's shares or other equity instruments. An example would be a bonus for staff that will be paid in cash, but is based on the change in the company's share price.

The basic rule for such transactions is:

> For cash-settled share-based payment transactions, the entity shall measure the goods or services acquired and the liability incurred at the fair value of the liability. Until the liability is settled, the entity shall remeasure the fair value of the liability at each reporting date and at the date of settlement, with any changes in fair value recognised in profit or loss for the period. (Para. 30, FRS 20.)

Where the rights are granted retrospectively, such as where a bonus is based on the share price over a year and determined at the end of that year, with no future service requirement, then the services are presumed to have been received and a liability recognised immediately.

Where the terms of the grant contain conditions related to the future, such as a continuing period of service, then the services received and the liability are recognised over the service period.

The liability is measured, both initially and at each subsequent reporting date, at its fair value. That fair value is determined using an option pricing model, taking account of the terms and conditions of the grant and the extent to which service has already been rendered.

As noted above, this treatment must also be applied by companies adopting the FRSSE for accounting periods beginning on or after 1 January 2007.

7.7.5 Equity-settled share-based payment transactions

Equity-settled share-based payment transactions are those where the company issues equity instruments in return for receiving goods or services.

The basic rule is that:

> For equity-settled share-based payment transactions, the entity shall measure the goods or services received, and the corresponding increase in equity, directly at the *fair value* of the goods or services received, unless that fair value cannot be estimated reliably. If the entity cannot estimate reliably the fair value of the goods or services received, the entity shall measure their value, and the corresponding increase in equity, indirectly, by reference to the fair value of the *equity instruments granted*. (Para. 10, FRS 20.)

At its simplest this means that if a company acquires goods which would normally cost £1,000, but rather than paying cash it issues shares to the vendor, then the proceeds of the issue of shares is £1,000.

In principle, the same accounting treatment applies where the company receives services. If it is clear that a company has received a service from a third party who is not an employee and the value of the service is determinable, then it is that value which is taken to be the proceeds of issue for the shares.

As a result, in the case of both goods and services received from non-employees, there is a rebuttable presumption that the fair value of the goods or services can be measured reliably.

However, with services there is a greater likelihood that this presumption that will be rebutted. Specifically in the case of services received from employees (and others providing similar services) FRS 20 requires that the equity instruments be valued. The value of the services is then deemed to be the value of the equity instruments rather than vice versa. The FRS notes that attempting to value an employee benefit package which includes items such as share options, without considering the value of those options, would be extremely difficult, if not impossible.

The extension of the requirement to those providing similar services to employees covers persons such as non-executive directors who may not legally be employees of the company, but where the work they undertake is similar to that undertaken by employees.

As noted at 7.7.2, UITF 41 is also potentially relevant, in respect of both goods and services. This UITF applies where there are unidentifiable goods or services, whether in isolation or combined with identifiable goods and services. In such a case, any identifiable goods and services are accounted for in the usual way, but the unidentifiable goods or services received are valued at the difference between the total fair value of the share-based payment and the fair value of the identifiable goods and services received. For equity-settled share based payments, this determination is made as at the grant date. The impact of UITF 41, and the changes to FRS 20 that replace it, could be reasonably summarised by saying that companies must value both the goods and services they have received and the instruments they have issued for those goods or services; they are then required to account for the higher of the two figures obtained.

With effect for accounting periods beginning on or after 1 January 2010, UITF 41 is withdrawn, and its requirements are included within the text of FRS 20 itself.

As noted above, companies adopting the FRSSE, in its 2008 version, are subject to very different requirements. They are not required to attempt to value rights granted, but are instead required to provide disclosure.

7.7.6 Timing of recognition

Where goods are received, there will usually be no problems with determining the date at which the equity instruments are to be recognised. If there are problems, these are likely to involve issues which are not directly affected by FRS 20 but which would also arise if payment were to be made in cash.

The situation is more complex in the case of services, and particularly in the case of services provided by employees. In such situations account needs to be taken of when the instruments vest. If the instruments vest immediately, then, in the absence of evidence to the contrary, it is to be assumed that the services have been received and the company will account for the instruments at the date of grant. For example, an employee bonus in the form of shares which vest immediately would be accounted for immediately. Put another way, there is an implicit assumption that such a bonus is directly related to past performance and should be recognised at the earliest opportunity.

Where the instruments do not vest immediately, and there is a specific period of future service, there is a presumption that the services will be received in the future, during the vesting period.

An example given in FRS 20 is that a company might grant share options to staff, but such grant might be conditional upon the staff completing three years' service. In this case, the implicit assumption is that the grant is connected with retention and that the services for which the grant has been made are received over the three years.

A further example provided is that of a grant conditional upon a performance target, where the vesting period is not defined but continues until that condition is met. In this case, the company assumes that the services will be rendered over the period until it expects that the performance condition will be met. The treatment differs slightly according to whether the condition is a market condition or not. In this context, a market condition means one where vesting is related to the market price of the company's equity instruments, such as the share price reaching a certain target. Where the condition is a market condition then the assumptions made at the date of grant concerning the expected length of the vesting period must be consistent with those used in valuing the instrument. These assumptions are not changed in future periods, even where it becomes clear that the situation has changed. Where the condition is not a market condition, for example, a grant based on internal targets for a division, the length of the vesting period should be altered in subsequent accounting periods if it becomes clear that the vesting period is likely to differ from previous estimates.

FRS 20 changed with effect for accounting periods beginning on or after 1 January 2009 in relation to the treatment of cancellations. The amended standard requires all cancellations in the vesting period to give rise to an accelerated charge of the unamortised balance in respect of the options. There is, therefore, no relevant difference between cancellations by the employer and cancellations by the employee.

This can give rise to some slightly odd results. For example, if continued employment were a vesting condition (as is common) and an employee were to resign from a company, this would breach the vesting conditions, and any previous charges would effectively be reversed. However, if the employee were first to leave the scheme and only subsequently to resign from the company, then there would be an accelerated charge to profit arising when the employee left the scheme. The distinction between the scenarios is unclear, yet the accounting treatments are radically different.

7.7.7 Measurement of fair value of instruments

As noted earlier, where services are received from employees, or where the presumption that the value of goods and services can be measured reliably is rebutted, then the transaction must be valued at the fair value of the equity instruments granted.

In such cases, the instruments granted must be valued at the measurement date, based on market prices wherever possible and taking into account the terms and conditions upon which those equity instruments have been granted. For services received from employees, the measurement date is the grant date. In other cases, it is the date at which the goods are obtained or the service is received.

Where market prices are available, the determination of value is obviously fairly straightforward. For example, if a company grants share options to employees and there are identical traded options in issue, then the value of the options at the measurement date would be the value of the traded options at that date.

In nearly all cases, this will not apply. It is relatively unusual for options to be granted to employees where there are identical traded options. Where a market price cannot be used directly, the company has to estimate the fair value of the equity instruments using a valuation technique intended to determine the price of those instruments at the measurement date in an arm's length transaction between knowledgeable, willing parties. The valuation technique used should be consistent with commonly used valuation methodologies for pricing financial instruments, and take account of all factors that knowledgeable, willing market participants would take into account in determining a price.

There are certain restrictions on the calculations.

(1) Vesting conditions, other than market conditions, such as those related to

continuing to be an employee or meeting targets, are ignored in determining the value of the instruments. Instead, vesting conditions other than market conditions are applied in determining the number of instruments likely to be issued. As a result, the amount initially recognised will take account of the best estimate of the number of instruments to be issued, and this amount will then be revised, if necessary, in future periods. Ultimately, the estimate is revised on the date on which the instruments vest.

(2) Market conditions, such as a target share price, are taken into account. This means, for example, that if employees are granted share options conditional on both remaining in service and a specified increase in the share price then there will be a charge in respect of such services if employees stay for the vesting period, even if the share price target is not met and as a result the options never vest.

(3) Where options have a reload feature, that is, there is an automatic re-grant of additional options where option holders exercise their options using the company's shares rather than cash to satisfy the exercise price, then these are ignored in valuing the options. (Instead, such reloads are treated as a new grant of option and are valued and accounted for accordingly where they are subsequently granted.)

FRS 20 changed with effect for accounting periods beginning on or after 1 January 2009. The changes were the UK version of changes made by the IASB to IFRS 2, the standard on which FRS 20 is based.

The change was to define and limit vesting conditions. These will be service conditions, for example, continued employment, or performance conditions, eg meeting a financial target such as a specified increase in profit over a specified period of time.

After instruments have vested, the values are not altered for any subsequent changes. For example, where there has been a charge in respect of share options which have vested then this is not reversed even if, for whatever reason, the options lapse unexercised.

In some cases it may not be possible to determine a reliable estimate of the fair value of instruments issued, when that value is required in order to value the transaction. In such cases the FRS requires the following.

(1) That the equity instruments are initially measured at their intrinsic values. This is determined as the difference between the fair value of the underlying shares and the price that is required to be paid. For example, an option at £1 for a share worth £1.25 has an intrinsic value of 25p.

(2) That at subsequent reporting dates and the date of final settlement any change in intrinsic value is recognised in the profit and loss account.

(3) That the goods or services received are recognised based on the number of

instruments that ultimately vest or are ultimately exercised. This procedure is undertaken in the same way as for other instruments with a vesting period, except that the requirements concerning market conditions do not apply. This means that, unlike in other cases where changes take place after the vesting date so that, for example, share options lapse, the amount previously recognised for goods and services is reversed.

Where companies have used this exception on the basis that they are not able to provide a reliable estimate of the value of the instruments at the measurement date, they will not be affected by the other provisions of the standard concerning changes to the option terms, since these will be taken into account in the determination of the intrinsic value initially, at each subsequent reporting date and on settlement. However, if the instruments are settled early, then this is treated as early vesting and the company should immediately recognise the amounts it would otherwise have deferred over the vesting period. In addition, where payments are made on settlement they are accounted for as if they were the repurchase of equity instruments, that is, as a deduction from equity. This applies up to the intrinsic value, with any amounts over and above this being recognised as an expense.

7.7.8 Changes in terms

Companies may change the terms and conditions on which equity instruments have been granted. For example, share options may be repriced. Where transactions are measured at values determined by reference to the value of the underlying instruments, generally, but not exclusively, with employees, then consideration needs to be given to whether and how those changes affect the accounting.

In all cases, companies should recognise, as a minimum, the fair value of the equity instruments granted at the measurement date, except where the equity instruments fail to vest as a result of a failure to meet a vesting condition that is not a market condition and which was part of the initial terms of issue. This applies even where there are changes that affect the instruments, or where they are cancelled or settled.

Where there are changes that increase the fair value of the instruments or are otherwise of benefit to the other party, then the effects of those changes also need to be recognised.

Where a company cancels or settles a grant of equity instruments during the vesting period, other than by failure to meet vesting conditions, then:

- this is treated as an acceleration of vesting, and the company has to recognise the amount that would otherwise have been recognised over the remainder of the vesting period;
- any payment made on cancellation or settlement is treated as a repurchase of

an equity instrument, up to the fair value of the equity instruments at the repurchase date, any amounts over and above this must be treated as an expense;

- if new equity instruments are granted at the same time, and the company identified them as replacement instruments, then the issue of those new instruments is treated as a modification of the conditions associated with the existing instruments. The incremental fair value is then calculated as the difference at the date of replacement between the fair value of the new instruments and the fair value of the old, less any amounts that have been treated as a deduction from equity, and
- where new equity instruments are granted at the same time, but are not identified as replacement instruments then the two transactions are treated separately.

Where a company purchases vested equity instruments, this is treated as a deduction from equity, except to the extent that the payment exceeds the fair value of the items repurchased, as measured at the date of repurchase. Any such excess is treated as an expense.

7.7.9 Cash alternatives

Companies may be involved in share-based payment transactions where either they or the other party has the choice as to whether the transaction is settled in cash (or another asset) or by the issue of equity instruments.

The basic rule in such cases is:

> . . . the entity shall account for that transaction, or the components of that transaction, as a cash-settled share-based payment transaction if, and to the extent that, the entity has incurred a liability to settle in cash or other assets, or as an equity-settled share-based payment transaction if, and to the extent that, no such liability has been incurred. (Para. 34, FRS 20.)

The accounting treatment depends on the basis of valuing the transaction and also which party has the right to choose how the transaction will be settled.

Where the other party has the right to determine whether settlement is in cash or equity instruments then split accounting is required. This means that the company is considered to have granted a compound instrument which contains:

- a debt element, being the right of the other party to require payment in cash, and
- an equity element, being the right of the other party to demand settlement in equity instruments.

Where such a transaction is valued directly, at the fair value of the goods or services received, then:

- the goods or services are recorded at their fair value;

- the debt element is recorded at the amount the third party can demand to be paid in cash or kind, and
- the equity element is the difference between these amounts.

Where the other party has the choice and a transaction is recorded at the value of the equity instruments issued, such as with transactions involving the service of employees, then both the debt and equity elements need to be valued. The value of the equity element takes account of the fact that the right to cash cannot also be exercised. The transaction value will then be the sum of both. In some cases, the equity element may have no value. This may be very deliberate and the instrument may have been structured in such a way that zero is the only possible value. For example, the other party may have a choice between taking shares or an amount of cash based on the value of those shares. In this case the value of the alternatives must be the same, so the equity element has a value of nil.

Where such a transaction is recorded as a mixture of debt and equity elements then the recognition of the goods and services received must also be split. Given that there are differences in the recognition rules for cash-settled and equity-settled share-based payment transactions, this may lead to goods or, particularly, services being recorded in different periods.

When such an arrangement is finally settled the liability is remeasured to fair value at the settlement date. If in fact equity instruments are issued on settlement, then the liability is deemed to be the consideration received for the issue. If the settlement is in the form of cash, then any existing equity component remains there. However, it can be reclassified with equity.

Where it is the company which has the choice as to whether to pay cash or issue equity instruments then the company has to determine whether it has a present obligation to settle in cash. Such a present obligation exists where:

- the choice has no commercial substance, such as where the company cannot issue shares, for example where it has no unissued authorised share capital or is prohibited by covenant from issuing further shares;
- the company has a past practice of paying in cash;
- the company has a stated policy of paying in cash, or
- the company generally settles in cash where the other party requests this, notwithstanding the absence of their legal right to insist on cash settlement.

Where this applies, the company treats the transaction as a cash-settled share-based payment transaction. Otherwise, the transaction is treated as an equity-settled share-based payment transaction.

Where a transaction treated as an equity-settled share-based payment transaction is settled then:

- if settlement is by issue of equity no further accounting is required, other than a transfer between reserves;

- if settlement is in cash this is treated as the repurchase of an equity interest, that is, as a deduction from equity, and
- if settlement is by the alternative with the highest fair value, whichever that is, the excess over the other option is not treated in accordance with the rules above, but is treated as an additional expense.

7.7.10   Groups and treasury shares

Despite the fact that FRS 20 is a relatively recent standard it has already been changed a number of times and affected by various UITFs. UITF 44 deals with the issue of treasury shares and groups. This is an issue that has then been revisited in the changes made to FRS 20, which are applicable for accounting periods beginning on or after 1 January 2010. UITF 44 is withdrawn when the changes to FRS 20 take effect

Shares acquired to settle equity rights

An entity may grant rights to equity instruments to employees where it chooses or is required to purchase the equity instruments to satisfy its obligations to employees. For example, a company may grant share options to staff where it either cannot issue any more shares, or where it chooses not to do so. Instead it will acquire the shares from current shareholders in order to satisfy the option requirements.

The question arises as to whether this is an equity-settled or cash-settled transaction. There is some logic behind both positions, given that there is no intrinsic difference between an option where shares are to be acquired or shares are to be issued. At the same time, the company will pay cash (or other assets) to satisfy its obligations. The consensus is that such transactions are equity-settled. This applies in all cases.

The acquisition of shares is then dealt with separately, and is outside the scope of FRS 20.

Groups

FRS 20 is fairly clear when dealing with the treatment of items in the financial statements of standalone companies or groups as a whole. But there are some issues which arise where a transaction involves more than one company in a group. While the consolidated financial statements may be straightforward, the treatment by each individual company in its own accounts was not clearly addressed in the original version of FRS 20 and has, therefore, needed to be addressed both by a UITF and by amendments to the standard.

For example, employees of subsidiaries may be granted rights to equity instruments of the parent, either by the subsidiary or directly by the parent itself.

For periods beginning prior to 1 January 2010, if the rights are granted by the parent then these are accounted for as equity-settled transactions within the parent's separate financial statements, the subsidiary's financial statements, and the group accounts.

Where this occurs then, in the subsidiary, the effective double entry is:

Dr Employee services

Cr Equity (capital contribution from parent)

In the parent, the double entry is:

Dr Investment in subsidiary

Cr Equity (instruments granted)

In the group accounts, the additional investment in subsidiary and the capital contribution are netted off, leaving just the charge for employee services and the equity in the parent.

Where the rights are granted to an employee of a subsidiary, and subsequently that employee transfers to another subsidiary whilst the rights remain unchanged, the transaction is valued at the date of the initial grant, and not revalued at the date of transfer.

Where a subsidiary grants rights over shares in its parent, itself, then the transaction is treated as cash-settled in the subsidiary's accounts, but as equity-settled in the group accounts.

The acquisition and subsequent disposal of parent company shares by the subsidiary is treated as a treasury share transaction in the group accounts.

From 1 January 2010, these requirements do not change substantially, but, in some cases, they could lead to a slightly different result.

The basic requirement for the entity that receives the goods or services is that the transaction should be treated as either an equity-settled or a cash-settled share based payment transaction, after the assessment of the nature of the awards granted and its own rights and obligations. The standard goes on to clarify that this may imply that the amount recognised by the entity which receives the goods or services may differ from the amount which is recognised either in another entity within the group or within the group as a whole.

For example, the parent might grant rights, under a cash-settled share-based payment scheme, to employees of a subsidiary, where the amount is payable by the parent. From the perspective of the subsidiary, this is an equity-settled share-based payment scheme. Whilst it is the subsidiary that is receiving the benefit, it has no obligation to make the payment. From the perspective of the parent and the group, however, this is a cash-settled share-based payment scheme. Therefore, the charge made by the subsidiary will depend on the values at the date of grant and (assuming no changes to the scheme) will not be amended later. The amount recognised by the group will be cash-settled and will, therefore, need to be reconsidered at each reporting date.

7.7.11 Disclosure

The disclosure objectives of FRS 20 are to ensure that companies provide information allowing users of the accounts to understand:

- the nature and extent of share-based payment arrangements that existed in the period;
- how the fair value of the goods or services received, or the fair value of the equity instruments granted, during the period was determined, and
- the effect of share-based payment transactions on the company's profit or loss for the period and on its financial position.

This involves, in summary, the following disclosures.

(1) A description of each type of share-based payment arrangement that existed in the period.

(2) The number and weighted average exercise price of share options outstanding at the beginning and end of the period, exercisable at the end of the period and granted, forfeited, exercised, or expired during the period, all separately.

(3) The weighted average share price, at the date of exercise, for those share options exercised during the period or the weighted average share price where options were regularly exercised.

(4) The range of exercise prices and weighted average remaining contractual life for options outstanding at the period end, divided into ranges where necessary.

(5) Where goods or services received have been valued on the basis of the value of the equity instruments granted then:

(a) for new options, the weighted average fair value of those options at the measurement date and information on how that value was determined, including the option pricing model used and the inputs to that model, how volatility was determined and an explanation of whether it was based on historical volatility and whether any other features were incorporated into the fair value;

(b) for new equity instruments other than options, the number and weighted average fair value at the measurement date and information on how that value was determined, including how fair value was determined if not based on observable market prices, whether and how dividends were included in the measurement and whether and how other features were incorporated into the fair value, and

(c) for equity instruments modified in the period, an explanation of the modifications, the incremental fair value granted and information on how this was measured.

(6) Where goods and services subject to share-based payment transactions have been measured directly then how that fair value was determined.

(7) Where the company has rebutted the presumption that the fair value of goods and services received can be measured reliably, then a statement of this fact and an explanation of how the presumption was rebutted.

(8) The total expense arising from share-based payment transactions in the period, where the goods or services received did not qualify for recognition as assets, including separate disclosure of the part of that total which relates to equity-settled share-based payment transactions.

(9) The total carrying amount of liabilities at the end of the year, arising as result of share-based payment transactions and the total intrinsic value at the end of the period for liabilities, where the other party's rights had vested by the end of the period.

For companies complying with the 2008 version of the FRSSE, equity-settled share-based payments are dealt with only through disclosure. Such companies are required to disclose the principal terms and conditions of any equity-settled share-based payment arrangements that exist during the period including:

- the number of shares involved and potentially involved;
- the number of employees involved and potentially involved;
- the grant date;
- any performance conditions and over what period they apply, and
- any option exercise prices.

Potential impact of the FRSME

The FRSME contains the same basic principles as FRS 20. Unlike the FRSSE, it requires a charge to be recorded in respect of equity-settled share-based payments. However, it lacks the (now voluminous) guidance included within or with FRS 20, and would, as a result, almost certainly introduce greater flexibility into the determination of share-based payment charges. It also glosses over issues arising, in relation to groups, noting that where a parent (which applies the FRSME or EU-adopted IFRS) grants share-based payment rights to employees of subsidiaries, those subsidiaries should record a reasonable allocation of the group charge. This ignores the accounting entries required and the problems where it is the subsidiary that grants the rights over the equity of the parent, both of which are problems that required amendments to FRS 20.

8 TAXATION

8.1 INTRODUCTION

This chapter will deal with both current and deferred taxation.

With regard to current taxes, the two taxes that will be considered in this chapter are value added tax (VAT) and corporation tax. Reference will also be made to overseas taxation, but solely in respect of disclosure. Employers' National Insurance contributions are dealt with in conjunction with staff costs in Chapter 7. This chapter deals solely with the accounting treatment and disclosure of taxation and not with the calculation of the underlying charge or liability.

Even ignoring charitable enterprises, some companies, even in the UK, do not pay tax on all of their profits. For example, UK shipping companies, subject to various restrictions, may elect to pay tax on their shipping activities based on their tonnage rather than their profits. In such cases, most of FRS 16 *Current Tax* and, in particular, FRS 19 *Deferred Tax* will not apply. Where profits are not, and will not in the future be, subject to taxation, then neither current nor deferred taxation is relevant.

The international standard that deals with taxation is IAS 12 *Income Taxes*. This deals with both current and deferred taxation, but does not deal with taxes such as VAT. The UK and international standards are broadly similar, and the accounting treatment of current taxation is likely to be much the same under both standards. There may also be cases where the calculation and treatment of deferred taxation will be the same, depending on the circumstances of the company, but there are also some areas of significant difference between UK and international practice. For example, IAS 12 may require deferred taxation to be calculated on revaluations and some other value adjustments, whereas this is rarely the case under FRS 19, whilst IAS 12 does not allow deferred tax amounts to be discounted.

Potential impact of the FRSME

It is the basic approach of IAS 12 that is reflected in the FRSME, so there are some potential changes to the treatment of deferred tax that would arise if the FRSME were to come into force. It is noteworthy that the FRSME is based primarily on IAS 12 itself, and not on the taxation-related requirements of the IFRS for SMEs which underpins most of the rest of the document. This is because the IFRS for SMEs anticipated some changes to IAS 12 that were proposed at the time it was being issued. Those changes were rejected and never reflected in IAS 12 itself.

8.2 VALUE ADDED TAX

8.2.1 Accounting for value added tax

The basic accounting treatment for VAT is set out in SSAP 5 *Accounting for Value Added Tax* and in paragraph 9.15 of the FRSSE (in the version effective April 2008).

Although VAT is collected at various stages of the production and distribution process, it is in most cases only borne by the final consumer. At each stage of the production and distribution process each party will simply be collecting part of the total VAT which it must then pass on to HM Revenue and Customs (HMRC). Each company will be able to claim back the VAT that it has incurred and will simply pass over the difference between the tax collected and the tax paid. As a result, for most types of expenditure, companies will not actually bear the cost of the tax.

As noted in SSAP 5, the fact that companies are usually only collecting VAT, rather than bearing it, has to be reflected in the accounting treatment adopted:

> VAT is a tax on the supply of goods and services, which is eventually borne by the final consumer, but collected at each stage of the production and distribution chain. As a general principle, therefore, the treatment of VAT in the accounts of a trader should reflect his role as a collector of the tax and VAT should not be included in income or in expenditure whether of a capital or of a revenue nature. (Para. 1, SSAP 5.)

Income and expenditure will normally be stated at their net amounts, with VAT being a liability, or less commonly an asset, in the company's balance sheet. This will represent the amount due to or from HMRC. However, if a company wishes, SSAP 5 allows turnover to be stated gross, that is, inclusive of the VAT amount. If a company chooses to use this option, it will need to make a deduction to arrive at the turnover exclusive of VAT. This is probably still acceptable, despite the fact that the Companies Act states that:

> 'turnover' in relation to a company, means the amounts derived from the provision of goods and services falling within the company's ordinary activities, after deduction of:
>
> (i) trade discounts;
> (ii) value added tax, and
> (iii) any other taxes based on the amounts so derived. (CA 2006, s. 474(1).)

(There is some similarity with the requirement in FRS 9 for group accounts to disclose the turnover of a group plus its joint ventures, and then to deduct the turnover attributable to joint ventures in order to arrive at the statutory measure of group turnover.)

The option to state both gross and net turnover probably seemed far more relevant when SSAP 5 was introduced in 1974, at the time that VAT was itself introduced. Very few, if any, companies now choose to show the gross turnover with a separate deduction for the applicable amount of VAT. The FRSSE states that turnover shown in the profit and loss account should exclude VAT on taxable outputs. It does not provide the option of disclosing gross turnover as well:

> Turnover shown in the profit and loss account shall exclude either VAT on taxable outputs or VAT imputed under the flat rate VAT scheme. (Para. 9.15, FRSSE 2008.)

The VAT balance will not always be a creditor, although it will be for the majority of companies. It is possible that the input VAT suffered in a period may be higher than the output tax due. The VAT balance will then be a debtor, and should be included as such in the balance sheet. This is most likely to occur where a company trades exclusively or primarily in goods subject to VAT at the zero rate. As when the balance is a liability, separate disclosure of the amount is not normally required.

IAS 12 does not deal with VAT, or similar taxes which are based on output, sales or turnover. It deals only with income taxes, which are defined as taxes based on taxable profits.

8.2.2   Companies that are not taxable persons

Not all companies are registered for VAT. A company may choose not to register if its turnover is below the current registration limit or if it trades exclusively in goods and services which are exempt from VAT. If a company is not registered for VAT, then it is effectively the final consumer of all the goods and services which it receives. As such it must suffer the full cost of the VAT and is not able to recover the VAT it has paid. In such cases, the full costs of each transaction should be recorded, inclusive of the VAT.

For example, where such a company makes a purchase at a cost of £117.50, inclusive of VAT, this is the amount it should record as the cost of that purchase. No attempt should be made to distinguish between the net cost and the VAT cost. One implication of this is that where two companies buy identical fixed assets, but one is a taxable person and the other is not, then the cost recorded in their financial statements will differ since one company will be able to recover the VAT, but the other will have to suffer the VAT as part of the cost.

8.2.3   Partially exempt businesses

A company is partially exempt where some of its outputs are taxable and some are exempt from VAT. A company in this position will be able to recover some, but not all, of the VAT which it incurs. The company will have established or adopted a method by which the proportion of irrecoverable VAT is calculated. In normal circumstances this method should also be applied to the costs incurred in the period to ensure that these are also stated inclusive of the VAT which is not recoverable.

The most important practical distinction is often between the irrecoverable VAT on fixed assets and the irrecoverable VAT on purchases and overheads incurred in the period. This is because the VAT on fixed assets can be included in the cost of those assets, and carried forward, while the VAT incurred in respect of costs of the period will normally need to be written off as an expense in the period. Both SSAP 5 and the FRSSE contain explicit requirements that irrecoverable VAT be included in the costs of fixed assets. In most cases, non-recoverable VAT will be known, since any amounts due will have been agreed with HMRC by the time financial statements are prepared. However, if VAT and accounting periods do not coincide, and financial statements are prepared quickly, then it may be necessary to make an estimate of the amount of VAT that will not be recoverable.

8.2.4 Non-deductible inputs

Where input tax is not recoverable, it should be included in the cost of the expense or the fixed asset. No separate disclosure of the amount of VAT involved is required. This applies to all companies, whether they are fully taxable, exempt or partially exempt.

Where any such expense is separately disclosable in financial statements (under some other standard or a statutory requirement), the amount disclosed should be inclusive of VAT.

8.2.5 Cash accounting

Some smaller companies may be eligible to use the cash accounting scheme for VAT. This will have little effect on the amounts included in their financial statements, although it may make the underlying accounting slightly more complicated. VAT should still be recorded on each transaction as it takes place and the company will need to maintain a separate record of cash receipts and payments including VAT, so that the amount due to or recoverable from HMRC can be calculated.

In such a case, even if the accounting and VAT periods are the same, the amount shown in the financial statements will not agree with the amount due to or from HMRC, but it will reflect the effect of all transactions which have been recorded in the period. This is because cash accounting is being used for VAT purposes, while accruals accounting is still required for the company accounts. Similarly, only if accrual accounting is adopted will the debtors' and creditors' figures in the balance sheet reflect the total amounts receivable and due, since such amounts are inclusive of VAT. The use of these methods will result in a form of (for want of a better term) deferred taxation, where the accounting effect of a transaction and its taxation effect will occur at different times.

8.2.6 Commitments

Where capital, or other, commitments are disclosed in financial statements, they should be shown inclusive of irrecoverable VAT, if any, which is to be incurred, but should not include any VAT which is expected to be recoverable.

Potential impact of the FRSME

In practice, the FRSME would have no impact on the accounting treatment of VAT. The FRSME does not address VAT at all, but the accounting treatments required by SSAP 5 are uncontentious and would not change. SSAP 5 is one of those standards that may have been necessary at the time – VAT was after all new – but now deals with questions to which the answers seem obvious.

8.3 CURRENT TAX

8.3.1 Introduction

Accounting for current tax is dealt with by FRS 16 *Current Tax*. The stated objective of FRS 16 is to ensure that reporting entities recognise current taxes in a consistent and transparent manner.

FRS 16 defines current tax as follows.

> The amount of tax estimated to be payable or recoverable in respect of the taxable profit or loss for a period, along with adjustments to estimates in respect of previous periods. (Para. 2, FRS 16.)

The taxable profit or loss is further defined as:

> The profit or loss for the period, determined in accordance with the rules established by the tax authorities, upon which taxes are assessed. (Para. 2, FRS 16.)

In the UK, the above definitions, in effect, mean that current tax is the corporation tax on a company's profits, excluding any effects of deferred taxation.

FRS 16 applies to all financial statements that are intended to give a true and fair view of a reporting entity's financial position and profit or loss (or income and expenditure) for a period. Where a company adopts the FRSSE, it will be exempt from FRS 16, although the FRSSE contains very similar requirements to the FRS.

IAS 12 also contains very similar requirements to FRS 16 in respect of current taxation.

8.3.2   Recognition of current tax

When dealing with the recognition requirements for current tax, FRS 16 takes account of the existence of the statement of total recognised gains and losses:

> Current tax should be recognised in the profit and loss account for the period, except to the extent that it is attributable to a gain or loss that is or has been recognised directly in the statement of total recognised gains and losses. (Para. 5, FRS 16.)

> Where a gain or loss is or has been recognised directly in the statement of total recognised gains and losses, the tax attributable to that gain or loss should also be recognised directly in that statement. (Para. 6, FRS 16.)

Current tax is most likely to be recognised in the statement of total recognised gains and losses where it relates either to an exchange difference recognised in that statement or to tax arising on disposal of a previously revalued fixed asset. In the latter case, the underlying gain itself would have been recognised in the statement of total recognised gains and losses in the earlier accounting period when the asset was revalued. The Companies Act 2006 also permits tax relating to a gain or loss credited or debited to the revaluation reserve to be taken to that reserve rather than to the profit and loss account.

FRS 16 notes that, in exceptional circumstances, it may be difficult to determine the amount of current tax that is attributable to gains or losses that have been recognised directly in the statement of total recognised gains and losses. Where this is the case the FRS states that the attributable tax should be based on a reasonable pro rata allocation, or another allocation that is more appropriate in the circumstances.

The FRSSE does not contain the same level of detail as FRS 16, but contains the same basic requirement in terms of allocating current tax, where relevant, between the profit and loss account and the statement of total recognised gains and losses.

IAS 12 also requires that current tax be charged to profit, to the extent that it arises in respect of items which have themselves been taken into account in the determination of profit. From 2009, the situation on items which are recognised outside of profit is a little more complex, reflecting the fact that IFRS financial statements now contain a statement of comprehensive income. Where gains or losses are treated as other comprehensive income, then the attributable tax must also be dealt with as other comprehensive income. This can either be done by having a separate tax charge (or credit) within other comprehensive income or by showing each individual category giving rise to a tax charge or credit net of attributable taxation.

8.3.3   *Dividends and interest*

When dealing with dividends and interest, it is important to distinguish between withholding tax and tax credits, as the two are treated differently under FRS 16.

A tax credit is defined as:

> The tax credit given under UK tax legislation to the recipient of a dividend from a UK company. (Para. 2, FRS 16.)

FRS 16 further notes that the tax credit is given to acknowledge that the income out of which the dividend has been paid has already been charged to tax, rather than because any withholding tax has been deducted at source. UK companies cannot reclaim tax credits on dividend income, though the dividend income from other UK companies is not itself taxable income for a UK company.

FRS 16 defines withholding tax as:

> Tax on dividends or other income that is deducted by the payer of the income and paid to the tax authorities wholly on behalf of the recipient. (Para. 2, FRS 16.)

Domestically within the UK, withholding tax most commonly applies to interest income and expenditure.

The FRS 16 requirements relating to the treatment of tax credits and withholding tax on outgoing and incoming dividends and interest are as follows.

> Outgoing dividends paid and proposed (or declared and not yet payable), interest and other amounts payable should be recognised at an amount that:
>
> (a)   includes any withholding taxes, but
> (b)   excludes any other taxes, such as attributable tax credits, not payable wholly on behalf of the recipient. (Para. 8, FRS 16.)

> Incoming dividends, interest or other income receivable should be recognised at an amount that:
>
> (a)   includes any withholding taxes, but
> (b)   excludes any other taxes, such as attributable tax credits, not payable wholly on behalf of the recipient.

The effect of any withholding tax suffered should be taken into account as part of the tax charge. (Para. 9, FRS 16.)

FRS 16 also notes that its requirements mean that the amount recognised as income will exclude not only tax credits but also underlying tax. Although FRS 16 does not formally define the term 'underlying tax', a footnote explains that a UK company receiving dividends from an overseas company may obtain relief for the tax (underlying tax) that the overseas company has paid on the profits from which the dividend has been paid. The UK company's taxable income will then be increased by the amount of the underlying tax attributed to the dividend and relief will be given against the resulting UK tax charge.

The FRSSE contains similar requirements to FRS 16.

The issue of withholding tax and tax credits is not dealt with in IAS 12.

8.3.4   Measurement of current tax

FRS 16 addresses the issue of whether to take into account changes in tax rates which occur after the balance sheet date, but before the financial statements are approved and which affect the calculation of the current year's tax charge:

> Current tax should be measured at the amounts expected to be paid (or recovered) using the tax rates and laws that have been enacted or substantively enacted by the balance sheet date. (Para. 14, FRS 16.)

The FRS explains that a UK tax rate can be regarded as having been substantively enacted if it is included in either:

(a)   a Bill that has been passed by the House of Commons and is awaiting only passage through the House of Lords and Royal Assent; or

(b)   a resolution having statutory effect that has been passed under the Provisional Collection of Taxes Act 1968. (Para. 15, FRS 16.)

As current UK practice is to specify the rate of corporation tax in advance, the tax rate to be used in the measurement of current tax is not at present a significant issue in the UK.

IAS 12 is identical in intent to FRS 16. The only difference is that, of course, IAS 12 is less precise when dealing with the meaning of 'substantively enacted' since it needs to deal with legislative procedures across a wide range of jurisdictions. It makes no reference to the specific procedures by which UK legislation is enacted.

8.3.5   Income and expenses subject to non-standard rates of tax

FRS 16 also deals with the treatment of income and expenses which are subject to non-standard rates of tax. It is intended to prohibit companies from grossing up profits and tax charges where they receive income which is subject to non-standard tax rates or which is not subject to any tax. The requirement is as follows.

> Subject to paragraphs 8 and 9 [which deal with dividends and interest], income and expenses should be included in the pre-tax results on the basis of the income or expenses actually receivable or payable. No adjustment should be made to reflect a notional amount of tax that would have been paid or relieved in respect of the transaction if it had been taxable, or allowable for tax purposes, on a different basis. (Para. 11, FRS 16.)

The FRS notes that the above requirement applies, for example, to non-taxable income, non-deductible expenditure and income and expenditure subject to non-standard rates of tax. However, the requirement applies only to notional tax, that is, tax which is not actually recovered or paid. FRS 16 points out that in specialised industries, such as leasing, profit from transactions is allocated to accounting periods on a post-tax basis with the tax charge and pre-tax profit for an accounting period being found by applying the effective rate of tax to the post-tax profit. FRS 16 states that such an approach will usually result in the actual pre-tax profit and tax charge being recorded over the life of the transactions, which is consistent with the requirements of the FRS.

IAS 12 does not deal with non-standard rates of tax, although it could easily be argued that the FRS 16 requirements are implicit in the remainder of that standard. On this interpretation, the FRS 16 requirement (itself preceded by and based on a UITF) is for clarification and avoidance of doubt. IAS 12 does deal with the issue of tax rates which vary dependent on distribution policy.

8.3.6 Transitional arrangements for ACT

Although ACT was abolished more than a decade ago, with effect from 6 April 1999, companies which at that date had unrelieved ACT carried forward are still covered by the shadow ACT regime. The effect of this regime is that the ACT carried forward at 6 April 1999 will become recoverable only to the extent that would have been the case had ACT continued to exist. Therefore, it is possible that ACT recoverable which had, for accounting purposes, been written off might in fact still be recovered. Conversely, ACT recoverable carried forward as an asset might become irrecoverable and need to be written off in the financial statements, although given the time since the abolition of ACT it would be surprising were this now to be encountered in anything other than extremely unusual circumstances.

To address this issue, FRS 16 includes the following transitional provision.

> Any unrelieved advance corporation tax (ACT) that at the date of implementation of the FRS is carried forward for relief against future taxable profits should be recognised on the balance sheet only to the extent that it is regarded as recoverable. Any change in the amount of ACT regarded as recoverable should be recognised as part of the tax expense (or income) for the period in the profit and loss account and separately disclosed on the face of the profit and loss account or in a note. (Para. 20, FRS 16.)

This is then supplemented by an appendix to the FRS, which restates the guidance formerly contained in SSAP 8 on the circumstances in which ACT can be regarded as recoverable.

> ACT is regarded as recoverable where the amount of the ACT previously paid on outgoing dividends can be:
>
> (a) set off against a corporation tax liability on the profits of the period under review or of previous periods;
> (b) properly set off against a credit balance on the deferred tax account; or

(c) expected to be recoverable taking into account expected profits and dividends (normally those of the next accounting period only). (Para. 1, Appendix II, FRS 16.)

Appendix II to FRS 16 states that, in deciding whether ACT should be carried forward as recoverable, regard should be had only to the immediate and foreseeable future, which it suggests should not normally extend beyond the next accounting period unless there is a deferred tax account.

ACT should be offset against a credit balance on the deferred tax account only if, in the period in which the underlying timing differences are expected to reverse, the reversal will create sufficient taxable profits to enable ACT to be recovered under the shadow ACT system.

IAS 12 does not deal with similar issues. However, again, the Appendix is a clarification of what is actually a fairly straightforward accounting issue.

8.3.7 *Financial Reporting Standard for Smaller Entities*

The FRSSE contains a simplified version of the requirements of FRS 16. It does not incorporate the FRS 16 requirements relating to income and expenses subject to non-standard rates of tax, formerly contained in UITF Abstract 16. Nonetheless, FRS 16 clearly represents best practice in this area.

Potential impact of the FRSME

The accounting treatment of current tax would change very little with the introduction of the FRSME. The only changes would, in most cases, be those that relate more to the general changes to the formats and presentation of financial statements that arise out of the FRSME rather than matters that relate directly to issues of current tax.

8.4 DISCLOSURES RELATING TO CURRENT TAX

8.4.1 *Companies Act 2006*

A Statutory Instrument to the Companies Act 2006 requires the following disclosures in respect of taxation.

2 Particulars must be given of any special circumstances which affect liability in respect of taxation of profits, income or capital gains for the financial year or liability in respect of taxation of profits, income or capital gains for succeeding financial years.

3 The following amounts must be stated:

(a) the amount of the charge for United Kingdom corporation tax;

(b) if that amount would have been greater but for relief from double taxation, the amount which it would have been but for such relief;

(c) the amount of the charge for United Kingdom income tax, and

(d) the amount of charge for taxation imposed outside the United Kingdom of profits, income and (so far as charged to revenue) capital gains.

These amounts must be stated separately in respect of each of the amounts which is:

... shown under the following items in the profit and loss account, that is to say 'tax on profit on ordinary activities' and 'tax on extraordinary profit or loss'. (Para. 67, Sch. 1 to The Large and Medium-sized Companies and Groups (Accounts and Reports) Regulations 2008 (SI 2008/410).)

The disclosure requirements applicable to larger companies have not been included in Sch. 1 to The Small Companies and Groups (Accounts and Directors' Report) Regulations 2008 (SI 2008/409), but small companies are still required to comply with the requirements of the FRSSE, which are stated later.

Although there is no such separate statutory heading, many companies disclose corporation tax as a separate sub-category of creditors. (There is a requirement to show amounts due in respect of taxation and social security separately from other creditors.)

8.4.2 FRS 16

FRS 16 requires the following major components of the current tax expense (or income) for the period in the profit and loss account and the statement of total recognised gains and losses to be disclosed separately:

- UK tax, and
- foreign tax.

Both should be analysed to distinguish between tax estimated for the current period and any adjustments recognised in respect of prior periods. The domestic tax should be disclosed both before and after double taxation relief.

Appendix I to FRS 16 provides the following pro forma which illustrates one method of showing (by way of note) the tax items required to be disclosed under companies' legislation and the FRS.

EXAMPLE		
	£000	*£000*
UK corporation tax		
Current tax on income for the period	a	
Adjustments in respect of prior periods	b	

8. Taxation

	£000	£000
	c	
Double taxation relief	(d)	
		e
Foreign tax		
Current tax on income for the period	f	
Adjustments in respect of prior periods	g	
		h
Tax on profit on ordinary activities		i

8.4.3 Financial Reporting Standard for Smaller Entities

The FRSSE requires that the following amounts be disclosed in respect of taxation.

- The material components of the current tax charge.
- Any special circumstances that affect the overall tax charge or credit for the period (or which may affect those of future periods).

The effects of a fundamental change in the basis of taxation should be included in the tax charge or credit for the period, and separately disclosed on the face of the profit and loss account.

8.5 DEFERRED TAX

8.5.1 Introduction

FRS 19 applies to all financial statements intended to give a true and fair view, other than those of entities that are preparing accounts in accordance with the FRSSE. The recognition rules under the FRSSE are similar, being based on those included in FRS 19.

8.5.2 Recognising deferred tax assets and liabilities

As a general rule, deferred tax:

- should be recognised in respect of all timing differences that have originated but not reversed by the balance sheet date, and
- should not be recognised on permanent differences.

Timing differences are defined as:

Differences between an entity's taxable profits and its results as stated in the financial statements that arise from the inclusion of gains and losses in tax assessments in periods different from those in which they are recognised in financial statements. Timing differences originate in one period and are capable of reversal in one or more subsequent periods. (Para. 2, FRS 19.)

Examples of timing difference given in the standard are where:

- tax deductions for the cost of a fixed asset are accelerated or decelerated, ie capital allowances are received before or after the cost of the fixed asset is recognised in the profit and loss account through depreciation or amortisation;
- pension liabilities are accrued in the financial statements but are allowed for tax purposes only when paid or contributed at a later date;
- interest charges or development costs are capitalised on the balance sheet, either as separate assets or as part of assets, but are treated as revenue expenditure and allowed as incurred for tax purposes;
- intra-group profits in stock, unrealised at group level, are reversed on consolidation;
- an asset is revalued in the financial statements but the revaluation gain becomes taxable only if and when the asset is sold;
- a tax loss is not relieved against past or present taxable profits but can be carried forward to reduce future taxable profits, and
- the unremitted earnings of subsidiary and associated undertakings and joint ventures are recognised in the group results but will be subject to further taxation only if and when remitted to the parent undertaking.

Permanent differences are defined as:

Differences between an entity's taxable profits and its results as stated in the financial statements that arise because certain types of income and expenditure are non-taxable or disallowable, or because certain tax charges or allowances have no corresponding amount in the financial statements. (Para. 2, FRS 19.)

Permanent differences will never reverse, and as such do not have any implications for deferred tax.

The general rule is then amplified by dealing with particular categories of difference.

Capital allowances

Under FRS 19:

'Deferred tax should be recognised when the allowances for the cost of a fixed asset are received before or after the cost of the fixed asset is recognised in the profit and loss account. However, if and when all conditions for retaining the allowances have been met, the deferred tax should be reversed. (Para. 9, FRS 19.)'

As the standard notes, if an asset is not being depreciated (and has not otherwise been written down to a value that is less than its cost) the timing difference is the amount of capital allowances received.

The basic rule applies to most categories of capital allowance. Most are received on a conditional basis, and are repayable (perhaps via a balancing charge) if the assets to which they relate are sold for more than their tax written-down value.

Where this does not apply, the treatment may differ. The standard acknowledges the possibility of cases where allowances are initially conditional, but after certain conditions are met, perhaps just the passing of time, the allowances become absolute. At that point, any deferred tax that had previously been recognised (on the excess of the allowance over any depreciation) would be reversed. It would not be acceptable to anticipate that an asset will be retained until the end of the expiry period for repayment and to use this as a basis for not providing for deferred tax. This may mean that companies obtaining such allowances would be required to build up a deferred tax liability over many years, releasing the total amount at the point at which the allowances cease to be conditional. Such an amount could easily be material in the year of release. There are also allowances, such as most industrial buildings allowances now, which are not conditional at all. Any disposal of the asset to which such allowances relate would not trigger a recovery of the allowances previously obtained (although there might be a chargeable gain in relation to the disposal of the asset). Such allowances will not give rise to deferred taxation.

Revaluations and gains on disposal

The accounting treatment for revaluations depends on whether any associated revaluation gains and losses pass through the profit and loss account or pass through the statement of total recognised gains and losses.

If assets are continuously revalued to fair value with changes in fair value being recognised in the profit and loss account then deferred tax should be recognised on any timing differences arising.

The most common examples will be where items are restated to their fair values at each balance sheet date, perhaps for companies which are complying with the measurement requirements of FRS 26, with the changes in value being recognised in the profit and loss account. Where such gains and losses are subject to current tax then the question of deferred tax will not arise. But where the tax charge does not take account of such fluctuations in value, deferred tax must be accounted for in full.

In other cases (which are much more common under UK GAAP), where the gains are recognised in the statement of total recognised gains and losses, deferred tax should not be recognised on timing differences arising when other non-monetary assets are revalued, unless, by the balance sheet date, the reporting entity has:

- entered into a binding agreement to sell the revalued assets, and
- recognised the gains and losses expected to arise on sale.

This means that, in practice, most revaluation gains will not give rise to any deferred tax charge, since the conditions will not normally have been met.

A binding agreement to sell does not exist if there is no more than simply an intention, or even an expectation, of sale.

In addition, FRS 19 requires that:

> Deferred tax should not be recognised on timing differences arising when non-monetary assets (other than those . . . [subject to the mark-to-market rules above]) are revalued or sold if, on the basis of all available evidence, it is more likely than not that the taxable gain will be rolled over, being charged to tax only if and when the assets into which the gain has been rolled over are sold. (Para. 15, FRS 19.)

Deferred tax must be provided where this condition is not met, ie where it is more likely than not that a tax charge will arise as the gain cannot be rolled over.

In addition, this provision applies only to gains which are rolled over, and, therefore, where the gain will not be taxed unless and until the assets into which the gain has been rolled over is sold. Where the gain is simply held over for a finite period, so that tax is deferred, but not avoided, the deferred tax must still be accounted for.

There may be cases where there has to be judgement made regarding the availability of rollover relief. This will arise when the entity has not yet reinvested the proceeds of sale in qualifying replacement assets but may still do so within the period allowed. All available evidence, including that provided by events occurring after the balance sheet date should be considered when judging whether it is more likely than not that the gain will be rolled over. This may change with time and needs to be reassessed continually until the entity either claims rollover relief or loses its right to do so. Any adjustment to recognise a previously unrecognised deferred tax provision (or to release a provision previously recognised) is a change in estimate, which, as always, should be charged or credited as part of the tax charge for the period in the profit and loss account or statement of total recognised gains and losses.

Unremitted earnings of subsidiaries, associates and joint ventures

As a general rule, it will not be necessary to provide for deferred tax on the unremitted earnings of subsidiaries, associates and joint ventures as:

> Tax that could be payable (taking account of any double taxation relief) on any future remittance of the past earnings of a subsidiary, associate or joint venture should be provided for only to the extent that, at the balance sheet date:
>
> (a) dividends have been accrued as receivable; or
> (b) a binding agreement to distribute the past earnings in future has been entered into by the subsidiary, associate or joint venture. (Para. 21, FRS 19.)

This will be unusual. Therefore, the deferred tax provision will often comprise only the tax that will become payable (taking account of double taxation relief)

231

on receipt of dividends accrued at the balance sheet date. It should also be noted that the likelihood of encountering dividends treated as receivable when not actually received are fairly slim, given that under FRS 21 dividends are not accrued until declared, either for payment or receipt.

The FRSSE, while lacking the detail of FRS 19, requires similar accounting treatments to be adopted.

Comparison with IAS 12

IAS 12 takes a very different approach to FRS 19. Rather than dealing with timing differences, IAS 12 deals with temporary differences. These are defined as:

> ... differences between the carrying amount of an asset or liability in the statement of financial position and its tax base ... (Para. 5, IAS 12.)

(Since accounting periods beginning on or after 1 January 2009, all international standards, including IAS 12, replace all references to the 'balance sheet' with a reference to the 'statement of financial position'. The phrase 'balance sheet' can still be used in financial statements prepared under IFRS if the preparing entity wishes.) The standard then goes on to divide temporary differences into taxable temporary differences and deductible temporary differences. The tax base is also defined as the amount attributable to an asset or liability for tax purposes. In the case of items that are not taxable, their tax base is equal to their carrying value.

The definition of temporary differences is much wider than that of timing differences used in FRS 19. In particular, it encompasses differences that arise when assets are revalued. IAS 12 requires companies to provide deferred tax in respect of all revaluations where the future recovery of the carrying amount will result in a taxable flow of economic benefits. Contrary to FRS 19, IAS 12 makes it clear that calculating deferred tax on revaluations is required even where the company has no intention of disposing of the asset, and where it will be possible to roll over any realised gain into the cost of new assets. This means that it is likely that a higher level of provision for deferred tax is required under IAS 12 than would be required under FRS 19, if a company has a policy of revaluing some or all of its classes of asset.

IAS 12 does allow potential deferred tax liabilities to be ignored where they arise in respect of goodwill for which amortisation is not deductible for tax purposes and the initial recognition of assets and liabilities which do not result from a business combination and which, at the time of the transaction, affect neither accounting nor taxable profit.

Potential impact of the FRSME

The FRSME sections dealing with deferred tax are largely based on IAS 12 (and not the IFRS for SMEs, as noted at **8.1**). Therefore, the difference in approach between FRS 19 and IAS 12 is very relevant in considering the potential impact of the FRSME. Simplistically, FRS 19 approaches deferred tax by looking at the differences between the amounts recognised in taxable and accounting profits, whilst IAS 12 looks at the difference between the relevant values of assets and liabilities for tax and accounting purposes.

The FRSME adopts the IAS 12 approach and therefore is based on asset and liability amounts, and not profit related differences.

In many cases, the result will be the same. For example, if a fixed asset is carried at cost, depreciated and attracts capital allowances, then the difference between the accumulated depreciation charges and accumulated capital allowances will be the same as the difference between its carrying value and tax written down value.

In some cases, the result will differ. However, some of the other differences between the FRSME and IFRS (in general) limit the impact of this. Revaluation of assets (where such revaluations are not taxable) is an obvious area where a 'balance sheet' approach and a 'profit and loss' approach will lead to different results. This is true under the FRSME, but of less relevance than it might otherwise be as the FRSME restricts the circumstances where assets may be revalued. For example, items of property, plant and equipment (tangible fixed assets) may not be revalued and must be stated at depreciated historic cost. This means that no difference between the two approaches actually arises. There are exceptions. The FRSME does propose to allow the revaluation of investment properties, and this means that deferred tax will need to be provided on revaluation gains, when this is not the case under current UK accounting practice (with some limited exceptions). Similarly, the differences in approach becomes manifest when dealing with charges in respect of share-based payments; particularly, if equity settled, as the deferred tax that arises through looking at accumulated accounting charges and tax benefits obtained bears no relationship to the deferred tax that arises if determined by looking at the carrying values and potential tax benefits.

8.5.3 Deferred tax assets

Consistent with FRS 18, FRS 19 has downgraded the application of prudence to the rules on the recognition of deferred tax assets.

> Deferred tax assets should be recognised to the extent that they are regarded as recoverable. They should be regarded as recoverable to the extent that, on the basis of all available evidence, it can be regarded as more likely than not that there will be suitable taxable profits from which the future reversal of the underlying timing differences can be deducted. (Para. 23, FRS 19.)

Suitable taxable profits are those that are:

- generated in the same taxable entity (or an entity whose profits would be available via group relief) and assessed by the same tax authority as the income or expenditure giving rise to the deferred tax asset;

- generated in the same period as that in which the deferred tax asset is expected to reverse, or in a period to which a tax loss arising from the reversal of the deferred tax asset may be carried back or forward, and
- of a type (such as capital or trading) from which the taxation authority allows the reversal of the timing difference to be deducted.

Account may be taken of tax planning opportunities, such as:

- accelerating taxable amounts or deferring claims for writing down allowances to recover losses being carried forward (perhaps before they expire);
- changing the character of taxable or deductible amounts from trading gains or losses to capital gains or losses or vice versa, or
- switching from tax free to taxable investments.

There is no limit to the amount by which deferred tax assets can be taken into account in being offset against deferred tax liabilities, so long as in practice the assets and liabilities could be offset if they were to reverse in the same accounting period.

Where deferred tax assets cannot be offset against deferred tax liabilities, it is necessary to consider the likelihood of there being other suitable taxable profits. All evidence should be considered, including, but not limited to, historical information about the entity's financial performance and position, which may provide the most objective evidence.

The existence of unrelieved tax losses at the balance sheet date should be taken as strong evidence that there will not be suitable taxable profits in future against which the losses (and other deferred tax assets) can be recovered. In such circumstances, the unrelieved losses (and other deferred tax assets affected) are recognised only if there is other persuasive and reliable evidence suggesting that suitable taxable profits will be generated.

In the case of unrelieved trading losses, such evidence may exist if the loss resulted from an identifiable and non-recurring cause and the reporting entity has otherwise been consistently profitable over a long period, with any past losses being more than offset by income in later periods.

If an unrelieved capital loss can be relieved only against future capital gains, there is likely to be persuasive and reliable evidence that there will be suitable taxable gains against which the loss can be relieved only to the extent that:

- a potential chargeable gain not expected to be covered by rollover relief is present in assets but has not been recognised as a deferred tax liability;
- plans are in place for the sale of these assets, and
- the carried-forward loss will be offset against the resulting chargeable gain for tax purposes.

If it is expected that it will take some time for tax losses to be relieved, the recoverability of the resulting deferred tax asset is likely to be relatively uncertain. In such circumstances, it may not be appropriate to recognise the deferred tax asset at all.

This needs to be reconsidered each year. Changes in circumstances may mean that items become, or cease to be, considered as recoverable. As these are changes in estimates, they should be taken into account in the tax charge or credit for the year, and should not be treated as prior period adjustments.

The rules under IAS 12 are broadly similar in terms of the recognition of assets, although as noted above the amounts of deferred tax that are calculated may differ significantly.

Potential impact of the FRSME

Given that the FRSME sections dealing with tax are based on IAS 12, there are few differences that would arise from current UK practice.

8.5.4   Recognition in the statements of performance

The basic rule is that deferred tax should be taken to the profit and loss account, unless the item which has given to the deferred tax has been taken to the statement of total recognised gains and losses, in which case the applicable amount of the deferred tax should be dealt with in that statement.

Accounting standards and legislation require or enable certain gains or losses to be credited or charged directly in the statement of total recognised gains and losses. The FRS requires any attributable deferred tax to be treated in the same way.

In exceptional cases, it may be difficult to determine the amount of deferred tax attributable to gains or losses recognised directly in the statement of total recognised gains and losses. In such circumstances, the attributable deferred tax is based on a reasonable pro rata allocation, or another allocation that is more appropriate.

Similar rules are in place under IAS 12, which distinguishes between deferred tax that should be taken to income and deferred tax that should be recognised as part of other comprehensive income. Again, this depends on the accounting treatment adopted for the underlying transaction.

Potential impact of the FRSME

The FRSME includes the same distinction between those items that should be recognised in profit and those that should be recognised elsewhere. This distinction between profit and other comprehensive income is very much the same as the UK GAAP distinction between profit and other recognised gains and losses. This does not mean that the presentation will always be unchanged, since if another requirement introduced by the FRSME were to move a transaction from profit to other comprehensive income or vice versa, then the placement of the tax effect would also change.

8.5.5 *Measurement*

FRS 19 requires that:

> Deferred tax should be measured at the average tax rates that are expected to apply in the periods in which the timing differences are expected to reverse, based on tax rates and laws that have been enacted or substantively enacted by the balance sheet date. (Para. 37, FRS 19.)

A UK tax rate is to be regarded as having been substantively enacted if it is included in either:

- a Bill that has been passed by the House of Commons and is awaiting only passage through the House of Lords and Royal Assent, or
- a resolution having statutory effect that has been passed under the Provisional Collection of Taxes Act 1968.

It will normally be necessary to calculate an average tax rate only if the enacted or substantively enacted tax rates are graduated, ie if different rates apply to different levels of taxable income. To calculate the average tax rate it is necessary to estimate the levels of profits expected in the periods in which the timing differences reverse.

This does not involve averaging rates relating to different types of item or items in different jurisdictions. For example, a group which has operations in a number of jurisdictions does not need to use an average tax rate: each part of its overall timing differences should be charged (or credited) to deferred tax at the relevant rates for each item.

As noted above when dealing with current taxation, IAS 12 contains similar rules in respect of the tax rates to be used, but obviously makes no reference to the specific manner in which UK tax rates are passed into law.

Potential impact of the FRSME

The FRSME would not change current practice.

8.5.6 *Discounting*

Companies are allowed, but not required, to discount their tax liabilities. In making this decision, account should be taken of FRS 18 and, in particular:

- materiality;

- the costs and benefits of discounting, and
- whether it is a common practice in the company's industry.

When a company decides to discount its deferred tax balances, it must be consistent in doing so.

Where underlying timing differences are themselves discounted, such as pension liabilities or investments in finance leases, then the deferred tax provisions to which they give rise already incorporate discounting. Therefore, they must not be discounted again.

Under FRS 19:

> If deferred tax balances are discounted, the discount period(s) should be the number of years between the balance sheet date and the date(s) on which it is estimated that the underlying timing differences will reverse. Assumptions made when estimating the date(s) of reversal should be consistent with those made elsewhere in the financial statements. The scheduling of the reversal(s) should take into account the remaining tax effects of transactions that have already been reflected in the financial statements. However, no account should be taken either of other timing differences expected to arise on future transactions or of future tax losses. (Para. 47, FRS 19.)

The example provided in the FRS is that of assets which are depreciated over their useful economic lives, but receive capital allowances early in their lives.

In this case, the timing of the reversal of accelerated capital allowances is determined:

- by scheduling all expected future movements in the accelerated capital allowances on assets that are held at the balance sheet date, taking account of future depreciation patterns and the expected timing of remaining capital allowances to be received, but
- without taking into consideration timing differences that might arise on fixed assets to be purchased in future.

The assumptions about future depreciation charges and residual value should be consistent with those used to account for the related fixed assets. It may be possible to use approximations or averages to simplify the calculations without introducing material errors.

Future expected tax losses must be ignored in undertaking these calculations.

The FRS provides guidance on the discount rates that must be used for the purposes of the calculations:

> If deferred tax balances are discounted, the discount rates used should be the post-tax yields to maturity that could be obtained at the balance sheet date on government bonds with maturity dates and in currencies similar to those of the deferred tax assets or liabilities. (Para. 52, FRS 19.)

The yields to maturity on government bonds can be obtained from the financial press or financial websites. The post-tax yield is estimated by deducting tax at the rate at which it would be paid by an entity holding the bond, based on enacted or substantively enacted tax rates and laws. In theory, undertaking this process properly requires a different discount rate to be applied to each year in which a timing difference is forecast to reverse and for each different tax jurisdiction. A degree of approximation will normally be acceptable.

The FRSSE also allows, but does not require, discounting. Furthermore, it does not provide the level of detail that is included in FRS 19.

IAS 12 takes a completely different approach and prohibits the discounting of deferred tax balances. It justifies this in the following terms.

> The reliable determination of deferred tax assets and liabilities on a discounted basis requires detailed scheduling of the timing of the reversal of each temporary difference. In many cases such scheduling is impracticable or highly complex. Therefore it is inappropriate to require discounting of deferred tax assets and liabilities. To permit, but not to require, discounting would result in deferred tax assets and liabilities which would not be comparable between enterprises. Therefore, this Standard does not require or permit the discounting of deferred tax assets and liabilities. (Para. 54, IAS 12.)

The logic of this is completely contrary to that used in FRS 19. However, it should be noted that due to the requirement to provide for deferred tax on revaluations under IFRS, there would be far more problems in scheduling the reversal of differences than in the UK where deferred tax is not currently provided on such items. The apparent contradiction is, therefore, not quite as strong as might at first appear. Nonetheless, the different approach on grounds of comparability between enterprises remains.

Potential impact of the FRSME

The FRSME, like IAS 12, prohibits discounting of deferred tax. This would obviously have no impact on those companies which have not chosen to discount deferred tax under FRS 19. For those entities, the minority, which have chosen to discount deferred tax, the likely effect of this change would be an increase in deferred tax liabilities.

8.5.7 *Presentation*

In terms of balance sheet presentation:

> With the exception of deferred tax relating to a defined benefit asset or liability recognised in accordance with FRS 17 'Retirement Benefits':
>
> (a) net deferred tax liabilities should be classified as provisions for liabilities and charges.
> (b) net deferred tax assets should be classified as debtors, as a separate subheading of debtors where material. (Para. 55, FRS 19.)

(FRS 19 was not updated to reflect the change in the statutory heading to 'provisions for liabilities', but this causes no confusion in practice.) Debit and credit balances should be offset within the above headings to the extent, and only to the extent, that they relate to taxes levied by the same tax authority and arise in the same entity or in a group of entities where the tax losses of one entity can reduce the taxable profits of another. Deferred tax in relation to defined benefit assets or liabilities recognised in accordance with FRS 17 are covered in Chapter 7.

In some cases, balances may need to be shown on the face of the balance sheet:

> Deferred tax liabilities and assets should be disclosed separately on the face of the balance sheet if the amounts are so material in the context of the total net current assets or net assets that, in the absence of such disclosure, readers may misinterpret the financial statements. (Para. 58, FRS 19.)

In terms of the profit and loss account, all deferred tax should be included within the heading 'tax on profit or loss on ordinary activities'.

8.5.8 Disclosures

The following disclosures must be provided.

(1) The notes to the financial statements should disclose the amount of deferred tax charged or credited within:

    (a) tax on ordinary activities in the profit and loss account, separately disclosing material components, including those attributable to:

        (i) changes in deferred tax balances (before discounting, where applicable) arising from:
the origination and reversal of timing differences;
changes in tax rates and laws, and
adjustments to the estimated recoverable amount of deferred tax assets arising in previous periods;

        (ii) where applicable, changes in the amounts of discount deducted in arriving at the deferred tax balance;

    (b) tax charged or credited directly in the statement of total recognised gains and losses for the period, separately disclosing material components, including those listed in (a) above.

(2) The total deferred tax balance (before discounting, where applicable), showing the amount recognised for each significant type of timing difference separately.

(3) The impact of discounting on, and the discounted amount of, the deferred tax balance.

(4) The movement between the opening and closing net deferred tax balance, analysing separately:

    (a)   the amount charged or credited in the profit and loss account for the period;

    (b)   the amount charged or credited directly in the statement of total recognised gains and losses for the period, and

    (c)   movements arising from the acquisition or disposal of businesses.

(5)   The amount of a deferred tax asset and the nature of the evidence supporting its recognition if:

    (a)   the recoverability of the deferred tax asset is dependent on future taxable profits in excess of those arising from the reversal of deferred tax liabilities, and

    (b)   the reporting entity has suffered a loss in either the current or preceding period in the tax jurisdiction to which the deferred tax asset relates.

(6)   Circumstances that affect the current and total tax charges or credits for the current period or may affect the current and total tax charges or credits in future periods. This disclosure to include the following.

    (a)   A reconciliation of the current tax charge or credit on ordinary activities for the period reported in the profit and loss account to the current tax charge that would result from applying a relevant standard rate of tax to the profit on ordinary activities before tax. Either the monetary amounts or the rates (as a percentage of profits on ordinary activities before tax) may be reconciled. Where material, positive amounts should not be offset against negative amounts or vice versa: they should be shown as separate reconciling items. The basis on which the standard rate of tax has been determined should also be disclosed.

    (b)   If assets have been revalued in the financial statements without deferred tax having been recognised on the revaluation gain or loss, or if the market values of assets that have not been revalued have been disclosed in a note – an estimate of tax that could be payable or recoverable if the assets were sold at the values shown, the circumstances in which the tax would be payable or recoverable and an indication of the amount that may become payable or recoverable in the foreseeable future.

    (c)   If the reporting entity has sold (or entered into a binding agreement to sell) an asset but has not recognised deferred tax on a taxable gain because the gain has been or is expected to be rolled over into replacement assets – the conditions that will have to be met to obtain the rollover relief and an estimate of the tax that would become payable if those conditions were not met.

    (d)   If a deferred tax asset has not been recognised on the grounds that there is insufficient evidence that the asset will be recoverable – the amount that has not been recognised and the circumstances in which the asset would be recovered.

    (e)   If any other deferred tax has not been recognised – the nature of the amounts not recognised, the circumstances in which the tax would become payable or recoverable and an indication of the amount that may become payable or recoverable in the foreseeable future.

Relevant 'standard' tax rates may vary. For example, a relevant rate for a group whose profits are earned primarily in the UK is the standard rate of corporation tax in the UK, even if some of the group's operations are conducted in other countries. The impact of different rates of tax applied to profits earned in other countries would be shown as a reconciling item. For groups based primarily overseas, a relevant rate might be an average rate of tax (weighted in proportion to accounting profits) applicable across the group.

The FRSSE contains far less in terms of disclosure. It requires disclosure of:

- the material components of deferred tax;
- the amount of the unwinding of the discount, if a company chooses to discount deferred tax balances;
- the deferred tax balance and its material components;
- the movement between the opening and closing net deferred tax balances and the material components of this movement, and
- if assets have been revalued, or if their market values have been disclosed in a note, the amount of tax that would be payable or recoverable if the assets were sold at the values shown.

9 EARNINGS PER SHARE

9.1 INTRODUCTION

9.1.1 The use of earnings per share

One of the most common simple indicators used in making investment decisions is the price/earnings (P/E) ratio, showing how many times the current earnings of a company are covered by its share price. This indicator is a very elementary form of cost benefit analysis. The price is a measure of costs and the earnings figure is a measure of benefit.

In order to use earnings as a surrogate for benefit, it is essential that the earnings figure used in the calculation is both comparable across companies, insofar as this is achievable, and also comparable over time. The first accounting standard in the UK to attempt to introduce this consistency was SSAP 3, *Earnings Per Share*. This was later amended by FRS 3, *Reporting Financial Performance*, and then replaced by FRS 14 *Earnings per Share*, which was then in turn replaced by FRS 22. The need for consistency in calculation is made clear in the stated objective of FRS 22:

> The objective of this Standard is to prescribe principles for the determination and presentation of earnings per share, so as to improve performance comparisons between different entities in the same reporting period and between different reporting periods for the same entity . . . (Para. 1, FRS 22.)

Despite this, it is not always easy to use the basic measure of earnings per share in order to make comparisons between companies. This is because the basic measure takes account of all of the events that have affected a company during the year, however unusual they may be, and the fact that accounting policies differ both between companies and across time. This limitation is acknowledged, at least in part, in FRS 22:

> . . . Even though earnings per share data have limitations because of the different accounting policies that may be used for determining 'earnings', a consistently determined denominator enhances financial reporting. The focus of this Standard is on the denominator of the earnings per share calculation. (Para. 1, FRS 22.)

It has been common for calculations of earnings per share not to be based on the measure required by accounting standards, but on some alternative method of calculation. Such measures often attempt to strip out the impact of unusual events which are unlikely to affect the earnings of companies in future accounting periods. As a result, they are considered by some users of financial statements to be more relevant than the measure required by FRS 22 or by IAS 33, the international standard on which FRS 22 is based. Nonetheless, FRS 22 now limits the use of such measures in financial statements, and relegates them to notes, not allowing them on the face of the profit and loss account.

9.1.2 Scope

With FRS 22, there is a fundamental difference between the purported and real scope of the standard. Earnings per share could, in principle, be calculated by any company. However, UK accounting standards limit the requirement for disclosure of earnings per share to companies in which there is the greatest level of public interest, since they have, or shortly will have, listed ordinary shares or listed instruments that may give rise to the issue of ordinary shares. Such a limited scope has been reflected in every standard since SSAP 3.

The term 'ordinary share' is defined as an equity instrument that is subordinate to all other classes of equity instrument. 'Equity instrument' is not defined within FRS 22, but the standard makes it clear that the same definition is used as applies under FRS 25, *Financial Instruments: Presentation*. Under FRS 25, an equity instrument is defined as any contract that evidences a residual interest in the assets of an entity after deducting all of its liabilities. Potential ordinary shares are financial instruments or other contracts that may entitle their holders to ordinary shares. Examples of potential ordinary shares include convertible debt (so long as conversion is into an equity instrument), convertible preference shares, warrants for ordinary shares, rights granted under employee share plans that may entitle employees to receive ordinary shares and rights to ordinary shares that are contingent upon the satisfaction of certain conditions resulting from contractual arrangements, such as the purchase of a business or other assets.

As a result, the standard would in theory apply to, for example, companies with ordinary shares or potential ordinary shares traded on AIM as well as companies with a full listing. But of course, most companies with a full listing or listed on AIM do not produce financial statements in accordance with UK GAAP at all, and as a result FRS 22 will not affect them. They will be complying with IFRS.

Listed companies which do not have subsidiaries and which are therefore not required to produce group accounts are still allowed to produce UK GAAP accounts, and so could be affected by the standard. The same applies to companies listed on AIM, where IFRS is also mandatory for group accounts but not for companies which are not required to produce group accounts. Single companies could continue to use UK GAAP if they wish. Despite this, there are now fairly few companies which are required to comply with FRS 22, and a small number that do so voluntarily.

Despite the limited number of companies that are required to comply with FRS 22, its theoretical scope since accounting periods beginning on or after 1 January 2009, has been:

(a) the separate or individual financial statements of an entity:

(i) whose ordinary shares or potential ordinary shares are traded in a public market (a domestic or foreign stock exchange or an over-the-counter market, including local and regional markets) or

(ii) that files, or is in the process of filing, its financial statements with a securities commission or other regulatory organisation for the purpose of issuing ordinary shares in a public market; and

(b) the consolidated financial statements of a group with a parent:

(i) whose ordinary shares or potential ordinary shares are traded in a public market (a domestic or foreign stock exchange or an over-the-counter market, including local and regional markets) or

(ii) that files, or is in the process of filing, its financial statements with a securities commission or other regulatory organisation for the purpose of issuing ordinary shares in a public market. (Para. 2, FRS 22.)

Potential impact of the FRSME

Companies which would fall within the proposed scope of the FRSME are not currently required to disclose earnings per share, nor would they be required to do so under the proposals. It will therefore have virtually no impact in this area.

The only requirement contained within the draft FRSME in relation to earnings per share is that if a company chooses to include such a measure in its financial statements, it will be required to describe the basis on which such information has been prepared and presented.

9.2   BASIC EARNINGS PER SHARE

9.2.1   Basic calculation

The basic calculation of earnings per share is extremely straightforward, so long as there are no complications such as the issue of shares during the period.

FRS 22 includes the following.

Basic earnings per share shall be calculated by dividing profit or loss attributable to ordinary equity holders of the parent entity (the numerator) by the weighted average number of ordinary shares outstanding (the denominator) during the period. (Para. 10, FRS 22.)

The FRS notes that companies may have more than one class of ordinary share in issue, although unlike previous standards it then provides little guidance on the accounting treatment to be adopted in such cases.

Earnings are included on the following basis.

For the purpose of calculating basic earnings per share, the amounts attributable to ordinary equity holders of the parent entity in respect of:

(a) profit or loss from continuing operations attributable to the parent entity; and
(b) profit or loss attributable to the parent entity

shall be the amounts in (a) and (b) adjusted for the after-tax amounts of preference dividends, differences arising on the settlement of preference shares, and other similar effects of preference shares classified as equity. (Para. 12, FRS 22)

This means that the full amount of any appropriation in respect of cumulative preference shares must be charged, even where the dividends cannot lawfully be paid as a result of an absence of distributable profits. For the avoidance of doubt, the standard points out that this does not include any preference dividends paid or declared in the current period in respect of previous periods, since these would already have been taken into account in the determination of earnings per share for earlier periods.

The earnings per share figures (calculated in accordance with FRS 22) should be disclosed on the face of the profit and loss account for each class of ordinary share that has a different right in the net profit for the period. The amounts should be given even where they are negative, when they should be described as losses per share. The amounts referred to are the earnings per share based on profit or loss from continuing operations, if relevant, and earnings per share based on total profit or loss. Companies should also disclose earnings per share on discontinued operations, which can be done either on the face of the profit and loss account or in the notes.

A very simple example will show the basic calculation.

EXAMPLE

The following figures are extracted from the financial statements of B plc for the year ended 31 December 2011.

	£000
Profit on ordinary activities before taxation	4,567
Tax on profit on ordinary activities	744
Profit on ordinary activities after taxation	3,823
Minority interest	469
Profit attributable to members of B plc	3,354
Dividends (note 1)	654
Retained profit for the financial year	2,700

Note 1		£000
Dividends	Ordinary	490
	Preference	164
Total		654

There are 11,000,000 shares in issue throughout the year.

Under FRS 22 the earnings per share figure is:

$$\frac{3,354,000 - 164,000}{11,000,000} = 29 \text{ pence}$$

Inevitably, matters are not always quite so simple and there are a number of problems that can arise. These primarily affect the number of shares in issue, although they may also have some impact upon the earnings.

9.3   EARNINGS

9.3.1   Preference shares

Basic earnings are always calculated after taking account of the dividends attributable to preference shareholders, since this amount is not available for distribution to the ordinary shareholders.

Cumulative preference dividends must, as set out above, always be taken into account for the purposes of determining earnings per share, even where they cannot legally be paid because the company does not have sufficient distributable profits. This means that the amount that should have been paid, if sufficient distributable profits were available, should always be taken as the figure for preference dividends, regardless of the amounts that have actually been paid in the year. Of course, this also means that where preference dividends are paid in a year, having been included as an appropriation in previous years, they have no effect upon earnings per share for that year.

If preference dividends are not cumulative, then they are charged in the profit and loss account (and used in the earnings per share calculation) only if they are paid out of distributable profits.

The example above included the deduction of preference dividends from the earnings for the purposes of calculating earnings per share.

9.3.2   Participating preference shares

Participating preference shares will normally rank for a dividend that can be divided into two parts. The fixed element in the dividend will normally be a stated percentage of the nominal value of the shares. This fixed element should be treated in exactly the same way as any normal preference dividend. There will also be a further element which will depend upon the profits generated by the company. This variable element may be limited or unlimited.

Where the variable element is limited, the full amount should be included in the calculation of earnings per share only when the conditions under which the shares participate in profits have been met. Where the variable element is unlimited, then a separate calculation needs to be performed of the extent to which the profits generated are attributable to the preference shareholders. Once this calculation has been performed, the total of the fixed and variable elements should then be deducted to arrive at the profits attributable to ordinary shareholders.

EXAMPLE

A company makes a profit of £1,000,000 during 2011. The company has 100,000 £1 preference shares in issue which are subject to the following conditions:

- there is a 5 per cent fixed dividend, and
- there is also an additional dividend of 7.5 per cent of any profits earned by the company in any year in excess of £500,000.

The calculation will fall into two parts:

		£
Fixed dividend	(100,000 × 5%) =	5,000
Variable dividends	((1,000,000 − 500,000) × 7.5%) =	37,500
Total		42,500

The full amount of £42,500 should be deducted from the earnings in order to arrive at the earnings attributable to the ordinary shareholders.

A more general rule is provided in Appendix A to FRS 22. This requires that where there are any participating equity instruments (or other rights to participate in undistributed earnings) then:

- profit or loss attributable to ordinary equity holders is adjusted by the amount of dividends declared in the period for each class of shares and by the contractual amount of dividends or similar that must be paid for the period;
- the remaining profit or loss is allocated to ordinary shares and participating equity instruments to the extent that each instrument shares in earnings as if all of the profit or loss of the period has been distributed, and
- the total amount of profit or loss allocated to each class of equity instrument is divided by the number of outstanding instruments to which the earnings are allocated to determine the earnings per share for that instrument.

9.3.3   Increasing rate preference shares

Preference shares may be issued with an increasing rate of dividend. There are various possible scenarios, such as issuing shares at a premium with compensation provided by the payment of dividends at above market rate in later periods. Where such shares are issued, the discount or premium on initial issue must be amortised to retained earnings using the effective interest rate method. This amortisation charge must be treated as a preference dividend for the purposes of calculating earnings per share.

It should be noted that, while the amount of this charge will not be flat (given that it is calculated on the effective interest rate method) it will normally be flatter than the amount of dividends actually paid. In fact, it will normally lead to a reducing charge as time goes on, whereas the actual dividends paid are increasing.

9.3.4   Repurchase of preference shares

Where preference shares are repurchased by a company, and the fair value of the consideration given exceeds the current carrying amount of the preference shares, this excess is a charge to retained earnings. This amount must be deducted in calculating the profit or loss attributable to ordinary equity holders of the company. Similarly, where preference shares are settled when the fair value of the consideration paid is less than the carrying value of the preferences shares, then the difference is added to the profit or loss attributable to ordinary shareholders.

9.3.5   Early conversion of preference shares

Where preference shares are convertible into ordinary shares, FRS 22 notes that there may be favourable changes to the original conversion terms or the payment of additional consideration, in order to persuade preference shareholders to convert their holdings. Where this applies, the excess of the fair value of the ordinary shares or other consideration over the fair value of the ordinary shares issuable under the original terms should be treated as a return to shareholders and deducted when calculating the profit or loss attributable to the ordinary equity holders.

9.3.6   Prior period adjustments

Comparative figures should always be provided for earnings per share. Where the profits, and, therefore, earnings of previous periods have been restated due to a prior period adjustment, the comparative figure for earnings per share will also need to be recalculated to take account of the changes.

9.4   THE EFFECT OF CAPITAL CHANGES

9.4.1   Changes in the number of shares in issue

Where there have been no changes in the number of shares in issue throughout a period, or subsequently to the date of approval of the financial statements, then the share figure used in calculating the earnings per share is that reflected in the balance sheet and no adjustments are necessary. Whenever there is a change in the number of shares in issue during a period, the earnings per share calculation will need to reflect this change. In some cases, it will also be necessary to adjust earnings per share figures for previous periods and to take account of changes which have taken place between the balance sheet date and the date on which the financial statements are approved.

The basic rule is given in FRS 22:

> For the purpose of calculating basic earnings per share, the number of ordinary shares shall be the weighted average number of ordinary shares outstanding during the period. (Para. 19, FRS 22.)

9.4.2 Issues at full market price

The simplest situation is where shares are issued at the full market price, whether the consideration is received in the form of cash or through other assets.

In this situation, the earnings per share calculation should be performed by taking the number of shares in issue at all points through the year, and adjusting for the period during which each number of shares was in issue. Strictly, this should be done on a daily basis, but the standard notes that a reasonable approximation of the weighted average will often be adequate. This means, for example, that it may not be necessary to use the precise dates of issue of shares if this will have little effect on the overall calculation. If a company were, say, to issue shares increasing its total number of shares by five per cent on the third day of a month, then it would normally be acceptable to perform the calculations based on whole months as the answer obtained is not going to be materially different from that obtained if the calculation were performed on a daily basis.

The use of the total number of shares in issue at the end of the year is not appropriate, since the cash or assets obtained from the issue would not have been available to generate earnings prior to the issue date.

EXAMPLE

A company has earnings of £1,200,000.

The company's accounting year ends on 31 December.

At 1 January 3 million ordinary shares were in issue.

On 30 June a further 2 million shares were issued, at full price.

Therefore, the company has 3 million shares in issue for the first half of the year and 5 million shares in issue for the second half of the year.

The weighted average number of shares in issue is:

3,000,000 × 6/12	1,500,000
5,000,000 × 6/12	2,500,000
	4,000,000

Earnings per share is therefore:

$$\frac{1,200,000}{4,000,000} = 30 \text{ pence}$$

Where shares are issued to unconnected non-shareholders, at below their market price, they should still be treated as if they were issued at the full market price. This does not apply in the case of the exercise of options or similar situations, for example, where shares are issued as the result of an employee share option scheme.

In determining the date from which newly issued shares are to be brought into the computation, FRS 22 does not usually take account of dividend rights, but focuses on the date on which additional resources were available to the company. The general point is made that shares should be included in the calculation according to the specific terms and conditions which are connected with their issues, and that this should take account of the substance of the transaction as well as its form.

Subject to this general requirement, the FRS provides the following guidance on some specific ways in which shares may be issued.

(1) Shares issued for cash should be included from when cash is receivable.

(2) Shares issued on the voluntary reinvestment of dividends should be included from the dividend payment date.

(3) Shares issued as a result of the conversion of a debt instrument, or in place of interest or repayments of principal on other financial instruments, should be included from the date interest ceases accruing.

(4) Shares issued in exchange for the settlement of a liability should be included from the settlement date.

(5) Shares issued as consideration for the acquisition of an asset other than cash should be included from the date on which the acquisition is recognised.

(6) Shares issued for the rendering of services to the company are included as the services are rendered.

In the case of shares issued in connection with a business combination, those shares should be brought into account from the date at which the combination is deemed to take place for accounting purposes. In the case of an acquisition, this means the acquisition date itself. The FRS itself does not deal with the situation in the case of a merger. This is because FRS 22 is based on the international standards and mergers are not allowed under IFRS 3, the international standard dealing with business combinations. As a result, Appendix C to FRS 22 deals with this issue and requires that the shares are effectively deemed to have always been in issue, which is consistent with the accounting treatment applied to the combination as a whole.

This may often be quite complex if the companies merging have had substantial changes in their capital structure in the periods prior to the merger, but still included in the current or comparative figures. The basic calculation set out earlier will have to be adjusted for all of the changes in capital structure which would normally have had an impact upon the disclosed earnings per share.

For example, if a company undertook an issue of shares at full price six months prior to a merger then this would need to be reflected in the earnings per share figure disclosed after the merger. This is best shown in an example.

EXAMPLE

Companies A and B merge on 30 September 2011. They both prepare accounts to 31 December.

At the start of 2011, Company B has a share capital of 1 million £1 shares. On 30 June 2011, it issues a further 500,000 shares at full market price.

As part of the merger, all shares in B are transferred to A.

Company A has a share capital of 10 million £1 shares at the start of the year. As a result of the merger, it issues a further 9 million shares.

The combined earnings for the year are £15 million.

The weighted average number of shares in issue can be calculated as follows:

'A' shareholders		10,000,000
'B' shareholders	(9,000,000 × 1/2)	4,500,000
	(9,000,000 × 1/2 × 2/3)	3,000,000
Total		17,500,000

Earnings per share: $\dfrac{15,000,000}{17,500,000}$ = 85.7 pence

---

Situations such as bonus issues prior to the merger will be relatively simple, since (as explained below) bonus issues always affect all accounting periods presented.

The main exception to the general rule that dividend rights are not taken into account when determining the number of shares is that partly paid shares should be treated as a fraction of ordinary shares to the extent that they were entitled to participate in dividends relative to fully paid up shares during the period. Where this is the case, to the extent that partly paid shares are not entitled to dividends, they should be treated as share warrants or options for the purposes of calculating diluted earnings per share.

9.4.3 Mandatorily convertible instruments

Where there is a convertible instrument in issue, which results in a mandatory conversion into ordinary shares, then the ordinary shares that will be issued are taken into account in determining earnings per share from the date the instruments are first issued. This applies even though conversion has not yet taken place.

9.4.4 Contingently issuable shares

Where there are ordinary shares that are issuable only if certain conditions are satisfied then they should be excluded from the computation of basic earnings per share until all of the conditions have been met. At this stage, the shares are no longer contingent.

For this purpose, where the only condition is the passage of time, then this is not a contingency, and they are treated as mandatorily convertible, on the basis that the passage of time is a certainty not a contingency.

9.4.5 Contingently returnable shares

Shares that are subject to recall are not treated as outstanding, and are excluded from the calculation of earnings per share, until the date by which they can be recalled is past.

9.4.6 Repurchase of shares

The repurchase of shares at full price is very similar to the issue of shares at full price, except of course that the number of shares is reduced rather than increased. The calculations required are effectively the same. As with the issue of shares, the number of shares outstanding at every point during the year is calculated on a time weighted basis.

Certain companies with listed securities have been allowed to hold some of their own shares in treasury since 1 December 2003. Previously, such shares would have had to have been cancelled, as they continue to be for most companies.

Where companies hold shares in treasury, then the shares are still treated as though they were cancelled for the purposes of determining earnings per share.

Of course, as noted above, there are very few companies which fall within the scope of the legal rules on treasury shares, yet are producing financial statements in accordance with UK GAAP and applying FRS 22.

The treatment of shares in the company that are held in an ESOP trust is dealt with at **9.5.3**.

9.4.7 *Changes that do not affect resources*

All the situations that have been considered so far involve a change in both the number of shares in issue and the resources available to the company. Therefore, in principle they should have an effect on both the numerator and the denominator in the calculation. This is not always the case, as the number of shares in issue may be altered without any change in the resources available to the company. For example, where a company makes a bonus issue (also known as a capitalisation or scrip issue) then the number of shares will increase but there will be no additional resources available to the company, and hence no reason why any additional earnings should be generated.

FRS 22 states:

> The weighted average number of ordinary shares outstanding during the period and for all periods presented shall be adjusted for events, other than the conversion of potential ordinary shares, which have changed the number of ordinary shares outstanding, without a corresponding change in resources. (Para. 26, FRS 22.)

Where a change such as a bonus issue takes place after the end of the year but before the financial statements are authorised for issue, the per share calculations should still be changed for the new number of shares, although this fact needs to be disclosed.

9.4.8 *Bonus issues*

A bonus issue is where shares are issued to existing shareholders pro rata to their existing shareholdings, without payment.

For the current year, the total number of shares after the issue is used in the earnings per share calculation. In effect, the bonus shares are treated as though they had always been in issue. This applies even where the new shares are issued after the period covered by the financial statements, although prior to their approval.

The comparative figures also need to be adjusted, in order to be comparable with the figures for the current year.

EXAMPLE

A company has earnings per share in 2010 of 30p, with an issued share capital of 300,000 ordinary shares.

In 2011, an additional 200,000 shares are issued as a bonus issue.

The earnings in 2011 are £100,000.

The 2011 earnings per share would be calculated as:

$$\frac{100,000}{(300,000 + 200,000)} = 20 \text{ pence per share}$$

In addition, the comparative figure needs to be adjusted.

The number of shares has increased during 2011 without having any effect on the earnings made by the company.

In order to make the 2010 earnings per share figure comparable it needs to be divided by the same number of shares as those for 2011.

This can be achieved by multiplying the 2010 earnings per share by 300,000/500,000 (or 3/5). The comparative figure is then:

$30 \times 3/5 = 18$ pence per share.

9.4.9 Share splits

Where ordinary shares are split into shares of smaller nominal value, the treatment is identical to that applied where there is a bonus issue. The effect is exactly the same: the number of shares in issue has increased without having increased the company's earning capacity.

9.4.10 Share consolidations

A consolidation of shares is where the number of shares is reduced by being converted into fewer shares of higher denomination, while there is no change in the resources available to the company. Like a share split or a bonus issue, this alters the number of shares, but does not alter the earning capacity of the company. As a result, the consolidation is treated as affecting all of the periods presented.

However, the FRS also considers a situation which was described in the exposure draft preceding FRS 14 as a 'synthetic share repurchase'. This occurs where a share consolidation is combined with a special dividend, and the overall effect is equivalent to a repurchase of shares at fair value. A special dividend is not defined by the standard, but its definition is implicit in the requirement set out above. In effect, it is a dividend of such a level above the normal level of dividends which, when combined with a share consolidation, is as if a full value share repurchase had taken place. This is an application of the principle of substance over form.

The weighted average number of shares in issue is adjusted in respect of the period from the date the special dividend is paid, since it is at this date the resources left the company.

This is best shown by an example.

EXAMPLE

Company A has 1,200,000 50p shares in issue at the start of its accounting year, which runs to 31 March.

The value of each share in the market is approximately £5 for the first three months of the company's accounting year.

On 20 June, the company undertakes a share consolidation, replacing every six shares with five new shares.

On 30 June the company pays a dividend of £1,200,000. Its normal level of dividends is approximately £180,000.

The number of shares in issue will be calculated as follows:

$(1,200,000 \times 3/12) =$ 300,000
$(1,000,000 \times 9/12) =$ <u>750,000</u>

                1,050,000

9.4.11 *Rights issues*

Rights issues can take place either at or below the market price of the shares already issued.

If the issue takes place at full value then it is treated in the same way as a normal issue at full price. This is, however, unusual and most rights issues will take place at a discount. The way FRS 22 looks at such an issue is to break it down into two elements:

- an issue at full price, and
- a bonus element.

The amount of the issue at full price is taken into account in determining the number of shares from the date of the issue. The bonus element is applied in the determination of the number of shares for all accounting periods presented.

In order to do this the number of ordinary shares in issue prior to the rights issue is adjusted by the following factor:

$$\frac{\text{Fair value per share immediately before the exercise of rights}}{\text{Theoretical ex-rights fair value per share}}$$

The ex-rights value is a theoretical price, being the price at which the share should, in theory, be quoted immediately after the rights issue. The theoretical price is used rather than the actual price, since the actual price could be affected by many other factors which are unconnected with the rights issue.

EXAMPLE

A company has 2 million shares in issue at 1 January. On 30 June it makes a rights issue of 1 for 5 at 50p.

The price of the shares immediately prior to the rights issue was £1.

Earnings for the year were £1,100,000.

The previous year's earnings were £950,000.

The company's accounting year ends on 31 December.

The theoretical ex-rights fair value per share is calculated by dividing the total cost of the shares (adding the original value to the proceeds from the rights issue) by the number of shares outstanding after the exercise of the rights:

$$\frac{(2,000,000 \times 1) + (400,000 \times 0.5)}{2,400,000} = 91.67\text{p}$$

The adjustment factor is calculated as:

$$\frac{1.00}{0.9167} = 1.0909$$

The weighted average share capital is then:

2,000,000 × 1.0909 × 6/12	1,090,900
2,400,000 × 6/12	1,200,000
	2,290,900

Therefore, the earnings per share figure for the current year would be £1,100,000/2,290,900 = 48 pence.

The earnings per share for the previous year would have been reported as £950,000/2,000,000, or 47.5 pence.

However, the comparative figure in the current year's accounts will be calculated as 950,000/(2,000,000 × 1.0909) = 43.54 pence.

9.5 DILUTED EARNINGS PER SHARE

9.5.1 The need for diluted earnings per share

The basic earnings per share is calculated on the basis of the actual amount of earnings and the actual number of shares in issue. Although both of these figures may need to be adjusted, and do not always agree with the amounts in the profit and loss account and balance sheet, they are still fundamentally the current figures.

Where no changes are expected in the number of shares in issue, this amount can also be considered to give some indication of the capacity of the business to generate earnings in the future. However, where changes in the number of shares can be anticipated, it might also be useful to have a measure which will take account of the effect that those changes will have. This is the diluted earnings per share. This measure is not perfect, since it only indirectly takes account of any future changes in earnings. Nonetheless, a measure of the potential impact of expected capital changes can have its value.

FRS 22 contains the following.

> For the purpose of calculating diluted earnings per share, an entity shall adjust profit or loss attributable to ordinary equity holders of the parent entity, and the weighted average number of shares outstanding, for the effects of all dilutive potential ordinary shares. (Para. 31, FRS 22.)

A potential ordinary share is defined as a financial instrument or other contract that may entitle its holder to ordinary shares.

The following are examples of potential ordinary shares:

- debt or equity instruments, including preference shares, that are convertible into ordinary shares;
- share warrants and options;
- rights granted under employee share plans that may entitle employees to receive ordinary shares as part of their remuneration and similar rights granted under other share purchase plans, and
- rights to ordinary shares that are contingent upon the satisfaction of certain conditions resulting from contractual arrangements, such as the purchase of a business or other assets, ie contingently issuable shares.

Diluted earnings per share, in respect of both total profit or loss and, where relevant, profit or loss from continuing operations, need to be shown on the face of the profit and loss account. Where there is a discontinued operation, diluted earnings per share must be disclosed, but this can be either on the face of the profit and loss account or in the notes. As with basic earnings per share, where a company has more than one class of ordinary share in issue then diluted earnings per share must be given for each class.

There is no materiality threshold for the disclosure of diluted earnings per share, and it has to be given in all cases. The only time when a company will not have to disclose diluted earnings per share is where it has no potential ordinary shares in issue in the period, or where it has such items but none of them are dilutive.

Diluted earnings per share should also be given where the basic earnings per share is a loss.

9.5.2 Basic calculation of diluted earnings per share

The basic principle for determining the diluted earnings per share is that the basic earnings per share figure is adjusted to take account of:

- the additional shares that would be issued if all the dilutive potential ordinary shares were converted, and
- the change in earnings that would take place directly as a result of conversion.

FRS 22 provides more guidance on the determination of the number of shares to be used in the calculation of diluted earnings per share:

> For the purpose of calculating diluted earnings per share, the number of ordinary shares shall be the weighted average number of ordinary shares calculated ... [for the purposes of determining basic earnings per share] ... plus the weighted average number of ordinary shares that would be issued on the conversion of all the dilutive potential ordinary shares into ordinary shares. Dilutive potential ordinary shares shall be deemed to have been converted into ordinary shares at the beginning of the period or, if later, the date of the issue of the potential ordinary shares. (Para. 36, FRS 22.)

The standard also deals with the adjustment of earnings:

> For the purpose of calculating diluted earnings per share, an entity shall adjust profit or loss attributable to ordinary equity holders of the parent entity, as calculated ... [for the purposes of basic earnings per share], by the after-tax effect of:
>
> (a) any dividends or other items related to dilutive potential ordinary shares deducted in arriving at profit or loss attributable to ordinary equity holders as calculated in accordance with paragraph 12;
>
> (b) any interest recognised in the period related to dilutive potential ordinary shares; and
>
> (c) any other changes in income or expense that would result from the conversion of the dilutive potential ordinary shares. (Para. 33, FRS 22.)

In calculating diluted earnings per share, account is taken only of those items which will have the effect of dilution:

> Potential ordinary shares shall be treated as dilutive when, and only when, their conversion to ordinary shares would decrease earnings per share or increase loss per share from continuing operations. (Para. 41, FRS 22.)

Potential ordinary shares which do not meet this condition are ignored.

9.5.3 Number of shares

In determining the number of ordinary shares that would be issued, it is important to look at the terms of the financial instruments or rights that created the potential ordinary shares.

Where there is more than one possibility, the calculation should always assume the most advantageous conversion rate or exercise price from the point of view of the holder of the potential ordinary share. While not part of the requirement, this will usually mean that this is less advantageous, that is, more dilutive, from the point of view of the company.

There may be times when this is not straightforward, particularly where the conditions are variable. For example, there may be cases where the number of shares to be issued varies with, say, the share price or earnings but the total value of the expected gain to the holder of potential ordinary shares will remain constant. If the variation is with the share price then FRS 22 requires that the number of shares to be used in the calculation of diluted earnings per share be based on current market price, or the average price over a period, depending upon the basis of the calculation included in the contract. If the variation is directly related to earnings, then it is possible that the diluted earnings per share will be the same at all possible points, but with a different numerator and denominator. In this case, the only approach would seem to be to assume a point at one end of the scale and then provide disclosure of the terms of conversion. The diluted earnings per share would still be the same whatever point on the scale were used.

Where a company issues a contract which can be settled in shares or cash, at the option of either the holder or the company, then there are different rules depending on which of these parties has the option. If it is at the option of the company, then it should be assumed that the contract will be settled in ordinary shares, and therefore will affect diluted earnings per share, if the effect is dilutive. If it is at the option of the holder then the more dilutive of cash settlement or equity settlement must be assumed. The basic approach to be adopted by FRS 22 is to break any potential issue of shares down into, potentially, two elements:

- a fair value issue, and
- a bonus issue.

The fair value issue is then ignored for the purposes of calculating diluted earnings per share, but account is taken of the effective bonus issue.

Items are only taken into account if they have the effect of dilution. If, for example, an option price is above the fair value of the shares then it is ignored.

FRS 22 states:

> For the purpose of calculating diluted earnings per share, an entity shall assume the exercise of dilutive options and warrants of the entity. The assumed proceeds from these instruments shall be regarded as having been received from the issue of ordinary shares at the average market price of ordinary shares during the period. The difference between the number of ordinary shares issued and the number of ordinary shares that would have been issued at the average market price of ordinary shares during the period shall be treated as an issue of ordinary shares for no consideration. (Para. 45, FRS 22.)

This approach works for most companies affected by the standard. However, FRS 22 also applies to companies that voluntarily disclose earnings per share and companies that are in the process of obtaining a listing for their ordinary shares. In neither case will there be a price for the company's shares, and it is therefore impossible to adopt precisely the approach given in the standard. We suggest that where companies are not able to comply with the standard they state the basis on which they have determined the value of their shares for the purposes of determining dilution.

The basic calculation of diluted earnings per share can be shown by an example.

EXAMPLE

A company has 5 million shares in issue throughout the year. During the year the average price of each share is £1.

Options have been granted to a number of directors to subscribe for shares at 85p per share. The number of options outstanding is 750,000.

These options were granted in a previous year.

Earnings for the year are £1 million.

The number of shares to be used for diluted earnings per share is:

	£
Shares used for basic earnings per share	5,000,000
Notional shares issued at no cost (see below)	112,500
Total	5,112,500

Diluted earnings per share is therefore:

$$\frac{1,000,000}{5,112,500} = 19.56 \text{ pence}$$

The number of full value shares is calculated as follows:

Proceeds of issuing shares

750,000 × 0.85	637,500
Share price	1

$$= 637,500 \text{ shares}$$

Which means the number of bonus shares must be:

$$750,000 - 637,500 = 112,500$$

Where there is a share option or other share-based payment arrangement to which FRS 20 applies, then both the issue price and the exercise price have to include the fair value of any goods or services that are to be supplied to the company, in the future, under the share option or share-based payment arrangement.

Where there are employee share options with fixed or determinable terms, or ordinary shares which have not yet vested, they are treated as options from the grant date in the calculation of diluted earnings per share, even though they may be contingent on vesting. Where employee share options are performance based they are treated as though they were contingently issuable shares.

With any contingently issuable shares, the number of shares included in the calculation of diluted earnings per share is based on the number of shares that would be issued if the end of the reporting period were the end of the contingency period. Where the conditions are effectively cumulative then the condition is assumed to remain unchanged for the remainder of the contingency period. For example, if shares are issuable if the cumulative profits over a five-year period are £5 million, then at the end of the first two years if the cumulative profits are £3 million then no further profits are assumed and the contingently issuable shares are ignored. Similarly, if the condition for issue were that ten new branches were opened, and seven new branches have been opened to date then the contingently issuable shares would be ignored in determining the diluted earnings per share.

If the number of shares depends on the share price then, as noted above, the share price used for the calculations depends on the share price at the end of the reporting period or over a specified period, depending on the terms of the contract.

The overall effect of the requirements is likely to be that, in practice, many contingently issuable shares will not be included in the determination of diluted earnings per share.

Restatement of prior period diluted earnings per share figures is not allowed, if the conditions are not met when the contingency period expires.

9.5.4   *Earnings*

With some potential ordinary shares any conversion would alter the number of shares in issue, but would also affect the earnings. As noted earlier, this needs to be taken into account when calculating diluted earnings per share.

For example, if a company has convertible debt in issue then conversion will increase the number of shares, but will also reduce the interest charge to the company, with a resultant increase in the earnings.

EXAMPLE

A company with a December year end has 2 million ordinary shares in issue at 1 January 2011.

In 2008, £300,000 of ten per cent convertible loan stock was issued, with the following terms.

Every £100 of stock can be converted to ordinary shares at the following rates:

	Shares
30 June 2011	120
30 June 2012	105

No conversion took place on 30 June 2011, and earnings for the year are £800,000.

The rate of corporation tax is 30 per cent.

Basic earnings per share is:

$$\frac{800,000}{2,000,000} = 40 \text{ pence}$$

Earnings for diluted earnings per share need to be calculated by starting from the normal earnings and then taking account of the effect of the loss of the interest charge if the stock were to be converted. Since interest is paid out of profits before tax, the tax effect of the conversion also needs to be taken into account.

		£
Basic earnings		800,000
Interest saved	(300,000 × 10%)	30,000
Less: tax	(30,000 × 30%)	(9,000)
		821,000
Original shares		2,000,000
New shares	(300,000 × 105/100)	315,000
		2,315,000

Diluted earnings per share is therefore:

$$\frac{821,000}{2,315,000} = 35.46 \text{ pence}$$

If we alter some of the assumptions, we can see how items which do not dilute are ignored.

The assumptions are the same as before, except that:

- the conversion rate for June 2012 is 80 shares;
- the interest rate on the stock is 15%, and
- earnings are currently £100,000.

Basic earnings per share will now be:

$$\frac{100,000}{2,000,000} = 5 \text{ pence}$$

Diluted earnings per share is:

Basic earnings		100,000
Interest saved	(300,000 × 15%)	45,000
Less: tax	(45,000 × 30%)	(13,500)
		131,500
Original shares		2,000,000
New shares	(300,000 × 80/100)	240,000
		2,240,000

Diluted earnings per share is therefore:

$$\frac{131,500}{2,240,000} = 5.87 \text{ pence}$$

In this case, there is no dilution, and therefore the diluted earnings per share would not be given.

9.6 DISCLOSURE AND PRESENTATION

It has already been noted that basic and, where applicable, diluted earnings per share should be stated in respect of overall profit or loss and profit or loss from continuing operations on the face of the profit and loss account for each class of ordinary share that has different rights to share in the net profit for the period. Comparatives are required for all figures, and the amounts must be given even if they are negative.

Where a company has discontinued operations, it must disclose the basic and diluted earnings per share in respect of such operations, but this may be done either on the face of the profit and loss account or in the notes to the financial statements.

Where comparative figures for diluted earnings per share are given, they must not be adjusted for any changes in the assumptions used for the conversion of potential ordinary shares into ordinary shares. For example, where there are contingently issuable shares, comparative figures would not be restated where the conditions have now been met, when they had not at the end of previous periods.

Companies must also disclose ordinary share or potential ordinary share transactions which occur after the end of the year, even where they have not been taken into account in determining the disclosed earnings per share. This disclosure is only required if they are of such importance that non-disclosure would affect the ability of the users of the financial statements to make proper evaluations and decisions. This is, in effect, an extension of the existing requirements to disclose non-adjusting post balance sheet events. Examples of the sorts of situation envisaged by the standard are:

- the issue of shares for cash;
- the issue of shares when the proceeds are used to repay debt or preference shares outstanding at the balance sheet date;
- the redemption of ordinary shares;
- the conversion or exercise of potential ordinary shares outstanding at the balance sheet date into ordinary shares;
- an issue of options, warrants or convertible instruments, and
- the achievement of conditions that would result in the issue of contingently issuable shares.

Companies must also disclose the following.

(1) The amounts used as the numerators in calculating basic and diluted earnings per share, and a reconciliation of those amounts to the profit or

loss for the period. This reconciliation must include the individual effect of each class of instruments that affects earnings per share.

(2) The weighted average number of ordinary shares used as the denominator in calculating basic and diluted earnings per share and a reconciliation of these denominators to each other. Again, this reconciliation must include the individual effect of each class of instruments that affects earnings per share.

(3) Details of instruments, including contingently issuable shares, that could potentially dilute basic earnings, but were not included in the calculation of diluted earnings per share because they are antidilutive for the period.

Where companies disclose any other measures of earnings per share, as many do, then these must be calculated using the same number of shares as used for the calculation of the basic and diluted earnings per share as required by FRS 22. The disclosure may now also only be provided in the notes to the financial statements. Both basic and diluted earnings per share must be provided in respect of such measures and the basis for determining the numerator must be stated, including whether it is before or after tax. Where a line item from the profit and loss account is not used, a reconciliation must be provided from a line item to the amounts used.

9.7 COMPARISON WITH INTERNATIONAL STANDARD

Notwithstanding the fact that FRS 22 is the UK version of IAS 33, there are some minor differences between the standards. The main differences are:

- an appendix to FRS 22 provides guidance on earnings per share on mergers, since mergers are still possible, albeit rare, under current UK practice, whereas they are now prohibited under international practice, so there is no guidance in IAS 33, and
- the references to other standards have been changed to the UK equivalents.

As noted above, the IFRS for SMEs does not require the disclosure of earnings per share. Therefore, the draft FRSME, which is based on the IFRS for SMEs, also contains no requirements in respect of earnings per share. However, under the proposals, were a company to disclose earnings per share voluntarily it would be required to disclose the basis on which the information had been prepared and presented.

10 FOREIGN CURRENCY TRANSLATION

10.1 INTRODUCTION

10.1.1 Relevant accounting standards

For the immediate future, and even putting to one side those companies that have adopted the FRSSE, the UK will have two sets of accounting standards dealing with foreign currency translation.

SSAP 20 was issued many years ago. For many UK companies, in fact the vast majority of companies which are not entitled to the FRSSE, it remains in force. In the unlikely situation that a company has to deal with hyperinflation, then it will also need to comply with UITF 9 if it continues to fall within the scope of SSAP 20.

However, FRS 23 *The Effects of Changes in Foreign Exchange Rates* and FRS 24 *Financial Reporting in Hyperinflationary Economies* have also been issued. These new standards have limited application since they apply only to those companies which are also complying with FRS 26, and cannot be applied where that condition is not met. The majority of companies that use UK GAAP are not required to adopt, and have not voluntarily adopted, FRS 26.

It is unusual to have parallel sets of accounting standards in issue. This issue has arisen since, for companies within its scope, FRS 26 now deals with the treatment of all financial instruments, including those that are connected with foreign exchange. Therefore, for those companies complying with that standard, the foreign exchange standards need to be consistent with it. All of these standards are based on their international equivalents, which were designed to be consistent with each other. Instead, the ASB has opted to have separate foreign currency standards for those entities which use FRS 26 and those which do not.

As a result, this chapter deals firstly with SSAP 20, and then with FRS 23 and FRS 24.

Potential impact of the FRSME

The FRSME, based on the IFRS for SMEs, is closer to FRS 23 than to SSAP 20. Whilst the differences are not vast, it means that there will be guidance on certain issues that are currently not dealt with in SSAP 20. In particular, there is much more guidance on the determination of the currency that should be used for the underlying accounting (the functional currency) and then coverage of associated issues such as how to deal with a change in functional currency. The

FRSME also deals with the currency in which the financial statements are actually shown, the presentation currency, which is not specifically covered in SSAP 20. Apart from such general differences, the procedures that need to be applied are much the same, particularly at the level of the individual reporting entity.

10.1.2 Objectives of foreign currency accounting

As noted in SSAP 20 *Foreign Currency Translation*, there are two ways in which a company can engage in foreign currency operations.

(1) It can do this directly by undertaking transactions which are themselves denominated in a foreign currency. Since financial statements are produced in one currency, the reporting currency, the results of these transactions will then need to be translated into the reporting currency in order for them to be incorporated in the financial statements.

(2) It can undertake foreign operations through its ownership or control of another enterprise. That enterprise will need to maintain its own accounting records in the appropriate foreign currency. Where consolidated accounts are required, the results of that foreign enterprise will then need to be translated into the reporting currency that is to be used for the group.

FRS 23 identifies precisely the same possibilities.

The objectives of the accounting treatment which should be used for foreign currency translation are set out in SSAP 20.

> The translation of foreign currency transactions and financial statements should produce results which are generally compatible with the effects of rate changes on a company's cash flows and its equity and should ensure that the financial statements present a true and fair view of the results of management actions. Consolidated statements should reflect the financial results and relationships as measured in the foreign currency financial statements prior to translation. (Para. 2, SSAP 20.)

Although the objectives may appear to be simple, the way in which they are to be achieved is often far from obvious.

SSAP 20 is divided into two fairly distinct parts, one dealing with individual companies and the other dealing with groups.

The FRSSE repeats much of SSAP 20 as it applies to individual companies. It also covers some, but not all, of the matters affecting groups.

The objective of FRS 23 is somewhat different, actually focussing far less on what the standard is intended to achieve and far more on how it might do so:

... The objective of this Standard is to prescribe how to include foreign currency transactions and foreign operations in the financial statements of an entity and how to translate financial statements into a presentation currency.

The principal issues are which exchange rate(s) to use and how to report the effect of changes in foreign exchange rates in the financial statements. (Paras. 1 and 2, FRS 23.)

10.1.3 Local currency under SSAP 20

SSAP 20 defines 'local currency' as:

... the currency of the primary economic environment in which [the company] operates and generates net cash flows. (Para. 39, SSAP 20.)

This is usually, but not necessarily, the same as the currency of the country in which the company is legally based. So for UK companies, the local currency may not always be sterling.

Under SSAP 20, 'foreign' currencies are those other than the 'local' currency and amounts denominated in foreign currencies should be translated into the local currency for inclusion in the financial statements. Therefore, the implication in SSAP 20 is that it is not acceptable to report in a currency other than the local currency.

It is perhaps worth noting that there is no specific requirement in UK legislation or standards to prepare and file accounts in sterling, although almost all companies do so because sterling is their local currency. However, a small number of UK companies report in another currency, most commonly the US dollar or the euro, on the basis that this is their local currency. The Registrar of Companies accepts financial statements prepared in a currency other than sterling, provided that the exchange rate used has been disclosed in the notes to the accounts. Given changes in the tax rules in respect of reporting in currencies other than sterling, the number of companies reporting in currencies other than sterling has increased in the last few years.

Potential impact of the FRSME

In practice, few companies would be affected by the introduction of the FRSME. Whilst the FRSME contains considerably more detail than SSAP 20 on determining the relevant currency, called the functional currency, and allows a free choice of the presentation currency, there are few companies that would need to change their basic currency, and it is highly unlikely that many would wish to take the opportunity to present the financial statements in another currency.

10.2 INDIVIDUAL COMPANIES UNDER SSAP 20

10.2.1 Transactions

The general principle for the recording of transactions is that they should be translated using the actual rate at the date on which the transaction took place:

> Subject to the [following] provisions ... each asset, liability, revenue or cost arising from a transaction denominated in a foreign currency should be translated into the local currency at the exchange rate in operation on the date on which the transaction occurred; if the rates do not fluctuate significantly, an average rate for a period may be used as an approximation. Where the transaction is to be settled at a contracted rate, that rate should be used. Where a trading transaction is covered by a related or matching forward contract, the rate of exchange specified in that contract may be used. (Para. 46, SSAP 20.)

This is quoted virtually verbatim in the FRSSE.

This principle may appear to be straightforward, but it actually raises nearly as many questions as it answers. In the first place, the standard provides no definition of the date of a transaction. The majority of the time, this does not present a problem, but in some cases it is not obvious. Certain standards provide guidance on the date on which a transaction takes place. Where a transaction in a foreign currency is also a transaction of a type covered in another standard, the requirement of that other standard should be followed. Whatever date is given by that standard should then also be used for the purposes of currency translation. Where this is not the case, one must return to basic principles, and consider FRS 5 and when the risks and benefits normally associated with ownership have passed, whether to or from the company.

The standard also allows a company to use the average rate for a period for translating transactions, on the condition that the rate has not fluctuated significantly in that period. The first problem that this raises is when a fluctuation is significant or insignificant. Neither SSAP 20 nor the FRSSE provides a definition of significance for this purpose. A company might decide to determine significance solely on the basis of the extent of fluctuations in the exchange rate itself. For example, it might decide that no significant fluctuations have taken place if the rate has not changed by more than, say, ten per cent.

However, and more reasonably, it could also determine significance on the basis of the likely effect that the fluctuations would have on its reported results. In this case the assessment of significance would be partly determined by the materiality of the transactions undertaken in that currency. Where a company undertakes very few transactions in a particular currency it may decide that even large movements in the exchange rate will have little effect on the reported results and that, therefore, an average rate can be used. Conversely, much smaller movements in a currency in which the company undertakes a large number of transactions may have a noticeable effect on the recorded results, and therefore the actual rate or, more realistically, a regularly updated average must be used.

There is also the practical problem of the recording of transactions. If a company maintains its own accounting records in a single currency, then it is almost certain to record each transaction at the actual rate on the date of the transaction. A smaller number of companies use an estimated average rate, usually based on the previous period, which is likely to be the previous week or month.

However, companies can also maintain accounting records in multiple currencies, using control accounts to ensure the integrity of the double entry. In these cases companies are likely to be very unwilling to use the actual rate, even if it is later shown that there have been significant fluctuations in the exchange rate. Where this applies, foreign currency transactions are almost certain to be material, as otherwise it is unlikely that the company would have considered it necessary to maintain accounting records in separate currencies. With a large number of transactions, the effort involved in translating each transaction at the correct rate, for the purposes of producing the financial statements, may be substantial. As a result, the method of translation is more likely to be affected by the nature of the accounting system, and practical considerations, than by any other considerations.

The average rate itself is also an ambiguous term. SSAP 20 discusses, but does not resolve, this problem. One issue concerns the length of time over which it should be calculated. Should it be calculated weekly, monthly, quarterly or even annually and then applied to all the transactions within each period? Another decision to be made is how frequently the individual rates within the chosen period need to be sampled. For example, in order to calculate an annual average, would it be acceptable to use the average of the closing rates on the last day, or middle day, of each month of the year? A third issue concerns the weighting of the sampled rates; if an annual average is used, should each month be weighted differently to reflect the different levels of activity of the company in each month?

In practice, materiality is likely to be the main determinant of how the average is constructed. Where a company undertakes very few transactions in a particular currency, but at regular intervals, then an annual average is unlikely to distort the reported results significantly. If a company undertakes a few transactions at irregular intervals, then the use of an average rate may have a substantial distorting effect on the results. An actual rate must then be used. Where a very high proportion of the company's transactions take place in a particular foreign currency, a weekly average would probably be the greatest level of approximation acceptable, unless currency fluctuations had been minimal. For the majority of companies the use of a monthly average is reasonable.

SSAP 20 and the FRSSE require that any rate included in a contract be used for recording a transaction. They also allow the rate in a related or matching forward contract to be used in translating a trading transaction, but do not require this rate to be used. This means that where a company has a forward contract, as well as an underlying transaction, there are two, or in practice more, rates at which the transaction might be recorded. The use of the actual or average rate is likely to lead to an exchange difference being recorded on the transaction by the time it is settled; the use of the contract rate is likely to mean that no such difference will be recorded. The absence of greater detail about which method should be used, and the absence of guidance on other forms of hedging, is a common criticism of SSAP 20. (Such problems do not arise where a company is complying with FRS 23, since such companies must also comply with the requirements of FRS 26 which deals with hedging in detail.)

Both SSAP 20 and the FRSSE refer only to trading transactions when dealing with the use of a matching forward contract. This must presumably mean that the rate in a forward contract cannot be used if the underlying transaction is not a trading transaction. The forward contract will be treated as though it was effectively used for speculation rather than hedging, which may not be a fair reflection of the situation. This could cause a problem if, for example, a company were to obtain financing in a foreign currency and then use forward contracts to manage the exchange rate risk.

When a transaction is recorded in one part of the year and then settled during a subsequent part, an exchange loss or gain will often result. This will be calculated by comparing the equivalent of the amount received or paid with the carrying value of the asset or liability. Such losses or gains should normally be treated as part of the profit or loss on ordinary activities before taxation.

10.2.2 Non-monetary assets

Once a non-monetary asset denominated in a foreign currency has been recorded in the balance sheet its value is set. The value of the asset is not changed to take account of any subsequent fluctuations in the exchange rate. However, there is an exception for certain equity investments financed by foreign currency borrowings (see **10.2.5** for details).

This raises the problem of when assets are non-monetary. Most cases are clear, but there are still some areas of ambiguity. For example, if a company owns investment assets denominated in a foreign currency, but which it intends to sell prior to maturity, is the asset monetary or non-monetary? The only method of determining if an asset is monetary or non-monetary is to consider if the stated value of the asset is intended to represent an amount receivable. Taking the example of the investment denominated in a foreign currency, it is probably not a monetary asset, as the company cannot treat the retranslated cost as the amount it expects to receive. A different situation would arise if the company intended to hold the instrument until maturity, when the amount would represent a receivable and should be retranslated accordingly.

Potential impact of the FRSME

It is unlikely that the introduction of the FRSME would affect many companies in this area. Both the FRSME and SSAP 20 distinguish between assets that are retranslated and those that are not. However, there are some differences between the two standards, and some items would fall to be retranslated under the FRSME that are not currently retranslated under SSAP 20. The differences are most likely to affect groups rather than individual companies, but might affect a company if it were (say) to acquire an overseas branch in a transaction which gave rise to goodwill.

10.2.3 *Monetary assets and liabilities*

SSAP 20 and the FRSSE require that, as a general rule, all monetary assets and liabilities should be retranslated at the closing rate at each balance sheet date.

They require that where a contracted rate is in existence then this should be used. This is consistent with the rule that a contracted rate must be used for translating the underlying transaction. However, as with transactions, the standards allow, but do not require the rate in a related or matching forward contract to be used for trading balances. The choice of method to use in such cases can have an effect on the profits recorded in each particular accounting period. Taking this together with the provisions on the recording of the initial transaction, it would appear that all of the methods in the following example would be acceptable accounting treatments.

EXAMPLE

A company purchases an asset for $100,000 on 30 September 2011, for which the company will pay on 1 March 2012. It also takes out a matching forward contract to purchase $100,000 on 1 March 2012 at a rate of £1 = $2.00. The exchange rate at 30 September is £1 = $1.9, and at 31 December, the company's accounting reference date, it is £1 = $2.1.

In accounting for the $100,000 liability, any of the following methods are acceptable under SSAP 20.

	30 Sep 2011 £		31 Dec 2011 £		1 Mar 2012 £
Recorded throughout at actual:					
	$100,000		$100,000		$100,000
@ $1.9	52,632	@ $2.1	47,619	@ $2.0	50,000
		Gain	5,013	Loss	(2,381)

Initially recorded at actual, retranslated at contract rate:

	$100,000		$100,000		$100,000
@ $1.9	52,632	@ $2.0	50,000	@ $2.0	50,000
		Gain	2,632	Gain	0

Initially recorded at actual, retranslated at actual:

	$100,000		$100,000		$100,000
@ $2.0	50,000	@ $2.1	47,619	@ $2.0	50,000
		Gain	2,381	Loss	(2,381)

Recorded throughout at contract:

	$100,000		$100,000		$100,000
@ $2.0	50,000	@ $2.0	50,000	@ $2.0	50,000
		Gain	0	Gain	0

The calculation, and recording, of profits and losses on exchange on short-term monetary items is usually uncontentious. The closing rate is assumed to be a reasonable estimate of the amount to be paid or received, and treated accordingly. However, there may be exceptions, and one is given in the example below.

EXAMPLE

In March 2011, a company makes a sale of €40,000 when the exchange rate is £1 = €1.60. Later, at the company's balance sheet date, the exchange rate is £1 = €1.28. By the time the cash is received, the exchange rate has reverted to £1 = €1.60.

Under SSAP 20 the company would record an exchange gain of £6,250 in the first accounting period.

= €(40,000/1.28) – (40,000/1.60)

= £31,250 – £25,000

= £6,250

However, an exchange loss of £6,250 would be recorded in the second period.

The outcome is that, in reality, the company has not made either a gain or a loss. Nonetheless, at the balance sheet date it was not known that the £ would revert to £1 = €1.60 and in complying with SSAP 20, the company would have to record both the initial profit and the subsequent loss.

Neither SSAP 20 nor the FRSSE mentions currency options. A currency option is the right to sell or acquire a specified amount of currency at a given rate at a given time or during a given period, but not an obligation. There will be an amount paid, the premium, for the option. This premium is not refundable. By applying the same basic logic used for forward contracts there are two possible methods of dealing with an option acquired to hedge against a foreign currency transaction:

- ignore it, and treat it as a separate asset in its own right, or
- include it in determining the exchange rate that will be applied in settling the transaction.

The separate treatment of the option would be allowed, and would always be required if a company purchased an option for speculative rather than hedging purposes. The accounting treatment would be to treat the premium as an asset. Then, at the balance sheet date, the company would need to consider if the option is likely to be exercised.

If the option will be exercised, then the costs of the premium would be carried forward. If it appears unlikely that the option will be exercised then the premium would be written off in full.

If the option is to be considered in conjunction with the underlying transaction, then the accounting treatment would be initially to record the premium as an asset. At the balance sheet date the company would need to consider if the premium is likely to be exercised. If it were, then the option rate could be used for the translation of the balance, and the amount of the premium should be deducted from the resulting amount. If it did not seem likely that it would be exercised then the premium would be written off in full immediately, and the balance would be translated at the closing rate. These treatments can be shown in the following example.

EXAMPLE

Two cases are considered:

(1)   An option with no underlying transaction to be hedged.

A company purchases an option to buy 500,000 dollars at £1 = $2.1. The cost of the premium is £300. The cost of exercising the option and purchasing the dollars is:

$500,000 /2.1 = £238,095

Consider the cases in which the exchange rate at the balance sheet date is either:

(a)   £1 = $2.05, or
(b)   £1 = $2.15.

(a)   If the exchange rate were $2.05 then the normal cost of purchasing the same amount of dollars will be £243,902 ($500,000 /2.05). The option clearly has a value, and can be carried forward at cost.

Assuming no further movements in the exchange rate, the company could buy the dollars under the option and sell them on at an immediate profit. Since an option is currency-related it could also be argued that the company can record the profit at the balance sheet date.

The option in the balance sheet would be revalued to £5,807 (= £243,902 − £238,095) and a profit of £5,507 (= £5,807 − £300) would be recognised.

Although this would not be consistent with the normal principles of accounting (or rather not accounting) for unrealised profits, it would be consistent with the provisions of SSAP 20 for dealing with exchange rate changes, and therefore acceptable.

(b)   However, if the exchange rate were $2.15 then the company could acquire the $500,000 on the open market, and pay £232,558 ($500,000/2.15). The

---

275

> option will not be exercised, and the amount of the premium should be written off.

(2) An option with an underlying dollar liability.

Alternatively, assume the same situation, except that immediately prior to the purchase of the option, the company acquires an underlying dollar liability of $500,000 (recorded when the exchange rate was £1 = $2.0) that must be met, then the treatment will be as follows.

The liability will initially be recorded at £250,000. Consider the cases in which the exchange rate at the balance sheet date is either:

(a) £1 = $2.05, or
(b) £1 = $2.15.

(a) If the exchange rate at the balance sheet date were $2.05 then the option will be exercised, because it is cheaper to purchase the dollars through the option than through the open market. The liability would be recorded at £238,095 being:

£238,095 = $500,000 /2.1 = the cost of exercising the option

However, the option could not then be treated as an asset with a value of £300, since it is necessary to use the option in order to obtain the advantageous rate of exchange ($2.1 rather than the current rate of $2.05). Therefore, it would be written off.

A profit will be recorded because the sterling value of the liability has fallen; the profit will be £11,905 (= £250,000 − £238,095), but this will be reduced by the cost of the option written off to £11,605 (= £11,905 − £300). The amount payable using the closing rate (£243,902 = $500,000 /2.05) can be ignored.

(b) If the exchange rate is $2.15 then the option will not be exercised. The liability should be recorded at £232,558 (= $500,000 /2.15). Also, the cost of the premium must be written off immediately.

An even more contentious area is that of long-term monetary items. SSAP 20 requires that:

> Exchange gains and losses on long-term monetary items should also be recognised in the profit and loss account; however, it is necessary to consider on the grounds of prudence whether, in ... exceptional cases ... the amount of the gain, or the amount by which exchange gains exceed past exchange losses on the same items to be recognised in the profit and loss account, should be restricted. (Para. 50, SSAP 20.)

SSAP 20 justifies this treatment by using the year-end rate as the best estimate of the future rate:

> When dealing with long-term monetary items, additional considerations apply. Although it is not easy to predict what the exchange rate will be when a long-term liability or asset matures, it is necessary, when stating the liability or the asset in terms of the reporting currency, to make the best estimate possible in the light of the information available at the time; generally speaking translation at the year end rate will provide the best estimate, particularly when the currency concerned is freely dealt in on the spot and forward exchange markets. (Para. 9, SSAP 20.)

This is consistent with the known properties of exchange rate movements, although it fails to take account of the impact of differential interest rates on future expected exchange rates.

However, the final and practical argument used by SSAP 20 is:

> Exchange gains on unsettled transactions can be determined at the balance sheet date no less objectively than exchange losses; deferring the gains whilst recognising the losses would not only be illogical by denying in effect that any favourable movement in exchange rates had occurred but would also inhibit fair measurement of the performance of the enterprise in the year. In particular, this symmetry of treatment recognises that there will probably be some interaction between currency movements and interest rates and reflects more accurately in the profit and loss account the true results of currency involvement. (Para. 10, SSAP 20.)

This practical argument is probably the best. The main alternative treatments available would probably be to:

- record only losses by reference to the closing rate, and to ignore apparent profits on the grounds of prudence under conditions of uncertainty, or
- ignore the closing rate entirely, and simply record items at the original transaction rate.

Neither method is acceptable under SSAP 20. The first method would ignore all trends that tend to increase the value of the business, and result in exaggerated profits in the year in which profitable transactions were finally settled. The second method would ignore all exchange rate trends altogether. Although the retranslation of all monetary items, including long-term ones, can lead to unsatisfactory results, it probably leads to fewer than the main alternatives.

The FRSSE has exactly the same requirements, but does not contain the justification for this treatment that has been included in SSAP 20.

As noted in paragraph 9 of the standard quoted above, SSAP 20 does allow one exception to the general rule that long-term monetary items should be translated at the closing rate. Where a company is faced with an apparent gain on long-term monetary items it needs to consider whether the gain should be restricted if there are doubts about the convertibility or marketability of the currency. This restriction can be justified on the grounds of prudence under conditions of uncertainty. The restriction can either be applied to the gain as a whole, or consideration can be given to restricting the gain to the amount of past losses on the item. However, such a situation is very rare and there are few cases where this exception could be invoked. (It was probably of somewhat greater relevance in 1983 when SSAP 20 was first issued.)

This matter is not covered in the FRSSE. This leaves open the question of whether in such a case the FRSSE would not allow any restriction on the gain to be recorded, or whether such restriction can still be made on the grounds of prudence, despite the absence of discussion of this matter in the standard. In our opinion it would still be acceptable to restrict the amount of the gain that has been recognised, as any other accounting treatment would be inconsistent with one of the basic accounting principles.

Potential impact of the FRSME

The FRSME would eliminate much of the flexibility that SSAP 20 allows, although it is worth mentioning that the flexibility in the standard is rarely used. The ability to translate items using rates in associated derivatives would disappear. Instead, the asset or liability itself would always be translated at the spot rate, and the derivative instrument being used would then be accounted for separately. That instrument would not be dealt with under the FRSME requirements in relation to foreign exchange, but the requirements in relation to financial instruments. This would also mean that the current option of virtually ignoring the existence of the derivative (other than for disclosure purposes) would be eliminated. It would need to be recorded, on the balance sheet, at its fair value on an ongoing basis. The accounting treatment of the changes in value would depend on whether hedge accounting was available and applied.

10.2.4   *Transactions between group companies*

Where transactions take place between companies within a group, SSAP 20 states that each company should calculate exchange gains and losses as normal and include them in their respective profit and loss accounts. Normally, such gains and losses will be automatically eliminated on consolidation. For example, so long as both parties to a trading transaction use the exchange rate on the same day for initial recording and settlement then the exchange gain arising in one company should be exactly offset by an exchange loss in another.

However, there may be an effect on recorded asset values, as shown in the following example.

EXAMPLE

A company owns stock with a cost of €1,000. At the balance sheet date the exchange rate is £1 = €1.60.

If the company retains the asset then the balance sheet value will be £625. Suppose, however, that the company sells the asset to another company in its group for €1,000 (ie with no profit and no loss in terms of €) for cash when the exchange rate is £1 = €1.80. In this case, the balance sheet value will be £556. The elimination of intra-group profits will not affect this transaction, as no profit was made. There will also be no exchange gain or loss recorded by either party.

10.2.5 Foreign equity investments financed or hedged by foreign currency borrowings

Normally, the value of a non-monetary asset, denominated in a foreign currency, is not changed to take account of subsequent fluctuations in the exchange rate (see **10.2.2**). However, when foreign equity investments are financed or hedged by foreign currency borrowings, both SSAP 20 and the FRSSE contain special rules for dealing with exchange differences in this situation:

> Where a company has used foreign currency borrowings to finance, or provide a hedge against, its foreign equity investments and the conditions set out in this paragraph apply, the equity investments may be denominated in the appropriate foreign currencies and the carrying amounts translated at the end of each accounting period at closing rates for inclusion in the investing company's financial statements. Where investments are treated in this way, any exchange differences arising should be taken to reserves and the exchange gains or losses on the foreign currency borrowings should then be offset, as a reserve movement, against these exchange differences. The conditions which must apply are as follows:
>
> (a) in any accounting period, exchange gains or losses arising on the borrowings may be offset only to the extent of exchange differences arising on the equity investments;
>
> (b) the foreign currency borrowings, whose exchange gains or losses are used in the offset process, should not exceed, in the aggregate, the total amount of cash that the investments are expected to be able to generate, whether from profits or otherwise; and
>
> (c) the accounting treatment adopted should be applied consistently from period to period. (Para. 51, SSAP 20.)

This is repeated in the FRSSE.

It should be noted that, perhaps surprisingly, this does not actually require that the investment and the borrowings be denominated in the same currency.

UITF 19 *Tax on Gains and Losses on Foreign Currency Borrowings that Hedge an Investment in a Foreign Enterprise* slightly amends the treatment allowed by SSAP 20. Where a company chooses to adopt the alternative treatment, the amounts should be shown after tax. This applies to the amounts allowed to be offset and the limit in respect of total proceeds from the investment.

Where companies are affected, they have to disclose the attributable tax and the gross amount of the transfer to or from reserves, as well as the net amount which will be the reserve movement. (The normal situation is that where such amounts are taken to the statement of total recognised gains and losses, there will be no immediate corporation tax charge, and the attributable taxation will, therefore, be deferred taxation. However, there are various exceptions to this general rule.)

The justification for the treatment required by SSAP 20 is that the eventual cash flows to be received by the investing company will be affected by changes in exchange rates in a way exactly opposite to the cash flows related to the loan. This is shown in the following example.

EXAMPLE

A company purchases an investment in a foreign company at a cost of £100,000, through a foreign currency loan to finance the purchase of the investment.

After one year the foreign company has made no profit or loss, but the value of the currency in which the investment was purchased has risen; both the loan and the investment now have a value of £120,000. After two years, still without profit or loss, the foreign investment is worth £140,000, as is the loan, and the investment is sold at this price, and the proceeds used to repay the loan.

If the SSAP 20 special rules were not applied, then in the first year the company would show an exchange loss of £20,000 on the loan. In the second year it would also show an exchange loss of £20,000 on the loan but a profit on disposal of £40,000. Applying SSAP 20 means that the company does not show a profit or loss in either of the two years, which provides a better reflection of the real financial position. However, it should be noted that if the interest payments on the foreign currency loan were denominated in that foreign currency, then the sterling cost of meeting these payments will have risen by 40 per cent over the two years.

The mechanics of the treatment can also be shown in a simple example.

EXAMPLE

A company makes an equity investment in a French company at a cost of €140,000 on 1 June 2011 when the exchange rate is £1 = €1.40. The company obtains a loan of €84,000 on the same day to partially finance the purchase. At the company's balance sheet date of 31 December 2011 the exchange rate is £1 = €1.50.

The asset would be recorded (using the rate of £1 = €1.40) at £100,000, and the loan (also using the rate of £1 = €1.40) at £60,000. At the balance sheet date both the investment and the loan would be retranslated at £1 = €1.50, to give £93,333 and £56,000 respectively. This would mean an exchange loss of £6,667 on the investment and a gain of £4,000 on the loan. These amounts could be offset against each other and the net loss of £2,667 taken directly to reserves.

If the company has not adopted this option under SSAP 20, then only the exchange gain on the loan of £4,000 would have been recorded, and this would have been treated as part of the profit or loss for the current year.

The amounts involved in this process may pose a problem. In the above example, the amount of the loan was only two-thirds of the cost of the investment. The question then arises of how small the borrowings can be in relation to the cost of the investment before it can no longer be treated as genuine finance, or a genuine hedge, for the investment. This is important since the standard normally treats equity investments as non-monetary assets which are not retranslated. Taking the provision to the extreme, a company might argue that its liability of $10,000 was being used as a hedge for an investment of $250,000, allowing it to retranslate the whole amount of the investment at each balance sheet date. It is difficult to set a general rule for such matters, but what seems reasonable is that if the amount of the borrowings accounts for less than 50 per cent of the value of the investment, then it should not be treated as financing or a hedge against the investment.

Further problems may arise if the borrowings are repaid. This may happen where the borrowings are intended as a hedge, but is clearly more likely if the borrowings were used as finance for the purchase. Two main questions arise.

(1) How should any exchange gain or loss on settlement be treated?

(2) How should the carrying value of the investment be calculated once the borrowings have been repaid?

Probably any terminal gain or loss should be available for offset in the same manner as applied when the borrowings were still in existence. The effect of the hedge will last up until the time at which the amount is repaid, not only at balance sheet dates which happen to fall within the period in which the hedge is in existence. An example of some of the potential treatments is given below.

EXAMPLE

For example, in 1998, a company takes out a loan of G100,000 to hedge against a foreign equity investment, of the same amount and made at the same time. At the time of the transactions, the rate is £1 = G1.6, and therefore both loan and investment are recorded at G100,000 /1.6 = £62,500.

At each subsequent balance sheet date, exchange movements on the investment are offset against the exchange movements on the loan. At the balance sheet date in 2010, the rate is £1 = G2.5. The loan and the investment are valued at £40,000.

During 2011, there are significant exchange fluctuations and the currency falls to £1 = G4. Given this situation, the loan is repaid, at a cost of £25,000 (= G100,000 /4).

Once the hedge has been eliminated there are a number of ways to treat the investment in the 2011 balance sheet.

(1) Retain the investment at the last balance sheet value of £40,000 (= G100,000 /2.5).

This treatment would be the simplest, but would not be consistent with the recommended treatment for accounting for gains and losses on repayment of the borrowings.

(2) Retranslate the investment at the rate when the borrowings were repaid.

This treatment is preferable as the investment is retranslated only during the period in which the hedge is in existence. Furthermore, since the investment and the loan are closely related, it seems fair to offset the gain on the loan since the last balance sheet (£15,000 = £40,000 − £25,000) against the loss on the investment.

(3) Restate the investment at its historic cost of £62,500 = G100,000 /1.6.

This approach seems to introduce an unnecessary complication into the accounting treatment. The net effect of all previous translations of the investment would be eliminated from reserves; however, the effect of the retranslation of the borrowings would not. This inconsistency would be particularly important if the investment were sold shortly after at a loss. The loss

---

on the disposal of the investment would pass through the profit and loss account in the year of disposal. However, the profit on the loan would have been treated as a movement on reserves.

(4) Continue to translate the investment at each balance sheet date.

The fourth treatment does not seem to be consistent with the intention of the provision, but it is not certain that it is prohibited. A very strict reading of the provision gives a result which is ambiguous. The standard states that exchange differences on the investment should be offset against the exchange differences on the borrowings. If there are no borrowings then this could be seen to be impossible. However, the standard also states 'where a company has used foreign currency borrowings'. The use of the past tense does not make it clear whether the borrowings must still be in existence at the time the method is applied.

Potential impact of the FRSME

The FRSME deals with the general principle of hedging in a different way. Its hedge accounting requirements are covered when dealing with financial instruments in general, rather than specifically in relation to foreign exchange. However, the FRSME will continue to allow hedge accounting for the foreign exchange risk on a net investment in a foreign operation at group level. At entity level, amounts will need to be recognised in profit or loss.

10.3 GROUP ACCOUNTS UNDER SSAP 20

10.3.1 *The net investment method*

The net investment method, also known as the closing rate method, should be used for the translation of the results of most foreign subsidiaries:

This method recognises that the investment of a company is in the net worth of its foreign enterprise rather than a direct investment in the individual assets and liabilities of that enterprise. The foreign enterprise will normally have net current assets and fixed assets which may be financed partly by local currency borrowings. In its day-to-day operations the foreign enterprise is not normally dependent on the reporting currency of the investing company. The investing company may look forward to a stream of dividends but the net investment will remain until the business is liquidated or the investment disposed of. (Para. 15, SSAP 20.)

As with many other areas, the FRSSE requires the same accounting policy to be adopted, but omits the justification for this treatment.

When this method is used, the amounts in the balance sheet of the foreign company are translated at the closing rate. An exchange difference will arise if this rate has changed from that used at the previous balance sheet date.

If an overseas subsidiary has an accounting reference date that differs from the group accounting date, then the question arises of whether the closing rate used should be that for the subsidiary's accounting date or the group accounting date. The use of the rate at the group accounting date is probably better, since the financial statements purport to be a reflection of the position at this time. Nonetheless, SSAP 20 does not state that this is required. If the subsidiary's profit and loss account is to be translated at an average rate, then the question will also arise as to whether this should be the average over its own accounting period or the group accounting period. In this case it might be better to use the average over the company's own accounting period. It seems to make little sense to apply an exchange rate based on rates outside the period covered by the company's results. In both cases there is no truly satisfactory answer, and it is clearly preferable that the accounting reference dates be the same if this is at all possible.

The amounts in the profit and loss account can be translated either at the closing rate, or at an average rate for the period.

The closing rate is probably more consistent with the underlying rationale for the method. However, the average rate will provide a better reflection of the results of the enterprise as they arise. A company must be consistent from year to year in using the average or closing rate for translation of the profit and loss account.

Exchange differences, other than those recorded in the accounts of the foreign enterprise, may arise in two main ways.

(1) If the closing rate is used for the translation of the profit and loss account, then an exchange difference will arise on the opening net assets, now translated at a different exchange rate to that used in the previous year.

(2) If the average rate is used for translating the profit and loss account, then there will also be a difference between the profit as recorded in the profit and loss account and the addition to net assets recorded in the balance sheet.

As with individual companies, SSAP 20 gives little guidance on the way in which the average rate should be calculated:

> No definitive method of calculating the average rate has been prescribed, since the appropriate method may justifiably vary between individual companies. Factors that will need to be considered include the company's internal accounting procedures and the extent of seasonal trade variations; the use of a weighting procedure will in most cases be desirable. Where the average rate used differs from the closing rate, a difference will arise which should be dealt with in reserves. (Para. 18, SSAP 20.)

One common method of calculating the average rate is to use a weighted average of the exchange rates at the mid-point of each month in the financial year.

Both of these types of exchange difference should be treated as movements on reserves (normally the profit and loss account) as they do not reflect transactions taking place in the year and their inclusion in the profit and loss account would distort the reported result:

> The results of the operations of a foreign enterprise are best reflected in the group profit and loss account by consolidating the net profit or loss shown in its local currency financial statements without adjustment (other than for normal consolidation adjustments). If exchange differences arising from the retranslation of a company's net investment in its foreign enterprise were introduced into the profit and loss account, the results from trading operations, as shown in the local currency financial statements, would be distorted. Such differences may result from many factors unrelated to the trading performance or financing operations of the foreign enterprise, in particular, they do not represent or measure changes in actual or prospective cash flows. It is therefore inappropriate to regard them as profits or losses and they should be dealt with as adjustments to reserves. (Para. 19, SSAP 20.)

(The logic of SSAP 20 is not as persuasive as it once was. The changes that the standard states should not be treated as profits or losses are now dealt with in the statement of total recognised gains and losses. Whilst this is not quite the same as recording a profit or loss, it is not that dissimilar, and somewhat contrary to the rationale provided in SSAP 20.)

The mechanics of the net investment method are best demonstrated by the following example.

EXAMPLE

Company A acquired a US subsidiary (Company B) on 26 June 2011 when the exchange rate was $1.55 = £1. The net assets of Company B at that time were $200,000. Company A owns 100% of the share capital of Company B, for which it paid $310,000. Company A uses the net investment method, with the average rate used for translation of the profit and loss account. During 2012, the average exchange rate was $1.65 = £1, whilst the closing rate was $1.60 at the end of 2011 and $1.62 at the end of 2012. Goodwill arising on this acquisition is to be amortised over a period of 20 years, with a full year's charge in the year of acquisition.

The companies had the following profit and loss accounts for the year 2012 and balance sheets at the 2012 year end, which will lead to the following consolidated results.

Profit and loss account for 2012

	A £	B $	@1.65 £	Total £
Turnover	529,487	325,830	197,473	726,960
Cost of sales	317,692	211,794	128,360	446,052
Gross profit	211,795	114,036	69,113	280,908
Dividend income	4,985			
Overheads	137,226	74,943	45,420	186,194
Profit before tax	79,554	39,093	23,693	94,714
Taxation	27,798	17,595	10,664	38,462

	A £	B $	@1.65 £	Total £
Profit after tax	51,576	21,498	13,029	56,252
Dividends	20,000	8,225	4,985	20,000
Retained profit	31,756	13,273	8,044	36,252
Profit b/f	475,261	251,266	152,282	–
Profit c/f	507,017	264,539	160,326	–

Notes:

(1) The total column here is Company A + Company B translated at the average rate of 1.65.

(2) Total overheads also include goodwill amortisation of £3,548.

(3) The intra-group dividends have been netted off and eliminated.

Balance sheet at 2012 year end

	A £	B $	@1.62 £	Total £
Tangible fixed assets	415,687	236,268	145,844	561,531
Investments	200,000			
Intangible fixed assets				
Goodwill				63,872
	615,687	236,268	145,844	625,403
Current assets	159,874	92,229	56,931	216,805
Current liabilities	122,844	20,570	12,698	135,542
Net current assets	37,030	71,659	44,233	81,263
Long-term liabilities	45,700	23,388	14,437	60,137
	607,017	284,539	175,640	646,529
Share capital	100,000	20,000		100,000
Profit and loss account	507,017	264,539		546,529
	607,017	284,539		646,529

Notes:

(1) The total column here on the net assets side is: Company A + Company B translated at the year-end rate, 1.62, with the investment in Company B replaced by the goodwill arising on consolidation.

(2) The goodwill on consolidation of £63,872 is £70,968 − £7,096, ie ($310,000 − $200,000) @ 1.55 less two years' amortisation [2 × 3,548 (= 70,968 ÷ 20)].

(3) The share capital total is that of Company A only.

(4) The profit and loss account is derived as follows:

The balance b/f to the beginning of 2012

	£	£
A Ltd – profit b/f, from profit and loss		475,261
B Ltd – the increase in profit and loss reserve from acquisition to beginning of 2012		40,912
At beginning 2012:		

	£	£
From profit and loss $251,266 translated at year end 2011 rate, 1.60	157,041	
On acquisition, 26 June 2011: Net assets $200,000 less share capital $20,000 translated at 1.55	116,129	
B Ltd – the change in shares from acquisition to beginning of 2012 = $20,000/1.60 – $20,000/1.55		(403)
Goodwill amortisation		(3,548)
		512,222

Movements during 2012

		£
A Ltd – retained profit, from profit and loss		31,756
B Ltd – retained profit, from profit and loss, translated at the average rate 1.65 = $13,273/1.65		8,044
Goodwill amortisation		(3,548)
Exchange difference on translating retained profit at the year end rate 1.62 in the balance sheet and at the average rate 1.65 in profit and loss = $13,273/1.62 – 8,044		148
Exchange difference on translating opening net assets at the closing rate of 1.62 in 2012 balance sheet and at 1.60. for the previous year $271,266/1.62 – $271,266/1.60		(2,093)
Opening net assets are derived:		
Closing net assets	$284,539	
Less retained profit for 2012	$(13,273)	
	$271,266	
Profit and loss account 2012 balance sheet		546,529

When SSAP 20 was issued, the normal treatment of purchased goodwill was immediate write-off. However, under FRS 10 *Goodwill and Intangible Assets*, purchased goodwill must be capitalised. This, therefore, raises the issue of whether the amount should be retranslated each year, or left at the original figure. It is better that goodwill is not recalculated, since it reflects the excess of the value of the business over that of its identifiable assets and liabilities at a particular point in time, ie the date of acquisition, and is recorded in the reporting currency then. However, retranslation is not prohibited by SSAP 20.

The net investment method should also be used for accounting for investments in overseas associates. In this case the same calculations will need to be performed, but the net assets will be included on the equity basis rather than on a line-by-line basis.

Potential impact of the FRSME

The FRSME deals with foreign exchange issue together, that is, it does not differentiate between the impact on entities and groups. In practice, the changes would be fairly limited in many cases, although the FRSME is more prescriptive in terms of the rates that must be used for financial statements. There would also be a potential difference in that goodwill arising in respect of a foreign operation would be treated as being in the currency in which it arose and therefore retranslated. As noted earlier, this is not a breach of SSAP 20 at the moment, which does not really deal with the question, although most companies choose not to retranslate.

10.3.2 The temporal method

The net investment method is based on the assumption that the foreign enterprise is a largely independent concern, which does not depend upon the parent company for its activities. In some cases this assumption does not hold, and an alternative accounting method must be applied:

> However, there are some cases in which the affairs of a foreign enterprise are so closely interlinked with those of the investing company that its results may be regarded as being more dependent on the economic environment of the investing company's currency than on that of its own reporting currency. In such a case the financial statements of the foreign enterprise should be included in the consolidated financial statements as if all its transactions had been entered into by the investing company itself in its own currency. For this purpose the temporal method of translation should be used; the mechanics of this method are identical with those used in preparing the accounts of an individual company ... (Para. 22, SSAP 20.)

No single factor determines the accounting treatment, instead it will be a balanced judgement based on a number of separate factors, including the following.

(1) The extent to which the cash flows of the foreign enterprise have a direct impact on those of the investing company, for example, the extent to which profits are remitted, in whatever form, as soon as they are earned.

(2) The extent to which the functioning of the foreign enterprise is dependent on the investing company. This might be affected by where the management of the foreign enterprise is based, and the degree of autonomy given to local managers and staff.

(3) The currency in which the majority of the transactions of the foreign enterprise are denominated.

(4) The major currency to which the foreign enterprise is exposed in its financing structure. SSAP 20 provides three examples of when the temporal method may be appropriate, if the foreign enterprise:

    (a) acts as a selling agency receiving stocks of goods from the investing company and remitting the proceeds back to the company;

    (b) produces a raw material or manufactures parts or sub-assemblies which are then shipped to the investing company for inclusion in its own products, or

    (c)   is located overseas for tax, exchange control or similar reasons to act as a means of raising finance for other companies in the group.

As SSAP 20 notes, the basic accounting treatment for enterprises recorded under the temporal method is to treat them as though they were part of the investing company. Clearly, if the foreign enterprise maintains its records in the investor's reporting currency this requirement can be literally applied. More commonly, the accounting records will be maintained in the local currency, and a series of approximations will be used to incorporate its results.

This will have the following effects, amongst others:

- most transactions will be translated at the average rate for an accounting period;
- stock will be stated at historical rate (usually an estimate) in the balance sheet and in the calculation of cost of sales in the profit and loss account, and
- fixed assets will be stated at the historical rate, and depreciation will be charged on the basis of the historical rate.

The previous example can be used to demonstrate the method, but with some additional assumptions.

EXAMPLE

The additional assumptions here are that: all of the fixed assets were acquired when the exchange rate was 1.55; depreciation accounts for 50 per cent of the overheads excluding goodwill amortisation; opening and closing stocks were purchased when the exchange rates were 1.59 and 1.64 respectively.

Profit and loss account for 2011

		A		B	Rate		B	Total
	£	£	$	$		£	£	£
Turnover		529,487		325,830	1.65		197,473	726,960
O Stock	56,984		19,400		1.59	12,201		
Purchases	359,845		215,394		1.65	130,542		
C Stock	(99,137)		(23,000)		1.64	(14,024)		
Cost of sales		(317,692)		(211,794)			(128,719)	(446,411)
Gross profit		211,795		114,036			68,754	280,549
Dividend income		4,985						
Depreciation		(68,613)		(37,471)	1.55		(24,175)	(92,788)
Goodwill amortisation								(3,548)
Other overheads		(68,613)		(37,472)	1.65		(22,710)	(91,323)

	A	B	Rate	B	Total
Profit before tax	79,554	39,093		21,869	92,890
Taxation	(27,798)	(17,595)	1.65	(10,664)	(38,462)
Profit after tax	51,576	21,498		11,205	54,428
Dividends	(20,000)	(8,225)	1.65	(4,985)	(20,000)
Retained profit	31,756	13,273		6,220	34,428

Balance sheet at 2011 year end

	A £	B $	Rate	B £	Total £
Tangible fixed assets	415,687	236,268	1.55	145,844	561,531
Investments	200,000				
Goodwill					63,872
	615,687	236,268		145,844	625,403
Stocks	99,137	23,000	1.64	14,024	113,161
Other current assets	60,737	69,229	1.62	42,734	103,471
Current liabilities	(122,844)	(20,570)	1.62	(12,698)	(135,542)
Net current assets	37,030	71,659		44,060	81,090
Long-term liabilities	(45,700)	(23,388)	1.62	(14,437)	(60,137)
	607,017	284,539		175,467	646,356
Share capital	100,000	20,000			100,000
Profit and loss account	507,017	264,539			546,356
	607,017	284,539			646,356

In practice, it will also be necessary to calculate the exchange difference on the net monetary assets or liabilities and to charge this to the profit and loss account, not as a movement on reserves. Comparatives are required for this purpose.

Potential impact of the FRSME

The temporal method does not exist under the FRSME. The logic is that it is unnecessary since the requirements in respect of the use of the functional currency mean that each component is necessarily dealt with in the appropriate currency for the purposes of consolidation. This also means that there are no potential issues that can arise due to a change in method, as dealt with overleaf. (Although it does mean that the issue of a change in functional currency may arise.) It also means that there is no guidance, nor need for guidance, in respect of branches.

10.3.3   Change of method

As a general principle, a group should be consistent over time and adopt the same accounting treatment for an overseas enterprise. However, this will not apply where there is a genuine change in the position of that enterprise, such that it is no longer appropriate to treat it in the same way as before.

For example:

- a parent company has previously held an overseas enterprise solely to act as its agent in another country, but reorganises its activities, granting the overseas enterprise a substantial degree of autonomy and control over its own operations, or
- a previously autonomous overseas enterprise becomes an effective branch of the company overseas.

In the first case the enterprise, previously recorded under the temporal method, would now have to be accounted for under the net investment method. In the second case the reverse would be true, and the net investment method should give way to the temporal method.

Where an enterprise has previously been accounted for under the net investment method, but this changes to the temporal method, there appear to be two possibilities:

- the amounts could be restated as if the temporal method had always been used, with a consequent adjustment to retained reserves, or
- the amounts at the time of the change in status could be treated as the starting point of the temporal method, with no adjustment needed to retained reserves.

The first method is unlikely to be applied in practice, as it may be extremely difficult. The company may need to reanalyse its balances and transactions over a considerable period in order to arrive at the correct result. There is also a much more important reason why this method may be inappropriate. The accounting change is not really a change in accounting policy, but a change in the underlying circumstances such that new policies need to be applied from this time. If the new method were applied retrospectively then the overseas enterprise would be treated as though it had always been an effective branch of the parent. This is not true. It is, therefore, suggested that the second, and by far the simplest, method be adopted.

Where there is a change from the temporal method to the net investment method, the consequent adjustment of the recorded values can be treated as a movement on reserves in the period in which the change in status takes place, or an adjustment to the opening retained reserves could be made to reflect the position at the previous balance sheet date. Using the same argument as for the change in the other direction, the adjustment should be made solely in the year of change, since this again reflects a change in status and not a change in accounting policy.

10.3.4 *Foreign branches*

SSAP 20 requires that foreign branches are treated like foreign enterprises. Each branch needs to be assessed in accordance with the criteria for the net investment method and the temporal method and accounted for accordingly:

> For the purpose of this statement, foreign operations which are conducted through a foreign branch should be accounted for in accordance with the nature of the business operations concerned. Where such a branch operates as a separate business with local finance, it should be accounted for using the closing rate/net investment method. Where the foreign branch operates as an extension of the company's trade and its cash flows have a direct impact upon those of the company, the temporal method should be used. (Para. 25, SSAP 20.)

A branch is defined in the following terms:

> A *foreign branch* is either a legally constituted enterprise located overseas or a group of assets and liabilities which are accounted for in foreign currencies. (Para. 37, SSAP 20.)

This is a very broad definition. It could, for example, allow a company owning a fleet of ships to treat each vessel as a separate branch.

This treatment can be applied in the individual financial statements of a company; it does not only apply to group accounts.

10.3.5 *Hyperinflation*

The obligatory section of SSAP 20 does not deal with hyperinflation, but it is mentioned in the explanatory notes to the standard. A problem may arise where a company has an investment in a subsidiary, associate or branch which maintains its own accounting records in the currency subject to hyperinflation. It is suggested that in such cases it may not be appropriate simply to translate the unadjusted financial statements, since this may not give a true and fair view of the financial position or the results of the enterprise. Instead, the financial statements should be adjusted to take account of current price levels prior to translation.

There are three main problems with this provision:

- it is not mandatory;
- the standard does not define hyperinflation, and
- the standard does not state how the financial statements should be adjusted prior to translation.

The Urgent Issues Task Force addressed this problem with the issue of UITF Abstract 9 *Accounting for Operations in Hyper-Inflationary Economies*. UITF 9 clearly takes account of the original international accounting standard dealing with this subject; indeed an appendix to the draft is a direct quotation from this standard, describing some of the characteristics of hyperinflation. The Abstract does not attempt to provide a single definition of hyperinflation, noting that:

> The question of what constitutes hyper-inflation is necessarily judgmental. (Para. 3, UITF 9.)

It does, however, state that, in all cases, adjustments to take account of the effects of hyperinflation are required where the cumulative rate of inflation over three years exceeds 100 per cent, and the operations in the hyperinflationary economy are material. (It should be noted that an inflation rate of 26 per cent per annum for three years would therefore fall within the definition of hyperinflation.) In other cases, adjustments are required if the distortions introduced by hyperinflation are likely to distort the view given by the financial statements of the group.

The other factors, taken from the original international standard and quoted in UITF 9, which may indicate there is hyperinflation are:

(a) the general population prefers to keep its wealth in non-monetary assets or in a relatively stable foreign currency. Amounts of local currency held are immediately invested to maintain purchasing power;

(b) the general population regards monetary amounts not in terms of the local currency but in terms of a relatively stable foreign currency. Prices may be quoted in that currency;

(c) sales and purchases on credit take place at prices that compensate for the expected loss of purchasing power during the credit period, even if the period is short;

(d) interest rates, wages and prices are linked to a price index ... (Para. 3, IAS 29.)

It is important to remember that UITF 9 applies only where the effect will be material. In other cases, the additional effort that will be required in order to comply with the pronouncement may be out of proportion to the benefit.

UITF 9 states that two methods should normally be used to deal with hyperinflation, but allows other methods if the suggested methods would not give an acceptable result.

The first method is to adjust the local currency financial statements to reflect current price levels before translating them for incorporation in the group accounts (or, in the case of a branch, in the company accounts). Any loss or gain on the net monetary position should be taken through the profit and loss account. This method has the disadvantage that it does not treat part of the group or company consistently with the remainder: why should only part of the group or company accounts be stated at their current value? However, consistency would come at a very high price. Either the accounts of the entity affected by hyperinflation would have to be stated at their original amounts, which would be virtually meaningless, or the remainder of the accounts would have to be stated on the basis of some form of current value accounting. The compromise reached in the pronouncement is the best that can be expected in the immediate future.

The second method uses a functional currency other than the main currency of the country in which the business operates. Items are translated into the functional currency, either at the time of initial recording or by the use of the temporal method, and it is the functional currency amounts that are translated and incorporated in the final group or company accounts. The example given is that of certain territories in Latin America, where the US dollar might be used as the functional currency. This proposal is consistent with the definition of hyperinflation included in the international standard, since one of the factors is the degree to which people try to keep assets in a foreign currency, and another the degree to which the local population tends to think of monetary amounts in terms of another currency.

Where neither of these methods is appropriate, UITF 9 states that companies should be allowed to use another method, so long as they state:

- the reasons why neither of the normal methods is appropriate, and
- the accounting policy that has been adopted to eliminate the distortions of hyperinflation.

The accounting policy will have to be stated in all cases, even where one of the two suggested methods is used.

The FRSSE does not deal at all with the matter of hyperinflation. The reason for this is, presumably, that few companies entitled to use the FRSSE are likely to have operations in hyperinflationary economies. This still leaves the problem of what small companies should do if, however unusual this may be, they are affected by hyperinflation. Where the amounts involved are material, it would seem that the only sensible option open to them is to comply with the requirements of UITF 9. This is not too onerous, given the flexibility that is included in the abstract.

Potential impact of the FRSME

The FRSME requirements on hyperinflation are somewhat more specific than those in UITF 9, being broadly the same as those included in FRS 24. This is unlikely to be of any relevance to many companies.

10.3.6 *Foreign equity investments financed or hedged by foreign currency borrowings*

SSAP 20 and the FRSSE contain a similar provision in respect of group accounts as individual company accounts when dealing with foreign equity investments financed or hedged by foreign borrowings.

UITF 19 altered the provision by requiring that the relevant amounts be calculated after tax (see **10.2.5**).

The provision is identical if the investment is in an investment other than a subsidiary or associate. The only additional condition is that the procedure must have been used in the individual company accounts if it is also to be used in the group accounts.

There are some differences if the procedure is to be used for an associate or an investment in a subsidiary. It does not appear to be necessary that the parent or investing company has used the procedure in its own accounts for it to be used in the group accounts. The standard contains the following rules.

> Where foreign currency borrowings have been used to finance, or provide a hedge against, group equity investments in foreign enterprises, exchange gains or losses on the borrowings, which would otherwise have been taken to the profit and loss account, may be offset as reserve movements against exchange differences arising on the retranslation of the net investments provided that:
>
> (a)   the relationships between the investing company and the foreign enterprises concerned justify the use of the closing rate method for consolidation purposes;
>
> (b)   in any accounting period, the exchange gains and losses arising on foreign currency borrowings are offset only to the extent of the exchange differences arising on the net investments in foreign enterprises;
>
> (c)   the foreign currency borrowings, whose exchange gains or losses are used in the offset process, should not exceed, in the aggregate, the total amount of cash that the net investments are expected to be able to generate, whether from profits or otherwise; and
>
> (d)   the accounting treatment is applied consistently from period to period. (Para. 57, SSAP 20.)

The closing rate, or net investment, method must be used in order for this provision to apply. It would be illogical to allow the use of this provision if the temporal method were applied, since the temporal method treats balances and transactions as if they were those of the company. Since a company could not offset exchange differences as a movement on reserves if it undertook the transactions itself, it should not be allowed to offset such differences if the transactions are undertaken by a company accounted for using the temporal method. However, the same argument could also be used against the use of the provision when the net investment method has been applied. It is fundamental to the preparation of group accounts that they are prepared as if the group were a single entity. Allowing any exchange differences to be taken to reserves is an exception to this general principle.

It should be noted that there is no such restriction on individual companies. A company with an investment in a foreign subsidiary may offset exchange gains and losses in its own financial statements even if the subsidiary is accounted for under the temporal method in the group accounts, and the offset is then not available.

There is also another important difference between the provision applying to individual companies and that for groups. The individual company provision only refers to the amount of the investment, but the group provision refers to the net investment. Net investment is defined in the standard:

> The *net investment* which a company has in a foreign enterprise is its effective equity stake and comprises its proportion of such foreign enterprise's net assets; in appropriate circumstances, intra-group loans and other deferred balances may be regarded as part of the effective equity stake. (Para. 43, SSAP 20.)

This definition excludes any goodwill attributable to the investment, since goodwill would not fall within the net assets of the enterprise. This may restrict the amount that can be offset, and in some cases to below the amount that was offset in the investing company's own financial statements. This is shown in the following example.

EXAMPLE

A company purchases a foreign subsidiary at a price equivalent to £1,000,000 at the ruling rate of exchange; the net assets of the subsidiary are equivalent to £600,000. The company takes out a loan equivalent to £1,000,000 denominated in a foreign currency to hedge against the investment.

In the first year of ownership the foreign company makes no profit and no loss, but exchange rate changes mean that the loan and investment now have a value of £1,050,000. In the investing company's own financial statements the gain and loss can be offset, leaving no net movement.

In the group accounts, however, the net assets of the subsidiary will be recorded at £630,000, six-tenths of the value of £1,050,000. The goodwill of £400,000 will have been offset against reserves on acquisition, or treated as an asset and amortised, but will no longer be available for offset against the loss on the loan. The group financial statements would therefore include a net loss on exchange of £20,000 (£50,000 loss on the loan less £30,000 gain on the asset).

Note that it is assumed that the subsidiary is reasonably expected to make sufficient profit in the future to justify the investing company retaining the investment at its full cost.

Potential impact of the FRSME

As noted above, when dealing with individual entities the FRSME deals with all hedging issues in a slightly different way to SSAP 20. However, it will allow exchange differences on a net investment in a foreign operation to be treated as part of other comprehensive income at group level. This contrasts with the treatment at entity level where such differences must be recognised in profit or loss.

10.4 FRS 23 AND FRS 24

10.4.1 *Introduction*

As noted above, FRS 23 and FRS 24 replace SSAP 20 and UITF 9, but only for companies which are also complying with FRS 26. For other companies, SSAP 20 and UITF 9 remain in force.

Potential impact of the FRSME

Most companies that will adopt the FRSME (if it comes into force) are probably currently covered by SSAP 20 and not FRS 23. However, for the small number of companies that are currently applying FRS 23 and then move to the FRSME, there will be very few changes in their accounting practices, as the FRSME requirements are basically an abbreviated version of FRS 23.

10.4.2 *Scope of FRS 23*

Apart from the scope of FRS 23 as set out above, the standard is also restricted in that it applies:

- to accounting for transactions and balances in foreign currencies, except that it does not apply to derivative transactions and balances that fall within the scope of FRS 26;
- in translating the results and financial position of foreign operations, whether those operations are included through consolidation, proportionate consolidation or the use of the equity method, and
- in translating results into a presentation currency.

The exclusion of derivatives covered by FRS 26 limits the application of the standard, and forms much of the justification for requiring SSAP 20 to remain in force for those companies which have not made the change to FRS 26. FRS 23 also does not deal with hedge accounting, since again this is covered by FRS 26.

10.4.3 *Functional currency*

One of the very basic ideas underlying FRS 23 is that of functional currency. Functional currency is defined as:

> . . . the currency of the primary economic environment in which the entity operates. (Para. 8, FRS 23.)

In most cases, this will be fairly obvious. Much of the guidance included in FRS 23 is intended to deal with those situations where the functional currency is not immediately clear. Nonetheless, functional currency is intended to be a matter of fact, and a company does not have a choice as to which functional currency it wishes to use.

Functional currency underpins FRS 23, and is of greater importance than local currency under SSAP 20. Effectively, basic accounting needs to take place in the functional currency. The FRS deals with the issue of where the underlying accounting records are maintained in a currency that is not the functional currency. While such a method is acceptable, the translation needs to take place such that after translation the same amounts appear as would have arisen had all of the underlying books and records been maintained in the functional currency. Given this, it seems far easier for companies to maintain their underlying records in their functional currency.

The primary guidance is that, in determining the functional currency, a company should consider:

- the currency that mainly influences sales prices for goods and services, usually the currency in which sales prices are denominated and settled;
- the currency of the country whose competitive forces and regulations mainly determine the sales prices of its goods and services, and
- the currency that mainly influences labour, material and other costs, again usually the currency in which such costs are denominated and settled.

Where these factors do not provide a definitive answer, then companies should also take account of:

- the currency in which funds for financing activities are generated, and
- the currency in which receipts from operating activities are usually retained.

When dealing with foreign operations then additional considerations come into play. Again, these are relevant only where the primary tests set out above do not provide a clear answer. A foreign operation is defined as:

> . . . an entity that is a subsidiary, associate, joint venture or branch of a reporting entity, the activities of which are based or conducted in a country or currency other than those of the reporting entity. (Para. 8, FRS 23.)

Once a foreign operation has been identified, then the question arises of the degree of autonomy that operation has. It is necessary to consider:

- whether the foreign operation's activities are carried out as an extension of the reporting entity, rather than autonomously;
- whether transactions with the reporting entity form a high or low proportion of the foreign operation's activities;
- whether cash flows of the foreign operation directly affect the cash flows of the reporting entity and are readily available for remittance, and
- whether cash flows from the activities of the foreign operation are sufficient to service existing and normally expected debt obligations, without requiring funding from the reporting entity.

In effect, the decision needs to be made whether the foreign operation is an autonomous business in its own right or akin to a branch, whatever legal status it may have. Where, for example, all of a foreign operation's sales are of goods supplied by its parent, on demand, and where all cash received is remitted back after deduction of costs, this would make the foreign operation an effective branch. Its functional currency would then be the functional currency of the entity of which it is a branch. If the business is independent, for example, raising its own finance, buying and selling locally and retaining funds, then its functional currency will be determined without taking account of the fact that it is classified as a foreign operation.

There is no place for the temporal method under FRS 23. This is on the basis that those entities to which it would have applied under SSAP 20 must have the functional currency as the functional currency of their parent, or equivalent. If this is the case, the temporal method is not necessary as there is no difference between the functional currency of the parent and the branch.

Once the functional currency has been determined then it is fixed. This is on the basis that functional currency is a matter of fact and is not subject to any choice. However, it is possible that activities change in such as way as to alter the functional currency of an entity. For example, a foreign operation might be set up as, in effect, a branch of a reporting entity. At some point in the future, the operation may acquire a sufficient level of autonomy that it is no longer to be treated as a branch and should be accounted for separately. At this point, the functional currency may change.

Where a functional currency changes, the change should be applied prospectively. This means that transactions taking place prior to the date of change are not deemed to have occurred under the new functional currency. This again reflects the fact that functional currency is a matter of fact, and any change must, therefore, have taken place at a given date. It would not be appropriate to treat the change as having occurred at any other time.

The procedure required is that all items are translated into the new functional currency using the exchange rate in place at the date of change. Any exchange differences that have previously been recognised through the statement of total recognised gains and losses are not recognised in profit at this time, but are deferred until disposal.

As a final point, where a functional currency is that of a hyperinflationary economy, then FRS 24 must be followed. It is not open to a company to avoid restatement by using another functional currency. This contrasts with the situation under UITF 9 where such an approach is amongst those acceptable.

10.4.4 *Foreign currency transactions*

The basic rule for the initial recording of foreign currency transactions under FRS 23 is that they should be recorded in the functional currency by applying the spot rate to the foreign currency amounts.

The date that should be used for determining the spot rate is the date that the transaction falls to be recorded in accordance with other standards.

However, FRS 23 allows a company to use an average rate for a period, say a week or a month, where the effect of using such an approximation will not lead to any material distortion.

At subsequent balance sheet dates:

- monetary items denominated in a foreign currency need to be translated using the closing rate;
- non-monetary items stated at historic cost are not retranslated, but remain at the exchange rate used at the date of the original transaction, and
- non-monetary items stated at fair value in a foreign currency are translated using the exchange rate at the date the fair value was determined.

This differs from SSAP 20 in a number of ways.

(1) SSAP 20 deals with translation where there are, for example, foreign exchange contracts in place, albeit that SSAP 20 allows a number of treatments. FRS 23 does not deal with this, on the basis that most derivatives and hedging fall within the scope of FRS 26.

(2) SSAP 20 does not deal with the issue of non-monetary items measured in a foreign currency. This is relevant since there are some industries where assets may be generally sold in one currency, which may not be the same as the functional currency of the company using those assets. The guidance in FRS 23 is, therefore, clearer. FRS 23 points out that as a result of these rules there may be circumstances where, for example, impairment losses are recognised in the functional currency where they would not be in the foreign currency or vice versa. This will apply where an exchange movement offsets any change in the underlying value of the asset.

FRS 23 deals separately with the issue of recognition of exchange differences. It points out that some exchange differences that may arise using the rules set out above will not be recognised in income, since they may require a different treatment under FRS 26. For example, exchange differences on items that form part of a cash flow hedge will normally be taken directly to the statement of total recognised gains and losses, to the extent that they are effective.

Most exchange differences arising at a balance sheet date, however, must be recognised in profit or loss in the period in which they arise. There are exceptions where:

- an exchange gain or loss arises on a gain or loss on a non-monetary item which itself passes through the statement of total recognised gains and losses, in which case the same treatment is adopted for the exchange movement, and
- an exchange difference arises on a monetary item that forms part of a reporting entity's net investment in a foreign operation where, in the group

accounts, that gain or loss should be recognised in the statement of total recognised gains and losses and recognised in income only on disposal.

Unlike SSAP 20, where an exchange difference arises on a monetary item that forms part of a reporting entity's net investment in a foreign operation that difference must be treated as part of profit, for the entity's own financial statements. It is only in the group accounts that such an item passes through the statement of total recognised gains and losses.

10.4.5   Presentation currency

The presentation currency is the currency in which the financial statements are presented. The most common situation is, naturally, that the presentation currency is the same as the functional currency, in which case no additional issues arise.

However, FRS 23 does not dictate or prohibit any currency being used as the presentation currency, and any currency can be used for this purpose. The most common situation is probably where group accounts must be prepared and there are various functional currencies for entities within the group. In this case, at least some of the entities must be translated into the presentation currency of the group.

Where the results and position of an entity need to be translated into a different presentation currency, and the functional currency is not that of a hyperinflationary economy:

- all assets and liabilities for each balance sheet presented are translated at the closing rate at each relevant balance sheet date;
- income and expenses are translated at the exchange rates at the date of the transactions, and
- all resulting exchange differences are recognised through the statement of total recognised gains and losses.

Where group accounts are being produced, and there is a minority interest, accumulated exchange differences attributable to minority interests are treated as part of the minority interests in the consolidated balance sheet.

In practice, income and expenses are likely to be translated at a rate, such as an average rate, that approximates the actual rates at the dates of transactions. This is accepted by FRS 23, so long as rates have not fluctuated significantly such that the use of an average rate is likely to lead to material distortion of the results.

As FRS 23 notes, the exchange differences that result will derive from:

- using the actual (or average) rate for transactions, whilst assets and liabilities are translated at the closing rate, and

- the retranslation of the opening net assets at a closing rate that differs from the closing rate of the previous period.

Such differences are not recognised in income and are treated through the statement of total recognised gains and losses. While FRS 23 is not entirely clear, the transitional provisions show that it is expected that these amounts are to be separately disclosed. This then raises the theoretical problem of the opening balance on the move to FRS 23. It would be impractical in many cases to determine what the cumulative amount would be since it could cover many years. As a result, FRS 23 allows the opening balance to be taken as zero.

Different procedures are applied where translation into the presentation currency is required but the functional currency is that of a hyperinflationary economy. In this case all amounts, that is, assets, liabilities, income, expenses, other gains and losses, are translated at the closing rate of the latest balance sheet date, except that comparatives are not restated, if the presentation currency is not hyperinflationary.

FRS 24 is applied prior to the translation.

FRS 23 also deals with a few issues which arise when consolidating a foreign operation.

(1) While normal consolidation adjustments are made, there will still be an exchange gain or loss in respect of intra-group balances. This is correct since, when stated in the presentation currency, the group is exposed to an exchange risk.

(2) Where the financial statements of a foreign operation are prepared as at a date that differs from the group balance sheet date, and no separate financial statements to the group date are prepared, then the exchange rate used should normally be that as at the balance sheet date of the foreign operation. However, that may need to be adjusted, as with all major changes between the balance sheet dates, if there is a major movement in the exchange rate.

(3) Goodwill and fair value adjustments arising on the acquisition of a foreign operation are treated as assets and liabilities of the foreign operation, so they are treated as being in that operation's functional currency and translated accordingly.

Point 3 was subject to a transitional provision. Companies must apply this treatment in respect of acquisitions occurring on or after the implementation date of the standard. However, for earlier transactions they had a choice of either adopting this treatment or of treating goodwill and fair value adjustments as assets of the reporting entity, that is, as non-monetary, which means that no retranslation is required, either at the date of the transition to FRS 23 or subsequently.

Where a foreign operation is disposed of through sale, liquidation, repayment of share capital or abandonment, any cumulative exchange differences which have been treated through the statement of total recognised gains and losses are recognised in profit or loss in calculating the profit or loss on disposal. There were some minor changes to the wording of the requirements, in relation to the treatment of accumulated exchange difference on a disposal, which apply for accounting periods beginning on or after 1 January 2009. However, there were no changes of substance. (The changes were made to ensure consistency of wording with the international standard on which FRS 23 is based, but the more substantial changes that were made to the international standard have not been reflected in FRS 23. This is because they arise as a consequence of changes to the international standard dealing with interests in subsidiaries, and that standard has not been adopted in the UK.)

FRS 23 provides only one method for translating into a presentation currency. There is no temporal method. As explained above, this is because the temporal method is not relevant since entities which would have had that method applied to them under SSAP 20 will, under FRS 23, find that their functional currency is that of the entity of which they are a branch. If that is the case, translation issues do not arise.

10.4.6 Hyperinflation

FRS 24 now deals with hyperinflation, for those companies which are also complying with FRS 26.

In broad terms, FRS 24 and UITF 9 can be compared as follows.

(1) The identification of hyperinflation will not change between the UITF and the standard. (Not surprising, given that the UITF quotes the international standard on which FRS 24 is based.)

(2) UITF 9 allows three methods of dealing with hyperinflation. FRS 24 allows only one, being the first mentioned in UITF 9. FRS 24 is far more specific in terms of the mechanics and application of this method.

Basically, FRS 24 requires all amounts, including comparatives, to be restated using the measuring unit current at the latest balance sheet date, and the gain or loss on the net monetary position to be treated as part of the profit or loss for the period.

Given that few UK companies will be affected by FRS 24, only a brief summary of the standard is provided.

Where historical cost financial statements are being prepared, the following adjustments are required for the balance sheet.

(1) Monetary items are not restated, since they are already current.

(2)   Assets and liabilities linked by agreement to changes in prices (ie index linked) are adjusted according to the agreement.

(3)   Non-monetary items are not restated if they are already carried at amounts current at the balance sheet date, such as those stated at fair value or net realisable value.

(4)   Other non-monetary items, those not already at current values, are restated and consideration is then given as to whether this figure should be reduced for impairment.

(5)   No adjustment is made for borrowing costs where to do so would lead to restatement of both a capital item and the capitalisation of borrowing costs.

(6)   All components of equity are restated by applying a general price index, except for revaluation surpluses, which are eliminated, and retained earnings, which is the resulting figure.

Estimates may be needed, particularly if a currency that was previously not hyperinflationary becomes hyperinflationary. This is accepted by the standard.

The profit and loss account is also restated, together with the gain or loss on the net monetary position. The cash flow statement also needs to be restated.

Comparatives are restated using the measuring unit current at the latest balance sheet date.

If hyperinflation ceases, the latest balance sheet figures are the basis for carrying amounts in subsequent periods. In effect, they become the new deemed cost.

10.5   DISCLOSURE

10.5.1   Companies Act

The Companies Act 2006 contains very little in the way of disclosure requirements concerning foreign currencies, except the following.

> Where any sums originally denominated in foreign currencies have been brought into account under any items shown in the balance sheet format or profit and loss account formats, the basis on which those sums have been translated into sterling (or the currency in which the accounts are drawn up) must be stated. (Para. 70, Sch. 1 to The Large and Medium-sized Companies and Groups (Accounts and Reports) Regulations 2008 (SI 2008/410).)

Oddly, the wording is slightly different for small companies (whilst having precisely the same effect), although, in both cases, it is interesting that the requirements at least reflect that financial statements under UK GAAP are not necessarily drawn up in sterling.

10.5.2 SSAP 20

SSAP 20 contains the following disclosure requirements.

(1) The method used in translating the financial statements of foreign enterprises and the treatment used for exchange differences should be disclosed.

(2) The net amount of exchange gains and losses on foreign currency borrowings, less deposits, identifying separately:

(a) any amounts offset on reserves, as a hedge or finance for foreign equity investments (including showing separately the gross amount of such movements and the tax effect, if any), and

(b) the net amount charged or credited to the profit and loss account.

(3) For all companies, or groups, the net movement on reserves arising from exchange differences.

The FRSSE does not contain any of the disclosure requirements of SSAP 20.

10.5.3 FRS 23

FRS 23 contains the following disclosure requirements.

(1) The amount of exchange differences recognised in profit or loss for the period, except for those arising on financial instruments measured at fair value through profit or loss in accordance with FRS 26.

(2) Net exchange differences recognised through the statement of total recognised gains and losses.

(3) A reconciliation of exchange differences recognised through the statement of total recognised gains and losses at the beginning and end of the period.

(4) When the presentation currency differs from the functional currency, a statement of that fact, together with the functional currency and the reasons for using a different presentation currency.

(5) When there is a change in the functional currency, of either the reporting entity or a significant foreign operation, then that fact and the reasons for the change in functional currency.

(6) When an entity displays financial statements, or other financial information, in a currency that is neither its presentation nor functional currency, and it has not used the method required by FRS 23 to translate from a functional to presentation currency then it must:

(a) clearly distinguish the information as supplementary, to distinguish it from the information that complies with Financial Reporting Standards;

(b)　disclose the currency in which the supplementary information is displayed, and

(c)　disclose the functional currency and the method of translation used for the supplementary information.

Where a company does not present its financial statements in accordance with the translation methods required by FRS 23, it should not state that its financial statements have been prepared in accordance with Financial Reporting Standards.

10.5.4　FRS 24

FRS 24 contains the following disclosure requirements.

(1)　The fact that financial statements and the corresponding figures for previous periods have been restated for the changes in the general purchasing power of the functional currency and, as a result, are stated using the measuring unit current at the balance sheet date.

(2)　Whether the financial statements are based on a historic cost or current cost approach.

(3)　The identity and level of the price index at the balance sheet date and the movement in the index during the current and previous period.

10.6　THE EURO

10.6.1　Accounting issues arising

With effect from 1 January 1999, the euro became the currency of the countries participating in European monetary union, called 'participating Member States', although national currencies still existed (as denominations of the euro) until the end of the transition period at the beginning of 2002. Although the UK has not yet joined the euro zone, and may never do so, its introduction raised major accounting issues for UK companies for the following reasons.

(1)　Companies may have incurred significant costs in adapting their information systems to deal with the euro. Such costs may be ongoing as companies decide that they wish to be able to deal with the euro, even though the UK remains outside the euro zone.

(2)　The irrevocable locking of national currencies of participating Member States impacted on cumulative exchange differences and anticipatory hedging instruments.

(3)　Some UK companies may adopt the euro as their functional (local) currency and will, therefore, be preparing their accounts in euros, which raises translation issues relating to comparatives.

UITF Abstract 21 *Accounting Issues Arising from the Proposed Introduction of the Euro*, issued in March 1998, deals with issues 1 and 2 above. The Appendix to UITF 21, issued in August 1998, deals with issues relating to 3 above, although its main focus is on companies whose functional currency is that of a country participating in monetary union.

Issues relating to costs incurred in connection with the introduction of the euro (point 1) are dealt with in Chapter 5 – *Reporting financial performance* and Chapter 11 – *Fixed assets*.

Entities which apply the FRSSE are exempt from complying with UITF 21, although the FRSSE incorporates the basic accounting principle regarding treatment of costs arising in preparing for the euro. Where the impact of the euro is likely to be significant, smaller entities should consider the matters addressed in the Abstract as a guide to best practice.

As a result of the introduction of FRS 23, there are effectively now two versions of UITF 21. The original version applies to those companies which continue to apply SSAP 20, whilst there are some changes that apply where companies have moved to FRS 23.

10.6.2 *Preparation of financial statements in euros*

Where a UK company has the majority of its assets, liabilities, income and expenses in the currencies of participating Member States, or where the major part of a group headed by a UK parent is situated in participating Member States, it may decide that its local or functional currency is the euro. Additionally, a UK company may decide that it will transact in euros wherever possible, thus effectively making the euro its local or functional currency. In such situations, the UK company will be able to prepare and file its financial statements in euros, and indeed should do so if it is to apply the principles underlying SSAP 20. Perhaps strangely, FRS 23 would not require this, since it is fairly indifferent to presentation currency, but it would be sensible for a company to do so.

As noted in the introduction to this chapter, there is no requirement for UK companies to prepare and file accounts in sterling and the Registrar of Companies accepts accounts prepared in other currencies, including the euro. A company may prepare its financial statements in euros if:

- a major part of its trading is conducted in euros, with assets retained in that currency, or
- its major assets and liabilities are located in the euro zone, a majority of shareholders are resident there, and distributions are made in euros.

Alternatively, companies may provide a convenient translation into euros along with their statutory accounts, or file an additional version of their accounts in euros.

10.6.3   Cumulative foreign exchange differences

Where a parent and subsidiary have previously reported in different national currencies of participating Member States, UITF 21 specifies that cumulative foreign exchange translation differences recognised in the statement of total recognised gains and losses in previous years should remain in reserves after the introduction of the euro and should not be reported in the profit and loss account. Although UITF 21 does not directly address the issue, the same principle could be applied when a UK parent switches to producing its accounts in euros and has subsidiaries in participating Member States.

10.6.4   Anticipatory hedges

At the time of the UITF, there was no UK standard dealing with measurement issues relating to anticipatory hedges. Anticipatory hedges are now dealt with in FRS 26, for companies complying with that standard.

Upon the introduction of the euro, the exchange risk between the currencies of participating Member States disappeared. The UITF considered this issue in the context of a company that had an accounting policy of deferring gains and losses on anticipatory hedges and recognising them in the profit and loss account in the same period as the income or expense being hedged. It concluded in UITF 21 that the introduction of the euro would have no impact on this accounting policy.

This also applies where FRS 26 is applied.

11 FIXED ASSETS

11.1 INTRODUCTION

11.1.1 Accounting standards

Tangible fixed assets are of major importance to many businesses. FRS 15 *Tangible Fixed Assets* deals with such assets in general although there are also other standards that deal with particular areas:

- SSAP 4 *Accounting for Government Grants*;
- SSAP 13 *Accounting for Research and Development*;
- SSAP 19 *Accounting for Investment Properties*;
- SSAP 21 *Accounting for Leases and Hire Purchase Contracts*, and
- FRS 30 *Heritage Assets*.

Of these standards, SSAP 4 is dealt with in Chapter 12 and SSAP 21 is covered in Chapter 16.

FRS 30 is the most recent standard. The standard is effective for accounting periods beginning on or after 1 April 2010, although early adoption is encouraged. Heritage assets are defined as assets with historic, artistic, scientific, technological, geophysical or environmental qualities that are held principally for their contribution to knowledge and culture; many, although not necessarily all, such assets would be fixed assets. FRS 30 came after two exposure drafts, which took very different approaches to the issue of heritage assets. The first draft, FRED 40, proposed extensive changes to accounting for such assets, including taking such assets outside the scope of FRS 15 and introducing a new category of asset. The proposals did not meet with widespread favour, and a very different approach was then put forward. The next draft, FRED 42, proposed dealing with the issue of heritage assets primarily by way of enhanced disclosure. It is FRED 42 that has led to FRS 30.

Potential impact of the FRSME

The FRSME proposes a number of changes to current practice concerning fixed assets, although many of the changes will affect a relatively small number of companies.

Among the main changes are:

- prohibiting the revaluation of property, plant and equipment;
- prohibiting the capitalisation of any borrowing costs incurred over the period of production of property, plant and equipment (and any other assets which might be affected), and
- somewhat more minor changes, such as requiring estimates of residual

values to be reconsidered where there is an indication that they might have altered.

There are fairly basic changes in relation to investment properties, where revaluation changes will be reflected in profit not as other gains or losses. (There is also a strictly unconnected change that will affect investment properties, in that deferred tax will need to be provided on the valuation changes.)

11.1.2   Definition

The following definition of fixed assets is included in statute:

> ... assets of a company which are intended for use on a continuing basis in the company's activities ... (CA 2006 s. 853(6).)

The balance sheet formats in Sch. 1 to The Large and Medium-sized Companies and Groups (Accounts and Reports) Regulations 2008 (SI 2008/410) list three types of fixed asset:

(I)   Intangible assets
(II)   Tangible assets
(III)   Investments

This chapter deals with both tangible and intangible assets. Investments are dealt with in Chapter 13. The definitions of intangible assets and tangible assets in FRSs 10 *Goodwill and Intangible Assets* and 15 are covered in the relevant sections dealing with each of these standards.

It is standard practice for an intangible asset to be treated as tangible where it relates to a right over a tangible fixed asset. For example, leasehold properties are normally treated as tangible fixed assets, and this is recognised in the statutory formats, even though, strictly, they should be treated as intangible. Since they represent a right with regard to a tangible fixed asset, this is a reasonable treatment. Similarly, computer software is also usually treated as a tangible asset, being a component of a computer system along with the hardware.

11.2   TANGIBLE FIXED ASSETS

11.2.1   FRS 15 Tangible Fixed Assets

FRS 15 became effective for accounting periods ending on or after 23 March 2000. This standard provided detailed requirements in many areas where these were previously lacking, especially in relation to determination of cost, capitalisation of interest and revaluations. However, much of the standard is based on what was already considered best practice and therefore, for many companies, its introduction did not have a major impact on the accounting treatment and disclosure of tangible assets.

11.2.2   Definition

FRS 15 provides the following definition of a tangible fixed asset.

> Assets that have physical substance and are held for use in the production or supply of goods or services, for rental to others, or for administrative purposes on a continuing basis in the reporting entity's activities. (Para. 2,FRS 15.)

The FRS 15 definition is very similar to that in the international standard IAS 16 *Property, Plant and Equipment*, which FRS 15 closely resembles in many, although not all, respects.

11.2.3   Determining the cost of tangible fixed assets

Tangible fixed assets should initially be measured at cost, whatever valuation policies are normally adopted by the company.

There is also a requirement that the amount originally recognised should not exceed the recoverable amount of the asset. Normally, this is very unlikely to be a problem. It may just occasionally be an issue where an asset is acquired and there is an immediate problem, such as a slump in demand for the ultimate product to be made using the new asset. Again, this is most likely where an asset takes a long time from order to delivery (or commencement of construction to completion). A problem of this sort is unlikely to be easily missed.

The issue of cost over-runs is separate. As noted below, abnormal production costs should not be included within the cost of fixed assets, so they should not lead to any consideration of the recoverable amount of the assets affected.

In many cases, determining the cost of a tangible fixed asset is straightforward. This is likely to be true where a tangible fixed asset:

- is purchased, rather than constructed, and
- can be used immediately by the enterprise.

To take a simple example, there is likely to be little difficulty in determining the cost of the office furniture purchased by a company. It will normally be the invoiced cost exclusive of VAT. Similarly, the cost of a motor car will be the invoiced cost, but in this case inclusive of the VAT, since input tax on motor cars cannot normally be reclaimed. For companies which are not registered for VAT, the cost will always be the VAT-inclusive cost of the asset. The only difficulty in such circumstances is likely to be where a company is partially exempt from VAT. In this case, the cost of each asset can often only be determined at the end of each VAT period, when the amount of VAT recovered is known.

However, there can be other difficulties, and these are most likely to arise if any of the following situations occur.

- Where the asset is constructed by the company rather than purchased from an outside organisation.
- Where there are substantial costs that are only indirectly associated with the purchase of the asset.
- Where the asset is acquired to replace or improve an existing asset.
- Where the asset is paid for in a foreign currency.

The basic rules on the calculation of the cost of an asset, whether a tangible fixed asset or otherwise, are given in Sch. 1 to The Large and Medium-sized Companies and Groups (Accounts and Reports) Regulations 2008 (SI 2008/410) and Sch. 1 to The Small Companies and Groups (Accounts and Directors' Report) Regulations 2008 (SI 2008/409):

(1) The purchase price of an asset is to be determined by adding to the actual price paid any expenses incidental to its acquisition.

(2) The production cost of an asset is to be determined by adding to the purchase price of the raw materials and consumables used the amount of the costs incurred by the company which are directly attributable to the production of that asset.

(3) In addition, there may be included in the production cost of an asset:

(a) a reasonable proportion of the costs incurred by the company which are only indirectly attributable to the production of that asset, but only to the extent that they relate to the period of production; and

(b) interest on capital borrowed to finance the production of that asset, to the extent that it accrues in respect of the period of production;

provided, however, in a case within paragraph (b), that the inclusion of the interest in determining the cost of that asset and the amount of the interest so included is disclosed in a note to the accounts. (Para. 27, Sch. 1 to The Large and Medium-sized Companies and Groups (Accounts and Reports) Regulations 2008 (SI 2008/410).)

The issue of cost measurement is addressed in FRS 15. Its requirements are, in places, slightly more restrictive than the statutory provisions.

The key requirements of the FRS are:

A tangible fixed asset should initially be measured at its cost.

Costs, but only those costs, that are directly attributable to bringing the asset into working condition for its intended use should be included in its measurement. (Paras. 6 and 7, FRS 15.)

This effectively prohibits the addition of some of the indirect costs that are allowed (but not required) to be included in the cost of a fixed asset under statute. By contrast, SSAP 9 requires the inclusion of indirect production overhead in the cost of an item of manufactured stock. This apparent inconsistency between FRS 15 in relation to the cost of a fixed asset and SSAP 9 in relation to the cost of stock is highlighted where a company capitalises as a fixed asset an item which was classified as stock at the time of its manufacture. Neither FRS 15, nor UITF Abstract 5 *Transfers from Current Assets to Fixed Assets* addresses this point. Therefore, it appears that, to comply with FRS 15, when such an item is transferred from current assets to fixed assets, the indirect production costs previously included in the cost of the item of stock, but which do not meet the FRS 15 criteria for inclusion in the cost of a fixed asset, should be written off.

FRS 15 states that directly attributable costs are the labour costs of own employees and the incremental costs to the company that would have been avoided only if the tangible fixed asset had not been constructed or acquired. The FRS points out that administration and other general overhead costs and employee costs not related to the specific asset are not directly attributable costs. It also provides examples of directly attributable costs:

- acquisition costs (including items such as stamp duty);
- the cost of site preparation and clearance;
- initial delivery and handling costs;
- installation costs;
- professional fees (such as legal, architects' and engineers' fees), and
- the present value of the estimated cost of dismantling and removing the asset and restoring the site, to the extent that it is recognised as a provision under FRS 12 *Provisions, Contingent Liabilities and Contingent Assets*.

FRS 15 states that abnormal costs (eg those relating to design errors, wasted resources or industrial disputes) should be excluded from the cost of assets. This is consistent with the approach adopted by SSAP 9 in relation to stocks. FRS 15 also states that operating losses that occur because a revenue activity has been suspended during the construction of a tangible fixed asset are not directly attributable costs.

FRS 15 contains specific requirements on the treatment of start-up or commissioning costs:

> The costs associated with a start-up or commissioning period should be included in the cost of the tangible fixed asset only where the asset is available for use but incapable of operating at normal levels without such a start-up or commissioning period. (Para. 14, FRS 15.)

The standard distinguishes between essential start-up and commissioning periods (when the asset is incapable of operating normally) and other periods prior to profitable commercial use. If a company builds a new production line, there may be a period during which the line needs to run at zero or low capacity simply in order for it to be tested. Commercially, the line is incapable of normal use even though it is physically complete. Therefore, the commissioning and start-up costs in this period should be capitalised. This contrasts with the situation where an asset is capable of operating normally, but does not do so initially because demand for the product produced or service provided by the asset has not yet built up. In this context, the FRS gives examples of hotels and bookshops which could operate at normal levels almost immediately, but where demand will build up slowly with full utilisation or sales levels being achieved only over a period of several months.

Prior to FRS 15, some companies tried to defer some of their initial costs in loss-making periods on the basis that the unprofitable periods were a necessary stage before they could operate profitably. This was effectively a use of the matching concept, on the basis that the costs associated with an asset should be matched with the revenues that the asset is used to generate. FRS 15 does not accept the matching argument and so does not permit such costs to be included in the cost of a tangible fixed asset. To further clarify the treatment of start-up costs in general, UITF Abstract 24 *Accounting for start-up costs* was issued in June 2000. As with all UITF abstracts, reporting entities applying the FRSSE are exempt, although the FRSSE contains the same basic rule as UITF 24. As a result, there should be no differences between larger and smaller companies as to whether start-up costs can be treated as assets.

Start-up costs are defined in Abstract 24 to include costs arising from one-time activities related to opening a new facility, introducing a new product or service, conducting business in a new territory, conducting business with a new class of customer, initiating a new process in an existing facility, starting a new operation and similar items. They also include relocation and reorganisation costs relating to part or all of an entity, costs related to organising a new entity, and expenses and losses incurred both before and after opening.

Abstract 24 requires that:

- start-up costs should be accounted for on a basis consistent with the accounting treatment of similar costs incurred as part of the entity's ongoing activities, and
- in cases where there are no such similar costs, start-up costs that do not meet the criteria for recognition as assets under a relevant accounting standard, such as FRS 10, FRS 15 or SSAP 13, should be recognised as an expense when they are incurred; they should not be carried forward as an asset. In the case of companies adopting the FRSSE, the test is whether items can be treated as assets in accordance with other provisions of that standard.

Where start-up costs meet the definition of exceptional items in FRS 3, they should be disclosed in accordance with that standard. The UITF also encourages entities to give additional disclosures regarding start-up costs in accordance with the ASB Statement *Operating and Financial Review*.

It is worth noting that the logic of UITF 24 (and FRS 15) is consistent with that of FRS 18 *Accounting Policies*. FRS 18 redefined the concept of accruals such that it no longer includes any direct reference to matching.

Potential impact of the FRSME

The basic rules on the determination of costs under the FRSME, whilst expressed in a very different way to those in FRS 15, will normally lead to precisely the same result.

11.2.4 Period of construction

FRS 15 contains specific requirements on when capitalisation should cease and on the treatment of start-up or commissioning costs:

> Capitalisation of directly attributable costs should cease when substantially all the activities that are necessary to get the tangible fixed asset ready for use are complete, even if the asset has not yet been brought into use. (Para. 12, FRS 15.)

The FRS goes on to state that the asset is ready for use when physical construction is complete. For example, a property development may be complete and available for letting even though tenants have not yet moved in. As with commissioning periods, this requirement is intended to avoid companies including costs for periods during which the asset was available for use even though it was not actually being used, or fully used.

This section of the FRS, perhaps surprisingly, does not deal with the issue of assets that can easily be sub-divided and may be available for use in parts. We consider that, in this case, a similar treatment to that required by FRS 15 for borrowing costs should be adopted. This means that a divisible asset should be considered as a group of separate assets and capitalisation should cease in respect of each part as it becomes available for use, even though other parts of the overall project may be unfinished.

11.2.5 Finance costs

As shown above, statute allows the capitalisation of interest and other finance costs where an asset is constructed, but does not require this. However, the legislation lacks detail and is of very little value in determining which accounting treatment is appropriate. It seems sensible that the requirement that the asset should be produced, rather than purchased, should be interpreted with respect to the substance of the transaction. For example, construction could include construction by contractors, as well as by the company itself. Items should be treated as constructed for this purpose if they are made to the company's requirements, rather than purchased in their existing form.

On this interpretation, where an asset is purchased and then altered, borrowing costs could be capitalised on the alteration costs, but not on the initial purchase. This principle has now been incorporated into FRS 15.

When the ASB first addressed the issue of the capitalisation of borrowing costs they made it clear that they wished capitalisation to be either prohibited or mandatory. They were not happy with the statutory approach which allows but does not require it. Despite this, the ASB accepted that capitalisation should remain optional. This is on the basis that prohibition is not a widely supported approach, but if capitalisation is to be mandatory then the issue of notional borrowing costs must be addressed. In commercial terms, lost interest (opportunity cost) is just as real a cost as interest paid. Yet the current framework for accounting does not allow for notional borrowing costs, and there is no consensus as to how the framework could be developed to deal with such costs.

As a result, FRS 15 has retained the option of capitalisation, rather than mandating or prohibiting it, but does require consistency of treatment once a policy has been determined:

> Where an entity adopts a policy of capitalising finance costs, finance costs that are directly attributable to the construction of tangible fixed assets should be capitalised as part of the cost of those assets. The total amount of finance costs capitalised during a period should not exceed the total amount of finance costs incurred during that period. (Para. 19, FRS 15.)

> An entity need not capitalise finance costs. However, if an entity adopts a policy of capitalisation of finance costs, then it should be applied consistently to all tangible fixed assets where finance costs fall to be capitalised in accordance with the above requirement. (Para. 20, FRS 15.)

The definition of finance costs in FRS 15 was originally based on that in FRS 4, *Capital Instruments*. As a result of the issue of FRS 25, *Financial Instruments: Presentation*, the reference to FRS 4 has been removed but the definition itself remains unchanged.

Where a company does adopt a policy of capitalisation, FRS 15 provides much more specific requirements than are contained in the statutory instruments supporting the Companies Act. These are largely based on the international standard IAS 23 *Borrowing Costs*, although the treatment is not the same as that which applies under the version of the international standard now in force. IAS 23, until 1 January 2009, was very similar to UK practice since, like FRS 15, it allowed capitalisation of interest, but did not require it. However, IAS 23 was revised. With effect for accounting periods beginning on or after 1 January 2009, it makes a policy of capitalisation of qualifying interest mandatory.

Directly attributable finance costs, like all other directly attributable costs, are those that would not have been incurred if the fixed asset had not been constructed.

The finance costs capitalised may be in respect of borrowings specifically to finance the asset or general borrowings of the company.

Where the company has borrowed funds specifically to finance the construction of a tangible fixed asset, the amount of finance costs capitalised is limited to the actual costs incurred on the borrowings during the period in respect of expenditures to date on that asset.

In many cases, the company may not undertake specific borrowings to finance the production of a fixed asset, but may finance it out of the company's general borrowings. Where this is done, FRS 15 states that the company should calculate a capitalisation rate based on the weighted average borrowing costs which the company incurred in the period, in proportion to the borrowings outstanding in the period. The borrowings used for this purpose exclude any borrowings which are specifically for the finance of other fixed asset constructions, and which therefore are being taken into account independently, or which are for other specific purposes such as hedging foreign investments. The capitalisation rate should then be applied to the weighted average carrying amount of the asset during the period. In the past, it has been common practice for companies to apply capitalisation to tranches of expenditure in the period, but this will arrive at precisely the same result. An illustration of the capitalisation of interest paid from general borrowings is given below.

EXAMPLE

A company with a 31 December year end finances the construction of a tangible fixed asset from its general borrowings. The amount of capitalised expenditure on the asset is given in row 1. The amount brought forward from the previous year (including interest) is £2,000. The balances of capitalised expenditure (excluding interest) during the year are: at 1 April £5,000; at 1 July £6,000; at 1 October £10,000; at 31 December £12,000.

The company's general borrowings are given in row 5. They stand at £10,000 on 1 January. The subsequent balances are: at 1 April £8,000; at 1 July £9,000; at 1 October £12,000; at 31 December £14,000. Borrowing costs over each quarter, shown in row 6, are £300, £280, £342 and £480 respectively.

		Annual average	*1 Jan b/f*	*1 April*	*1 July*	*1 Oct*	*31 Dec c/f*
1	Capitalised expenditure	5,750	2,000	5,000	6,000	10,000	12,000
2	Weights			0.25	0.25	0.25	0.25	
	Capitalised interest for the year						206
	Total						12,206
3	Tranches	5,750	2,000	3,000	1,000	4,000	2,000
4	Weights		1	0.75	0.5	0.25	
5	Total borrowings outstanding		10,000	8,000	9,000	12,000	14,000
6	Borrowing costs during the period		300	280	342	480	
7	Capitalisation rate	0.0358	0.03.	0.035	0.038	0.04.	

Interest capitalisation costs for the year, £206, are calculated by multiplying:

- the annual average balance of expenditure, £5,750, by
- the annual average capitalisation rate, 0.0358.

The costs are then added to the other capitalised expenditure, £12,000, to be carried forward to the next year. The details of the calculations are as follows.

- *The annual average capitalised expenditure, £5,750*

  Since each of the balances £2,000, £5,000, £6,000 and £10,000 last for three months, the annual average is their time-weighted average, using weights in row 2.

  Alternatively, the average can be found from the tranches of expenditure, shown in row 3. The weights are shown in row 4: the initial balance of £2,000 remains for the whole year and has a weight of 1; similarly, the subsequent expenditure of £3,000 which takes place on 1 April has a weight of 0.75; the other expenditures of £1,000 and £4,000 have weights of 0.5 and 0.25 respectively.
- *The capitalisation rate, 0.0358*

  The capitalisation rate (row 7) for each quarter is given by dividing the borrowing costs (row 6) by the borrowings outstanding (row 5). The rates for each quarter are then averaged using the weights in row 2.

The borrowings that should be taken into account will vary, according to the way in which a company's or group's activities are financed. Where, for example, borrowings are undertaken separately by all of the companies in a group then each company should only take account of its own borrowings. Where funds are, in effect, pooled within a group and finance is thus considered on a group basis then a capitalisation rate may be determined at group level. In all cases, the intention is to ascertain a capitalisation rate which is a fair reflection of the costs that have been incurred in the financing of the asset construction, however that has been arranged.

Capitalisation of finance costs should only start when:

- finance costs are being incurred;
- expenditure is being made on the asset, and
- activities necessary to get the asset into use are in progress.

FRS 15 makes it clear that the activities referred to are wider than the actual construction. This means that, for example, where land is purchased and work has started on drawing up architect's plans and obtaining any necessary permits, then this would constitute relevant activities for the purpose of capitalisation. However, this condition is intended to prohibit companies from acquiring assets and then capitalising interest when they are merely holding the assets ready for use or development, rather than in the process of actually developing them.

Capitalisation should be suspended if there are any major periods during which the asset is not under construction. Such breaks in development may be planned (for example, where a company chooses to discontinue development as there is perceived shrinking demand) or may be externally imposed. However, FRS 15 requires that when such breaks arise, they should result in capitalisation of interest being suspended.

Capitalisation must cease when the asset is available for use, as with all other categories of cost that may be capitalised. Where an asset can be used in parts, then capitalisation should cease in respect of each part as that part is completed. FRS 15 illustrates this point by means of two contrasting situations. It cites a business park comprising several buildings, each of which can be used individually as an example of an asset of which parts are usable while construction continues on other parts. By contrast, an example of an asset that needs to be completed before any part can be used is an industrial plant involving several processes that are carried out in sequence at different parts of the plant within the same site, such as a steel mill.

FRS 15 includes the following disclosure requirements where a policy of capitalisation of finance costs is adopted:

> Where a policy of capitalisation of finance costs is adopted, the financial statements should disclose:
>
> (a) the accounting policy adopted;
> (b) the aggregate amount of finance costs included in the cost of tangible fixed assets;
> (c) the amount of finance costs capitalised during the period;
> (d) the amount of finance costs recognised in the profit and loss account during the period; and
> (e) the capitalisation rate used to determine the amount of finance costs capitalised during the period. (Para. 31, FRS 15.)

Potential impact of the FRSME

The FRSME prohibits the capitalisation of borrowing costs. For those entities, albeit few in number, that are regularly involved in the production of assets which take a long time to produce and where the costs of financing that production period can be substantial, this could lead to significant adjustments to their financial statements, both in terms of asset values and reported profits in periods in which such assets are being produced.

11.2.6   Subsequent expenditure

A common problem is that of additional expenditure on an asset or group of assets. There is often a far from clear dividing line between expenditure incurred to maintain the standard of an asset (repairs and maintenance) and an actual improvement or addition.

FRS 15 states that:

Subsequent expenditure to ensure that the tangible fixed asset maintains its previously assessed standard of performance should be recognised in the profit and loss account as it is incurred. (Para. 34, FRS 15.)

The standard points out that without such expenditure the depreciation expense would be increased because the useful economic life or residual value of the asset would be reduced.

FRS 15 identifies three circumstances in which subsequent expenditure should be capitalised:

   (a)   where the subsequent expenditure provides an enhancement of the economic benefits of the tangible fixed asset in excess of the previously assessed standard of performance.

   (b)   where a component of the tangible fixed asset that has been treated separately for depreciation purposes and depreciated over its individual useful economic life, is replaced or restored.

   (c)   where the subsequent expenditure relates to a major inspection or overhaul of a tangible fixed asset that restores the economic benefits of the asset that have been consumed by the entity and have already been reflected in depreciation. (Para. 36, FRS 15.)

The first situation would cover, for example, an extended life programme which would enable an asset to be used for considerably longer than had originally been expected. This involves such an alteration in the nature of the original asset that it warrants separate capitalisation. Similarly, if enhancements to an asset increase its productive capacity, then the additional costs incurred should be capitalised.

An example of the second situation would be the replacement of a roof on a building. A roof may have a shorter life than the remainder of the building and be considered a separate asset. Each time the roof is replaced this should be treated as a disposal, at nil proceeds, and the acquisition of a new asset. The guidance notes with the FRS point out that this treatment should only be adopted for items which are both relatively irregular (meaning at least less frequently than annually) and material. Where ongoing replacement and refurbishment takes place, the costs should be written off to the profit and loss account as incurred.

The third situation has been included in FRS 15 for consistency with FRS 12 *Provisions, Contingent Liabilities and Contingent Assets*, which is covered in Chapter 17. FRS 12 prohibited the previously common practice of setting up a provision for anticipated major inspection or overhaul costs which occur every few years, such as aircraft engine overhauls or drydocking of vessels. Instead of making a provision, FRS 12 states in its guidance notes that such expenditure should be capitalised and depreciated over the period to the next overhaul. This approach of capitalisation is formalised in FRS 15. A practical difficulty arises in that the first overhaul will not occur until several years into the asset's life. Therefore, when a new asset is purchased or constructed, the amount capitalised needs to be divided into the core asset and the cost of a deemed or 'built-in' overhaul. The latter element would normally be based on the estimated cost of the first overhaul, and would be depreciated over the period until that overhaul occurs, upon which it would be treated as a disposal and replaced by the actual cost of the overhaul.

Potential impact of the FRSME

The FRSME does not generally deal with the specific issue of subsequent expenditure on the basis that it contains principles which determine whether or not costs incurred qualify for recognition as items of property, plant and equipment, and are equally applicable whether it is the initial or subsequent expenditure that is being considered. It does make specific reference to the treatment of significant planned overhauls, and would not cause any significant change in this area.

11.2.7   Assets purchased in a foreign currency

Where an asset is purchased in a foreign currency, it is the exchange rate at the date on which the transaction is originally recorded that should be used for calculating the cost of the asset. If the exchange rate on this date differs from that on the invoice date, the exchange gain or loss should be taken directly to the profit and loss account. It should not be treated as an addition to, or deduction from, the cost of the asset.

11.2.8   The FRSSE

The FRSSE incorporates a simplified version of FRS 15's requirements relating to the cost of tangible fixed assets.

The FRSSE incorporates the basic requirement that a tangible fixed asset should initially be measured at its cost, then written down to its recoverable amount if necessary. The FRSSE also states that only costs that are directly attributable to bringing the tangible fixed asset into working condition for its intended use should be included in the cost of an asset. However, the FRSSE omits the detailed FRS 15 requirements relating to the costs to be included or excluded and makes no reference to start-up or commissioning periods.

In common with FRS 15, the FRSSE permits an accounting policy of capitalising finance costs. Where such a policy is adopted, the FRSSE requires that finance costs that are directly attributable to the construction of tangible fixed assets should be capitalised as part of the cost of those assets. The total amount of finance costs capitalised during a period should not exceed the total amount of finance costs incurred during that period. The FRSSE makes no reference to specific or general borrowings or to the use of a capitalisation rate.

The FRSSE requires that capitalisation of directly attributable costs, including finance costs, should be suspended during extended periods in which active development is interrupted. Capitalisation should cease when substantially all the activities that are necessary to get the tangible fixed asset ready for use are complete, even if the asset has not yet been brought into use.

The FRSSE contains slightly simpler rules than FRS 15 regarding subsequent expenditure, by omitting any reference to major inspection or overhaul of assets.

11.3   DEPRECIATION OF TANGIBLE FIXED ASSETS

Whether assets should be depreciated, and if so, the method which should be chosen depends on the rationale underlying the concept of depreciation. In simple terms, there are four major justifications for depreciation:

- the allocation of the original cost of an asset over its estimated useful life;
- the measurement of loss in value during the period;
- to provide a current valuation in the balance sheet, and
- to provide for the maintenance of the company's capital.

In many circumstances, all of the rationales will lead to the same decision concerning whether to depreciate an asset or not. However, there will be some circumstances in which the decision will be affected.

Potential impact of the FRSME

The basic requirement for depreciation is the same in both the FRS 15 and the FRSME, and in many cases the result of applying both standards would be precisely the same. There are some differences between the standards and these are dealt with separately below.

11.3.1   The requirement for depreciation

Depreciation is required for virtually all fixed assets unless, like land, they have an infinite useful economic life. Under the Companies Act 2006:

> In the case of any fixed asset which has a limited useful economic life, the amount of
>
> (a)   its purchase price or production cost; or
> (b)   where it is estimated that any such asset will have a residual value at the end of the period of its useful economic life, its purchase price or production cost less that estimated residual value;
>
> must be reduced by provisions for depreciation calculated to write off that amount systematically over the period of the asset's useful economic life. (Para. 18, Sch. 1 to The Large and Medium-sized Companies and Groups (Accounts and Reports) Regulations 2008 (SI 2008/410) and Para. 18, Sch. 1 to The Small

Companies and Groups (Accounts and Directors' Report) Regulations 2008 (SI 2008/409).)

In some cases even land should be deemed not to have an infinite useful economic life, such as land which is subject to depletion by the extraction of minerals.

The need for depreciation is not always seen as obvious. One of the problems that has been faced by those dealing with depreciation has been that of assets which have been increasing in value. Most people who disagree with depreciation in these cases would seek to rely on the exact wording of the Companies Act, arguing that the residual value of these assets will exceed the purchase price or production cost, and therefore there is no amount which needs to be depreciated.

Unfortunately, the ASC (the predecessor body to the ASB) created much of the problem themselves with the original SSAP 12 (the standard which dealt with depreciation prior to FRS 15) and again when they issued the exposure draft which eventually became the revised SSAP 12. In their definition of depreciation they included the phrase 'fall in value', and stated that this was one of the reasons why depreciation was required. The seemingly obvious corollary of this was that depreciation need not be provided if an asset were increasing rather than falling in value. The draft also mentioned that there might be cases in which an asset were maintained to such a standard as not to require depreciation and that it might be appropriate in some circumstances to reinstate fully depreciated assets. By the time the exposure draft became the revised standard the ASC had clarified their own thoughts on the matter, and provided the following definition of depreciation:

> ... the measure of the wearing out, consumption or other reduction in the useful economic life of a fixed asset whether arising from use, effluxion of time or obsolescence through technological or market changes. (Para. 10, SSAP 12.)

No mention was made of fall in value. Indeed, there was no mention of value. All reference to assets maintained at such a high level as to make depreciation inappropriate were omitted. The revised definition of depreciation showed that, in the opinion of the ASC at least, it was nothing more than a specific application of the accruals concept (as then defined in SSAP 2). The original cost of an asset was to be spread over its life; or, put another way, the cost of the asset was to be matched with the benefits to which it had given rise.

The ASB has included a very similar definition of depreciation in FRS 15 to that provided by the ASC in SSAP 12:

> The measure of the cost or revalued amount of the economic benefits of the tangible fixed asset that have been consumed during the period.

> Consumption includes the wearing out, using up or other reduction in the useful economic life of a tangible fixed asset whether arising from use, effluxion of time

or obsolescence through either changes in technology or demand for the goods and services produced by the asset. (Para. 2, FRS 15.)

The ASB has very clearly decided that the need for depreciation is based on the cost of using assets, and that changes in value are not relevant:

> The fundamental objective of depreciation is to reflect in operating profit the cost of use of the tangible fixed assets (ie amount of economic benefits consumed) in the period. This requires a charge to operating profit even if the asset has risen in value or been revalued. (Para. 78, FRS 15.)

Statute does give one case in which depreciation, and most of the other normal rules concerning fixed assets, can be ignored:

> Subject to sub-paragraph (2), assets which fall to be included:
>
> (a)   amongst the fixed assets of a company under the item "tangible assets"; or
> (b)   . . .
>
> may be included at a fixed quantity and value.

> Sub-paragraph (1) applies to assets of a kind which are constantly being replaced, where:
>
> (a)   their overall value is not material to assessing the company's state of affairs; and
> (b)   their quantity, value and composition are not subject to material variation. (Para. 26, Sch. 1 to The Large and Medium-sized Companies and Groups (Accounts and Reports) Regulations 2008 (SI 2008/410) and Para. 26, Sch. 1 to The Small Companies and Groups (Accounts and Directors' Report) Regulations 2008 (SI 2008/409).)

The revaluation of an asset does not eliminate the requirement that it should be depreciated, if it has a limited useful economic life. As the Companies Act 2006 states:

> Where the value of any asset of a company is determined on any basis . . . [under the alternative accounting rules] . . . that value must be, or (as the case may require) be the starting point for determining, the amount to be included in respect of that asset in the company's accounts, instead of its purchase price or production cost or any value previously so determined for that asset;

> The depreciation rules apply accordingly in relation to any such asset with the substitution for any reference to its purchase price or production cost of a reference to the value most recently determined for that asset on any basis mentioned . . . [under the alternative accounting rules] (Para. 33, Sch. 1 to The Large and Medium-sized Companies and Groups (Accounts and Reports) Regulations 2008 (SI 2008/410) and Para. 33, Sch. 1 to The Small Companies and Groups (Accounts and Directors' Report) Regulations 2008 (SI 2008/409).)

Under statute it is permissible to split the depreciation in the profit and loss account between that attributable to the historical cost and that attributable to the amount of the revaluation. However, this is not an acceptable practice under FRS 15 or the FRSSE.

Nonetheless, the amount of the additional depreciation as a result of the revaluation can be transferred as a movement on reserves, between the revaluation reserve and the profit and loss account. This will mean that the profit and loss account has been diminished only to the extent of cumulative depreciation on the historic cost.

FRED 17 (the exposure draft that preceded FRS 15) proposed that the additional depreciation charge following a revaluation should not only affect future years, but the current year also, even when the revaluation occurred at the year end. The rationale for this was that the profit and loss account should be consistent with the balance sheet. However, the proposal attracted adverse comment, as it would potentially have involved charging depreciation based on a value at a point in time (such as the balance sheet date) subsequent to that over which the year's depreciation had accrued. In FRS 15, the ASB modified its earlier proposal:

> Where an asset has been revalued the current period's depreciation charge is based on the revalued amount and the remaining useful economic life. Ideally, the average value of the asset for the period should be used to calculate the depreciation charge. In practice, however, either the opening or closing balance may be used instead, provided that it is used consistently each period. (Para. 79, FRS 15.)

This means that, unusually for an FRS, considerable flexibility of approach is permitted. Where a closing (or average) valuation is used as the basis for the year's depreciation charge, it is unclear whether this should also be based on the life remaining at the year end (or midway through the year). In our view, as depreciation accrues over the year, we believe it is best to use the remaining useful economic life as at the start of the year, regardless of whether the opening, closing or average valuation is used as the basis of calculation.

Prior to FRS 15, the approach would have been to charge the year's depreciation based on the book value during the year. It is likely that most companies will do this, especially when asset values are rising, as this is likely to lead to the lowest reported charge in the profit and loss account.

In FRS 15, the ASB has addressed the impact of subsequent expenditure on the need for depreciation:

> Subsequent expenditure on a tangible fixed asset that maintains or enhances the previously assessed standard of performance of the asset does not negate the need to charge depreciation. (Para. 86, FRS 15.)

The ASB points out that it is assumed when calculating the useful economic life of an asset that subsequent expenditure will be undertaken to maintain the previously assessed standard of performance. Without such expenditure the depreciation expense would be increased because the useful economic life or residual value of the asset would be reduced. Where the subsequent expenditure is capitalised, the ASB accepts that this may extend the useful economic life but points out that this extension cannot be indefinite and does not negate the need to charge depreciation.

FRS 15 also introduced a formal requirement for 'component depreciation':

> Where the tangible fixed asset comprises two or more major components with substantially different useful economic lives, each · component should be accounted for separately for depreciation purposes and depreciated over its individual useful economic life. (Para. 83, FRS 15.)

With large or complex assets, it is therefore necessary to consider whether the asset as a whole will be consumed at the same rate or whether some parts will have a shorter life than others. In the latter case, those components should be depreciated over their individual lives. However, this requirement is intended to apply only to major components that will be replaced relatively infrequently. Routine maintenance should not be treated as a separate component of the asset. Where a component is replaced, this is then treated as a disposal and replacement asset, under the FRS 15 requirements relating to subsequent expenditure, which were covered earlier in this chapter.

Potential impact of the FRSME

The FRSME contains similar requirements in relation to components, albeit that they are couched in quite different terms.

11.3.2 Depreciation of buildings

For many years, the depreciation of buildings has been a controversial issue. The ASC included the following statement in SSAP 12.

> Buildings are no different from other fixed assets, in that they have a limited useful economic life, albeit usually significantly longer than that of other types of assets. They should, therefore, be depreciated having regard to the same criteria. (Para. 24, SSAP 12.)

In spite of this statement, many companies do not currently depreciate their buildings. The main reason companies give is that they maintain them to such a standard that no depreciation is required. Other reasons given are that frequent revaluation renders the charging of depreciation of little value, that the market value exceeds the book value and that the amount of depreciation is not material.

The ASB proposed in FRED 17 that the grounds for non-depreciation of buildings outlined above were unacceptable and that buildings should always be depreciated. This proposal met with considerable hostility, partly because it was seen to lack commercial realism, but also because it appeared inconsistent with FRS 10, in which the ASB had recently permitted non-amortisation of goodwill and intangible assets.

The ASB, therefore, modified its stance and has included the following in FRS 15:

> For tangible fixed assets other than non-depreciable land, the only grounds for not charging depreciation are that the depreciation charge and accumulated depreciation are immaterial. The depreciation charge and accumulated depreciation are immaterial if they would not reasonably influence the decisions of a user of the accounts. (Para. 90, FRS 15.)

This statement is not itself specific to land and buildings, but is much less likely to apply to other categories of asset, although a potential example would be antique furniture or works of art included in fixtures and fittings.

FRS 15 also points out that the uncharged depreciation must not be material in aggregate as well as for each tangible fixed asset. Depreciation may be immaterial because of very long useful economic lives or high residual values (or both). The ASB has listed conditions in FRS 15 under which non-depreciation may be justified. These may be summarised as follows.

(1) The entity has a policy and practice of regular maintenance and repair (which is charged in the profit and loss account) such that the previously assessed standard of performance is maintained.

(2) The asset is unlikely to suffer from economic or technological obsolescence.

(3) Where estimated residual values are material:

    (a) the entity has a policy and practice of disposing of similar assets well before the end of their economic lives, and

    (b) the disposal proceeds of similar assets (after excluding the effect of price changes since the date of acquisition or last revaluation) have not been materially less than their carrying amounts.

The above conditions are most likely to apply to 'trophy assets' such as, for example, a high-class hotel in a highly-desirable area or a listed historic building.

The ASB has also included an additional requirement for impairment reviews in FRS 15:

> Tangible fixed assets, other than non-depreciable land, should be reviewed for impairment, in accordance with FRS 11, at the end of each reporting period when either:
>
> (a) no depreciation charge is made on the grounds that it would be immaterial (either because of the length of the estimated remaining useful economic life or because the estimated residual value of the tangible fixed asset is not materially different from the carrying amount of the asset); or
>
> (b) the estimated remaining useful economic life of the tangible fixed asset exceeds 50 years. (Para. 89, FRS 15.)

This is broadly consistent with FRS 10's approach for intangible assets and goodwill, although FRS 10 mandates annual reviews where useful economic lives exceed 20 years rather than 50 years.

Potential impact of the FRSME

This is not addressed specifically in the FRSME, but in practice there may be little change in accounting. This is because the same basic principle of using residual values in determining the depreciable amount applies under the FRSME, and where the residual value is very high, then the amount of appropriate depreciation may be low. The FRSME also requires residual values to be re-estimated where there is an indication that they may have changed significantly. In some cases, the residual values may have risen.

11.3.3   Methods of depreciation

FRS 15 contains the following requirement:

> The depreciable amount of a tangible fixed asset should be allocated on a systematic basis over its useful economic life. The depreciation method used should reflect as fairly as possible the pattern in which the asset's economic benefits are consumed by the entity. The depreciation charge for each period should be recognised as an expense in the profit and loss account unless it is permitted to be included in the carrying amount of another asset. (Para. 77, FRS 15.)

FRS 15 goes on to mention that the method chosen should result in a depreciation charge throughout the asset's useful economic life and not just towards the end of its useful economic life or when the asset is falling in value. The FRS mentions two methods of depreciation: straight-line and reducing balance and goes on to state that where the pattern of consumption of an asset's economic benefits is uncertain, a straight-line method of depreciation would usually be adopted.

FRS 15 provides a list of factors to consider in determining the useful economic life, residual value and depreciation method of an asset. These may be summarised as:

- the expected usage of the asset, assessed by reference to its expected capacity or physical output;
- the expected physical deterioration of the asset through use or effluxion of time;
- economic or technological obsolescence, for example arising from changes or improvements in production, or a change in the market demand for the product or service output of that asset, and
- legal or similar limits on the use of the asset, such as the expiry dates of related leases.

FRS 15 contains the following definition of residual value:

The net realisable value of an asset at the end of its useful economic life. Residual values are based on prices prevailing at the date of the acquisition (or revaluation) of the asset and do not take account of expected future price changes. (Para. 2, FRS 15.)

The estimate, therefore, needs to be made at the time that the asset is acquired or later, when it is revalued. In addition, the estimate should be made using current prices; the company should not attempt to estimate what the value is likely to be at the time of final disposal.

For example, if a company purchases a machine that is expected to last for five years, then the residual value should be based on the current price for such a machine which is five years old. This can of course be impossible where an asset is of a type that has not been in existence for the period of its estimated useful economic life. In such cases, the directors need to make an estimate of its value.

FRS 15 contains the following requirements relating to the review of both useful economic lives and residual values.

The useful economic life of a tangible fixed asset should be reviewed at the end of each reporting period and revised if expectations are significantly different from previous estimates. If a useful economic life is revised, the carrying amount of the tangible fixed asset at the date of revision should be depreciated over the revised remaining useful economic life. (Para. 93, FRS 15.)

Where the residual value is material it should be reviewed at the end of each reporting period to take account of reasonably expected technological changes based on prices prevailing at the date of acquisition (or revaluation). A change in its estimated residual value should be accounted for prospectively over the asset's remaining useful economic life, except to the extent that the asset has been impaired at the balance sheet date. (Para. 95, FRS 15.)

FRS 15 states that when residual value is revised, it should be restated in terms of the price level that existed when the asset was purchased (or revalued) where this is practicable. Events or changes in circumstances that cause the residual value to fall may also be indicative of an impairment of the asset, thus necessitating an impairment review in accordance with FRS 11.

There are no standard useful economic lives for particular types of fixed asset and each company needs to arrive at an estimate based on its own circumstances. The main test is that of reasonableness. For example, computer equipment should usually be written off over a short period, as it is not likely to be in use for many years. Buildings may be in use for a very long period, and may be written off over a period such as 50 years. The only time when the period is not a matter of judgement is where the life of the asset is known with certainty, as with a short lease.

Where there is a change in the estimate of the useful economic life of an asset, the net book value of the asset must be written off over the revised remaining useful economic life. The amount involved should not be material, or this is prima facie evidence that the company has not been complying with the requirement for regular reviews of asset lives.

An adjustment to asset lives should never be treated as giving rise to a prior year adjustment, as it is deemed to be a change in an accounting estimate and not a change in accounting policy or a fundamental error.

FRS 15 allows a change in the method of depreciation provided that it will give a fairer representation of the company's results and financial position. As with a revision of the economic life of the asset, such a change is not a change in accounting policy and therefore cannot be treated as a prior year adjustment. The net book value should be written off over the remaining useful economic life, starting with the year in which the change of depreciation method is adopted. The FRSSE contains a similar requirement.

EXAMPLE

A company has a fixed asset which it purchased seven years ago at a cost of £28,000.

It has been depreciated for six years on the basis of 15 per cent on the reducing balance.

It has now been decided that it should be written off on the straight-line basis over the four remaining years of its useful life.

The current carrying amount of the asset will be as follows:

	£
Cost	28,000
Depreciation year 1	(4,200)
Book value at end of year 1	23,800
Depreciation year 2	(3,570)
Book value at end of year 2	20,230
Depreciation year 3	(3,035)
Book value at end of year 3	17,195
Depreciation year 4	(2,579)
Book value at end of year 4	14,616
Depreciation year 5	(2,192)
Book value at end of year 5	12,424
Depreciation year 6	(1,864)
Book value at end of year 6	10,560

The balance at the end of the sixth year then needs to be written off over the next four years. The annual charge for depreciation will therefore be 10,560 (÷ 4 = £2,640).

The following methods are the most commonly used for calculating depreciation.

Straight line

This is the simplest method. The cost, less residual value, is written off in equal parts over the asset's life. The basic formula for the annual depreciation charge is:

$$\frac{\text{Original depreciable value of asset}}{\text{Total life of asset}}$$

For example, if an asset is purchased for £78,000, and is expected to last for eight years with a residual value of £5,000 then the depreciable amount is £78,000 − £5,000 = £73,000, giving an annual depreciation charge of £73,000/8 = £9,125.

Reducing balance

The main argument for this method is that the total cost of owning the asset is loaded towards the early years of the asset's life. As the depreciation charge starts to fall this is likely to be replaced by a higher cost for repairs and maintenance, and the benefit obtained from the asset will be reduced. In many cases, companies choose this method because it reflects falls in market value more accurately than straight line. This is not necessarily a good basis for a choice of accounting method. The formula for the annual charge is:

Current carrying value of asset × Percentage charge

In most cases the percentage depreciation rate to be applied is not calculated in order to arrive at any particular residual value at the end of the estimated useful economic life. The percentage chosen is often simply a reasonable figure estimated by the directors. Nonetheless, residual values (unless zero) can be used to calculate a reducing balance rate.

EXAMPLE

An asset is purchased for £78,000, and is expected to last for eight years. The residual value at the end of the period is expected to be £5,000.

In order to arrive at a residual value of £5,000 in eight years, the percentage charge p needs to be such that $£78,000 \times (1 - p)_8 = 5,000$.

Therefore, $(1 - p)_8 = 0.064102564$. This gives a value for $1 - p$ of 0.709348125, giving a value of p of roughly 29 per cent per annum on the reducing balance.

Where the residual value has not been calculated, which is the most common procedure in practice, the reducing balance percentage will simply be a rate felt to be reasonable by the directors.

Sum of the digits

This is a variation on the reducing balance method, with the same basic justification. The depreciation charge falls by a fixed amount each year. The basic formula for the annual depreciation is:

$$\frac{\text{Original value of asset} \times \text{Remaining life of asset} + 1}{(\text{Original life of asset} \times [\text{Original life of asset} + 1])/2}$$

EXAMPLE

An asset is purchased for £73,000 and is expected to last for eight years.

The denominator of the formula is $(8 \times 9)/2 = 36$

The depreciation over its life would be:

		£
Year 1	73,000 × 8/36 =	16,222
Year 2	73,000 × 7/36 =	14,194
Year 3	73,000 × 6/36 =	12,167
Year 4	73,000 × 5/36 =	10,139
Year 5	73,000 × 4/36 =	8,111
Year 6	73,000 × 3/36 =	6,083
Year 7	73,000 × 2/36 =	4,056
Year 8	73,000 × 1/36 =	2,028
Total		73,000

Double declining balance

As with reducing balance and sum of the digits, the depreciation charge reduces as the age of the asset increases.

The formula for the annual depreciation charge is:

$$\frac{(\text{Current asset value}) \times 2}{\text{Original life of asset}}$$

The figure of 2 could be changed to 3, to become the triple declining balance method (and so on).

Unit of production

The asset is written off in line with its estimated lifetime output. This is often appropriate for assets used in extractive industries. The formula is:

$$\frac{\text{Original value} \times \text{Value of annual output}}{\text{Expected lifetime value of output}}$$

Annuity method

In this method, account is taken of the cost of capital involved in the asset. The objective is that the total of the interest and depreciation charge for each year should be relatively constant. Therefore, when the asset is new, and the outstanding debt is high, the depreciation is low. The method could be appropriate for major items of fixed assets, where they are funded by external sources.

The fundamental problem with this method is that it is not clear why the estimate of capital consumption should be affected by the way in which the asset is financed. Therefore, the basis for this method of depreciation is weak. In addition, this method may be seen as imprudent, since it relies upon the assumption of future profitability.

The ASB clearly regards the annuity method of depreciation as unsatisfactory as many years ago it issued an exposure draft *Amendment to FRS 15 'Tangible fixed assets' and FRS 10 'Goodwill and intangible assets': Interest methods of depreciation.* This proposed limited amendments to prohibit the use of the annuity method or other interest methods of depreciation. The ASB proposed an exception to this prohibition where a tangible asset is leased out to another party under an operating lease. Even then, the ASB proposed to attach the following conditions to the use of interest methods of depreciation.

(1) The lease term must represent a significant portion of the useful economic life of the asset.

(2) It must be reasonably expected that, at any point in time during the lease term, the net present value of the future net cash inflows to be received by the lessor under the lease arrangement, together with the estimated net realisable value of the tangible fixed asset at the end of the lease term, will not be less than the carrying value of the tangible fixed asset.

(3) The terms and conditions of the lease must ensure that the lessee is unable to cancel the lease before the end of the lease term without the receipt by the lessor of adequate compensation.

The ASB also noted in the exposure draft that, in rare cases, it may be appropriate to adopt a method of depreciation that has the effect of back-end loading the depreciation charge, where it can be demonstrated that the resulting allocation of depreciation reflects the expected pattern of consumption of economic benefits, without regard to the time value of money.

The exposure draft has not been followed up, but this is probably because there is little evidence that such methods are commonly used, rather than that the ASB changed its mind about the principle.

Potential impact of the FRSME

It is unlikely that depreciation methods will change under the FRSME. However, in some cases, depreciable amounts may alter as the FRSME requires residual values to be altered where there is an indication that they may have changed significantly. Under FRS 15, residual values are only determined at the date an asset is acquired. (FRS 15 also requires current residual values to be used where an asset is revalued, but this will not be of any relevance under the FRSME as it prohibits revaluation.)

11.3.4 Renewals accounting

FRS 15 introduced new requirements in relation to renewals accounting, which was an area not previously specifically addressed by accounting standards. Renewals accounting is a method of providing for depreciation of an infrastructure system, such as a railway or pipeline network. Although some assets or components of an infrastructure system may be separately identifiable and therefore accounted for and depreciated over their useful economic lives, the remaining assets in the system may be, in effect, a single asset (the 'infrastructure asset'), which is continually being renewed to maintain its operation.

Renewals accounting involves treating the level of annual expenditure required to maintain the operating capacity of the infrastructure asset, as set out in an asset management plan, as the depreciation charged for the period. This charge is then deducted from the carrying amount of the asset (as part of accumulated depreciation). Actual expenditure is capitalised (as part of the cost of the asset) as incurred.

FRS 15 specifies the circumstances in which renewals accounting may be used as a method of estimating depreciation:

(a) the infrastructure asset is a system or network that as a whole is intended to be maintained at a specified level of service potential by the continuing replacement and refurbishment of its components; and

(b) the level of annual expenditure required to maintain the operating capacity (or service capability) of the infrastructure asset is calculated from an asset management plan that is certified by a person who is appropriately qualified and independent; and

(c) the system or network is in a mature or steady state. (Para. 97, FRS 15.)

The FRS states that evidence that a system or network is in a mature and steady state is provided when the annual cost of maintaining that system is relatively constant, and also points out that the carrying amount of that part of the infrastructure asset that is replaced or restored by the subsequent expenditure should be eliminated.

Under FRS 15, renewals accounting is not required; instead the expenditure to maintain the operating capacity of the infrastructure assets could be recognised in accordance with the requirements relating to subsequent expenditure, with depreciation being calculated in the conventional manner.

Potential impact of the FRSME

The FRSME does not deal with renewals accounting.

11.3.5   The FRSSE

The depreciation requirements in the FRSSE broadly follow those in FRS 15. The principal differences are that the FRSSE does not address non-depreciation, other than in relation to non-depreciable land, and does not explicitly require annual impairment reviews where the remaining useful economic life exceeds 50 years or where depreciation is omitted as immaterial. The FRSSE requires residual values and useful economic lives to be reviewed regularly rather than annually although the treatment of a revision is consistent with FRS 15. The FRSSE makes no reference to renewals accounting, as this is highly unlikely to be relevant to small companies.

11.4   REVALUATION OF TANGIBLE FIXED ASSETS

11.4.1   Companies Act 2006

Prior to the introduction of FRS 15, there was no accounting standard dealing with revaluations of tangible fixed assets in general, although SSAP 12, *Accounting for Depreciation*, did address the depreciation of revalued assets. Thus, the main source of guidance had been that contained in the alternative accounting rules in the Companies Act 1985, which have now been replaced by similar rules under the Companies Act 2006.

FRS 15 introduced extensive requirements relating to revaluations, which are covered separately below.

The revaluation of fixed assets is allowed by the alternative accounting rules of the Companies Act:

> Tangible fixed assets may be included at a market value determined as at the date of their last valuation or at their current cost. (Para. 32(2) Sch. 1 to The Large and Medium-sized Companies and Groups (Accounts and Reports) Regulations 2008 (SI 2008/410) and Para. 32(2) Sch. 1 to The Small Companies and Groups (Accounts and Directors' Report) Regulations 2008 (SI 2008/409).)

Where an asset is revalued, the amount of the revaluation, including depreciation previously charged and no longer required, should be credited to the revaluation reserve.

Where the value of the asset subsequently falls, the amount of the decrease in value should be taken from the revaluation reserve. If the amount of the fall in value exceeds the original amount of the revaluation then it is normal to deduct the excess from the profit and loss account. This can be seen in the following example. However, under statute it appears possible to reduce the revaluation reserve by more than the amount previously included in relation to a revalued asset, which may lead to a debit balance, providing the fall in value is expected to be temporary.

EXAMPLE

A company owns an asset. The net book value is currently £70; the original cost is £100 and the accumulated depreciation is £30. The asset is then revalued at £160. The increase of £90 is credited to the revaluation reserves; accumulated depreciation is set to zero and £60 is added to the value of the asset.

Subsequently, the asset is depreciated by £20, giving a net book value of £140. Consider the treatment of two situations in which the asset falls in value.

(1)   The asset is revalued to £90.

In this case, £50 will be debited to revaluation reserves; the depreciation set to zero and the asset value is reduced by £70.

(2)   The asset is revalued to £40.

In this case, the depreciation is set to zero and the asset value is reduced by £120. However, only £90 is debited to revaluation reserves since this is the amount of the original increase, and £10 is charged to profit and loss.

Once a revaluation has taken place, the use of the revaluation reserve is very limited:

An amount may be transferred:

(a)   from the revaluation reserve:

(i)   to the profit and loss account, if the amount was previously charged to that account or represents realised profit, or

(ii)   on capitalisation,

(b)   to or from the revaluation reserve in respect of the taxation relating to any profit or loss credited or debited to the reserve.

The revaluation reserve must be reduced to the extent that the amounts transferred to it are no longer necessary for the purposes of the valuation method used ...

The revaluation reserve must not be reduced except as mentioned in this paragraph. (Para. 35, (3) and (5) Sch. 1 to The Large and Medium-sized Companies and Groups (Accounts and Reports) Regulations 2008 (SI 2008/410) and Para. 35, (3) and (5) Sch. 1 to The Small Companies and Groups (Accounts and Directors' Report) Regulations 2008 (SI 2008/409).)

11.4.2   FRS 15 requirements in relation to revaluation

FRS 15 introduced far more rigour into revaluation practices in the UK than had previously existed. It does not eliminate the choice that companies have between stating their fixed assets at cost or at valuation. However, it does prohibit occasional revaluations and will eliminate the 'cherry-picking' that occurred previously, whereby companies either chose to revalue only when asset values were high or selected particular assets to revalue (for example, because their value had increased).

FRS 15 requires that companies which choose to revalue classes of asset do so on a regular basis. The intention behind this is that the carrying value should be the current value at the balance sheet date.

The principle underlying the ASB's approach is that of value to the business or 'deprival value'. Asset values should be based on the cost of replacing the economic benefits inherent in an asset were the company to be deprived of it. This approach is based on that set out in the ASB's *Statement of Principles for Financial Reporting*, and is also explained in Appendix IV to FRS 15. It may be shown diagrammatically. See below.

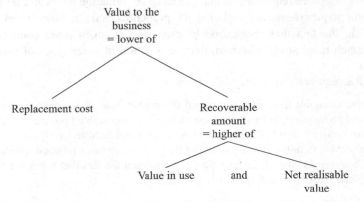

If a company is to continue in its existing business at its current or a greater volume, the value to the business of a tangible fixed asset will normally be its replacement cost, unless the asset is impaired, in which case its recoverable amount will be lower. Therefore, if the company were to be deprived of the asset, it would normally seek to replace its productive capacity or utility to the business. Therefore, 'replacement cost' means the cost of replacing the capability of the asset.

The determination of recoverable amount has already been addressed by the ASB in FRS 11, which is covered in a separate section of this chapter. FRS 15 focuses mainly on the method and frequency of valuations whereby a reasonable approximation to replacement cost may be obtained, without imposing an excessive burden on companies in terms of frequency or complexity of valuations.

The basic FRS 15 requirement in relation to revaluation is as follows:

> Tangible fixed assets should be revalued only where the entity adopts a policy of revaluation. Where such a policy is adopted then it should be applied to individual classes of tangible fixed assets (in accordance with paragraph 61), but need not be applied to all classes of tangible fixed assets held by the entity. (Para. 42, FRS 15.)

The FRS goes on to state that:

> Where a tangible fixed asset is subject to a policy of revaluation its carrying amount should be its current value as at the balance sheet date. (Para. 43, FRS 15.)

Current value is defined as:

> The current value of a tangible fixed asset to the business is the lower of replacement cost and recoverable amount. (Para. 2, FRS 15.)

FRS 15 does not provide a definition of 'replacement cost' as such. Instead, it provides extensive requirements and guidance on valuation bases and frequency. Different requirements are included for properties and for other fixed assets, reflecting the fact that revaluation of properties is much more common, and often much more straightforward, than revaluation of other types of asset.

The FRS requires consistency of treatment:

> Where a tangible fixed asset is revalued all tangible fixed assets of the same class should be revalued. In those rare cases where it is impossible to obtain a reliable valuation of an asset held outside the UK or the Republic of Ireland the asset may be excluded from the class of assets for the purposes of this paragraph. However, the carrying amount of the tangible fixed asset and the fact that it has not been revalued must be stated. (Para. 61, FRS 15.)

FRS 15 defines a class of tangible fixed assets as:

> A category of tangible fixed assets having a similar nature, function or use in the business of the entity. (Para. 2, FRS 15.)

FRS 15 restates the categories of tangible asset which are set out in statute, but goes on to point out that these are broad categories, and that a company may use narrower classes that meet the definition of a class of tangible fixed assets and are appropriate to their business. The FRS gives an example of the sub-categorisation of land and buildings into specialised properties, non-specialised properties and short leasehold properties.

For definitions of specialised properties and non-specialised properties, the FRS refers to definitions that were originally set out in technical material produced by the Royal Institution of Chartered Surveyors (RICS). In broad terms, specialised properties are ones with a very specific use and which, as a result, are not normally sold for continuous use in the same type of business, for example oil refineries, chemical works, dock installations, schools, hospitals, and properties of an abnormal size, specification or location such that there would be no ready market for them. The RICS definitions are no longer current, but there is little evidence that this causes problems in practice.

Potential impact of the FRSME

The FRSME would cause a complete change in this area; it prohibits revaluation of property, plant and equipment. This renders all of the guidance in FRS 15, on the detail of revaluation, redundant.

11.4.3 Frequency of valuations

FRS 15 does not require a full formal valuation each year, but does set out the following requirements for various types of asset.

(1) *Properties:*

    (a) full valuation every five years, with an interim valuation in year three, and in other years where it is likely that there has been a material change in value, or

    (b) rolling valuation of the portfolio on a five-year basis, with interim valuations on the remaining four-fifths of the portfolio where it is likely that there has been a material change in value (this approach is appropriate only where the property portfolio either consists of a number of broadly similar properties likely to be affected by the same market factors, or can be divided on a continuing basis into five groups of a broadly similar spread).

(2) *Other tangible fixed assets:*

    (a) for assets, for example company cars, where there is an active second-hand market or where an appropriate index exists, annually by the directors (the index must be appropriate to the class of asset, its location and condition, and take into account technological change; and have a proven record of regular publication and use and be expected to be available in the foreseeable future), otherwise

    (b) valuation should be performed by a qualified valuer at least every five years, with an update in year three, also performed by a qualified valuer and, in addition, the valuation should be updated in the intervening years where it is likely that there has been a material change in value (if a qualified internal valuer is used for the five-yearly valuation, the valuation should be subject to review by a qualified external valuer).

FRS 15 also provides considerable detail on what is expected of full and interim valuations of properties:

A full valuation of a property normally involves, inter alia, the following:

(a) detailed inspection of the interior and exterior of the property (on an initial valuation this will involve detailed measurement of floor space etc, but this would need to be reperformed in future full valuations only if there was evidence of a physical change to the buildings);

(b) inspection of the locality;

(c) enquiries of the local planning and similar authorities;

(d) enquiries of the entity or its solicitors; and

(e) research into market transactions in similar properties, identification of market trends, and the application of these to determine the value of the property under consideration. (Para. 47, FRS 15.)

A full valuation of a property is conducted by either:

(a) a qualified external valuer; or

(b) a qualified internal valuer, provided that the valuation has been subject to review by a qualified external valuer. The review involves the valuation of a sample of the entity's properties by the external valuer and comparison with the internal valuer's figures leading to expression of opinion on the overall accuracy of the valuation, based upon analysis of this sample. The external valuer must be satisfied that the sample represents a genuine cross-section of the entity's portfolio. (Para. 48, FRS 15.)

An interim valuation of a property is conducted by a qualified (external or internal) valuer and consists of:

(a) research into market transactions in similar properties, identification of market trends, and the application of these to determine the value of the property under consideration (as in paragraph 47(e));

(b) confirmation that there have been no changes of significance to the physical buildings, the legal rights, or local planning considerations; and

(c) an inspection of the property or the locality by the valuer to the extent that this is regarded as professionally necessary, having regard to all the circumstances of the case, including recent changes to the property or the locality and the date on which the valuer previously inspected the property. (Para. 49, FRS 15.)

Furthermore, FRS 15 also defines qualified internal and external valuers:

A person conducting the valuation who holds a recognised and relevant professional qualification and having recent post-qualification experience, and sufficient knowledge of the state of the market, in the location and category of the tangible fixed asset being valued. An internal valuer is a director, officer or employee of the entity. An external valuer is not an internal valuer and does not have a significant financial interest in the entity. (Para. 2, FRS 15.)

The FRS provides such a level of detail as to leave little scope for judgement or discretion on the part of management. Although many companies which revalue their assets do use the services of qualified valuers, the frequency of valuations required by FRS 15 may be considerably greater than companies would otherwise wish, thus potentially increasing the cost of revaluations. This may deter some companies from maintaining a policy of revaluations.

The main area where some judgement may be required concerns what constitutes a 'material change in value' requiring a valuation in a year where one would not normally be undertaken. Even here, FRS 15 is not silent, although its guidance borders on stating the obvious:

> A material change in value is a change in value that would reasonably influence the decisions of a user of the accounts. In assessing whether a material change in value is likely, the combined impact of all relevant factors (eg physical deterioration in the property, general movements in market prices in the area etc) should be considered. (Para. 52, FRS 15.)

11.4.4 Basis of valuations

FRS 15 also specifies the basis of valuations:

> The following valuation bases should be used for revalued properties that are not impaired:
>
> (a) non-specialised properties should be valued on the basis of existing use value (EUV), with the addition of notional directly attributable acquisition costs where material. Where the open market value (OMV) is materially different from EUV, the OMV and the reasons for the difference should be disclosed in the notes to the accounts.
> (b) specialised properties should be valued on the basis of depreciated replacement cost.
> (c) properties surplus to an entity's requirements should be valued on the basis of OMV, with expected directly attributable selling costs deducted where material. (Para. 53, FRS 15.)

Again, in relation to properties, the FRS has drawn on technical material that was originally produced by RICS for the definitions of existing use value (EUV) and open market value (OMV). In many cases, EUV and OMV will be similar. Differences may arise due, for example, to planning restrictions which prevent another occupier from using the property in a different manner, or because a property may have a greater value if converted or redeveloped for other uses. The definitions used in FRS 15 are no longer current under the RICS guidance, although as noted above there is little indication that this gives rise to substantial problems in practice.

Notional directly attributable acquisition costs should be taken into account, where they are material, because, if the company were to purchase the property at its valuation, these costs would still be incurred and would be capitalised under the FRS 15 provisions dealing with the measurement of an asset's cost. Notional directly attributable acquisition costs include normal dealing costs, such as professional fees, non-recoverable taxes and duties. They do not include enhancement expenditure, such as site improvements, costs involved in obtaining planning consent, the cost of site preparation and clearance, or other costs that would already be reflected in EUV.

The FRS also deals with properties that are bought and sold, and therefore valued as businesses. The EUV of such properties takes account of trading potential, but excludes personal goodwill created by the present owner or management, which is not expected to remain with the business in the event of the property being sold.

A practical problem arises with non-specialised properties where the owning company adapts the basic property to suit its particular needs. For example, a retailer may purchase a bare shop and fit its own signs, frontage and fittings, and make structural changes to meet its requirements. These 'adaptation works' would be of little or no value to any other purchaser of the property. In such cases, FRS 15 states that the adaptation works and shell of the property may be treated separately, with only the shell of the property revalued using EUV. In such a case, the adaptation works are held at depreciated replacement cost or depreciated historical cost.

Because of the nature of specialised properties, a market value is not available and they are therefore valued at depreciated replacement cost. Again, in the case of properties, FRS 15 refers to original RICS guidance for a detailed definition. The FRS states that the objective of depreciated replacement cost is to make a realistic estimate of the current cost of constructing an asset that has the same service potential as the existing asset.

For tangible assets other than properties, FRS 15 contains far less detail on valuation bases, as such assets are revalued by a much smaller proportion of companies than are properties. FRS 15 does, however, include the following specific requirement.

> Tangible fixed assets other than properties should be valued using market value, where possible. Where market value is not obtainable, assets should be valued on the basis of depreciated replacement cost. (Para. 59, FRS 15.)

The FRS states that notional directly attributable acquisition costs should be added to market value where material. For other tangible fixed assets that are surplus to requirements, expected selling costs should be deducted if material. Where market value is not obtainable, depreciated replacement cost should be used, with the assistance of a qualified valuer. The reference in the FRS to a qualified valuer is likely to deter many businesses from revaluing tangible assets other than properties, on grounds of cost, unless market values are ascertainable or current values are particularly significant to users of the accounts.

FRS 15 defines depreciated replacement cost as:

> The cost of replacing an existing tangible fixed asset with an identical or substantially similar new asset having a similar production or service capacity, from which appropriate deductions are made to reflect the value attributable to the

remaining portion of the total useful economic life of the asset and the residual value at the end of the asset's useful economic life.

Costs directly attributable to bringing the tangible fixed asset into working condition for its intended use, such as costs of transport, installation, commissioning, consultants' fees, non-recoverable taxes and duties, are included in depreciated replacement cost. The deductions from gross replacement cost should take into account the age and condition of the asset, economic and functional obsolescence, and environmental and other relevant factors. (Para. 2, FRS 15.)

The FRS points out that depreciated replacement cost provides a realistic estimate of the value attributable to the remaining service potential of the total useful economic life of the asset. Practical difficulties may arise, however, for example because of changing technology, as, were a company to replace an asset, it would do so by means of a very different one. This may make it difficult or time-consuming (and therefore expensive) to obtain a reliable valuation, especially where assets are highly specialised or have very long useful economic lives.

11.4.5   Reporting gains and losses on revaluation

In relation to revaluation gains, FRS 15 largely reflects what was already considered best practice:

> Revaluation gains should be recognised in the profit and loss account only to the extent (after adjusting for subsequent depreciation) that they reverse revaluation losses on the same asset that were previously recognised in the profit and loss account. All other revaluation gains should be recognised in the statement of total recognised gains and losses. (Para. 63, FRS 15.)

Note that the gain recognised in the profit and loss account on reversal of a previous loss should be reduced by the amount of depreciation that would have been charged had the loss previously taken to the profit and loss account not been recognised in the first place. This achieves the same overall effect as if the original downward revaluation had not occurred.

In relation to revaluation losses, previous practice was often to take these through reserves and the statement of total recognised gains and losses, even where this results in a debit balance on the revaluation reserve. FRS 15 states that:

> All revaluation losses that are caused by a clear consumption of economic benefits should be recognised in the profit and loss account. Other revaluation losses should be recognised:
>
> (a) in the statement of total recognised gains and losses until the carrying amount reaches its depreciated historical cost; and
> (b) thereafter, in the profit and loss account unless it can be demonstrated that the recoverable amount of the asset is greater than its revalued amount, in which case the loss should be recognised in the statement of total recognised

> gains and losses to the extent that the recoverable amount of the asset is greater than its revalued amount. (Para. 65, FRS 15.)

The first point that arises here is what constitutes 'a clear consumption of economic benefits'. The FRS gives examples of physical damage or a deterioration in the quality of the service provided by the asset and points out that this is really an impairment loss rather than a downward revaluation.

The second point is that FRS 15 does not completely rule out a loss compared to depreciated historical cost being taken through the statement of total recognised gains and losses, and therefore, presumably, to revaluation reserve. However, this is likely to arise only in exceptional circumstances where the current value of an asset is temporarily depressed, eg because of a slump in the market, but the asset still has significant value to the business in terms of its expected future income-generating potential.

FRS 15 provides the following example.

EXAMPLE

Reporting revaluation gains and losses

Assumptions

A non-specialised property costs £1 million and has a useful life of ten years and no residual value. It is depreciated on a straight-line basis and revalued annually. The entity has a policy of calculating depreciation based on the opening book amount. At the end of years 1 and 2 the asset has an EUV of £1,080,000 and £700,000 respectively. At the end of year 2, the recoverable amount of the asset is £760,000 and its depreciated historical cost is £800,000. There is no obvious consumption of economic benefits in year 2, other than that accounted for through the depreciation charge.

Accounting treatment under modified historical cost

	Year 1 £000	Year 2 £000
Opening book amount	1,000	1,080
Depreciation	(100)	(120)
Adjusted book amount	900	960
Revaluation gain (loss):		
recognised in the STRGL	180	(220)
recognised in the profit and loss account	–	(40)
Closing book amount	1,080	700

In year 1, after depreciation of £100,000, a revaluation gain of £180,000 is recognised in the statement of total recognised gains and losses, in accordance with paragraph 63.

In year 2, after a depreciation charge of £120,000, the revaluation loss on the property is £260,000. According to paragraph 65, where there is not a clear consumption of economic benefits, revaluation losses should be recognised in the statement of total

---

recognised gains and losses until the carrying amount reaches its depreciated historical cost. Therefore, the fall in value from the adjusted book amount (£960,000) to depreciated historical cost (£800,000) of £160,000 is recognised in the statement of total recognised gains and losses.

The rest of the revaluation loss, £100,000 (ie the fall in value from depreciated historical cost (£800,000) to the revalued amount (£700,000)), should be recognised in the profit and loss account, unless it can be demonstrated that recoverable amount is greater than the revalued amount. In this case, the recoverable amount of £760,000 is greater than the revalued amount of £700,000 by £60,000. Therefore, £60,000 of the revaluation loss is recognised in the statement of total recognised gains and losses, rather than the profit and loss account, giving rise to a total revaluation loss of £220,000 (£60,000 + £160,000) that is recognised in the statement of total recognised gains and losses. The remaining loss (representing the fall in value from depreciated historical cost of £800,000 to recoverable amount of £760,000) of £40,000 is recognised in the profit and loss account.

FRS 15 also contains a 'no-netting-off' rule:

> In determining in which performance statement gains and losses on revaluation should be recognised, material gains and losses on individual assets in a class of asset should not be aggregated. (Para. 67, FRS 15.)

This is consistent with the approach taken in SSAP 19 in relation to investment properties.

11.4.6   Reporting gains and losses on disposal

At present, FRS 15 maintains the previous practice of presenting gains and losses on disposal in the profit and loss account:

> The profit or loss on the disposal of a tangible fixed asset should be accounted for in the profit and loss account of the period in which the disposal occurs as the difference between the net sale proceeds and the carrying amount, whether carried at historical cost (less any provisions made) or at a valuation. Profits or losses on the disposal of fixed assets should be shown in accordance with FRS 3 'Reporting Financial Performance'. (Para. 72, FRS 15.)

FRS 15 also states the rather obvious point that where an asset (or a component of an asset) is replaced, its carrying amount is removed from the balance sheet (by eliminating its cost (or revalued amount) and related accumulated depreciation).

11.4.7   The FRSSE

The FRSSE includes a simplified version of the FRS 15 requirements relating to revaluations, which misses out much of the detail contained in the FRS. The FRSSE permits the adoption of a policy of revaluation, which must then be applied to all assets within a class, but which need not be applied to all classes of asset. The FRSSE repeats the FRS 15 definition of classes of assets, ie those having a similar nature, function or use in the business.

Where an entity adopts a policy of revaluation under the FRSSE, the valuations must be performed:

- by an experienced valuer, ie one who has recognised and relevant recent professional experience, and sufficient knowledge of the state of the market in the location and category of the tangible fixed asset being valued (rather than by a 'qualified valuer' as required by FRS 15), and
- at least every five years.

Interim valuations by an experienced valuer should be carried out if there is likely to have been a material change in value in the intervening years. Unlike FRS 15, there is no mandatory requirement for an interim valuation at the end of the third year where there is no indication of any material change.

The bases of revaluation are simplified, being market value or best estimate thereof for all tangible fixed assets (unless the directors judge this to be inappropriate, in which case current value should be used instead).

The treatment of revaluation losses is also simplified. Revaluation losses caused only by changing market prices should be recognised in the statement of total recognised gains and losses until the carrying amount reaches depreciated historic cost. All other revaluation losses should be recognised in the profit and loss account. There is also no statement to the effect that material gains and losses within a class should not be aggregated.

11.5   DISCLOSURE

11.5.1   The Companies Act 2006

The formats in Sch. 1 to The Large and Medium-sized Companies and Groups (Accounts and Reports) Regulations 2008 (SI 2008/410) show the four standard categories of tangible fixed asset.

(1)   Land and buildings.

(2)   Plant and machinery.

(3)   Fixtures, fittings, tools and equipment.

(4)   Payments on account and assets in course of construction.

For small companies, this is reduced to the following.

(1)   Land and buildings.

(2)   Plant and machinery, etc.

Since all of the sub-categories are assigned Arabic numerals in the format they can, or rather must, always be altered to provide a more appropriate reflection of the types of asset held by the individual company.

Where the special nature of the company's business requires it, the company's directors must adapt the arrangement, headings and sub-headings otherwise required in respect of items given an Arabic number in the balance sheet or profit and loss account format used. (Para. 4, Sch. 1 to The Large and Medium-sized Companies and Groups (Accounts and Reports) Regulations 2008 (SI 2008/410) and Para. 4, Sch. 1 to The Small Companies and Groups (Accounts and Directors' Report) Regulations 2008 (SI 2008/409).)

For example, motor vehicles is a common sub-category in practice.

Sub-analysis of land and buildings is required for companies other than small companies:

In relation to any amount which is ... shown in respect of the item 'land and buildings' in the company's balance sheet there must be stated:

(a) how much of that amount is ascribable to land of freehold tenure and how much to that of land of leasehold tenure; and

(b) how much of the amount ascribable to land of leasehold tenure is ascribable to land held on long lease and how much to land held on short lease. (Para. 53, Sch. 1 to The Large and Medium-sized Companies and Groups (Accounts and Reports) Regulations 2008 (SI 2008/410).)

For these purposes, a long lease is one which still has at least 50 years to run at the balance sheet date. A short lease is any other lease. Where a company holds land in Scotland, similar rules apply, but the terms used are in accordance with Scottish rather than English law.

For fixed assets, the general requirement to show comparatives is replaced by the requirement to show the movements in each asset category over the period:

In respect of each item which is ... shown under the general item "fixed assets" in the company's balance sheet the following information shall be given:

(a) the appropriate amounts in respect of that item as at the date of the beginning of the financial year and as at the balance sheet date respectively;

(b) the effect on any amount shown in the balance sheet in respect of that item of:

(i) any revision of the amount in respect of any assets included under that item made during that year on any basis ... [in accordance with the alternative accounting rules] ... ;

(ii) acquisitions during that year of any assets;

(iii) disposals during that year of any assets; and

(iv) any transfers of assets of the company to and from that item during the year ...

In respect of each item ... [included above] there must also be stated:

(a) the cumulative amount of provisions for depreciation or diminution in value of assets included under that item as at each date mentioned ... [above];

(b) the amount of any such provisions made in respect of the financial year;

(c) the amount of any adjustments made in respect of any such provisions during that year in consequence of the disposal of any assets; and

(d) the amount of any other adjustments made in respect of any such provisions during that year;

shall also be stated. (Para. 51, Sch. 1 to The Large and Medium-sized Companies and Groups (Accounts and Reports) Regulations 2008 (SI 2008/410).)

The depreciation charge for the period must also be shown in a note to the profit and loss account.

Where a charge has been made to reduce the value of a fixed asset due to a permanent diminution in value, this charge must be disclosed either on the face of the profit and loss account or in the notes. It may be shown either separately or in aggregate.

Identical disclosure must also be made where a provision has been written back since it is no longer necessary.

If the amount shown for any fixed asset includes capitalised borrowing costs then this fact must be stated, together with the amount involved.

Where there has been a change in the method of depreciation, the effect needs to be stated, together with the reason for the change. In certain circumstances, the effect of an adjustment to the method may be treated as an exceptional item. In such cases, the nature and amount of the adjustment must be given.

Where the alternative accounting rules have been used, additional disclosures are required:

The items affected and the basis of valuation adopted in determining the amounts of the assets in question in the case of each such item must be disclosed in a note to the accounts.

In the case of each balance sheet item affected (except stocks) either:

(a) the comparable amounts determined according to the historical cost accounting rules; or

(b) the differences between those amounts and the corresponding amounts actually shown in the balance sheet in respect of that item;

must be shown separately in the balance sheet or in a note to the accounts. (Para. 34, Sch. 1 to The Large and Medium-sized Companies and Groups (Accounts and Reports) Regulations 2008 (SI 2008/410) and Para. 34, Sch. 1 to The Small Companies and Groups (Accounts and Directors' Report) Regulations 2008 (SI 2008/409).)

Where any fixed assets of the company (other than listed investments) are included under any item shown in the company's balance sheet at an amount determined ... [under the alternative accounting rules], the following information must be given:

(a) the years (so far as they are known to the directors) in which the assets were severally valued and the several values; and

(b) in the case of assets that have been valued during the financial year, the names of the persons who valued them or particulars of their qualifications for doing so and (whichever is stated) the bases of valuation used by them. (Para. 52, Sch. 1 to The Large and Medium-sized Companies and Groups (Accounts and Reports) Regulations 2008 (SI 2008/410) and Para. 49, Sch. 1 to The Small Companies and Groups (Accounts and Directors' Report) Regulations 2008 (SI 2008/409).)

The 'comparable amounts' cover both the aggregate net amount and the amount of the cumulative provisions for depreciation. The effect on the depreciation charge for the period must also be stated.

Where assets have been revalued, the revaluation reserve must be separately disclosed but may be described under another name.

11.5.2 FRS 15 disclosure requirements

For tangible fixed assets in general, FRS 15 includes the following disclosure requirements. These do not apply to heritage assets which fall within the scope of FRS 30, where separate disclosure requirements apply.

'The following information should be disclosed separately in the financial statements for each class of tangible fixed assets:

(a) the depreciation methods used;
(b) the useful economic lives or the depreciation rates used;
(c) total depreciation charged for the period;
(d) where material, the financial effect of a change during the period in either the estimate of useful economic lives . . . or the estimate of residual values . . . ;
(e) the cost or revalued amount at the beginning of the financial period and at the balance sheet date;
(f) the cumulative amount of provisions for depreciation or impairment at the beginning of the financial period and at the balance sheet date;
(g) a reconciliation of the movements, separately disclosing additions, disposals, revaluations, transfers, depreciation, impairment losses, and reversals of past impairment losses written back in the financial period; and
(h) the net carrying amount at the beginning of the financial period and at the balance sheet date. (Para. 100, FRS 15.)'

The FRS states that when a tangible fixed asset is revalued, the carrying amount of the asset is restated at its revalued amount, accumulated depreciation at the date of revaluation is eliminated, and the cost or revalued amount of the asset is restated at its revalued amount. However, the FRS permits an alternative presentation where the valuation is calculated on a depreciated replacement cost basis. Instead of following the usual presentation, both the cost or revalued amount and the accumulated depreciation at the date of revaluation may be restated, so that the carrying amount of the asset after revaluation equals its revalued amount.

Where depreciation methods or useful economic lives have been revised, FRS 15 contains the following.

> Where there has been a change in the depreciation method used, the effect, if material, should be disclosed in the period of change. The reason for the change should also be disclosed. (Para. 102, FRS 15.)

Where any class of tangible fixed assets has been revalued, FRS 15 requires the following disclosures.

> In addition to the disclosures required by paragraphs 53(a), 61 and 72, where any class of tangible fixed assets of an entity has been revalued the following information should be disclosed in each reporting period:
>
> (a) for each class of revalued assets:
>
>   (i)   the name and qualifications of the valuer(s) or the valuer's organisation and a description of its nature;
>
>   (ii)   the basis or bases of valuation (including whether notional directly attributable acquisition costs have been included or expected selling costs deducted);
>
>   (iii)   the date and amounts of the valuations;
>
>   (iv)   where historical cost records are available, the carrying amount that would have been included in the financial statements had the tangible fixed assets been carried at historical cost less depreciation;
>
>   (v)   whether the person(s) carrying out the valuation is (are) internal or external to the entity;
>
>   (vi)   where the directors are not aware of any material change in value and therefore the valuation(s) have not been updated ... a statement to that effect; and
>
>   (vii)   where the valuation has not been updated, or is not a full valuation, the date of the last full valuation.
>
> (b) in addition, for revalued properties:
>
>   (i)   where properties have been valued as fully-equipped operational entities having regard to their trading potential, a statement to that effect and the carrying amount of those properties; and
>
>   (ii)   the total amount of notional directly attributable acquisition costs (or the total amount of expected selling costs deducted), included in the carrying amount, where material. (Para. 74, FRS 15.)

The FRSSE requires disclosure of the depreciation methods, useful economic lives or depreciation rates and, where material, financial effect of changes to useful economic lives or residual values, but omits the remainder of FRS 15's disclosure requirements, leaving just the statutory disclosures in place.

11.5.3 FRS 15 transitional provisions

Most transitional provisions included in accounting standards have a very short period of relevance, affecting only one or two accounting periods. Those included in FRS 15 are different in that, while they had to be implemented at a specific point in the past, they will continue to affect company accounts for many years to come.

Prior to FRS 15, there were no detailed rules on when a company had to, or could choose to, revalue assets. As a result, practice was inconsistent and some companies simply revalued assets occasionally. It was open to the ASB when bringing in FRS 15 to require companies to eliminate the effects of such previous inconsistency, by either reverting to cost or continuing to revalue on a regular basis. However, for some companies, this was felt to lead to an unacceptable increase in compliance costs because of the potential for a need for greater involvement of qualified valuers if companies with previous revaluations were forced to revalue in the future. Therefore, FRS 15 includes transitional provisions:

> Where, on implementation of the FRS for the first time, an entity does not adopt a policy of revaluation, but the carrying amount of its tangible fixed assets reflects previous revaluations, it may:
>
> (a) retain the book amounts (subject to the requirement to test the assets for impairment in accordance with FRS 11 where there is an indication that an impairment may have occurred). In these circumstances the entity should disclose the fact that the transitional provisions of the FRS are being followed and that the valuation has not been updated and give the date of the last revaluation; or
> (b) restate the carrying amount of the tangible fixed assets to historical cost (less restated accumulated depreciation), as a change in accounting policy. (Para. 104, FRS 15.)

FRS 15 also deals with reclassifications of assets into separate components on first implementation of the standard:

> Where, on adoption of the FRS, entities separate tangible fixed assets into different components with significantly different useful economic lives for depreciation purposes, in accordance with paragraphs 36-41 and 83-85, the changes should be dealt with as prior period adjustments, as a change in accounting policy. (Para. 108, FRS 15.)

The UITF issued Abstract 23 *Application of the transitional rules in FRS 15* to clarify the application of the transitional provisions in relation to separation of assets into components. The abstract states that the prior period adjustment required when an entity adopts component depreciation, ie treats the major components of an asset separately for depreciation purposes, should not also include any changes in useful economic lives or residual values of the other components of the asset. Any such changes should be accounted for under FRS 15 as revisions of accounting estimates. Abstract 23 limits the prior year adjustment on separating assets into components to the effects of treating separately only those components in respect of which:

- any provision for repairs and maintenance was itself eliminated by prior year adjustment on implementation of FRS 12, or
- there has been a change from a previous policy of writing off as incurred

relevant repairs and maintenance expenditure to a policy where such expenditure is capitalised because it replaces a separately depreciated component.

As noted above, unlike many other transitional provisions, those of FRS 15 are likely to have an impact for some time to come. In particular, the use of previous valuations as, in effect, deemed cost on the implementation of FRS 15 may continue to affect company accounts for many years, until there is a policy change or until disposal of the affected assets.

11.6   INVESTMENT PROPERTIES

11.6.1   Introduction

Investment properties are a separate category of tangible fixed assets, dealt with by SSAP 19 *Accounting for Investment Properties*. The ASB originally intended to include investment properties within the scope of FRS 15, but also decided to leave SSAP 19 in place pending the development of a new international standard on investment properties.

In April 2000, the IASC issued its new standard, IAS 40 *Investment Property*. Under IAS 40, an enterprise must choose between two models.

(1)   A fair value model, under which investment property is measured at fair value and changes in fair value are recognised in the profit and loss account.

(2)   A cost model, under which investment property is measured at depreciated cost (less any accumulated impairment losses). An enterprise that chooses the cost model should disclose the fair value of its investment property.

The ASB has not yet issued new proposals on investment properties, and given its plans for UK GAAP, it is extremely unlikely to do so. There has been a revised version of IAS 40, which has been effective since accounting periods commencing on or after 1 January 2005, and indeed further changes were made to the standard which apply to accounting periods beginning on or after 1 January 2009. The 2005 and 2009 versions do not change the basic requirements of the standard, and continue to allow both the cost and fair value models to be used. The 2005 revision clarified the treatment in some areas, for example, by using similar principles to IAS 16 in determining costs, and in providing further guidance in respect of property interests held by a lessee under an operating lease. The 2009 revision amended the definition of investment properties, and, in particular, properties acquired with the intention of being developed as investment properties are now deemed to be investment properties from acquisition.

11.6.2 Investment properties and depreciation

There is a general presumption that fixed assets should be depreciated, unless they have an infinite useful economic life. The requirement that fixed assets be depreciated applies even where the value of an asset is increasing, so long as it has a finite useful economic life.

The requirement, however, is appropriate only where an asset is held for use within a business. Under current rules, depreciation is simply a specific application of the accruals concept. When an asset is depreciated we are attempting to match the cost of that asset with the revenues which it is generating, or at least helping to generate. Where an asset is not being used in order to generate revenues then charging depreciation serves no useful purpose; there is no income with which the cost could be matched. The only result of charging depreciation would be that the final profit on disposal of the asset would be higher than would otherwise be the case (or the loss reduced, or a loss turned into a profit). Depreciation would not meet the objective of matching revenues with costs, it would simply allocate profits to separate accounting periods on an almost random basis.

SSAP 19 argues that in cases where assets are not held for use, then it is the current value (the open market value) of such assets that is important, not their depreciated original cost. It is, therefore, also the current value that needs to be included in the financial statements in order to provide a proper understanding of the position of the company. The calculation of a depreciation charge would not be useful to the user of the financial statements. This is because any income stream from renting the property does not provide a fair reflection of the ultimate value of the asset to the business.

For example, there may be rental income obtained prior to the disposal of the asset, but if this is not intended to be the major source of revenue from holding that asset then matching this income with the depreciation charge would not be meaningful. It would not be difficult to argue that any apparent matching could be misleading. Similarly, in these circumstances the user of the financial statements is likely to be far more interested in the current value of the asset, and the potential that this gives for realising a gain, than in a depreciated historical cost amount which gives little or no idea of the asset's current value.

Most companies that hold investment properties, as defined by SSAP 19 and the FRSSE, are likely to be specialist investment companies, such as investment trusts or property investment companies, but other companies are not excluded. The treatment required by both standards applies to all types of company which hold investment properties.

The introductory notes to SSAP 19 state that depreciation should not be applied where 'a significant proportion of the fixed assets of an enterprise' are investment properties.

In the text of SSAP 19 itself, no mention is made of the fact that a company or enterprise must hold a significant proportion of its assets in the form of investment properties for the other provisions of the standard to apply. This is, presumably, on the basis that accounting standards are only intended to apply to material items, and that such a reference would therefore be superfluous. Companies with substantial property holdings, only a small part of which consists of investment properties, might not wish to adopt different accounting treatments for each class. In deciding what is material, consideration must be given to both the profit and loss account and the balance sheet. Depreciation charges on properties are often quite low as a proportion of their total value, and so may not be material to the reported profit. However, they accumulate and may eventually have a material effect on the net asset value. Consideration needs to be given to both if investment properties are to be deemed immaterial. Despite these problems, we suggest that companies should only apply the special provisions if investment properties are material. If this view is accepted, properties should only be treated in accordance with SSAP 19 and the FRSSE if they form a major part of the fixed assets of a company. Where a company holds a small number of investment properties, and the holding of such properties cannot be deemed to be a major part of the company's business, then there is little benefit in following the provisions of the standard.

11.6.3 Definition of investment property

SSAP 19 defines an investment property as:

> ... an interest in land and/or buildings:
>
> (a) in respect of which construction work and development have been completed; and
> (b) which is held for its investment potential, any rental income being negotiated at arm's length. (Para. 7, SSAP 19.)

This definition has also been included in the FRSSE.

The first condition does not entirely preclude a company from constructing a property which is intended to be used for investment purposes. Instead, it means that it should not be accounted for as an investment property during the period of construction. During this period, the property should be stated at cost and included in fixed assets in the balance sheet under 'payments on account and assets in course of construction'. The description of the property or properties can be altered and a more appropriate phrase used if required. (This treatment was also the same under IFRS until 2009. From 2009, under IAS 40, properties acquired with the intention of being developed as investment properties are now considered to fall within that category from the date on which they were acquired.)

A property cannot be treated as an investment property if it is occupied by the company, or let to any company in the same group. There is no strict prohibition upon a company letting an investment property to an associated undertaking, or any other business with which it is connected but which does not form part of its group. However, in these circumstances great care would need to be taken to ensure that the rental income was actually negotiated at arm's length. The burden of proof would be placed on the directors to justify their treatment in such a case.

Potential impact of the FRSME

The FRSME adopts a slightly different approach to the definition of an investment property. It makes no mention of any requirement for the property to have been completed, so an investment property in the course of construction is an investment property. (This is consistent with the IAS on which the requirements in the IFRS for SMEs were broadly based, and which was changed to allow this.)

The definition is partly negative, being any interests in land and buildings held for rental income or capital appreciation, or both, that is not used in the business or held for sale in the ordinary course of business. The FRSME definition also specifically allows assets held under a finance lease to be investment properties. Oddly, given the definition, the FRSME also allows properties held under operating leases to be treated as investment properties so long as the value of the property interest can be determined without undue cost or effort on an ongoing basis. It makes it very clear that the value of an interest in a property under an operating lease is the fair value of that lease and not the value of the property.

11.6.4   Basic accounting treatment

Investment properties should not normally be subject to any charge for depreciation. Instead, they should be included in the balance sheet at their open market value, as determined each year.

The valuation need not be undertaken by a professionally qualified valuer, or even someone independent of the company, but the following details must be disclosed.

(1)   The name of the person who made the valuation, or particulars of his or her qualifications.

(2)   The bases used for the valuation of the properties.

(3)   If the person making the valuation is an employee of the company, then this fact also needs to be stated.

The introduction to SSAP 19 also suggests, without making it a requirement, that more stringent conditions should be applied by 'major enterprises'. Major enterprises are not defined, although the example given in the introduction is that of a public company. It seems reasonable to assume that a major enterprise might also be one which exceeds the criteria for defining a medium-sized company under the Companies Act by a factor of ten, since this definition is used elsewhere in SSAPs, for example SSAP 13.

The more stringent conditions are:

- that the valuation should be carried out by a person who holds a recognised professional qualification, and has recent post-qualification experience of dealing with the location and category of properties involved, and
- that an external valuation should be undertaken at least every five years.

The change in the value of investment properties should not be dealt with through the profit and loss account but should instead pass through a separate investment revaluation reserve.

In principle, both increases and decreases in value should pass through the investment revaluation reserve. However, a problem arises where any investment property falls below its original cost, due to the effect of the statutory requirement that permanent diminutions in the value of a fixed asset should be charged to the profit and loss account.

> Provisions for diminution in value must be made in respect of any fixed asset which has diminished in value if the reduction in its value is expected to be permanent (whether its useful economic life is limited or not), and the amount to be included in respect of it must be reduced accordingly ... (Para. 19 (2), Sch. 1 to The Large and Medium-sized Companies and Groups (Accounts and Reports) Regulations 2008 (SI 2008/410) and Para. 19 (2), Sch. 1 to The Small Companies and Groups (Accounts and Directors' Report) Regulations 2008 (SI 2008/409).)

This used to mean that there was a possible conflict between SSAP 19, which seemed to imply that a portfolio approach should be adopted for investment properties, and statute which effectively prohibited such an approach. While various methods were developed to avoid this problem, no single solution gained total acceptance.

This problem was resolved, in part, with the amendment of SSAP 19 by the ASB. Increases in the value of an investment property have never caused a problem, since they have always been dealt with in the revaluation reserve. Similarly, to the extent that any fall in value simply eliminates previous increases above cost then again the amount involved has always been deducted from the reserve. SSAP 19 now requires two different treatments for the amount by which any diminution in value takes the recorded value of the asset below its original historic cost:

- if the fall in value is expected to be permanent, then the amount should be taken to the profit and loss account, as required by statute, or
- if the fall in value is expected to be temporary, then the amount should be dealt with in the revaluation reserve, even if this means that the reserve has a debit balance either in respect of the individual property or in total.

Since statute does not require provisions to be made at all for temporary diminutions in the value of fixed assets, this treatment is not in breach of statute.

The only problems that have not been resolved by the amendment of the standard are those that relate to a change in the assessment of the nature of the provision. The simplest case is where a permanent provision is now considered to be temporary. No change should be made until the asset has actually started to increase in value, since SSAP 19 always requires that investment properties are stated at their current value. When the asset's value increases then, to the extent that amounts were originally charged to the profit and loss account, they should be credited to the profit and loss account. If the asset value increases beyond its original historic cost then amounts should be credited to the revaluation reserve. This treatment is effectively required by the Companies Act 2006, since it states that:

> Where the reasons for which any provision was made in accordance with ...
> [the rules on permanent diminutions in value] ... have ceased to apply to any
> extent, that provision must be written back to the extent that it is no longer
> necessary ... (Para. 20 (1), Sch. 1 to The Large and Medium-sized Companies
> and Groups (Accounts and Reports) Regulations 2008 (SI 2008/410) and Para. 20
> (1), Sch. 1 to The Small Companies and Groups (Accounts and Directors' Report)
> Regulations 2008 (SI 2008/409).)

The slightly more difficult situation is where a temporary diminution is now considered to be permanent. In this case the amount of the diminution below original cost should be transferred from the revaluation reserve to the profit and loss account.

The changes introduced to SSAP 19 reflect the fact that an additional financial statement has been introduced since SSAP 19 was first published, and that the statement of total recognised gains and losses is now available to clarify some of the movements in the financial statements that have not passed through the profit and loss account.

SSAP 19 states that investment trust companies and property unit trusts need not charge deficits to the profit and loss account where they exceed the balance of the investment revaluation reserve. However, they should show the amount of the deficit prominently in their financial statements. Pension funds, and insurance companies, when dealing with long-term business, should not pass any movements in respect of changes in the value of investment properties through a revaluation reserve, since such movements should instead pass through the relevant fund account.

Potential impact of the FRSME

The FRSME requires interests in investment properties to be stated at their fair value so long as that fair value can be measured reliably without undue cost or effort. An important difference between SSAP 19 and the FRSME is that

357

changes in that value are reflected in profit or loss, and not taken to a separate investment property revaluation reserve.

Where a reliable fair value cannot be obtained without undue cost or effort, the interest in an investment property should be stated at cost under the FRSME, and treated as property, plant and equipment, that is, it would be depreciated in the normal way.

11.6.5   Short leasehold investment properties

There is currently an exception to the general rule that depreciation should not be charged on investment properties. Where the property in question is a leasehold property and the lease has an unexpired term of 20 years or less then depreciation should be charged in accordance with normal practice. (It should be noted that the definition of a 'short leasehold', for the purposes of SSAP 19, differs from that normally used. SSAP 19 adopts different treatments for leases of fewer than and those of more than 20 years, whereas statutory disclosure requirements for larger companies distinguish between leases of fewer than and those of more than 50 years.)

The reason given by the standard for the exception is that in such cases it would be unfair if the fall in value were taken through the investment revaluation reserve, with the rental income being passed through the profit and loss account. Although there is undoubtedly some logic behind this suggestion, the same problem could also be held to apply to any investment property where there is significant rental income prior to disposal.

The standard does not mention the problem of accounting for a property held on a lease which originally had a term of longer than 20 years, but which has only 20 years to run from the current accounting period.

The best solution is that the revalued amount should be depreciated, rather than the original cost. If the property's value prior to depreciation is below cost, then the accounting treatment is simply to charge the annual depreciation to the profit and loss account. If the value was originally above cost, and therefore there is an amount included in the revaluation reserve in respect of the property, then we suggest that:

- depreciation is charged to the profit and loss account on the basis the company normally adopts for leasehold properties, and
- a transfer should be made from the revaluation reserve to the profit and loss account as a movement on reserves equal to the depreciation charge.

This transfer from the revaluation reserve should continue annually until the revaluation reserve includes no amounts in respect of the property. After that, depreciation should simply be charged to the profit and loss account as normal.

The financial statements should disclose the change in accounting treatment when the 20-year threshold is reached.

Potential impact of the FRSME

The FRSME takes a slightly different approach. Such an interest could, if the various normal conditions are met, be treated as an investment property. However, the FRSME requires all value changes to be taken to profit. There is therefore no question of depreciation being charged, but of course the value of the leased interest is (all other things being equal) likely to fall as the end of the lease approaches and this will be charged as a cost.

11.6.6   Non-compliance with statute

Until 2005, both SSAP 19 and the FRSSE stated that the valuation of investment properties was an example of the true and fair override and a departure from the normal practice under the Companies Act 1985 of depreciating fixed assets with a limited useful life. When the change to the rules on diminutions in value was introduced, the ASB also took the opportunity of noting that UITF Abstract 7 *True and Fair Override Disclosures* should be considered when drafting the wording in the notes to the accounts dealing with non-compliance with the Companies Act 1985.

However, from 2005 this problem has changed. From this time the Companies Act 1985 allowed the statement of investment properties at fair value if such properties fall within the definition of an investment property under international accounting standards, but required that changes in value be taken to the profit and loss account. This position has been carried forward into the Companies Act 2006. Therefore, any company which continues to adopt a policy of revaluation via a revaluation reserve will still be in breach of a statutory requirement, but this now relates solely to the treatment of the surplus not its recognition.

11.7   HERITAGE ASSETS

11.7.1   Introduction

FRS 30, *Heritage Assets*, is effective for accounting periods beginning on or after 1 April 2010.

The standard is based on FRED 42. Contrary to the ASB's original intentions, as reflected in FRED 40, it is primarily a disclosure standard. The significant changes to accounting practice that the ASB had proposed in FRED 40, which would have seen heritage assets as a separate category of asset with their own accounting requirements, have not been followed through.

Potential impact of the FRSME

The original draft of the FRSME did not deal with heritage assets. (The IFRS for SMEs on which the FRSME is based also does not deal specifically with heritage assets.) However, in the process of developing the proposed Financial Reporting Standard for Public Benefit Entities (FRSPBE), the ASB decided that the requirements previously included in FRS 30 should be included in the FRSME rather than the FRSPBE. As a result, the FRSME in effect now contains the same requirements as in FRS 30, other than some changes made to reflect the terminology and approach of that standard. This means that there would be no substantial changes from FRS 30 if the FRSME were to come into force.

11.7.2   Objectives and definition

FRS 30 has two stated objectives.

The first, which applies in all cases, is to enhance disclosure in respect of heritage assets regardless of the accounting treatment that is being adopted. The second is conditional; that heritage assets should be reported in a balance sheet where information on their cost or value is available.

A heritage asset is defined as:

> A tangible asset with historical, artistic, scientific, technological, geophysical or environmental qualities that is held and maintained principally for its contribution to knowledge and culture. (Para. 2, FRS 30)

It is noteworthy that this is affected by the use to which the asset is put and not by the intrinsic nature of the asset. For example, where a historic building is used by a business as its head office, then it would not fall within the definition of a heritage asset.

11.7.3   Disclosure

The disclosure requirements of FRS 30 apply, with very limited exceptions, to all heritage assets, whether they are included in the balance sheet or otherwise.

The primary requirement is that financial statements should contain an indication of the nature and scale of heritage assets held by the entity. The other disclosure requirements are all intended to further this primary requirement.

The financial statements should set out the entity's policy for the acquisition, preservation, management and disposal of heritage assets. This must include a description of the records maintained by the entity, of its collection of heritage assets, and information on the extent to which access to the assets is permitted.

This information, which does not directly relate to accounting, may be provided within the financial statements, but may also be provided in another document. If this option is taken, then there must be a reference to that other document in the financial statements.

The accounting policy for heritage assets must be stated, including details of the measurement bases that have been used.

Where heritage assets are not reported in the balance sheet, reasons for this exclusion must be stated, and the notes should explain the significance and nature of the assets not reported in the balance sheet. While FRS 30 does not make the recognition of heritage assets in the balance sheet mandatory in all cases, it is intended to encourage entities to record such assets wherever possible. Therefore, there is no requirement to explain why heritage assets are included in a balance sheet, only why they are not.

Where heritage assets are reported in the balance sheet, the following disclosures should be provided:

- the carrying amount of heritage assets at the beginning of the financial period and balance sheet date, including an analysis between those classes or groups of heritage assets that are reported at cost and those that are reported at valuation, and
- where assets are reported at valuation, sufficient information to assist in an understanding of the valuations being reported and their significance, to include:
- the date of the valuation;
- the methods used to produce the valuation;
- whether the valuation was carried out by external valuers and, where this is the case, the valuer's name and professional qualification, if any, and
- any significant limitations on the valuation.

Where heritage assets are not included in the balance sheet, the financial statements should disclose any information that is available to the entity that would be useful in assessing the value of those assets.

The financial statements should contain a summary of transactions relating to heritage assets, disclosing, for the current period and each of the previous four periods:

- the cost of acquisitions of heritage assets;
- the value of heritage assets acquired by donation;
- the carrying amount of heritage assets disposed of in the period and the proceeds received, and
- any impairment recognised in the period.

This summary should show, separately, transactions in assets that are reported in the balance sheet and those that are not.

There is a transitional provision in relation to this. If it is not practicable to get information for periods prior to the comparative period, then this information need only be given for the comparative period, if there is a statement that it is not practicable to go back further. Obviously, where this exemption is taken, the number of periods will increase year on year until data for five years is being provided.

There is a presumption that valuations can be obtained for assets acquired by donation. However, in exceptional cases, where it is not practicable to obtain such a valuation, the reasons should be stated. Disclosure should also be provided on the nature and extent of significant donations of heritage assets.

All of the disclosures may be presented in aggregate for groups or classes of heritage assets, provided this does not obscure significant information. Separate disclosures should be provided for assets reported at cost and assets at valuation. Amounts in respect of assets not reported in the balance sheet should not be aggregated with amounts for assets that are recognised at cost or valuation.

The standard is accompanied by various examples of disclosures that might be provided by entities which hold heritage assets.

11.7.4 Recognition and measurement

On recognition and measurement, the basic approach required by the standard is that heritage assets should be reported as tangible fixed assets and recognised and measured in accordance with FRS 15 *Tangible Fixed Assets*.

However, the standard then deals with various modifications to this basic requirement.

Where information is available on the cost or value of heritage assets:

- they should be presented in the balance sheet, separately from other tangible fixed assets;
- the balance sheet or notes should identify, separately, those classes of heritage assets that are being reported at cost and those at valuation, and
- changes in valuation should be recognised in the statement of total recognised gains and losses, except for impairment losses.

The carrying amount of heritage assets should be reviewed where there is evidence of impairment, for example, where they have suffered physical deterioration or doubts arise as to authenticity. Any impairment should be dealt with in accordance with FRS 11 *Impairment of Fixed Assets and Goodwill*.

FRS 30 notes that where assets have previously been capitalised or are recently purchased, information on cost or value will always be available. In other cases, attempts should be made to obtain such information, but where it cannot be obtained at a cost commensurate with the benefits to users of the financial statements, then the assets will not be recognised in the balance sheet and the assets will be covered solely by disclosure.

Given the wide nature of items that might be heritage assets, the standard is permissive in terms of valuation. Unlike FRS 15, FRS 30 allows valuations by any method that is appropriate and relevant. Similarly, there is no requirement for valuations to be carried out or verified by external valuers, nor any minimum period between valuations. The standard does, however, note that where heritage assets are reported at valuation, the carrying amount should be reviewed with sufficient frequency to ensure valuations remain current.

Given that the accounting treatment for heritage assets falls broadly within FRS 15, depreciation may be necessary. Nonetheless, FRS 30 points out that depreciation need not be provided on heritage assets which have indefinite lives.

For assets received by donation, the default rule is that they should be reported in the profit and loss account at valuation. Where, exceptionally, it is not practicable to obtain a valuation for a donated heritage asset, such assets will be dealt with solely by disclosure.

11.8 INTANGIBLE FIXED ASSETS

11.8.1 Introduction

There is a very wide range of intangible fixed assets, including:

- research and development;
- development costs, other than research and development;
- goodwill;
- brand names;
- patents and trade marks;
- exploration costs in extractive industries;
- licences;
- copyright and other publishing rights;
- deferred charges;
- technical know-how, and
- publishing rights and titles.

However, most companies do not have intangible fixed assets in their balance sheet.

FRS 10 *Goodwill and Intangible Assets* applies to all intangible assets with the exception of:

- oil and gas exploration and development costs;
- research and development costs, and

- any other intangible assets that are specifically addressed by another accounting standard.

SSAP 13 *Accounting for Research and Development* continues to apply to research and development costs, and is addressed in a separate section of this chapter.

Goodwill is primarily discussed in Chapter 21.

Two UITF Abstracts are also relevant to accounting for intangible assets. These are:

- Abstract 24 *Accounting for start-up costs*, which is covered in the section of this chapter dealing with FRS 15, and
- Abstract 27 *Revision to estimates of the useful economic life of goodwill and intangible assets*, which is covered with goodwill in Chapter 21.

There is also a consultation paper issued by the ASB dealing with business combinations, impairment and intangible assets. The ASB is not convinced that the proposals, which are those originally put forward by the IASB and are now IFRS 3, represent any improvement over current UK rules, and in some cases feel that the proposals are weaker than existing UK practice. There are no immediate plans to alter UK accounting practice, and, in the light of the ASB's plans for UK GAAP, there is very little chance that the consultation paper will ever lead to a UK standard.

11.8.2 Categories of intangible assets

The formats included in Sch. 1 to The Large and Medium-sized Companies and Groups (Accounts and Reports) Regulations 2008 (SI 2008/410) contain the following categories of intangible fixed asset.

(1) Development costs.

(2) Concessions, patents, licences, trade marks and similar rights and assets.

(3) Goodwill.

(4) Payments on account.

For small companies under Sch. 1 to The Small Companies and Groups (Accounts and Directors' Report) Regulations 2008 (SI 2008/409) this is reduced to:

(1) Goodwill.

(2) Other intangible assets.

Since all of these items have been assigned an Arabic numeral they may all be changed so as to be more appropriate to the individual company.

11.8.3   Recognition

Statute does not provide specific recognition criteria for intangible assets as a whole. However, it provides basic criteria for the recognition of concessions, patents, trade marks and similar rights and assets:

> Amounts in respect of assets are only to be included in a company's balance sheet under this item if either:
>
> (a)   the assets were acquired for valuable consideration and are not required to be shown under goodwill; or
>
> (b)   the assets in question were created by the company itself. (Note (2) to balance sheet formats, Sch. 1 to The Large and Medium-sized Companies and Groups (Accounts and Reports) Regulations 2008 (SI 2008/410).)

There are similar rules for small companies.

FRS 10 has the same basic requirements for recognition of intangible assets, although it does state quite clearly that qualifying assets should appear on the balance sheet:

> An intangible asset purchased separately from a business should be capitalised at its cost. (Para. 9, FRS 10.)

The definition of an intangible asset in FRS 10 is fairly straightforward:

> Non-financial assets that do not have physical substance but are identifiable and are controlled by the entity through custody or legal rights. (Para. 2, FRS 10.)

In this context, identifiable means that the assets are capable of being sold or otherwise disposed of separately, without disposing of a business of the company.

The FRS 10 definition is based, of course, on the recognition criteria for assets under FRS 5, *Reporting the Substance of Transactions*:

> Evidence that an entity has rights or other access to benefits (and hence has an asset) is given if the entity is exposed to the risks inherent in the benefits. (Para. 17, FRS 5.)

> Where a transaction results in an item that meets the definition of an asset or liability, that item should be recognised in the balance sheet if:
>
> (a)   there is sufficient evidence of the existence of the item (including where appropriate evidence that a future inflow or outflow of benefit will occur), and
>
> (b)   the item can be measured at a monetary amount with sufficient reliability. (Para. 20, FRS 5.)

FRS 10 then expands upon some of these matters. It points out that access to expected benefits is not sufficient to allow an item to be treated as an asset in the balance sheet. For example, a company may have highly trained and efficient staff from whom it expects to generate significant benefit in the future. However, since staff are normally free to leave the company without penalty there is insufficient control to warrant capitalisation. This could be contrasted with the position regarding, say, footballers, who are under contract to a club and for whom a transfer fee was paid. In this case there may be both the expected benefit and the control which will allow the players to be treated on the balance sheet.

Under the historical cost accounting rules, the initial amount to be included will be the purchase price or production cost.

The statutory rules on the calculation of the purchase price or production cost are the same as those for tangible fixed assets:

> (1)   The purchase price of an asset is to be determined by adding to the actual price paid any expenses incidental to its acquisition. (Para. 27 (1), Sch. 1 to The Large and Medium-sized Companies and Groups (Accounts and Reports) Regulations 2008 (SI 2008/410) and Para. 27 (1), Sch. 1 to The Small Companies and Groups (Accounts and Directors' Report) Regulations 2008 (SI 2008/409).)

The production cost is also, in principle, calculated in the same way as for tangible assets. However, the Companies Act guidance is not easily applicable to intangible assets, since it refers to the cost of raw materials and consumables used in the production of the asset. FRS 10 does not really address the issue of identification of cost of intangible fixed assets.

Potential impact of the FRSME

The FRSME does contain recognition criteria for intangible assets. This is unlikely to lead to any change in practice since those criteria are similar to the general asset recognition criteria that already apply under FRS 5, albeit that there are no such criteria in FRS 10.

11.8.4   Amortisation

Where an intangible asset has a limited useful economic life it will fall within the scope of the amortisation rules of the Companies Act 1985.

> In the case of any fixed asset which has a limited useful economic life, the amount of:
>
> (a)   its purchase or production cost; or
> (b)   where it is estimated that any such asset will have a residual value at the end of the period of its useful economic life, its purchase price or production cost less that estimated residual value;
>
> must be reduced by provisions for depreciation calculated to write off that amount systematically over the period of the asset's useful economic life. (Para. 18 (1), Sch. 1 to The Large and Medium-sized Companies and Groups (Accounts and Reports) Regulations 2008 (SI 2008/410) and Para. 18 (1), Sch. 1 to The Small Companies and Groups (Accounts and Directors' Report) Regulations 2008 (SI 2008/409).)

FRS 10 provides far more guidance than statute on the determination of the useful economic lives of intangible fixed assets:

> There is a rebuttable presumption that the useful economic lives of purchased goodwill and intangible assets are limited to periods of 20 years or less. This presumption may be rebutted and a useful economic life regarded as a longer period or indefinite only if:
>
> (a) the durability of the acquired business or intangible asset can be demonstrated and justifies estimating the useful economic life to exceed 20 years; and
>
> (b) the goodwill or intangible asset is capable of continued measurement (so that annual impairment reviews will be feasible). (Para. 19, FRS 10.)

(Goodwill is dealt with in Chapter 21 on group accounts.)

Where an intangible asset has a limited useful economic life, FRS 10 requires that it be amortised on a systematic basis over that life. Where, exceptionally, an intangible asset does not have a finite useful economic life then FRS 10 requires that it is not amortised. This is a breach of the Companies Act requirement, and as such represents a use of the true and fair override. If this is the case, then the company will have to provide the disclosure necessary under FRS 18.

The situation is even more restricted where the legal rights to an asset are for a finite period. In this case, the amortisation period must be the same as the period for which the rights run, unless it can be clearly demonstrated that the legal rights are renewable and the renewal is assured.

In determining the depreciable amount, account also needs to be taken of the residual value. FRS 10 contains a strong presumption that the residual value of most intangible fixed assets will be zero. A residual value may only be assigned if there is a legal or contractual right to a fixed sum at the end of the period of use, or if there is a readily ascertainable market value for the residual asset.

As with all other fixed assets, the useful economic life needs to be reconsidered on a regular basis. Under FRS 10, this should be done annually. Revisions to the useful economic life of an intangible asset are accounted for prospectively as revisions of accounting estimates.

Assuming that an asset needs to be amortised, FRS 10 states that the method of amortisation chosen should reflect the expected pattern of depletion of the asset. There is a very strong presumption that the straight-line method should be used, unless another method can be clearly shown to be more appropriate.

Impairment of intangible assets is covered separately later in this chapter.

Potential impact of the FRSME

The FRSME contains broadly similar requirements in relation to amortisation, although it also has a requirement that where the useful economic life of an intangible asset cannot be reliably estimated, it should be taken to be ten years. In the case of goodwill, the period is five years. The FRSME also contains a rebuttable presumption that the residual value of an intangible asset is zero. This presumption can be rebutted only where a third party has committed to acquire the asset at the end of its life or there is, and is expected to continue to be, an active market for the asset from which a market price can be taken.

11.8.5 Alternative accounting rules

Under the alternative accounting rules, intangible fixed assets, other than goodwill, may be included at their current cost. Where this is applied, the financial statements must refer to the basis on which the intangible assets have been valued. The following information must also be given:

- the comparable amount determined under the historical cost accounting rules, or
- the difference between the historical cost amount and the amount shown in the balance sheet.

The amount stated still needs to be amortised each year, by reference to the balance sheet value rather than the historical cost. However, under statute it is acceptable to amortise only the historical cost, on the condition that the amount of the difference between the historical cost amortisation and amortisation on the basis of the amount in the balance sheet is stated.

FRS 10 limits revaluation of intangible assets to those which have a readily ascertainable market value and requires that where it is one of a class of intangible fixed asset then all members of that class should be revalued. Where an intangible fixed asset is revalued, revaluation must be a consistent policy thereafter.

As noted above, an asset is considered to have a readily ascertainable market value where two conditions are satisfied. The asset must be:

- one of a relatively homogeneous population of assets that are equivalent in all material respects, and
- one in which there is an active market, evidenced by frequent transactions.

Goodwill cannot be revalued. These limitations also prohibit the capitalisation of internally generated brands. It would not be possible to argue that a brand was one of a homogeneous population, or it would have no value.

Potential impact of the FRSME

The FRSME prohibits the revaluation of an intangible asset in all cases.

11.8.6   Disclosure

The statutory disclosures for all classes of intangible fixed assets are basically the same as for tangible fixed assets. The movements in the cost (or valuation) and the accumulated amortisation must be shown in a note to the balance sheet. The information given must include, in respect of cost:

* the cost or revalued amount at the beginning and end of the year;
* the effect of any revision due to a revaluation made during the year;
* acquisitions made during the year;
* disposals made during the year, and
* any transfers of items between categories.

Similar information must also be given in respect of accumulated amortisation:

* the cumulative amount of any provisions for amortisation at the beginning and end of the year;
* the provision for amortisation made during the year;
* the amount of amortisation released on disposals during the year, and
* any other adjustments made to the accumulated amortisation during the year.

If the alternative accounting rules have been applied, then the financial statements must also state:

* the years in which the assets were valued, and the values at that time, and
* if the amounts have been valued during the year, then the names of the persons who valued them, or details of their qualifications for performing the valuation, and the basis of valuation used.

Under FRS 10, the following additional disclosures are required in respect of intangible fixed assets:

* the method used to value intangible assets;
* each class of intangible asset must be shown separately in the statutory disclosures;
* the methods and periods of amortisation of intangible assets and the reasons for choosing those periods;
* where an amortisation period is shortened or extended following a review of the remaining useful economic lives of intangible assets, the reason and the effect, if material, in the year of change;
* where there has been a change in the amortisation method used, the reason and the effect, if material, in the year of change, and
* where an intangible asset is amortised over a period that exceeds 20 years from the date of acquisition or is not amortised, the grounds for rebutting the 20-year presumption should be given, with a reasoned explanation based on the specific factors contributing to the durability of the intangible asset.

11.8.7 The FRSSE

Companies adopting the FRSSE are exempt from complying with FRS 10, except in relation to purchased goodwill arising on consolidation where group accounts are being prepared voluntarily. The FRSSE includes a simplified version of FRS 10's requirements in relation to intangible assets (and goodwill arising in an individual company's books). The main differences are as follows:

- internally generated intangible assets should not be capitalised (even in the limited cases in which FRS 10 would permit this);
- there is an absolute prohibition on useful lives exceeding 20 years, which also means that no automatic annual impairment reviews will be required, and
- intangible assets may not be revalued (even in the cases that would be allowed by FRS 10).

The FRSSE does not incorporate the additional disclosure requirements of FRS 10, although the statutory disclosures noted above do still apply.

11.9 RESEARCH AND DEVELOPMENT

11.9.1 Introduction

The statutory balance sheet formats include an item covering development costs, but this does not mean that all development costs that have been incurred can necessarily be treated as a fixed asset.

> Notwithstanding that an item in respect of "development costs" is included under "fixed assets" in the balance sheet formats set out in Part I of this Schedule, an amount may only be included in a company's balance sheet in respect of development costs in special circumstances. (Para. 21 (1), Sch. 1 to The Large and Medium-sized Companies and Groups (Accounts and Reports) Regulations 2008 (SI 2008/410) and Para. 21 (1), Sch. 1 to The Small Companies and Groups (Accounts and Directors' Report) Regulations 2008 (SI 2008/409).)

Since there is an accounting standard dealing with this subject (SSAP 13 *Accounting for Research and Development*), it is generally accepted that where a company is able to include an amount in its balance sheet under the provisions of that standard then that will be deemed to be sufficient to comply with the 'special circumstances' provision included in the legislation. The FRSSE is consistent with SSAP 13.

Potential impact of the FRSME

The FRSME prohibits the capitalisation of both research and development expenditure. Whilst this is the same as the SSAP 13 treatment of research, it is fundamentally different in relation to development costs.

The FRSME does allow the capitalisation of research and development expenditure where it forms part of the cost of another asset that meets the recognition criteria relevant to that category of asset.

11.9.2 Definitions

SSAP 13 provides the following definition of research and development, and of the various sub-categories included within it:

> Research and development expenditure means expenditure falling into one or more of the following broad categories (except to the extent that it relates to locating or exploiting oil, gas or mineral deposits or is reimbursable by third parties either directly or under the terms of a firm contract to develop and manufacture at an agreed price calculated to reimburse both elements of expenditure):
>
> (a) *pure (or basic) research*: Experimental or theoretical work undertaken primarily to acquire new scientific or technical knowledge for its own sake rather than directed towards any specific aim or application;
> (b) *applied research*: Original or critical investigation undertaken in order to gain new scientific or technical knowledge and directed towards a specific practical aim or objective;
> (c) *development*: Use of scientific or technical knowledge in order to produce new or substantially improved materials, devices, products or services, to install new processes or systems prior to the commencement of commercial production or commercial applications, or to improve substantially those already produced or installed. (Para. 21, SSAP 13.)

Where research and development is undertaken on behalf of a third party who will reimburse the costs, either directly or indirectly through the price charged, then SSAP 13 does not apply. The costs incurred do not form part of the intangible fixed assets of the company, in any circumstances, but instead will be treated as either stock or long-term contract work in progress and accounted for accordingly. For these purposes, the costs incurred are not treated as research and development.

The distinction between pure and applied research may not always be absolutely clear in practice, and pure research may evolve and become applied research as the whole project progresses. For the accountant this does not cause any problem, since the accounting treatment required by SSAP 13 in both cases is identical.

There may also be difficulties in establishing the precise division between applied research and development. Again, such difficulties are unlikely to be fundamental, since separate criteria are established for when development costs can be included in a balance sheet as an intangible fixed asset. These criteria are separate from the criteria for deciding whether or not an item should be described as development.

SSAP 13 contains a list of items, not intended to be comprehensive, that would normally be considered to be research and development:

(a) experimental, theoretical or other work aimed at the discovery of new knowledge, or the advancement of existing knowledge;
(b) searching for applications of that knowledge;
(c) formulation and design of possible applications for such work;
(d) testing in search for, or evaluation of, product, service or process alternatives;
(e) design, construction and testing of pre-production prototypes and models and development batches;
(f) design of products, services, processes or systems involving new technology or substantially improving those already produced or installed;
(g) construction and operation of pilot plants. (Para. 6, SSAP 13.)

As the list progresses there is a gradual move from pure research to development.

The first item, for example, is clearly pure research, since it is undertaken with a view to the acquisition of new knowledge. Similarly, the final item is clearly development, since when a pilot plant is produced the project must be aimed very specifically at the production of a new product or service. A logical division might be that items (a) to (d) are research, since they all appear to be speculative and without a definite commercial application, and that items (e) to (g) are development, since they all appear to be at the stage prior to commercial production.

SSAP 13 also provides a list of typical items that would not fall within the definition of research and development:

(a) testing and analysis either of equipment or products for purposes of quality or quantity control;
(b) periodic alterations to existing products, services or processes even though these may represent some improvement;
(c) operational research not tied to a specific research and development activity;
(d) cost of corrective action in connection with break-downs during commercial production;
(e) legal and administrative work in connection with patent applications, records and litigation and the sale or licensing of patents;
(f) activity, including design and construction engineering, relating to the construction, relocation, rearrangement or start-up of facilities or equipment other than facilities or equipment whose sole use is for a particular research and development project;
(g) market research. (Para. 7, SSAP 13.)

11.9.3 *Fixed assets used in research and development*

There is essentially no distinction between tangible fixed assets used in research and development and other tangible fixed assets. The accounting treatment is the same. Where tangible fixed assets are acquired or constructed for use in research and development activities, they should be capitalised and written off over their useful economic lives.

11.9.4   Accounting treatment for research

Whether the research is pure or applied, research costs should be written off through the profit and loss account in the year in which they are incurred. In no circumstances should they be treated as a fixed asset of the company.

This does not imply that such research will have no commercial benefit for the company. It simply indicates that such costs should not be recorded on the balance sheet because of the following factors, based on the recognition criteria in FRS 5.

(1)   It would often be impossible to allocate the benefit of such research to particular accounting periods, and as such the simplest treatment is to write off the costs as incurred. With hindsight, of course, it is often easy to see where the benefits of research have been gained, but this is of little value when preparing financial statements at the time the expenditure is incurred.

(2)   It would not usually be prudent to carry forward such costs to match against future income, because when a project is only at the research stage there is unlikely to be any guarantee that there will ever be any future income.

11.9.5   Recognition of development costs

Given the 'special circumstances' provision included in the legislation, it is reasonable to assume that all development costs should be written off in the year in which they are incurred unless there are very good and justifiable reasons why they should be carried forward.

The introduction to SSAP 13 stresses that the accounting treatment of research and development is derived from the basic concepts applied to all areas of accounting, as they were defined in SSAP 2 at the time that SSAP 13 was issued:

> The accounting policies to be followed in respect of research and development expenditure must have regard to the fundamental accounting concepts including the "accruals" concept by which revenue and costs are accrued, matched and dealt with in the period to which they relate and the "prudence" concept by which revenue and profits are not anticipated but are recognised only when realised in the form either of cash or of other assets the ultimate cash realisation of which can be established with reasonable certainty. It is a corollary of the prudence concept that expenditure should be written off in the period in which it arises unless its relationship to the revenue of a future period can be established with reasonable certainty. (Para. 1, SSAP 13.)

Although the accruals and prudence concepts are no longer defined in the same way now that FRS 18 *Accounting Policies* (covered in Chapter 2) has superseded SSAP 2, the principles stated above are still valid in relation to the treatment of research and development costs.

It is, therefore, always necessary to start from the assumption that development costs will be written off as incurred. This provides that basic justification for the very stringent conditions contained in SSAP 13 for treating development costs as an intangible fixed asset.

Companies may always choose to write off development expenditure as it is incurred, even if they meet the conditions in SSAP 13 for carrying forward the costs. The policy of capitalisation is allowed by the standard, but it is not required. By contrast, the international standard which now deals with development costs, IAS 38 *Intangible Assets*, states that development costs should be capitalised if the criteria in that standard are met.

Even when the development stage has been reached, it is often difficult to guarantee that future income will be sufficient to cover the costs that have been incurred. In such circumstances the prudent treatment is to write the cost off. However, where development has reached a sufficient stage, such that the future commercial success of the project is relatively certain, then to write off the cost would no longer be an appropriate treatment. In such a case it is the matching concept that must take precedence. Since prudence no longer acts as a limiting factor, it is now necessary to attempt to ensure that the costs of development are matched with the income generated by the development. It is appropriate to record the development costs as an asset and to write them off over the accounting periods expected to benefit from their application.

SSAP 13 sets specific conditions, (a) to (e), which must be met in order for development expenditure to be treated as an intangible fixed asset:

Development expenditure should be written off in the year of expenditure except in the following circumstances when it may be deferred to future periods:

(a) there is a clearly defined project, and
(b) the related expenditure is separately identifiable, and
(c) the outcome of such a project has been assessed with reasonable certainty as to:

    (i) its technical feasibility, and
    (ii) its ultimate commercial viability considered in the light of factors such as likely market conditions (including competing products), public opinion, consumer and environmental legislation, and

(d) the aggregate of the deferred development costs, any further development costs, and related production, selling and administration costs is reasonably expected to be exceeded by related future sales or other revenues, and
(e) adequate resources exist, or are reasonably expected to be available, to

enable the project to be completed and to provide any consequential increases in working capital. (Para. 25, SSAP 13.)

These conditions are discussed in turn.

Condition (a), that there should be a clearly defined project, is largely intended to provide an additional form of differentiation of research from development. Where the project cannot be clearly defined it provides a very strong indication that it has not yet reached the stage at which its commercial success can be assessed with any degree of certainty.

Condition (b) relates to the previous condition. There may be a connection between the extent to which the project is defined and the degree to which the costs can be differentiated. Where the project has not reached the stage at which it is thought necessary to differentiate its costs this may also indicate that it is not yet sufficiently developed for an assessment of its commercial prospects.

Condition (c) is broken into two parts; the first part is a necessary requirement of the second, since it could never be assumed that a project was reasonably certain of commercial viability if it were not already proven that the project was technically feasible. Technical feasibility will always need to be assessed by experts in the relevant field. Commercial viability simply implies that it will be legal to use or sell the product and that there will be a market for the goods involved, if they are for sale rather than use.

Condition (d) is probably the most stringent. If strictly interpreted it can also be seen to have undesirable consequences. Put simply, the revenues reasonably expected to be generated in the future, or the savings in cost, must exceed all of the costs that have been or will be incurred in the production of the goods or service for sale or use. The rationale for the condition is that unless the project will be profitable, then the expenditure will have no value to the company. This is an application of the prudence principle and similar to the normal rule that stocks must be stated at the lower of their cost and net realisable value.

However, at the time of the development, the company may not be in a position to have such reasonable expectations over the life cycle of the product being developed. For example, the development may be driven by strategic considerations, and so far as the company can estimate currently, the investment may make a small loss. This would mean that the whole of the development costs incurred may need to be written off. The international accounting standard IAS 38 (as revised) contains more realistic conditions for treating development expenditure as an asset including:

(d) how the intangible asset will generate probable future economic benefits. Among other things, the entity can demonstrate the existence of a market for the output of the intangible asset or the intangible asset itself or, if it is to be used internally, the usefulness of the intangible asset; (Para. 57, IAS 38.)

This is then supplemented by the statement:

To demonstrate how an intangible asset will generate probable future economic benefits, an entity assesses the future economic benefits to be received from the asset using the principles in IAS 36, *Impairment of Assets*. If the asset will generate economic benefits only in combination with other assets, the entity applies the concept of cash-generating units in IAS 36. (Para. 60, IAS 38.)

Therefore, under international standards, the amount of an asset recognised is restricted to the recoverable amount. Although deferred development costs fall within the scope of FRS 11 *Impairment of Fixed Assets and Goodwill*, the conditions in SSAP 13 are such that, strictly, no asset may be recognised unless a profit is anticipated. SSAP 13 states that:

In the foregoing circumstances development expenditure may be deferred to the extent that its recovery can reasonably be regarded as assured. (Para. 26, SSAP 13.)

However, despite the inclusion of the phrase 'to the extent', this does not modify the accounting treatment required, and adds nothing to the standard. The standard still states that revenues must exceed costs.

EXAMPLE

A company has incurred development costs of £1,000,000. The future total costs of producing and selling the goods developed are expected to be £2,000,000. Consider the treatment of the expenditure under two situations:

(a) the future revenue expected at this stage of the project is £2,999,999;
(b) the future revenue expected at this stage of the project is £3,000,001.

	(a) £	(b) £
Under SSAP 13 the two treatments would be:		
Total expected revenue	2,999,999	3,000,001
Total expected costs	(3,000,000)	(3,000,000)
Expected profits	(1)	1
Balance sheet amount capitalised	0	1,000,000
Under IAS 38, the treatments would be:		
Balance sheet value capitalised	999,999	1,000,000

The example quoted is, quite obviously, exaggerated. Nonetheless, it does indicate a very important problem with SSAP 13. At the time of the development, the company may not be able to justify reasonable expectations about the profitability of the project. A company will need to have financial projections covering a number of years. All projections are uncertain, and considerable prudence will need to be exercised in their creation. It is possible that a projection will only be admissible if there has been extensive market research, or if the underlying assumptions can be proven in some other way.

Since companies should comply with accounting standards, the requirements of SSAP 13 should be followed, even where they lead to the result shown above. In borderline cases it might be possible to rely upon the true and fair exemption, and to fail to apply SSAP 13 as it would not lead to a meaningful or useful result. Reliance upon truth and fairness to fail to comply with an accounting standard is, however, an extreme measure and should be used only where absolutely necessary. Full disclosure in accordance with FRS 18 *Accounting Policies* would be required.

Condition (e) for capitalisation in paragraph 25 of SSAP 13 is simply a criterion of prudence. If it is not certain that a company has, or will obtain, sufficient funds to complete the project then it should not record an intangible asset. This condition could be seen as unnecessary, since if it is not met then the previous condition could also not be met. Where it is far from certain that a company will be able to complete a project, it must also be far from certain that future revenues (if any) will exceed the costs already incurred or to be incurred.

These conditions are not only applied at the stage at which initial capitalisation is considered. They also need to be considered each year, and a new assessment made of whether or not each condition is still being met. Where it becomes clear that the conditions are no longer being met, the development costs should be written off in the current period.

This annual reconsideration contrasts with the original SSAP 13, which required that where development costs had previously been written off, but the conditions used to justify their write-off no longer applied, then the amounts involved should still not be reinstated. This is not an acceptable practice under the Companies Act 1985.

> Where the reasons for which any provision was made . . . have ceased to apply to any extent that provision must be written back to the extent that it is no longer necessary.

> Any amounts written back . . . which are not shown in the profit and loss account must be disclosed (either separately or in aggregate) in a note to the accounts. (Para. 20, Sch. 1 to The Large and Medium-sized Companies and Groups (Accounts and Reports) Regulations 2008 (SI 2008/410) and Para. 20,, Sch. 1 to The Small Companies and Groups (Accounts and Directors' Report) Regulations 2008 (SI 2008/409).)

As a result, if the reasons for such provisions can no longer be justified, then those provisions have to be written back.

SSAP 13 requires that where a company adopts a policy of capitalising development expenditure that meets the criteria then it must apply the same policy to all projects that meet the criteria. This is nothing more than a statement of the concept of consistency.

11.9.6 Amortisation

SSAP 13 requires that where development costs are recognised as an asset they should be amortised over the periods expected to benefit from their use. Amortisation should commence when commercial production begins, or when the good or service developed comes into use.

The standard suggests that it may be appropriate to charge amortisation in line with the sale or use of the product, service, process or system. This seems to be the most appropriate method, where it can be used. In other cases, it may be necessary to charge over the period expected to benefit using some other method, as with most other fixed assets.

11.9.7 Valuation

SSAP 13 does not mention the possibility that the company may wish to state its development costs at valuation rather than historical cost, although the tone of the standard indicates that such a treatment would not be acceptable.

Development costs should never be stated at a valuation. The only possible basis for the valuation of such an asset is likely to be discounted future earnings. As noted earlier in this chapter, the inclusion of an asset valued on the basis of discounted future earnings is likely to distort the profits recorded in particular accounting periods, and should therefore be avoided.

11.9.8 Disclosure

The disclosure requirements for research and development include all of the statutory requirements for intangible fixed assets, which were stated above.

In addition, SSAP 13 requires that the accounting policy for research and development should be stated. Where the amounts involved are material – and of course accounting standards do not apply to immaterial items – then the statement of this policy would already be required by FRS 18.

Movements on deferred development expenditure and the amounts carried forward at the beginning and end of the period should also be disclosed.

The amount of research and development expenditure which has been charged in the profit and loss account, analysed between the current year's expenditure, and any amounts amortised from deferred expenditure, must also be disclosed by some companies.

The companies that must provide this disclosure are:

- public limited companies;

- banking and insurance companies;
- parent undertakings of public limited companies, or banking and insurance companies, and
- companies that exceed the criteria set in the Companies Act 2006 for a medium-sized company, multiplied in each case by 10.

For accounting periods beginning on or after 6 April 2008, these limits are turnover of £259 million and a balance sheet total of £129 million, and 2,500 employees.

11.9.9 Website development costs

UITF Abstract 29 *Website Development Costs* has been mandatory since accounting periods ending on or after 23 March 2001. The Abstract clarifies when a company should recognise the costs of developing a website as an asset for its own use, and sets out strict criteria to be satisfied if costs are to be capitalised.

The Abstract divides website development costs into four main categories:

- planning costs, which should be treated as an expense when incurred;
- application and infrastructure development costs, including purchase of a domain name, hardware costs and software costs, which are largely covered by the existing fixed assets requirements in FRS 10 *Goodwill and Intangible Assets* (eg a domain name) and FRS 15 *Tangible Fixed Assets* (eg hardware and software costs);
- design costs to develop the design of individual web pages, and
- content costs, ie expenditure on preparing, accumulating and posting the website content.

Abstract 29 requires capitalisation of development costs, excluding planning costs, provided that strict criteria are met to ensure that there is a sufficiently certain relationship between the expenditure and the future economic benefits. Expenditure to maintain or operate a website once it has been developed should be charged to the profit and loss account as incurred.

Website design and content development costs should be capitalised only to the extent that they lead to the creation of an enduring asset delivering benefits at least as great as the amount capitalised. If the criteria are not satisfied, the costs should be expensed. The main criteria are that:

- the expenditure should be separately identifiable;
- the technical feasibility and commercial viability of the website must have been assessed with reasonable certainty;
- the website must be expected to generate sales or other revenues directly (eg through online sales, advertising or subscription fees) and the expenditure must make an enduring contribution to the development of the revenue-generating capabilities of the website;

- there should be a reasonable expectation that the present value of the future cash flows to be generated by the website will be no less than the amounts capitalised, and
- adequate resources should exist, or be reasonably expected to be available, to enable the project to be completed and to meet any consequential need for increased working capital.

These are clearly based on the criteria for capitalisation of development costs set out in SSAP 13, although with some changes to make them appropriate for website development costs.

Capitalised website costs should be treated as tangible fixed assets in accordance with FRS 15, and depreciated over their estimated useful economic lives, which are likely to be short. It is also possible that the components of the asset may have different lives, eg the design or content may require more frequent replacement than the infrastructure. The costs capitalised should be reviewed for impairment if there is an indication that the carrying amounts may not be recoverable.

If a website is used only for advertising or promotion of the company's own products or services, it is unlikely that there will be sufficient evidence to demonstrate that revenues will be generated directly from the site.

11.10 IMPAIRMENT OF FIXED ASSETS AND GOODWILL

11.10.1 Introduction

There is a long-standing statutory requirement for fixed assets to be written down if there has been a permanent diminution in value:

> Provisions for diminution in value must be made in respect of any fixed asset which has diminished in value if the reduction in its value is expected to be permanent (whether its useful economic life is limited or not), and the amount to be included in respect of it must be reduced accordingly.

> Any provisions ... which are not shown in the profit and loss account shall be disclosed (either separately or in aggregate) in a note to the accounts. (Para. 19 (2) and (3), Sch. 1 to The Large and Medium-sized Companies and Groups (Accounts and Reports) Regulations 2008 (SI 2008/410) and Para. 19 (2) and (3), Sch. 1 to The Small Companies and Groups (Accounts and Directors' Report) Regulations 2008 (SI 2008/409).)

Although legislation has never set out how to apply this requirement in detail, SSAP 12 did provide more specific requirements in relation to tangible assets. These included a requirement to write an asset down to its recoverable amount if there had been a permanent diminution. However, there was no requirement to write down assets where there had been a temporary diminution in value. This led inevitably to problems in practice in determining whether a diminution was temporary or permanent. Additionally, there was no detailed guidance on how to calculate recoverable amount or how to present write-downs.

The need for a comprehensive standard dealing with diminutions (or impairments as they have become known) intensified when the ASB addressed the issues of goodwill and intangible assets. Many large companies had adopted a practice of not amortising intangibles such as brands, but instead operated a policy of annual review to identify possible diminution in value by reference to forecasts of future cash flows. There was also widespread opposition to the mandatory amortisation of capitalised goodwill, with many large companies arguing that they should be allowed to apply the same approach as for capitalised brands, ie no amortisation but annual reviews to identify possible diminutions. Consequently, the ASB developed a standard to deal with the issue as part of its goodwill and intangibles project, but also included other assets within its scope as many of the issues arising also applied to tangible assets (and to investments).

In 1998, the ASB issued FRS 11 *Impairment of Fixed Assets and Goodwill* to address the problems outlined above and to complement FRS 10 *Goodwill and Intangible Assets*. FRS 11 became mandatory for accounting periods ending on or after 23 December 1998. The standard made major changes to procedures for dealing with impairments, which FRS 11 defines as a reduction in the recoverable amount of a fixed asset or goodwill below its carrying amount.

The standard does not impose any general requirement to conduct impairment reviews annually, but does require such reviews where there is an indication that an asset or group of related assets may be impaired. In simple terms, FRS 11 requires that assets be stated at the lower of their carrying amount and their recoverable amount. The latter is defined as the higher of:

- net realisable value, and
- value in use, which is the present value of the future cash flows obtainable as a result of an asset's continued use, including those resulting from its ultimate disposal.

FRS 11 glosses over the previous distinction between permanent and temporary diminutions in value, made under statute, since in all cases there is a need to consider future cash flows from the asset. However, in limited cases, the presentation of an impairment loss will differ according to its cause.

Potential impact of the FRSME

The FRSME requirements are broadly similar to the requirements of FRS 11, although often far less specific – matters dealt with in considerable detail in FRS 11 are dealt with briefly and at a very high level in the FRSME. There are some basic differences, and, in particular, the FRSME contains no requirement for annual impairment reviews (as FRS 11 may, where goodwill or intangible are deemed to have long or indefinite lives, although of course that situation itself cannot, or is extremely unlikely to arise, under the FRSME), but at the same time is then fairly specific in setting out what actually needs to be done in determining whether there is any indication of impairment.

11.10.2   Scope of FRS 11

FRS 11 applies to all financial statements that are intended to give a true and fair view of a reporting entity's financial position and profit or loss (or income and expenditure) for a period. The applicability of FRS 11 to entities applying the FRSSE is dealt with separately below. FRS 11 applies to purchased goodwill that is recognised in the balance sheet and all fixed assets, except:

- financial assets within the scope of the FRS dealing with disclosures of derivatives and financial instruments, which is now normally FRS 29 (covered in Chapter 13);
- investment properties as defined in SSAP 19 *Accounting for Investment Properties*, and
- an entity's own shares held by an ESOP.

Since FRS 11 was, rather obviously, issued prior to FRS 13 it did not make reference to that standard. As a result, no change to the scope of FRS 11 was required on the issue of FRS 25, and no further change required on the move to FRS 29.

Note that, as investments in subsidiaries, associates and joint ventures are nearly always outside the scope of FRS 29, these investments fall within the scope of FRS 11, whereas most other investments do not. This could be particularly significant where a parent company recognises an impairment of goodwill or an intangible asset recognised on consolidation of a subsidiary. Such an impairment may also necessitate reviewing the carrying value of the investment in the subsidiary in the parent's own balance sheet.

The scope of FRS 11 has also been effectively limited by FRS 30. With respect to heritage assets, FRS 11 applies only where there is an indication of impairment as dealt with in FRS 30. This standard provides, as examples, where the asset has suffered physical deterioration or breakage or new doubts arise as to its authenticity. The other indicators of impairment given in FRS 11, such as declines in market value, are not seen as being necessarily relevant given that, by definition, heritage assets are not held in order to benefit (or suffer) from changes in their market value. Unhelpfully, the ASB's notes on the development of FRS 30 make it clear that the standard does not specify or restrict the other circumstances in which an impairment review is required, and instead note that this is a matter of 'professional judgement'.

11.10.3   *Requirement for impairment reviews*

FRS 11 includes the following general requirement:

> A review for impairment of a fixed asset or goodwill should be carried out if events or changes in circumstances indicate that the carrying amount of the fixed asset or goodwill may not be recoverable. (Para. 8, FRS 11.)

The ASB points out that impairment occurs because something has happened either to the fixed assets themselves or to the economic environment in which the fixed assets are operated. FRS 11 lists possible indications of impairment, which are summarised as follows.

(1)   Operating losses or net cash outflows in the current period, together with either past losses or cash outflows or the expectation of future losses or cash outflows, in the business in which the fixed asset or goodwill is involved.

(2)   A significant decline in the fixed asset's market value.

(3)   Evidence of obsolescence or physical damage to the asset.

(4)   A significant adverse change in the business or market, such as a new competitor, changes in the statutory or regulatory environment, or a fall in any 'indicator of value' (such as turnover) used to measure the fair value of a fixed asset on acquisition.

(5)   A commitment by management to undertake a significant reorganisation.

(6)   A major loss of key employees.

(7)   A significant increase in market interest rates or other market rates of return that are likely to affect materially the fixed asset's recoverable amount.

Note that, from (1), above, a track record of problems, or current problems that are expected to continue, is required for there to be indications of impairment; not simply an isolated loss. In (7), above, a change in short-term interest rates can usually be ignored. However, long-term rates are more likely to affect the required returns from assets and therefore impact on net present value calculations.

In the case of goodwill and intangible assets falling within its scope, FRS 10 includes two additional requirements. Firstly, FRS 10 requires annual impairment reviews where the useful economic life of the assets or goodwill exceeds 20 years from initial recognition or is indefinite. This applies regardless of whether there is any indication of impairment. Secondly, where intangible assets or goodwill are amortised over a period of 20 years or less from initial recognition, FRS 10 requires a 'first year review'. The first year review is itself conducted in two stages at the end of the first full year following initial recognition of the intangible asset or goodwill. In the first stage, any possible impairment is identified by comparing post-acquisition performance in the first year with pre-acquisition forecasts used to support the purchase price. Then, if the initial review indicates that the post-acquisition performance has failed to meet pre-acquisition expectations or if any other previously unforeseen events or changes in circumstances indicate that the carrying values may not be recoverable, a full impairment review must be carried out in accordance with FRS 11.

FRS 15 introduces a further requirement for annual impairment reviews of tangible assets, other than non-depreciable land, which are either not depreciated on the grounds of immateriality or which have a remaining useful economic life exceeding 50 years. As with the FRS 10 requirements for annual impairment reviews, these reviews must be performed even when there is no indication of impairment.

11.10.4 *Procedure for performing impairment reviews*

The basic procedure for an impairment review is contained in the standard:

> The impairment review should comprise a comparison of the carrying amount of the fixed asset or goodwill with its recoverable amount (the higher of net realisable value and value in use). (Para. 14, FRS 11.)

The logic behind this is that companies will make use of an asset in the best way possible. They will either dispose of it or continue to use it, depending on which generates the greatest present value.

The procedures for a full impairment review are potentially complex and time-consuming: it is vital to stress that they are not required as a matter of course. Even where they are performed there may be no need to undertake detailed calculations of value in use (which are dealt with below). FRS 11 points out that simple calculations may make it very clear that the amount involved exceeds the carrying value, in which case no further impairment review is needed. Alternatively, these calculations may indicate that value in use is below the net realisable value of the asset, in which case the net realisable value of the asset is the relevant amount to compare with the carrying amount. It may also be possible to argue that, where there is an active market for the type of asset in question, the net realisable value may be a close approximation to value in use.

The deferred tax balances that would arise in each case should also be taken into account in determining whether value in use or net realisable value is the appropriate figure to use. This will often be relevant only where a company has previously revalued assets, although it may also be important in reducing the amount of write-downs due to impairment, as the potential tax benefit may increase.

11.10.5   Net realisable value

Net realisable value is defined as:

> The amount at which an asset could be disposed of, less any direct selling costs. (Para. 2, FRS 11.)

Direct selling costs may include such items as legal costs or stamp duty or the cost of removing a sitting tenant from a building. Indirect costs, such as the costs connected with the reorganisation of a business, must not be taken into account in determining the net realisable value.

The determination of net realisable value may prove to be a problem, but not really one with which the accountant can help. Valuations may need to be undertaken, either internally by the business or externally.

11.10.6   Value in use

Value in use is defined as:

> The present value of the future cash flows obtainable as a result of an asset's continued use, including those resulting from its ultimate disposal. (Para. 2, FRS 11.)

To calculate value in use, it is necessary to identify the asset (or group of assets), the cash flows and a suitable discount rate. Each of these will be considered in turn.

Assets and income-generating units

Some assets may generate an income stream that is largely independent of the company's other income streams, a possible example being a vessel. However, FRS 11 notes that it will rarely be practicable to determine the cash flows associated with a single asset, as most assets are used in combination with others and with goodwill. As a result, it is expected that most calculations of value in use will take account of groups of assets rather than assets on their own. The groups of assets to be used for the purposes of impairment reviews are referred to as 'income-generating units'. These are defined as:

> A group of assets, liabilities and associated goodwill that generates income that is largely independent of the reporting entity's other income streams. The assets and liabilities include those directly involved in generating the income and an appropriate portion of those used to generate more than one income stream. (Para. 2, FRS 11.)

The carrying value of the income-generating unit is the net of the carrying amounts of all of the assets, liabilities and goodwill allocated to that unit.

Note that, under FRS 11, any asset where there is already an intention to sell should be treated as an income-generating unit in its own right, although in this case there is no distinction between the value in use of an asset and its net realisable value.

The main text of the standard gives rather more detail on the identification of income-generating units:

> Income-generating units should be identified by dividing the total income of the entity into as many largely independent income streams as is reasonably practicable. Except as permitted . . . each of the identifiable assets and liabilities of the entity, excluding deferred tax balances, interest-bearing debt, dividends payable and other items relating wholly to financing, should be attributed to (or apportioned between) one (or more) income-generating unit(s). (Para. 27, FRS 11.)

Items that will generate cash flows equal to their carrying value in the balance sheet may be excluded from the income-generating units, and the income they will generate excluded from the value in use calculation. This makes no difference in practice as, were they to be included, the results would be the same. This means, for example, that many debtors can be excluded from the calculations.

In determining how to break down a total business between income-generating units, a balance has to be drawn between:

- on the one hand, wanting to make the groups as small as possible to ensure that any necessary write-downs are allocated to the businesses affected, but
- on the other hand, the fact that each group of assets has to be capable of generating its own cash flows, largely independent of the others.

The division into income-generating units may follow the way in which management organises the business, for example into product groupings. However, FRS 11 points out that where a division does not have an external market for its product, it will not be a separate income-generating unit. The standard also notes that where a division does have an external market for its product, impairment calculations should be based on the market price, not any internal transfer price.

For some businesses, there may be only one income-generating unit for the company as a whole, for example, where the company is in a single business and the cash flows of any divisions that it may have are all interdependent and not separately identifiable.

Practical considerations may also apply. One of the examples provided with the standard is that of a chain of restaurants. It might be possible to undertake impairment reviews on a restaurant-by-restaurant basis. However, there is little likelihood that such reviews will give rise to material impairments. As a result, it would be acceptable to group together different restaurants that are exposed to similar economic factors, for example, by region.

The allocation of assets and liabilities into income-generating units will often be a complex exercise. For many businesses there will be only a relatively small number of such streams, but even in such cases there may still be problems in the allocation of general assets which are used by the company as a whole and not by any particular part of its business. Some items, one example given in the standard being head office assets and liabilities, may need to be apportioned between the income-generating units. The standard does not give a single methodology by which such an allocation can be made and the requirement is that it should be reasonable. However, in some cases it may not be possible to make a sensible allocation. In this case:

> If it is not possible to apportion certain central assets meaningfully across the income-generating units to which they contribute, these assets may be excluded from the individual income-generating units. However, an additional impairment review should be performed on the excluded central assets. In this review, the income-generating units to which the central assets contribute should be combined and their combined carrying amount (including that of the central assets) should be compared with their combined value in use. (Para. 32, FRS 11.)

One of the practical problems that is faced is that of the allocation of goodwill, except where a specific goodwill balance is attributable to one income-generating unit:

> Capitalised goodwill should be attributed to (or apportioned between) income-generating units or groups of similar units. If they were acquired as part of the same investment and are involved in similar parts of the business, individual units identified for the purpose of monitoring the recoverability of assets may be combined with other units to enable the recoverability of the related goodwill to be assessed. (Para. 34, FRS 11.)

This requirement (together with that in respect of central items that cannot be allocated) may mean that multi-level impairment reviews need to be undertaken. An initial impairment review will need to be done at the level of each income-generating unit. A further review may then be required where various income-generating units are combined together to deal with the allocation of central items, the allocation of goodwill, or both.

Cash flows

In order to calculate the present value of income-generating units the future cash flows must be estimated. The standard is fairly precise in giving rules for this, particularly when dealing with longer-term items:

> The expected future cash flows of the income-generating unit, including any allocation of central overheads but excluding cash flows relating to financing and tax, should be based on reasonable and supportable assumptions. The cash flows should be consistent with the most up-to-date budgets and plans that have been formally approved by management. Cash flows for the period beyond that covered by formal budgets and plans should assume a steady or declining growth rate. Only in exceptional circumstances should:

(a) the period before the steady or declining growth rate is assumed extend to more than five years; or

(b) the steady or declining growth rate exceed the long-term average growth rate for the country or countries in which the business operates. (Para. 36, FRS 11.)

If a company wishes to use a higher growth rate for a longer period, it must be able to demonstrate that, for example, the industry is going to perform better in the future than the general economy and that the business will be able to perform as well as its sector.

While this part of the standard appears reasonable in theory, it may prove very problematic in practice. While most small companies will, if they wish, be able to ignore the detailed requirements of the standard by adopting the FRSSE, there are still a considerable number of larger businesses that do not have the formal projections and budgets that are expected by the standard. In the absence of such information, companies may either rely upon net realisable value (which may lead them to make unnecessary write-downs) or prepare such projections for the first time, obviously having no track record of accurate projection.

There are certain cash flows that must be ignored in estimating the future cash flows for the purposes of impairment calculations:

- cash outflows or costs savings associated with reorganisations for which no provision has been made, and
- future capital expenditure that will improve or enhance the income-generating units or assets in excess of their originally assessed standard of performance, or the benefits of this expenditure.

FRS 11 allows an exception for the reorganisation and additional capital costs that may be associated with the acquisition of a newly acquired income-generating unit such as a subsidiary. Account may be taken of such costs (and more importantly the future benefits they will bring) so long as they were anticipated in plans in existence at the time of performing an impairment review in the first full year after the acquisition took place. This is crucial in industries such as shipping, as it is only on this basis that companies will be entitled to take account of future drydocking costs in performing their calculations. Without this exception, companies would be forced to make projections that ignored future major refurbishment of assets. While this would cut the costs going forward, it would even more dramatically reduce the projected income. It does mean that additional capital expenditure that was not anticipated at the date of acquisition (such as an extended life programme) may not be taken into account in the calculations until the work has been done. This is really no different from current practice.

Discount rate

Once the cash flows have been determined, the next stage is to decide upon the discount rate that should be used in arriving at the present value of those cash flows. The standard deals with this in the following terms.

> The discount rate used should be an estimate of the rate that the market would expect on an equally risky investment. It should exclude the effects of any risk for which the cash flows have been adjusted and should be calculated on a pre-tax basis. (Para. 41, FRS 11.)

Note that the above represents a change from FRED 15 (the exposure draft which preceded FRS 11) which had proposed that calculations be performed on a post-tax basis. FRS 11 does not provide a single method by which the discount rate may be determined, but mentions that some of the approaches that might be used are:

- the rate implicit in market transactions in respect of similar assets;
- the weighted average cost of capital (WACC) of a listed company with a similar risk profile for its cash flows, and
- the WACC for the entity, adjusted for the specific risk profile of each unit.

If the final approach is adopted, FRS 11 points out that if it were used for all of the income-generating units (including those in which there is no indication of impairment) this would have to arrive at the entity's WACC in total. Also, where the calculations for units include cash flows where a higher than average growth rate has been assumed for periods more than five years in the future, the discount rate should be higher to compensate for the increased risk. As with forecasting cash flows, the approach adopted in the standard may appear reasonable in theory, but is likely to prove impractical for many businesses to apply, as they will lack the necessary information and expertise.

The standard also mentions that it may be possible to adjust the cash flows for risk, and then use a risk-free rate as a discount rate. The important thing is that risk is not double-counted. Whether or not inflation adjustments are made will depend upon whether the projected cash flows are stated in current prices. These requirements may have some theoretical validity, but they are often going to be difficult to implement in practice.

The sensitivity of impairment calculations to changes in the discount rate is illustrated in the following example.

EXAMPLE

A company has an asset which is an income-generating unit in itself. The net book value is currently £70,000 and its net realisable value is £50,000. The asset is expected to have a remaining useful economic life of 10 years, with no scrap value. The forecast annual net cash flows are £10,000, which may be assumed to occur at the end of each year. The appropriate discount rate is 10 per cent.

In this example, value in use may be calculated using the following annuity formula:

$$\frac{1}{r(1 + r)^n}$$

Where:

r = discount rate, expressed as a decimal number of periods

n = number of periods

Impairment will be assessed as follows:

Value in use (VIU) $= £10,000 \times \left[\frac{1}{0.1} - \frac{1}{0.1(1 + 0.1)^{10}} \right]$

                   $= £61,446$

Net realisable value (NRV)	= £50,000
Therefore, recoverable amount	= £61,446 (higher of VIU and NRV)
Carrying value	= £70,000
Therefore, impairment loss	= £8,554 (70,000 − 61,446)

The written-down value of £61,446 would then be depreciated over the remaining useful economic life of the asset.

Note that if the discount rate had been 5 per cent, there would have been no impairment, as the value in use would have been £77,217, calculated as follows:

$$£10,000 \times \left[\frac{1}{0.05} - \frac{1}{0.05(1 + 0.05)^{10}} \right] = £77,217$$

11.10.7 Allocation of impairment losses

If the impairment review gives rise to losses, in the absence of an obvious impairment to an individual asset, these should be recognised as follows:

- first, against goodwill in the income-generating unit;
- secondly, against any capitalised intangible assets in the unit, and
- finally, against tangible fixed assets in the unit on a pro rata or more appropriate basis.

The approach taken by FRS 11 is to write down assets with the most subjective values first. This is subject to the requirements that:

- intangible assets with a readily ascertainable market value should not be written down to below their net realisable value, and
- tangible assets with a net realisable value that can be measured reliably should not be written down to below that amount.

The distinction between these two may seem trifling on first reading, but the phrase 'readily ascertainable market value' used when referring to intangible assets is defined as:

... the value that is established by reference to a market where:

(a) the asset belongs to a homogeneous population of assets that are equivalent in all material respects; and

(b) an active market, evidenced by frequent transactions, exists for that population of assets. (Para. 2, FRS 11.)

This, therefore, limits the application of the exception to intangible assets in a way that it does not for tangible assets.

Where an impairment loss is recognised, there should also be a reconsideration of the useful economic life of the assets. (This may of course be required even where there is no such impairment.)

FRS 11 does not give guidance on what should be done with any remaining deficiency after appropriate amounts have been written off goodwill, intangible and tangible fixed assets. Under FRS 12, no further provision can be made as this would amount to a provision for future operating losses. (In such cases, the business might well be in very severe financial difficulties, and accounting may be the least of their problems.)

11.10.8   Acquired and existing businesses merged

There is an implicit assumption in much of FRS 11 that each income-generating unit remains independent. Of course, this may not be true.

One possibility is that an acquired business is merged with an existing business unit. The goodwill attributable to the combined unit will then consist of the purchased goodwill on the acquisition and the internally-generated (and therefore unrecorded) goodwill on the existing business with which it was merged. Given that the business units have merged, it will not be possible to undertake separate impairment reviews for the two elements in the future. FRS 11 requires the following procedures to be applied to deal with this.

(1) The amount of the internally-generated goodwill attributable to the original business must be calculated as at the date the business units were merged.

(2) This amount must then be added to the actual carrying values of the assets and liabilities when undertaking the impairment review.

(3) If any impairment review is undertaken immediately after the merger (as may be required by FRS 10) then the impairment should be allocated solely to the purchased goodwill.

(4) Any subsequent impairments should be allocated pro rata between the goodwill attributable to the existing business and the purchased goodwill.

(5) The element of impairments allocated to the existing business should be allocated first to the notional goodwill (and therefore to the extent that this

is sufficient to cover the impairment there will be no write-down in the financial statements).

(6) Only the impairments allocated to purchased goodwill and the fixed assets should be recognised in the financial statements.

This approach involves another implicit assumption: that the amortisation pattern of the notional goodwill is identical to that of the purchased goodwill. This assumption seems reasonable: if the units have merged then it is difficult to see how to construct an argument that the existing goodwill could be distinguished in any way from the purchased goodwill, including in respect of its useful economic life.

It is worth stressing that this procedure means that the calculation of the internally-generated goodwill at the date of merger is required, even if there is no indication of impairment. The reason for this is that if there is a subsequent impairment, this information is necessary in order to allocate the impairment properly.

11.10.9 *Subsequent monitoring*

After an impairment review where recoverable amount was based on value in use, regardless of whether an impairment was actually recognised, cash flows must be monitored for five years, by comparing the actual figures with the original forecasts. If the actual cash flows are significantly lower than the original forecasts, the original calculation should be reperformed using the actual cash flows, but retaining the other original assumptions. If this review identifies that an impairment loss would have arisen had the actual cash flows been used in the original calculation, the loss should be recognised in the current year.

However, where, by performing an impairment review, the company is able to demonstrate that the earlier reversal has now reversed, no loss need be recognised provided that the rules on reversal do not prohibit its recognition. Where such a reversal has occurred, and is allowed to be recognised, there is a requirement to disclose the unrecorded impairment.

11.10.10 *Reversal of past impairments*

For tangible assets and for investments within the scope of FRS 11, impairment losses may be reversed if the value increases due to changes in economic conditions or the expected use of the asset. In effect, the circumstances are the reverse of the indications of impairment. The standard notes that the circumstances would include increases in the recoverable amount as a result of further capital investment or a reorganisation, where the benefits had been excluded from the original calculation of value in use. FRS 11 does not permit recognition of a reversal where this arises due to the passage of time (because, as future cash inflows become closer, their discounted value increases) or the occurrence of forecast cash outflows (which would then drop out of any net present value calculation).

In the cases of intangible assets and goodwill, reversal is allowed only if:

- an external event caused the recognition of the impairment loss in previous periods, and subsequent external events clearly and demonstrably reverse the effects of that event in a way that was not foreseen in the original impairment calculations, or
- the intangible asset in question has a readily-ascertainable market value, and this has increased.

Note that the external event giving rise to the initial impairment referred to above must have reversed. The FRS gives an example where purchased goodwill is impaired because a company's product is overtaken by a technologically more advanced model introduced by a competitor. If the company then recovers the situation by making a technological breakthrough of its own, this does not permit recognition of the reversal of the goodwill impairment as the original event itself (ie the entry of the new competitor's product) has not reversed.

In any event, the impairment can only be reversed to the extent that the assets return to the amount at which they would have been stated had no impairment been recognised, that is, taking account of notional depreciation or amortisation. While (subject to other standards) the assets may be written up above this amount, this is a revaluation and not the reversal of an impairment loss.

11.10.11 Presentation and disclosure

In the case of assets that have not previously been revalued, all impairment losses should be recognised in the profit and loss account. They should be charged within the relevant statutory heading in arriving at operating profit and may also be an exceptional item.

For previously revalued assets, impairment losses should be reflected in the profit and loss account if they arise as a result of the clear consumption of economic benefit. This is an operating cost similar to depreciation and may arise, for example, as a result of physical damage or a deterioration in the quality of the service provided by the asset. Other impairments should be reflected in the statement of total recognised gains and losses, to the extent that they relate to previous revaluations of the same assets, and in the profit and loss account to the extent that they take the carrying value below depreciated historic cost. This treatment should also be mirrored when a reversal takes place. Where a loss is recognised in the statement of total recognised gains and losses it should be included as a separate line on the face of that statement.

In the notes to the financial statements in accounting periods after the impairment:

- impairment losses on assets treated at historic cost should be treated as additional depreciation, and should not involve writing down the cost;
- for revalued assets carried at market value the loss should be included within the revalued carrying amount, and
- for revalued assets held at depreciated replacement cost, any impairment charged to the profit and loss account should be treated as additional depreciation and any charge to the statement of total recognised gains and losses should be deducted from the carrying amount.

For accounting periods beginning before 1 January 2010, where losses have taken account of value in use of a fixed asset or income-generating unit, then the discount rate used must be disclosed. Where a risk-free rate was used, then there should be an indication of how the cash flows were adjusted to take account of risk. Where, in measuring value in use, the period before a steady or declining long-term growth rate has been assumed extends to more than five years from the balance sheet date, then the length of the period must be stated, with justification. Where, in measuring value in use, the growth rate used has exceeded the long-term average, the financial statements should disclose the growth rate assumed and the circumstances justifying it.

For periods beginning on or after 1 January 2010, these disclosures are extended slightly. The discount rate used must be disclosed in all cases, where discounted cash flows have been used in measuring an impairment loss, irrespective of whether they have been used in determining the value in use or the net realisable value of the asset or income generating unit. There is no change to the requirement to provide an indication of how cash flows have been adjusted to take account of risk, where a risk-free rate has been used, except that this also applies whenever discounted cash flow techniques have been applied. In addition, the period over which management has projected cash flows and the growth rate used to extrapolate cash flow projections must always be disclosed. This is in addition to the previous requirements to state and justify an increasing growth rate for a period of more than five years, or where the growth rate exceeds the long term average.

Where an impairment loss would have been recognised in a previous period had the forecasts of future cash flows been more accurate but the impairment has reversed and the reversal of the loss is permitted to be recognised, the impairment now identified and its subsequent reversal should be disclosed.

Where a reversal has been recorded in the current period, the reasons must be stated, including any changes in the assumptions on which the calculation of recoverable amount has been based.

11.10.12   The FRSSE

Entities adopting the FRSSE are exempt from complying with FRS 11, except that, where group accounts are prepared, FRS 11 must additionally be applied in full to purchased goodwill arising on consolidation, as required by FRS 10.

For individual company accounts, the FRSSE includes the main principles of FRS 11 concerning the requirements for impairment write-downs and reversals, but omits all of the detail.

The FRSSE includes the basic definitions of recoverable amount and net realisable value from FRS 11, together with the requirement that fixed assets and goodwill should not be carried in the balance sheet at more than their recoverable amounts. The FRSSE does not specify when an impairment review should be conducted, but gives obsolescence and a fall in demand for the product as examples of when the net book amount may not be recoverable in full. The FRSSE requirements apply to the same types of fixed asset as FRS 11.

The FRSSE includes the same core recognition requirements for impairment losses, and the same restriction on the recognition of reversals of impairment losses for intangible assets and goodwill, as are contained in FRS 11.

The FRSSE makes no reference to income-generating units and there is no guidance on how to calculate recoverable amount. This appears to leave open the possibility of using a more flexible approach to estimating value in use than would be permitted under FRS 11. It is worth noting that the FRSSE does not allow the recoverable amount to be based on net realisable value in circumstances where FRS 11 would not allow this.

12 GOVERNMENT GRANTS

12.1 INTRODUCTION

12.1.1 Accounting for government grants

SSAP 4 *Accounting for Government Grants*, as revised, provides the main guidance in this area. Company law does not deal directly with the issue, although some of the provisions that are included in the statutory instruments supporting the Companies Act 2006 have an effect on the way in which government grants can be recorded in financial statements.

SSAP 4 notes that government assistance can take many different forms; for example, cash grants, direct investment in enterprises, subsidised loans and advice. It also notes that the nature of government assistance tends to change over time: for example, assistance in the form of consultancy and advice has been increasingly popular for a number of years, with less reliance placed upon direct cash grants. Direct cash assistance, while still available, is no longer the only form of aid. As a result, the standard, while taking particular account of the forms of assistance most common at the time it was written, also sets general principles which can be applied in all circumstances. It is almost inevitable that forms of assistance will continue to change since that which is deemed socially, economically or politically desirable by the government is subject to regular change. The standard is attempting to ensure that it will still be relevant even when there are further changes in the nature of assistance available to companies.

However, in terms of defining appropriate accounting treatments, SSAP 4 uses a strict definition of government grants, which excludes non-financial assistance:

> Government grants are assistance by government in the form of cash or transfers of assets to an enterprise in return for past or future compliance with certain conditions relating to the operating activities of the enterprise. (Para. 22, SSAP 4.)

This definition has been repeated in the FRSSE.

Disclosure is required for other forms of assistance, where this is possible, but it is not intended that they should be recorded in the financial statements. While there may be some value in attempting to quantify the benefits associated with non-financial assistance it is unlikely that it would give rise to assets which should be included in financial statements in accordance with the current accounting framework. It might well be difficult to justify the inclusion of assets, in particular, given the restrictive nature of the definition of an asset provided in FRS 5, *Reporting the Substance of Transactions*, and the restrictions placed on the recognition of assets under that standard.

Government grants also do not include beneficial tax arrangements, such as accelerated depreciation or reduced tax rates. Such arrangements are not mentioned in SSAP 4, but are explicitly excluded in IAS 20, the international standard that deals with government grants for companies complying with IFRS other than entities adopting the IFRS for SMEs. Beneficial tax arrangements may fall to be disclosed as part of the reconciliation of the tax charge required by FRS 19, *Deferred Tax*, or as part of deferred tax, depending on the nature of the arrangement.

Charitable companies are subject to different requirements, as they need to consider the SORP *Accounting by Charities*, as well as accounting standards and the requirements of company law. Charitable companies are outside the scope of this book.

Under IFRS, accounting for government grants, other than those associated with agriculture, is dealt with by IAS 20 *Accounting for Government Grants and Disclosure of Government Assistance* and section 24 of the IFRS for SMEs. While SSAP 4 and IAS 20 are broadly similar, there are some differences in practice. In particular, IAS 20 allows capital grants to be treated as deferred income or deducted from the costs of assets acquired. While SSAP 4 also allows both, in principle, it then goes on to point out that companies are not allowed to treat capital grants as reductions in the cost of assets as this would entail a breach of the statutory requirements. The IFRS for SMEs does not differentiate between capital and revenue grants, and applies the same accounting basis for both. The logic of the IFRS for SMEs would appear to be closer to that of SSAP 4 than IAS 20, since the absence of specific requirements on recognition of capital grants might be taken to imply that separate recognition is more appropriate.

The IASB is proposing to replace IAS 20, at least eventually, and it is noticeable that the current version of this standard requires treatments which are not entirely consistent with the treatment of grants under IAS 41 in relation to agriculture. The IASB is fully aware of the inconsistency, and initially at least preferred the logic underpinning IAS 41, in relation to grants, to that underpinning IAS 20. However, there has been some change in the IASB's view and it is aware of some conceptual issues affecting the treatments required by IAS 41. In addition, the IASB also made a decision to wait in revising IAS 20, as it was working on provisions, contingent assets and contingent liabilities and considered that the results of that work could have an impact on the appropriate treatment of government grants. This break in progress has now continued for some years. Notwithstanding that it is not yet entirely clear what changes may be made to IAS 20, the IASB still gives various reasons for wishing to change IAS 20.

(1) It is not convinced that the recognition requirements of IAS 20 always result in an accounting treatment that is consistent with the IASB Framework. In particular, the IASB notes that there may be cases where a

deferred credit is shown where this does not meet the Framework's definition of a liability.

(2) The recognition requirements of IAS 20 are not consistent with more recent pronouncements of standard-setting bodies relating to government grants and other non-reciprocal transfers.

(3) IAS 20 contains options. In some cases those options can be used in such a way as to understate the position of an entity. The IASB also considers that the options, whatever their merits may be in particular cases, reduce the comparability of financial statements and therefore warrant reconsideration.

Potential impact of the FRSME

The FRSME is based on the IFRS for SMEs, and as such the comments made above concerning the IFRS for SMEs are relevant. In particular, the FRSME does not distinguish between capital and revenue grants, treating them as part of a single category.

The FRSME contains similar exclusions to IAS 20 in relation to beneficial tax arrangements such as investment tax credits, accelerated depreciation allowances and reduced tax rates. Whilst not mentioned in SSAP 4, these should already be considered to be outside of the scope of the definition of government grants.

12.1.2   *Grants from other bodies*

SSAP 4 is obligatory only when dealing with government grants. However, the definition of 'government' in the standard, which is repeated in the FRSSE, is deliberately widely drawn:

> Government includes government and inter-governmental agencies and similar bodies whether local, national or international. (Para. 21, SSAP 4.)

Therefore, grants do not need to come from central government in order to fall within the definition. They can also come from local or regional government bodies and international bodies. In particular, this definition would include any grants received from the European Union or any of its connected bodies.

In other cases, for example, where a company obtains a grant from a private or charitable body, SSAP 4 and the FRSSE are simply indicative of best practice. Nonetheless, there would normally need to be a good reason not to follow their requirements.

Potential impact of the FRSME

The FRSME may well have little impact on this matter, but does not define government. It does define a state to include regional and local government as well as national.

12.2   REVENUE GRANTS

12.2.1   Recognition

Government grants can, with some degree of over-simplification, be divided into revenue grants and capital grants. Revenue grants are basically those grants that relate either to specific periods or to activities which are undertaken by a company. Capital grants are those grants that are received in order to enable the company to purchase an asset for continuing use in the business; that is, a fixed asset.

Accounting for both types of government grant under SSAP 4 is determined by the application of the accruals and prudence principles, both of which were taken from SSAP 2, *Disclosure of Accounting Policies*. In basic terms, grants should be matched with the expenditure to which they are intended to contribute, but must also be recognised only when the conditions for their receipt have been fulfilled.

SSAP 4 has not been amended since the withdrawal of SSAP 2 and its replacement by FRS 18, *Accounting Policies*. This does not give rise to any fundamental problems, but it does mean that its logic is not as entirely consistent with other areas of accounting practice as it used to be.

12.2.2   Prudence

The general requirement for prudence is stated in SSAP 4:

> [The requirements of matching income to expenditure] ... are subject to the proviso that a government grant should not be recognised in the profit and loss account until the conditions for its receipt have been complied with and there is reasonable assurance that the grant will be received. (Para. 24, SSAP 4.)

While this is in practice consistent with the requirements of FRS 18, which continues to require a degree of certainty in respect of the recognition of both assets and income, it is couched in terms which are clearly not based upon that standard. The concept of matching is of far less relevance in determining accounting practices than was the case when SSAP 4 was produced, and is not considered primary under FRS 18 in the same way as it was under SSAP 2.

The receipt of a government grant is not normally without conditions. In order to ensure that grants are used for the purposes for which they were intended, the government (as defined above) normally imposes conditions which must be satisfied. These may either relate to a period of time (for example, an asset must be retained by the company for a stated period) or to a specific event. If the company does not comply with these conditions then the grant may need to be repaid.

At each balance sheet date the company should consider whether there has been a breach of the conditions or if such a breach is likely in the future. If there has been a breach, normally no further income should be recognised, and the amount of income that has already been recognised should be charged to the profit and loss account, and a provision for repayment created:

> The repayment of a government grant should be accounted for by setting off the repayment against any unamortised deferred income relating to the grant. Any excess should be charged immediately to the profit and loss account. (Para. 27, SSAP 4.)

Where it appears that a grant may need to be repaid, it will normally be treated simply as an expense in the period in which it becomes clear that repayment is likely. Where appropriate, it may be necessary to treat such a charge as an exceptional item in accordance with FRS 3.

In some cases, a company may fail to comply with the conditions of the grant, but the body that originally made the grant will not seek to recover the amounts paid. This might arise, for example, because the company has complied with the main parts of the terms of the grant and the breaches are minor and do not affect the substance of the grant. In such cases it is acceptable not to provide for repayment, but the company should obtain written confirmation that it will not need to repay all or part of the grant it has received.

Where a company is a going concern, prudence does not necessarily require a company to defer income until full compliance with all of the conditions of the grant has taken place. For example, a company may have a grant that is conditional on its maintaining, or increasing, its current level of employment for a stated number of years. In such cases, it would not be necessary to wait until the last year before recognising income. The company should record income on a systematic basis over the relevant period, and only defer recognition where there are reasons for believing that the company will not be able to comply with the conditions attached to the grant.

A company will always need to assess the likelihood, no matter how remote, of having to repay a grant, unless it has complied with all of the relevant conditions. Where necessary the company should disclose the potential liability to repay the grant as a contingent liability in accordance with FRS 12 *Provisions, Contingent Liabilities and Contingent Assets* or the FRSSE. This means that disclosure will need to be made unless the likelihood of repayment is remote, or of course if the amount is trivial.

12.2.3 Accruals

The recognition principle that should be applied when the requirements of prudence are satisfied is stated in SSAP 4:

> Government grants should ... be recognised in the profit and loss account so as to match them with the expenditure towards which they are intended to contribute. (Para. 4, SSAP 4.)

This is clearly based on SSAP 2, but as noted above is still consistent in practice with FRS 18.

As the standard notes, the simplest case is that in which a grant is received that is specifically to reimburse identified expenditure. In this case, the amount of the grant is taken to income as and when the expenditure is recorded.

A much more difficult situation is where the terms of the grant are not related to specific expenditure, but are either in more general terms, or related to two or more separate criteria. SSAP 4 gives the example of a grant that is affected both by capital expenditure and the number of jobs created by a project. The general rule under SSAP 4 is that such grants should be recorded as income on the basis of the circumstances that give rise to the payment of the instalments of the grant. If an instalment is made when evidence is given that a certain amount of expenditure has been incurred, then the income from that instalment should be treated in the same accounting period as that expenditure. Where the grant is paid on another basis, such as in line with the number of jobs created, then an attempt should be made specifically to identify, or fairly estimate, the costs of achieving that objective. The grant should be treated as income in line with the recognition of the costs that have been incurred and allocated to achieving the objective.

EXAMPLE

A company obtains a grant of £20,000 to assist in the preparation of a research report. The grant will be received when the final report is submitted. During 2011 the company incurs staff costs of £15,000 in performing the basic research. At the end of the year it is clear that the report will be completed, and that the grant will be received. Additional costs of £25,000 are incurred in 2012.

The grant should be treated in relation to the underlying total expenditure. In this case it would mean that income of £7,500 would be recorded in 2011:

$$20,000 \times \frac{15,000}{15,000 + 25,000} = 7,500$$

This would be matched with the costs incurred during the year of £15,000. The balance of £12,500 would then be recorded as income in 2012.

Of course, this method requires knowledge of 2012 expenditure at the end of 2011, or rather when the financial statements for 2011 are prepared. Depending on the status of the company this may be up to nine months after the balance sheet date, but,

---

nonetheless, will still be before the next year is complete. Therefore, an estimate of the 2012 expenditure may be necessary to make the allocation for the 2011 accounts.

The standard accepts that there may be times when the basis for payment of instalments of the grant may not be directly related to the expenditure that it is intended to reimburse. Evidence about such matters may be obtained from the terms of the grant or in the correspondence with the grant-making body. For example, a company may receive a grant that is intended to meet capital costs, retraining expenditure and recruitment costs. For convenience, the payment of instalments of the grant may be made as capital expenditure is incurred. In such a case, the way in which matching is generally applied to government grants should be broken in favour of matching which reflects the economic substance. This is because the basis of payment is for convenience only and is not directly related to the costs that the grant is intended to reimburse. We could even go so far as to say the actual payments are made on an arbitrary basis. Therefore, recognising income as the actual payments are received would not lead to proper matching of the income from the grant with the costs it is intended to cover.

Where a grant is meeting a range of separate types of expenditure, it should be allocated to each form of expenditure in proportion to the cost of that type of expenditure to the total. Some grants may need to be divided between capital and revenue elements, and each part treated appropriately.

Once the expenditure to be reimbursed has been identified then the treatment of income is relatively straightforward.

> Once the relationship between the grant and the related expenditure has been established, the recognition of the grant in the profit and loss account will follow. The grant should be recognised in the same period as the related expenditure. (Para. 12, SSAP 4.)

Where grants are received in respect of expenditure which has already been incurred it should be taken to income as received.

Where grants are received to cover the general costs of a period, rather than any specific costs, they should be treated as income in the period in respect of which they are paid. If the period is not specified in the terms of the grant they should be treated as income as they are received.

If there are amounts in respect of grants which have not been taken to income at the balance sheet date they should be treated as deferred income.

The treatment of a grant for tax purposes should not affect the accounting treatment of the grant. If a grant is subject to tax, and that tax arises in different periods from those in which the underlying expenditure is incurred, then a timing difference will be created, which should be treated in accordance with FRS 19 *Deferred Tax* or the FRSSE.

The basic treatment of revenue grants is the same under both IAS 20 and the IFRS for SMEs. There is also a statement, SIC 10, from the former Standing Interpretations Committee, which clarifies that, under IAS 20, grants received for which there are no particular operating conditions to be satisfied are still government grants, and therefore should be taken to income and not treated as capital transactions.

Potential impact of the FRSME

There are no substantial differences of principle between the FRSME and SSAP 20. The basic requirements proposed in the FRSME are that:

- where a grant does not contain specified future performance conditions on the recipient, it should be recognised in income when the grant proceeds are receivable, and
- where a grant does contain specified future performance conditions on the recipient, it should be recognised in income only when the performance conditions are met.

Where grants are received before the criteria for revenue recognition have been met, they should be treated as a liability.

12.3   CAPITAL GRANTS

12.3.1   Recognition

The same basic principle applies to capital grants as to revenue grants: subject to the requirements of prudence, they should be taken to income at the same time as the expenditure they are intended to meet. The only difference is in the mechanics of how this is achieved.

In practice, prudence is less likely to be a problem with capital grants. Where a grant is received for the purchase of fixed assets then it will normally be received only when the expenditure has been made, and the main condition of the grant has therefore been met. However, there may be conditions attached to the retention of the asset for a specified period, and these still need to be considered.

12.3.2   Accounting treatment

In the case of a company, the accounting treatment is as follows.

- The fixed asset is initially recorded at its full cost, ignoring the receipt of the grant, and depreciated over its useful economic life.
- The grant is recorded as deferred income and taken to income over the same period, and on the same basis, as the cost of the asset is depreciated.

EXAMPLE

A company purchases a fixed asset at the beginning of the 2011 financial year at a cost of £100,000. The asset has a useful economic life of 12 years, and is to be depreciated on the straight-line basis. The company receives a grant of £30,000 towards the cost.

The accounting treatment would be as follows:

Year	Asset value in balance sheet £	Deferred income £	Depreciation £	Grant income £	Net charge £
2011	91,667	(27,500)	8,333	(2,500)	5,833
2012	83,334	(25,000)	8,333	(2,500)	5,833
2013	75,001	(22,500)	8,333	(2,500)	5,833
2014	66,668	(20,000)	8,333	(2,500)	5,833
2015	58,335	(17,500)	8,333	(2,500)	5,833
2016	50,002	(15,000)	8,333	(2,500)	5,833
2017	41,669	(12,500)	8,333	(2,500)	5,833
2018	33,336	(10,000)	8,333	(2,500)	5,833
2019	25,003	(7,500)	8,333	(2,500)	5,833
2020	16,670	(5,000)	8,333	(2,500)	5,833
2021	8,337	(2,500)	8,333	(2,500)	5,833
2022	0	0	8,337	(2,500)	5,837
			100,000	(30,000)	70,000

In theory, it is also possible to deduct the amount of the grant from the total cost of the asset and to depreciate the net amount. The net charge to the profit and loss account in each year would be exactly the same, and the net assets of the company would also not be affected. However, this treatment seems to be prevented by the Companies Act:

> Paragraph 17 of Schedule 4 [to the Companies Act 1985] requires that, subject to any provision for depreciation or diminution in value, the amount to be included in the balance sheet in respect of any fixed asset shall be its purchase price or production cost. Paragraph 26(1) states that the purchase price of an asset shall be determined by adding to the actual price paid any expenses incidental to its acquisition. The CCAB has received Counsel's opinion that these paragraphs have the effect of prohibiting enterprises to which the legislation applies from accounting for grants made as a contribution towards expenditure on fixed assets by deducting the amount of the grant from the purchase price or production cost of the related asset. (Para. 34, SSAP 4.)

This did not change with the introduction of the Companies Act 2006, since the same problems arise under Sch. 1 to The Large and Medium-sized Companies and Groups (Accounts and Reports) Regulations 2008 (SI 2008/410). Given that the substance of the issue remains exactly the same, the ASB has not considered it necessary to change the reference.

This is made even clearer in the FRSSE:

. . . the option to deduct government grants from the purchase price or production costs of fixed assets is not available to companies governed by the accounting and reporting requirements of UK companies legislation. (Para. 6.54 FRSSE.)

This means that such a treatment can be adopted by unincorporated enterprises which comply with accounting standards, whether the normal standards or the FRSSE, but may not be used by a company. As noted above, this treatment is also acceptable under IAS 20, the international equivalent of SSAP 4.

Where a company is provided with an asset, rather than with a contribution towards the cost of an asset which it has purchased or is to purchase, SSAP 4 states that:

Where a government grant takes the form of a transfer of non-monetary assets, the amount of the grant is the fair value of the assets transferred. (Para. 16, SSAP 4.)

The implication of this is that the asset should be capitalised at its fair value, and the grant treated as deferred income and taken to income over the same period as the asset is depreciated. The net effect of this treatment is that there will be no charge in the profit and loss account, and there will also be no change to the net assets of the company. (Since an unincorporated body is allowed to deduct the amount of a grant from the cost of a fixed asset, this implies that it would be acceptable for such a body to ignore the receipt of the asset, since the net cost is zero.)

SSAP 4 does not state what it means by fair value. IAS 20 defines fair value as:

. . . the amount for which an asset could be exchanged between a knowledgeable, willing buyer and a knowledgeable, willing seller in an arm's length transaction. (Para. 3, IAS 20.)

This definition could also be used for SSAP 4.

If a company disposes of an asset in respect of which there is still a deferred income balance, and where the grant does not need to be repaid as a result, then the balance on the deferred income account should be taken into account in calculating the profit or loss on disposal.

If an asset against which a government grant has been received becomes impaired, then the release of the grant to the profit and loss account should be matched with the impairment write-down.

EXAMPLE

A company sells an asset which originally cost £20,000, which has been depreciated by £17,000 and on which there is still deferred income of £1,500. The proceeds of disposal are £2,500.

The profit on the transaction will be £1,000, calculated as follows:

	£
Cost	20,000
Accumulated depreciation	(17,000)
Net book value	3,000
Less: deferred income remaining	(1,500)
Net amount transferred	1,500
Proceeds	2,500
Net amount transferred	(1,500)
Profit	1,000

Where a capital grant is repaid, the repayment should be accounted for first from the balance on the deferred income account. Any additional amount should be charged directly to the profit and loss account.

Potential impact of the FRSME

As noted earlier, the FRSME does not distinguish between revenue and capital grants. The only mention it makes that is more likely to be relevant to capital than revenue grants is its statement that all grants should be measured at the fair value of the assets received or receivable. This could apply in both cases, but capital grants are more likely to be in a form other than cash.

The statutory issue identified in relation to government grants and that affects SSAP 4 would continue to apply if the FRSME were to be introduced. Companies would therefore still be required to treat capital acquisitions which are wholly or partially grant funded gross, with the balance being initially treated as a liability, that is, as deferred income.

12.4   DISCLOSURE

The disclosure of government grants is important for investors to estimate the source of the reported earnings. If a company has received grants which have affected the profits reported in the financial statements, but which are not expected to be available in the future, then this will affect the user's assessment of the underlying profitability of the company.

The following information should be disclosed in the financial statements.

(1)   The accounting policy for government grants, including the periods over which capital grants are taken to income, if this is practical. If it is not, since the company receives a wide range of capital grants, then a general statement that they are taken to income over the same period as the depreciation periods for the assets they are intended to cover will be sufficient.

(2) The effect of government grants on the results of the period and the financial position of the company.

(3) If the results of the period have been materially affected by government assistance in a form other than grants, such as free advice, subsidised loans or guarantees, then a statement of the nature of the assistance should be provided. Where it can be measured, the financial effect of the assistance received should also be stated. For example, this would be unlikely to prove possible if the company had received free consultancy in the period. However, if it had received a subsidised loan then it should be possible to make a reasonable estimate of the difference between the interest paid and the amount that would have been paid if the loan had been on normal commercial terms.

The first of these disclosure requirements is not specifically included in the FRSSE. Instead, it is covered by the general requirement that companies state their accounting policies.

With regard to revenue grants, IAS 20 discusses the two possible approaches to presentation:

● showing the gross income receivable as grants, either separately or within another heading such as 'other income', or
● treating the grants as a reduction in expenses.

The IAS allows both methods to be used. SSAP 4 does not address this issue. Instead, by requiring the effect on the period to be disclosed, it ensures that sufficient information is available however the grants have been presented.

Companies should also consider disclosing a contingent liability in respect of grants which may need to be repaid if they have not already complied fully with the conditions for receipt of the grant, and if the likelihood of repayment is not remote.

Potential impact of the FRSME

The disclosure requirements included in the draft FRSME differ somewhat from those in SSAP 20, although there is overlap. The FRSME requires disclosure of:

● the nature and amounts of government grants recognised in the financial statements;
● unfulfilled conditions and other contingencies attaching to government grants that have not been recognised in income; and
● an indication of other forms of government assistance from which the entity has directly benefited.

The FRSME excludes from the definition of government grants those forms of government assistance that cannot reasonably have a value placed upon them, and transactions with government that cannot be distinguished from the normal trading transactions of the entity. The first of these categories would still be caught by the disclosure requirement set out earlier.

12.5 POSSIBLE CHANGES

In January 2000, the ASB published as a discussion paper a special report, *Accounting by Recipients for Non-reciprocal Transfers, Excluding Contributions by Owners*, prepared by the G4+1 group of international standard-setters. The paper examines how items such as government grants and charitable donations should be accounted for by those who receive them.

A non-reciprocal transfer occurs when an entity receives assets from another, or its liabilities are forgiven, without giving approximately equal value in return, for example, government grants and gifts and donations (including those made in kind) that are made to charitable organisations. The paper does not address the accounting for contributions made by owners (for example, new shares).

The paper's principal conclusion is that non-reciprocal transfers should usually be recognised as assets (or reductions in liabilities) and credited to income when they become receivable. If implemented, this would be a radical departure from the approach currently required in the UK by SSAP 4, but would be consistent with the approach currently adopted under accounting rules for charities. The departure from matching is not surprising given the changes that have taken place since the introduction of SSAP 4, and, in particular, the replacement of SSAP 2 with FRS 18.

Since the issue of the discussion paper, the IASB has made some progress on accounting for government grants. In January 2003, the IASB decided to withdraw IAS 20, but did not decide on a replacement. In February 2004, the IASB reconsidered its decision to amend IAS 20, and agreed that it would be premature to issue a new standard given the ongoing work on revenue recognition.

Since then, the IASB has considered government grants in the light of the treatment of grants in IAS 41 *Agriculture*. They originally tentatively decided the following.

(1) To distinguish between conditional and unconditional grants, with recognition of income depending on the category into which a grant falls. They have also decided to define a condition as a stipulation, with commercial substance, that entitles government to the return of the granted resources if a specified event either does or does not occur.

(2) To specify that an entity should recognise a government grant as an asset (but not necessarily as income) at the earlier of:

    (a) having an unconditional right to receive the government grant, regardless of where there are conditions attached to retaining the grant, and

(b)   receiving the government grant.

(3)   To amend the definition of a government grant, to remove references to 'conditions' since this would not fit with a framework that distinguished between conditional and unconditional grants.

(4)   To delete references to loans at nil or low interest rates, and to government guarantees, due to conflicts between IAS 20 and IAS 39, (a change which has been made separately).

(5)   To require entities receiving government grants in connection with the acquisition of assets to test those assets for impairment on initial recognition, with some clarification of the process for doing so.

(6)   To propose retrospective application of any changes, in accordance with IAS 8, but after having sought views as to whether such a requirement could cause difficulties.

There appears to have been some change in the IASB's thinking on this issue, and it now seems less clear that the model incorporated in IAS 41 is to be adopted more widely. In addition, the IASB has also considered the issue of emissions trading, and has added this to the project dealing with government grants.

As noted earlier, the IASB project has now been held up by the ongoing work on provisions, contingent assets and contingent liabilities. It is not yet clear when the IASB will recommence work on government grants.

13 INVESTMENTS, CAPITAL INSTRUMENTS AND FINANCIAL INSTRUMENTS

13.1 INTRODUCTION

This chapter will deal with investments, capital instruments and financial instruments. It does not deal with investment properties, which are covered in Chapter 11. This chapter also does not deal with the treatment of subsidiaries, associates and joint ventures in group accounts, which is covered in Chapter 21.

Any differences in treatment which are required for small companies are given in the relevant section.

Of all areas of UK accounting, this is probably the one that has been subject to the greatest change in recent years. Perhaps strangely, many companies have been fairly unaffected by many of the changes that have taken place.

This is because some of the changes are as a result of standards that are optional, for most companies at least, and which the majority of companies can therefore ignore if they wish. The key standard is FRS 26 (IAS 39) *Financial Instruments: Recognition and Measurement*. This standard has been mandatory for listed companies which are not using IFRS since accounting periods beginning on or after 1 January 2005. It is optional for other companies, since it applies only to those companies which choose to adopt the fair value rules of the Companies Act 2006, which have now been introduced into law as a result of an EU directive. Even where it is adopted, it came into force only for accounting periods beginning on or after 1 January 2006. It has also changed, many times, since being introduced. Very few companies have voluntarily chosen to adopt the fair value rules of the Companies Act 2006, and, therefore, the accounting standards that go along with it.

FRS 26 is a very long and complex standard. This chapter, whilst summarising the basic requirements of the standard, does not attempt to cover the standard in depth, on the basis that it applies to only a very limited number of companies.

FRS 25 (IAS 32) *Financial Instruments: Presentation*, which does apply to many more companies, has applied since January 2005, although it too has changed a number of times since it was originally introduced. For one thing, it has changed title, having referred to disclosure as well when first brought into force. Originally, it had disclosure requirements, which were optional for most companies and mandatory only for companies complying with FRS 26. These were removed when FRS 29 was issued. The presentation requirements have been mandatory for all companies, other than those adopting the FRSSE, since accounting periods beginning on or after 1 January 2005.

FRS 25 also replaced much of FRS 4, *Capital Instruments*. That standard remains in issue, but many of its paragraphs have been deleted and its original rationale has been removed. FRS 4 now deals solely with the issue of the allocation of costs associated with liabilities to accounting periods and information on sources of finance.

FRS 25 deals with all types of financial instruments other than:

- interests in subsidiaries, quasi-subsidiaries, associates, partnerships and joint ventures;
- pension schemes;
- contracts for contingent consideration in a business combination, for the acquirer;
- insurance contracts, except for embedded derivatives in insurance contracts that are within the scope of FRS 26;
- financial instruments a company issues with a discretionary participation feature, as dealt with in FRS 26, with regard to most aspects of the standard, and
- most instruments covered by FRS 20, except that treasury shares purchased, sold, issued or cancelled in connection with employee share option plans and similar are subject to the same rules as other treasury shares.

Finally, FRS 29 has been in force since accounting periods beginning on or after 1 January 2007. However, like the previous disclosure section of FRS 25 this is mandatory only for companies which are also complying with FRS 26, which in practice is a very small minority of companies adopting UK GAAP. Like the other standards that deal with the area of financial instruments, this standard has changed a number of times since it was first introduced. This standard also changed with effect for accounting periods beginning on or after 1 January 2009, even though the changes were not actually made until May 2009.

Potential impact of the FRSME

The FRSME adopts a dual approach to the area of financial instruments. It contains two sections covering the area; one dealing with basic financial instruments and the other dealing with more complex instruments. Unusually for the FRSME, the second part is optional, in that a company has the alternative of complying with IAS 39, the international standard which forms the basis of (and is therefore virtually identical to) FRS 26. (This ignores the fact that IAS 39 is itself supposed to be abolished with effect for accounting periods beginning on or after 1 January 2013, when it is expected to be replaced with IFRS 9.) Even if a company takes this option, it would still be able to provide only the disclosures required by the FRSME, and would not have to provide the disclosures contained within IFRS 7, the standard on which FRS 29 is based.

The changes that would be introduced by the FRSME in this area differ from the changes that would affect many other areas. It is not really possible to contrast the FRSME requirements with the current UK GAAP requirements on an issue-by-issue basis. As a result, rather than commenting on specific areas of change, a brief summary of the proposals has been included at the end of this chapter.

13.2   INVESTMENTS

13.2.1   Definition of investment

The term 'investment' is not defined in statute, although an indication of its intended scope is provided by the items that are included under this heading in the statutory instruments made under the Companies Act 2006.

As with some other areas where UK guidance is not particularly explicit, it can be useful to look at international standards. In this case, there is no useful definition under current international standards but an old standard, International Accounting Standard 25, provided a useful definition:

> . . . an asset held by an enterprise for the accretion of wealth through distribution (such as interest, royalties, dividends and rentals), for capital appreciation or for other benefits to the investing enterprise such as those obtained through trading relationships. (Para. 3, IAS 25.)

(IAS 25 has long been defunct, and replaced by IASs 39 and 40, which deal with financial instruments and investment properties respectively, with effect for accounting periods beginning on or after 1 January 2001.) The definition given in IAS 25 then goes on to exclude specifically stocks and tangible fixed assets. This definition still allows for considerable latitude in deciding which items may be described as investments.

13.3   FIXED AND CURRENT ASSET INVESTMENTS

The formats contained in Sch. 1 to The Large and Medium-sized Companies and Groups (Accounts and Reports) Regulations 2008 (SI 2008/410) and Sch. 1 to The Small Companies and Groups (Accounts and Directors' Report) Regulations 2008 (SI 2008/409) indicate the items that are expected to fall within each category. Both lists are given below.

Format for larger companies

B. Fixed assets

III   Investments

(1)   Shares in group undertakings

(2) Loans to group undertakings

(3) Participating interests

(4) Loans to undertakings in which the company has a participating interest

(5) Other investments other than loans

(6) Other loans

(7) Own shares

Format for small companies

(1) Shares in group undertakings and participating interests

(2) Loans to group undertakings and undertakings in which the company has a participating interest

(3) Other investments other than loans

(4) Other investments

C. Current assets

III Investments

(1) Shares in group undertakings

(2) Own shares

(3) Other investments

Format for small companies

(1) Shares in group undertakings

(2) Other investments

The value of both of these lists is reduced, since each contains a category of other investments. The only thing this shows clearly is that the categories given are not assumed to be exhaustive.

There is no intrinsic difference between a fixed asset investment and a current asset investment. What distinguishes them is merely the purpose for which the investment is held.

In order to be treated as a fixed asset an investment must fall within the definition of such an asset given in the Companies Act 2006:

> ... assets of a company which are intended for use on a continuing basis in the company's activities. (CA 2006, s. 853 (6).)

In the case of investments, it is not obvious how this definition could strictly apply, since investments are not 'used' in the way that other possible fixed assets can be used. In order for the definition to make sense, the term 'use' needs to be interpreted widely, for example, as in 'used to generate income'.

A very rough guide to the difference between a current asset and fixed asset investment is as follows:

- it is a fixed asset if there is no intention, or requirement, to sell in the year following acquisition, and
- it is a current asset investment if there is an intention, or requirement, to sell in the year following acquisition.

Since the difference between a fixed and a current asset investment relates not to the intrinsic economic substance of the instrument itself, but to the intentions of the holder, it is perfectly understandable for investments to be reclassified from one category to another. Consequently, this practice is significantly more common than for any other type of fixed or current asset. This may occur where there has been a change in intention, or where there has been a change in circumstances. For example, where a company owns redeemable shares in another company, they may be treated as a fixed asset investment until redemption is imminent, when they might be transferred and treated as a current asset.

13.4   FIXED ASSET INVESTMENTS

13.4.1   At cost

In common with all fixed assets, investments have, in the past, usually been stated at cost less any necessary write-downs, although there have always been many exceptions to this general rule. This is likely to continue to be true, for the majority of companies. It differs for those companies, the minority, that have chosen to adopt the fair value rules of the Companies Act 2006, and are, therefore, required to comply with FRS 26. FRS 26 requires most investments (not that the standard defines investments, as it also covers many financial instruments that would not fall within any definition of investments) to be stated at fair value. The main exception to this is that FRS 26 allows unquoted equity investments whose fair value cannot be reliably measured, or derivative assets linked to such instruments, to be stated at cost less impairment. It is slightly more questionable whether certain instruments, such as bonds with a limited duration and which the owning company intends to hold to maturity, should be described as investments, but these may also be stated at amortised cost. (There are some fairly strict conditions that need to be met if this treatment is to be allowed.)

For companies not adopting the fair value requirements, the rules on depreciation or amortisation need to be considered when dealing with investments as with all other categories of fixed asset. However, they will not usually apply, as investments will not normally have a finite useful economic life, and therefore will not count as depreciable assets. Some items, such as the limited life bonds mentioned above, may have a finite life. In this case, they are not depreciated, but their accounting treatment is normally on an amortised cost basis determined using the effective interest rate. This reflects the limited period over which such instruments are to be held.

In determining the cost of an investment, any expenses incidental to its acquisition, such as stamp duty and broking fees, may be included. However, interest on loans used to fund the purchase may not be included, because interest charges can only be capitalised where they relate to funding the cost of producing an asset, and not to funding its purchase.

Since individual shares, or similar types of investment, may not be specifically identifiable we need to have a basis on which cost can be allocated to a holding. Naturally, this has an effect only where there is a part disposal of the holding. It makes no difference which basis is used so long as the company only increases or retains its stake, or disposes of the holding in full. Under the Companies Act 2006 investments are subject to the same rules on calculation of cost as items of stock. Where a portfolio of shares in one company is built up through piecemeal acquisition and disposal, the following methods may be used for determining the cost of the investment at any time:

- first in first out (FIFO);
- last in first out (LIFO), or
- weighted average, or any other similar method.

While LIFO is not normally an acceptable method for the valuation of stocks, it is less clear that it is unacceptable for investments. In an investment context, LIFO would represent an investment strategy of building up a core holding over time whilst trading to make marginal adjustments to the portfolio. It should be noted that the tax treatment of share disposals should not drive the accounting treatment. Therefore, the deferred tax account may have to be used if there are differences in treatment.

If the value shown in the company's balance sheet differs materially from the 'relevant alternative amount', then that amount also needs to be disclosed. The 'relevant alternative amount' is assumed to be the replacement cost, unless the directors believe that the most recent actual purchase price would give a fairer representation. This requirement may be amended where FRS 29 applies, since in those cases there will be a requirement to disclose the fair value of the items. This requirement applies both under FRS 29 and Sch. 1 to The Large and Medium-sized Companies and Groups (Accounts and Reports) Regulations 2008 (SI 2008/410).

Although depreciation is usually not required, for the reason stated above, there may still be a diminution in the value of a fixed asset investment for companies that are not stating investments at their fair value. Investments are now one of the few areas where the pre-FRS 11 *(Impairment of Fixed Assets and Goodwill)* rules on diminution still apply.

If such a diminution is expected to be temporary then the company is not required to make any provision for the loss, but it is allowed to do so:

> Where a fixed asset investment of a description falling to be included under item B. III of either of the balance sheet formats set out in Part I of this Schedule has diminished in value provisions for diminution in value may be made in respect of it and the amount to be included in respect of it may be reduced accordingly. (Para. 19 (1), Sch. 1 to The Large and Medium-sized Companies and Groups (Accounts and Reports) Regulations 2008 (SI 2008/410) and Para. 19 (1) Sch. 1 to The Small Companies and Groups (Accounts and Directors' Report) Regulations 2008 (SI 2008/409).)

Where a diminution in value is expected to be permanent then the company is required to write down the value of the investment. This must be disclosed, either separately or in aggregate, either in the profit and loss account or in the notes. However, it is not acceptable to maintain an investment at below original cost if the reason for creating the provision for diminution in value has ceased to apply:

> Where the reasons for which any provision was made ... have ceased to apply to any extent, that provision must be written back to the extent that it is no longer necessary.

> Any amounts written back ... which are not shown in the profit and loss account must be disclosed (either separately or in aggregate) in a note to the accounts. (Para. 20 (1) and (2), Sch. 1 to The Large and Medium-sized Companies and Groups (Accounts and Reports) Regulations 2008 (SI 2008/410) and Para. 20 (1) and (2), Sch. 1 to The Small Companies and Groups (Accounts and Directors' Report) Regulations 2008 (SI 2008/409).)

As noted above, in many cases, it is still these statutory rules that will apply, despite the introduction of FRS 11. FRS 11 excludes from its scope any fixed assets which fall within the scope of FRS 25.

Most investments will be treated as financial assets under FRS 25. These are defined as:

> any asset that is

(a) cash;

(b) an equity instrument of another entity;

(c) a contractual right:

    (i) to receive cash or another financial asset from another entity; or

    (ii) to exchange financial assets or financial liabilities with another entity under conditions that are potentially favourable to the entity; or

(d) a contract that will or may be settled in the entity's own equity instruments and is:

(i) a non-derivative for which the entity is or may be obliged to receive a variable number of the entity's own equity instruments; or

(ii) a derivative that will or may be settled other than by the exchange of a fixed amount of cash or another financial assets for a fixed number of the entity's own equity instruments. For this purpose the entity's own equity instruments do not include instruments that are themselves contracts for the future receipt or delivery of the entity's own equity instruments. (Para. 11, FRS 25.)

FRS 25 now excludes from its scope all interests in subsidiaries, quasi-subsidiaries, associated undertakings, partnerships and joint ventures. As a result, investments of this type are covered by the FRS 11 rules on impairment. These rules are dealt with in Chapter 11.

FRS 11 does not, in effect, distinguish between temporary and permanent diminutions in the value of fixed assets and adopts a single approach to measuring the value of all assets.

For those items that fall outside the scope of FRS 11, the distinction between temporary and permanent diminutions in value continues to be relevant. This distinction, rarely straightforward when dealing with any type of asset, is particularly difficult to apply when dealing with investments. The basic rationale is that financial statements should not necessarily be affected by short term fluctuations in asset values. Even if this is considered reasonable, the distinction between a temporary fall and a long-term decline is rarely clear (except subsequently and with hindsight), particularly when applied to assets such as investments which often have no clear life. In nominal terms at least, many assets may have the potential for recovery to their original values, even where this reflects a genuine loss of economic value. Trying to decide when a loss is permanent rather than temporary, and therefore requires to be reflected, is often a matter of considerable judgement.

13.4.2 *At valuation*

Even for companies that have not adopted FRS 26, an alternative to showing fixed asset investments at their cost is to use a valuation. This is allowed by statute:

> Investments of any description falling to be included under item B. III of either of the balance sheet formats set out in Part I of this Schedule may be included either
>
> —
>
> (a) at a market value determined as at the date of their last valuation; or
> (b) at a value determined on any basis which appears to the directors to be appropriate in the circumstances of the company;
>
> But in the latter case particulars of the method of valuation adopted and of the reasons for adopting it must be disclosed in a note to the accounts. (Para. 32 (3), Sch. 1 to The Large and Medium-sized Companies and Groups (Accounts and Reports) Regulations 2008 (SI 2008/410) and Para. 32 (3), Sch. 1 to The Small

Companies and Groups (Accounts and Directors' Report) Regulations 2008 (SI 2008/409).)

This allows considerable flexibility in the valuation of investments. It is surprising that under the Companies Act where market value is to be used, the stated value need not be that at, or even at a date close to, the accounting reference date. It simply needs to be at the date of the last valuation. This is very different to the rules on tangible fixed assets included within FRS 15 which require, in principle, values to be continually current, even if that standard compromises this principle somewhat as a result of the costs of obtaining valuations. Statute provides very little guidance on the methods which may be used by the directors in arriving at their valuation. Therefore, the quality of the information provided by the balance sheet in this case is limited, since the recorded amount may be neither the current value nor the historic cost.

Where a revaluation has taken place, and FRS 26 is not being applied, any increase in value must be taken to a revaluation reserve, and cannot be included in the profit and loss account. The method for calculating the profit on the disposal of an investment is given in both FRS 3, *Reporting Financial Performance* and the FRSSE. The profit must be calculated by comparing the net sale proceeds with the carrying value of the investment.

However, investments are rarely depreciable, and therefore many of the accounting problems that can arise with revaluation surpluses do not apply.

FRS 26 takes an entirely different approach to the valuation of financial assets. This is covered separately.

13.5   CURRENT ASSET INVESTMENTS

For companies that have not adopted fair value accounting and FRS 26, current asset investments are normally stated at the lower of their purchase price and net realisable value. The purchase price is inclusive of any incidental costs of their acquisition.

As with fixed asset investments, where necessary, the cost of current investments may be determined by using a cost flow assumption such as FIFO or LIFO, so long as disclosure is made of the replacement cost or latest actual purchase price.

Where a current asset investment has previously been written down to its net realisable value, but the provision which has been made proves not to have been required, then the provision must be eliminated or reduced, as appropriate.

Current asset investments may also be stated at their current cost. Current cost is generally accepted to be the lower of net current replacement cost and recoverable amount. Recoverable amount is itself the higher of net realisable value and value in use. In the case of a normal current asset investment, value in use is unlikely to apply. Value in use implies that the asset is held as part of an ongoing trading relationship, which in turn implies that the investment should be treated as a fixed rather than current asset investment. Value in use is covered in greater detail in Chapter 11.

The very different rules that apply where a company has adopted FRS 26 are covered separately.

13.6   DISCLOSURE OF INVESTMENTS

13.6.1   All categories of fixed asset

For fixed asset investments the disclosure requirements are the same as those which apply to all categories of fixed asset:

> In respect of each item which is ... shown under the general item "fixed assets" in the company's balance sheet the following information shall be given
>
> (a)   the appropriate amounts in respect of that item as at the date of the beginning of the financial year and as at the balance sheet date respectively;
> (b)   the effect on any amount shown in the balance sheet in respect of that item of
>
>> (i)   any revision of the amount in respect of any assets included under that item made during that year on any basis mentioned in paragraph 32;
>> (ii)   acquisitions during that year of any assets;
>> (iii) disposals during that year of any assets; and
>> (iv)   any transfers of assets of the company to and from that item during that year. (Para. 51 (1), Sch. 1 to The Large and Medium-sized Companies and Groups (Accounts and Reports) Regulations 2008 (SI 2008/410) and Para. 48 (1), Sch. 1 to The Small Companies and Groups (Accounts and Directors' Report) Regulations 2008 (SI 2008/409).)

(The reference to para. 32 covers the alternative accounting rules if the company has chosen to state the investments at a valuation.)

Similar disclosures of the movement on the depreciation account are also required, in the rare cases when this applies.

13.6.2   All categories of investment

There are also a number of specific disclosure requirements in respect of all investments, whether treated as fixed or current:

> In respect of the amount of each item which is or would but for paragraph 4 (2)(b) be shown in the company's balance sheet under the general item "investments"

(whether as fixed assets or as current assets) there must be stated how much of that amount is ascribable to listed investments.

Where the amount of any listed investments is stated for any item in accordance with subparagraph (1), the following amounts must also be stated:

(a) the aggregate market value of those investments where it differs from the amount so stated; and

(b) both the market value and the stock exchange value of any investments of which the former value is, for the purposes of the accounts, taken as being higher than the latter. (Para. 54, Sch. 1 to The Large and Medium-sized Companies and Groups (Accounts and Reports) Regulations 2008 (SI 2008/410) and Para. 50, Sch. 1 to The Small Companies and Groups (Accounts and Directors' Report) Regulations 2008 (SI 2008/409).)

Listed investment is further defined as:

... an investment as respects which there has been granted a listing on:

(a) a recognised investment exchange other than an overseas investment exchange, or

(b) a stock exchange of repute outside the United Kingdom.

(2) "Recognised investment exchange" and "overseas investment exchange" have the meaning given in Part 18 of the Financial Services and Markets Act 2000. (Para. 8, Sch. 10 to The Large and Medium-sized Companies and Groups (Accounts and Reports) Regulations 2008 (SI 2008/410) and Para. 5, Sch. 8 to The Small Companies and Groups (Accounts and Directors' Report) Regulations 2008 (SI 2008/409).)

If fixed asset investments have been included at a valuation other than market value then the following details must be given:

● the method of valuation that has been used, and
● the reasons for adopting that method of valuation.

If fixed asset investments (other than listed investments) have been stated at a valuation then the accounts must disclose the years, so far as this is known to the directors, in which the assets were valued. If the valuation took place in the year then the name or qualification of the person who valued them should be given, together with the basis of the valuation.

Where an investment is 'significant' then additional details need to be given. For these purposes 'significant' means:

(a) it amounts to 20% or more of the nominal value of any class of shares in the undertaking, or

(b) the amount of the holding (as stated or included in the company's accounts) exceeds one-fifth of the amount (as so stated) of the company's assets. (Para. 4(2), Sch. 4 to The Large and Medium-sized Companies and Groups (Accounts and Reports) Regulations 2008 (SI 2008/410) and Para. 5 (2), Sch. 2 to The Small Companies and Groups (Accounts and Directors' Report) Regulations 2008 (SI 2008/409).)

If this applies, as well as the name, there must be stated:

(a) if the undertaking is incorporated outside the United Kingdom, the country in which it is incorporated;

(b) if it is unincorporated, the address of its principal place of business.

There must also be stated:

(a) the identity of each class of shares in the undertaking held by the company, and

(b) the proportion of the nominal value of the shares of that class represented by those shares. (Para. 5 (2) and (3), Sch. 4 to The Large and Medium-sized Companies and Groups (Accounts and Reports) Regulations 2008 (SI 2008/410) and Para. 6 (2) and (3), Sch. 2 to The Small Companies and Groups (Accounts and Directors' Report) Regulations 2008 (SI 2008/409).)

13.7 PARTICIPATING INTERESTS

Investments in, and income from, participating interests need to be disclosed separately from all other types of investment except by small companies. A 'participating interest' means:

> . . . an interest held by an undertaking in the shares of another undertaking which it holds on a long-term basis for the purpose of securing a contribution to its activities by the exercise of control or influence arising from or related to that interest. (Para. 11(1) of Sch. 10 to The Large and Medium-sized Companies and Groups (Accounts and Reports) Regulations 2008 (SI 2008/410).)

The rules for determining when a participating interest exists are very similar to those used for identifying an associated undertaking. A holding of 20 per cent or more of the shares of an undertaking is presumed to be a participating interest unless the contrary is shown. The definition of a participating interest specifically excludes a subsidiary company.

However, some participating interests may also be classified as associated undertakings. This arises because the legal definition of an associate is dependent upon the fact that the investment falls within the category of a participating interest:

> An "associated undertaking" means an undertaking in which an undertaking included in the consolidation has a participating interest and over whose operating and financial policy it exercises a significant influence, and which is not
>
> (a) a subsidiary undertaking of the parent company, or
>
> (b) a joint venture dealt with in accordance with paragraph 18. (Para. 19(1) of Sch. 6 to The Large and Medium-sized Companies and Groups (Accounts and Reports) Regulations 2008 (SI 2008/410).)

The reference to paragraph 18 covers unincorporated joint ventures that are being dealt with by proportional consolidation. This treatment is prohibited by FRS 9 *Associates and Joint Ventures*, and is therefore in practice of no relevance.

There may be particular difficulty in identifying which participating interests are also associates. The key factor is therefore whether or not it is 'influence' or 'significant influence' which is being exercised. For group accounts purposes, where a company has both associated undertakings and participating interests then the statutory formats are amended, showing associated undertakings separately, as follows:

B. Fixed assets

III Investments

3(i)   Interests in associated undertakings

3(ii)   Other participating interests

Similar changes should be made to the profit and loss account format.

If a company has participating interests, although it does not own 20 per cent or more of the capital of the undertakings concerned, then there is no additional disclosure beyond the separate categorisation of the investment and income.

Where the company owns 20 per cent or more of the capital then additional disclosure is required:

(a)   the aggregate amount of the capital and reserves of the undertaking as at the end of its relevant financial year, and

(b)   its profit or loss for that year. (Para. 6 (1), Sch. 4 to The Large and Medium-sized Companies and Groups (Accounts and Reports) Regulations 2008 (SI 2008/410).)

However, there are a number of exceptions to this disclosure rule. The information is not required if:

(a)   the company is exempt by virtue of section 400 or 401 of the 2006 Act from the requirement to prepare group accounts (parent company included in accounts of larger group), and

(b)   the investment of the company in all undertakings in which it has such a holding as is mentioned in sub-paragraph (1) is shown, in aggregate, in the notes to the accounts by way of the equity method of valuation. (Para. 13 (1), Sch. 4 to The Large and Medium-sized Companies and Groups (Accounts and Reports) Regulations 2008 (SI 2008/410).)

Information also need not be given in respect of an undertaking if:

(a)   the undertaking is not required by any provision of the 2006 Act to deliver a copy of its balance sheet for its relevant financial year and does not otherwise publish that balance sheet in the United Kingdom or elsewhere, and

(b)   the company's holding is less than 50% of the nominal value of the shares in the undertaking. (Para. 6 (2), Sch. 4 to The Large and Medium-sized Companies and Groups (Accounts and Reports) Regulations 2008 (SI 2008/410).)

13.8 FRS 4 CAPITAL INSTRUMENTS

FRS 4 continues to exist as a separate standard. However, ever since FRS 25 was issued, FRS 4 has been basically limited to dealing with the allocation of finance costs to accounting periods.

13.9 DISCLOSURE OF CAPITAL INSTRUMENTS

13.9.1 Capital and reserves format

The formats of Sch. 1 to The Large and Medium-sized Companies and Groups (Accounts and Reports) Regulations 2008 (SI 2008/410) contain the following division of capital and reserves:

(I)   Called up share capital
(II) Share premium account
(III) Revaluation reserve
(IV) Other reserves

    (1) Capital redemption reserve

    (2) Reserve for own shares

    (3) Reserves provided for by the articles of association

    (4) Other reserves

(V)   Profit and loss account

For small companies there is no sub-division of other reserves.

A note to the format mentions that the amount of allotted share capital and the amount of called up share capital which has been paid up shall be shown separately.

13.9.2 Companies Act requirements – share capital

The following additional information must also be provided in the notes to the accounts under the Companies Act 2006.

(1) Where shares of more than one class have been allotted, the number and aggregate nominal value of shares of each class that have been allotted.

(2) Where shares are held as treasury shares, the number and aggregate nominal value of the treasury shares and, where shares of more than one class have been allotted, the number and aggregate nominal value of the

shares of each class held as treasury shares. (This applies only to those companies which are allowed to hold treasury shares.)

(3)   Where any part of the allotted share capital consists of redeemable shares:

    (a)   the earliest and latest dates on which the company has the power to redeem those shares;

    (b)   whether redemption of the shares is obligatory, or whether the choice is given to the company or the shareholder, and

    (c)   whether there is any premium payable on redemption, and if so, the amount.

(4)   Where the company has allotted any shares during the year:

    (a)   the classes of each share allotted, and

    (b)   for each class of share, the number allotted, their aggregate nominal value, and the consideration received by the company for the allotment.

(5)   For companies other than small companies, where there is any contingent right to the allotment of shares in the company:

    (a)   the number, description and amount of shares in relation to which the right is exercisable;

    (b)   the period during which it can be exercised, and

    (c)   the price to be paid for the shares allotted.

The requirement to disclose authorised share capital was removed by the Companies Act 2006. (There is a slight oddity in that the requirement to disclose authorised share capital was abolished for accounts covering periods beginning on or after 6 April 2008. The requirement for companies to have an authorised share capital did not disappear until 1 October 2009. Those companies which already had an authorised share capital at 1 October 2009 still have one, unless they have taken the appropriate steps to remove it, although the provision has been moved from their Memorandum to their Articles by process of law. It is also worth mentioning that IFRS do contain a requirement to disclose authorised share capital, if a company has one.)

A contingent right to the allotment of shares in the company means either an option to subscribe for shares, or any other right to require the company to allot shares, whether this is through the conversion of a security or otherwise. It would therefore include, for example, options, warrants and convertible bonds.

The need to provide information on contingent rights to shares is in addition to the need to disclose specific details about any such rights granted to directors.

13.9.3   Equity and debt

FRS 25 takes a substance over form approach to equity and debt instruments:

The issuer of a financial instrument shall classify the instrument, or the component parts, on initial recognition as a financial liability, a financial asset or an equity instrument in accordance with the substance of the contractual arrangement and the definitions of a financial liability, a financial asset and an equity instrument. (Para. 15, FRS 25.)

For example, a share that is redeemable will be treated as a liability if:

- redemption is to take place at a fixed date;
- redemption is to take place on the occurrence or non-occurrence of a future event which is outside of the control of the entity, or
- redemption may take place at the request of the holder.

The only time that a redeemable share will form part of equity is if redemption can take place solely at the option of the company.

The defining characteristic in all these, and all similar cases, is whether there is an obligation to deliver cash or another financial asset, or to exchange financial assets or financial liabilities under conditions that are potentially unfavourable. (Strictly, it is also necessary to consider whether there is any requirement to settle a balance by using the entity's own equity instruments in cases where the number of instruments is variable or whether it is a derivative that requires a fixed amount of cash or other financial assets to be exchanged for a fixed amount of equity instruments. Such cases will be rare.)

Going back to redeemable shares, if, say, the redemption can take place at the request of the holder then the company can be required to transfer cash or other financial assets. This makes it a liability of the company. If redemption is solely at the company's option then there is no such obligation, since it is within the company's control whether or not such redemption, and consequently payment of cash or other financial assets, takes place.

In addition, FRS 25 deals with components of instruments. This means that in some cases an instrument may need to be split between equity and debt elements.

For example, where a company issues convertible debt, and conversion is into items that are equity instruments, then that convertible debt contains both equity and debt elements. On issue, the elements need to be split between:

- the debt element, and
- the conversion rights, which are a component of equity.

The manner in which this is done is to value the debt element by determining the fair value of a similar instrument excluding the equity element. For example, a company may issue convertible debt on the basis that the interest rate it can obtain is lower than would be obtainable if the conversion rights were not in place. The company would then apply the interest rate it would have obtained in the absence of the conversion rights to the cash flows associated with the debt including the conversion rights. This will inevitably lead to a lower figure. This lower figure is then used as the debt element and accounted for as a liability. The difference between the debt figure and the proceeds represents the equity element and is taken directly to reserves. This does not pass through the statement of total recognised gains and losses, since it does not form part of a gain but is instead effectively advance consideration in respect of the equity shares that may eventually be issued.

There is also a transitional provision in FRS 25 that deals with the issue. The default rule in FRS 25 is that the standard should be applied retrospectively. This means that compound instruments already issued need to be adjusted. However, FRS 25 requires this only where the liability element of a compound instrument was outstanding at the date of transition to FRS 25.

FRS 25 was changed with effect for accounting periods beginning on or after 1 January 2010. The issue dealt with in this change relates to items that had previously been treated as liabilities, but which had many of the characteristics of equity.

The first issue dealt with in the 2010 changes was that of puttable financial instruments. A puttable instrument is one that gives the holder the right to put the instrument back to the issuer for cash (or other financial assets) or which is automatically put back to the issuer on the occurrence of an uncertain future event or the death or retirement of the holder.

Under the previous rules, all such puttable instruments had been treated as financial liabilities. This is because they include an obligation on the issuer to transfer economic resources at the request of the holder, or in circumstances which are outside the control of the issuer.

In 2010, this changes and now a puttable financial instrument is treated as equity if all of the following conditions are met:

- the instrument entitles the holder to a pro rata share of net assets in the event of the issuer's liquidation;
- the instrument is in the class of instruments that is subordinate to all other classes of instrument, without any conversion being required;
- all of the instruments in the class are identical (ie all puttable, and with the same formula used to determine the share of net assets);
- there are no contractual obligations (other than the repurchase or redemption right) to deliver cash or other assets, or to exchange financial assets or liabilities under conditions that are potentially unfavourable, and the instrument cannot be settled by transfer of the issuer's own equity instruments;
- the total cash flows attributable to the instrument over its life are based on profits, losses, changes in net assets and changes in fair values of the recognised and unrecognised net assets of the issuer, and
- there are no other financial instruments or contracts of the issuer that have

cash flows based substantially on profits, losses, changes in net assets and changes in fair values of the recognised and unrecognised net assets of the issuer and that will substantially restrict or fix the return to the holders of the puttable financial instruments.

Finally, where there are non-financial contracts with other holders of instruments, these are ignored for the purposes of the later tests, if they are on the same terms as would apply if the party were not an instrument holder. (Put another way, arm's length non-financial contracts that happen to be with holders of other financial instruments are ignored.)

Taken together, these conditions mean that the holder is the last in line and really does have the final category of interest in the net assets.

The second issue is that of instruments, or parts of instruments, that impose on the issuer an obligation to deliver a pro rata share of net assets only on liquidation. This may arise for reasons outside of the control of the issuer (for example, with a company with a predetermined finite life) or where it is uncertain but at the option of the holder.

The conditions for such instruments to be treated as equity are broadly the same as for puttable instruments, but:

- no reference is made to other contractual obligations to transfer cash or other financial assets, and
- no reference is made to the cash flows over the life of the instrument.

Some instruments may fall into, or out of, the categories above. For example, whether an instrument is subordinate to all other instruments may change when another instrument is issued or redeemed.

Where this results in a reclassification, that reclassification is accounted for from the date of the change.

If an instrument becomes a liability, having previously been an equity instrument:

- the liability is initially recorded at the fair value at the date of reclassification, and
- any difference between the carrying value of the equity instrument and fair value of the financial liability at the date is itself taken to equity.

If an instrument becomes equity, having previously been a liability, then the equity instrument is measured at the carrying value of the financial liability at the date of reclassification.

There was a further change to FRS 25, which applied to accounting periods beginning on or after 1 February 2010 (so, strictly, there were three versions of the standard in the course of three months). Early adoption is allowed.

This amendment further changed the distinction between equity and liabilities by treating rights issues exclusively as equity, even if they are denominated in a foreign currency, so long as certain conditions are met. Under the current requirements, rights, option, or warrants to acquire a fixed number of the entity's own equity instruments for a fixed amount of any currency are themselves equity instruments if the rights, options or warrants are offered pro rata to all existing owners of the same class of the entity's own non-derivative equity instruments.

This change, which reflects a similar change in IAS 32, the international standard on which FRS 25 is based, was introduced to avoid the previous anomaly that a rights issue in a foreign currency gave rise to an embedded derivative liability.

13.9.4 Dividends and other appropriations

As noted above, under FRS 25 the underlying nature of the instrument is used in determining whether an instrument which is legally in the form of a share should be treated as equity or a liability. Where the instrument forms part of equity then dividends continue to be treated as an appropriation of profit. However, where it is determined that a share should be treated as a liability, payments in respect of that share, still legally dividends, are accounted for as an expense. FRS 25 states that these may either be presented with interest on other liabilities, or separately. It recommends that they be treated separately, since they will often have different characteristics. The example of such a difference given in FRS 25 is that of tax deductibility, but where a company does not have distributable profits there is also the issue of whether payment can lawfully be made. Where there are arrears of cumulative fixed dividends on shares treated as liabilities then such arrears should, under FRS 25, be treated as liabilities like any other.

13.9.5 Reserve movements

There is also a statutory requirement to show movements on any reserve accounts. The information that must be given when there is a movement on any reserve account is:

- the amount of the reserve at the beginning and end of the year;
- any amounts transferred to or from the reserve during the year, and
- the source or application of any amounts transferred.

13.9.6 Debt finance – Companies Act requirements

Amounts of debt will normally be treated as creditors. In the statutory formats it is most common for them to fall within debenture loans or bank loans and overdrafts. However, in practice it is rarely these descriptions that are used. It is normally more appropriate to describe each form of debt separately in the note to the accounts.

If the company is using balance sheet format 1, then it needs to divide its creditors between amounts falling due within and after more than one year on the face of the balance sheet. If it is using format 2, which is fairly rare, then it need only provide this analysis in a note to the accounts.

Although the most common division of the balance sheet, under format 1, is to show only capital and reserves on the bottom half, this is not required by the Companies Act. Companies may show debt on the bottom half of the balance sheet if they wish. However, in such cases they must take care to ensure that it is not implied that these are amounts of capital and reserves.

The balance sheet items must be presented in the order given in the formats – where a company chooses the alternative form of presentation it is in effect inserting the balance sheet total in an unusual place.

Under the Companies Act 2006, debenture is defined as follows:

> . . . "debenture" includes debenture stock, bonds and any other securities of a company, whether or not constituting a charge on the assets of the company. (CA 2006, s. 738.)

The Companies Act 2006 requires the following disclosures where a company, other than a small company, has debentures in issue.

(1) Where the company has issued any debentures during the year:

    (a) the classes of debentures issued, and

    (b) for each class of debentures, the amount issued and the consideration received by the company for the issue.

(2) Where any of the company's debentures are held by a nominee of the company, the nominal amount of the debentures and the amount at which they are stated in the accounting records.

There are also statutory disclosure provisions that apply to all forms of creditors, where relevant.

(1) The aggregate amount of any debts which are payable or repayable otherwise than by instalments and fall due for payment or repayment more than five years after the balance sheet date, and any amounts payable after more than five years, and which form part of a balance payable by instalments.

(2) The terms of payment or repayment and the rate of interest payable for any item included in the two categories above (however, where this would result in a statement of excessive length then the company may alternatively provide a general indication of the terms of repayment and the applicable interest rates).

(3) The aggregate amount of any debts in respect of which any security has been given by the company, and an indication of the nature of the security.

The fact that the rate of interest on debt is variable does not exempt a company from disclosure. It will normally be possible to state how the interest rate is calculated; for example, by reference to a given premium over base rates or LIBOR (London inter-bank offered rate).

13.10 SHARE CAPITAL AND RESERVES

13.10.1 *Issue of share capital*

Share capital, when fully called up, is always stated at its par or nominal value. Any excess of value received over this amount is treated as share premium. Shares cannot legally be issued at a discount.

Under FRS 25, and as set out above, some shares will be treated as liabilities. Where this applies, the whole amount received is treated as the initial liability and the distinction between share capital and premium is ignored, for accounting purposes. (The legal prohibition on issuing shares at a discount to nominal value will, of course, continue to apply, as will the other restrictions which apply to items that are legally part of share capital.)

Where share capital is issued in a foreign currency, and this is different from the currency in which the results are reported, the situation is a little more complicated. This matter is not unambiguously addressed in SSAP 20, although FRS 23 is perhaps a little clearer. The problem of rights issues, in relation to equity instruments denominated in a foreign currency, and the changes that came into effect for accounting periods beginning on or after 1 February 2010, have been dealt with above, but this amendment does not affect the underlying issue. When the share capital is issued it will be translated at the exchange rate at the date of issue. The question then arises of whether or not the stated value of the shares should be retranslated, at the closing rate, at each balance sheet date or retained at the original value.

The answer will depend on the nature of the shares.

Where the shares are part of equity, in accordance with FRS 25, by definition, the company does not have a financial liability. As a result, the appropriate treatment is to crystallise the carrying value at the exchange rate at the date at which the shares were issued. Future changes in exchange rates will have no effect on the stated value of the shares. Most companies follow this treatment.

Where shares fall to be treated as liabilities, in accordance with FRS 25, they are basically no different to any other liability in another currency. There is an obligation on the company to transfer economic resources. If the shares are denominated in a foreign currency, then that obligation alters as exchange rates move and, therefore, the shares should be retranslated at each balance sheet date.

13.10.2   *Warrants*

Where warrants in respect of equity are issued, the proceeds should be treated as part of shareholders' funds. The amount received will be shown in the reconciliation of the movements in shareholders' funds.

Where a warrant is exercised then the amount of the proceeds should include both the value of the additional consideration received and the amount that had previously been recognised on the issue of the warrant. At the time at which a warrant is exercised the reconciliation of the movement in shareholders' funds will only show the amount of the additional consideration received.

If a warrant lapses without having been exercised then this represents a gain to the existing shareholders and should be included in the statement of total recognised gains and losses. This will also require an adjustment to the reconciliation of the movement in shareholders' funds, since the amount will need to be deducted from shareholders' funds before being reintroduced as a gain.

Were warrants to be issued in respect of items that would themselves be treated as liabilities then they would simply be an advance on those liabilities.

13.10.3   *Conversion of debt*

Where debt is converted into shares, the carrying amount of the debt at the date of conversion should be treated as the consideration received for the shares. This, therefore, automatically includes any amounts of interest or other finance costs that have been accrued on the debt, but which are no longer payable once conversion takes place. The amount of the deemed consideration will need to be shown in the reconciliation of the movement in shareholders' funds.

Assuming that the debt was always convertible (rather than simply converted in lieu of payment when no such right previously existed), there will also be an existing balance within equity. This will be the amount of the value originally ascribed to the conversion rights when the convertible debt was issued.

For those entities which are within the scope of, or are in fact applying, FRS 26, these rules change slightly with effect for accounting periods beginning on or after 1 July 2010. UITF 47 deals with the issue of the extinguishment of debt through issuing capital. UITF 47 is dealt with at **13.14.1**. However, in summary, it requires a broadly similar accounting treatment to that set out above, but requires the equity issued to be valued at its own fair value (if this can be reliably determined) and the fair, rather than carrying value of the debt (if it cannot). UITF 47 does not apply where the conversion of debt into equity is in accordance with the original terms of the instrument. It also contains exemptions in relation to existing equity holders and entities under common control.

13.10.4 Share splits

A company may issue new shares in place of its existing shares, usually in smaller denominations. As there is no additional consideration, there is no accounting effect, except that the description of the shares will change and the new details will need to be given in the financial statements.

13.10.5 Bonus issues and scrip dividends

Where a company has a balance of distributable profits, a share premium account, a revaluation reserve or a balance on any capital redemption reserve, then these balances may be used to issue additional shares to existing members. The accounting treatment for such a bonus issue is extremely straightforward, and involves reducing the profit and loss account or capital redemption reserve and increasing the amount of the share capital. If the profit and loss account is used, the company is simply allocating some of the distributable profits to the capital base of the company. If the capital redemption reserve is used, then there is no change in the capital base of the company, since the capital redemption reserve is, like share capital, not distributable.

Some companies offer their shareholders additional shares instead of a cash dividend. Such issues are often referred to as a scrip dividend. The consideration for the issue should be taken as the value of the cash alternative, and treated as an appropriation of profit. The deemed consideration may need to be treated through both the share capital and share premium accounts.

Scrip dividends are often treated for legal purposes as bonus issues. If this is the case then the appropriation of profit should be written back as a movement on reserves, and a transfer should be made from distributable reserves (usually the accumulated profit and loss account) to the share capital account for the nominal value of the shares issued with any excess over this amount being taken to the share premium account.

Where a company has offered a scrip dividend, but is preparing financial statements before it knows the level of acceptance, it should treat the whole amount as a liability to pay cash dividends. In the next accounting period it will then, effectively, treat any amount of scrip dividend as if it were the conversion of debt.

13.10.6 Share premium

Where a company issues shares at above their par value, it will normally have to create, or add to, a share premium account to deal with the difference. It does not matter whether the consideration is received in the form of cash or otherwise. Once a share premium account has been created it is, with some exceptions, treated under statute almost as if it were share capital of the company. This means that the reserve is undistributable.

However, there are certain circumstances in which a company need not set up, or add to, a share premium account. These reliefs are usually known as merger relief and group reconstruction relief. Where the relief is available, the company that has issued the shares may ignore the amount of the effective premium in calculating the value at which the consideration received is to be stated in its financial statements, or it may transfer the effective premium to another reserve.

EXAMPLE

A company issues 100,000 £1 shares in order to acquire shares in another company with a value of £250,000.

Normally, a share premium account would need to be set up, at an amount of £150,000, and the investment acquired would need to be stated at the full cost of £250,000. If merger relief is available then no share premium account need be created and the investment acquired can be stated at a cost of £100,000. However, companies are not required to state the shares at nominal value. If they wish, they can state the assets at their full effective cost (£250,000) and transfer the excess of the value over the issued share capital (£100,000) to a separate, distributable, reserve.

Merger relief, which should not be confused with merger accounting, is available where one company has secured 90 per cent of the equity of another company under an arrangement by which the acquiring company will issue shares, and the consideration for those shares will be:

- the issue or transfer to the acquiring company of shares in the other company, or
- the cancellation of shares in the other company not already held by the acquiring company.

In these circumstances the company need not transfer any premium on the shares to a share premium account. The shares that are issued or transferred to the acquiring company, or cancelled, need not all be equity shares, as long as the condition that the acquiring company must obtain 90 per cent of the equity capital has been met.

Merger relief is available only for the particular transaction in which the 90 per cent threshold is breached, but the acquiring company does not have to acquire all the shares in a single transaction. For example, a company could acquire all the equity shares in another company by purchasing one-fifth of those shares in five separate transactions in return for the issue of its own shares. Merger relief would only be available on the final transaction.

Where the company which is being acquired has an equity share capital consisting of more than one class of share, the 90 per cent condition must be satisfied in relation to each class for merger relief to be available.

For the purposes of determining when 90 per cent of the shares are held by the acquiring company, any shares held by the acquiring company's parent, subsidiary or fellow subsidiary are deemed to be held by the acquiring company.

A similar form of relief is also available for certain group reconstructions. The relief is available if a wholly owned subsidiary allots shares to its parent, or a fellow wholly owned subsidiary, in return for the transfer of assets from another group company rather than cash. The relief is limited to the difference between the normal amount that would need to be treated as share premium and the 'minimum premium value'. The minimum premium value is the difference between the aggregate nominal value of the shares allotted and the 'base value' of the consideration.

The base value of the consideration is the amount by which the base value of the assets transferred exceeds the base value of any liabilities assumed by the company which issued the shares.

For these purposes, the base value of assets is the lower of the cost of the assets to the company that has transferred them and their book value immediately prior to the transfer and the base value of liabilities is their book value immediately prior to transfer.

EXAMPLE

A group issues 50,000 £1 shares to its parent in return for the transfer of fixed assets with a fair value of £130,000, and a net book value of £60,000.

The company would need to set up a share premium account for the excess of the net book value over the nominal amount of the shares issued, which in this case would amount to £10,000. It would not have to treat the additional £70,000 as share premium.

Once a share premium account has been created its uses are restricted, but it can be used for:

- writing off the company's preliminary expenses;
- writing off the expenses or commission paid, or the discount allowed on any issue of shares or debentures of the company;
- providing for any premium payable on the redemption of debentures by the company, or
- issuing additional bonus shares.

FRS 25 does not change the legal position in respect of share premiums. However, it does have implications for accounting, since if shares are issued which fall within debt under FRS 25 then no share premium will be created as far as the financial statements are concerned. The legal requirements will therefore need to be applied by companies maintaining records of amounts appearing within liabilities.

13.10.7   Revaluation reserve

Where any asset of a company is revalued in accordance with the alternative accounting rules of Sch. 1 to The Large and Medium-sized Companies and Groups (Accounts and Reports) Regulations 2008 (SI 2008/410), the amount of the revaluation should be taken to a separate revaluation reserve. This reserve must be shown separately in the company's balance sheet.

Until the Companies Act 1989, there were no clear statutory prohibitions on the uses to which the revaluation reserve could be put. The Companies Act 1989 restricted the uses of the revaluation reserve. Apart from changes, whether positive or negative, due to revaluations it can only be:

- transferred to the profit and loss account, if the amount was previously charged to that account, or if it represents realised profit;
- capitalised, that is, used to issue fully or partly paid bonus shares to members of the company, or
- transferred to or from the revaluation reserve in respect of the taxation relating to any profit or loss credited or debited to the reserve.

The revaluation reserve cannot be reduced for any other reason.

These rules have been carried forward into Sch. 1 to The Large and Medium-sized Companies and Groups (Accounts and Reports) Regulations 2008 (SI 2008/410).

Where amounts are credited or debited to the revaluation reserve, the tax treatment should be disclosed in a note to the accounts. The accounting treatment arising from the disposal of revalued assets, and changes in the value of assets, are covered in Chapter 11.

13.10.8   Rights of companies to acquire or redeem their own shares

The Companies Act 2006 contains a general principle that companies may not acquire their own shares:

> A limited company must not acquire its own shares, whether by purchase, subscription or otherwise, except in accordance with the provisions of this Part. (CA 2006, s. 658 (1))

However, the exceptions are so wide as to render the general principle of very little importance and the Companies Act 2006 has, in practice, extended the possibilities. Nonetheless, where a company holds its own shares it cannot use them in the unfettered way normally allowed.

The conditions under which a company can acquire its own shares are if:

- they are redeemable shares and have been redeemed;
- they comply with the rules on purchase of own shares;
- the shares are obtained without providing valuable consideration, and are fully paid;
- it obtains the shares as part of a reduction of capital with the agreement of the courts;
- the shares are purchased in accordance with a court order connected with a change in the company's objects;
- the shares are purchased in accordance with a court order connected with an objection to the re-registration of the company as a private company;
- it purchases the shares in accordance with a court order granted as relief to unfairly prejudiced members, or
- it acquires the shares due to forfeiture or surrender, when authorised by the articles of association, for failure to pay any sum payable in respect of the shares.

13.10.9   Redeemable shares

A company is allowed to issue redeemable shares if the following conditions apply:

- it is authorised to do so by its articles of association;
- there are also irredeemable shares in issue at the time the redeemable shares are issued, and
- the shares can be redeemed only when they are fully paid, and where payment is to be made on redemption.

In general, shares can only be redeemed out of distributable profits or out of the proceeds of a fresh issue of shares, and any premium paid on redemption must be made out of distributable profits of the company.

If redeemable shares were initially issued at a premium, then any premium payable on their redemption may be paid out of the proceeds of a fresh issue of shares up to the lower of:

- the aggregate of the premiums received on the shares to be redeemed when they were originally issued, or
- the current amount on the company's share premium account, including any sum transferred to that account on the issue of new shares.

The share premium account may be reduced by this amount.

When shares are redeemed they must be cancelled, but this does not involve a reduction in the authorised share capital of the company.

Where a company is issuing new shares at the same time as it redeems shares, it can ignore the number of shares to be redeemed in calculating the number of shares it is allowed to issue while staying within its authorised amount.

Where shares are redeemed out of a company's profits, the amount by which the share capital has been reduced on redemption must be transferred to a capital redemption reserve.

Where shares are redeemed from the proceeds of a fresh issue, then the transfer to the capital redemption reserve is limited to the amount by which the proceeds of the fresh issue fall short of the nominal amount of the shares redeemed.

The capital redemption reserve is not distributable, but may be used to issue fully paid bonus shares to members of the company. A number of examples can be used to illustrate the application of these provisions.

EXAMPLE

Consider the simplest case, in which a company redeems shares at par without a fresh issue of shares, and in which there was no premium on the original issue of the shares. The company's balance sheet appears as follows:

	£
Net assets	10,000
Ordinary £1 shares	2,500
Redeemable £1 shares	2,500
Profit and loss account	5,000
	10,000

The entries required will be:

Dr Redeemable shares	2,500	
Dr Profit and loss account	2,500	
Cr Cash		2,500
Cr Capital redemption reserve		2,500

The capital of the company must be maintained through the transfer to the capital redemption reserve.

The balance sheet will then be:

	£
Net assets	7,500
Ordinary £1 shares	2,500
Capital redemption reserve	2,500
Profit and loss account	2,500
	7,500

If the company had instead redeemed the shares from the proceeds of a fresh issue, then the situation would differ. The situation is the same except that a new issue of 1,000 £1 ordinary shares takes place at the same time at par.

The entries will then be:

Dr Redeemable shares	2,500	
Dr Cash (proceeds of issue)	1,000	
Dr Profit and loss account	1,500	
Cr Ordinary shares		1,000
Cr Cash (redemption costs)		2,500
Cr Capital redemption reserve		1,500

The balance sheet would then be:

	£
Net assets	8,500
Ordinary £1 shares	3,500
Capital redemption reserve	1,500
Profit and loss account	3,500
	8,500

The situation is slightly more complicated where there is a premium on redemption.

A company has the following balance sheet:

	£
Net assets	10,000
Ordinary £1 shares	2,500
Redeemable £1 shares	1,000
Share premium	1,000
Profit and loss account	5,500
	10,000

The share premium arose on the ordinary shares. The shares are redeemed at £1.50 per share.

The entries will be:

Dr Redeemable shares	1,000	
Dr Profit and loss account	1,500	
Cr Cash		1,500
Cr Capital redemption reserve		1,000

The balance sheet would then be:

	£
Net assets	8,500
Ordinary £1 shares	2,500
Share premium	1,000
Capital redemption reserve	1,000
Profit and loss account	4,000
	8,500

Exactly the same entries would be made if the premium had arisen on the redeemable shares. However, if there is a fresh issue of shares to finance the redemption then the situation may be different.

Taking the same situation as in the previous example, the company also issues 1,000 new £1 ordinary shares at par and it is assumed that the share premium arose on the redeemable shares.

The entries will now be:

Dr Redeemable shares	1,000	
Dr Share premium	500	
Dr Profit and loss account	1,000	
Dr Cash (proceeds of share issue)	1,000	
Cr Ordinary shares		1,000
Cr Cash (redemption costs)		1,500
Cr Capital redemption reserve		1,000

Which would result in the following balance sheet:

	£
Net assets	9,500
Ordinary £1 shares	3,500
Share premium	500
Capital redemption reserve	1,000
Profit and loss account	4,500
	9,500

13.10.10 Purchase of own shares

The accounting procedures for the purchase by a company of its own shares are the same as those for redemption out of capital.

Companies may purchase their own shares with the agreement of the courts in a number of circumstances, noted above. They can also purchase their own shares without the authority of the courts if they comply with certain requirements. In order to purchase its own shares a company must have that authority in its articles of association, and it may not purchase shares if, as a result of the purchase, there would only be redeemable shares in issue.

Different rules apply to 'off market' and market purchases. A purchase is off market if it either does not take place on a recognised investment exchange, or takes place on a recognised investment exchange but not under a marketing arrangement. A marketing arrangement means that the shares are listed on the exchange or that the shares can be traded in that exchange without time limit and without prior permission being required for transactions.

If the purchase is to be off market, then all of the following conditions must be satisfied:

- the terms of the proposed contract must have been authorised by a special resolution of the company;
- if the company is a public company, the authority for the purchase must have a date of expiry, which must not be more than 18 months from the date of the original resolution, or the date on which the authority was renewed;
- the decision to allow the authority cannot have been decided as a result of a vote from the party whose shares are to be purchased, and
- a copy of the contract, if it is to be in writing (or a memorandum setting out the terms of the contract, if it is not to be in writing), must have been available for inspection by members of the company at the company's registered office for not less than 15 days prior to the meeting, and a copy must also be available at the meeting.

Any memorandum of terms must include the names of any members holding shares to which the proposed contract relates, and such names must be attached to any written contract if they are not included in the contract itself.

The same rules apply to a special resolution to alter, revoke or renew such authority, except that a copy of the original contract or memorandum must also be available for inspection by members of the company, together with any previously revised contracts or memoranda.

A company can also enter a contingent purchase contract for off market purchases. A contingent purchase contract is one under which the company may become entitled to purchase the shares if stated conditions are met. The requirements for a contingent purchase contract are the same as those for an authority for off market purchases.

Companies must meet all of the following conditions for a market purchase of their shares:

- the purchase must have been authorised in a general meeting of the company;
- the authority must state the maximum number of shares to be acquired;
- the authority must state both the minimum and maximum price which may be paid for the shares, which can be either absolute amounts or an objective formula for their calculation, and
- the authority must state the date on which it will expire, which may not be more than 18 months from the date of the resolution.

A purchase may still be made after the expiry of such authority, but only if the contract was entered into prior to its expiry, and this was not prohibited by the resolution.

Whichever way a company chooses to purchase its own shares, there is a wide range of requirements concerning publicity. Within 28 days of such a purchase, the company must inform the Registrar of the number and nominal value of the shares it has purchased. If the company is a public company then it must also state the total amount paid and the maximum and minimum prices paid for individual shares. Any contract or memorandum of terms for off market purchases, or contingent purchase contract, must be retained by the company at its registered office for ten years from the date of the last purchase, and it must be available for inspection by members, or the general public in the case of a public company. The disclosure requirements in the company's annual report are covered in Chapter 3.

The amount paid for the purchase by a company of its own shares must be taken from the company's distributable profits or the proceeds of a fresh issue.

13.10.11 *Purchase or redemption of shares out of capital*

A private company may also, in certain circumstances, redeem or purchase shares otherwise than out of distributable profits or the proceeds of a fresh issue of shares.

Under the Companies Act 1985, there needed to be a permissible capital payment. The Companies Act 2006 continues to allow a permissible capital payment but also extends this, from October 2008, so that private companies are now able to reduce their capital without going down the permissible capital payment route.

Under the old procedures, the excess of the amount required for redemption over the proceeds of a fresh issue and the amount of distributable profits is referred to as a permissible capital payment.

If the permissible capital payment, plus the proceeds of any fresh issue of shares, is less than the nominal amount of the shares purchased or redeemed, then the difference must be transferred to the capital redemption reserve.

If the permissible capital payment, plus the proceeds of any fresh issue of shares, is more than the nominal amount of the shares purchased or redeemed, then the difference should be deducted from the capital redemption reserve, the share premium account, the share capital of the company or the revaluation reserve.

Under the Companies Act 2006, if the statutory conditions are satisfied, a purchase of own shares need not result in a capital redemption reserve.

13.10.12 *Treasury shares*

Treasury shares are a relatively recent addition to UK accounting practice, although they have been available in many other countries for many years.

Listed companies may, subject to various restrictions, acquire their own shares (in accordance with the normal legal rules) but rather than those shares being cancelled they are treated as treasury shares.

Where this occurs, the treasury shares are treated as a deduction from equity, effectively a negative reserve.

No gain or loss is recognised on the purchase, sale, issue or cancellation of those shares, since in all cases the transactions are deemed to be capital transactions with shareholders.

The legal position does need to be monitored, as it may have accounting implications. For example, the ability to hold treasury shares lapses if a company ceases to be listed. Where this occurs, there needs to be an accounting entry since at this stage the shares are cancelled and the issued share capital is accordingly reduced.

Where a subsidiary owns shares in a parent company, they will be treated as an asset in the subsidiary's accounts but will be adjusted as above in the group accounts.

UITF 38 applies the same accounting policy in respect of own shares held in an ESOP trust or similar.

13.10.13   Distributable profits

Companies can make distributions only out of profits available for this purpose. Distributions include all payments to members, whether in cash or assets, other than:

- issues of shares as fully or partly paid bonus shares;
- the redemption or purchase of shares out of capital;
- the reduction of share capital by reducing or extinguishing amounts owed on share capital not paid up, or by paying off paid up share capital;
- distributions on the winding up of the company, and
- repayments of debts due to members, not in their capacity as members.

Except in the case of investment companies, distributions can be made only out of the accumulated realised profits of a company which have not previously been distributed or capitalised less any accumulated realised losses, as far as not written off in a previous reduction or reorganisation of capital.

Public companies may also not make distributions if this would mean that their net assets would fall below the aggregate of their called up share capital and undistributable reserves.

Undistributable reserves are the share premium account, the capital redemption reserve, accumulated unrealised profits less accumulated unrealised losses and any other reserves not distributable as a result of the memorandum and articles of association of the company.

The Companies Act is singularly unhelpful in defining realised profits and losses as:

> ... such profits or losses of the company as fall to be treated as realised in accordance with principles generally accepted at the time when the accounts are prepared, with respect to the determination for accounting purposes of realised profits or losses. (CA 2006, s. 853 (4).)

It is only possible to assume that it means 'in accordance with accounting standards' and, presumably, UITF consensus pronouncements. In areas not covered by accounting standards, or similar, it might be difficult to prove that any treatments were sufficiently generally accepted to ensure compliance with the Act.

Guidance on distributable profits has been issued by the Institute of Chartered Accountants in England and Wales and Institute of Chartered Accountants of Scotland in the form of *Guidance on the determination of realised profits and losses in the context of distributions under the Companies Act 2006 (Tech 02/10).* (This guidance covers issues that arise under IFRS as well as those that arise under UK GAAP.)

Statute does provide some specific guidance, as follows.

(1) Development costs included in a company's balance sheet should be treated as realised losses, unless there are special circumstances justifying the directors in not treating them as realised losses, and this is included in a note to the accounts.

(2) Provisions are to be treated as realised losses, except for provisions for the diminution in value of a fixed asset arising from a revaluation of all of the fixed assets of the company, or all of its fixed assets other than goodwill. A revaluation is deemed to take place where the directors have considered the matter, but have decided that some or all of the assets are worth at least their book value, but that it is not necessary to revalue them. If a deemed revaluation is to be effective, the directors must note in the accounts that they:

    (a) have considered the value of the fixed assets, without revaluing them;

    (b) are satisfied that the aggregate value of those assets is not less than their net book value, and

    (c) are treating their consideration of the value of the fixed asset as a revaluation.

(3) Where fixed assets have been revalued, and the annual depreciation charge is accordingly higher than it would otherwise have been, then an amount

equal to the cumulative additional depreciation is to be treated as a realised profit.

(4) Where there is no record of the cost of an asset, or that information cannot be obtained without undue expense or delay, then its cost is taken to be its value in the earliest available record of the company.

Where a company makes a distribution in the form of an asset other than cash, then any unrealised profit included in its book value can be treated as a realised profit. Effectively, the profit is treated as being realised when the asset is distributed.

In addition, where a company appropriately uses a mark-to-market basis for assets, usually investments, then the profits calculated on this basis can be considered to be realised and therefore distributable.

Investment companies are subject to similar rules, except that they can distribute only the excess of their accumulated realised revenue profits over their accumulated revenue losses, whether realised or not, except for those losses that have been eliminated through a reduction or reorganisation of capital. There are also some additional requirements for investment companies. An investment company may not make a distribution if:

- its assets would no longer be at least one and a half times its liabilities;
- its shares are not listed on a recognised investment exchange, other than an overseas investment exchange, or
- during the preceding accounting period it distributed any of its capital profits, or if it used unrealised revenue profits, or capital profits, whether realised or unrealised, in paying up debentures or amounts unpaid on its issued shares.

Despite having been otherwise replaced many years ago, SSAP 22 *Accounting for Goodwill* may also affect the distributable profits of a company. This matter was covered in Appendix 2 to the standard. FRS 10 reproduces the text of the Appendix to SSAP 22, as this will continue to apply to goodwill previously written off which is not reinstated on implementation of the new standard. However, in order for this to still be relevant now, the notional period for amortisation of goodwill would have to be extremely long, given that FRS 10 has applied since December 1998.

Goodwill that arises in group accounts will have no effect on distributable profits, since distributions are always made by reference to individual company accounts. However, goodwill can also arise in company accounts. Where a company purchased a business before FRS 10 took effect, it was allowed to write off goodwill to reserves. This did not represent a realised loss. Companies in this position are allowed to use 'notional' amortisation of the goodwill for the purposes of determining the distributable profits. This means that the company undertakes a separate calculation of what the goodwill amortisation would have been, had the goodwill been capitalised. This figure is then used in place of the amount written off to calculate distributable profits.

Distributable profits are normally determined by reference to the last annual accounts of the company. If the audit report on the accounts was qualified, then no distribution may be made if the qualification states that the financial statements do not give a true and fair view. If the qualification is on the basis that the financial statements were not properly prepared, then the auditors must state, or have stated, that the subject of the qualification is not material for the purposes of determining the legality of the distribution.

Where a company's last annual accounts do not show realised profits sufficient to justify the proposed distribution, then interim accounts must be prepared. If the company is a private company then these interim accounts need merely be sufficient to justify the distribution, and need not be audited. If the company is a public company then the accounts still need not be audited, but there are additional requirements:

- they must have been properly prepared, in accordance with the normal requirements for annual accounts, in respect of all material items which may affect the legality of the distribution, and the balance sheet must have been signed by a director;
- the balance sheet and profit and loss account must give a true and fair view, and
- the accounts must be delivered to the Registrar; and if they are not in English, then a certified translation must also be delivered to the Registrar.

If a new accounting rule means that a company may be able to recognise and realise a gain, or treat a previously recognised gain as realised, then it is open to the company to prepare interim accounts, for the purpose of being able to make a distribution, during the first period when the new accounting rule will be applied.

Conversely, where a new accounting standard is to be implemented, but has not yet, and that standard will require a loss to be accounted for which was previously either just disclosed or even ignored, then the new standard can be ignored before the accounting period in which it is first applied. This stops companies having the problem of distributions becoming retrospectively unlawful. However, in the first period in which the new standard is applied the new rule has to be applied to interim distributions. It is not open to the company to ignore the new rule until the end of the accounting period.

Where a company wishes to make a distribution before it has prepared its first annual accounts, it must prepare initial accounts. There are no specific requirements if the company is a private company, but the accounts must obviously be sufficient to justify the distribution. If the company is a public company then the initial accounts must be prepared, audited and filed in the same way as if they were annual accounts.

13.11 DEBT

13.11.1 The nature of debt

As noted above, FRS 25 takes a 'substance over form' approach to debt and equity. This means that items are treated as equity only where they consist of a residual interest and there is no obligation for the company to transfer economic resources. Where there is such an obligation, for example where shares can be redeemed at the option of the holder or where they will be redeemed at a fixed date, then they form a part of debt.

13.11.2 Initial recording

Although FRS 25 deals with whether or not an item is debt, FRS 4 continues to deal with some of the aspects of accounting for items where they are categorised as debt.

When debt is issued it should initially be stated at the amount of the net proceeds. The net proceeds are defined as:

> The fair value of the consideration received on the issue of a capital instrument after deduction of issue costs. (Para. 11, FRS 4.)

Where the consideration is not in cash then the debt should be stated at the fair value of the asset received.

Issue costs are defined as:

> The costs that are incurred directly in connection with the issue of a capital instrument, that is, those costs that would not have been incurred had the specific instrument in question not been issued. (Para. 10, FRS 4.)

This prohibits companies from including any general costs of obtaining finance from the amount of the instrument received. Only those costs which have been directly incurred in obtaining the particular instrument can be treated as issue costs. Under the provisions of FRS 4 dealing with the allocation of finance costs, the effect of this treatment is that issue costs are amortised over the life of the debt.

The FRSSE does not use the term 'issue costs', but replaces this with 'arrangement fees'.

13.11.3 Apportionment of finance costs

Finance costs on debt need to be allocated to appropriate accounting periods. Finance costs are defined as:

The difference between the net proceeds of an instrument and the total amount of the payments (or other transfers of economic benefits) that the issuer may be required to make in respect of the instrument. (Para. 8, FRS 4.)

This term is used throughout FRS 4, since it is less specific than terms such as 'interest'. It refers to any differences between the amounts that were initially received and the amounts that must ultimately be paid. While this includes interest, it is not limited to it.

FRS 4 requires that finance costs be allocated to accounting periods so as to give a constant rate of charge on the carrying amount, an idea that should be familiar from lease accounting.

Where the amount of future payments is not known with certainty, then a best estimate of the amount should be made, although this issue is not fully addressed in FRS 4.

EXAMPLE

A company has a loan of £200,000. Interest on the loan is to be charged at the rate of ten per cent per annum. The company is to repay the loan in equal quarterly instalments over a period of four years. The loan will be paid off in the following way:

Year	Quarter	Opening balance £	Interest £	Repayments £
1	1	200,000.00	4,822.74	15,214.33
	2	189,608.41	4,572.16	15,214.33
	3	178,966.24	4,315.54	15,214.33
	4	168,067.44	4,052.73	15,214.33
2	1	156,905.84	3,783.58	15,214.33
	2	145,475.09	3,507.94	15,214.33
	3	133,768.70	3,225.66	15,214.33
	4	121,780.02	2,936.57	15,214.33
3	1	109,502.26	2,640.50	15,214.33
	2	96,928.43	2,337.30	15,214.33
	3	84,051.41	2,026.79	15,214.33
	4	70,863.87	1,708.79	15,214.33
4	1	57,358.32	1,383.12	15,214.33
	2	43,527.12	1,049.60	15,214.33
	3	29,362.38	708.04	15,214.33
	4	14,856.09	358.24	15,214.33
			43,429.28	243,429.28

In this case the application of the rules in FRS 4 is quite straightforward. In total, the company has repaid £243,429.28 on an initial loan of £200,000. The difference is the interest that it has paid over the life of the loan. The interest has been charged to the loan on the basis of the outstanding balance at each point. The charge to the profit and loss account has gradually reduced, as the company pays off more and more of the capital element of the loan.

EXAMPLE

At the other extreme we could use the example of a zero coupon bond.

A company issues such a bond for proceeds of £200,000, and will repay £292,820 in four years. The difference between the initial receipt and the ultimate payments will equate to the total finance cost, which in this case we would not normally describe as interest. The effective rate of charge is ten per cent, exactly the same as in the first example.

Year	Balance £	Finance cost £	Payment £
At issue	200,000	20,000	0
1	220,000	22,000	0
2	242,000	24,200	0
3	266,200	26,620	0
4	292,820	0	292,820

Since there are no payments until the end of the period the level of charge increases over the life of the instrument, as the balance increases. A higher proportion of the total charge is made in the later stages of the instrument's life.

In principle, the accounting treatment that should be adopted under the FRSSE for arrangement fees is the same as that adopted under FRS 4 for issue costs. However, the FRSSE stresses that it may not be necessary to adopt this treatment where the amounts involved are not especially material:

> Where an arrangement fee is such as to represent a significant additional cost of finance when compared with the interest payable over the life of the instrument, the treatment set out in paragraph 12.2 [being the allocation of the charge at a constant rate on the carrying amount] should be followed. Where this is not the case it should be charged in the profit and loss account immediately it is incurred. (Para. 12.4, FRSSE.)

13.11.4   Amending the value of debt

At the end of each year companies should:

- increase the amount of debt by the finance costs allocated to the period, and
- reduce the amount of debt by the payments made during the period.

Despite this, accrued finance costs may be disclosed as accruals, and not added to the carrying amount of debt so long as they have been incurred in the current accounting year and will be paid in the next.

13.11.5   Determining the term of debt

The basic rule is that the term of debt should be taken to be the period from the date on which the instrument is issued to the date at which it will:

- expire;
- be redeemed, or

- be cancelled.

Where there are options included in the conditions of the debt then the situation is more complicated:

- if either of the parties has a right to redeem or cancel the instrument then the term should only run to the date at which the instrument might be cancelled or redeemed, unless it is certain that they will not exercise their option, or
- if either of the parties has the right to extend the life of the instrument then the period of extension should be ignored unless there is certainty that it will be extended.

13.12 FRS 26

13.12.1 Introduction and scope

FRS 26, which deals with the recognition, derecognition and measurement of financial instruments, is an unusual standard in that for many companies it is optional. It has had to be applied by listed companies still preparing UK accounts for accounting periods commencing on or after 1 January 2005. Other companies have had to apply it since 1 January 2006 if they adopt the fair value accounting rules now included in the Companies Act 2006.

Most UK companies have not adopted FRS 26, nor is there very much likelihood that they will do so. As a result, the following sections provide only a summary of the main requirements of the standard and omit a vast amount of the detail.

When applied, FRS 26 deals with all financial instruments, other than:

- interests in subsidiaries, quasi-subsidiaries, associates, partnerships and joint ventures;
- leases, except that the impairment rules apply to investments in finance leases and the standard does apply to derivatives embedded in leases;
- assets and liabilities arising under pension schemes;
- equity instruments, as defined by FRS 25, issued by the company;
- most rights and obligations under insurance contracts;
- contracts for contingent consideration in a business combination covered by FRS 7, for the acquirer;
- contracts between an acquirer and a vendor in a business combination to buy or sell an acquiree in future;
- most loan commitments that cannot be settled in cash or other financial instruments, and
- most financial instruments covered by FRS 20; and
- rights to payments to reimburse a company for expenditure it is required to make to settle a liability recognised as a provision under FRS 12.

13.12.2 Non-financial contracts

FRS 26 deals only with financial instruments. However, when dealing with a contract for a non-financial item, consideration needs to be given as to whether or not the contract may still fall within the scope of the standard. The basic rules are set out in FRS 26:

> This Standard shall be applied to those contracts to buy or sell a non-financial item that can be settled net in cash or another financial instrument, or by exchanging financial instruments, as if the contracts were financial instruments, with the exception of contracts that were entered into and continue to be held for the purpose of the receipt or delivery of a non-financial item in accordance with the entity's expected purchase, sale or usage requirements. (Para. 5, FRS 26.)

Where a contract appears to be for non-financial items, it can still be settled net in cash or other financial instruments under FRS 26 if:

- the terms permit either party to settle in cash or other financial instruments;
- the terms do not so permit, but the company has a practice of settling similar contracts net in cash or other financial instruments by exchanging financial instruments, whether with the counterparty to the contract or otherwise;
- the company has a practice of taking delivery of non-financial items and selling them within a short period in order to obtain a profit from short-term price or margin fluctuations, and
- the non-financial item is readily convertible to cash.

These rules are intended to deal with contracts which deal with non-financial items, but in fact or in practice are entered into as though they were financial instruments. For example, companies may enter into various contracts involving commodities when they have no need for the commodities that are the subject of the contract, or have no such commodities expected to be available.

13.12.3 Embedded derivatives

A derivative is defined as a contract with the following characteristics:

(a) its value changes in response to the change in a specified interest rate, financial instrument price, commodity price, foreign exchange rate, index of prices or rates, credit rating or credit index, or other variable, provided in the case of a non-financial variable that the variable is not specific to a party to the contract (sometimes called the "underlying");

(b) it requires no initial net investment or an initial net investment that is smaller than would be required for other types of contracts that would be expected to have a similar response to changes in market factors; and

(c) it is settled at a future date. (Para. 9, FRS 26.)

Embedded derivatives are components of a host contract that behave economically in a way that differs from that of the remainder of the host contract. Basically, an embedded derivative is a derivative that is included in any type of contract, rather than entered into as a derivative in its own right.

Embedded derivatives need to be separated from the host and accounted for separately under FRS 26, if:

- the economic characteristics and risks are not closely related to the economic characteristics and risks of the host contract;
- a separate instrument with the same terms would be a derivative, and
- the hybrid is not measured at fair value, with changes in fair value recognised in profit or loss.

The first two criteria would appear to define an embedded derivative. The third appears more a matter of practicality, since there is little point in separately identifying an embedded derivative if the whole of the contract within which it is embedded is stated at fair value through profit or loss.

If it is not possible to determine the value of an embedded derivative separately then the hybrid is treated as a financial asset or liability and classified as held for trading.

Examples of embedded derivatives are:

- put options on equity instruments;
- call options on equity instruments, as far as the holder is concerned although not from the point of view of the issuer;
- an option to extend the term of a debt, unless the interest rate will be reconsidered at the same time;
- equity-indexed interest or principal payments;
- commodity-indexed interest or principal payments;
- equity conversion features in debt instruments, and
- credit derivatives whereby a party can assume (or transfer) the credit risks associated with debt without taking over the debt.

13.12.4   Measurement at recognition

Financial assets and liabilities are initially recognised at their fair value, plus, in the case of items that are not categorised as at fair value through profit or loss, direct acquisition or issuance costs.

In most cases, the fair value is the amount paid or received, that is, the cost. However, there may be cases where this does not apply. For example a company may receive a long term loan from a shareholder, whether another company or even an individual, which has nil or low interest. In this case the fair value of the liability acquired is less than the proceeds. The difference, being the discount obtained, should normally be taken to equity as a capital contribution.

13.12.5 Subsequent measurement

Subsequently, financial assets are valued on different bases according to their classification.

All financial assets fall into the four categories set out below. They are measured according to the rules set out, although in some cases this may be altered where the instruments are being used for hedging purposes.

Financial assets at fair value through profit or loss

This includes trading items, which are items acquired with the intention of selling in the short term, or part of a portfolio where there has been evidence of short-term profit taking. Derivatives are always considered to be held for trading unless they are a hedge.

It also includes any other assets which are so designated on initial recognition. The option to designate any other financial assets to fall within this category is available only where:

- failure to do so would result in a measurement or recognition inconsistency that would arise from measuring assets or liabilities or recognising gains and losses on them on different bases;
- a group of financial assets, financial liabilities or both is managed and its performance evaluated on a fair value basis, in accordance with a documented risk management or investment strategy and information about the group is provided internally on that basis to key management, or
- the item included an embedded derivative, unless that embedded derivative does not significantly affect cash flows or it is clear on initial recognition that separation is prohibited.

As the title rather suggests, such items are stated at fair value, with all value changes going through profit or loss. When fair value is referred to, this means excluding any deduction for transaction costs that would be incurred on sale.

Held-to-maturity investments

This includes assets with fixed or determinable payments and a fixed maturity that the enterprise both can and will hold to maturity, other than loans and receivables, items designated as at fair value through profit or loss and those designated as available for sale.

This excludes most items of a class where any sale has taken place in the current and previous two years, except those virtually at maturity or forced by non-recurring circumstances.

Loans and receivables

This includes assets with fixed or determinable payments that are not quoted in an active market except those that are created or acquired with the intention of immediate or short-term sale, those designated as at fair value through profit or loss and those for which the holder may not recover substantially all of its initial investment.

Available for sale

All other financial assets fall into the category of available for sale.

Available-for-sale assets are stated at fair value.

The general rule is that financial assets are stated at fair value, but there are exceptions for:

- loans and receivables which are stated at amortised cost using the effective interest method;
- held to maturity investments which are stated at amortised cost using the effective interest method, and
- unquoted investments in equity instruments whose fair value cannot be reliably measured, or derivatives that are linked to such instruments.

In all cases, financial assets should be written down where an impairment review indicates that this is necessary.

Hedging provisions may cut across these requirements.

Financial liabilities are subsequently stated at amortised cost using the effective interest method, except for financial liabilities designated as at fair value through profit or loss, including all derivative liabilities other than those linked with unquoted equity investments whose value cannot be measured reliably.

13.12.6   Reclassifications

There is a general principle of FRS 26 that items cannot be reclassified into, or out of, the category 'at fair value through profit or loss'.

However, an exception to this general principle has been in place since late 2008. At that time the IASB agreed to some limited changes to IAS 39 to eliminate inconsistencies between IFRS and US GAAP. Given that FRS 26 is the UK version of FRS 26, the UK standard was also changed. These changes derive from market conditions in 2008.

FRS 26 continues to prohibit:

- all reclassifications into the fair value through profit or loss category;

- the reclassification of derivatives out of the fair value through profit or loss category, and
- the reclassification of any financial instrument out of the fair value through profit or loss category which, upon initial recognition, had been designated as at fair value through profit or loss.

However, some financial assets which were included in the fair value through profit or loss category, because they were initially considered to be held for trading, may now be reclassified. Such a reclassification is, generally, allowed only in rare circumstances. The market conditions in place around the end of 2008 can be considered such rare circumstances.

There is also a more specific exemption for items that (other than the fact they were initially considered to be held for trading) would have qualified as loans and receivables. Such a reclassification is allowed, even outside of the 'rare circumstances' situation. Instead, the entity must simply have the intention and ability to hold the financial asset for the foreseeable future or to maturity.

Where such reclassifications are undertaken, the asset is reclassified at its fair value at the date of reclassification. All fair value changes up to this point continue to be included in accumulated profits, so at the date of reclassification no changes are made to profits or losses that have already been recognised.

The fair value of the reclassified asset then becomes its deemed cost, or amortised cost, on the date of reclassification.

Where a financial asset fell within the definition of loans and receivables, but was treated as available for sale, it may also now be reclassified to loans and receivables. The requirements are similar to those for assets held for trading. So, the entity must have the intention and ability to hold the financial asset for the foreseeable future or to maturity. Again, there is no 'rare circumstances' criterion.

The mechanics are also similar, so reclassification takes place at the fair value at the date of reclassification. This value becomes the asset's deemed cost, or amortised cost, on the date of reclassification. The main difference is the treatment of previous changes in value. Such changes will not have been taken to profit, but recognised directly in equity (except for any previous impairment losses or foreign exchange movements). The treatment of previous value changes which have not affected profit will depend on whether the financial asset has a fixed maturity: if it does, then such gains or losses will be amortised over the remaining life of the asset, using the effective interest method; if it doesn't, then the gains or losses will be recognised only on sale or other disposal.

Both of these are overridden if there is a subsequent impairment, when any gains or losses that have previously been dealt with in equity will be reclassified to profit or loss.

Assets which have been reclassified in accordance with any of the new exemptions set out above are subject to special rules on the application of effective interest rates.

As a general rule, where assets are affected by effective interest rates and estimates of future cash flows are changed then this will affect the carrying amount of financial assets and liabilities.

This, however, does not apply in the case of assets reclassified under the new rules, and to the extent that such changes in expected cash flows derive from increases in the estimate of recoverable cash receipts. Where such a change in estimate is made, the carrying amount of the assets is not affected immediately.

Instead, the change in expected cash flows is treated as an adjustment to the effective interest rate from the date the estimate is altered. This means the benefit of the increased cash inflows will be spread over the life of the asset, not recognised immediately.

Where an asset ceases to be held to maturity, it is reclassified as available for sale and measured at fair value. This can occur where items of a similar nature are sold, such that no such items can be treated as held to maturity.

Where an asset or liability moves from being stated at fair value to stated at amortised cost, then its previous fair value becomes its deemed cost. Any gain or loss previously included in equity is:

- in the case of an asset becoming held to maturity, amortised to profit or loss over the period to maturity, and
- in other cases, left in equity until disposal.

The same applies where it becomes impossible to continue to state an asset at fair value, when a measure of fair value had previously been available. This might arise where a company is delisted.

Where an asset is part of a class which is normally stated at fair value, but where it was previously stated at cost since no reliable measure of value was available, it should be remeasured if a reliable measure becomes available. The simplest example of this is where an unquoted company becomes quoted and a market price becomes available for the first time.

13.12.7   Gains and losses

Ignoring hedging:

- gains or losses on items designated at fair value through profit or loss are treated as part of profit or loss;
- gains or losses on available-for-sale assets are recognised through the statement of total recognised gains and losses, except impairment losses and exchange gains and losses, until derecognition;
- interest calculated on the effective interest method is recognised in profit or loss;
- dividends on equity investments are recognised in profit or loss, when the right to recover payment is established, and
- impairment losses are recognised in profit or loss on items stated at amortised cost, together with normal amortisation and interest charges, as well as any gains or losses arising on derecognition.

13.12.8 Impairment

Impairment needs to be considered annually.

In order for impairment to be recognised, there needs to be an objective indication of impairment. However, the standard is not attempting to limit the grounds on which impairment provisions may be made, where there is any type of indication of a problem. It appears more to be trying to ensure that companies are not able to make excessive and unjustified impairment provisions.

For items carried at amortised cost, impairment is taken to profit or loss. Impairment is measured as the difference between the carrying amount and the present value of future estimated cash flows.

For items carried at fair value, impairment involves recognising the impairment in profit or loss, even where previously recognised in equity, and prior to derecognition.

Reversals may be accounted for, although in the case of available-for-sale financial assets which are equity instruments any reversal may not pass through profit or loss.

13.12.9 Hedging

Hedging means designating one or more hedging instruments so that their change in fair value offsets, in whole or in part, changes in the fair value of the hedged item.

There are three types of hedge:

- fair value;
- cash flow, and
- of a net investment in a foreign operation.

A hedge exists only if:

- at the inception of the hedge there is documentation of the hedging relationship, setting out full details;
- the hedge is expected to be highly effective;
- for cash flow hedges, a proposed transaction is highly probable;
- the effectiveness of the hedge can be measured, and
- the hedge is actually assessed as being effective.

Fair value hedges should be taken to the profit and loss account in full. This includes both sides, and is irrespective of the accounting treatment normally adopted.

Cash flow hedges and hedges of net investments in a foreign operation should be dealt with through equity, to the extent that they are considered effective, and through the profit and loss account to the extent that they are ineffective.

13.13   FRS 29

13.13.1   Introduction

FRS 29 is based on IFRS 7. For companies complying with FRS 26, it has been mandatory since accounting periods beginning on or after 1 January 2007. However, for all other companies it is optional.

FRS 29 has seen substantial change since it was issued. Changes were made in 2009, further changes in 2010, and there are current proposals to amend the standard still further.

13.13.2   Scope

FRS 29 is intended to apply to all types of financial instruments, other than:

- interests in subsidiaries, quasi-subsidiaries, associates, partnerships and joint ventures, unless held for resale;
- employers' rights and obligations in respect of employee benefit plans;
- contracts for contingent consideration in a business combination, for the acquirer;
- insurance contracts, except for embedded derivatives in insurance contracts, and
- financial instruments, contracts and obligations under share-based payment transactions.

The FRS is intended to apply to both recognised and unrecognised financial instruments.

There is also an amendment to the scope for companies which do not apply the FRS 26 requirements on measurement. In this case, the disclosures are to be amended in line with the accounting policies actually adopted for the relevant transactions.

13.13.3   Significance of financial instruments

The first key disclosure requirement is that companies should provide information on the significance of financial instruments for their financial position and performance.

This is then broken down into a number of specific minimum disclosures.

Classification

Companies should disclose the carrying amount of each of the following:

- financial assets at fair value through profit and loss, showing separately those classified as trading and those designated as at fair value through profit or loss;
- held to maturity investments;
- loans and receivables;
- available-for-sale financial assets;
- financial liabilities at fair value through profit or loss, showing separately those classified as held for trading and those designated by the entity as at fair value through profit or loss, and
- financial liabilities measured at amortised cost.

Where financial liabilities are designated as at fair value through profit and loss, then the company also needs to disclose:

- the amount of any change in fair value that is not attributable to changes in the benchmark interest rate, and
- the difference between the carrying amount and the amount contractually required to be paid at maturity.

The standard provides a method for estimating the amount of any change in a liability that is not attributable to changes in the benchmark interest rate.

Reclassification

If the company has reclassified a financial asset as one measured at cost or amortised cost rather than at fair value then the reason for this reclassification also has to be disclosed.

Collateral

In respect of collateral, companies will have to disclose:

- the carrying amount of financial assets pledged as collateral for liabilities;

- the carrying amount of financial assets pledged as collateral for contingent liabilities, and
- terms and conditions relating to assets pledged as collateral.

Allowance account for credit losses

When an allowance account has been used to reduce the carrying amount of financial assets impaired by credit losses, then a reconciliation should be provided of changes in the account during the period for each class of financial asset.

An allowance account is basically what used to be known as a bad debt provision.

Defaults and breaches

If there have been any defaults of principal, interest, sinking fund or redemption provisions during the period on loans payable or any other breaches when those breaches can permit the lender to demand repayment then companies will have to disclose:

- details of those defaults;
- the amount recognised at the balance sheet date in respect of the loans payable on which the defaults occurred, and
- where amounts are shown as above, then whether the default has been remedied or the loans renegotiated before the date the financial instruments were authorised for issue.

In addition, there is a specific exemption from these requirements for breaches in respect of short-term trade payables on normal credit terms, so companies will not need to provide disclosure simply because they fail to pay a trade creditor in accordance with the relevant terms of trade.

Income, expense, gains and losses

Companies are required to disclose the following.

(1) Net gains or losses on:

    (a) financial assets and liabilities at fair value through profit or loss, showing separately those on items classified as trading and those designated as at fair value through profit or loss;

    (b) available-for-sale financial assets, showing separately amounts recognised in equity, and the amount removed from equity and recognised in profit or loss for the period;

    (c) held to maturity investments;

    (d) loans and receivables, and

    (e) financial liabilities measured at amortised cost.

(2) How the income statement amounts above are determined.

(3) Total interest income and total interest expense, for financial assets and liabilities not at fair value through profit or loss.

(4) Fee income and expense (other than amounts included in determining the effective interest rate) arising on financial assets and liabilities and from trust and other fiduciary activities that result in the holding or investing of assets on behalf of individuals, trusts, retirement benefit plans and other institutions.

(5) Interest income on impaired assets.

Impairment

Companies will have to disclose the amount of any impairment loss by class of financial asset.

Accounting policies

While not precise in terms of the details that need to be disclosed, FRS 29 notes that the following matters will need to be included:

- the criteria for determining, on initial recognition, whether a financial instrument is at fair value through profit or loss;
- the criteria for designating financial assets as available for sale;
- whether regular way purchases and sales of financial assets are accounted for at trade date or settlement date;
- when an allowance account is used to reduce the carrying amount of financial assets impaired by credit losses:
- the criteria for determining when the carrying amount is directly reduced and when the allowance account is used;
- the criteria for writing off amounts charged to the allowance account against the carrying amount of impaired financial assets;
- the criteria for determining that an impairment loss has occurred, and
- the policy for determining when financial assets are no longer past due.

Where fair value accounting is not being used, more disclosure is necessary. This includes the treatment that has been adopted in respect of:

- costs of acquisition or issuance;
- premiums and discounts;
- changes in the estimated amount of determinable future cash flows;
- changes in circumstances that result in significant uncertainty about the timely collection of all contractual amounts due from monetary financial assets;
- declines in the fair value of financial assets below their carrying amount, and
- restructured financial liabilities.

Where fair value accounting is being used, then companies should disclose whether fair values are based on market prices, on independent appraisals, on discounted cash flows or through the use of some other method.

Where discounted cash flow or other methods are being used then the assumptions should be stated.

Companies should also disclose the basis for reporting in the income statement realised and unrealised gains and losses, interest, and other items of income and expense associated with financial assets and liabilities.

Hedge accounting

In addition, for each class of hedge, companies will need to disclose:

- a description of the hedge;
- a description of the financial instruments designated as hedging instruments, and their fair values at the balance sheet date;
- the nature of the risks being hedged, and
- for cash flow hedges, the periods in which cash flows are expected to occur, when they are likely to enter into the determination of profit or loss, and a description of any forecast transaction for which hedge accounting had previously been used but which is no longer expected to occur.

If a gain or loss on a hedging instrument has been recognised directly in equity then:

- the amount that was recognised in equity in the period;
- the amount that was removed from equity and included in profit or loss for the period, and
- the amount that was removed from equity and included in the initial cost or carrying amount of a non-financial asset or liability that was a hedged highly probable forecast transaction.

Fair values

For each class of financial asset and liability, companies must disclose the fair value of that class. This must be done in such a way as to enable direct comparison with the amounts which are shown in the balance sheet.

No disclosure is required in respect of items such as short-term trade debtors, where the carrying value is a reasonable approximation to fair value.

Similarly, no disclosure of fair values is required in respect of investments in unquoted equity instruments, or derivatives which are based on them, where fair value cannot be measured reliably, nor in respect of discretionary participation features where the fair values cannot be measured reliably.

Where fair values are not given on the basis that they cannot be measured reliably, then the following alternative disclosures should be provided:

- a statement that fair value information has not been given, as it is not possible to measure the fair values reliably;

- a description of the financial instruments involved, their carrying amount and an explanation of why fair value cannot be measured reliably;
- information about the market for the instruments;
- information about whether and how the company intends to dispose of the instruments, and
- where financial assets whose fair value could not previously be measured are sold, then that fact, the carrying amount at the time of sale and the amount of gain or loss that has been recognised.

Fair value disclosures are now based on a hierarchy. This fair value hierarchy reflects the significance of the inputs that have been used in making the measurements.

There are the following levels:

- instruments with unadjusted quoted prices in active markets for identical assets or liabilities – Level 1;
- instruments valued using inputs other than quoted prices for the instruments, but where those inputs are observable either directly or indirectly – Level 2, and
- instruments using valuation techniques for which any significant input is not based on observable market data – Level 3.

Instruments fall into the lowest level of the hierarchy for which there is a significant input. So, for example, an instrument which contains one significant unobservable input will fall into category 3, even if all of the other inputs that are used in its valuation are based on observable data. Judgement will sometimes be required in determining whether or not an input is significant.

For items which are stated at fair value in the balance sheet, the following disclosure is required:

- the level of the fair value hierarchy into which the fair value measurements are categorised, and
- any significant movements between Level 1 and Level 2, separately in each direction.

For Level 3 items, a reconciliation from the opening to closing balances is also needed showing separately:

- the total gains or losses for the period recognised in profit or loss and a description of where they are presented in the profit and loss account, or statement of total recognised gains and losses;
- total gains or losses that have been recognised in the statement of total recognised gains and losses;
- purchases, sales, issues and settlements, each separately, and
- transfers into and out of Level 3, and the reasons for those transfers;
- the total unrealised gains and losses on Level 3 items held at the balance sheet date, together with a description of where such gains and losses are included in the profit and loss account, and

- for Level 3 items, a sensitivity analysis, showing the impact of any reasonably possible change in any significant input, which is not based on observable market data. This applies where the impact would be to change fair value significantly, which should itself be assessed by reference to profit or loss, and total assets or total liabilities, or, when changes in fair value are recognised in other comprehensive income, total equity.

All of the quantitative disclosures should usually be shown in the form of a table.

Where an entity has designated a loan or receivable (or group of loans or receivables) as at fair value through profit or loss it must disclose:

- the maximum exposure to credit risk at the balance sheet date;
- the amount by which any related credit derivatives or similar instruments mitigate that maximum exposure to credit risk;
- the amount of change, both during the period and cumulatively, in the fair value attributable to changes in the credit risk of the financial asset determined either:

  - as the amount of change in fair value that is not attributable to changes in market conditions that give rise to market risk, or
  - using an alternative method the entity believes more faithfully represents the amount of change in its fair value that is attributable to changes in the credit risk of the asset, and

- the amount of the change in the fair value of any related credit derivatives or similar instruments that has occurred during the period and cumulatively since the loan or receivable was designated.

The standard notes that changes in market conditions that give rise to market risk include changes in an observed (benchmark) interest rate, commodity price, foreign exchange rate or index of prices or rates.

13.13.4   Risk

Qualitative disclosures

For each risk arising from financial instruments, the following should be disclosed:

- the exposure to risk and how that risk arose;
- the company's objectives, policies and processes for managing the risk, and the methods used to measure the risk, and
- any changes in these items from the previous period.

FRS 29 is amended with effect for accounting periods beginning on or after 1 January 2011. There are no specific changes to the qualitative disclosures, but a paragraph has been added to the standard which stresses that the qualitative disclosures are intended to complement the quantitative disclosures, and to allow users to link the information in such a way as to form an overall picture of the nature and extent of the risks that arise from financial instruments.

Quantitative disclosures

For each risk arising from financial instruments, the following should be disclosed:

- summary quantitative data about the extent to which the company is exposed to the risk at the reporting date, based on the information provided to key management, and
- details of concentrations of credit risk.

There is a minor change to this disclosure that applies with effect for accounting periods beginning on or after 1 January, in that the definition of key management is amended to make reference to the definition in FRS 8.

Where quantitative data at the balance sheet date is unrepresentative, then further information that is representative.

Details of concentrations of risk need to be provided. Such details must include:

- how management determines concentrations of risk;
- a description of the shared characteristics used to identify each concentration, and
- the amount of the risk exposure associated with all financial instruments sharing that characteristic.

Credit risk

For accounting periods beginning prior to 1 January 2011, companies are required to disclose, for each class of financial asset with credit risk:

- the maximum credit risk exposure at the balance sheet date, ignoring collateral;
- a description of collateral pledged as security and other credit enhancements and, unless impracticable, their fair value, and
- information about the credit quality of financial assets with credit risks that are neither past due nor impaired.

For accounting periods beginning on or after 1 January 2011, this changes so that:

- there is no requirement to disclose the maximum exposure to credit risk on financial instruments where this is the same as the carrying amount, and
- the description of collateral must indicate the financial effect of that collateral, for example, a quantification of the extent to which collateral or similar credit enhancements mitigate the credit risk in relation to the maximum credit risk.

Where assets are past due or impaired:

- an analysis of the age of financial assets that are past due at the reporting date but not impaired;
- an analysis of financial assets that are impaired at the reporting date, including the factors the company considered in determining the financial assets are impaired, and
- in respect of these items, a description of collateral pledged as security and other credit enhancements and, unless impracticable, their fair value.

The third of these disclosures is abolished with effect for accounting periods beginning on or after 1 January 2011.

When a company obtains assets during the period by taking control of collateral pledges as security or calling on other credit enhancements (such as guarantees) then:

- the nature of the assets obtained;
- the fair value of the assets obtained less the cost of obtaining them, and
- when the assets are not readily convertible into cash and the company does not plan to use them in its operations, then its policies for disposing of such assets.

This disclosure is also changed with effect for accounting periods beginning on or after 1 January 2011, when it is made clear that the disclosure is required only for those assets which are held at the reporting date.

There are also further disclosures that are required in relation to credit risk, among other matters, where loans or receivables (or groups of loans or receivables) have been designated as at fair value through profit or loss. These are dealt with above when dealing with disclosures in relation to fair values.

Liquidity risk

Companies must disclose:

- a maturity analysis for financial liabilities that shows the remaining contractual maturities, and
- a description of how they manage the liquidity risk.

With effect for accounting periods beginning on or after 1 January 2009, there is a requirement to split the maturity analysis between derivative and non-derivative liabilities. An explanation of those analyses, and information on potential differences in outflows, must also be provided.

Market risk

Companies must disclose:

- a sensitivity analysis for each type of market risk at the reporting date, showing the effect of reasonable possible changes in the relevant risk variable (such as interest or exchange rates) on profit or loss and, when changes in fair value are being reflected in equity, on equity;

- the methods and assumptions used in preparing the sensitivity analysis, and
- changes from the previous period in the methods and assumptions that are being used.

If the sensitivity analysis is unrepresentative of a risk inherent in a financial instrument, then additional information to include:

- a description of the risk, and
- the effect of changes in the relevant risk variable on profit or loss and, when changes in fair value are reflected in equity, on equity.

13.13.5   *Capital*

Companies must disclose the following.

(1)   Qualitative information about their objectives, policies and processes for managing capital, including but not limited to:

   (a)   a description of what they regard as capital;

   (b)   when the company is subject to externally imposed capital requirements, then the nature of those requirements and how those requirements are incorporated into the management of capital, and

   (c)   how they are meeting their objectives for managing capital.

(2)   Summary quantitative data about what they regard as capital and any capital targets set by management.

(3)   Any changes in any of the items above from the previous period.

(4)   Whether during the period they complied with capital targets set by management and any externally imposed capital requirements to which they are subject.

(5)   Where the company has not complied with the capital targets set by management or with externally imposed capital requirements then the consequences of such non-compliance.

These disclosures are to be based on the information that is provided to key management personnel.

Where a company is subject to various separate capital requirements, and information on an aggregate basis would not provide useful information, then the information should be disaggregated. Otherwise, aggregate information will normally be sufficient.

13.13.6   *Reclassifications*

FRS 26 was amended in 2008 to allow certain reclassifications of financial instruments which had previously been prohibited (see **13.12.6**).

Where a company takes advantage of the reclassification changes, it is required to provide certain disclosures under FRS 29:

- the amount reclassified into and out of each category;
- for each period until derecognition, the carrying amounts and fair values of all financial assets that have been reclassified in the current and previous periods;
- if a financial asset was reclassified in accordance with the rare circumstances criterion, then the rare situation and the facts and circumstances indicating that the situation was rare;
- for the period when the financial asset was reclassified, the fair value gain or loss on the financial asset recognised in profit or loss or the statement of total recognised gains and losses in that period and in the previous period;
- for each period following the reclassification (including the period in which the financial asset was reclassified) until derecognition of the financial asset, the fair value gain or loss that would have been recognised in profit or loss or the statement of total recognised gains and losses if the financial asset had not been reclassified, and the gain, loss, income and expense recognised in profit or loss, and
- the effective interest rate and estimated amounts of cash flows the entity expects to recover, as at the date of reclassification.

13.13.7 Proposals for change

The ASB has issued an exposure draft of proposed changes to FRS 29 dealing with transfers of financial assets. This is the UK version of the changes that were made to IFRS 7 in October 2010, and would ensure that the standards remain, in substance, identical.

The disclosure must be given in a single note to the financial statements, and provided for all transferred financial assets that are not derecognised and for any continuing involvement in a transferred asset.

For the purposes of these proposed disclosure requirements, an entity transfers all or a part of a financial asset if, and only if, it either:

- transfers the contractual rights to receive the cash flows of that financial asset, or
- retains the contractual rights to receive the cash flows of that financial asset, but assumes a contractual obligation to pay the cash flows to one or more recipients.

The proposed amendments contain objectives-based disclosure requirements supplemented by specific disclosures. The final disclosure requirement is for any additional information necessary to meet the disclosure objectives.

The proposed amendment notes that continuing involvement should be taken to exclude:

- normal representations and warranties relating to fraudulent transfer, reasonableness, good faith and fair dealing;
- forward, option and other contracts to reacquire the transferred financial asset for which the price is the fair value of the transferred financial asset, or
- arrangements where, in effect, the transferring party acts solely as collection agent.

Where transferred financial assets are not derecognised or are only partially derecognised, it is proposed that entities will have to disclose:

- the nature of the transferred assets;
- the nature of the risks and rewards of ownership to which the entity is exposed;
- a description of the nature of the relationship between the transferred assets and the associated liabilities, including restrictions arising from the transfer on the reporting entity's use of the transferred assets;
- when the counterparty to the associated liabilities has recourse only to the transferred assets, a schedule setting out the fair value of the transferred assets and associated liabilities and the net position;
- when the entity continues to recognise all of the transferred assets, the carrying amounts of the transferred assets and the associated liabilities, and
- when the entity continues to recognise the assets to the extent of its continuing involvement under FRS 26, the total carrying amount of the original assets before the transfer, the carrying amount of the assets that the entity continues to recognise, and the carrying amount of the associated liabilities.

Where transferred financial assets are derecognised entirely, but entities have continuing involvement with those assets, it is proposed that entities will have to disclose:

- the carrying amount of the assets and liabilities that represent the entity's continuing involvement in the derecognised financial assets, and the line items in which they are recognised;
- the fair value of the assets and liabilities representing the continuing involvement in the derecognised financial assets;
- the amount that best represents the entity's maximum exposure to loss from its continuing involvement in the derecognised financial assets, and how this was determined;
- the undiscounted cash outflows that would or may be required to repurchase derecognised financial assets or other amounts payable to the transferee in respect of the transferred assets. If variable, this should be based on conditions at each reporting date;
- a maturity analysis of the undiscounted cash outflows that would or may be required to repurchase the derecognised financial assets or other amounts payable to the transferee in respect of the transferred assets, showing the remaining contractual maturities of the entity's continuing involvement, and
- qualitative information that explains and supports the quantitative disclosures above.

For all types of continuing involvement, under the proposals entities will have to disclose:

- the gain or loss recognised at the date of transfer of the assets;
- income and expenses recognised, both in the reporting period and cumulatively, from the entity's continuing involvement in the derecognised financial assets, and
- if the total amount of proceeds from transfer activity (that qualifies for derecognition) in a reporting period is not evenly distributed throughout the reporting period then:

  - when the greatest transfer activity took place within that reporting period;
  - the amount recognised from transfer activity in that part of the reporting period, and
  - the total amount of proceeds from transfer activity in that part of the reporting period.

The example provided of a sub-period is the last five days before the end of a reporting period.

13.14 RECOGNITION AND DERECOGNITION

13.14.1 Recognition

The original version of FRS 26 dealt only with the measurement requirements derived from IAS 39. With effect for accounting periods beginning on or after 1 January 2007, the recognition and derecognition requirements also came into force.

The recognition requirements are usually straightforward. The basic requirement is that companies should recognise financial assets and liabilities when they become a party to the contractual provisions of the instrument.

Derecognition is a much more complex issue. Financial assets are derecognised when and only when:

- the contractual rights to the cash flows from the asset expire, or
- it transfers the financial asset.

A transfer of a financial asset takes place only where the company:

- transfers the contractual rights to receive the cash flows of the financial assets, or
- retains the contractual rights to receive the cash flows, but assumes a contractual obligation to pay the cash flows to one or more recipients in a transaction that meets the following conditions:

  - the requirement to pay on cash flows exists only to the extent that amounts are received from the original assets (even if short term advances are made, so long as they are recoverable);

- the company cannot sell or pledge the original assets other than as security to the new recipients for the obligation to provide them with cash flows, and
- the company must pass on cash flows it receives from the original assets to the recipients without material delay.

These requirements can be applied to a group of financial assets, as single financial asset, or a discrete part of a financial asset.

Where a transfer has taken place, the company needs to consider whether it has retained the risks and rewards associated with ownership. If it has, then the assets are derecognised, although there may be separate assets or liabilities which require to be recognised as a result of the transaction. Where the risk and rewards have been retained, the asset continues to be recognised. Where the situation is less clear, then the company may be required to continue to recognise the assets in part.

Financial liabilities are derecognised only when the obligation is discharged, is cancelled or expires.

UITF 47 deals with the specific issues that arise where financial liabilities are extinguished as a result of the company issuing equity instruments, sometimes referred to as 'debt for equity swaps'. The UITF is limited, in that it applies only to those companies which are within the scope of, or which voluntarily apply, FRS 26. The UITF is based on IFRIC 19, which deals with the same issues under IFRS.

Under the UITF:

- where equity instruments are issued to a creditor, this will count as an extinguishment of the financial liability and the creditor should be removed from the balance sheet;
- the equity instruments should be recorded, and measured at their fair value, but if this cannot be reliably measured, then the fair value of the financial liability extinguished should be used, and
- the difference between the carrying amount of the financial liability extinguished and the fair value of the equity instruments issued (or the fair value of the financial liability, where the fair value of the equity instruments could not be reliably measured) should be included in profit or loss for the period.

There are exceptions to the basic requirement, and UITF 47 should not be applied where:

- the creditor is also a direct or indirect shareholder and is acting in its capacity as a direct or indirect existing shareholder;
- the creditor and the entity are controlled by the same party or parties before

and after the transaction, and the substance of the transaction includes an equity distribution by, or contribution to, the entity; or

- the issue of equity is in accordance with the original terms of the financial liability (as with a convertible bond, for example).

Where only part of a financial liability has been extinguished, consideration needs to be given to the FRS 26 requirements in respect of modification of debt, and in particular whether some of the consideration paid relates to a modification of the remaining debt. In such cases, the consideration needs to be allocated between the part of the liability extinguished and the part that remains outstanding. If the modification is substantial, then this would need to be treated as the extinguishment of one debt and the creation of another.

The UITF is effective for accounting periods beginning on or after 1 July 2010, the same date as the IFRIC on which it is based. Early adoption is allowed, although where the UITF is adopted early this fact must be disclosed.

13.15 POTENTIAL IMPACT OF THE FRSME

Financial Instruments are dealt with in sections 11 and 12 of the FRSME. Section 11 applies to basic financial instruments and section 12 applies to all other financial instruments; those which are slightly more complex. Companies that are only party to basic financial instruments may be able, in practice, to ignore section 12, but would have to check this.

Companies will have to make an accounting policy choice as to whether in accounting for their financial instruments they wish to apply:

- the requirements of section 11 and section 12 (to the extent relevant) in full, or
- the recognition and measurement provisions of IAS 39, 'Financial Instruments: Recognition and Measurement' as adopted by the EU and the disclosure requirements of sections 11 and 12.

13.15.1 Basic financial instruments

Scope

Section 11 applies to all financial instruments that fall within the category of basic financial instruments, other than:

- investments in subsidiaries, associates and joint ventures that are accounted for in accordance with other sections of the FRSME;
- own equity;
- leases, although the derecognition requirements of section 11 would apply to lease receivables recognised by a lessor and lease payables recognised by a lessee, and

- employers' rights and obligations under employee benefit plans.

Section 11 of the FRSME does not quite define a basic financial instrument, but instead provides a list of items that would qualify, being:

(a) cash;

(b) many debt instruments (such as accounts, notes, or loans receivable or payable), with further tests applied;

(c) commitments to receive loans that:

    (i) cannot be settled net in cash, and

    (ii) when the commitments are executed, are expected to meet the basic debt instrument conditions, and

(d) investments in non-convertible preference shares and non-puttable ordinary shares or preference shares.

The additional conditions that must be met for a debt instrument to fall within the scope of section 11 are that:

(a) returns to the holder are:

    (i) a fixed amount;

    (ii) a fixed rate of return over the life of the instrument;

    (iii) a variable return that, throughout the life of the instrument, is equal to a single referenced quoted or observable interest rate (such as LIBOR), or

    (iv) some combination of such fixed rate and variable rates (such as LIBOR plus specified basis points), provided that both the fixed and variable rates are positive;

(b) there is no contractual provision that could, by its terms, result in the holder losing the principal amount or any interest attributable to the current period or prior periods, which does not apply simply because the debt is subordinated;

(c) contractual provisions that permit the issuer (the debtor) to prepay a debt instrument or permit the holder (the creditor) to put it back to the issuer before maturity are not contingent on future events, and

(d) there are no conditional returns or repayment provisions except for the variable rate return and prepayment provisions covered above.

The draft provides examples of instruments that would normally meet the conditions, including trade accounts and notes receivable and payable, bank loans, and loans to and from subsidiaries and associates which are due on demand.

It also provides examples of instruments that would not fall within this category, including investments in equity, options and forwards contracts, and investments in convertible debt.

Recognition and initial measurement

The draft requires a company to recognise a financial instrument when it becomes party to the contractual provisions of that instrument.

The default rule for the initial measurement of a financial asset or financial liability is the transaction price (including transaction costs if the amortised cost model is being used). However, if the arrangement is a financing transaction deferred beyond the normal business terms or is financed at a rate of interest that is not a market rate, then it needs to be measured at the present value of the future payments discounted at a market rate of interest of a similar debt instrument.

Subsequent measurement

After initial recognition:

- qualifying debt instruments are stated at amortised cost calculated using the effective interest method, net of impairment in the case of assets;
- commitments to receive a loan are measured at cost less impairment, although the draft notes that cost may be nil, and
- investments in non-convertible preference shares and non-puttable ordinary or preference shares should be stated at fair value with changes recognised in profit or loss, if their fair value can be measured reliably, and at cost less impairment if their fair value cannot be measured reliably.

Where investments are stated at fair value, the following hierarchy should be used:

- the quoted price (usually the current bid price) for an identical asset in an active market;
- the price of a recent transaction for an identical asset, so long as there has not been a significant change in economic circumstances or a significant lapse of time since the transaction took place, and as adjusted if the company can show the last price was not a good estimate of fair value, and
- if the market for the asset is not active and recent transactions of an identical asset on their own are not a good estimate of fair value, then a value determined using a valuation technique.

Impairment of financial assets must be considered at the end of each reporting period. An impairment loss must be recognised if there is objective evidence of impairment. The draft provides various indicators of impairment, including:

- significant financial difficulties of the issuer;
- breaches of contract, such as default in interest or principal payments, and
- a probability that the debtor will enter bankruptcy or similar.

When measuring impairment, the method of measurement depends on the basis of the carrying amount of the asset:

- for items carried at amortised cost, but not carrying variable interest, the impairment loss is the difference between the carrying amount and the present value of the estimated future cash flows discounted at the original effective interest rate;

- for items carried at amortised costs with variable interest, the impairment loss is the difference between the carrying amount and the present value of the estimated future cash flows discounted at the current effective interest rate, and
- for items carried at cost less impairment, the impairment loss is the difference between the carrying amount and the best estimate of the amount that would be received for the asset if it were sold at the reporting date.

An impairment loss is only reversed in a subsequent period if the event that reverses the impairment loss occurred after the impairment was recognised. The reversal must not result in a carrying amount of the financial asset that exceeds what the carrying amount would have been had the impairment not been recognised. The reversal is recognised in profit or loss.

Derecognition

Financial assets are derecognised when:

- the contractual rights to the cash flows have expired or are settled;
- the company transfers substantially all the risks and rewards of ownership of the financial asset, or
- the company has retained some significant risks and rewards of ownership, but has transferred control of the asset to another party, so that the party can sell the asset unilaterally, in which case the company derecognises the asset and recognises separately any rights or obligations created by the transfer.

Where an asset is not derecognised, as risks and rewards have not been transferred, a financial liability is recognised for any consideration received.

Financial liabilities are derecognised when they are extinguished, that is when the obligation is discharged, cancelled or expires.

Disclosures

The draft FRSME contains a wide range of disclosure requirements in relation to basic financial instruments. These are based on the IFRS for SMEs, other than in relation to financial instruments at fair value which are required by the EU where fair value accounting is adopted.

13.15.2   Other financial instruments

As noted above, section 12 of the FRSME deals with financial instruments other than basic financial instruments. This section is optional, as companies could also choose to adopt the requirements of IAS 39, which are the same as the requirements of FRS 26.

Section 12 applies to all financial instruments except:

(a) basic financial instruments covered by Section 11;

(b) interests in subsidiaries, associates and joint ventures;

(c) employers' rights and obligations under employee benefit plans;

(d) rights under insurance contracts, unless the insurance contract could result in a loss to either party as a result of contractual terms that are unrelated to:

  (i)   changes in the insured risk;

  (ii) changes in foreign exchange rates, or

  (iii) a default by one of the counterparties.

(e) own equity;

(f) leases, unless the lease could result in a loss to the lessor or the lessee as a result of contractual terms that are unrelated to:

  (i)   changes in the price of the leased asset;

  (ii) changes in foreign exchange rates, or

  (iii) a default by one of the counterparties.

(g) contracts for contingent consideration in a business combination, for the acquirer.

Most contracts to buy or sell a non-financial item such as a commodity, inventory or property, plant and equipment would also be excluded, since they are not financial instruments. However, it would apply to contracts that can be settled net in cash or another financial instrument, or by exchanging financial instruments, unless those contracts were entered into and continue to be held for the purpose of the receipt or delivery of a non-financial item in accordance with the company's expected purchase, sale or usage requirements.

Recognition and measurement

Items within the scope of this section are, like basic financial instruments, to be recognised when the company becomes a party to the contractual provisions of the instrument. They are measured at fair value both on initial recognition and (in most cases) subsequently. On initial recognition, the transaction price should normally be the fair value. This excludes transaction costs.

The only exception to subsequent measurement at fair value is equity instruments that are not publicly traded and whose value cannot be measured reliably, or contracts linked to such instruments. In both cases, the instruments should be stated at cost less impairment. Where an instrument falls into this category, having previously had a determinable fair value, the fair value at the last date this was reliably measurable is treated as its cost.

Changes in fair value should be recognised in profit or loss.

Other matters

Section 12 does not deal in depth with issues such as impairment of items held at amortised cost or derecognition instead stating that the same principles should be applied as in Section 11 for basic financial instruments.

Hedge accounting

The draft FRSME allows hedge accounting only if all of the following conditions are met.

- The entity designates and documents the hedging relationship so that the risk being hedged, the hedged item and the hedging instrument are clearly identified and the risk in the hedged item is the risk being hedged with the hedging instrument.
- The hedged risk is one of the risks specified in the draft.
- The hedging instrument is one of the instruments specified in the draft.
- The entity expects the hedging instrument to be highly effective in offsetting the designated hedged risk. The effectiveness of a hedge is the degree to which changes in the fair value or cash flows of the hedged item that are attributable to the hedged risk are offset by changes in the fair value or cash flows of the hedging instrument.

The risks specified are:

- interest rate risk of a debt instrument measured at amortised cost;
- foreign exchange risk in a firm commitment or a highly probable forecast transaction;
- price risk of a commodity that the company holds, or in a firm commitment or highly probably forecast future transaction to purchase or sell a commodity, or
- foreign exchange risk in a net investment in a foreign operation.

In order to qualify, a hedging instrument must:

- be an interest rate swap, foreign currency swap, or a foreign currency forward exchange contract;
- be expected to be highly effective in offsetting the designated hedged risk;
- involve a party external to the reporting entity;
- have a notional amount equal to the designated amount of the principal or notional amount of the hedge item;
- have a specified maturity date not later than the date that is relevant to the item being hedged, and
- have no prepayment, early termination or extension features.

The treatment of hedges depends upon the nature of the instrument and the item being hedged.

For a hedge of the fixed interest rate risk of a recognised financial instrument or commodity price risk of a commodity held, the company will recognise the hedging instrument as an asset or liability and the change in the fair value of the hedging instrument in profit or loss, and recognise the change in the fair value of the hedged item related to the hedged risk in profit or loss and as an adjustment to the carrying amount of the hedged item. In the case of a hedge of the fixed interest rate risk of a debt instrument measured at amortised cost, the company also has to recognise the profit or loss on the periodic net cash settlements on the interest rate swap in the period in which the net settlements accrue.

Hedge accounting for a hedge of the fixed interest rate risk of a recognised financial instrument, or commodity price risk of a commodity held, is discontinued if the hedging instrument expires or is sold or terminated, or if the hedge fails to meet the hedge accounting conditions, or if the company revokes the designation of the hedge. Where hedge accounting is discontinued and the hedged item is an asset or liability carried at amortised cost that has not been derecognised, then any gains or losses that have been recognised as adjustments to the carrying amount of the hedged item are amortised into profit or loss using the effective interest method over the remaining life of the hedged instrument.

Where the hedged risk is any of:

- the variable interest rate risk in a debt instrument measured at amortised cost;
- the foreign exchange risk in a firm commitment or a highly probable forecast transaction;
- the commodity price risk in a firm commitment or highly probable forecast transaction, or
- the foreign exchange risk in a net investment in a foreign operation,

then the change (or portion of the change) in the fair value of the hedging instrument that was effective is recognised in other comprehensive income. Any excess is recognised in profit or loss. The hedging gain or loss that is initially recognised in other comprehensive income is reclassified to profit or loss when the hedged item is recognised in profit or loss or when the hedging relationship ends. In the case of a hedge of the variable interest rate risk of a debt instrument measured at amortised cost, the company also has to recognise in profit or loss the periodic net cash settlements on the interest rate swap in the period in which the net settlements accrue.

Hedge accounting is discontinued in the same circumstances as set out above, with the addition of a requirement to discontinue if, in a hedge of a forecast transaction, the forecast transaction ceases to be highly probable. Where hedge accounting is discontinued, any gains or losses previously recognised in other comprehensive income are reclassified to profit or loss.

This section of the draft also requires various disclosures in relation to hedge accounting, as well as requiring the same disclosures in respect of instruments falling within Section 12 as for those falling within Section 11.

14 STOCKS

14.1 INTRODUCTION

For companies that hold stock, the accounting treatment adopted will usually have a direct and significant effect on the reported profit for a period, and stock will often be one of the more important items on the company's balance sheet. The rules for accounting for stock are contained in SSAP 9 *Stocks and Long-term Contracts*, the FRSSE and the Companies Act 2006. Many of the statutory rules that apply to stocks also apply to other current assets.

The rules for stock appear to be straightforward, and in practice they often are. However, there are some problems:

- SSAP 9 and the FRSSE provide more latitude than one might expect in respect of such an important constituent of a balance sheet;
- the requirements of SSAP 9, the FRSSE and the Companies Act 2006 are not always consistent, and
- determining the amounts to include in the cost of stock can be very difficult in practice, however clear the rules may be in theory.

Under IFRS, stocks, described using the American term inventories, are covered by IAS 2. In general, the UK and international standards are similar and indeed are getting closer. The requirements in relation to inventories in the IFRS for SMEs are also very similar to the requirements in IAS 2 and, therefore, SSAP 9, although, as with the FRSSE, those rules are set out in somewhat less detail.

Potential impact of the FRSME

As noted above, there are few major differences between the approach adopted in SSAP 9 and that adopted in the IFRS for SMEs. As a result, the introduction of the FRSME would not cause a major change in accounting practice.

14.2 ACCOUNTING TREATMENT FOR STOCK

14.2.1 Constituents of stock

Contrary to what we might expect, SSAP 9 does not provide a definition of stock, in the sense that we would normally describe a definition. In place of such a definition it includes a list of the types of item that should be included under this heading:

Stocks comprise the following categories:

(a) goods or other assets purchased for resale;

(b) consumable stores;

    (c)   raw materials and components purchased for incorporation into products for sale;

    (d)   products and services in intermediate stages of completion;

    (e)   long-term contract balances; and

    (f)   finished goods. (Para. 16, SSAP 9.)

There is also no definition within the Companies Act 2006. Instead, Sch. 1 to The Large and Medium-sized Companies and Groups (Accounts and Reports) Regulations 2008 (SI 2008/410) simply provides a list of the sub-categories that should be used for disclosure purposes:

I Stocks

(1)   Raw materials and consumables

(2)   Work in progress

(3)   Finished goods and goods for resale

(4)   Payments on account. (Extract from balance sheet format, CA 1985, Sch. 4.)

For small companies statute is even less helpful, with only two categories of stocks: one is stocks and the other payments on account.

Despite this lack of a clear definition of stock, there is little evidence that companies experience major difficulties in determining which items should be treated as stock. This is not to say that the statutory categories, or those used within SSAP 9, can simply be applied without amendment. In many cases the categories are supplemented by additional items.

Examples of additional categories that have been used by companies are current intangible assets, and development land and properties. The addition of a category to those included in statute is acceptable, if:

- the assets involved cannot be classified as fixed assets, and
- costs have been incurred in their production or purchase, and
- there is the intention of realisation, use or sale in the near future.

In addition, companies should adapt the standard headings provided by statute if this will provide a fairer reflection of the categories of stock they hold.

However, it should be noted that companies should not reclassify fixed assets as stock if this is simply because the company has decided to sell the assets but has not done so by the balance sheet date. They continue to be fixed assets, even though they are held for disposal.

There are some important points that arise from the items included under the heading of stocks in SSAP 9, but which apply equally to small companies that have adopted the FRSSE.

(1)   Items do not need to be intended for resale in order to be included within stocks. The purpose of carrying stocks in the balance sheet is to recognise an asset, ie to recognise that the company has rights or other access to

future economic benefits arising from a past transaction or event. The past transaction or event will usually be that costs have been incurred in purchasing or producing the item; the future economic benefit may be obtained from selling the item directly, from using it to generate revenue indirectly (for example, through the use of materials in subsequent production) or from the avoidance of a future outlay. Direct sale is, therefore, only one of the possibilities, albeit the one that is most commonly encountered. To account for stock, it is only necessary that the costs which have been incurred should be of value and used up in a subsequent accounting period. This means, for example, that consumable stores, such as fuel, can often still be treated as part of stock, even though they will not be sold on by the company, as the future benefit arises indirectly through their subsequent use by the company in revenue-generating activities.

(2)   Stock also need not be tangible. The first category in the quote from para. 16 of SSAP 9 refers to 'other assets', as well as goods, whilst the section on work in progress specifically refers to 'services in intermediate stages of completion'. This allows, for example, professional service companies (or limited liability partnerships) to account for the value of work in progress in their balance sheets.

14.2.2   *Matching and prudence*

SSAP 9 makes reference to, and applies, the accruals (or matching) and prudence concepts as they were originally set out in SSAP 2 *Disclosure of Accounting Policies* at the time SSAP 9 was issued. SSAP 2 has since been superseded by FRS 18 *Accounting Policies*, which deals with these concepts in a very different manner. FRS 18 itself is covered in Chapter 2. However, although both matching and prudence have been significantly altered by FRS 18, this does not affect the basic principles of SSAP 9 itself.

The introduction to SSAP 9 emphasises the importance of the matching principle in the recognition of profit:

> The determination of profit for an accounting year requires the matching of costs with related revenues. The cost of unsold or unconsumed stocks will have been incurred in the expectation of future revenue, and when this will not arise until a later year it is appropriate to carry forward this cost to be matched with the revenue when it arises; the applicable concept is the matching of cost and revenue in the year in which the revenue arises rather than in the year in which the cost is incurred. (Para. 1, SSAP 9.)

FRS 18 makes no reference to matching in the text of the standard itself. However, the appendix to the FRS does acknowledge that the matching principle still operates:

> [Accruals, as defined in FRS 18, and FRS 5's asset and liability definitions] provides a discipline within which the matching process can operate, while still

resulting in the simultaneous recognition of revenues and costs that result from the same transactions or events. (Para. 9, Appendix IV, FRS 18.)

Therefore, although the way in which accruals and matching are expressed in accounting standards has changed since SSAP 9 was issued, the basic principles to which SSAP 9 refers still, in effect, apply. Matching may no longer be directly relevant, but the accounting treatment it dictated for stocks still applies. When goods or services are sold, the profit on the transaction needs to be calculated by comparing the revenue received with the costs that were incurred in order to allow the transaction to take place. This basic objective can only be achieved if the costs of goods and services to be sold in subsequent accounting periods are carried forward at the end of each accounting period.

However, in recognising and measuring assets representing stocks, the prudence principle may act as a limiting factor. This will apply to stock where there is uncertainty about whether future revenues will meet all of the costs that have been, or will be, incurred by the time of the sale.

The explanatory material in FRS 18 includes the following statement in relation to prudence.

> Often there is uncertainty, either about the existence of assets, liabilities, gains, losses and changes to shareholders' funds, or about the amount at which they should be measured. Prudence requires that accounting policies take account of such uncertainty in recognising and measuring those assets, liabilities, gains, losses and changes to shareholders' funds. In conditions of uncertainty, appropriate accounting policies will require more confirmatory evidence about the existence of an asset or gain than about the existence of a liability or loss, and a greater reliability of measurement for assets and gains than for liabilities and losses. (Para. 37, FRS 18.)

This means that the loss must be included in the stated value of the stock as soon as it is anticipated, even though the loss will not be realised until a subsequent accounting period.

The combination of these two principles provides the basic accounting treatment for stock, required by SSAP 9 and the FRSSE, which is that it should be stated at the lower of its cost and net realisable value. A virtually identical rule is contained in the relevant statutory instrument under the Companies Act 2006, which applies to all current assets and not just stock:

23 Subject to paragraph 24, the amount to be included in respect of any current asset must be its purchase price or production cost.

24 (1) If the net realisable value of any current asset is lower than its purchase price or production cost the amount to be included in respect of that asset must be the net realisable value.

(2) Where the reasons for which any provision for diminution in value was made in accordance with sub-paragraph (1) have ceased to apply to any extent, that provision must be written back to the extent that it is no longer necessary. (Sch. 1, The Large and Medium-sized Companies and

Groups (Accounts and Reports) Regulations 2008 (SI 2008/410) and Sch. 1, The Small Companies and Groups (Accounts and Directors' Report) Regulations 2008 (SI 2008/409).)

The second part of para. 24 has little relevance for stocks, although it may have important implications for the accounting treatment of long-term contract work in progress, which is covered in Chapter 15.

Potential impact of the FRSME

The draft of the FRSME contains the same basic requirement in terms of the treatment of stock, albeit that it uses different terms; inventories should be measured at the lower of cost and estimated selling price less costs to complete and sell.

14.3 COST OF STOCK

14.3.1 Calculation of cost

Calculating the cost of stock can be a very simple or an extremely complicated exercise.

In the simplest case, goods are bought and then sold on in the same condition, that is, without any work having been done on them. This might be a typical situation for a wholesaler or retailer. The cost of stock will then simply be the cost of the goods that were purchased for resale, plus the costs (if any) of bringing the goods to the site at which they are to be sold. The other costs that are incurred are the costs of selling, marketing and distributing the goods, which should not be included in the cost of stock.

Sometimes, the calculation will be considerably more complicated. In a manufacturing business, for example, there will usually be indirect costs and overheads. It is clear that these costs can be attributed to production as a whole, but far from clear how they should be allocated to particular units of production.

SSAP 9 defines the cost of stock as:

> ... that expenditure which has been incurred in the normal course of business in bringing the product or service to its present location and condition. This expenditure should include, in addition to cost of purchase ... such costs of conversion ... as are appropriate to that location and condition. (Para. 17, SSAP 9.)

The two phrases 'cost of purchase' and 'cost of conversion' used in this definition are clarified further:

> *Cost of purchase* comprises purchase price including import duties, transport and handling costs and any other directly attributable costs, less trade discounts, rebates and subsidies. (Para. 18, SSAP 9.)

Cost of conversion comprises:

(a)   costs which are specifically attributable to units of production, eg, direct labour, direct expenses and sub-contracted work;

(b)   production overheads . . . ;

(c)   other overheads, if any, attributable in the particular circumstances of the business to bringing the product or service to its present location and condition. (Para. 19, SSAP 9.)

The FRSSE repeats the definition of the cost of stock from SSAP 9. It does not repeat the definitions of costs of conversion or purchase. Despite this, it is very clear that the intention of the FRSSE is that the recorded costs should be the same as under the full standard. The sub-definitions included in SSAP 9 are intended as amplifications and clarifications of the basic requirement, and should not be seen as additional.

The rules in SSAP 9 on the determination of the cost of stock are consistent with the rules contained in The Large and Medium-sized Companies and Groups (Accounts and Reports) Regulations 2008 (SI 2008/410). Statute requires that the purchase price of any asset, including stock, should include any expenses that were incidental to its acquisition. This is similar to the requirement in the standard to include all costs incurred in bringing the goods to their present location and condition. Where an asset is produced, rather than purchased, SSAP 9 requires that any directly attributable overheads are added to the cost of the raw materials and consumables used in its production. Statute also allows, but does not require, the inclusion of reasonable indirect production overheads and interest in the cost of assets, including stocks. In both cases, the cost included must only be in respect of the period of production. Where interest is included in the cost of an asset, that interest must be disclosed.

It has sometimes been argued that the omission of certain categories of overhead from the cost of stock is prudent. While the adoption of this policy would reduce the reported value of stock this would be arbitrary rather than prudent. This argument is rebutted in Appendix 1 to SSAP 9, which goes on to argue that prudence should be applied through the requirement that stock be stated at the lower of cost and net realisable value, not through the deliberate omission of relevant costs. (It would also be a breach of FRS 18, which takes some pains to limit the application of prudence in situations where there is no material uncertainty.)

The calculation of the cost of stock for a company that produces goods usually involves two parts:

•   the calculation of the direct costs attributable to each unit, and

•   the calculation of the proportion of the total overhead costs that can be attributed to each unit.

The identification of direct costs is often the simpler part of the exercise. Direct costs would include items such as:

- costs of the basic raw materials;
- costs of additional raw materials and components;
- costs of direct labour, and
- production overheads that vary directly with the level of production (variable production overheads).

The reported stock value must not include any amounts in respect of distribution costs. This is expressly prohibited by para. 27 (4) of Sch. 1 to The Large and Medium-sized Companies and Groups (Accounts and Reports) Regulations 2008 (SI 2008/410) and Sch. 1 to The Small Companies and Groups (Accounts and Directors' Report) Regulations 2008 (SI 2008/409). For these purposes 'distribution costs' should be interpreted widely, to include all costs connected with the marketing and selling of the goods, as well as distribution costs from the site of sale to customers.

Potential impact of the FRSME

The draft FRSME contains fairly similar requirements to those included in SSAP 9. It states that the costs of inventories should include all costs of purchase, costs of conversion and other costs incurred in bringing the inventories to their present location and condition. While this does not refer to the normal course of business, as does SSAP 9, it is not clear that such a difference actually has any impact. The definitions of costs of purchase and costs of conversion are also very similar.

The FRSME is somewhat more explicit in allowing the change in the fair value of the hedging instrument in a hedge of a fixed interest rate risk or commodity price risk to be reflected in the cost of a commodity held as inventory. This matter is not dealt with in SSAP 9, although that is more likely to reflect the vintage of the standard than any matter of principle.

Borrowing costs are an area of difference between current practice and the FRSME. SSAP 9 allows borrowing costs to be included in the costs of stocks, although this is fairly rare, as is also allowed by the Companies Act 2006. The FRSME would not allow this, reflecting its general prohibition on borrowing costs being added to the cost of any asset. Going slightly further, the FRSME points out that where inventories are purchased on deferred settlement terms this may contain an unstated financing element; for example, where the agreed price differs from that on normal credit terms. Where this is the case, the difference must be split out and treated as interest and must not be included in the cost of inventories.

14.3.2 *Inclusion of overheads*

For a company involved in the production of goods, the more complicated part of the costing exercise is usually determining the amount of indirect production overhead that can be allocated to each unit of production. SSAP 9 defines production overheads in the following terms:

> Overheads incurred in respect of materials, labour or services for production, based on the normal level of activity, taking one year with another. For this purpose each overhead should be classified according to function (eg production, selling or administration) so as to ensure the inclusion, in cost of conversion, of those overheads (including depreciation) which relate to production, notwithstanding that these may accrue wholly or partly on a time basis. (Para. 20, SSAP 9.)

The ASC acknowledged that the allocation of overheads to production is often a very difficult exercise. In order to provide some guidance in this area, they drafted an appendix to SSAP 9 which deals with overhead allocation. The appendix does not form part of the standard, and it therefore does not have obligatory status. In the appendix, the ASC notes that there is often no single method by which overheads can be allocated:

> The costing methods adopted by a business are usually designed to ensure that all direct material, direct labour, direct expenses and sub-contracted work are identified and charged on a reasonable and consistent basis but problems arise on the allocation of overheads which must usually involve the exercise of personal judgement in the selection of an appropriate convention. (Para. 3, Appendix 1, SSAP 9.)

This raises two problems:

- the determination of the costs to be allocated, and
- the method of allocation to be used.

The appendix notes that it is only the normal costs of conversion that can be included in the value of stock. For example, it is acceptable to include the costs of the average level of wastage inherent in production, usually described as the normal loss. The costs of wasted materials are effectively spread over the level of good production. Any amounts over and above this normal level of wastage should not be included, and should be charged directly to the profit and loss account.

Although the costs of having idle capacity should not be included in the costs of stock, this does not imply that calculations need to be performed on the unrealistic assumption that 100 per cent efficiency is always achieved in production. It is a normal, achievable, level of activity that should be used in calculating the cost of stock. The appendix provides guidance on some of the factors that need to be considered in the interpretation of the 'normal' level of activities:

(a) the volume of production which the production facilities are intended by their designers and by management to produce under the working conditions (eg single or double shift) prevailing during the year;

(b) the budgeted level of activity for the year under review and for the ensuing year;

(c)   the level of activity achieved both in the year under review and in previous years. (Para. 8, Appendix 1, SSAP 9.)

Where there is a very short-term change in the level of activity, this should not affect the calculation of the normal level of activity. Clearly, where such a change persists, it will need to be taken into account in a redefinition of the normal level. It is worth noting that the requirement that only normal costs should be included in the value of stock is, arguably, not consistent with the production of financial statements under the historical cost convention. Where unusually high costs have been incurred in the production of stock, those costs still form part of the actual historical cost. (This is entirely separate from the requirement that stocks should not be stated at more than their net realisable value.) Nonetheless, such a treatment is still prohibited by SSAP 9 and the FRSSE.

Apart from eliminating the effect of any abnormal costs incurred, all overheads also need to be categorised by their function. For example, costs may be divided between costs which are incurred in production and administration. Whether or not the overhead is time or volume-related is not relevant.

The original allocation of costs to functions may not allow the final result to be determined without further allocation. Some of the costs may relate to central service departments, which in turn provide their services to a number of functions. The costs of these departments then need to be allocated to each of those functions. For example, the work of the accounts department will be partly attributable to production, partly to marketing and distribution and partly to general administration. That part of the overall cost of each central service department that can reasonably be allocated to production can be included in calculating the value of stock.

The costs of the general management of the enterprise as a whole need to be distinguished from the costs of management of each particular function. Such general management costs cannot normally be included in the calculation of the cost of stock. However, a particular problem may arise in a smaller organisation where a clear distinction between general and functional management cannot be drawn. In a case such as this, it would lead to understatement of the stock cost if the general management cost were to be simply ignored in the calculation of the stock value. Instead, some basis for allocation of the general management costs needs to be found. It may be extremely difficult to find a wholly objective basis, and the allocation is likely to use a greater degree of judgement than is required in a larger enterprise. A possible basis for the allocation of such costs would be, for example, the amount of time that management spend dealing with each function.

The basic rules on the inclusion of overheads, and other costs, in stock are the same under IAS 2 IAS 2 and the IFRS for SMEs.

Potential impact of the FRSME

As stated earlier, the IFRS for SMEs is very similar to SSAP 9; naturally so is the FRSME. The FRSME provides a little more guidance than SSAP 9 when dealing with periods of abnormally high activity, such that costs are likely to be overstated due to too much fixed overhead being allocated to each unit of production. In this case, costs must be restricted to those actually incurred. SSAP 9 concentrates rather more on the opposite situation, where the underlying costs themselves are abnormally high, but the requirements in both the actual and proposed standard are nonetheless consistent. The difference in emphasis does not reflect a difference in requirements.

14.3.3   Cost flow assumptions

Once the total production overhead to be allocated has been calculated, two problems still remain.

(1) How should the total production overheads be allocated to the different products produced by the enterprise?

(2) How should the costs attributable to each type of product be allocated to each particular unit?

The first problem (the allocation to different products) needs to be resolved by determining an appropriate overall costing method, such as job costing, batch costing, process costing or standard costing. The choice of method will usually depend upon the nature of the production process. For example, job costing will be most appropriate where individual items are produced to meet a particular customer's specifications.

The second problem (the allocation of costs to particular units of production) applies to all businesses which deal with homogeneous goods, whether they are involved in their production or sale. It involves determining the most appropriate cost flow convention to apply in the calculation of the stock cost. Even when it is possible to determine the total amount of production overhead that needs to be allocated, an assumption must be made regarding the flow of costs. This is necessary in order to determine how much of that overhead should be allocated to the cost of the sales made in the period and how much should be carried forward by inclusion in the value of stock. Normally, the cost flow convention that is employed is closely related to the physical flow of goods. Possible conventions include:

- unit cost;
- FIFO (first in first out);
- LIFO (last in first out);
- weighted average cost, and
- base stock.

These are discussed in turn.

The benchmark treatment under IAS 2, in circumstances where unit cost cannot be used, is that FIFO or weighted average be used. Until surprisingly recently, IAS 2 also allowed the use of LIFO, but this was prohibited in 2005 when the revised version of IAS 2 came into force.

Potential impact of the FRSME

The FRSME requires the use of unit cost where goods or services are not interchangeable and are produced for specific projects. For other inventories, it allows the use of FIFO or weighted average cost. Perhaps, oddly, it feels it necessary to specifically state that it prohibits the use of LIFO.

For reasons of practicality, the FRSME will also allow the use of standard costing, the retail method (selling price less estimated margin) and the most recent purchase price. In all cases, these methods are acceptable only where they approximate cost.

14.3.4 Unit cost

In those cases where it can be used, unit cost is the best method of costing. Since the cost of each stock item is the actual cost that has been incurred in its production, it does not involve the inevitable assumptions and averaging procedures that affect all of the alternative methods. Unit cost is a practical method of determining cost for wholesalers and retailers who deal in low-volume high-value goods, where there are virtually no problems with the allocation of overheads. In such cases, the only costs to be included will normally be those of purchase and transportation inwards. There may be cases where other costs need to be included, for example, costs of necessary storage, but this would be unusual.

In manufacturing or producing companies, this method often cannot be used, since the costs of maintaining the necessary information would be out of all proportion to the benefit. Where there is a high volume of production it may be impossible, or at least impractical, to determine the individual costs to be attributed to each unit of production. This effectively means that unit cost can be applied only by companies which produce at a low volume or where each unit produced is made to order. Unit cost is acceptable both under accounting standards and the Companies Act 1985.

14.3.5 First in first out

FIFO is another accepted method of valuing stock items. The underlying assumption is that the goods which are produced or purchased first are sold first. The items that remain in stock at the end of the period are those which have been produced or purchased at the most recent levels of cost. For most businesses this is a realistic assumption and should reflect the physical flow of goods from production or purchase to sale. The profit and loss account should provide a very close approximation to the actual costs incurred in the production or purchase of each unit of sales.

Where FIFO is being used, stock will be stated at the most recent costs that have actually been incurred. It is the fact that these costs must have actually been incurred that distinguishes FIFO from replacement cost methods of stock valuation. It is not acceptable simply to apply the latest purchase price or production cost to all of the units held in stock. This method would not state stock at the actual cost incurred in its purchase or production, and would in most cases lead to an overstatement of the profit that has been earned during the period.

14.3.6   Last in first out

LIFO involves the opposite assumption to FIFO. Under this method it is assumed that the latest goods to be produced or purchased will be the first ones to be sold. The justification for this treatment is that it normally ensures that the profit on each sale is calculated by comparing a current level of revenue with a realistic current level of cost. The problem is that the cost shown in the balance sheet is unlikely to be the actual cost of the goods held by the business, and the costs shown in the profit and loss account are unlikely to reflect the physical flow of goods.

As a general rule, the profits shown using LIFO will be lower than those shown using FIFO. However, there is an important exception. If there is a considerable decrease in the level of stocks held in a period, then some of the old costs will be matched with current income, which will lead to a high level of profit being reported.

Statute specifically allows the use of LIFO as a method for the determination of the cost of stock. SSAP 9 does not absolutely prohibit its use, but it does place a considerable burden on the directors of the company to justify their action:

> This standard requires the use of a method which provides a fair approximation to the expenditure actually incurred. The use of some of the methods allowed by paragraph 27 of the Schedule [Sch. 4, CA 1985] will not meet this requirement.
>
> In particular, the use of the LIFO method can result in the reporting of current assets at amounts that bear little relationship to recent costs. This may result in not only a significant misstatement of balance sheet amounts but also a potential distortion of current and future results. This places a special responsibility on the directors to be assured that the circumstances of the company require the adoption of such a valuation method in order for the accounts to give a true and fair view. (Paras. 38 and 39, SSAP 9.)

The reference to the Schedule to the Companies Act 1985 is not changed by the move to the Companies Act 2006.

Given the strength of this statement, it is perhaps not surprising that so few companies in the UK adopt this method of valuing their stock. The complexity of the accounting records required in order to use a LIFO system also means that it is unlikely to have widespread appeal.

As noted above, IAS 2 now prohibits the use of the LIFO method of stock valuation.

14.3.7 Weighted average

Under the weighted average cost method, the total costs of production (or total costs of purchase) over a period are divided equally between all of the goods produced (or purchased) in that period. A period for the purposes of the use of this method need not be the same as the company's accounting period. For example, while a company may produce financial statements on an annual basis it may use a monthly basis for the calculation of the cost of its stock; however, the company will then have to make an additional assumption about the flow of units between the months.

Weighted average is an acceptable method under both the Companies Act 1985 and accounting standards. It is subject to some of the same criticisms as LIFO, and, in particular, it is not likely to reflect the actual costs incurred in the production or purchase of each actual unit of sales. Nonetheless, in practice, the differences that will result are unlikely to be large unless there is a very high rate of inflation, or if the period used for averaging purposes is excessively long. Weighted average is a relatively common costing method in the UK.

14.3.8 Base stock

The base stock method involves stating a fixed quantity of stock at a fixed price. This base stock level is deemed to be the minimum amount of stock needed by a company to continue to operate and is, in effect, treated as though it were a fixed asset of the enterprise. All amounts of stock over and above this base level must be valued using a separate cost flow assumption. The base stock method is acceptable under the Companies Act 2006 if:

- the amount involved comprises 'raw materials and consumables' rather than any other category of stock;
- the overall value of the stock is not material in assessing the state of affairs of the company, and
- the quantity, value and composition of the stock are not subject to material valuation.

As with LIFO, base stock is not absolutely prohibited by SSAP 9, but the dangers of its use are mentioned. It is made clear that it is rarely likely to result in amounts appearing in the balance sheet at recent cost levels. This implies that the presentation of current assets is likely to be misleading.

However, since company law only allows the use of the base stock method where the amount involved is 'not material to assessing the company's state of affairs' it will also not conflict with SSAP 9 or the FRSSE in such cases, since accounting standards do not apply to immaterial items.

14.3.9 Non-allocative methods

All the above methods involve the allocation of historical expenditure in order to estimate the cost of stock. In contrast to these normal methods, there are also four other main ways in which the value of stock can be determined. These methods are different because they use procedures which are not based on the allocation of historical expenditure on stock. They are:

- standard cost;
- selling price less estimated profit margin;
- replacement cost, and
- current cost.

14.3.10 Standard cost

Put simply, standard costing involves the creation of cost standards for the quantity and price of inputs of labour, materials and overheads to be used in the manufacture of products. Cost standards could be loosely described as detailed budgets. The standards are normally set prior to production, by reference to product specifications, expected levels of cost, operating volumes and efficiency. The standards are then altered as the experience of actual production grows. The alteration of a standard does not necessarily imply that the original standard was incorrectly calculated. Standards are often altered, particularly with a relatively new product, to reflect the increased experience and expertise of the staff involved in production. As experience grows, the rate of production will often increase, and methods of using materials and other resources more efficiently may be found.

At the end of a period the profit actually earned can be analysed by reference to the 'standard' profit on the volume of sales achieved and variances from this standard amount. For example, if staff are paid at a higher wage rate than was originally expected, then there will be an adverse variance arising from the labour cost attributable to production. Similarly, if fewer materials are used for the actual volume of production than would have been expected from the standard, then this will give rise to a favourable variance.

The use of standard costs for valuing stock is acceptable. When standard costs are used they must be reviewed frequently to ensure that they continue to bear a reasonable relationship to actual cost. If variances are large and frequent then this indicates that it is the standards themselves that do not accurately reflect the costs involved in production, and so need to be revised. Standard costing, where properly operated, has the advantage that it applies the requirement that costs carried forward be based on the normal level and manner of operating, and not on unusual circumstances.

14.3.11   Estimated margin

SSAP 9 also allows the cost of stock to be determined by applying the estimated profit margin to the selling price. This is on the condition that it is possible to demonstrate that this provides a reasonable approximation of the actual cost. This is a puzzling condition because it is possible to show that this method provides a reasonable approximation to actual cost only if the actual cost is known independently. If this is the case, then no approximation is required.

This method is used by some organisations with fixed margins, usually because it is the only practical method they can adopt. It is sometimes described as the 'retail method', as its most common use is by retailers.

14.3.12   Replacement cost

Where the historical cost convention is being used, replacement cost is not an acceptable method of valuing stock. This is because it does not provide the actual cost that has been incurred and is likely to overstate the profits for the period. However, replacement cost is one of the factors that need to be considered if the alternative accounting rules are being applied and stock is to be stated at its current cost.

14.3.13   Current cost

Under the Companies Act 2006, stock may also be stated at its current cost if the alternative accounting rules are adopted. Current cost is the lower of replacement cost and net realisable value. Where current cost is used, the amount of any unrealised profit or loss arising as a result must usually be credited or debited to the revaluation reserve.

In practice, the use of the current cost of stocks is rare.

14.3.14   By-products

By-products are not usually subject to the normal rules for stock valuation. In order to be treated as a by-product an item should:

- have no material value of its own, and
- have no cost which could be determined separately from the cost of the principal product.

In such cases it is acceptable to state the by-products at their net realisable value. Their net realisable value should also be deducted from the costs attributed to the main product.

Potential impact of the FRSME

The FRSME deals with the cost of both joint products and by-products. The treatment for joint products is rather vague, in that the FRSME simply states that costs shall be allocated on a rational and consistent basis, but it does then give the example of using the relative sales value either at the stage the products become separable or at the completion of production. The treatment of by-products is the same as that included in SSAP 9, on the basis that by-products are nearly always immaterial.

14.3.15   Effect of use of different cost flow assumptions

An example will illustrate the different results that can be obtained by the use of different cost flow assumptions.

EXAMPLE

A company has no stock at the beginning of the period. During the year it purchases 1,000 items, at various prices, of which 150 are still in stock at the end of the year. The transactions during the year are:

		Number	Number	Price £	Value £	Cumulative number of units
1 January	Purchase	100		50	5,000	100
23 February	Purchase	200		55	11,000	300
15 March	Sale		150	100	15,000	150
4 May	Purchase	300		60	18,000	450
7 June	Sale		250	105	26,250	200
28 July	Purchase	200		70	14,000	400
15 August	Sale		200	105	21,000	200
9 November	Purchase	200		80	16,000	400
17 December	Sale		250	120	30,000	150
Total		1,000	850			

The sales value is not affected by the cost flow assumption used, and will in all cases be £92,250. Similarly, the total cost of purchases will be £64,000. However, the stock value and cost of sales will be greatly affected by the cost flow assumption adopted. The examples used are FIFO, LIFO and weighted average.

● *FIFO*

150 items are left in stock. FIFO assumes that it is the stock from the most recent purchase, and therefore the value of the stock will be 150 × £80 = £12,000.

In this case, the gross profit will be:

	£	£
Turnover		92,250
Purchases	64,000	
Less: closing stock	12,000	
Cost of sales		52,000
Gross profit		40,250

● *LIFO*

150 items are left in stock. LIFO assumes that it is the stock from the earliest purchases that is still in stock, taking account of the minimum levels of stock held at any particular time. At no point since 23 February has the stock level fallen below 150, and therefore the items in stock comprise the whole of the 100 items purchased on 1 January and 50 of the items purchased on 23 February. The cost is therefore (100 × £50) + (50 × £55) = £7,750.

The gross profit will be:

	£	£
Turnover		92,250
Purchases	64,000	
Less: closing stock	7,750	
Cost of sales		56,250
Gross profit		36,000

● *Weighted average*

150 items are left in stock. The total purchase cost is spread across all of the items purchased in the period. The cost of stock is therefore £64,000 × 150/1,000 = £9,600.

The gross profit will be:

	£	£
Turnover		92,250
Purchases	64,000	
Less: closing stock	9,600	
Cost of sales		54,400
Gross profit		37,850

This is an exaggerated example, and costs are unlikely to increase this dramatically (at least in the UK) over such a short period. As a result, the difference between the weighted average and the FIFO profits is likely to be exaggerated. The difference between the LIFO and FIFO profits is more plausible, if we assume that a company has seen continuous increases in stock over a considerable period.

14.3.16 Service industries

We have already noted that there is no requirement for stocks to be tangible, and that this allows service companies to carry forward work that has not yet been completed as part of their work in progress.

Unbilled work in service industries may be calculated by the time spent, if this is the basis for charging, or in some other way, such as where a surveyor may obtain a stated percentage of a total contract's value.

While SSAP 9 has not itself been changed, the treatment of work in progress in service industries has been altered by Application Note G to FRS 5 *Reporting the Substance of Transactions*, and, more specifically UITF 40 *Revenue Recognition and Service Contracts*. The implications of the Application Note and UITF are dealt with inChapter 4, but, in summary, it is now less likely that amounts will be treated as work in progress stated at cost. Cost will continue to form the basis for the recognition of work in progress where there is a critical event, outside of the control of the company, which must take place before the company is entitled to income and which has not taken place at the balance sheet date.

Where this applies, care needs to be taken to ensure that the amount included as work in progress does not include any element of profit. If time has been recorded in the accounting system, then it will often have been recorded at rates that include an element of profit. The profit element must be eliminated in order to arrive at cost. Charge rates will normally be based on some multiple of direct cost, and so this calculation may need to be performed in reverse in order to arrive at the cost. Where the income is calculated by reference to a given percentage of the total value of the project undertaken, it is likely to be considerably more complicated to determine the cost, and this will have to be done by estimating the profit to be earned and then deducting the profit element from the value of the work performed to date.

Net realisable value also needs to be considered. Costs should not be included in respect of time or work where that cost is not expected to be recovered. This has an impact when considering the interaction with UITF 40. Under UITF 40, income is not recognised where a critical event is required for the income to be earned and that critical event has not yet taken place. As a result, this would appear to increase the risk that such event will not occur, meaning that the net realisable value of the work in progress will be nil. However, the fact that a critical event has not occurred by the balance sheet date does not mean the same as saying that the critical event is not expected to occur. As a result, it does not follow that work in progress on such critical event work cannot be recognised as an asset.

14.4   NET REALISABLE VALUE

14.4.1   Definition

SSAP 9 defines net realisable value as:

The actual or estimated selling price (net of trade but before settlement discounts) less:

(a) all further costs to completion; and
(b) all costs to be incurred in marketing, selling and distributing. (Para. 21, SSAP 9.)

This is repeated in the FRSSE.

The most important aspect of this definition is what it omits; no reference is made to the value at which the goods could be sold in their current state. Net realisable value is not the same as the current market price of the goods involved, in their current state. It is fairly common for companies to hold stocks of goods that they could not sell for the price they paid. Some of these goods may actually have no commercial value in their present state. However, this is not relevant if those goods are to be included in other finished items which will realise at least the total costs that have been incurred in their production. The first appendix to SSAP 9 makes this point clear:

> ... no reduction falls to be made when the realisable value of material stocks is less than the purchase price, provided that the goods into which the materials are to be incorporated can still be sold at a profit after incorporating the materials at cost price. (Para. 19, Appendix 1, SSAP 9.)

The definition of net realisable value included in SSAP 9 is consistent with the going concern concept. While it might seem prudent to value stocks on the basis of their actual realisable value at the balance sheet date, it would conflict with the requirement that the accounts should be drawn up on the basis that the company will continue in existence. Since there is no likelihood that the goods will actually be sold on in their present state, the amount they would realise, were this to happen, is not a relevant consideration.

A simple example of this situation is work in progress for a company that is a going concern. Where an asset is partially completed it may have no or negligible value in its present state. It will no longer have any value as raw materials, since they may no longer be in a usable form. At the same time the good is incomplete and cannot be sold. The only value the item may have is its scrap value, if any. This does not mean that the total costs incurred in producing all work in progress should be written off, as long as the items currently under production will be completed.

Potential impact of the FRSME

The requirements included in the draft FRSME are the same as those in SSAP 9, albeit that the term 'net realisable value' is not used.

14.4.2 Application of net realisable value

Net realisable value should be considered either for individual items, or for groups of similar items. It is unacceptable to consider the value of stock as a whole, or even by major category, and then to determine if the total cost or total net realisable value is lower. This is an example of the asymmetry of the application of prudence under conditions of uncertainty; while the value of stock must take account of any anticipated losses, it should not take account of any anticipated gains.

It is acceptable for a company to start by using a pre-determined formula to perform the initial calculation of the net realisable value of its stock. For example, the formula might take account of the age of the stock held, the scrap value of the goods involved, the current level of trading and previous experience. Nonetheless, the simple application of any formula will never be sufficient to provide the final result. In all cases, consideration must be given to any special factors that may affect the value of the stock. Each item, or group of items, must be considered individually. Events that have occurred after the balance sheet date must be taken into account in determining the net realisable value of stock. For example, a company should consider the price that it has received on its sales in the next accounting period and any new competing products that may affect the value or volume of sales.

The first appendix to SSAP 9 provides a list of situations in which net realisable value may fall below cost:

> The principal situations in which net realisable value is likely to be less than cost are where there has been:
>
> (a)   an increase in costs or a fall in selling price;
> (b)   physical deterioration of stocks;
> (c)   obsolescence of products;
> (d)   a decision as part of a company's marketing strategy to manufacture and sell products at a loss;
> (e)   errors in production or purchasing. (Para. 20, Appendix 1, SSAP 9.)

The list is not intended to be exhaustive. The standard also points out that where the company is holding excess stocks then it is more likely that some of these situations may apply. For example, the stocks are more likely to deteriorate physically or to become obsolete. The company may also be tempted to sell the goods at a lower price in order to reduce the costs of holding stock.

Where the net realisable value of finished goods falls below their cost, this may also have an effect on the net realisable value of raw materials and components to be used in their manufacture.

Where spares are held for sale, the appendix also provides a list of three factors that should be considered when determining their net realisable value:

(a) the number of units sold to which they are applicable;

(b) the estimated frequency with which a replacement spare is required;

(c) the expected useful life of the unit to which they are applicable. (Para. 18, Appendix 1, SSAP 9.)

In such cases the demand for the spares is derived from the demand for the underlying product, and the net realisable value calculation should take account of this information.

Consumable stores, and other goods that are not directly intended for resale, must also be stated at the lower of their cost and net realisable value. In such cases the strict application of the definition of net realisable value would result in a figure of zero, since there is no selling price. It is very unlikely that the ASC intended this result, which would not always provide a fair reflection of the costs that have been incurred but not yet used up. Such stocks should be stated at the lower of their actual cost and replacement cost, so long as the goods involved are expected to be used. They should be written off in full if there is any serious doubt as to their value.

Nonetheless, it is fairly common for companies to write off the full cost of such goods at the time of purchase. This is acceptable if the level of such stocks, or the fluctuation in that level, is not material. As has already been noted, it is also consistent with a strict interpretation of SSAP 9.

14.5 CONSIGNMENT STOCKS

14.5.1 The basics

Consignment stocks are similar to stocks held subject to reservation of title, as the stock is held by one party to the arrangement, but the legal title to the stock is held by the other. However, there are important differences. For example, the legal title may be transferred at a time other than when cash is paid, the price may not always be fixed in advance, and there may be a financing charge.

The ASB addresses the issue of consignment stocks in the application notes to FRS 5 and provides a very brief summary of the issue in the FRSSE. FRS 5 outlines the main features of a consignment stock, in the context of the motor trade.

(1) The manufacturer supplies goods to the dealer, but the legal title to the goods does not pass at the date of the transfer, but when some future event takes place. Events which might give rise to the transfer of legal title include:

(a) the expiry of an agreed period of time from the date of the original supply of the goods;

(b) sale to a third party, or

(c)   the adoption of the goods in some other form.

It is very common for two or more conditions to be included, for example, the transfer of legal title may take place at the earlier of the date of sale to a third party or after a specified period of time. Until the relevant event takes place, the dealer can usually return the goods to the manufacturer, or the manufacturer can ask for the goods to be returned from the dealer.

(2)   The price to be paid by the dealer will normally be fixed in one of three ways:

(a)   at the date of the original supply;
(b)   by using the list price at the date of the transfer of legal title, or
(c)   by reference to the period of time for which the stock has been held.

(3)   The dealer may need to place a deposit with the manufacturer, or to pay a financing charge. The deposit or charge may be fixed or variable, and is often set by reference to the previous sales record of the dealer.

There will also normally be other conditions in the agreement dealing with, for example, insurance and inspection, but, as the ASB notes, these are not usually of great importance in determining the accounting treatment.

As with all areas where the principle of substance over form may need to be applied, the key questions are concerned with the allocation of the commercial risks and benefits of ownership of the assets, and this is quite a separate matter from the legal rights of the parties. There are exceptions, but, unfortunately, there is usually no single factor on which such an assessment may be made, and all of the factors will need to be considered. The final decision will depend upon the relative importance, in practice, of each of the factors. When we consider the various factors we may obtain results that point to different accounting treatments; some factors may indicate that the stock should be treated as an asset by the dealer and some that it should be dealt with by the manufacturer. We always need to decide which of the factors should take precedence. This is the most difficult part of the exercise, since the various factors must be weighted according to their commercial effect, and, unfortunately, this is the one area where general guidance cannot really be given.

Having outlined the main features, FRS 5 then analyses four major factors that should normally be used in determining which party should treat the stock as an asset:

- the manufacturer's right of return;
- the dealer's right of return;
- the stock transfer price and deposits, and
- the dealer's right to use the stock.

The list of relevant factors is not limited to these, and other items may also need to be considered in any particular case. As stated above, the most important fact is that the final result should be based on those factors which are most likely to have commercial effect in practice, and not simply on the mathematical balance of all the factors. These factors are now discussed, in turn.

14.5.2   Manufacturer's right of return

Under a consignment stock arrangement, the manufacturer will normally have a right to require the return of the goods, or to require the goods to be passed on to a third party. It is not the legal right that determines the accounting treatment; it is the commercial effect of that right.

The question to be answered is not 'can the manufacturer require the return of the goods?', but 'is there any likelihood that the manufacturer will ask for the return of the goods?' Just because there is a legal right to require the return of the goods does not mean that this is the normal course of events.

The first source of evidence is likely to be the previous record of the dealer and the manufacturer. Is it common for goods to be returned at the manufacturer's request or is this unusual? As the standard states, if there is a high rate of return at the request of the manufacturer, then this indicates that the dealer may not have control over the assets, and, therefore, that the dealer should not treat the goods as stock. Conversely, where the rate of return is very low, then this indicates that the stock should appropriately be dealt with in the accounts of the dealer. Since each arrangement needs to be judged on its own merits, the record for the type of goods in question may be the relevant one, rather than that for all goods acquired from the manufacturer.

Another consideration is any financial arrangement connected with the right of return. If the dealer is provided with some form of compensation when the right to require return is exercised, this indicates that the dealer is the effective owner of the stock. Similarly, where no consideration is provided for the return of the stock, this makes it more likely that the stock is held by the manufacturer rather than the dealer.

14.5.3   Dealer's right of return

Apart from the right of the manufacturer to require return, the right of the dealer to return the goods must be considered. In many ways this will be done in much the same way as with the manufacturer's rights: not 'can they', but 'will they'. The main source of evidence will, again, be the historical record. Considering the dealer's right of return effectively involves looking at the risks associated with the stock. Two of the most important of these risks are the risk of obsolescence and the risk that the goods become unsaleable. This means that, in addition to the factors noted below, the actual risk of obsolescence and the risk of being unable to sell the goods are relevant factors. The nature of the goods, and the current position of the market in which they are sold, will therefore be important.

The stock is probably not that of the dealer in any of the following situations:

- the right of return is regularly exercised;
- although the right of return is not usually exercised, there is a high likelihood that it will be used for the particular goods in question, or
- the manufacturer provides a financial incentive to deter the return of the goods, when without such an incentive there is a high likelihood that the goods would be returned.

The second point is not mentioned in the paragraph of FRS 5 dealing with the dealer's right of return, but is nonetheless an important consideration which is mentioned elsewhere in the draft. It is important to remember not only to look at the historical record as a means of assessing the likelihood of events that will occur in the future. If there is some good reason to distinguish between previous experience and what is likely to happen in future, then this should be done. This may necessitate distinguishing between different classes of transaction with the same manufacturer. This will inevitably involve more work, but will also come up with a more reasonable result.

Factors which indicate that the goods are those of the dealer rather than the manufacturer include:

- the dealer having no right to return the stock (this alone would be virtually conclusive evidence that the stock is that of the dealer);
- a record of very few returns to the manufacturer, and
- a significant penalty to the dealer if goods are returned.

14.5.4   Stock transfer price and deposits

The arrangements for the transfer price affect two things:

- whether or not the dealer is protected from changes in the price, and
- which party bears the risk of slow movement of the stock.

It is important to decide which is likely to be the most important in practice. This is because the nature of the arrangement will not always give rise to the same result when looked at in these two different ways.

(1)   For example, if there is a fixed price that will be paid by the dealer only when the goods are sold on, or otherwise transferred, then the price risk is likely to lie with the dealer. As with a normal purchase, changes in the manufacturer's list price will have no effect on the price to be paid by the dealer.

(2)   If the risk of slow movement lies with the manufacturer and not the dealer; if the goods are not sold for a considerable time then it is the manufacturer who must wait for a return after having already incurred the costs of production. The dealer will only have to incur the cost when there is a sale, and income will be received. This indicates that the goods are still those of the manufacturer.

Since the different viewpoints give rise to different results, it is necessary to determine whether the risk of price changes or slow movement is likely to have the greater commercial effect. Where the basic price is fixed at the date of the original transfer, but is increased by a factor depending on the period for which the stock is held by the dealer, then the dealer suffers both the price risk and the slow movement. This will be true however the effective interest charge is calculated, whether directly, by reference to average sales periods, or in some other manner. It may, however, depend on the level of the effective interest charge. The dealer bears the slow movement risk if the factor approximates to commercial rates, but this may not be true if the effective interest charge is only a nominal amount. Where the dealer has to pay the manufacturer's list price at the date of the ultimate sale, then the price risk lies with the manufacturer, but it is more difficult to determine the slow movement risk.

The main risk is likely to lie with the manufacturer since they will obtain no direct compensation for the fact that their income has been deferred, while the dealer is likely to be able to pass on any price changes to the ultimate customer.

As FRS 5 notes, the existence of a deposit complicates the analysis. The main question is whether or not the deposit means that the dealer, rather than the manufacturer, bears the slow movement risk. This will naturally depend on the amount of the deposit and the main terms of the arrangement. Put simply, the higher the level of the deposit the more the risk of slow movement is passed on to the dealer.

14.5.5   *Dealer's right to use the stock*

The fact that a dealer has the right to use the stock held under a consignment stock arrangement is unlikely to be a major factor in determining which party should treat the stock as an asset. However, where the dealer exercises this right, this normally causes the legal title to be transferred, and therefore it should be treated as an acquisition of the stock by the dealer, unless it has already been determined that the stock is that of the dealer.

14.6   SPECIALIST INDUSTRIES

There are certain industries where specialist procedures with regard to the costing and valuation of stock have evolved. For example, farming is an industry where normal calculations may not be applicable. Whilst it may be possible to identify the costs that have been incurred in growing crops (such as seed, fertiliser and pesticides), it is often more difficult to determine the costs of, for example, livestock. In some cases it is a common practice to value such stock by reference to their sales value, and then to adjust this value to take account of the margin of profit. Taking the more specific example of bloodstock held for stud purposes, it is common practice for a valuation to be undertaken by an independent valuer, and for this valuation to be incorporated in the financial statements. Detailed consideration of the valuation practices adopted in specialist industries is outside the scope of this work.

There is a specific international accounting standard, IAS 41, which deals with agriculture. Under IAS 41, biological assets and agricultural produce should normally be stated at their fair value less estimated point of sale costs. Biological assets are living animals or plants, and agricultural produce is the harvested product of biological assets. With reference to animals, harvest is a euphemism for slaughter.

Potential impact of the FRSME

The FRSME contains separate rules for biological assets and agricultural products at the point of harvest. These are measured at fair value less estimated costs to sell, and not in accordance with the requirements which apply to the majority of inventories. This builds on IAS 41, as mentioned above.

14.7   DISCLOSURE

14.7.1   *Accounting policy*

The financial statements should disclose the accounting policy that has been adopted for the valuation of stocks. SSAP 9 states that a suitable description of the amount at which stocks have been included is 'at the lower of cost and net realisable value' (para. 12, SSAP 9). However, this alone is not really sufficient, as more detail will be required to enable the user to determine how cost has been calculated. We have already seen that there is no single method that is used in all cases, and to omit the disclosure of the method of calculating costs is to omit valuable information. It is also a requirement of FRS 18, *Accounting Policies*, that companies state those estimation techniques that have had a material impact. The basis of determining the costs of stock is an estimation technique. (The FRSSE does not require the routine disclosure of estimation techniques.) Nonetheless, many companies do not currently provide this information. However, this information does not need to go into great detail, as shown by the examples below.

EXAMPLE

Estimated margin disclosure

Stocks have been valued at the lower of cost and net realisable value. The cost of the stock is calculated by deducting the appropriate departmental gross profit margin from the normal selling price.

Disclosure of prudential valuation policy

Stocks and work in progress are valued at the lower of cost and net realisable value. Cost is defined as the actual cost of raw materials and an appropriate proportion of labour and overheads in the case of work in progress and finished goods. Provision is made for obsolete and slow-moving items and for unrealised profits on items of inter-company manufacture. The net realisable value of long-term contracts (those extending over more than one year) has incorporated estimated costs to completion. A prudent level of profit attributable to the contract activity is taken up only if the final outcome of such contracts can be reliably assessed. Full provision is always made for any losses in the year in which they are first foreseen.

Disclosure which mentions the exclusion of distribution and administration expenses

Finished products are valued at the lower of purchase price, manufacturing cost and net realisable value. Distribution and administration expenses are not included in the valuation. Work in progress is valued at the cost of materials plus manufacturing labour and overheads. Raw materials are valued at purchase price but are reduced to net replacement cost if this is lower. Account is always taken of any slow-moving or obsolete items.

Where different bases have been adopted for the valuation of different types of stock, this also needs to be disclosed.

Potential impact of the FRSME

The FRSME requires disclosure of the accounting policy, and is also explicit about the requirement to state the cost formula that has been used.

The FRSME also requires disclosure of:

- the amount of inventories recognised as an expense in the period;
- any impairment losses recognised or reversed in profit or loss, and
- the total carrying amount of inventories that have been pledged as security for liabilities.

14.7.2   Classification

Stocks should be sub-classified in accordance with the formats provided by statutory instruments to the Companies Act 2006. A simpler analysis is allowed for small companies as shown below.

Stocks

(1)   Raw materials and consumables.

(2)   Work in progress.

(3)   Finished goods and goods for resale.

(4)   Payments on account.

Format for small companies

(1) Stocks.

(2) Payments on account.

As noted above, companies can and do alter the basic classifications so that they are more appropriate to the business.

Potential impact of the FRSME

The FRSME contains a requirement that inventories be split between the following categories for the purposes of disclosure.

- Those held for sale in the ordinary course of business.
- Those in the process of production for such sale.
- Those in the form of materials or supplies to be consumed in the production process or in the rendering of services.

This is not quite the same as the current requirements under SSAP 9, or indeed statute, although there is some overlap.

It also contains a general requirement that inventories be analysed between categories appropriate to the entity, without specifying what those categories might be.

14.7.3 Replacement cost

Where there is a material difference between the value of stock as included in the balance sheet and the replacement cost (or the most recent actual purchase price or production cost prior to the balance sheet date) of the stock, that difference should be disclosed in a note to the financial statements. The directors should determine whether it is the replacement cost, latest purchase price or latest production cost that is the most appropriate standard of comparison.

This disclosure is not required if the items of stock in the balance sheet are stated at their actual cost, that is, a cost flow assumption (such as FIFO, LIFO or weighted average) has not been used.

Strictly, no statement need be made where there is no material difference between the recorded cost and the replacement cost, latest production cost or latest purchase price, even where a cost flow assumption has been used in determining the cost of stock. Some companies still choose to make such a disclosure, since it may assist in the interpretation of the financial statements.

14.7.4 Interest

Interest and financing costs are not usually included in stocks. However, there are exceptions. In certain industries the period between the commencement of manufacturing or production and sale is considerable. In these cases, the interest on capital borrowed to finance the production may be included in the costs of stock. For example, in whisky distilling, 'stocks of maturing whisky and other spirits' may include substantial amounts in respect of interest, since such stocks may be held for many years.

The inclusion of interest in the valuation of assets is considered further in Chapter 11.

Potential impact of the FRSME

As noted earlier, the FRSME prohibits the inclusion of borrowing or interest costs in the cost of inventories.

15 LONG-TERM CONTRACT WORK IN PROGRESS

15.1 INTRODUCTION

Long-term contract work in progress is simply one form of stock that can be held by a company. As a result, many of the basic principles that should be applied to normal stocks must also be applied when dealing with long-term contract work in progress. Principles such as:

- the ascertainment of attributable direct cost;
- the inclusion of overheads, and
- the capitalisation of borrowing costs,

will apply in the same way as for all other items of stock.

In this chapter we will not consider those items which are the same as for all other types of stock, as they have been covered in Chapter 14. The most important difference between long-term contract work in progress and other items of stock is the time that is taken in completing long-term contract work in progress. It might not be clear why this should have a major effect on the accounting treatment that should be adopted. Why should an apparently purely quantitative difference have a qualitative effect? When we come to consider the matter more closely it becomes clear that there is an important distinction. The accounting treatment adopted for the majority of stocks is appropriate because sales and purchases take place quite close to each other, and because transactions are not usually individually material. When these conditions are not in place then we need to reconsider the accounting treatment we should adopt. If we applied the normal rules for stock valuation to long-term contract work in progress then we would find that this would often result in profit and loss accounts that provided little meaningful or useful information. The reported turnover for a company would tell us little about that company's level of activity. The reported profit or loss would similarly not reflect the underlying profitability of that business. In these circumstances, we need a better way of accounting for long-term contracts. It is also worth pointing out the 'contract' element of long-term contract work in progress. If stocks simply happen to be held for a long time, but are to be sold in the normal way, then they are not subject to any different accounting treatment than for stocks that are held only in the short term. The fact that there is a contract makes it more reasonable that profits be recognised prior to completion, since stocks are not being held in the normal hope and expectation of profit as there is more support than is normally the case. It is for these reasons that SSAP 9 allows for different treatments; both the long-term nature and the existence of a contract.

While the basic accounting treatment of long-term contracts has not been altered in recent years, there were some changes to recognition of income arising as a result of the introduction of Application Note G *Revenue Recognition* to FRS 5, *Reporting the Substance of Transactions*. The application note contains a separate section dealing with long-term contractual performance. It is also worth pointing out that part of the analysis above is no longer entirely valid, given the Application Note and UITF 40, *Revenue Recognition and Service Contracts*. Notwithstanding comments to the contrary, UITF 40 changed the accounting treatment for many short-term service contracts, where the service is provided on a time basis. As a result, the treatment of even short-term service contracts is often more akin to long-term contracts than that for other types of stock. The time criterion is actually of less relevance than it used to be.

Long-term contract work in progress, described as construction contracts, is covered by IAS 11. The principles of the UK and international standards are the same. There is part of an exposure draft, FRED 28 *Construction and Service Contracts*, which was originally proposed as a replacement for that part of SSAP 9 dealing with long-term contract work in progress. Other than the name, it did not propose major changes to the accounting treatment of long-term contracts. The exposure draft was based on the international standard. As noted in the previous chapter, this exposure draft has now been in issue for a very long time and, given the ASB's proposals in relation to the future of UK GAAP, is very unlikely to lead to a revision to SSAP 9.

Potential impact of the FRSME

The FRSME, like the IFRS for SMEs on which it is based, does not have a separate section dealing with long-term contracts, or construction contracts as they are described in the draft standard. Instead, they are dealt with in the section on revenue recognition. Despite this, the actual accounting treatment that would be applied under the FRSME does not differ that much in principle from the accounting treatment currently required under UK GAAP.

15.2   DIFFERENCES FROM NORMAL STOCK

15.2.1   Definition

SSAP 9 contains the following definition of a long-term contract:

> A contract entered into for the design, manufacture or construction of a single substantial asset or the provision of a service (or of a combination of assets or services which together constitute a single project) where the time taken substantially to complete the contract is such that the contract activity falls into different accounting periods. A contract that is required to be accounted for as long-term by this accounting standard will usually extend for a period exceeding one year. However, a duration exceeding one year is not an essential feature of a long-term contract. Some contracts with a shorter duration than one year should

be accounted for as long-term contracts if they are sufficiently material to the activity of the period that not to record turnover and attributable profit would lead to distortion of the period's turnover and results such that the financial statements would not give a true and fair view, provided that the policy is applied consistently within the reporting entity and from year to year. (Para. 22, SSAP 9.)

This definition, which is repeated in the FRSSE, contains some very important points that affect the accounting treatment of long-term contracts:

- they take place under a contract, with a known purchaser, and
- they consist of a substantial single project, or a group of related projects that can reasonably be treated as one, where the activity normally falls into two or more accounting periods.

The existence of a contract with a known purchaser is crucial as, without this, revenue would not be sufficiently certain to permit recognition prior to completion of work, which SSAP 9 specifically requires for long-term contracts. It is important not to confuse long-term contracts with other long-term work in progress where there is no contract with a known purchaser, for example, a speculative property development.

Since long-term contracts are by definition substantial, their recording will almost certainly have a material effect on the results reported for the accounting period. As they also fall into two or more accounting periods, the allocation of the profit on the contract as a whole will also significantly affect the results for any particular period.

In the absence of specific guidance, long-term contracts could be treated in the same way as stock. This would imply that turnover should only be recorded when the contract is completed, and that profit should be calculated and taken at this point. This treatment could be described as the 'completed-contract' method. Such a treatment would undoubtedly be prudent, but prudent almost to the point of absurdity.

As noted in the introduction, there would be two obvious implications.

(1) The recorded turnover would bear little relationship to the level of activity undertaken by the company in each accounting period. Instead, it would be determined largely by the number of contracts that had been completed. For example, a high level of turnover might be shown in an accounting period simply because a major contract had been completed in that period, even though very little work had been performed on that contract during the year.

(2) The profits shown would not be related to the level of activity, but again to the number of contracts that had been completed.

As already mentioned, this treatment is prudent, and consistent with the treatment of normal stocks. However, this treatment fails to comply with the most basic of requirements for financial statements; it does not give a true and fair view of the position of the company or of its activities during the year. SSAP 9 states the case in precisely those terms:

> Separate consideration needs to be given to long-term contracts. Owing to the length of time taken to complete such contracts, to defer recording turnover and taking profit into account until completion may result in the profit and loss account reflecting not so much a fair view of the results of the activity of the company during the year but rather the results relating to contracts that have been completed in the year. It is therefore appropriate to take credit for ascertainable turnover and profit while contracts are in progress ... (Para. 7, SSAP 9.)

It is the elimination of the arbitrary allocation of profits to accounting periods that SSAP 9 intends to achieve when dealing with long-term contracts.

It should be noted that the definition does not simply include contracts which will extend over more than one year. As the standard states, whilst many contracts will continue over such a period, it is not an essential part of the definition. The test that should be applied is whether or not turnover and profit should be recorded in order to ensure that the reported results provide a true and fair view of the activities of the business in the relevant period. Once a policy has been adopted, it must be applied consistently from year to year.

The basic differences from normal stock are therefore:

- turnover should be recorded as a contract progresses, and not only when it is completed, and
- profit should be recorded as it arises, and not taken solely on completion of each contract.

In both cases, the treatment will be subject to the requirements of prudence.

The requirements of the FRSSE are identical to those of SSAP 9, although the FRSSE omits the justification and discussion.

Potential impact of the FRSME

The definition of a construction contract in the FRSME is much shorter than that found in SSAP 9, and does not make reference to the period over which the contract is likely to be in place. This probably reflects the approach generally taken to revenue recognition in the FRSME, which is the percentage of completion method for services, which does not really differ from the approach required for construction contracts. This is also true under current UK GAAP, but less so at the time SSAP 9 was introduced, hence the detailed definition. The FRSME defines a construction contract as:

> A contract specifically negotiated for the construction of an asset or a combination of assets that are closely interrelated or interdependent in terms of their design, technology and function or their ultimate purpose or use.

This still deals with the main aspect of such contracts; that they are for the construction of one or more items for a particular customer and therefore should be considered differently from items constructed for future sale.

The accounting treatment required by the FRSME is also broadly similar to that required under SSAP 9.

15.3 ACCOUNTING TREATMENT

15.3.1 *Determining turnover*

SSAP 9 contains the general requirement that turnover should be recorded as the contract progresses, and not simply taken as a single sum at the contract's completion. The turnover recorded in any particular accounting period will then be the total attributable turnover to date, less any amounts which have already been recorded as turnover. Unfortunately, due to the very different industry practices, the guidance provided in the standard on the ascertainment of the amount of turnover is of little practical use:

> Companies should ascertain turnover in a manner appropriate to the stage of completion of the contracts, the businesses and the industries in which they operate. (Para. 8, SSAP 9.)

It is, presumably, the vagueness of the guidance provided in SSAP 9 that has led the ASB to include a section on the recognition of revenues under long-term contracts in Application Note G to FRS 5.

It is perhaps unfair to berate the ASC for the lack of guidance in SSAP 9, given that slightly more guidance is provided in Appendix 1 to the standard. The simplest case dealt with in SSAP 9 is where a contract is divided into separate identifiable parts:

> In some businesses, long-term contracts for the supply of services or manufacture and supply of goods exist where the prices are determined and invoiced according to separate parts of the contract. (Para. 22, Appendix 1, SSAP 9.)

In such cases, the turnover can easily be identified as each stage of the total contract is completed. Where this method can be applied, it is probably the best method available. However, this does not address the core problem. In such cases turnover and profit would be taken as each part of the contract is completed, even without the specific requirements of SSAP 9.

Another simple case is that of a 'cost-plus' contract, where the value of the contract is specified as the total cost incurred plus an agreed percentage. In such a case, turnover should be ascertained by adding the agreed percentage to the costs incurred to date. The costs used for the calculation should only be those costs that are recoverable. Other costs should be written off as incurred and not included when determining the level of turnover.

Unfortunately, the situation is often more complicated, and there is no obvious single method of ascertaining the amount of turnover that should be recorded. Until the issue of Application Note G to FRS 5, what had been required was that the method chosen should be:

- reasonable with regard to the nature of the contract;
- broadly in accordance with the methods which are generally adopted within that particular type of industry, and
- applied consistently both between different contracts and over time.

With the introduction of Application Note G to FRS 5 the situation was slightly clarified, and it was made clearer that turnover should be determined by reference to the stage of completion of the contract, which may or may not be directly related to the costs that have been incurred.

The first appendix to SSAP 9 states that the use of a valuation may be an appropriate method of determining the turnover to be recorded. Ideally, such a valuation should be undertaken by an independent surveyor, but there is no requirement for this in the standard or in the appendix. Application Note G stresses the importance of valuation, lending weight to the comments in Appendix 1 to SSAP 9. Application Note G, in the analysis section, but consistent with the section on required accounting, states:

> A seller should recognise turnover in respect of its performance under a long-term contract when, and to the extent that, it obtains the right to consideration. This should be derived from an assessment of the fair value of the goods or services provided to its reporting date as a proportion of the total fair value of the contract. In some contracts, this proportion will correspond with the proportion of expenditure incurred in comparison with total expenditure; however this will not always be the case. For all contracts, the guiding principle is to consider the stage of completion of the contractual obligations, which reflects the extent to which the seller has obtained the right to consideration (as defined in paragraph G3). As a result, different stages of contracts may vary in their relative profitability. (Para. G18, Application Note G to FRS 5.)

The application note goes on to state that the fair values used should normally represent those applicable at the inception of the contract. This will not apply where the contract terms specify that changes in prices will be passed on to the customer. (The right to consideration, referred to above, is basically defined as a seller's right to the amount received or receivable in exchange for its performance.)

Even since the introduction of Application Note G to FRS 5, there is still no single method by which turnover can be determined, although some methods that have been used in the past will no longer be acceptable, or may only be acceptable in more limited circumstances. Methods that continue to be acceptable are based on multiplying (i) an estimate of the percentage of completion by (ii) the agreed value of the contract. This gives a figure for cumulative turnover. The turnover shown in any particular accounting period will be the total attributable turnover to date, less amounts which have already been recorded in earlier accounting periods.

(1) A valuation by an independent surveyor should provide the relevant percentage of completion of the contract. This percentage should then be applied to the total expected value of the contract to give the total attributable turnover to date.

EXAMPLE

A surveyor estimates, at the end of 2010, that 60 per cent of a contract is complete. Thus, 60 per cent of the turnover should have been recorded at the year end. If the agreed value of the contract were £100,000, then £60,000 turnover should have been recorded in the company accounts. If £20,000 were recorded in the previous year, then £40,000 should be recorded in the 2010 accounts.

	End of year 2009	End of year 2010
Agreed value of contract £	100,000	100,000
Stage of completion	20%	60%
Turnover to date £	20,000	60,000
Turnover recorded for the year £	20,000	40,000

---

(2) Where the survey takes place shortly before the accounting reference date it may still be possible to use the amount certified, so long as the work undertaken in the intervening period is not material. Where the valuation has taken place considerably before the period end, the management of the company may need to make an adjustment to the amount to reflect the additional work performed. The valuation may also mention a level of retention, for the receipt of progress payments. This retention should be ignored in calculating the attributable turnover. This is made clear in Application Note G to FRS 5, which states that:

> ... This right does not necessarily correspond to amounts falling due in accordance with a schedule of stage payments which may be specified in a contractual arrangement. Whilst stage payments will often be timed to coincide with performance, they may not correspond exactly. Stage payments reflect only the agreed timing of payment, whereas a right to consideration arises through the seller's performance. (Para. G3, Application Note G to FRS 5.)

(3) In the absence of an independent surveyor's valuation, the management of the company should make their own estimate of the percentage of completion of the contract, and then apply this percentage to the contract value to arrive at the turnover. The mechanics of applying such a calculation are the same as those where a surveyor is used.

(4) The percentage of completion may also be estimated by considering the proportion of costs incurred to date. The estimate of turnover to date will then be:

$$\frac{\text{Costs to date}}{\text{Total expected costs}} \times \text{Total expected value of the contract}$$

However, this method needs to be applied with considerable caution. It has only ever been appropriate where the costs are incurred relatively evenly over the contract period and if there is a clear proportional relationship between the level of costs incurred to date and the degree of completion of the contract. If costs are not incurred evenly, for example, if there is a high initial outlay, then this method should not be used. This has been made even clearer by Application Note G to FRS 5, which states:

> '... The amount of turnover recognised should be derived from the proportion of costs incurred only where these provide evidence of the seller's performance and hence the extent to which it has obtained the right to consideration. (Para. G21, Application Note G to FRS 5.)'

(5) Where the formula in 3 above is not appropriate, it may be possible to amend the formula to provide a fairer reflection of progress, for example:

$$\frac{\text{Labour costs to date}}{\text{Total expected labour costs}} \times \text{Total expected value of the contract}$$

This would be appropriate where the labour cost is a fairer reflection of the contract's progress than the total costs. It is still subject to the conditions set out in Application Note G to FRS 5 and quoted above. This method may only be used where it is demonstrable that the labour costs provide a fair reflection of the progress of the contract. If this cannot be shown, then this method is not permissible.

Other methods may also be used, if none of the above provides a reasonable basis for calculating the appropriate amount of turnover.

It should be noted that there seems to have been some misunderstanding of the implications of SSAP 9, and, in particular, mistaking one way of determining revenue and profit for the general principle. Application Note G to FRS 5 was published together with comments on the development of the Application Note. These state:

> It was also suggested that the guidance in the Exposure Draft [which preceded Application Note G] could change existing practices as set out in SSAP 9, on the grounds that the Exposure Draft advocated a move away from measuring performance as the proportion of costs incurred to date in comparison with total expenditure.

> SSAP 9 does not require costs incurred to date to be used in measuring turnover in a long-term contract. Paragraph 9 notes that the profit taken up needs to reflect the proportion of work carried out at the accounting date. There will be contracts where costs incurred to date do reflect the work performed and in such circumstances it would be appropriate to use the proportion of costs incurred in comparison with total expenditure in measuring revenue; however, this will not always be the case. The incurrence of costs by a seller, does not, in itself, justify the recognition of revenue. The Application Note therefore re-emphasises that the key principle in recognising revenue is the seller's performance of its contractual obligations. (Paras. 31 and 32, The Development of the Application Note, Application Note G to FRS 5.)

The ASB were clearly not impressed.

It is also important to note that turnover should be allocated across the various accounting periods in which a contract is in progress, independently of the calculation of any attributable profit. In the early stages of a contract's completion it may be inappropriate to record any attributable profit, as the profitable outcome of the contract cannot be ascertained with sufficient certainty. This does not mean that turnover should not be recorded, it simply means that the transfer to cost of sales will equal the amount of turnover recorded.

Potential impact of the FRSME

The FRSME contains the same basic requirement in terms of recognising revenue in relation to construction contracts, but like SSAP 9 (even after the de facto amendments by FRS 5) is quite short on guidance as to how this might be determined. It mentions some of the same basic approaches that might be used in order to determine the progress of the contract.

15.3.2   Determining attributable profit

Normally, profit is not calculated directly. In most cases the turnover attributable to a transaction and the cost of sales are known. Profit is, in effect, the balancing figure. With long-term contracts such a procedure cannot always be applied. We need to calculate the turnover, which as we have seen is far more complex than with normal sales transactions. It has been common practice to calculate the profit attributable, leaving the transfer from costs incurred to cost of sales as the balancing figure. The costs incurred, which are not transferred, have been classified as the work in progress.

SSAP 9 implies that the procedure followed is the normal one:

> The procedure to recognise profit is to include an appropriate proportion of total contract value as turnover in the profit and loss account as the contract activity progresses. The costs incurred in reaching that stage of completion are matched with this turnover, resulting in the reporting of results that can be attributed to the proportion of work completed. (Para. 9, SSAP 9.)

Despite this, SSAP 9 provides no method by which costs to be treated as cost of sales could be calculated, but instead deals with the method of working out the attributable profit.

The situation has changed with the introduction of Application Note G to FRS 5, despite the fact that this note does not deal directly with the question of profit recognition. It does deal indirectly with the issue of profit recognition when it states, as already quoted above:

> As a result, different stages of contracts may vary in their relative profitability. (Para. G18, Application Note G to FRS 5.)

If this is the case, then methods which simply pro-rate total expected profits, however such pro-rating takes place, will not be acceptable.

SSAP 9 defines attributable profit as:

> That part of the total profit currently estimated to arise over the duration of the contract, after allowing for estimated remedial and maintenance costs and increases in costs so far as not recoverable under the terms of the contract, that fairly reflects the profit attributable to that part of the work performed at the accounting date. (There can be no attributable profit until the profitable outcome of the contract can be assessed with reasonable certainty.) (Para. 23, SSAP 9.)

SSAP 9 provides no more useful guidance on the determination of attributable profit than it does on the determination of turnover.

There are always two parts to the calculation of attributable profit:

- deciding when a profit can prudently be recorded, and
- once profit can be recorded, calculating the amount to be included.

The basic test for recording attributable profit is that it should only be recorded once the profitable outcome of the contract can be assessed with reasonable certainty. Appendix 1 to SSAP 9 includes the following:

> In determining whether the stage has been reached at which it is appropriate to recognise profit, account should be taken of the nature of the business concerned.

> It is necessary to define the earliest point for each particular contract before which no profit is taken up, the overriding principle being that there can be no attributable profit until the outcome of a contract can reasonably be foreseen. (Para. 24, Appendix 1, SSAP 9.)

This has not been affected by the issue of Application Note G to FRS 5.

Although a company should set criteria for assessing 'reasonable certainty' there will still inevitably be an element of subjectivity. A simple, and common, way of determining this point is to set a basic percentage of completion which is necessary before the profitable outcome is likely to be fairly certain. A figure of 30 per cent, or one-third, is often used. However, this must always be used solely as a rule of thumb, it should never be applied indiscriminately. Where a contract is approaching this level of completion, individual consideration must be given to the circumstances and a final decision reached.

The calculation of the total profit to be earned over the life of the contract must be made prudently. For example, it should take account of any expected increase in direct costs or overheads, and the possible costs of rectification or guarantee work. However, prudence should not be excessive, and companies must not deliberately understate their profits on contracts by making extreme assessments of future costs.

Once a company has decided that it can reasonably attribute some profit to the work undertaken to date, it then needs to calculate how much. The principles that should be applied are the same as those that are used for determining turnover:

- the method should be reasonable with regard to the nature of the contracts;
- the method should be broadly in accordance with the methods which are generally adopted within that particular type of industry, and
- the method must be applied consistently both between different contracts and over time.

However, there are also additional factors. The most important of these is that any known inequalities in the profitability of the contract over time should be taken into account. This has been stressed by Application Note G to FRS 5, which makes specific reference to uneven profitability.

The simplest cases are, again, where a contract can be divided into parts which are separately invoiced or where it is a cost-plus contract.

Where the parts of a project are separately invoiced then profit can be calculated by reference to each part. They can effectively be treated as separate projects.

In a cost-plus contract it is equally simple to determine profit; it is the addition to costs allowed under the contract.

In other cases, as with turnover, there are a number of methods that may be used to arrive at the attributable profit. Where possible, the method used for calculating the attributable profit should be consistent with the method used for calculating turnover. Since the method used to arrive at turnover is intended to provide a fair reflection of the progress of the contract it will often also provide a fair reflection of the profit earned.

Among possible methods of calculating attributable profit are:

1. $$\frac{\text{Surveyor's valuation}}{\text{Total expected value of the contract}} \times \text{Expected profit}$$

2. $$\frac{\text{Company valuation}}{\text{Total expected value of the contract}} \times \text{Expected profit}$$

3. $$\frac{\text{Costs to date}}{\text{Total expected costs}} \times \text{Expected profit}$$

4. $$\frac{\text{Labour costs to date}}{\text{Total expected labour costs}} \times \text{Expected profit}$$

These are, not surprisingly, very similar to the methods used in arriving at turnover. The problems with using costs or labour costs are the same, and again have been affected by the issue of Application Note G to FRS 5. Cost based methods of determining profit should not be used where it is not clearly demonstrable that costs do provide a fair reflection of the progress of the contract.

The following example illustrates the use of a surveyor's valuation to estimate sales and profit.

EXAMPLE

	End of year 1	*End of year 2*
Agreed value of contract £	100,000	100,000
Total estimated costs £	70,000	70,000
Total estimated profit £	30,000	30,000
Surveyor's valuation £	25,000	40,000
Percentage complete	25%	40%
Sales to date £	25,000	40,000
Sales recorded for the year £	25,000	15,000
Profit to date £	7,500	12,000
Profit recorded for the year £	7,500	4,500
Costs to date £	20,000	30,000
Costs written off to cost of goods sold, for the year £	17,500	10,500
Work in progress £	2,500	2,000

A company has a contract for an agreed sum of £100,000; the estimated costs are £70,000, leaving a profit of £30,000. Profit and sales are to be recognised as the contract progresses towards completion, based on a surveyor's assessment. It is not expected that the estimate of costs will change over the contract period.

At the end of the first year, a surveyor estimates that the contract is valued at £25,000 and is therefore 25 per cent complete. Therefore, sales of £25,000 and a profit of £7,500 (25 per cent of £30,000) will be recorded by the company. The costs written off to costs of goods sold will then need to be £17,500. Since the company has incurred costs of £20,000 on the project during the period, work in progress will be £2,500.

At the end of the second year, a surveyor estimates that the contract is valued at £40,000 and is, therefore, 40 per cent complete. The cumulative sales will be £40,000 and the cumulative profit will be £12,000 (40 per cent of £30,000). The sales for the period will be £15,000 (£40,000 − £25,000) and the profit for the period will be £4,500 (£12,000 − £7,500). The costs written off to costs of goods will then need to be £10,500. Since the company has incurred extra costs of £10,000 on the project during the second year (bringing the total costs to date to £30,000), work in progress will be reduced by £500 to £2,000.

However, in each case these calculations will give only a base figure, which may need to be amended. This arises because profits are often not generated evenly over the life of the contract, and this must be taken into account. For example, it may be known in advance that a project falls into two or more distinct parts where the level of expected profit differs. Where the profitability of the contract fluctuates considerably by reference to factors other than those which indicate the percentage of completion of the contract, then a formula reflecting these special factors should be used. Then there will be little connection between the profit formula and the turnover formula. The following example shows the treatment when costs and profit do not move together.

EXAMPLE		
	End of year 1	*End of year 2*
Agreed value of contract £	100,000	100,000
Total estimated costs £	70,000	70,000
Total estimated profit £	30,000	30,000
Surveyor's valuation £	20,000	36,000
Sales to date £	20,000	36,000
Sales recorded for the year £	20,000	16,000
Percentage complete	25%	40%
Costs to date £	17,500	28,000
Costs recorded for the year £	17,500	10,500
Profit to date £	6,000	10,800
Profit recorded for the year £	6,000	4,800
Work in progress £	3,500	2,800

A company has a contract for an agreed sum of £100,000; the estimated costs are £70,000, leaving a profit of £30,000. Profit and sales are to be recognised as the contract progresses towards completion, based on a surveyor's assessment; however, profits are not to be recognised in proportion to costs. It is not expected that the estimate of costs will change over the contract period.

At the end of the first year, the surveyor's valuation is £20,000 (20 per cent of the eventual value) even though 25 per cent of the costs have been incurred. The following items will be recognised in the company accounts:

Item	Amount £	Rationale
Sales	20,000	20% of 100,000
Profit	6,000	20% of 30,000
Costs	17,500	25% of 70,000
Split into:		
Cost of sales	14,000	
Work in progress	3,500	

Since profits are recognised later than costs, then £3,500 of the costs incurred are not charged to the profit and loss, but remain as work in progress.

At the end of the second year, the surveyor's valuation is £36,000 (36 per cent of the eventual value) even though 40 per cent of the costs have been incurred. The following items will be recognised in the company accounts:

Item	Amount £	Rationale
Sales to date	36,000	36% of 100,000
Sales already recognised	20,000	
Sales	16,000	
Profit to date	10,800	36% of 30,000
Profit already recognised	6,000	
Profit	4,800	

Item	Amount £	Rationale
Costs to date	28,000	40% of 70,000
Costs already recognised	17,500	
Costs	10,500	
Split into:		
Costs of sales	11,200	
Work in progress	(700)	

In the second year, the differential between the recognition of profit (36 per cent) and the incurring of costs (40 per cent) is smaller than in the first year. Therefore, £700 of the work in progress is transferred to the profit and loss account.

Uneven profits over the life of a contract are also generated when there are unexpected variations in cost, as shown in the following example.

EXAMPLE

	At the beginning	After 1 year	Potential, after 2 years at completion
Agreed value £	2,000,000	2,000,000	2,000,000
Percentage complete	0%	50%	100%
Costs to date £	0	850,000	1,700,000
Costs to completion £	1,500,000	800,000	0
Total expected costs	1,500,000	1,650,000	1,700,000
Total expected profit	500,000	350,000	300,000
Periodic profit after 1 year		175,000	
		or 150,000	

A company undertakes a project which lasts for two years. The total contract value is £2,000,000 and costs are expected to be £1,500,000. At the commencement of the project, the profit is expected to accrue evenly over the contract life.

After one year the project is 50 per cent complete. However, costs incurred are £850,000, and the estimate has been revised such that the costs to completion are now expected to be £800,000. The new estimated profit is, therefore, £350,000, and not £500,000 as originally anticipated.

Since the project is half complete it might be thought that half of the profit should be attributed, £175,000. However, this would not take account of the variation in profitability. The profit taken should perhaps be £150,000, since it might be anticipated that a further overrun of £50,000 will take place in the second year.

In practice, the profit taken might be even less than £150,000, since costs in the second year may rise even further, to beyond £850,000. Therefore, £150,000 should be the maximum profit recognised during the first year.

One of the basic intentions of SSAP 9 is to ensure that the profit recorded in each accounting period is a fair reflection of the activity in that period. In practice, this will often not be true for two main reasons.

(1)   The profit shown in each period will reflect changed expectations of the total profitability of the contract, which do not relate solely to the period in question. Some of the amounts used in calculating the attributable profit at

previous balance sheet dates may have been revised, and the effect of this revision will partly be recorded in the current year. The amounts involved should not normally be material, since no profit should be recorded unless the outcome of the contract can be foreseen with reasonable certainty.

(2) When profit is first taken on a contract it may include amounts attributable to earlier years. For example, a contract is intended to last for five years. After the first and second years it is considered that the outcome of the contract cannot be foreseen with sufficient certainty to allow profit to be recorded. In the third year, the profit can be reasonably estimated. The amount of profit recorded in the third year will include amounts which are strictly applicable to the previous two years, but which were not recorded in those years on the grounds of prudence.

Potential impact of the FRSME

The FRSME provides very little in the way of detail concerning the determination of profits over the life of a construction contract, simply noting that it should be recognised when the outcome of the contract can be estimated reliably. The basic approach, and indeed some of the specific guidance provided, is very similar to that included in SSAP 9.

15.3.3 Anticipated losses

The prudence concept is not symmetrical. Where a contract is expected to result in a profit then that profit should be allocated fairly over the periods in which the contract is in progress. Where a loss is expected then the rule in SSAP 9 is considerably different:

> If it is expected that there will be a loss on a contract as a whole, all of the loss should be recognised as soon as it is foreseen (in accordance with the prudence concept). (Para. 11, SSAP 9.)

SSAP 9 defines anticipated losses as:

> Losses which are currently estimated to arise over the duration of the contract (after allowing for estimated remedial and maintenance costs and increases in costs so far as not recoverable under the terms of the contract). This estimate is required irrespective of:
>
> (a) whether or not work has yet commenced on such contracts;
> (b) the proportion of work carried out at the accounting date;
> (c) the amount of profits expected to arise on other contracts. (Para. 24, SSAP 9.)

Where very substantial contracts are expected to result in a loss it may be necessary to include any administration overheads that will be incurred in the calculation of the loss. The total amount of the anticipated loss should be deducted from the work in progress figure. Where the loss is higher than the amount of work in progress then it should be shown separately as an accrual, either within creditors or under provisions for liabilities and charges.

Potential impact of the FRSME

The FRSME also requires that losses should be recognised immediately on a contract where it is probable that total contract costs will exceed total contract revenues.

15.4   DISCLOSURE

The disclosure requirements for long-term contracts are fully set out in SSAP 9:

Long-term contracts should be disclosed in the balance sheet as follows:

(a)   the amount by which recorded turnover is in excess of payments on account should be classified as "amounts recoverable on contracts" and separately disclosed within debtors;

(b)   the balance of payments on account (in excess of amounts (i) matched with turnover; and (ii) offset against long-term contract balances) should be classified as payments on account and separately disclosed within creditors;

(c)   the amount of long-term contracts, at costs incurred, net of amounts transferred to cost of sales, after deducting foreseeable losses and payments on account not matched with turnover, should be classified as "long-term contract balances" and separately disclosed within the balance sheet heading "stocks". The balance sheet note should disclose separately the balances of:

(i)   net costs less foreseeable losses; and

(ii)   applicable payments on account;

(d)   the amount by which the provision or accrual for the foreseeable losses exceeds the costs incurred (after transfers to cost of sales) should be included within either provisions for liabilities and charges or creditors as appropriate. (Para. 30, SSAP 9.)

In addition, a company should also disclose the policy it has used in arriving at the figures for turnover and attributable profit. This requirement is not stated in the FRSSE, but is implicit in the general requirement to disclose accounting policies.

Appendix 3 to SSAP 9 provides examples of the disclosure, and is worth reproducing in full.

	Project number					Balance sheet total	Profit & loss account
	1	**2**	**3**	**4**	**5**		
Recorded as turnover – being value of work done	145	520	380	200	55		1,300
Cumulative payments on account	(100)	(600)	(400)	(150)	(80)		
Classified as amounts recoverable on contracts	45			50		95DR	
Balance (excess) of payments on account		(80)	(20)		(25)		
Applied as an offset against long-term contract balances – see below		60	20		15		
Residue classified as payments on account		(20)	–		(10)	(30)CR	
Total costs incurred	110	510	450	250	100		
Transferred to cost of sales	(110)	(450)	(350)	(250)	(55)		(1,215)
	–	60	100	–	45		
Provision/accrual for foreseeable losses charged to cost of sales				(40)	(30)		(70)
		60	100		15		
Classified as provision/ accrual for losses				(40)		(40)CR	
Balance (excess) of payments on account applied as offset against long-term contract balances		(60)	(20)		(15)		
Classified as long-term contract balances		–	80		–	80DR	
Gross profit or loss on long-term contracts	35	70	30	(90)	(30)		15

Project 1

Profit and loss account – cumulative	£
Included in turnover	145
Included in cost of sales	(110)
Gross profit	35

Balance sheet

The amount to be included in debtors under 'amounts recoverable on contracts' is calculated as follows:

	£
Cumulative turnover	145
Less: cumulative payments on account	(100)
Included in debtors	45

In this case, all the costs incurred to date relate to the contract activity recorded as turnover and are transferred to cost of sales, leaving a zero balance in stocks.

NB If the outcome of the contract could not be assessed with reasonable certainty, no profit would be recognised. If no loss is expected, it may be appropriate to show as turnover a proportion of the total contract value using a zero estimate of profit.

Project 2

Profit and loss account – cumulative	£
Included in turnover	520
Included in cost of sales	(450)
Gross profit	70

Balance sheet

As cumulative payments on account are greater than turnover there is a credit balance, calculated as follows:

	£
Cumulative turnover	520
Less: cumulative payments on account	(600)
Excess payments on account	(80)

This credit balance should firstly be offset against any debit balance on this contract included in stocks and then any residual amount should be classified under creditors as a payment received on account as follows:

	£
Total cost incurred to date	510
Less: cumulative amounts recorded as cost of sales	(450)
	60
Less: excess payments on account (above)	(80)
Included in creditors	(20)

The amount to be included in stocks is zero and the credit balance of 20 is classified as a payment received on account and included in creditors.

The balance sheet note on stocks should disclose separately the net cost of 60 and the applicable payments on account of 60.

Project 3

	£
Profit and loss account – cumulative	
Included in turnover	380
Included in cost of sales	(350)
Gross profit	30

Balance sheet

As with Project 2, cumulative payments on account are greater than turnover and there is a credit balance calculated as follows:

	£
Cumulative turnover	380
Less: cumulative payments on account	(400)
Excess payment on account	(20)

This credit balance should firstly be offset against any debit balance on this contract included in stocks and the residual amount, if any, should be classified under creditors as a payment received on account.

The amount to be included in stocks under long-term contract balances is calculated as follows:

	£
Total costs incurred to date	450
Less: cumulative amounts recorded as cost of sales	(350)
	100
Less: excess payments on account (above)	20
Included in long-term contract balances	80

The balance sheet note on stocks should disclose separately the net cost of 100 and the applicable payments on account of 20.

Project 4

	£
Profit and loss account – cumulative	
Included in turnover	200
Included in cost of sales	(290)
Gross loss	(90)

Balance sheet

The amount to be included in debtors under 'amounts recoverable on contracts' is calculated as follows:

	£
Cumulative turnover	200
Less: cumulative payments on account	(150)
Included in debtors	50

The amount to be included as a provision/accrual for foreseeable losses is calculated as follows:

	£
Total costs incurred to date	250
Less: transferred to cost of sales	(250)
Foreseeable losses on contract as a whole	(40)
	(290)
Classified as provision/accrual for foreseeable losses	(40)

Note that the credit balance of 40 is not offset against the debit balance of 50 included in debtors.

Project 5

	£
Profit and loss account – cumulative	
Included in turnover	55
Included in cost of sales	(85)
Gross loss	(30)

Balance sheet

As cumulative payments on account are greater than turnover there is a credit balance, calculated as follows:

	£
Cumulative turnover	55
Less: cumulative payments on account	(80)
Excess payments on account	(25)

The credit balance should firstly be deducted from long-term contract balances (after having deducted foreseeable losses) and the residual balance included in creditors under payments received on account as follows:

	£
Total costs incurred to date	100
Less: transferred to costs of sales	(55)
Foreseeable losses on contract as a whole	(30)
	(85)
	15
Less: excess payments on account (above)	(25)
Included in creditors	(10)

The balance sheet note on stocks should disclose separately the net cost of 15 and the applicable payments on account of 15.

Potential impact of the FRSME

The FRSME does not contain disclosure requirements as extensive as those include in SSAP 9; it requires disclosure of only:

- the amount of contract revenue recognised as revenue in the period;
- the methods used to determine the contract revenue recognised in the period, and
- the methods used to determine the stage of completion of contracts in progress.

The FRSME also requires that companies present gross amounts due from customers, and gross amounts due to customers, separately as assets and liabilities.

15.5   PROPOSALS FOR CHANGE

As noted earlier, there is strictly a UK exposure draft, FRED 28, which proposes to replace the sections of SSAP 9 dealing with long-term contracts with a standard based on the equivalent international standard, IAS 11 *Construction Contracts*. In practice, and against the background of the ASB's proposals for UK GAAP, there is very little chance that such a standard will ever be issued.

At the international level, there are proposals to change the basis on which revenue is recognised. These proposals, whilst still be to be finalised, would appear to involve the deferral of both revenue and profit recognition from that which is under current UK and international practice. They do that by moving away from the percentage of completion approach that underlies both sets of standards and towards a method that relies more upon the extent to which items have been transferred to the ultimate customer under the contract. Given that performance of the work must necessarily precede delivery (or the transfer of rights) to the customer, this could, at best, result in amounts that are similar to those currently seen and, in many cases, would lead to later recognition of revenue and profits.

Even if the revenue proposals are adopted for international standards, it is not clear whether they would then also be reflected in the IFRS for SMEs and then ultimately in the FRSME.

16 LEASES AND HIRE PURCHASE CONTRACTS

16.1 INTRODUCTION

16.1.1 *The purchase and hire of assets*

When a company wishes to use a fixed asset in its business then it will sometimes buy that asset outright. There are a number of ways in which the business might pay for the asset.

The asset might be paid for out of cash resources that the business already holds. The asset might be paid for out of an agreed overdraft facility with the business's bankers. For substantial assets, in particular, the business might pay for the asset out of the proceeds of a loan to be secured on the asset or, alternatively, it might pay for the asset from the proceeds of an unsecured loan.

In all of these cases, even where the loan is secured on the asset, there is no major accounting problem. The asset will undoubtedly be treated as part of the fixed assets of the company, and the other side of the transaction will be recorded as a liability or as the reduction in the cash balance as appropriate.

The reason why no accounting problem arises is because the two relevant factors that might affect the accounting treatment are linked together in that the company has acquired:

- the legal title to the asset, and
- the benefits and risks of ownership.

In cases where these two primary elements of the use of an asset are split, or may appear to be split, the accounting treatment is much more complicated. For example, if one party has the benefits of ownership, but another party holds the legal title, in which party's balance sheet should the asset reside? This situation in which the two primary elements are split is dealt with in SSAP 21 *Accounting for Leases and Hire Purchase Contracts* and in the FRSSE.

SSAP 21 does not deal with:

> . . . lease contracts concerning the rights to explore for or to exploit natural resources such as oil, gas, timber, metals and other minerals. Nor does it apply to licensing agreements for items such as motion picture films, video recordings, plays, manuscripts, patents and copyrights. (Introduction, SSAP 21.)

16.1.2 Basic accounting treatment

Without considering the details and complications that are likely to be involved, the accounting treatment required by SSAP 21 is essentially that when one party has the use of an asset (the lessee) and another party has the legal title to the asset (the lessor) then:

- if the risks and rewards of ownership remain with the lessor (because, for example, the lessee is simply hiring the asset for some short period), then the lessor accounts for the asset as a fixed asset and records the income from hire, and the lessee records the hire payments – this case is known as an operating lease, and
- if the risks and rewards have been transferred to the lessee, then the lessee accounts for the asset as a fixed asset and the lessor accounts for the amount that will be received from the lessee – this case is known as a finance lease.

This principle, which underlies SSAP 21 and the FRSSE, is a clear example of the fundamental principle of substance over form, which is applied in more general terms by FRS 5, although FRS 5 tends to refer to risks and benefits rather than risks and rewards. In both cases the economic substance of the transaction is recorded, even though in one case this agrees with the legal form and in the other it does not. An important question in accounting for these transactions is to identify the economic substance of the agreement between the parties.

The principle underlying SSAP 21 does not meet with universal approval. In particular, it requires a decision to be made as to the party with whom the majority of risks and benefits lie. It is that party which then accounts for the underlying asset. Many would argue that this approach ignores the fact that all lease agreements involve a sharing of such items. This more nuanced approach is lost within SSAP 21, which takes an "all or nothing" approach. As a result, in December 1999, the ASB published a discussion paper, *Leases: Implementation of a New Approach*, which proposed that, in future, a single accounting treatment should apply to all leases. This would mean the abolition of the current 'all or nothing' approach to lease accounting. Instead, all leases would be capitalised. Since 1999, this project has moved on, albeit slowly, and the IASB has published both a discussion paper and an exposure draft, broadly along the lines of the 1999 paper, to change the international standard. Given the involvement of the ASB in the IASB project, they would presumably support the current proposals, in principle at least.

Potential impact of the FRSME

The requirements of the FRSME are based, ultimately, on IAS 17, the international standard dealing with leases. There are differences in the detail between the requirements in the FRSME and SSAP 21, but the principles are the same, and in particular there is a distinction between finance and operating leases even though the tests are not quite the same.

The differences between SSAP 21 and both IAS 17 and the IFRS for SMEs are dealt with at **16.2.4**. Given that the FRSME is effectively a UK version of the IFRS for SMEs, the same differences apply.

16.2 IDENTIFYING THE NATURE OF THE AGREEMENT

16.2.1 Leases and hire purchase contracts

SSAP 21 deals with three types of arrangement:

- hire purchase contracts;
- finance leases, and
- operating leases.

Hire purchase contracts are usually the easiest to identify, and it is perhaps for this reason that the standard says least about them.

Leases, taken as a whole, are also usually easy to identify, although SSAP 21 does provide a definition:

> ... a contract between a lessor and a lessee for the hire of a specific asset. The lessor retains ownership of the asset but conveys the right to the use of the asset to the lessee for an agreed period of time in return for the payment of specified rentals. (Para. 14, SSAP 21.)

Taken literally, this is an extremely poor definition, since the first part is circular. A lease is defined in terms of a contract between a lessee and a lessor, but there are lessees and lessors only where there are leases. However, this should not give rise to major practical problems. It is perhaps worth noting that a 'lease' need not use that term in its title. For example, in the shipping industry a bare-boat charter will often fall within the definition of a lease.

The more difficult problem is that of defining the division between an operating and a finance lease. SSAP 21 states, with an element of optimism:

> Leases can appropriately be classified into finance leases and operating leases. The distinction between a finance lease and an operating lease will usually be evident from the terms of the contract between the lessor and the lessee. (Para. 6, SSAP 21.)

While this may be evident from the conditions included in the lease, it is not always obvious. Two very simple extreme examples will indicate the basic difference between the two types of arrangement.

(1) A company hires an asset for a period of one year, paying a rental of £1,500. The asset would normally be expected to be in use for a period of approximately ten years, and has a capital cost of £8,000. It is clear that the

risks and rewards of ownership lie with the lessor. It is primarily a hiring arrangement and not a financing arrangement.

(2) A company hires an asset for ten years, paying an annual rental of £1,300. The asset would normally be expected to be in use for ten years, the capital cost of the asset is £10,000, and market interest rates are approximately six per cent. It is clear that the risks and rewards of ownership have been transferred in this case. In effect, the lessee is paying the whole of the capital cost of the asset and will retain its use for the whole of its useful economic life. This is a finance lease.

However, in practice the situation is rarely so simple.

16.2.2 Operating leases

The definition of an operating lease in SSAP 21 (and the FRSSE) is wholly dependent upon the definition of a finance lease:

> An operating lease is a lease other than a finance lease. (Para. 17, SSAP 21.)

Slightly more useful guidance is provided in the introductory notes to the standard:

> An operating lease involves the lessee paying a rental for the hire of an asset for a period of time which is normally substantially less than its useful economic life. The lessor retains most of the risks and rewards of ownership of an asset in the case of an operating lease. (Para. 7, SSAP 21.)

Nonetheless, this is still a somewhat negative definition. Therefore, it is still necessary to identify an operating lease by first applying the test to determine whether it is a finance lease.

16.2.3 Finance leases

SSAP 21 provides the following definition of a finance lease:

> A finance lease is a lease that transfers substantially all the risks and rewards of ownership of an asset to the lessee. It should be presumed that such a transfer of risks and rewards occurs if at the inception of a lease the present value of the minimum lease payments including any initial payment, amounts to substantially all (normally 90 per cent or more) of the fair value of the leased asset. The present value should be calculated by using the interest rate implicit in the lease ... If the fair value of the asset is not determinable, an estimate thereof should be used.

> Notwithstanding the fact that a lease meets the above conditions, the presumption that it should be classified as a finance lease may in exceptional circumstances be rebutted if it can be clearly demonstrated that the lease in question does not transfer substantially all the risks and rewards of ownership (other than legal title) to the lessee. Correspondingly, the presumption that a lease which fails to meet the conditions [above] is not a finance lease may in exceptional circumstances be rebutted. (Paras. 15 and 16, SSAP 21.)

The first part of this definition is included in the FRSSE.

In using this definition, two of the terms, namely the minimum lease payments and the implicit interest rate, must then be further defined. The minimum lease payments are:

> ... the minimum payments over the remaining part of the lease term (excluding charges for services and taxes to be paid by the lessor) and:
>
> (a) in the case of the lessee, any residual amounts guaranteed by him or by a party related to him; or
>
> (b) in the case of the lessor, any residual amounts guaranteed by the lessee or by an independent third party. (Para. 20, SSAP 21.)

It is important to note that the definition of minimum lease payments is slightly different for the lessee and the lessor. This means that there may be cases in which the two parties are considering the same lease, but are taking into account a different pattern of cash flows. The result of this is that it is possible for the same lease to be treated as an operating lease by one party, but as a finance lease by the other, even where the same information is available to both parties.

The implicit interest rate is defined as follows:

> The interest rate implicit in a lease is the discount rate that at the inception of a lease, when applied to the amounts which the lessor expects to receive and retain produces an amount (the present value) equal to the fair value of the leased asset. The amounts which the lessor expects to receive and retain comprise (a) the minimum lease payments to the lessor ... plus (b) any unguaranteed residual value, less (c) any part of (a) and (b) for which the lessor will be accountable to the lessee. If the interest rate implicit in the lease is not determinable, it should be estimated by reference to the rate which a lessee would be expected to pay on a similar lease. (Para. 24, SSAP 21.)

This definition is not included in the FRSSE.

The introductory notes to SSAP 21 stress that the difference between an operating and a finance lease is solely one of degree, not of fundamental difference. As it points out, all leases transfer some of the risks and rewards of ownership; the problem is then, when does 'some' become 'substantially all'?

SSAP 21 stresses that, like all accounting standards, it applies only to material items. Therefore, in some cases, companies may not need to determine whether a lease is a finance lease and can take the simpler option of assuming that it is an operating lease. However, the effect of materiality, in moving the accounting treatment towards an operating lease, is not as great as might be imagined. This arises because materiality issues should be considered in the context of both the profit and loss account and the balance sheet.

For example, if materiality were only considered by looking at the effect on the profit and loss account, then this might mean that many companies could treat leases as operating leases; the difference between the annual rental charge, and the charge if treated as a finance lease, may not be large. However, the balance sheet effect must also be considered, since the inclusion of the capital value of an asset (and the associated liability) may have a significant effect on the view given by the balance sheet.

Once a lease has been determined to be material, it is then necessary to determine if all or substantially all of the risks and rewards of ownership have been transferred. This will classify an agreement as either an operating lease or a finance lease.

Unfortunately, the standard manages to convey the impression that the '90 per cent test' is the key rule and that it is this rule which can be broken only in exceptional circumstances. This impression is not helped by the imprecise way in which the characteristics of a finance lease are stated. In practice, it has been common to interpret these conditions somewhat mechanistically as relating to the figure of 90 per cent. As the ICAEW has noted:

> Some leases are therefore arranged so that the minimum lease payments are fractionally below 90% of the fair value, say 88% or 89%, yet in commercial reality substantially all the risks and rewards of ownership have passed to the lessee. The 90% test is then used by the lessee to justify classification as an operating lease and thus exclusion from the balance sheet of both the asset and related finance. (Para. 21, FRAG 9/92.)

There is a certain irony in the fact that a standard based on the fundamental principle of substance over form has historically been interpreted in a way best described as 'legalistic'.

However, this requirement should be interpreted within the overall context of substance over form, a position strengthened by the arguments of FRS 5. The primary test for a finance lease should be that the present value of the minimum lease payments amounts to substantially all of the fair value of the leased asset. Although this may be guided by and implemented using the 90 per cent rule, it is simply a rule of thumb, and not the primary test itself. More importantly, deviations from this rule of thumb should not be interpreted as exceptions; these exceptions should relate to the primary test of whether substantially all the risks and rewards of ownership are transferred.

16.2.4 International Accounting Standard 17 and the IFRS for SMEs

IAS 17 provides an interesting contrast to the approach to classification adopted in SSAP 21. Both standards define a finance lease in terms of the passing of the risks and rewards of ownership. IAS 17, however, makes no reference to particular percentages of the fair value being included in the minimum lease payments. Instead, IAS 17 provides examples of situations which would normally lead to a lease (or hire purchase) being classified as a finance lease:

(a)   the lease transfers ownership of the asset to the lessee by the end of the lease term;

(b)   the lessee has the option to purchase the asset at a price that is expected to be sufficiently lower than the fair value at the date the option becomes exercisable for it to be reasonably certain, at the inception of the lease, that the option will be exercised;

(c)   the lease term is for the major part of the economic life of the asset even if title is not transferred;

(d)   at the inception of the lease the present value of the minimum lease payments amounts to at least substantially all of the fair value of the leased asset; and

(e)   the leased assets are of such a specialised nature such that only the lessee can use them without major modifications.. (Para. 10, IAS 17.)

IAS 17 also provides other indicators of situations which individually or in combination could also lead to a lease being classified as a finance lease:

(a)   if the lessee can cancel the lease, the lessor's losses associated with the cancellation are borne by the lessee;

(b)   gains or losses from the fluctuation in the fair value of the residual accrue to the lessee (for example, in the form of a rent rebate equalling most of the sales proceeds at the end of the lease); and

(c)   the lessee has the ability to continue the lease for a secondary period at a rent that is substantially lower than market rent. (Para. 11, IAS 17.)

The approach to lease classification set out in IAS 17 avoids the key weakness of the SSAP 21 approach, ie excessive reliance on the '90 per cent test'. In this respect, the IAS more closely reflects the application of the concept of substance over form than SSAP 21 does.

The likely impact of the differences is that some leases treated as operating leases under SSAP 21 may become finance leases under IAS 17. Apart from simply changing the financial statements this could cause problems for companies with, for example, covenants in loan contracts referring to maximum levels of borrowings. In particular, the fact that a lease will normally be classified as a finance lease where the lease term is for the major part of the economic life of the assets may make a substantial difference in the classification of leases between the two standards.

The IFRS for SMEs uses precisely the same tests for lease classification as IAS 17, although with less discussion around the conditions.

Potential impact of the FRSME

As noted above, the FRSME is based on the IFRS for SMEs. As a result, the differences noted also apply in relation to SSAP 21 and the FRSME.

16.2.5 Applying the '90 per cent test'

Having already argued that total reliance should not be placed on the 90 per cent threshold and that, therefore, there is no such test, it will, nonetheless, be assumed for all of the following examples that it does provide a fair reflection of the allocation of risks and rewards .

In order to be able to calculate the present value of the minimum lease payments we first need to define some of the terms.

The lease term is:

> ... the period for which the lessee has contracted to lease the asset and any further terms for which the lessee has the option to continue to lease the asset, with or without further payment, which option it is reasonably certain at the inception of the lease that the lessee will exercise. (Para. 19, SSAP 21.)

The contractual term of the lease is often referred to as the primary term, and any further period during which the lessee has the right to continue to lease the asset as the secondary term.

In determining whether the lessee is likely to proceed with the lease in the secondary term, a number of factors must be considered. The main consideration is likely to be the cost of the lease at the time. If the secondary term rental is estimated to be at the market rate at the time it becomes payable, then one cannot normally assume that it is reasonably certain that the lease will continue. Where the secondary lease charge is below estimated market rates then it is more likely that the lease will continue.

However, the purpose to which the leased asset is to be put must also be considered. If an asset is leased for a specific project, and the primary lease term is equal to the life of that project, then it is unlikely that the lease will be extended even at rates below market rates. The situation might differ if the lessee was allowed also to act as lessor to a third party during this secondary period, and considered that this might be profitable.

Fair value is also defined by the standard as:

> ... the price at which an asset could be exchanged in an arm's length transaction less, where applicable, any grants receivable towards the purchase or use of the asset. (Para. 25, SSAP 21.)

The fair value is normally a simple matter for the lessor to calculate, as it will often be the cost, but the lessee may need to estimate the fair value.

The date of the inception of a lease may also be an important consideration, and is defined as:

> ... the earlier of the time the asset is brought into use and the date from which rentals first accrue. (Para. 29, SSAP 21.)

The date of inception is not necessarily the same as the date on which the lease agreement is signed.

The unguaranteed residual value must also be taken into account:

> Unguaranteed residual value is that portion of the residual value of the leased asset (estimated at the inception of the lease), the realisation of which by the lessor is not assured or is guaranteed solely by a party related to the lessor. (Para. 26, SSAP 21.)

It is worth noting that in some cases it may not be necessary to estimate the residual value at the end of the lease term, and then to discount this figure. This is possible because the procedure for the estimation of the final residual value (which takes place at the inception of the lease) uses the predicted future prices at the end of the lease term. As long as there is no reason to expect a major change in the market, the current value of an asset of equivalent age to that of the asset at the end of the lease term should be a suitable estimate of the present value of the expected residual value.

It is now possible to consider some examples of the application of the 90 per cent test.

EXAMPLE

Company A (the lessee) leases an asset from company B (the lessor). The following details of the transaction are relevant:

- the cost of the asset to company B was £50,000; this is the market price and is also known to company A;
- company A is to pay company B an annual rental, payable in advance, of £7,500 for 10 years, and
- at the end of the lease term company B expects the asset to have a value of £15,000, but none of that amount has been guaranteed.

We first need to calculate the implicit interest rate in the lease. The interest rate is 13.2245 per cent. This is the rate at which the present value of all the payments to the lessor plus the discounted residual value is equal to the value of the asset.

Time	Discount factor £	Payments £	Residual value £	Present value of payments £	Present value of residual £	Total £
0	1.000	7,500		7,500		7,500
1	0.883	7,500		6,624		6,624
2	0.780	7,500		5,850		5,850
3	0.689	7,500		5,167		5,167
4	0.608	7,500		4,564		4,564
5	0.537	7,500		4,031		4,031
6	0.475	7,500		3,560		3,560
7	0.419	7,500		3,144		3,144
8	0.370	7,500		2,777		2,777

Time	Discount factor £	Payments £	Residual value £	Present value of payments £	Present value of residual £	Total £
9	0.327	7,500		2,451		2,451
10	0.289		15,000		4,332	4,332
				45,668	4,332	50,000

Implied interest rate is 13.2245%

Ratio of lease payments to fair value 91.336%

Note: Since the rental is payable in advance, the payments are made at the beginning of each period; therefore, the first payment is not discounted.

As common sense would suggest, the meaning of the implied interest rate is the rate of interest being paid to the lessor. This is why the rate can also be seen as one which equates the present value of what the lessee is paying (£45,668) and the present value of the net cost to the lessor (£50,000 − £4,332).

From this table it is also possible to determine whether the lease is a finance lease. The ratio of the minimum lease payments (£45,668) to the fair value of the leased asset (£50,000) is:

45,668/50,000 = 91.33%.

Judging by the 90 per cent test, it looks as if substantially all the risk and rewards of ownership have been transferred to the lessee. Therefore, the agreement should be treated as a finance lease.

The next example shows how the same lease can be treated as a finance lease by one party and an operating lease by the other.

EXAMPLE

Company A (the lessee) leases an asset from company B (the lessor). The following details of the transaction are relevant:

- the cost of the asset to company B was £50,000; this is the market price and is also known to company A;
- company A is to pay company B an annual rental, payable in advance, of £6,500 for 10 years;
- the residual value is estimated to be £20,000 and the manufacturer of the asset, who is unconnected with company A, has guaranteed £10,000 of this.

This gives an interest rate implicit in the lease of 10.773 per cent. The cash flow plan below distinguishes between the guaranteed and the unguaranteed parts of the residual value.

Time	Discount factor £	Payments £	Residual value £	Present value of payments £	Present value of residual £	Total £
0	1.000	6,500		6,500		6,500
1	0.903	6,500		5,868		5,868
2	0.815	6,500		5,297		5,297

Time	Discount factor £	Payments £	Residual value £	Present value of payments £	Present value of residual £	Total £
3	0.736	6,500		4,782		4,782
4	0.664	6,500		4,317		4,317
5	0.600	6,500		3,897		3,897
6	0.541	6,500		3,518		3,518
7	0.489	6,500		3,176		3,176
8	0.441	6,500		2,867		2,867
9	0.398	6,500		2,588		2,588
10	0.359		10,000[1]		3,595	3,595
10	0.359		10,000[2]		3,595	3,595
				42,810	7,190	50,000

[1] Guaranteed
[2] Not guaranteed

Implied interest rate is	10.773%
Ratio of lessee's payments to fair value	85.62%
Ratio of lessor's receipts to fair value	92.81%

From the viewpoint of the lessee, the minimum lease payments are £42,810; since this is 85.62 per cent of the fair value of £50,000, the 90 per cent rule would suggest that the agreement should be classified as an operating lease.

However, from the lessor's viewpoint, the payments to be received should include the guaranteed residual value of £10,000. The payments received by the lessor are £46,405, and this is 92.81 per cent of the fair value. The 90 per cent rule would indicate that the agreement should be classified as a finance lease.

The reason for this difference is that the lessee has not guaranteed any part of the residual value and, therefore, there is a difference between the payments by the lessee and the payments received by the lessor.

It might be argued that the results in the above example are the product of too much reliance being placed on the 90 per cent test, better described as a rule of thumb. Nevertheless, the example does illustrate the different perspectives of lessor and lessee which can arise, even when judged by the 'transfer of substantial risks and rewards' criterion.

In addition, it is worth noting that the same information may not be available to both parties to the transaction. In the above examples, it is assumed that the lessee has access to the market price of the asset. If, however, this has to be estimated by the lessee, a different classification may be made to that made by the lessor. As noted above, where there is a guaranteed residual value but the guarantee is provided by a party other than the lessee, then there may be an appropriate difference in classification between the two parties. The lessee might consider a lease to be an operating lease, quite correctly, whilst the lessor might consider it to be a finance lease, equally correctly. Where there is no such guaranteed residual then, in principle, the classification should be the same between the two parties. In practice, this may not always occur if the lessee uses a different estimate of the residual value, or if the lessee has to estimate the cost.

16.2.6   Hire purchase contracts

Hire purchase contracts are defined in the following terms in SSAP 21:

> A *hire purchase contract* is a contract for the hire of an asset which contains a provision giving the hirer an option to acquire legal title to the asset upon the fulfilment of certain conditions stated in the contract. (Para. 18, SSAP 21.)

Since hire purchase contracts have obvious similarities with leases they are treated by the standard in almost the same way.

> Those hire purchase contracts which are of a financing nature should be accounted for on a basis similar to that set out below for finance leases. Conversely, other hire purchase contracts should be accounted for on a basis similar to that set out below for operating leases. (Para. 31, SSAP 21.)

However, there are potentially important distinctions, and these will be covered when dealing with finance leases.

16.3   ACCOUNTING FOR OPERATING LEASES

16.3.1   Basic treatment

We have already established that an operating lease is, effectively, the hire of an asset for a certain period of time in return for rental payments. The accounting treatment mirrors this underlying position.

16.3.2   Lessees

Lessees should charge the rentals under an operating lease on a straight-line basis over the term of the lease. SSAP 21 also states that another method of spreading the total charge may be used if the basis is systematic and rational, and more appropriate in the circumstances. Unfortunately, SSAP 21 provides no guidance on when this might be, or on which methods might be acceptable.

It might be tempting to think that the closest analogy is with fixed assets and that, therefore, other acceptable methods might be similar to the common methods of depreciation, such as reducing balance or sum of the digits. However, by definition an operating lease is not a fixed asset of the business, and the parallel should not be followed too closely. Nonetheless, where a company can show that another method of allocating the payments would be preferable to the straight-line method it is entitled to use it.

Lessees should also disclose the following.

(1)   The total of operating lease rentals charged in the profit and loss account, divided between the hire of plant and machinery and the hire of other

assets (this is no longer a statutory requirement, but continues to be included in SSAP 21).

(2)   The accounting policy adopted for dealing with operating leases.

(3)   The amounts which the company must pay in respect of operating leases in the next year, analysed between leases expiring within one year, in the second to fifth years inclusive, and after more than five years, and divided between amounts in respect of land and buildings and other operating leases.

For companies adopting the FRSSE, the above disclosures are simplified. Disclosure 1 is not required and for disclosure 3 no analysis is required between leases in respect of land and buildings and other leases.

An example of this disclosure is given below.

EXAMPLE

At 31 December 2011 the company had annual commitments under non-cancellable operating leases as set out below.

	2011		2010	
	Land and buildings *£000*	*Other* *£000*	*Land and buildings* *£000*	*Other* *£000*
Operating leases which expire:				
within one year	30	100	25	90
within two to five years inclusive	80	50	75	40
in over five years	20	20	110	10
	130	170	210	140

16.3.3   Lessors

Assets held for use in operating leases should be carried in the balance sheet of the lessor and depreciated over their useful economic lives.

Rental income from operating leases, excluding charges made for additional services such as insurance or maintenance, should be recognised on a straight-line basis over the period of the lease, even if rental payments are not received on this basis. However, SSAP 21 also allows another basis to be used if it provides a better reflection of the benefit from the leased asset.

In this case it would be fair to assume that a company should be allowed to recognise income on a basis that is consistent with the method used for depreciation of the fixed asset, since this will provide the best matching of costs and income. However, this is not required by the standard.

Any initial direct costs incurred in setting up a lease arrangement may be apportioned over the period of the lease on a systematic and rational basis. This basis should be the same as that used for the recognition of income.

Lessors should disclose:

- the gross amount of assets held for use in operating leases, and the accumulated depreciation;
- the accounting policy adopted for operating leases, and
- the aggregate rentals receivable in an accounting period in respect of operating lease rentals.

The last of these disclosures is not required for companies complying with the FRSSE.

16.3.4   Operating lease incentives

In February 2001, the ASB issued UITF Abstract 28 *Operating lease incentives*. This has been mandatory since accounting periods ending on or after 22 September 2001 and superseded Abstract 12 *Lessee accounting for reverse lease premiums and similar incentives*. Abstract 28 made no major changes to accounting requirements for lessees, the main impact being to extend the requirements to accounting by lessors.

The central requirement is that all incentives for the agreement of a new or renewed operating lease should be recognised as an integral part of the net payment agreed for the use of the leased asset, irrespective of the incentive's nature or form or the timing of payments.

This means that the lease rentals, net of any incentive, should be recognised as rental expenses by lessees and rental income by lessors over the period of the leases or, if appropriate, the period to the next rent review. A straight-line basis should be used unless another systematic basis is more representative of the time pattern of benefits under the lease.

For example, a company enters into a five-year lease, with no rent review over the period. There is no payment in the first year, but the annual lease payments thereafter are £10,000. The total cost over the period of the lease is £40,000. As the lease is for five years, this gives rise to an annual charge of £8,000. A liability is recorded in respect of this amount, which then reduces over the next four years, to zero, as the charges continue to be £8,000 per annum while the payments are £10,000.

16.4 ACCOUNTING FOR FINANCE LEASES BY LESSEES

16.4.1 *Initial recording*

The basic principle for accounting for finance leases by lessees is that they should record the asset in the balance sheet, as well as the corresponding liability. More strictly, what are being recorded are:

- the rights over the asset, rather than the underlying asset itself, and
- the discounted value of the future rental payments.

When the lease commences, the lessee should record the present value of the minimum lease payments as both an asset and a liability, calculated using the interest rate which is implicit in the lease. Companies complying with the FRSSE should use the fair value of the asset, unless this is clearly out of line with the lease payments.

In practice, SSAP 21 also often allows the company to use the fair value of the asset, stating that this will often be a sufficiently close approximation to the present value of the minimum lease payments, and, as noted above, small companies can nearly always use this amount. By definition, the present value of the minimum lease payments will normally be at least 90 per cent or more of the fair value (subject to the fact that the 90 per cent rule should not be seen as the only matter to be considered).

However, there is an exception to the general rule that a company can use either the fair value of the asset or the present value of the minimum lease payments. This arises when the cost to the lessor and therefore to the lessee is substantially below the fair value:

> The combined benefit to a lessor of regional development and other grants together with capital allowances, which reduce tax liabilities, may enable the minimum lease payments under a finance lease to be reduced to a total which is less than the fair value of the asset. In these circumstances, the amount to be capitalised and depreciated should be restricted to the minimum lease payments. A negative finance charge should not be shown. (Para. 34, SSAP 21.)

It should be noted that in this case it is the actual amount of the minimum lease payments that is referred to, and not their present value. Where this provision is used, the lessee will capitalise the actual amount of the minimum lease payments, and reduce the outstanding balance by the amounts paid. There will be no finance charge. The only charges recorded in the profit and loss account of the lessee will be the amount of the depreciation of the asset.

16.4.2   Depreciation

Once the asset has been recorded in the balance sheet it must be depreciated. SSAP 21 provides no detail of the depreciation methods to be used, but they should be the same as the methods used for similar assets which are owned by the company.

However, SSAP 21 does state how the period for depreciation should be calculated.

> An asset held under a finance lease should be depreciated over the shorter of the lease term and the useful economic life of the asset. However, in the case of a hire purchase contract which has the characteristics of a finance lease, the asset should be depreciated over its useful life. (Para. 36, SSAP 21.)

This reflects the fact that, under a hire purchase contract, title to the asset will pass at the end of the contract term. There is no need to limit the depreciation period to reflect any risk that the benefit of the assets will cease to accrue to the company.

16.4.3   Allocation of finance charges

When the leased asset is acquired by the company, both sides of the balance sheet will reflect the present value of the rental payments. With most business expenses incurred during the period, the payments are shown as a reduction in assets and also as a reduction in the owners' equity (through the charge to the profit and loss account). With rental payments, the situation is slightly different because the present value of the liability is decreased by the rental payments. Therefore, instead of the full rental payment being charged to the profit and loss account, some of this is treated as a repayment of the liability, and the remaining amount is treated as a financing item which is charged to the profit and loss account.

SSAP 21 provides the following guidance on the allocation of finance charges under the lease:

> Rentals payable should be apportioned between the finance charge and a reduction of the outstanding obligation for future amounts payable. The total finance charge under a finance lease should be allocated to accounting periods during the lease term so as to produce a constant periodic rate of charge on the remaining balance of the obligation for each accounting period, or a reasonable approximation thereto. (Para. 35, SSAP 21.)

The strict method of allocation is known as the actuarial method, but at least two other methods are also acceptable. The sum of the digits method will often produce results that are fairly close to the actuarial method, and would thus fall within the definition of a reasonable approximation. The straight-line method is theoretically weak, but as the Guidance Notes issued with SSAP 21 state:

... it may be appropriate in certain cases to use the straight-line method. This is the simplest of the methods illustrated. It does not attempt to produce a constant periodic rate of change, but if used in connection with a relatively small lease it may produce figures which in any year are not significantly different from those which would be produced by one of the other methods. What is a small lease will depend on the size of the company. (Para. 32, Guidance Notes to SSAP 21.)

This is an example of the application of materiality to the area of leases. Where the effect will be minor, it is acceptable to use a very rough allocation of the finance charges to each accounting period. The FRSSE reiterates that the straight-line method will often be acceptable.

The basic example below will be used to illustrate the use of each of these methods.

EXAMPLE

A company leases an asset. The lease commences on the first day of the company's accounting year. The fair value of the asset (which is equal to the present value of the minimum lease payments) is £25,000. The lease agreement specifies that there are 20 quarterly payments, in advance, of £1,600 each. There is no residual value.

(1) The *implicit interest rate method* is that which discounts the 20 payments of £1,600 to the fair value of £25,000: this is 2.766 per cent per quarter. At the beginning of the lease, the liability is £25,000, but this is decreased at the same time by the first payment of £1,600. At the end of the quarter, the interest on the balance of £23,400 at 2.766 per cent amounts to £647; this is then added to the liability to be carried forward to the next period.

The total interest paid over the period of the lease is £7,000, and this is also equal to the total payments of £32,000 less the value of the asset employed, £25,000.

The finance charge for each year is then simply the sum of the finance charges for each of the four quarters in the year; this is charged to the profit and loss account. However, note that since payments are made in advance, there will be no interest charge in respect of the final period of the lease, as final payment will have been made at the beginning of that period. In the final year the finance charge will be (126 + 85 + 43) = £254.

Quarter	Liability at beginning of quarter (capital b/f) £	Payment at beginning of quarter £	Interest accrued on liability during quarter @ 2.766% £	Liability at end of quarter (capital c/f) £
1	25,000	(1,600)	647	24,047
2	24,047	(1,600)	621	23,068
3	23,068	(1,600)	594	22,062
4	22,062	(1,600)	566	21,028
5	21,028	(1,600)	537	19,965
6	19,965	(1,600)	508	18,873
7	18,873	(1,600)	478	17,751
8	17,751	(1,600)	447	16,598
9	16,598	(1,600)	415	15,413
10	15,413	(1,600)	382	14,195
11	14,195	(1,600)	348	12,943

Quarter	Liability at beginning of quarter (capital b/f) £	Payment at beginning of quarter £	Interest accrued on liability during quarter @ 2.766% £	Liability at end of quarter (capital c/f) £
12	12,943	(1,600)	314	11,657
13	11,657	(1,600)	278	10,335
14	10,335	(1,600)	242	8,977
15	8,977	(1,600)	204	7,581
16	7,581	(1,600)	165	6,146
17	6,146	(1,600)	126	4,672
18	4,672	(1,600)	85	3,157
19	3,157	(1,600)	43	1,600
20	1,600	(1,600)	0	0
		(32,000)	7,000	

The reduction in the liability in the balance sheet will be the total payments made, less the finance charges, as shown in the calculations. The liability at the end of each financial year will be:

	£
Year 1	21,028
Year 2	16,598
Year 3	11,657
Year 4	6,146
Year 5	0

(2) The *sum of the digits method* is an approximation to the (actuarial) implicit interest rate method. We first need to identify the number of lease payment periods (n), defined as the number of periods between the beginning of the lease and the last payment; it is the number of periods over which interest accrues. In this example, the number of periods is 19, since payments are made in advance. Of course, if payments were made in arrears there would be 20 lease payment periods.

Using the value of $n = 19$ in the formula

$$\frac{n(n + 1)}{2}$$

gives a value of 190, which is the denominator in the allocation of the finance charge of £7,000 over the life of the lease. Each of the 19 values is then used as the numerator in the calculations, from 19 down to 1. The finance charges which arise from this method are as follows.

Quarter	Liability at beginning of quarter (capital b/f) £	Payment at beginning of quarter £	Formula for interest accrued (sum of digits)	Interest on liability accrued during qtr £	Liability at end of quarter (capital c/f) £
1	25,000	(1,600)	(19/190) × 7,000 =	700	24,100
2	24,100	(1,600)	(18/190) × 7,000 =	663	23,163
3	23,163	(1,600)	(17/190) × 7,000 =	626	22,189
4	22,189	(1,600)	(16/190) × 7,000 =	590	21,179
5	21,179	(1,600)	(15/190) × 7,000 =	553	20,132
6	20,132	(1,600)	(14/190) × 7,000 =	516	19,048
7	19,048	(1,600)	(13/190) × 7,000 =	479	17,927

Quarter	Liability at beginning of quarter (capital b/f) £	Payment at beginning of quarter £	Formula for interest accrued (sum of digits)	Interest on liability accrued during qtr £	Liability at end of quarter (capital c/f) £
8	17,927	(1,600)	(12/190) × 7,000 =	442	16,769
9	16,769	(1,600)	(11/190) × 7,000 =	405	15,574
10	15,574	(1,600)	(10/190) × 7,000 =	369	14,343
11	14,343	(1,600)	(9/190) × 7,000 =	332	13,075
12	13,075	(1,600)	(8/190) × 7,000 =	295	11,770
13	11,770	(1,600)	(7/190) × 7,000 =	257	10,427
14	10,427	(1,600)	(6/190) × 7,000 =	221	9,048
15	9,048	(1,600)	(5/190) × 7,000 =	184	7,632
16	7,632	(1,600)	(4/190) × 7,000 =	147	6,179
17	6,179	(1,600)	(3/190) × 7,000 =	111	4,690
18	4,690	(1,600)	(2/190) × 7,000 =	73	3,163
19	3,163	(1,600)	(1/190) × 7,000 =	37	1,600
20	1,600	(1,600)			0
		(32,000)			7,000

In this case the charge for the final year would be $(111 + 73 + 37) = £221$. The liability in the balance sheet in each of the years will be:

	£
Year 1	21,179
Year 2	16,769
Year 3	11,770
Year 4	6,179
Year 5	0

As can be seen, the sum of the digits method is sometimes quite a reasonable approximation to the actuarial method, and is also simple to calculate.

(3)   The final, and simplest, method is the *straight-line method*. Using this method there is little point in determining the quarterly charge, since we only need to consider the charge per accounting period. Given that this is a lease for five years, the annual finance charge is simply the total interest (£7,000) divided by 5, which is equal to £1,400 per annum (£350 per quarter). The inevitable result of the use of this method is that the charge is lower than it should be in the earlier years, and higher than it should be in the later years. The straight-line method should not be used, except when the effect is not material.

16.4.4   Variation clauses

A finance lease may contain an interest variation clause, such that the rental payable will be affected by changes in interest rates. The Guidance Notes to SSAP 21 suggest that in such a case no adjustment need be made to the original calculations, but that the effect should be recorded over the remainder of the lease term. A simplified example illustrates how this might be done.

EXAMPLE

A company leases an asset with a fair value of £10,000. The lease agreement is that the company will pay for the asset in five annual instalments of £3,000, payable in arrears. There is an interest variation clause in the lease. The implicit interest rate, calculated with respect to the current payments of £3,000, is 15.239 per cent per annum (calculation not shown). The initial calculations using the actuarial method are given below.

Year	Liability at beginning of year (capital b/f) £	Payment at end of year £	Interest accrued on liability during year @ 15.239% £	Liability at end of year (capital c/f) £
1	10,000	(3,000)	1,524	8,524
2	8,524	(3,000)	1,299	6,823
3	6,823	(3,000)	1,040	4,863
4	4,863	(3,000)	741	2,604
5	2,604	(3,000)	396	0
		(15,000)	5,000	

It should be noted that since, in this example, payments are being made in arrears, the format of the calculation differs from that used where payments are made in advance. Specifically, the interest accrued on the liability during the year is 15.239 per cent of £10,000, since the payment of £3,000 is not made until the end of the period.

During the life of the lease, general interest rates fall, and after two years the rental decreases to £2,900 per annum. The revised calculation will be as follows:

Year	Liability at beginning of year (capital b/f) £	Payment at end of year £	Interest accrued on liability during year @ 15.239% £	Liability at end of year (capital c/f) £
1	10,000	(3,000)	1,524	8,524
2	8,524	(3,000)	1,299	6,823
			Interest accrued on liability during year @ 13.210%	
3	6,823	(2,900)	901	4,824
4	4,824	(2,900)	637	2,561
5	2,561	(2,900)	339	0
		(14,700)	4,700	

The decline in the annual payment to £2,900 reduces the total finance charge on the lease from £5,000 to £4,700. The implicit interest rate declines to 13.21 per cent; this is the rate which, at the beginning of year 3, discounts the three payments of £2,900 to the value of the liability at that point, £6,283. The interest rate inherent in the lease is, in effect, being treated as an accounting estimate. Where the estimate changes the effect is spread forward, but is not spread back.

A lease may also contain a tax variation clause, which will change the rentals payable if there are changes to tax rules or rates. The basic calculations should be as for an interest variation clause, except that where the reduction in rentals exceeds the future finance charges, then the excess should be applied to reduce future charges for depreciation. For example, a company may have already charged £1,000 in finance charges, but due to a change in rentals arising from a tax variation clause the total finance element of the total repayments will only be £900. The £100 difference should be deducted from the recorded value of the asset to reduce future depreciation. This treatment is basically consistent with that required where tax benefits for the lessor at the inception of the lease mean that the actual minimum lease payments are less than the fair value of the asset. As has been seen, in such cases it is the actual amount of the minimum lease payments that should be capitalised.

16.4.5 Disclosure

SSAP 21 requires the disclosure of fixed assets held under finance leases, but allows this disclosure to be given in one of two ways.

Firstly, the company may show the gross amounts of assets held under finance leases, divided into the major classes of assets, together with the total depreciation allocated to each major class of fixed assets under finance leases during the period.

Secondly, and more commonly in practice, a company may integrate the disclosure of leased and owned assets. Where this alternative is adopted, the company must state the net book value of assets held under finance leases included in the total. The depreciation allocated to assets held under finance leases should also be disclosed.

If the second alternative is adopted, a note similar to the following will be provided:

> The net book value of fixed assets of £x includes an amount of £y in respect of assets held under finance leases and hire purchase contracts.

Companies using the FRSSE need only allocate finance leases between land and buildings and other assets, not by major class.

The amounts of obligations under finance leases, net of finance charges allocated to future periods, should be disclosed separately either on the face of the balance sheet or in the notes to the accounts. This amount will normally need to be divided between:

- creditors: amounts falling due within one year, and
- creditors: amounts falling due after more than one year.

The net obligations under finance leases should be analysed, in a note to the accounts, between amounts payable in the next year, amounts payable in the second to fifth years inclusive and amounts payable after this time. The analysis may be presented separately, or included with similar obligations. If it is included with similar obligations then it is the total amount of these obligations that needs to be analysed in this way. If a company chooses to provide separate disclosure, then it may also show the gross obligations in respect of the relevant periods, and then deduct the total of future finance charges to arrive at the balance sheet amount. This disclosure need not be made by companies adopting the FRSSE.

Disclosure should be made of the amounts of any commitments under finance leases which have been entered into before the balance sheet date, but where the inception of the lease takes place in the next accounting period.

The company should disclose the accounting policy adopted for finance leases.

16.5   ACCOUNTING FOR FINANCE LEASES BY LESSORS

16.5.1   Initial recording

The lessor does not record the underlying asset in the balance sheet. Instead, it records the amounts due from the lessee. More strictly:

> The amount due from the lessee under a finance lease should be recorded in the balance sheet of a lessor as a debtor at the amount of the net investment in the lease after making provisions for items such as bad and doubtful rentals receivable. (Para. 38, SSAP 21.)

The net investment in a lease is further defined as:

(a)   the gross investment in a lease; less
(b)   gross earnings allocated to future periods. (Para. 22, SSAP 21.)

The gross investment is defined as:

> . . . the total of the minimum lease payments and any unguaranteed residual value accruing to the lessor. (Para. 21, SSAP 21.)

It is notable that, using these definitions, there will still be a balance on the lease after all the lease payments have been made. This amount is equal to the residual value of the underlying asset, or rather that part of it which will accrue to the lessor.

These definitions also make the situation appear to be more difficult than it really is. In practice, the net investment in a lease at its inception will normally be the cost of the asset to the lessor, less any government or similar grants received or receivable. An amendment to SSAP 21 eliminates the previous option, to gross up a tax-free grant and include the amount in profit before tax; the grant should be treated as non-taxable income.

Lessors are also allowed to take account of any initial direct costs in setting up the lease. The company may write off such costs immediately, or allocate them over the period of the lease on a systematic basis.

16.5.2 Allocation of income

Although the balance sheet amount is based on the net investment in the lease, the allocation of income to separate accounting periods should not be based on this amount, for finance leases, but instead on the net cash investment in the lease. Surprisingly, this contrasts with one of the changes contained in IAS 17, which now prohibits the net cash investment method and allows only the net investment method. For a hire purchase contract the allocation of income should be based on the net investment in the contract. There is no guidance in the FRSSE on the allocation of income.

The difference between the net investment and the net cash investment in the lease is that the latter takes account of other factors, taxation in particular, which are ignored in the calculation of the net investment. A definition is provided by the standard:

> The net cash investment in a lease at a point in time is the amount of funds invested in a lease by a lessor, and comprises the cost of the asset plus or minus the following related payments or receipts:
>
> (a)   government or other grants receivable towards the purchase or use of the asset;
> (b)   rentals received;
> (c)   taxation payments and receipts, including the effect of capital allowances;
> (d)   residual values, if any, at the end of the lease term;
> (e)   interest payments (where applicable);
> (f)   interest received on cash surpluses;
> (g)   profit taken out of the lease. (Para. 23, SSAP 21.)

The standard also allows a company to use another method, where it provides a reasonable approximation. This will often be related to the materiality of the finance lease income in terms of the company's total operations.

There are two main methods by which a company may take account of the net cash investment in the lease:

- the actuarial method after tax, and
- the investment period method.

These cases can be illustrated with the same basic data as for the original lessee calculation above.

EXAMPLE

The actuarial method after tax

A company leases an asset. The lease commences on the first day of the company's accounting year. The fair value of the asset (which is equal to the present value of the minimum lease payments) is £25,000. The lease agreement specifies that there are 20 quarterly payments of £1,600, in advance. There is no residual value. The following assumptions apply.

- the rate of corporation tax is 35 per cent, and the company always makes sufficient profits to pay tax, which is paid nine months after the end of each accounting period;
- the lessor receives capital allowances, and the rate of capital allowance is 25 per cent of the written down value of the asset, and
- interest on funds borrowed to finance the purchase of the asset is payable at 1.5 per cent per quarter.

1	2	3	4	5	6	7	8
	Net cash investment brought	Cash	Rental	Net cash investment at beginning of	Interest	Profit taken out	Net cash investment carried
Qtr	forward	flows	receipts	year	@ 1.50%	@ 0.90%	forward
	£	£	£	£	£	£	£
1	0	(25,000)	1,600	(23,400)	(351)	(211)	(23,962)
2	(23,962)		1,600	(22,362)	(335)	(201)	(22,898)
3	(22,898)		1,600	(21,298)	(319)	(192)	(21,809)
4	(21,809)		1,600	(20,209)	(303)	(182)	(20,694)
					(1,308)	(786)	
5	(20,694)		1,600	(19,094)	(286)	(172)	(19,552)
6	(19,552)		1,600	(17,952)	(269)	(162)	(18,383)
7	(18,383)		1,600	(16,783)	(252)	(151)	(17,186)
8	(17,186)	406	1,600	(15,180)	(228)	(137)	(15,545)
					(1,035)	(622)	
9	(15,545)		1,600	(13,945)	(209)	(126)	(14,280)
10	(14,280)		1,600	(12,680)	(190)	(114)	(12,984)
11	(12,984)		1,600	(11,384)	(171)	(102)	(11,657)
12	(11,657)	(237)	1,600	(10,294)	(154)	(93)	(10,541)
					(724)	(435)	
13	(10,541)		1,600	(8,941)	(134)	(80)	(9,155)
14	(9,155)		1,600	(7,555)	(113)	(68)	(7,736)
15	(7,736)		1,600	(6,136)	(92)	(55)	(6,283)
16	(6,283)	(756)	1,600	(5,439)	(82)	(49)	(5,570)
					(421)	(252)	
17	(5,570)		1,600	(3,970)	(60)	(36)	(4,066)
18	(4,066)		1,600	(2,466)	(37)	(22)	(2,525)
19	(2,525)		1,600	(925)	(14)	(8)	(947)
20	(947)	(1,170)	1,600	(517)	(8)	(5)	(530)
					(119)	(71)	
21	(530)		1,600	(530)	(8)	(5)	(543)
22	(543)			(543)	(8)	(5)	(556)
23	(556)			(556)	(8)	(5)	(569)
24	(569)	569		0	0		0
					(24)	(15)	
		(26,188)	32,000		(3,631)	(2,180)	

There are a number of points to be made about these calculations.

(1) Column 5, the net cash investment at the beginning of the period is the sum of columns 2 to 4.

(2) Column 6 (the interest cost of financing the purchase of the asset) is 1.5 per cent of the net cash investment at the beginning of the period. Column 7 (the profit taken out of the lease) is 0.9 per cent of the net cash investment at the beginning of the period.

(3) The cash flows in column 3 are the initial purchase cost, and then the tax cash flows. The tax cash flows are calculated by applying the rate of 35 per cent to the rental income, less the interest charge, less the capital allowances. Tax is paid nine months after the balance sheet date and the amounts involved are therefore those in the previous financial year. In the final period it is assumed that there is no income from sale of the asset, and so the amount not already dealt with through capital allowances is allowed in full. No account has been taken of the interest charge for the final period, £15, which would be allowed in the next year.

(4) The rate of profit taken on the lease (0.9 per cent) has been calculated by trial and error. It is based on a constant percentage of the average net cash investment in the lease.

The information to be included in the profit and loss account can be derived from this information:

Year	1 £	2 £	3 £	4 £	5 £	6 £	Total £
Rental	6,400	6,400	6,400	6,400	6,400		32,000
Capital element of lease receipts	(3,879)	(4,405)	(5,004)	(5,588)	(6,171)	47	(25,000)
Gross earnings	2,521	1,995	1,396	812	229	47	7,000
Interest	(1,308)	(1,035)	(724)	(421)	(119)	(24)	(3,631)
Pre-tax profit	1,213	960	672	391	110	23	3,369
Taxation	406	(237)	(756)	(1,170)	569	0	(1,188)
	1,619	723	(84)	(779)	679	23	2,181
Deferred tax	(834)	(102)	519	1,032	(608)	(8)	(1)
Net profit	785	621	435	253	71	15	2,180

(There are minor rounding differences, including a £1 balance on deferred tax. Since interest is calculated for all six years, there is also an apparent capital payment in year 6. In practice, these would probably be eliminated.)

The pre-tax profit is arrived at by grossing up the net profit at the appropriate rate of taxation, in this case 35 per cent.

EXAMPLE

The investment period method

An alternative method of allocating the finance lease income is to use the investment period method. This method allocates the gross earnings in proportion to the net cash investment in the lease. For example, in the table below £676 in column 6 is $(23,400/242,157) \times 7,000$.

The example uses the same figures as in the example for the actuarial method.

Either the average net cash investment, or the net cash investment at the end of each quarter, can be used for this calculation. This is because the interest and profit taken out are a constant percentage of the average net cash investment, and so would have no effect on the answer.

The difference in gross earnings between the two methods is not material.

Where a company undertakes very little leasing then, on the grounds of materiality, it may be possible to use a very approximate method. In theory, it may even be possible to use the straight-line method, although it is difficult to imagine that this would ever be acceptable in practice. The sum of the digits method may be an acceptable approximation in restricted circumstances.

1	*2*	*3*	*4*	*5*	*6*	*7*	*8*	*9*
	Net cash investment brought		*Rental*	*Net cash investments at beginning*	*Gross*	*Interest*	*Profit taken out*	*Net cash investment carried*
Qtr	*forward*	*Cash flows*	*receipts*	*of period*	*earnings*	*@ 1.50%*	*@ 0.90%*	*forward*
	£	£	£	£	£	£	£	£
1	0	(25,000)	1,600	(23,400)	676	(351)	(211)	(23,962)
2	(23,962)		1,600	(22,362)	646	(335)	(201)	(22,898)
3	(22,898)		1,600	(21,298)	616	(319)	(192)	(21,809)
4	(21,809)		1,600	(20,209)	584	(303)	(182)	(20,694)
					2,522	(1,308)	(786)	
5	(20,694)		1,600	(19,094)	552	(286)	(172)	(19,552)
6	(19,552)		1,600	(17,952)	519	(269)	(162)	(18,383)
7	(18,383)		1,600	(16,783)	485	(252)	(151)	(17,186)
8	(17,186)	406	1,600	(15,180)	439	(228)	(137)	(15,545)
					1,955	(1,035)	(622)	
9	(15,545)		1,600	(13,945)	403	(209)	(126)	(14,280)
10	(14,280)		1,600	(12,680)	367	(190)	(114)	(12,984)
11	(12,984)		1,600	(11,384)	329	(171)	(102)	(11,657)
12	(11,657)	(237)	1,600	(10,294)	298	(154)	(93)	(10,541)
					1,397	(724)	(435)	
13	(10,541)		1,600	(8,941)	258	(134)	(80)	(9,155)
14	(9,155)		1,600	(7,555)	218	(113)	(68)	(7,736)
15	(7,736)		1,600	(6,136)	177	(92)	(55)	(6,283)
16	(6,283)	(756)	1,600	(5,439)	157	(82)	(49)	(5,570)
					810	(421)	(252)	
17	(5,570)		1,600	(3,970)	115	(60)	(36)	(4,066)
18	(4,066)		1,600	(2,466)	71	(37)	(22)	(2,525)
19	(2,525)		1,600	(925)	27	(14)	(8)	(947)
20	(947)	1,170	1,600	(517)	15	(8)	(5)	(530)
					228	(119)	(71)	
21	(530)			(530)	16	(8)	(5)	(543)
22	(543)			(543)	16	(8)	(5)	(556)
23	(556)			(556)	16	(8)	(5)	(569)
24	(569)	569		0	0	0	0	0
					48	(24)	(15)	
		(26,188)	32,000	(242,157)	7,000	(3,631)	(2,180)	

16.5.3 Hire purchase

The calculations for a hire purchase contract are considerably simpler than those for a finance lease, since the net investment in the lease can be used in place of the net cash investment in the lease. This means that the treatment by the lessor is the mirror image of the treatment by the lessee, and the same calculations will be performed. The two main methods that will be used are the actuarial method before tax, and the sum of the digits method.

The Guidance Notes to SSAP 21 state that the sum of the digits method tends to front-load income, and that this becomes more pronounced the higher the total finance charges are as a proportion of the amount financed. For this reason, the notes suggest that the sum of the digits method will not be appropriate for a finance lease over a long period, say seven years. The two methods are compared in the examples on the following pages.

EXAMPLE

A company has made two leases. One is for 3 years; the asset cost £10,000 and annual receipts are £4,000 (in arrears). The other is for 15 years; the asset also cost £10,000 and the annual receipts are £1,292 (in arrears).

Lease 1

Actuarial method:

Year	Capital brought forward £	Finance @ 9.7% £	Receipts at end of period £	Capital carried forward £
1	10,000	970	(4,000)	6,970
2	6,970	676	(4,000)	3,646
3	3,646	354	(4,000)	0
		2,000		

Sum of the digits:

Year	Capital brought forward £	Formula for finance £	Finance £	Receipts at end of period £	Capital carried forward £
1	10,000	2,000 × 3/6	1,000	(4,000)	7,000
2	7,000	2,000 × 2/6	667	(4,000)	3,667
3	3,667	2,000 × 1/6	333	(4,000)	0
			2,000		

Lease 2

Actuarial method:

Year	Capital brought forward £	Finance @ 9.696% £	Receipts at end of period £	Capital carried forward £
1	10,000	970	(1,292)	9,678
2	9,678	938	(1,292)	9,324
3	9,324	904	(1,292)	8,936

Year	Capital brought forward £	Finance @ 9.696% £	Receipts at end of period £	Capital carried forward £
4	8,936	866	(1,292)	8,510
5	8,510	825	(1,292)	8,043
6	8,043	780	(1,292)	7,531
7	7,531	730	(1,292)	6,969
8	6,969	676	(1,292)	6,353
9	6,353	616	(1,292)	5,677
10	5,677	550	(1,292)	4,935
11	4,935	479	(1,292)	4,122
12	4,122	400	(1,292)	3,230
13	3,230	313	(1,292)	2,251
14	2,251	218	(1,292)	1,177
15	1,177	114	(1,292)	0
		9,380		

Sum of the digits:

Year	Capital brought forward £	Formula for finance £	Finance £	Receipts at end of period £	Capital carried forward £
1	10,000	9,380 @ 15/120 =	1,173	(1,292)	9,881
2	9,881	9,380 @ 14/120 =	1,094	(1,292)	9,683
3	9,683	9,380 @ 13/120 =	1,016	(1,292)	9,407
4	9,407	9,380 @ 12/120 =	938	(1,292)	9,053
5	9,053	9,380 @ 11/120 =	860	(1,292)	8,621
6	8,621	9,380 @ 10/120 =	782	(1,292)	8,111
7	8,111	9,380 @ 9/120 =	704	(1,292)	7,523
8	7,523	9,380 @ 8/120 =	625	(1,292)	6,856
9	6,856	9,380 @ 7/120 =	547	(1,292)	6,111
10	6,111	9,380 @ 6/120 =	469	(1,292)	5,288
11	5,288	9,380 @ 5/120 =	391	(1,292)	4,387
12	4,387	9,380 @ 4/120 =	313	(1,292)	3,408
13	3,408	9,380 @ 3/120 =	235	(1,292)	2,351
14	2,351	9,380 @ 2/120 =	156	(1,292)	1,215
15	1,215	9,380 @ 1/120 =	77	(1,292)	0
			9,380		

It is clear that in the first case the sum of the digits provides an acceptable approximation to the actuarial method. In the second case it does not.

It was common practice to argue that the sum of the digits method was an acceptable method partly on the grounds of practicality, by taking into account the time and costs involved in using the actuarial method. This argument now has very little validity. Modern computer programs mean that even very complicated leases can be analysed using the actuarial method in a very short time.

16.5.4   Variation clauses

The effect of variation clauses on the lessee has already been considered; obviously they will also affect the calculations of the lessor. The same basic principle should be applied. Whether the clause is a tax variation clause or an interest variation clause, the effect should be taken into account in the allocation of earnings for future periods. It should not be used to alter the calculations that have already been performed for past periods. The rental that is charged is assumed to be an accounting estimate, and treated accordingly.

16.5.5   Disclosure

Lessors should disclose the net investment in finance leases and hire purchase contracts at each balance sheet date. Since the amount will often be receivable partly after more than one year, the sum involved will also need to be disclosed.

EXAMPLE

	2006	2005
	£	£
Debtors		
Net investment in finance leases	1,200	1,100

The amounts receivable under finance leases and hire purchase contracts comprise:

	2006	2005
	£	£
Finance leases	900	820
Hire purchase contracts	300	280
	1,200	1,100

Included in the totals receivable is £900 (2000: £800) which falls due after more than one year.

Disclosure should also be made of:

- the accounting policy adopted for finance leases;
- the aggregate rentals receivable under finance leases in the period, and
- the costs of assets acquired for use in finance leases.

The second of these disclosures is not required by companies complying with the FRSSE.

Gross earnings under leases should be included as the turnover of the lessor. However, since the term turnover is inappropriate, it is better to describe it in some other way, such as gross earnings under finance leases.

16.6 OTHER MATTERS

16.6.1 Manufacturer/dealer lessors

A manufacturer or dealer lessor should not recognise a profit on sale at the start of an operating lease. This is because no sale has been recorded.

A profit on sale can be recorded on a finance lease, but this should be restricted to the difference between the fair value of the asset and the cost of the asset, after taking account of any grants received or receivable.

EXAMPLE

A dealer normally buys an asset for £1,500, and sells it for £2,000. There is also an alternative method of purchasing the asset, by five annual payments of £450, payable in advance. Average interest rates on finance leases are 11 per cent.

The 'fair value' of the asset is therefore £1,846, calculated as below.

Year	Capital brought forward £	Payments at beginning of period £	Finance charge @ 11% £	Capital carried forward £
1	1,846	(450)	154	1,550
2	1,550	(450)	121	1,221
3	1,221	(450)	85	856
4	856	(450)	44	450
5	450	(450)	0	0
		(2,250)	404	

The company can reasonably record the profit as the difference between the cost and this value, being £346. It should not record a profit of £500 on the original transaction, and then reduce finance lease income as a result.

Exactly the same principle would apply if a company were to offer an apparently interest-free financing arrangement. For example, if we change the previous example, and state that the company normally sells the asset for £2,250, equal to five instalments of £450, this would have no effect on the calculations. The company could not use the normal sales value in the calculation of the initial profit, and then use an interest rate of zero per cent. This would not provide a fair reflection of the income over the whole period during which payments are made. Instead, it would use a reasonable estimate of the interest rate (derived from its own normal rate, or that applied by others on similar transactions) and calculate the effective sale proceeds accordingly.

16.6.2   Sale and lease back

The existence of a sale and lease back transaction has no effect on the accounting treatment adopted by the lessor (the buyer). The transaction should be accounted for in the normal way. Although the cost of the asset may not be its market value, the effect of this will automatically be spread over the period of the lease.

However, the lessee must take account of the special nature of the transaction, and this may affect the accounting treatment.

The first thing that must be done by the lessee is to determine if the lease is a finance lease or an operating lease. The fact that it is a sale and lease back transaction will have no effect on this calculation.

If the transaction has given rise to a finance lease then:

> . . . any apparent profit or loss (that is, the difference between the sale price and the previous carrying value) should be deferred and amortised in the financial statements of the seller/lessee over the shorter of the lease term and the useful life of the asset. (Para. 46, SSAP 21.)

For example, a company owns an asset with a book value of £10,000. It sells the asset for £12,000 and leases it back under a finance lease. The new carrying value will therefore be £12,000. The apparent profit of £2,000 should not be treated as income, but recorded as a deferred credit and then taken to income over the shorter of the lease life and the estimated useful economic life of the asset.

An alternative method is to leave the asset at its original value, and to set up the amount received on sale as a creditor. The repayments are then treated partly as a repayment of the amount of the principal, and partly as the interest on the principal. This treatment is preferable since, as the Guidance Notes to SSAP 21 state:

> This treatment will reflect the substance of the transaction, namely that it represents the raising of finance secured on an asset which is held and not disposed of. (Para. 155, Guidance Notes, SSAP 21.)

Where the sale and lease back transaction has given rise to an operating lease then different considerations apply. The company has disposed of the main risks and rewards of ownership. Where the disposal proceeds are equal to the fair value of the asset then the profit or loss on disposal should be recorded immediately, as this represents the genuine realisation of a profit or loss. However, this is not the only possibility:

   (b)   if the sale price is below fair value, any profit or loss should be recognised immediately except that if the apparent loss is compensated by future rentals at below market price it should to that extent be deferred and amortised over the remainder of the lease term (or, if shorter, the period during which the reduced rentals are chargeable);

(c) if the sale price is above fair value, the excess over fair value should be deferred and amortised over the shorter of the remainder of the lease term and the period to the next rent review (if any). (Para. 47, SSAP 21.)

Some examples from the Guidance Notes.

(1) A company is carrying an asset at a value of £70, although it has a fair value of £100. It sells it for £120, and then leases it back with an annual rental of £28 for five years. A profit of £30 (fair value less book value) should be recorded immediately, but the additional profit of £20 should be deferred and taken to income over the five-year period.

(2) A company is carrying an asset with a book value of £70, but a fair value of £80. The asset is sold for £80 and rented for five years at an annual cost of £20. The profit on sale should be recognised immediately, and the difference between the sale proceeds and the fair value should be ignored.

(3) A company is carrying an asset at a book value of £95. The asset has a fair value of £100. The sale price is £80, and the company pays an annual rental to hire back the asset for £20 for five years. The company has made an apparent loss, but if the annual rental has been reduced to take account of this, then the loss of £15 should be deferred and charged to income over the lease term of five years.

16.6.3   Sub-leases and back-to-back leases

A company may be both a lessee and a lessor for the same asset. In this case the company is known as an intermediate party.

This will normally have no effect on the method of accounting used by the ultimate lessee and the ultimate lessor.

The particular situation needs to be analysed to determine the commercial nature of the arrangement. The key question is usually whether or not the intermediate party really has the risks and rewards of ownership. For example, if the ultimate lessee defaults, then will the intermediate party still be liable to the ultimate lessor?

If the answer to the question is 'yes', then the intermediate party should prepare accounts as both lessee and lessor. Its balance sheet will include the obligation under finance lease, and either the net investment in finance leases or assets held for use in operating leases. (The reverse situation is not logically possible: a company could not be an operating lease lessee but then use the asset as lessor in a finance lease, since it could not transfer the risks and rewards of ownership which it does not possess.) Alternatively, the company could also be an operating lessee and lessor, but in this case the situation would be very straightforward, as the net income would simply be the difference between the two rentals.

However, if the answer is 'no', then the intermediate party should normally record neither. In such a case the intermediate party is effectively an agent acting on behalf of one of the parties to the underlying transaction. Rather than recording the two leases, it should account for the net income alone. This might include an initial arrangement fee, and the difference between rentals payable and receivable.

16.7 PROPOSALS FOR CHANGE

In December 1999, the ASB published a discussion paper *Leases: Implementation of a New Approach*. This paper presents a position paper developed by the G4+1 international group of accounting standard-setters, which includes the ASB and the IASC. The international position paper builds on a previous special report on leasing issued by the G4+1 in 1996, which concluded that the present distinction between operating and finance leases was arbitrary and unsatisfactory.

The key proposal in the position paper was to introduce a single accounting treatment for all leases in place of the two different treatments currently required for operating leases and finance leases. The paper pointed out that the main deficiency of the present approach is that it does not provide for the recognition in the lessee's balance sheet of material assets and liabilities arising from operating leases. The main recommendations put forward were as follows.

(1) The objective for lessees should be to record, at the beginning of a lease term, the fair values of the rights and obligations conveyed by a lease. Therefore, leases which are currently treated as operating leases would give rise to assets and liabilities in the lessee's balance sheet but only to the extent that rights and obligations are contained in the lease. Where the lease is for a small proportion of the asset's life, only that proportion would be reflected in the lessee's balance sheet.

(2) Lessees would generally measure the fair value of the rights obtained under a lease at the present value of the minimum lease payments, plus any other liabilities incurred.

(3) Lessors should report financial assets (which would represent amounts receivable from the lessee) and residual interests in the leased items as separate assets because the two are subject to different risks.

In issuing the position paper as a discussion paper, the ASB noted in its foreword that, whilst it does not agree with the position paper on every point, it believed that the paper merited serious consideration as a basis for a new accounting standard.

The ASB also highlighted issues which are of particular relevance in the UK:

- accounting for buildings held on long leases;
- accounting for investment properties currently stated at fair value under SSAP 19 *Accounting for Investment Properties*, and
- the method of income recognition that should be applied by lessors.

A decade later the IASB, jointly with FASB, issued a discussion paper on leases. In 2010, the IASB and FASB issued an exposure draft proposing substantial changes to lease accounting, the fruits of which should be seen in the second half of 2011.

The exposure draft is long and complex, and the IASB continues to debate its precise points, but in principle the proposals are consistent with those made back in 1999. Some of the main proposals included in the draft (or discussed in subsequent IASB meetings) are:

- that the current distinction between finance and operating leases be abolished, insofar as it relates to whether or not assets and associated liabilities are recorded in a balance sheet;
- that all leased assets and associated liabilities be recorded in a lessee's balance sheet, other than in respect of short-term leases being those which do not and cannot extend beyond one year;
- that, possibly, a distinction between finance and operating leases survives in relation to the pattern of recognising costs, so that operating lease charges in total will continue to be charged on a straight line basis in nearly all cases, and
- that leases, which also contain service components, be allocated between the service and asset elements. (This already applies, but is not as relevant in practice today as it would be in future, as many of the affected leases are operating leases so no assets and liabilities associated with them are recognised.)

17 PROVISIONS, CONTINGENT LIABILITIES AND CONTINGENT ASSETS

17.1 INTRODUCTION

17.1.1 FRS 12 Provisions, Contingent Liabilities and Contingent Assets

FRS 12 deals with the general issue of provisions, contingent liabilities and contingent assets.

There are other UK standards which deal with specific types of provision:

(1) FRS 3 *Reporting Financial Performance*, which originally dealt with provisions arising on discontinuance (covered in Chapter 5). This is an area where FRS 12 provides more specific requirements, in effect superseding those which were originally set out in FRS 3.

(2) FRS 5 *Reporting the Substance of Transactions*, which defines, and establishes recognition criteria for liabilities (covered in Chapter 2). These principles also apply to provisions covered by FRS 12.

(3) FRS 7 *Fair Values in Acquisition Accounting*, which deals with the recognition of provisions on acquisition (covered in Chapter 21).

(4) FRS 17 *Retirement Benefits*, which deals with pension provisions and similar (covered in Chapter 7).

(5) FRS 19 *Deferred Tax* which deals with provisions in respect of deferred taxation (covered in Chapter 8).

There is also UITF 45 which deals with the very specific issue of liabilities arising from participation in the market for electrical and electronic equipment, and the EU requirements in respect of the collection, treatment, recovery and environmentally sound disposal of waste equipment.

As dealt with further below, FRS 12 contains a general exclusion from its scope for any provisions (or indeed contingent liabilities or assets) which are covered by a more specific accounting standard. FRS 12 is, therefore, a 'back-stop' standard which deals only with matters that are outside the scope of other standards.

Although, as in most other areas, lacking the detail of the main standard, the FRSSE requires treatments similar, in respect of provisions, contingent liabilities and contingent assets, to those required by FRS 12.

FRS 12 is very similar to the current version of the international standard dealing with similar matters, IAS 37, which is also entitled *Provisions, Contingent Liabilities and Contingent Assets*. It was basically produced as part of the same project. As a result, and putting to one side the possible changes to IAS 37 that have been proposed, companies that move to IFRS, at the moment, are unlikely to find that the change involves any significant alteration to their treatment of provisions and contingencies.

It could now be argued that there are two versions of FRS 12 in force. The first is the original standard, as amended by some subsequent pronouncements. This applies to nearly all companies using UK GAAP. However, for those companies which have adopted FRS 26, there is a slight difference in the scope of the standard and some items, such as guarantees, may be treated differently. FRS 26 is covered in Chapter 13.

There is also an exposure draft, FRED 39, of proposed revisions to FRS 12, as well as consequential changes to FRS 17. The exposure draft, which arises out of the business combinations project undertaken by the IASB, although it did not give rise to a new international standard when a revised standard on business combinations was issued in January 2008, is dealt with at the end of this chapter. The IASB has also made recent further proposals to change IAS 37, although these are consistent with the main thrust of their earlier proposals.

Potential impact of the FRSME

The FRSME takes the same basic approach as FRS 12 when dealing with provisions, contingent asset and contingent liabilities and would therefore be unlikely to lead to substantial change.

17.1.2   Objective of FRS 12

The ASB's stated objective in FRS 12 is as follows:

> The objective of this FRS is to ensure that appropriate recognition criteria and measurement bases are applied to provisions, contingent liabilities and contingent assets and that sufficient information is disclosed in the notes to the financial statements to enable users to understand their nature, timing and amount. (Para. 1, FRS 12.)

The ASB's stated objective appears laudable in itself. However, a major factor behind this stated objective was the ASB's desire to eliminate what it saw as one of the last bastions of creative accounting. Prior to FRS 12, some companies had used the creation and subsequent release of excessive provisions to smooth reported profits over a number of years. Such provisions were often known as 'big-bath' provisions. When a company had an especially good year it made ultra-prudent provisions across the board. This meant that in leaner years it could release some of the unnecessary provisions and flatter its results. The earnings trends of the company then appeared to be far more stable than they really were. The ASB considered, perhaps fairly, that neither prudence nor the accruals concept (as it was then defined in SSAP 2, *Disclosure of Accounting Policies*) were intended to allow this artificial smoothing of company results.

17.1.3   The ASB's approach to provisions

The central thrust of the ASB's approach to provisions was to abolish them as a distinct category of item in the financial statements and to define provisions as a sub-class of liabilities. This appears reasonable as provisions have often been thought of as obligations to pay someone at some point in the future, but which lack the certainty that is normally required to describe them as liabilities. This approach does not mean treating provisions as something entirely distinct from liabilities, but involves accepting that they are of a similar basic nature, but at different points on a scale. However, on closer examination of FRS 12, it rapidly becomes clear that this standard brought about a significant change in accounting practice.

FRS 12 went far beyond stamping out the abuses of 'big-bath' provisioning, and prohibited provisions in many areas where they had been long-established, and long-accepted, practice. Examples include provisions for major asset overhaul costs, as with ships or aircraft, provisions for the anticipated costs of dealing with changes in legislation that necessitate staff retraining, or provisions for self-insurance. In each of these cases, provisions had previously been justified on the grounds of applying the fundamental accounting concepts of accruals and prudence (as they were then set out in SSAP 2); but in each case provisions are prohibited by FRS 12. In its desire to eliminate abuses and to align accounting for provisions with other areas of financial reporting (and with its *Statement of Principles*) the ASB downgraded the importance of accruals and prudence. This was subsequently made even clearer in FRS 18.

17.2   COMPANIES ACT REQUIREMENTS

17.2.1   Provisions

The Companies Act 2006 formats include a heading for 'Provisions for liabilities' and include the following statement:

> References in these regulations to provisions for liabilities . . . are to any amount retained as reasonably necessary for the purpose of providing for any liability the nature of which is clearly defined and which is either likely to be incurred, or certain to be incurred but uncertain as to amount or as to the date on which it will arise. (Para. 2, Sch. 9 The Large and Medium-sized Companies and Groups (Accounts and Reports) Regulations 2008 (SI 2008/410) and Para. 2, Sch. 7, The Small Companies and Groups (Accounts and Directors' Report) Regulations 2008 (SI 2008/409).)

These requirements have changed. The reference to provisions being for items 'the nature of which is clearly defined' is clearly consistent with FRS 12, in attempting to prohibit any vague and unspecified liabilities. Such reference has not always been there.

However, the above requirement provides no detailed guidance on when to recognise provisions and none at all on their measurement. Both of these issues are dealt with by FRS 12.

The effect of FRS 12 is to limit provisions to circumstances where a liability exists under the ASB's recognition criteria. Mere likelihood, or even certainty, of incurring a loss in future is insufficient grounds for recognising a provision under FRS 12.

The statutory disclosure requirements relating to provisions are covered below under the section dealing with disclosures.

17.2.2   Contingent liabilities

The Companies Act 2006 contains the following rule regarding contingent liabilities:

> (2)   The following information must be given with respect to any other contingent liability not provided for –
>
>   (a)   the amount or estimated amount of that liability;
>   (b)   its legal nature; and
>   (c)   whether any valuable security has been provided by the company in connection with that liability and if so, what. (Para. 63 (2), Sch. 1 to The Large and Medium-sized Companies and Groups (Accounts and Reports) Regulations 2008 (SI 2008/410) and Para. 57 (2), Sch. 1 to The Small Companies and Groups (Accounts and Directors' Report) Regulations 2008 (SI 2008/409).)

This requirement provides a basic disclosure rule for contingent liabilities but leaves several questions unanswered. For example, how should contingent assets be treated? How should the amounts disclosed be measured? Do all contingent liabilities need to be disclosed? FRS 12 addresses these issues.

Some commentators believe that statute requires that all contingent liabilities be disclosed. However, this would lead to excessive and potentially meaningless disclosure. Furthermore, the non-disclosure of remote contingencies (as stipulated by FRS 12) can be justified under statute, since statutory requirements do not apply to immaterial items, and remote contingencies can be regarded as immaterial by nature.

17.3   THE SCOPE OF FRS 12

FRS 12 applies to all financial statements that are intended to give a true and fair view in accounting for provisions, contingent liabilities and contingent assets, except:

- those resulting from financial instruments that are carried at fair value (FRS 12 applies to instruments, including guarantees, which are not carried at fair value);
- those resulting from executory contracts, ie those where neither party has performed any of its obligations or both parties have partially performed their obligations to an equal extent, except where the contract is onerous;
- those arising in insurance entities from contracts with policyholders, or
- those covered more specifically by another FRS or SSAP.

Those companies complying with FRS 26 are subject to a slightly different scope. The first exception is omitted in this case, although the standard then still does not apply to financial instruments which are within the scope of FRS 26.

Reporting entities applying the FRSSE are exempt from FRS 12, although its general principles have been included in the FRSSE.

Where another FRS or a SSAP (or, in practice, a UITF) deals with a more specific type of provision, contingent liability or contingent asset, that other standard is applicable rather than FRS 12. Examples include provisions for deferred tax (FRS 19) and pension costs (FRS 17). However, as SSAP 21, *Accounting for Leases and Hire Purchase Contracts* contains no specific requirements dealing with operating leases that have become onerous, FRS 12 applies in such cases.

FRS 12 deals with provisions for liabilities. It does not apply to items that arise in the context of adjustments to the carrying amounts of assets, but which are often referred to as provisions. Examples of these include depreciation, impairment, bad and doubtful debts and stock write-downs.

FRS 12 does apply to provisions for restructuring, including discontinued operations. Where a restructuring meets the definition of a discontinued operation, additional disclosures may be required by FRS 3 *Reporting Financial Performance*. These disclosures are covered in Chapter 5.

Potential impact of the FRSME

The FRSME has a slightly different list of exclusions. However, not all of the differences between standards would lead to differences in practice. For example, the FRSME does not exclude insurance contracts from the scope of the requirements, but insurance companies would not be entitled to use the FRSME at all. The scope on the FRSME does make specific mention of leases (although applying to onerous operating leases), construction contracts, employee benefit obligations and income tax.

17.4 RECOGNITION OF PROVISIONS

17.4.1 *Meaning of 'provision' and related terms*

FRS 12 defines a provision as:

> A liability of uncertain timing or amount. (Para. 2, FRS 12.)

This simple definition makes it abundantly clear that, in the ASB's view, provisions are a particular class of liability and not something distinct from liabilities.

FRS 12 also restates the definition of a liability, introduced by FRS 5:

> Obligations of an entity to transfer economic benefits as a result of past transactions or events. (Para. 2, FRS 12.)

Provisions can, however, be distinguished from other liabilities, such as trade creditors and accruals, because of the degree of uncertainty as to their timing or amount.

An obligation (which is required for a liability) necessarily involves a commitment to a third party, though the exact identity of the third party need not be known (for example, it could be the public at large). The obligation must exist at the balance sheet date and must have arisen from an obligating event, which is defined as follows:

> An event that creates a legal or constructive obligation that results in an entity having no realistic alternative to settling that obligation. (Para. 2, FRS 12.)

As the obligation may be legal or constructive, this definition does not restrict provisions to situations in which there is a strict legal requirement. However, the term 'no realistic alternative' does rule out situations where management has discretion to take a different course of action to avoid incurring a particular cost.

A legal obligation is defined as:

> An obligation that derives from:
>
> (a)   a contract (through its explicit or implicit terms);
> (b)   legislation; or
> (c)   other operation of law. (Para. 2, FRS 12.)

This definition is relatively straightforward to apply, although not all legal requirements give rise to provisions as not all will arise from obligating events. For example, a legal requirement to incur expenditure in the future does not of itself create an obligation existing at the balance sheet date.

FRS 12 defines a constructive obligation as:

> An obligation that derives from an entity's actions where:
>
> (a) by an established pattern of past practice, published policies or a sufficiently specific current statement, the entity has indicated to other parties that it will accept certain responsibilities; and
>
> (b) as a result, the entity has created a valid expectation on the part of those other parties that it will discharge those responsibilities. (Para. 2, FRS 12.)

This definition is less straightforward to apply, as what constitutes 'an established pattern of past practice' or 'a valid expectation' is more a matter of judgement than what constitutes a legal obligation. The term 'no realistic alternative' in the definition of an obligating event does restrict constructive obligations to situations where there is a requirement that has much the same commercial effect as a legal obligation. For example, there is likely to be a constructive obligation where failure to do something would result in unacceptable damage to a company's reputation or future business.

One particular example, already mentioned in Chapter 7, is that of staff bonuses. Bonuses might be included in a contract of employment, in which case, they would arise as a result of a legal obligation and would usually be fairly straightforward. The more complex, and common, situation is where there is no contractual entitlement to bonuses. In such a situation, a company would need to make provision for bonuses relating to a financial year, but paid after that year, where it had a constructive obligation for such bonuses. So when does a constructive obligation exist? A policy or statement made before the end of the year that bonuses will be paid, even though not legally binding, would usually be sufficient. The even more common situation is probably where no such statement is explicitly made, but the company has a past practice of paying such bonuses. This may qualify under the 'pattern of past practice' criterion. Again, there can be problems as to the limits. A company that has been paying such bonuses for ten years has almost certainly created an expectation that it will continue to do so. Where a company pays such a bonus for the first time, without having previously stated that it will do so, it will not have established such a pattern. The problem is the dividing line between the two scenarios, which would need to take account of how long the practice had been established, what had previously been said about the basis for deciding upon bonuses and any other matters that might affect the perception of potential recipients.

17.4.2 General recognition principles

The basic recognition requirement in FRS 12 is as follows:

> A provision should be recognised when:
>
> (a) an entity has a present obligation (legal or constructive) as a result of a past event;
>
> (b) it is probable that a transfer of economic benefits will be required to settle the obligation; and

(c) a reliable estimate can be made of the amount of the obligation.

If these conditions are not met, no provision should be recognised. (Para. 14, FRS 12.)

Note that all three components of this requirement must be present if a provision is to be recognised. Each element of this requirement will be considered in turn.

Potential impact of the FRSME

The FRSME has exactly the same basic conditions that need to be met in order for a provision to be made, albeit that slightly different words are used. It is difficult to imagine any situations where a different accounting treatment would result.

17.4.3   Present obligation

At the balance sheet date, a present obligation must exist if a provision is to be recognised. In most cases, the existence or otherwise of a legal or constructive obligation will be clear from past events, or the lack of them. However, this will not always be the case as there may be a dispute with another party as to whether there is an obligation, for example, where a legal case is in progress. FRS 12 sets out the following requirement in such cases:

> In rare cases it is not clear whether there is a present obligation. In these cases, a past event is deemed to give rise to a present obligation if, taking account of all available evidence, it is more likely than not that a present obligation exists at the balance sheet date. (Para. 15, FRS 12.)

This requirement is much the same as the previous requirement in SSAP 18, *Accounting for Contingencies* to provide for contingent losses where these are probable. However, under FRS 12, such items are no longer defined as contingencies. In applying this requirement, companies should consider all available evidence, including that provided by events after the balance sheet date, which may confirm the existence or otherwise of an obligation. Other factors to consider in relation to a legal claim include:

- the opinions of legal experts, whether internal to the company or external;
- other expert opinions where they are relevant to the outcome of the case, and
- the company's experience, if any, of similar claims.

If, on the basis of the available evidence, it appears more likely than not that no present obligation exists, then no provision is recognised. Instead, the item will fall within the definition of a contingent liability.

17.4.4   Past event

The past event must be an obligating event, as defined by FRS 12. The event must itself create the obligation to transfer economic benefits and must be a past event, that is, it must have occurred and created the obligation by the balance sheet date. This requirement is more restrictive than it might at first appear, and prevents provisions from being made in many instances where this had previously been accepted practice.

FRS 12 makes it clear that the past event must be independent of the company's future actions:

> It is only those obligations arising from past events existing independently of an entity's future actions (ie the future conduct of its business) that are recognised as provisions. (Para. 19, FRS 12.)

This requirement means that, unless an obligating event has occurred, no provision is recognised for costs that need to be incurred to operate in the future. This applies even if the company cannot continue in business without incurring such costs. An example is major asset overhauls or refurbishment, such as periodic drydocking of a ship, which is often a legal requirement if the vessel is to continue operating. The ASB's view is that the future requirement to incur the expenditure exists only as a result of the intention to continue to use the asset. In the ASB's view, management could decide to dispose of the asset rather than overhaul or refurbish it. Instead of providing for the expected cost over the period to the next overhaul, the ASB states that depreciation of the asset should take into account the expected consumption. This means that part of the asset's cost is depreciated over the period to the next major overhaul. The costs of that overhaul are then treated as an addition to the asset and depreciated in turn.

The standard is drawing a distinction between events that give rise to a present obligation, and an obligation that is expected (or even known) to arise in the future. A known or expected obligation to do something in the future, but which does not arise as a result of an event in the past, does not give rise to a provision.

Examples of past events that do create an obligation are environmental damage, such as that caused by quarries, and decommissioning costs of oil or gas installations. However, an obligation will arise only in cases where there is a legal or constructive requirement to rectify damage that has already been caused at the balance sheet date. Obligations may also arise some time after the damage has been caused, for example, because of a change in the law or a public commitment to rectify past damage.

A constructive obligation may arise from a public statement of policy by a company. For example, subsequent failure to adhere to a published clean-up policy could cause unacceptable damage to a company's reputation or future business, even where there is no legal requirement to rectify environmental damage. Another example of such a constructive obligation is where a retail store has a policy of providing refunds that goes beyond the company's legal requirements.

The requirement that provisions need the company to have a present obligation arising as a result of a past event means that management intent is insufficient. This is clearly directed at reducing the scope for smoothing earnings.

17.4.5 Probable transfer of economic benefits

To minimise the possibility of confusion or misinterpretation, FRS 12 contains the following statement, regarding the meaning of 'probable':

> . . . a transfer of economic benefits or other event is regarded as probable if the event is more likely than not to occur, ie the probability that the event will occur is greater than the probability that it will not. (Para. 23, FRS 12.)

The ASB acknowledges that, by their nature, and as a result of the way that they are defined in the standard, the existence and amount of provisions cannot be determined precisely. In some cases, there may be a certain requirement to transfer economic benefits, but significant uncertainty as to the amount. An example is where liability under a legal dispute has been accepted, but the amount of any damages has not been determined. In other cases, an obligation may exist, but there may be some doubt as to whether any transfer of economic benefits will be required. Here, an estimate of the likelihood of a transfer taking place must be made, in which the concept of prudence needs to be applied, but without being over-prudent.

A company may have a large number of similar obligations, for example, product guarantees. For each item in isolation, the probability of a transfer of economic benefits (for example, via a refund) is small, but there may be a high probability that a transfer will be required in respect of the population as a whole. In such cases, FRS 12 requires that the class of obligations be considered as a whole in estimating the probability of a transfer.

17.4.6 Reliable estimate of the obligation

The uncertain nature of provisions makes some degree of estimation almost inevitable. However, many items in financial statements depend to some degree on estimates, and the need to make estimates when dealing with provisions is not of itself grounds for not recognising a provision. The ASB points out in FRS 12 that where a company can determine a range of possible outcomes, a sufficiently reliable estimate can be made. The ASB does, however, acknowledge the possibility of an exception:

> In the extremely rare case where no reliable estimate can be made, a liability exists that cannot be recognised. That liability is disclosed as a contingent liability. (Para. 26, FRS 12.)

FRS 12 provides no example of such an extremely rare case. In effect, 'extremely rare' means 'almost never'.

17.5   MEASUREMENT OF PROVISIONS

17.5.1   Best estimate

FRS 12 includes the following requirement:

> The amount recognised as a provision should be the best estimate of the expenditure required to settle the present obligation at the balance sheet date. (Para. 36, FRS 12.)

This requirement is consistent with the recognition principle in FRS 12 that a provision requires the existence of an obligation at the balance sheet date. It, therefore, seems appropriate to measure the liability at the amount that the company would rationally pay to settle the obligation then existing or to transfer it to a third party. In many cases, the company's rational course of action will not be to settle or transfer the obligation at the balance sheet date, because it would be either impossible or prohibitively expensive to do so. The actual transfer of economic benefits in settlement may occur at a later time as the rational course of action will usually be to settle an obligation on the best terms available to the company (including both the amount and timing of payment).

The provision should be calculated on a pre-tax basis and the tax consequences dealt with under FRS 19 *Deferred Tax*. FRS 19 is covered in Chapter 8.

In situations where the provision relates to a large population of items, such as product guarantees, an 'expected value' approach needs to be adopted. This means that the provision is estimated by weighting all possible outcomes by their associated probabilities. FRS 12 includes the following example of this.

EXAMPLE

An entity sells goods with a warranty under which customers are covered for the cost of repairs of any manufacturing defects that become apparent within the first six months after purchase. If minor defects were detected in all products sold, repair costs of £1 million would result. If major defects were detected in all products sold, repair costs of £4 million would result. The entity's past experience and future expectations indicate that, for the coming year, 75 per cent of the goods sold will have no defects, 20 per cent of the goods sold will have minor defects and 5 per cent of the goods sold will have major defects ... An entity assesses the probability of a transfer for the warranty obligations as a whole.

The expected value of the cost of repairs is:

(75% of nil) + (20% of £1 million) + (5% of £4 million) = £400,000

Where a potential provision relates to a single item, or a small group of items, it will not usually be acceptable to use an expected value approach. In such cases, the expected value may not even be a possible outcome. (However, as noted at the end of this chapter, this is not quite the same approach that is proposed in FRED 39.)

In making a 'best estimate' it is appropriate to take into account additional information provided by post-balance sheet events. This would include the actual number of defects and the amount of repair costs for goods sold during the year which arise in the period after the balance sheet date.

Potential impact of the FRSME

The FRSME contains the basic requirement that amounts should be based on the best estimate of the outcome. However, in doing this, it places greater emphasis on the fact that this is the amount that a company would rationally pay to settle the obligation at the end of the reporting period or to transfer it to a third party at that time. Like FRS 12, it requires the weighting of the various possibilities when a company is dealing with a large population of items. When dealing with a single item, the FRSME notes that the individual's most likely outcome may be the best estimate, but then goes on to note that this will not always be the case. Where there are various possible outcomes, then they will all need to be considered. If other possible outcomes are mostly higher (or lower) than the most likely outcome, then the best estimate will need to be amended accordingly.

17.5.2 Risks and uncertainties

FRS 12 requires that:

> The risks and uncertainties that inevitably surround many events and circumstances should be taken into account in reaching the best estimate of a provision. (Para. 42, FRS 12.)

Risk is a measure of the variability of outcome. Risk assessment is, inevitably, a matter of judgement. Care is needed on the one hand to avoid understating provisions and on the other hand to avoid excessively prudent provisioning (which may facilitate a smoothing of profit).

17.5.3 Present value

In many cases, the expected expenditure in settlement of an obligation will occur within a relatively short period after the balance sheet date, for example, within one year. In such situations, the difference between the nominal amount of the expected expenditure and its present value at the balance sheet date will be immaterial, and thus present values can, in effect, be ignored.

However, it is possible for the actual transfer of economic benefits in settlement of an obligation to occur a significant time after the obligation itself arose. An extreme example of this is the cost of decommissioning an oil rig. Here, a legal obligation arises when the rig is constructed but the actual decommissioning does not occur until the end of the rig's useful economic life, which may be many years later. To reflect the time value of money, FRS 12 includes the following requirement:

> Where the effect of the time value of money is material, the amount of a provision should be the present value of the expenditures expected to be required to settle the obligation. (Para. 45, FRS 12.)

This reflects the ASB's ever-increasing requirement for the use of discounting in financial statements. The unwinding of the discount should be included as other finance costs adjacent to interest.

As with other areas where discounting is required, such as in impairment calculations, there may be practical difficulties in application. In particular, many businesses are likely to experience significant difficulties in determining an appropriate discount rate. On this point, FRS 12 states that:

> The discount rate (or rates) should be a pre-tax rate (or rates) that reflect(s) current market assessments of the time value of money and the risks specific to the liability. The discount rate(s) should not reflect risks for which future cash flow estimates have been adjusted. (Para. 47, FRS 12.)

If the expected expenditure has been weighted for the risks involved, a risk-free discount rate should then be used to avoid double-counting. Where expected expenditures are expressed in constant prices, a real discount rate should be used.

Potential impact of the FRSME

The FRSME also requires provisions to be discounted using an appropriate pre-tax discount rate, or rates, where this is material.

17.5.4   Future events

Future events may have a significant impact on the expenditure expected to be required to settle an obligation. Examples of such events include changes in technologies, efficiency improvements and changes in legislation. To minimise the scope for abuse, for example, by making over-optimistic estimates of the likely impact of future events, FRS 12 includes the following requirement:

> Future events that may affect the amount required to settle an obligation should be reflected in the amount of a provision where there is sufficient objective evidence that they will occur. (Para. 51, FRS 12.)

The key issue is what constitutes 'sufficient objective evidence'. Such evidence may be provided by technically qualified, objective observers. It is more likely to be sufficient if it relates to cost reductions due to experience in applying existing technology than to the expected development of new, and as yet unproven, methods. Regarding legal changes, sufficient evidence may not exist until an Act of Parliament has been passed.

Potential impact of the FRSME

The FRSME reflects the current FRS 12 comments in relation to future events.

17.5.5 Expected disposal of assets

FRS 12 states that:

> Gains from the expected disposal of assets should not be taken into account in measuring a provision. (Para. 54, FRS 12.)

The reason for this exclusion is that it is normally considered imprudent to recognise gains until they are realised. It may be possible for a gain to be recognised by applying the principles of accounting for assets (covered in Chapter 11), for example, by revaluing an asset or by reversing a previous impairment loss in accordance with FRS 11. For consistency, the FRS 3 requirements relating to calculation of provisions for the sale or termination of an operation have been amended to remove expected profits from the disposal of assets from the calculation.

Potential impact of the FRSME

This issue is not mentioned in the FRSME, but it is difficult to imagine that such expected gains could be taken into account in the determination of the amount of a provision whilst complying with the standard.

17.6 APPLICATION OF THE RECOGNITION AND MEASUREMENT RULES

17.6.1 Future operating losses

Before the introduction of FRS 12, provision for future operating losses had already been barred by FRS 7 in the context of acquisition accounting. The recognition criteria in FRS 12 are such as to ban general provisions for expected losses, as these do not give rise to present obligations arising from past events. However, the ASB has made doubly sure that there can be no misunderstanding by including the following requirement in FRS 12:

> Provisions should not be recognised for future operating losses. (Para. 68, FRS 12.)

The ASB does point out that the expectation of future losses may indicate an impairment of assets, as dealt with by FRS 11 *Impairment of Fixed Assets and Goodwill* (considered in Chapter 11). At first sight, this appears to be an inconsistent application of the prudence concept. Whilst an expense may be recognised for an asset write-down, the same underlying cause (an expectation of losses) does not permit the recognition of an expense if the other side of the entry is to provisions for liabilities rather than allowances for depreciation or impairment. This illustrates how the ASB's accounting standards are now driven by its principles of asset and liability recognition, with the concepts of prudence and accruals adopting a secondary role, mainly with regard to measurement.

Potential impact of the FRSME

Whilst not specifically mentioned in the FRSME, it is very clear from the general comments on the requirement for a past event that such provisions would be prohibited. The FRSME notes that provisions cannot be made for any obligations that will arise from a company's future actions, no matter how likely they are to occur.

17.6.2 Restructuring

FRS 12 defines a restructuring as follows:

> A programme that is planned and controlled by management, and materially changes either:
>
> (a)   the scope of a business undertaken by an entity; or
> (b)   the manner in which that business is conducted. (Para. 2, FRS 12.)

Examples of events that may fall under the definition of restructuring include:

- sale or termination of a line of business;
- closure of business locations or the relocation of business activities;
- changes in management structure, and
- fundamental reorganisations that have a material effect on the nature and focus of the company's operations.

Prior to the issue of FRS 12, provisions for restructuring had been one of the most fertile areas for 'big-bath' provisioning. The ASB has, therefore, set out strict rules to limit the circumstances in which such provisions may be made, in addition to the general recognition and measurement criteria in FRS 12. FRS 3 *Reporting Financial Performance* placed restrictions on provisions for discontinuance, the principles of which have now been extended to restructurings in general. The FRS 12 requirements apply to the recognition and measurement of provisions on discontinuance, as well as other restructurings. In the case of a discontinuance, FRS 3 still provides additional disclosure requirements. FRS 3 is covered in Chapter 5.

The key issue is identifying when an obligation has arisen. Prior to FRS 12, many companies set up restructuring provisions based on management intentions, such as board decisions. These had often not been made public, let alone implemented, at the balance sheet date. In such cases, no legal or constructive obligation existed. This has now been prohibited as FRS 12 requires a legal or constructive obligation at the balance sheet date arising from a past event as a condition for recognising a provision. Possibly because of the difficulties of identifying when a constructive obligation exists, FRS 12 sets out the following specific requirement:

A constructive obligation to restructure arises only when an entity:

(a) has a detailed formal plan for the restructuring identifying at least:

  (i)   the business or part of a business concerned;
  (ii) the principal locations affected;
  (iii) the location, function, and approximate number of employees who will be compensated for terminating their services;
  (iv) the expenditures that will be undertaken; and
  (v)   when the plan will be implemented; and

(b) has raised a valid expectation in those affected that it will carry out the restructuring by starting to implement that plan or announcing its main features to those affected by it. (Para. 77, FRS 12.)

FRS 12 also provides extensive guidance on how to apply the above requirement in practice. A public announcement is sufficient only if it gives rise to a valid expectation that the company will carry out the restructuring. The implementation of the plan must begin as soon as possible and be completed in a time-frame that makes significant changes to the plan unlikely. A management or board decision taken before the year end does not give rise to a constructive obligation at the balance sheet date unless the company has already begun implementation or made a public announcement of the main features sufficient to establish a constructive obligation.

Where a provision for restructuring is recognised, FRS 12 also includes a specific measurement requirement:

A restructuring provision should include only the direct expenditures arising from the restructuring, which are those that are both:

(a) necessarily entailed by the restructuring and
(b) not associated with the ongoing activities of the entity. (Para. 85, FRS 12.)

This means that the provision should not include other costs indirectly related to the restructuring, such as retraining or relocating staff in a continuing operation. These costs are deemed to relate to future business conduct not the restructuring itself. Provisions for future losses of the restructured operation are also not permitted, unless they relate to onerous contracts.

Where an operation is to be sold, the FRS specifies that:

No obligation arises for the sale of an operation until the entity is committed to the sale, ie there is a binding sale agreement. (Para. 83, FRS 12.)

A decision to sell does not itself create an obligation unless there is a contract. Without a binding agreement, there is no past event independent of the company's future actions, as management may change its mind or be unable to find a purchaser. However, where a sale is envisaged this may indicate that assets are impaired, necessitating a review for impairment under FRS 11 *Impairment of Fixed Assets and Goodwill*.

In some cases, a company may start to implement a restructuring programme, or announce a restructuring programme to those affected, after the balance sheet date but before the financial statements are authorised for issue. In such cases, no provision for restructuring is permitted. However, FRS 21 then requires that details of the restructuring be provided in the notes to the financial statements if the restructuring is material, and non-disclosure could influence the economic decisions of users taken on the basis of the financial statements.

Potential impact of the FRSME

Restructuring is not specifically mentioned in the FRSME. It does contain requirements in relation to past events, noting that provisions cannot be made on the basis of future events, however likely or even virtually certain they are to occur, that should normally lead to a similar result. However, at the margin there might be cases where the result would differ from that under current practice, in the absence of the detailed rules currently in place.

17.7 OTHER MATTERS RELATING TO PROVISIONS

17.7.1 Reimbursements

In some cases, another party, such as an insurance company or a supplier under a warranty, may meet all or part of a company's expenditure to settle a provision. On this point, FRS 12 contains the following requirements:

> Where some or all of the expenditure required to settle a provision is expected to be reimbursed by another party, the reimbursement should be recognised only when it is virtually certain that reimbursement will be received if the entity settles the obligation. The reimbursement should be treated as a separate asset. The amount recognised for the reimbursement should not exceed the amount of the provision.
>
> In the profit and loss account, the expense relating to a provision may be presented net of the amount recognised for a reimbursement. (Paras. 56 and 57, FRS 12.)

This test is very different from that normally applied to a contingent asset as set out below, even though many of the same words are used. In general, an asset can be recognised only if virtually certain (and therefore not contingent), whereas a liability is recognised if an obligation and a transfer of economic benefit are both more likely than not to occur. In the case of a potential reimbursement, there is still a 'virtually certain' test, but the test is whether or not it is virtually certain that reimbursement will be received if payment is made.

For example, a company might consider that it has a 75 per cent chance of having to meet costs of £1m, but is 100 per cent certain that this is covered by insurance, if the liability arises. In this case, both an asset and a liability would be recorded. This involves accounting for an asset only 75 per cent likely to crystallise. This seems unusual but avoids the anomaly that would arise if the company were required to account for a loss which if it were to arise, would then certainly be met by insurance (which would then give rise to a profit.) This can be contrasted with the situation where, for example:

- a company believes it has a 75 per cent chance of obtaining a benefit of £1m, with no associated loss. In this case the contingent asset would be disclosed but not recorded, and
- a company believes it has a 75 per cent chance of having to meet costs of £1m, but then considers it only has a 75 per cent chance of this being covered by insurance. In this case, the company would accrue for the loss, but not the reimbursement. The reimbursement, if any, would then be recognised only when recovery were made, or sufficiently certain.

Where an asset is recognised, it is presented separately from the liability as, if the asset is not recovered, the company would still remain liable for its obligation. In cases where the company will not be liable if a third party fails to pay, then it no longer has a liability and neither the liability nor the asset are recorded.

FRS 12 contains a limit to the amount that may be recognised as a reimbursement, stating that this must not exceed the amount of the provision. No such limitation is stated in the FRSSE.

Potential impact of the FRSME

The FRSME contains brief guidance on the treatment of reimbursements (as a UK addition to the text of the IFRS for SMEs). This is not quite as clearly drafted as FRS 12, since it refers to 'on settlement of the obligations' where FRS 12 states 'if the entity settles the obligation'. There does not appear to be a difference in intended meaning.

17.7.2 Onerous contracts

In contrast to provisions for expected losses in general, onerous contracts represent an expectation of losses where the ASB's recognition criteria for provisions are met. In practice, the most common situation where this arises is with a lease on a property that is no longer being used by a business. Although SSAP 21 *Accounting for Leases and Hire Purchase Contracts* deals with most aspects of lease accounting, it does not address the issue of leases for assets that have become surplus to the needs of a business, especially leases of commercial property. Executory contracts, such as leases, are excluded from the scope of FRS 12 unless the contract has become onerous.

FRS 12 defines an onerous contract as:

A contract in which the unavoidable costs of meeting the obligations under it exceed the economic benefits expected to be received under it. (Para. 2, FRS 12.)

The existence of a contract at the balance sheet date means that the FRS 12 recognition requirement for a present obligation arising from a past event is satisfied. There will also be a probable transfer of economic benefit in the case of an onerous contract as, by definition, the unavoidable costs must exceed the benefit expected. The third criteria for recognition of a provision will also be met as the contract should provide sufficient information to make a reliable estimate of the amount involved. The unavoidable costs under a contract reflect the least net cost of exiting from the contract, ie the lower of the cost of fulfilling it and compensation or penalties arising from failure to fulfil it.

Practical difficulties arise in applying FRS 12 to onerous leases because of the possibility of sub-letting redundant premises. If a sub-lease exists at the balance sheet date where there will be no significant net cost to the company, the lease will not be onerous and will, therefore, fall outside the scope of FRS 12. However, if a sub-lease exists where the rentals are significantly lower than those under the main lease, the contract will be onerous. The example of an onerous lease in FRS 12 is unhelpful on the point of sub-leases as it specifically excludes the possibility of sub-letting.

FRS 12 does not directly address the issue of whether, and if so how, to take into account rentals receivable under a sub-lease when measuring a provision for an onerous lease. However, by applying the argument that the sub-lessee is in effect meeting part of the company's obligation under a lease, the principles set out in FRS 12 relating to reimbursements may be applied to this situation.

As the company will normally retain the liability for the full rentals under the main lease, even if the sub-lessee defaults, it appears, on a very strict interpretation of FRS 12, that the future rentals under the sub-lease cannot be netted off against the obligation under the main lease. Instead, provision should be made for the present value of the entire rental obligation under the main lease, with a separate asset being recognised for rentals under the sub-lease, provided that this asset is considered virtually certain. This then raises the question of whether it is correct to recognise an asset for future rentals receivable. However, failure to do so whilst at the same time recognising the provision in full would be inconsistent and would present a misleading picture of the company's financial position.

An alternative, and far better, view is that the rentals under a sub-lease should be taken into account in making the best estimate of the amount required to settle the obligation at the balance sheet date, and that provision should therefore be made only for the net amount. Such a treatment was illustrated in the exposure draft which preceded FRS 12, but was not carried through into the final standard as the ASB's offset rules would generally appear to preclude such a treatment. Given that the FRS 12 requirement is to make provision for the onerous nature of the contract, it would appear to be an exception to this general rule. Only the net estimate need be provided.

The situation is more complicated if no sub-lease actually exists at the balance sheet date. The problem is that using the ASB's general recognition criteria the 'asset' of future expected rentals lacks the certainty required in order to be recognised. FRS 12 states that a provision should be measured at the amount which a company would rationally pay to settle the obligation existing at the balance sheet date. It therefore seems sensible and commercially realistic to take into account the possibility of sub-letting. Similarly, the definition of an onerous contract refers to the 'unavoidable' costs but the 'expected' benefits. If a lessee company were to negotiate a payment in return for being released from a lease, both the lessee and lessor would take into account the possibility of sub-letting or re-letting the asset when determining the amount of the payment. On a very strict reading, under the measurement rules in FRS 12 this approach is not allowed, and the FRS appears to lack commercial realism on this point. If this view is taken, the FRS 12 requirements relating to onerous contracts could lead to a company making a significant provision in one year, when a building becomes redundant, and then reversing that provision in the following year when a sub-lease is granted which means that the main lease is no longer onerous.

However, this view does not seem consistent with the general intention of the FRS 12 rules. As stated above, a contract is onerous where the 'expected' benefits do not equal the unavoidable costs. If a company were, for example, to have a ten-year lease of a property with lease payments required of £100,000 per annum, and expect to receive income of £120,000 per annum, even though no sub-lease had yet been created, the contract would not be onerous and no provision would be required. The same would apply even if the expected income were £100,000. To state that a provision for ten years' rent (ie £1,000,000 before discounting) if the expected rentals fell to £99,999 is surely absurd. As noted above, it is also not consistent with the requirement that provisions be stated at the amount which a company would rationally pay to settle the obligation existing at the balance sheet date. This amount would take account of the potential rental income.

In summary, the most sensible interpretation of FRS 12 is that provision on onerous contracts should be made to the extent, and only to the extent, that they are onerous. This should be an estimate of the actual expected losses. Where a company may be able to sub-let, but has not yet done so, then prudence has a role in determining the amount of the expected benefit, as with all situations of uncertainty. The best approach would be to take a very prudent view of the potential rentals receivable. But this does not imply any requirement to provide for the whole amount of the expected costs without taking account of the expected benefits.

Potential impact of the FRSME

The FRSME also requires provision to be made for onerous contracts.

17.7.3 Dilapidations

Many operating leases for buildings, and some for other assets, contain requirements for the lessee to restore the leased asset to its original condition, to make good wear and tear or to repair damage caused during the lease. Prior to the introduction of FRS 12, it was common for lessees to make provisions for such costs over the lease term. Although FRS 12 prohibits provisions for major repairs and refurbishment of fixed assets, the main text of the FRS does not specifically address the issue of provisions made by lessees. The only reference to this matter in FRS 12 is in an appendix:

> In some operating leases the lessee is required to incur periodic charges for maintenance of the leased asset or to make good dilapidations or other damage occurring during the rental period. The principle illustrated in example 11 [which prohibits provisions for major refurbishment of assets] does not preclude the recognition of such liabilities once the event giving rise to the obligation under the lease has occurred. (Para. 39, Appendix VII, FRS 12.)

To determine whether a provision should be made for repairs, it is necessary to apply the FRS 12 recognition criteria. The key issue is whether there is a present obligation as a result of a past event. This criterion will be satisfied where the lease terms specifically require the lessee to pay for repairs or dilapidations, and identifiable wear or damage has occurred at the balance sheet date. The provision made should then cover the estimated repair cost of that wear or damage, but not expected future wear or damage that has not yet occurred.

Making provisions for dilapidations and similar costs appears inconsistent with the approach adopted by the ASB in relation to repairs and refurbishment of fixed assets which have suffered wear or damage where there is also a legal requirement to carry out repairs. In the latter case, the ASB's view is that the company could sell the asset and thus avoid the obligation. Although a lessee may be able to avoid actually incurring repair costs by sub-letting the asset, in most cases, the terms of the main lease will mean that the lessee under it will remain liable in the event of the sub-lessee defaulting. Therefore, an obligation still exists which is independent of the company's future actions.

Potential impact of the FRSME

The FRSME does not deal specifically with dilapidations, although neither does FRS 12 in its basic text. Given that the underlying requirements are the same, the FRSME should arrive at the same result.

17.7.4   Changes in provisions

Because of the uncertainties inherent in the estimates required where provisions are made, or not made, FRS 12 includes the following requirement:

> Provisions should be reviewed at each balance sheet date and adjusted to reflect the current best estimate. If it is no longer probable that a transfer of economic benefits will be required to settle the obligation, the provision should be reversed. (Para. 62, FRS 12.)

Where discounting is used, the carrying amount of a provision increases in each period to reflect the passage of time and this increase is recognised as an interest expense.

Potential impact of the FRSME

The FRSME also requires reconsideration of all provisions at each balance sheet date, although it refers to the end of each reporting period.

17.7.5   Use of provisions

As a further guard against 'big-bath' provisioning, FRS 12 contains the following restriction:

> A provision should be used only for expenditures for which the provision was originally recognised. (Para. 64, FRS 12.)

If a provision is no longer required for its originally intended purpose, it should be reversed and not used to conceal the impact of other unrelated expenditure.

Potential impact of the FRSME

The FRSME contains the same requirement that provisions be used only for the purpose for which they were originally intended.

17.7.6   Recognising an asset when recognising a provision

In some cases, an obligation may arise from a past event before a company has obtained economic benefits from the event concerned. An example is where a quarrying company establishes a new quarry and has a legal obligation to restore the land once quarrying is completed. When the quarry is initiated, the company has yet to realise the economic benefits from extraction of the rock. In such a case, FRS 12 requires that the debit entry corresponding to the liability recognised is added to the fixed asset for the cost of establishing the quarry rather than being expensed immediately. The cost passes to the profit and loss account as the asset is depreciated.

This situation should be contrasted with that of environmental damage which occurs as the associated economic benefits are obtained, for example, where a chemical works causes land contamination, which it is obliged to rectify, as chemicals are produced. In this case, a provision is required for damage which has arisen at the balance sheet date and the economic benefits, ie production of chemicals, have been obtained at that time. Therefore, there is no associated future benefit and the provision is charged immediately to the profit and loss account.

Potential impact of the FRSME

The FRSME also recognises that there are cases where a provision can be recognised as part of the cost of an asset rather than as an expense.

17.7.7   National Insurance contributions on share option gains

In July 2000, the ASB issued UITF Abstract 25 *National Insurance Contributions on Share Option Gains*. As with all UITFs, it does not apply to companies adopting the FRSSE.

The Social Security Act 1998 introduced a National Insurance charge on certain share option gains. The charge applies to gains under non-approved schemes on options granted after 5 April 1999. The gain subject to NI is the difference between the share price at the date the options are exercised and the exercise price which is paid by the employee. The charge applies to any schemes where the shares are 'readily convertible assets': that is, where they can be sold on a stock exchange or where arrangements are in place, or expected to be in place, that allow the employees to obtain cash for their shares.

The issue addressed by the Abstract is whether or not the employer should accrue for the estimated liability between the date of grant and the date of exercise. A secondary question of how any such accrual should be calculated also arises.

Abstract 25 requires companies to make provision for National Insurance contributions on outstanding share options that are expected to be exercised. The provision is calculated by applying the latest enacted NI rate to the difference between the market value of the underlying shares at the balance sheet date and the option exercise price. Where the exercise of the option is linked to a performance period, recognition of the provision should be spread over that period. Where there is no performance period, or the performance period has already ended, the amount should be fully adjusted using the market price of the shares. Because FRS 12 requires the principal assumptions affecting provisions to be disclosed, the Abstract states that companies may need to disclose the share price used in their calculations, and the effect of any significant movement in that price.

The amounts charged in making the provision should be taken to the profit and loss account, as staff costs, except to the extent that they may be capitalised in accordance with the Companies Act 2006 and accounting standards.

Since Abstract 25 was issued, The Child Support, Pensions and Social Security Act 2000 has been passed. This allows employers and employees to agree that the NI charge should be payable by the employee. There are two possibilities if such an agreement is reached.

(1) There is an agreement between the employee and the employer that the employee will assume the liability. In this case, the company should account for a separate asset and liability. Prudence will, of course, mean that no asset can be reflected unless it is virtually certain.

(2) There is a joint election between the employee and the employer to the effect that the employee will assume the liability. In this case, there is no cost to the company, and no charge or provision will appear in the company's financial statements.

Potential impact of the FRSME

The FRSME does not contain specific guidance on this issue.

17.8 DISCLOSURES

FRS 12 includes extensive disclosure requirements relating to provisions, the main points of which are as follows. For each material class of provision, a company should disclose:

- the carrying amount at the beginning and end of the period;
- additional provisions made during the year, including increases to existing provisions;
- amounts used during the year;
- unused amounts reversed during the year, and
- the increase in the discounted amount arising from the passage of time and the effect of any change in the discount rate.

Comparative information is not required.

Companies must also provide:

- a brief description of the nature of the obligation, and the expected timing of any resulting transfers of economic benefits;
- an indication of the uncertainties about the amount or timing of the transfers of economic benefits; this may include the major assumptions that have been made, and
- the amount of any expected reimbursement, stating the amount of any asset that has been recognised for that expected reimbursement.

Disclosure is not required where it would seriously prejudice negotiations with other parties in respect of the matter for which the provision was made. An example of this is where a legal dispute is in progress and where disclosure of details might be perceived by the other party as an admission of liability. The amount still needs to be recorded, but disclosure can then be limited to the general nature of the provision and the fact of, and reason for, non-disclosure of the details. This disclosure exemption does not apply where disclosure may be prejudicial to the interests of the company itself, for example, by damaging its reputation or causing embarrassment to its senior management.

The FRSSE omits all FRS 12 disclosure requirements relating to provisions, leaving only the statutory disclosures in place.

Potential impact of the FRSME

The FRSME contains similar disclosure requirements to FRS 12 and UK statute. It also contains the same exemption in relation to situations where disclosure may be seriously prejudicial.

17.9 CONTINGENT LIABILITIES AND CONTINGENT ASSETS

17.9.1 *The need to disclose contingent liabilities and contingent assets*

Users of financial statements need to be made aware not only of matters that have been resolved, or where resolution is virtually certain, but also of matters of uncertainty which exist at the balance sheet date where the criteria for recognition of a liability or asset in the financial statements are not met at that time, as such matters may have a material effect on the results or position of the business in the future.

The information provided by disclosures relating to contingent liabilities and contingent assets may be vital to the user. The user can then make an assessment of the effect of the possible outcomes and gain a far better understanding of factors affecting the business's position and performance. If the financial statements did not include such information, they would not give a true and fair view of the business to the user, and would be misleading by omission.

17.9.2 *Meaning of 'contingent liability'*

FRS 12 defines a contingent liability as:

   (a)   A possible obligation that arises from past events and whose existence will be confirmed only by the occurrence of one or more uncertain future events not wholly within the entity's control; or

(b) a present obligation that arises from past events but is not recognised because:

(a) it is not probable that a transfer of economic benefits will be required to settle the obligation; or

(b) the amount of the obligation cannot be measured with sufficient reliability. (Para. 2, FRS 12.)

Note that, from this definition, a contingent liability may arise in one of two main ways: a possible obligation or a present obligation where a transfer of economic benefits is not probable. That is, a contingent liability can exist only if there is at least a possible obligation that exists at the balance sheet date.

Although this definition differs from that previously contained in SSAP 18, the implications of this are limited. Items defined as contingent liabilities under SSAP 18 and for which provision needed to be made are no longer defined as contingent liabilities under FRS 12. They are now simply considered to be liabilities.

Potential impact of the FRSME

The FRSME contains a very similar definition of a contingent liability.

17.9.3 Recognition of contingent liabilities

The recognition requirement in FRS 12 is simple:

. An entity should not recognise a contingent liability. (Para. 27, FRS 12.)

Contingent liabilities arise where the conditions for recognising a provision (ie a type of liability) are not present due to the degree of uncertainty relating either to the existence of an obligation or to the likelihood of transfer of economic benefits. Recognition of a provision requires both a present obligation and a probable transfer of economic benefit.

Where a company is jointly and severally liable for an obligation, the part of the obligation that is expected to be met by other parties is usually treated as a contingent liability and a provision is recognised for the part of the obligation for which a transfer of economic benefits is probable.

The inherent uncertainties underlying a contingent liability are such that they should be monitored continuously to identify whether a possible obligation has become actual or a transfer of economic benefits has become probable. If it becomes probable that a transfer of future economic benefits will be required for an item previously dealt with as a contingent liability, a provision is recognised in the financial statements of the period in which the change in probability occurs.

Potential impact of the FRSME

The requirements of the FRSME are very similar to those included in FRS 12.

17.9.4   *Disclosure of contingent liabilities*

FRS 12 contains the following requirement:

> Unless the possibility of any transfer in settlement is remote, an entity should disclose for each class of contingent liability at the balance sheet date a brief description of the nature of the contingent liability and, where practicable:
>
> (a) an estimate of its financial effect, measured in accordance with [the requirements relating to measurement of provisions];
> (b) an indication of the uncertainties relating to the amount or timing of any outflow; and
> (c) the possibility of any reimbursement. (Para. 91, FRS 12.)

Where it is not practicable to give all of the above information, this fact should be stated.

The level of disclosure should be sufficient to enable the user to obtain a good understanding of the contingent liability. With, for example, litigation on which considerable progress has been made, the level of disclosure required may be extensive.

Disclosure is not required where it would seriously prejudice negotiations with other parties in respect of the matter which gave rise to the contingent liability. Disclosure can then be limited to the general nature of the matter and the fact of, and reason for, non-disclosure of the details.

Inevitably, there is reluctance on the part of many companies to provide disclosure of some types of contingent liability. For example, a company:

- may not wish to make and disclose an estimate of the possible effect of losing a court case, as this might appear to be evidence that it expects to lose the case, or
- may be unwilling to provide details of the existence and financial effect of a breach of law or regulations which it has committed, and which might result in a cost to the company.

In the second case there is the paradoxical position that disclosure of a contingent liability might mean that it would cease to be contingent and would become a provision. Disclosure is still required under statute and FRS 12 unless the amounts involved are immaterial or the likelihood of the liability actually arising is extremely remote.

The FRSSE merely requires disclosure of a brief description of any contingent liabilities and, where practicable, an estimate of the financial effect, except where their existence is remote. The detailed FRS 12 disclosure rules are not restated in full in the FRSSE.

Potential impact of the FRSME

The FRSME contains virtually identical requirements to those of FRS 12.

17.9.5 Effect of events after the balance sheet date

In general, events after the balance sheet date should be taken into account in determining whether a contingent liability exists, because a liability is contingent only if there is uncertainty relating to the outcome at the time the financial statements are approved. Therefore, if the matter has been resolved by the time the financial statements are approved, there will normally be no contingent liability disclosure.

However, an exception arises where a company has a number of similar contingent liabilities in existence at each balance sheet date, for example, bills of exchange discounted with recourse. In such cases, it is common practice to disclose the amount existing at the balance sheet date, even though the bills may have been honoured by the third party in the period since the balance sheet date. So that the reader is not misled, the amount which has ceased to be contingent in the period since the balance sheet date should also be disclosed. By providing such disclosures, which are not strictly required by FRS 12, companies can improve the comparability of information in the financial statements. This enables companies to avoid the potential problem of apparent fluctuations in the level of such liabilities from year to year which arises because of variations in the time taken to approve the accounts rather than changes in the actual amounts existing at the balance sheet date.

17.9.6 Remote contingent liabilities

FRS 12 does not include an explanation of why remote contingent liabilities should not be disclosed. SSAP 18 did provide such an explanation, which was that disclosure could be misleading where the probability of the ultimate outcome having a material effect on the financial statements was remote. The same argument could be used in support of the FRS 12 requirement, although, as noted below, an extremely prudent view of what is meant by remote should be adopted.

No specific guidance is provided in FRS 12 on the meaning of 'remote'. Since accountants are required to be prudent, remote should be interpreted as meaning virtually impossible. This means that the probability of an event occurring should be so small that it can be ignored. To understand this fully, it may be useful to consider the situation of a company which has provided a guarantee to a third party which, if it were to be called on to honour, would undermine the going concern basis. In such a situation, even a five or ten per cent chance that the guarantee will be enforced may not be considered remote as it could, potentially, destroy the entire company.

However, the major problems are likely to be measuring the factors which affect the probability of the event, rather than determining exactly what we mean by remote. We suggest that an extremely prudent policy should be applied when determining the probability of occurrence of an event. Many companies adopted such an approach in the past when applying SSAP 18 and have disclosed contingent liabilities even when their likelihood is very close to remote. In such cases the possible financial effect is often not stated since the low probability of occurrence will normally make estimating the financial effect with any degree of precision almost impossible.

Potential impact of the FRSME

The FRSME also requires, without justifying, the exclusion of remote contingent liabilities.

17.9.7 Meaning of 'contingent asset'

FRS 12 defines a contingent asset as:

> A possible asset that arises from past events and whose existence will be confirmed only by the occurrence of one or more uncertain future events not wholly within the entity's control. (Para. 2, FRS 12.)

This definition appears to mirror part (a) of the definition of a contingent liability set out at **17.9.2**, but, in fact, 'possible' in the context of contingent assets has a different meaning to that for contingent liabilities, as discussed below.

17.9.8 Recognition of contingent assets

The recognition requirement for contingent assets is also simple:

> An entity should not recognise a contingent asset. (Para. 31, FRS 12.)

The key distinction between contingent liabilities and contingent assets lies in the degree of probability involved. Contingent liabilities arise where an obligation, or the transfer of economic benefits, is possible, which in this context means not more likely than not. By contrast, 'possible' in the context of a contingent asset means anything less than virtually certain. This is an application of the prudence concept, although FRS 12 does not specifically mention 'prudence' in this context:

> Contingent assets are not recognised in financial statements because it could result in the recognition of profit that may never be realised. However, when the

realisation of the profit is virtually certain, then the related asset is not a contingent asset and its recognition is appropriate. (Para. 33, FRS 12.)

Where realisation of a profit is virtually certain, there is no justification for omitting the related asset as to do so would be excessively prudent.

Contingent assets should be monitored continuously so that any change in the probability of an outcome is reflected appropriately in the financial statements.

There is a very slight twist in the accounting treatment required where there is a change in the probability of a contingent asset being realised. FRS 12 notes that:

...If it has become virtually certain that an inflow of economic benefits will arise, the asset and the related profit are recognised in the financial statements of the period in which the change occurs... (Para. 35, FRS 12.)

Where the change occurs at most points during the year, the accounting treatment this implies is entirely reasonable. The oddity can arise where certainty is obtained after the end of a financial year, but before the financial statements have been issued. In this situation the wording would imply that the financial statements should not reflect the asset or associated gain, notwithstanding that the underlying situation existed at the balance sheet date and that the realisation of the gain is known with virtual certainty when the financial statements are prepared.

Potential impact of the FRSME

The FRSME also prohibits the recognition of contingent assets.

17.9.9 Disclosure of contingent assets

FRS 12 contains the following requirement:

Where an inflow of economic benefits is probable, an entity should disclose a brief description of the nature of the contingent assets at the balance sheet date and, where practicable, an estimate of their financial effect, measured using the principles set out for provisions ... (Para. 94, FRS 12.)

In this context, probable means more likely than not. Care is needed to avoid giving misleading indications of the likelihood of a profit arising.

The FRSSE incorporates a simplified version of this requirement, by omitting the reference to measurement principles.

Potential impact of the FRSME

The FRSME also requires disclosure of contingent assets. Oddly, it does not specifically state that the description should be brief.

17.10   PROPOSALS FOR CHANGE

17.10.1   FRED 39

FRED 39 has been issued by the ASB. This exposure draft is the UK version of an international draft that was developed as part of the second phase of the IASB's business combinations project, a project undertaken jointly with the US Financial Accounting Standards Board (FASB). Despite this, if implemented, it will change the accounting treatment adopted even where there has been no combination. IFRS 3, the main result of the IASB's business combinations project, was issued in January 2008. A new standard on provisions was not issued at the same time, and this has subsequently been deferred. However, there is little indication that the IASB has fundamentally changed its view of how provisions and contingencies should be treated. This is made clear by the issue, in January 2010, of specific proposals to alter IAS 37, the international standard that covers the same areas as FRS 12.

The chances that FRED 39 will ever become a UK accounting standard are exceedingly slim. However, it does go some way towards showing how IFRS might develop, which might then affect the FRSME.

17.10.2   Terminology

The draft proposes significant changes in terminology.

In particular:

- it proposes that the phrase 'provision' cease to be a defined term, and be replaced with the phrase 'non-financial liability', however, it will allow the phrase 'provision' to continue to be used in financial statements;
- it proposes removing the current definition of a provision, and replacing it with a definition of a non-financial liability, which will be simply any liability that falls outside the definition of a financial liability under FRS 25, *Financial Instruments: Presentation*, and
- it proposes eliminating the terms 'contingent liability' and 'contingent asset'.

17.10.3   Contingent liabilities and assets

The proposed elimination of the terms 'contingent assets' and 'liability' amounts to more than a change in terminology. There is a substantial difference between the accounting treatments and disclosure currently required and that proposed under the FRED.

Under FRS 12, a contingent liability is deemed to relate to a possible obligation. Contingent liabilities are currently not accounted for, on the basis that there is no probable outflow of economic resources or because the amount of the obligation cannot be measured with sufficient reliability. Disclosure is required for such contingent liabilities unless the likelihood of any outflow of economic resources is remote. In effect, the current standard combines the effect of the existence of a liability with the effect of the likelihood of an outflow.

The draft takes a different approach and splits the two impacts. In basic terms, the existence of a liability is assessed separately from any uncertainty that may affect the amount that will be required to settle such a liability. As a result, it argues that it is not the obligation that is contingent but the amount that is needed to settle the obligation that is contingent. This then means that the uncertainty about future events, which under the current standard affects whether or not a liability is recorded, would instead simply affect the amount of the liability to be recorded.

A similar logic is applied to what are currently treated as contingent assets.

17.10.4 Provisions

Consistent with the analysis of contingent assets and liabilities, the draft eliminates the current recognition criterion based on probability. Instead, it argues that there is an unconditional obligation, which may then involve an uncertainty as to the amount that will be required to meet the unconditional obligation.

The example given in the introduction to the standard deals with the issue of product warranties. Under FRS 12, a company needs to consider the likelihood of a claim arising under the warranty. Under the draft, the company accepts that there is an unconditional obligation to meet warranty claims. Any uncertainty relates solely to the amount that is needed to meet that unconditional obligation.

In terms of measurement, the change in approach has a profound impact upon the amounts that will be recorded, as it relates to individual items or small populations of items.

Under FRS 12, when dealing with a large population of similar items an expected value approach would be used. Again using the example of an identical warranty on a large number of items sold, this estimate, based on the information available to the company, would lead to a provision being made based on the estimated value of claims. While it would not be possible to determine on which items a claim might be made, experience would normally allow a company to make a provision based on past experience, as amended by current experience. This would not change under the draft in practice, even though the rationale might change.

The draft does make a fundamental change in relation to one-off items. Under FRS 12 the company would assess the likelihood of a claim arising and should normally provide the best estimate of the amount that may be payable. For example, a company is aware of a claim being made against it, in the amount of £1 million. However, after obtaining all relevant information concerning the claim, including expert advice where relevant, it determines that there is only a ten per cent chance of that amount actually having to be paid. To make the situation even starker, the amount is inclusive of costs and all costs will be met by the other party if the company is successful in defending the claim.

Under FRS 12, the most likely amount payable is zero. Therefore, no provision would be made. Since ten per cent is not remote, the company would be required to disclose the existence of a contingent liability (assuming that the amount is material).

Under the draft, the company would instead have to account for the amount at the best estimate of the amount that the company would rationally pay in order to settle the liability. Ignoring any impact of the time value of money, taking account of the amount involved and the likelihood of payment, that amount would be £100,000. A provision for this amount (called a non-financial liability) would then need to be made.

This is the expected value. As noted above, it is already used routinely for large populations, but not for individual items or small populations.

These proposals have changed slightly in the IASB's proposals issued in January 2010. Under these proposals, the key question becomes whether or not there is an obligation. If we assume that the assessed likelihood of a claim being successful is only ten per cent, then this would indicate that the company does not believe it has an obligation. In such a case, and as at present, no liability would be recorded.

17.10.5   Constructive obligations

FRS 12 already deals with constructive obligations, and requires them to be treated in the same way as legal obligations.

However, the current proposals are intended to clarify the requirements. In particular, the draft proposes:

- to amend the definition of a constructive obligation to make clear that the actions taken by the company must result in other parties having a valid expectation that they can rely on the company to discharge its responsibilities, and
- to provide more guidance on whether or not a constructive obligation has been incurred.

The draft sets three criteria that must be satisfied if a constructive obligation is to be recognised:

- the company must have indicated to other parties that it will accept particular responsibilities;
- the other parties must reasonably be able to expect the company to perform those responsibilities, and
- the other parties will either benefit from the company's performance or suffer harm from any non-performance.

While this will not change the accounting treatment in all cases, it may provide rather more clarity in borderline situations.

17.10.6 Onerous contracts

FRS 12 requires provision to be made for onerous contracts, being defined as a contract where the unavoidable costs of meeting the obligations exceed the economic benefits it is expected to produce. There is little else in the standard dealing with the detail of this.

The draft proposes that:

- a contract should not be considered as onerous where it will become onerous only as a result of a company's action and that action has not yet been taken, and
- in the case of an onerous operating lease, the unavoidable costs of meeting the obligation should be based on the unavoidable lease commitment less any sublease rentals that the company could reasonably receive, regardless of whether or not the entity intends to sublease the property.

The logic for the second proposal is that if the company were to negotiate an exit from the lease obligation the value of sublease income to be generated would enter into the determination of an appropriate value. This does not depend on whether or not the company intends to sublet.

17.10.7 Restructuring

The draft proposes changing the current requirements in respect of provisions for restructuring by:

- specifying that a liability in respect of restructuring is recognised only on the same basis as a liability would be recognised if the same item were to arise independently of a restructuring;
- amending FRS 17 to deal with employee termination benefits;
- requiring that a liability for costs that will continue to be incurred under a contract for its remaining term without equivalent benefit is recognised when the company ceases using the right conveyed by the contract, in

addition to any onerous contract liability that may already have been recorded, and

- requiring the costs of terminating a contract before the end of its term to be recognised when the contract is terminated in accordance with its terms.

17.10.8   ASB view

As noted earlier, while FRED 39 is published by the ASB it is simply a UK version of an international exposure draft. As a result, the ASB does not necessarily endorse the views that are contained within the draft. Specifically, the ASB has raised a number of questions about the draft in its own introduction, questions which have been echoed and expanded in response to the draft.

Among the issues raised by the ASB are the following.

(1)   The approach to non-financial liabilities is an 'exit value' approach. This means the amount that a company would rationally pay in order to settle an obligation. The ASB notes that as the proposals are intended to apply to all non-financial liabilities this implies a policy of measuring liabilities at exit values. Whether or not this is appropriate, it is a basic change which would be better considered as part of the review of the underlying framework of accounting, rather than in a specific standard.

(2)   The re-analysis of contingent items and the removal of the probability recognition criterion mean that many more liabilities will fall to be recognised, since there is no recognition threshold. The ASB is concerned that: even items that are very unlikely to give rise to any outflows will fall to be recognised, making it difficult to ensure that all such liabilities have been recorded; there will be far more subjectivity in determination of amounts; and, notwithstanding the continuation of the disclosure exemptions, the disclosure of such information may be prejudicial in negotiations.

(3)   The changes on restructuring, which in effect require it to be broken into components which may be recognised at different times, may mean the overall impact is lost.

The comments on the proposals, and on the business combinations proposals in general of which this forms just a part, have not been positive. As a result, it is uncertain whether the changes proposed will lead to equivalent changes in standards and, if so, when.

18 EVENTS AFTER THE BALANCE SHEET DATE

18.1 INTRODUCTION

18.1.1 FRS 21

FRS 21 *Events After the Balance Sheet Date*, has been effective since accounting periods beginning on or after 1 January 2005. It replaced SSAP 17, *Accounting for Post Balance Sheet Events*. FRS 21 is the UK version of the equivalent international standard, IAS 10 (although the title of the international standard has since been changed to refer to events after the end of the reporting period, to reflect the fact that the phrase 'balance sheet' is no longer used in IFRS).

Potential impact of the FRSME

There are no differences in principle between the current UK accounting requirements and those contained within the draft FRSME. This reflects the relatively uncontentious nature of the area, and the existing similarities in treatment between UK GAAP and IFRS. There are differences in terminology and in some of the details of the requirements.

18.1.2 Adjustment and disclosure

FRS 21 defines events after the balance sheet date as:

> ... those events, favourable and unfavourable, that occur between the balance sheet date and the date when the financial statements are authorised for issue. Two types of events can be identified:
>
> (a) those that provide evidence of conditions that existed at the balance sheet date (adjusting events after the balance sheet date); and
> (b) those that are indicative of conditions that arose after the balance sheet date (non-adjusting events after the balance sheet date). (Para. 3, FRS 21.)

The standard contains considerable guidance on when financial statements are deemed to be authorised for issue. This guidance is intended to deal with the many different procedures there may be for the issuance of financial statements in different countries. In the UK, it will continue to be the date on which the financial statements are approved by the board of directors.

The standard also requires that financial statements disclose the date that they were authorised for issue.

There is also a requirement to state if the entity's owners or others have the power to amend the financial statements after issue. This is not relevant in the UK, where financial statements are not subject to the same approval processes as in some other countries, although, strictly, it could be argued that there is a procedure for the directors amending the financial statements subsequently, as a result of the regulations dealing with revision of defective accounts. Such disclosure would not appear to be the intention behind the requirement and no disclosure of this possibility is therefore made in financial statements.

Potential impact of the FRSME

There is no difference in substance between the current requirements and those contained in the draft FRSME. The same distinction between adjusting and non-adjusting events applies, and the definitions are virtually the same, other than (like IFRS) the draft FRSME refers to events after the end of the reporting period rather than after the balance sheet date.

While not amounting to a relevant difference, the draft FRSME does point out that events after the end of the reporting period include all events up to the date when the financial statements are authorised for issue, even if those events occur after the public announcement of profit or loss or other selected financial information. Given the proposed scope of the FRSME, few companies falling within its compass are likely to make such public announcements.

The FRSME contains similar disclosures in relation to the date of authorisation of financial statements for issue, who provided that authorisation, and whether any parties have the right to amend the financial statements after issue.

18.2 ADJUSTING EVENTS

18.2.1 *Basic treatment*

The basic treatment for adjusting events is set out in FRS 21:

> An entity shall adjust the amounts recognised in its financial statements to reflect adjusting events after the balance sheet date. (Para. 8, FRS 21.)

Since adjusting events simply provide more information about the position that already existed at the balance sheet date, they need to be included in the assessment of the amounts to be shown in the financial statements. However, they do not normally need to be separately disclosed, unless they are required to be disclosed under some separate requirements, such as where they are of such size or impact that they fall to be treated as exceptional items.

FRS 21 provides a list of items that might be adjusting events after the balance sheet date.

(1) The settlement after the balance sheet date of a court case that confirms the

company has a present obligation at the balance sheet date. Where such a case is settled, the company may need to restate any provision that it had already made in accordance with FRS 12, or recognise such a provision if none had previously been created. FRS 21 makes it clear that, where the cause of action arose prior to the balance sheet date, it is not acceptable simply to disclose a contingent liability since the settlement provides evidence of the existence of an obligation. Of course the situation may be more complicated than FRS 21 implies, such as where a company loses a case, but believes that it has good grounds for appeal. Nonetheless, losing an action, even if only in a court of first instance, provides very strong evidence of the amount of any provision that should be made.

(2) Information received after the balance sheet date indicating that an asset was impaired at the balance sheet date, or that the amount of any previous impairment may need to be adjusted. The two specific examples given in the FRS are the bankruptcy of a debtor, which in nearly all cases will confirm that the debt was already irrecoverable at the balance sheet date, and the sale of stocks, which usually provides evidence of their net realisable value at the balance sheet date. In both of the cases specifically mentioned, the assumption is rebuttable in the sense that, in extreme cases, it may be possible to prove that the events giving rise to the loss arose after the balance sheet date. Such cases will be extremely rare.

(3) The determination, after the balance sheet date, of the cost of assets purchased or the proceeds of assets sold, before the balance sheet date. It is possible to make a sale or purchase prior to the end of the year where the final price has yet to be agreed. For example, a third party valuation may be required to establish the final amount payable or receivable. That valuation will then be treated as an adjusting event.

(4) The discovery of fraud or errors showing the financial statements are incorrect.

(5) The determination after the balance sheet date of the amount of a profit-sharing or bonus scheme, if the company had a legal or constructive obligation at the balance sheet date to make payments as a result of events up to that date.

The list is not intended to be exhaustive.

The last example given above (although the order adopted is not that in the standard) is potentially the most complex. The situation is fairly straightforward where there is, for example, a publicised bonus or profit-sharing scheme with clearly defined rules. While the amount payable may not be known at the balance sheet date itself, the basis of calculation is known, such as a percentage of profit, and once the figure is determined provision may be made. This will apply whether or not the scheme involves a legal obligation as even when it does not the staff members eligible will have an expectation of receiving a bonus or profit share, based on the company's stated policies. This is enough to create a constructive obligation.

The situation becomes more complex where such a 'scheme' is informal. If, for example, a company has no stated policy on bonuses, employment contracts make no mention of them, but in fact the company has paid bonuses for a number of years then this may also create a constructive obligation. However, such a case is not so clear cut and it is not obvious how long such a practice has to continue before a constructive obligation is created. Simply having paid a bonus for one year almost certainly creates no such obligation; having paid one consistently for ten years almost certainly does. But what about two years? Or three years? Obviously, the simplest situation for the accountant is for a company to have a stated policy, whether legally binding or otherwise, since this will allow a provision to be made even where no bonuses have been paid in the past. Companies may, however, prefer not to commit themselves, in which case each situation needs to be assessed on its individual merits.

It should be noted that FRS 21 is relevant only in so far as it determines the accounting treatment once it has been established that an obligation, arising as a result of past events, existed at the balance sheet date. It is FRS 12 that will determine whether or not there is any such obligation.

Potential impact of the FRSME

The treatment under the FRSME is the same as under extant UK GAAP. The draft FRSME is rather briefer than the FRS, in that it combines the requirement to update amounts recognised with the requirement to update related disclosures into one section, whereas the FRS deals with them separately. There is no distinction in this difference.

Even the list of examples in the FRSME covers the same areas as in the FRS. There are differences in terminology, but in all cases the accounting treatment to be applied is the same.

18.2.2   Adjusting disclosure

FRS 21 does not just deal with situations where an adjustment is required to the amounts appearing in the financial statements. It also deals with any further information about circumstances existing at the balance sheet date that may require changes to the disclosure provided in the financial statements:

> If an entity receives information after the balance sheet date about conditions that existed at the balance sheet date, it shall update disclosures that relate to those conditions, in the light of the new information. (Para. 19, FRS 21.)

Such information may or may not also affect the amounts included. The example given in the standard is of changing circumstances affecting a contingent liability. The amount recorded may need to be amended as new information is received but so may the nature of the disclosure.

Potential impact of the FRSME

The requirements of the draft FRSME are the same as those contained in the FRS. As noted earlier, the disclosure requirements are included in the same paragraph of the FRSME whereas they are separated in the FRS. In practice, this is of no relevance.

18.2.3 Adjusting events and going concern

FRS 21 states that:

> An entity shall not prepare its financial statements on a going concern basis if management determines after the balance sheet date either that it intends to liquidate the entity or to cease trading or that it has no realistic alternative but to do so. (Para. 14, FRS 21.)

Where the assumption of going concern is not appropriate, then, as the FRS mentions, the effect is so pervasive that there is a fundamental change in the basis of accounting and not just additional disclosure. In effect, the distinction between adjusting and non-adjusting events becomes largely irrelevant. This applies even where the company could continue, but after the end of the year a decision has been made to liquidate.

Potential impact of the FRSME

The draft FRSME does not deal as explicitly with this matter as the FRS. Management is required to make the same assessment, but there is no explicit reference as to whether this must reflect any decisions that have been made after the end of the reporting period.

18.3 NON-ADJUSTING EVENTS

18.3.1 Disclosure

By definition, non-adjusting events do not give rise to any alterations to the amounts appearing in the financial statements.

Non-adjusting events which need to be disclosed are those which, unequivocally, fall into the next accounting period, but which are material and could influence the economic decisions of users taken on the basis of the financial statements. Normal ongoing transactions therefore do not require disclosure.

Where a non-adjusting event does require disclosure, the financial statements should disclose:

- the nature of the event, and
- an estimate of the financial effect of the event, or a statement that no such estimate can be made.

FRS 21 provides some assistance, with a list of possible non-adjusting events that might warrant disclosure:

- major business combinations after the balance sheet date, or the disposal of a major subsidiary;
- the announcement of a plan to discontinue an operation;
- major purchases or disposal of assets, or expropriation of major assets by government;
- the destruction of a major production plant by a fire after the balance sheet date;
- announcing or commencing a major restructuring;
- major transactions in ordinary shares or potential ordinary shares (disclosure of such transactions may also be required by FRS 22);
- abnormally large changes after the balance sheet date in asset prices or foreign exchange rates;
- changes in tax rates or tax laws enacted or announced after the balance sheet date that have a significant effect on current and deferred tax assets and liabilities;
- entering into significant commitments or contingent liabilities, for example by issuing significant guarantees, and
- commencing major litigation arising solely out of events that occurred after the balance sheet date.

Most of these events are likely to lead to significant differences between the amounts included in the profit and loss account of the subsequent period and of the current accounting period.

One of the points of disclosing non-adjusting post balance sheet events is to warn the user of the financial statements that there are other events which they should consider when using the current year's profit and loss account as an indicator of future results. Given that FRS 3 *Reporting Financial Performance* defines ordinary activities so widely, it is not useful to think of non-adjusting items as outside of ordinary activities; they are more akin to exceptional items which occur after the balance sheet date.

Potential impact of the FRSME

The basic disclosure requirements of the FRSME are very similar to those under current UK GAAP.

The list of examples of such events is also virtually the same, with the only differences being those that reflect differences in terminology and accounting treatments that may be required under other parts of the draft standard that are not quite the same as under current UK GAAP. However, the draft FRSME also includes two further examples of non-adjusting events which are intended to clarify the distinction between these and adjusting events. The first deals with declines in the market values of investments where this relates to circumstances that arise subsequently to the end of the reporting period and do not represent circumstances existing at the end of that period. The second deals with a favourable settlement or judgement in relation to a court case which arises after the end of the period. This is considered to be a contingent asset at the reporting date. This is distinguished from agreement on the amount of damages where judgement had been reached prior to the end of the reporting period; in this situation it would be treated as an adjusting event on the basis that the only reason for not recognising the asset was not any question as to the existence of an asset, simply an inability to measure that asset reliably.

18.3.2 Dividends

FRS 21 states that:

> If an entity declares dividends to holders of equity instruments (as defined in FRS 25 *(IAS 32) Financial Instruments: Presentation*) after the balance sheet date, the entity shall not recognise those dividends as a liability at the balance sheet date. (Para. 12, FRS 21.)

This is consistent with FRS 12, since there is no obligation arising as a result of a past event at the balance sheet date.

This means that final dividends are not accrued in financial statements, and a liability for a final dividend on ordinary shares arises if, and only if, it is approved by the members in general meeting.

Companies are required to disclose that such dividends have been declared since the balance sheet date.

The statement quoted above is supplemented by a further paragraph, explaining that dividends which are declared after the balance sheet date are not recognised as a liability at the balance sheet date because 'they do not meet the criteria of a present obligation in FRS 12'. With effect for accounting periods beginning on or after 1 January 2009, this changed to 'because no obligation exists at that time'. Apparently, the previous wording had sometimes been interpreted to mean that there were cases where a liability could be recorded as a result of a constructive obligation. This was obviously never intended by the ASB (or more relevantly the IASB who actually drafted the standard on which FRS 21 is based). With the new wording there is presumably nobody who could argue that dividends, or rather dividends which need to be approved, can still be recorded as a liability prior to approval.

Potential impact of the FRSME

The accounting treatment under the FRSME is exactly the same. The FRSME does allow companies to present the amount of the dividend as a segregated component of retained earnings at the end of the reporting period.

18.3.3 Window dressing

SSAP 17 *Accounting for Post Balance Sheet Events*, the standard in force prior to FRS 21, dealt with window dressing, defined as a company undertaking a transaction during the year with the primary purpose of altering the appearance of its balance sheet. It required that where such transactions took place and were reversed after the balance sheet date, they be treated as non-adjusting but disclosed.

No such requirement is included in FRS 21, although it might still be necessary to consider whether a reversal could be of such significance as to require disclosure as a non-adjusting event in its own right, or whether disclosure is necessary under the broadest of requirements, the FRS 5 *Reporting the Substance of Transactions*, requirement to provide such information as is necessary in order that financial statements give a true and fair view.

19 CASH FLOW STATEMENTS

19.1 INTRODUCTION

Cash flow statements are intended to complement the other primary financial statements. While information about profits and other gains or losses is obviously very important in assessing the progress of a company, it is equally important to gain an understanding of how those gains and losses, and other transactions of the company, have been reflected in its cash flows.

As a basic principle, all enterprises that prepare financial statements intended to give a true and fair view are required by FRS 1 *Cash Flow Statements*, to include a cash flow statement. There are a number of exceptions to this general rule, and the following enterprises need not prepare a cash flow statement:

- registered companies which are entitled to file abbreviated accounts as a small company with the Registrar, regardless of whether or not they actually do so;
- other enterprises that would fulfil the criteria to qualify as a small company if they were registered under the Companies Act 2006;
- 90 per cent (or more) subsidiaries so long as they are included in group accounts which are publicly available;
- mutual life assurance companies;
- open-ended investment companies, subject to certain conditions, and
- pension funds.

As a result of the above exemptions for smaller companies, and other smaller entities, the FRSSE does not require a cash flow statement. However, the FRSSE does suggest that cash flow information may still be important for small companies. As a result, the FRSSE contains a simplified form of cash flow statement that it suggests be used, without making this a requirement. This statement is dealt with at the end of this chapter.

Potential impact of the FRSME

The FRSME also requires a cash flow statement or, strictly, a statement of cash flows.

This is quite different to the cash flow statement required by FRS 1, and is based on the statement required by IAS 7 for those entities adopting IFRS.

The FRSME statement does not just deal with cash, but (like the original FRS 1) also includes cash equivalents. These are highly liquid items which are close to being cash, usually taken as being items which have a maturity of no more than three months from the date on which they are made.

The FRSME statement also looks very different, having only three categories of cash flow, being operating, investing and financing.

Of course, for many entities, the individual amounts shown in a statement of cash flows prepared in accordance with the FRSME might well be the same as those shown in a cash flow statement prepared in accordance with FRS 1.

19.2 THE OBJECTIVE OF THE CASH FLOW STATEMENT

19.2.1 Statement of objective

FRS 1 includes the following statement of its objective:

> The objective of this FRS is to ensure that reporting entities falling within its scope:
>
> (a) report the cash generation and cash absorption for a period by highlighting the significant components of cash flow in a way that facilitates comparison of the cash flow performance of different businesses; and
>
> (b) provide information that assists in the assessment of their liquidity, solvency and financial adaptability. (Para. 1, FRS 1.)

The first objective is met by standardising the headings that must be used within the cash flow statements, requiring a common format to be used.

The second objective is met more generally by the requirements for the cash flow statement and the accompanying notes, rather than by any specific requirement.

19.3 DEFINITION

Those items which can be included in a cash flow statement are very severely restricted by FRS 1:

> Cash in hand and deposits repayable on demand with any qualifying financial institution, less overdrafts from any qualifying financial institution repayable on demand. Deposits are repayable on demand if they can be withdrawn at any time without notice and without penalty or if a maturity or period of notice of not more than 24 hours or one working day has been agreed. Cash includes cash in hand and deposits denominated in foreign currencies. (Para. 2, FRS 1.)

This means that many items which companies may conventionally consider to be cash are not considered to be this for the purposes of producing a cash flow statement. More specifically, it may also mean that items which appear as part of cash at bank and in hand in the balance sheet may also fail to meet the definition of cash. Such items are most likely to be dealt with in the cash flow statement in the section dealing with management of liquid resources.

In addition, the definition of cash in FRS 1 as revised is much stricter than the definition which was included in the original FRS 1. That standard allowed companies to produce a cash flow statement based on both cash and cash equivalents. While cash was defined very strictly, in fact even more strictly than under the current version of FRS 1, in practice it was the much wider definition of cash and cash equivalents that mattered. The revision to FRS 1 extended the definition of cash itself, but eliminating the use of cash equivalents has meant that fewer items qualify to be dealt with in a cash flow statement. The cash flow statement is now precisely what it says it is, and deals only with movements in a narrowly defined category of cash.

Potential impact of the FRSME

As noted above, the FRSME, unlike FRS 1, allows the use of cash equivalents, defined as short-term, highly liquid investments held to meet short-term cash commitments rather than for investment or other purposes. While not part of the definition, the FRSME notes that this will normally apply only to items which have a maturity of three months or less from the date on which they are acquired.

19.4 THE FORMAT OF THE CASH FLOW STATEMENT

19.4.1 Basic format

The cash flows of an enterprise should be disclosed under nine basic headings:

- operating activities;
- dividends from joint ventures and associates;
- returns on investment and servicing of finance;
- taxation;
- capital expenditure and financial investment;
- acquisitions and disposals;
- equity dividends paid;
- management of liquid resources, and
- financing.

The last two categories may be combined as long as the company shows the cash flows relating to each separately, and separate sub-totals are provided.

FRS 1 makes it clear that not all of the detailed information needs to be shown on the face of the cash flow statement:

... the individual categories of inflows and outflows under the standard headings set out in paragraphs 11-32 should be disclosed separately, where material, in the cash flow statement or in a note. (Para. 8, FRS 1.)

An example of a simple cash flow statement is shown below.

EXAMPLE

In this example, the company has a cash outflow (before management of liquid resources and financing) of £2,323, which is partly financed by:

- a share issue of £800;
- a debt issue of £600, and
- a sale of short-term deposits of £850.

This means that during the period there has been a decrease in cash of £73.

Cash flow statement for the year ended 31 December 2011

	£000	(£000)
Cash flow from operating activities		17,065
Dividends from joint ventures and associates		200
Returns on investment and servicing of finance		2,776
Taxation		(2,665)
Capital expenditure and financial investment		(750)
Acquisitions and disposals		(16,439)
Equity dividends paid		(2,510)
Cash inflow (outflow) before the use of liquid resources and financing		(2,323)
Management of liquid resources		850
Financing		
Cash flow from issue of shares	800	
Cash flow from increase in debt	600	
		1,400
Increase (decrease) in cash in the period		(73)

In general, cash flows should be shown gross, either on the face of the cash flow statement or in a note.

However, cash flows from operating activities may be shown net. This exemption is necessary since the standard allows a company to calculate the net effect of these cash flows by making adjustments to operating profit. This is known as the indirect method and, in practice, is the method most commonly used by companies.

Furthermore, cash flows relating to the management of liquid resources or financing may be reported net if:

- they relate in substance to a single financing transaction, or
- they are due to short maturities and high turnover occurring from rollover or reissue.

The first exemption avoids companies having to disclose repayments of loans and the receipt of further finance, when in reality the loan has been extended.

The second exemption is necessary to avoid the situation where companies would otherwise have to disclose regular rollovers of what is, in practice, the same money. For example, if a company regularly rolls over short-term deposits it would not make sense for the company to have to disclose large amounts in respect of both the acquisition and disposal of investments.

Potential impact of the FRSME

The FRSME is based on the IFRS for SMEs, and the cash flow statement in that standard is ultimately based on that required by IAS 7. The most obvious difference from FRS 1 is that there are only three categories of cash flow in a FRSME statement of cash flows, being operating, investing and financing. Therefore, even where the amounts shown are the same, as they would sometimes be, the statements would look quite different.

19.4.2 Operating cash flows

FRS 1 states that:

> Cash flows from operating activities are in general the cash effects of transactions and other events relating to operating or trading activities, normally shown in the profit and loss account in arriving at operating profit. (Para. 11, FRS 1.)

It then goes on to make it clear that this should include any cash flows associated with operating items relating to provisions, whether or not those provisions were charged in arriving at the operating profit.

The standard allows two alternative methods of disclosing the operating cash flows of an enterprise: the direct method and the indirect method.

Potential impact of the FRSME

The FRSME also allows the use of the direct or indirect method for operating cash flows.

19.4.3 The gross or direct method

Under the direct method, the operating receipts and payments are separately disclosed. For example, the financial statements would show separately:

- the amounts of cash paid to suppliers during the period;
- the amounts of cash actually received from customers during the period, and
- the amounts of cash paid to employees in respect of wages and salaries, and amounts paid on their behalf to the tax authorities.

Where this method is used, the financial statements must still provide a reconciliation between the operating profit and the operating cash flow. The contents of this reconciliation are considered in the next section.

The gross or direct method is relatively rare. Most companies do not use this method and prefer to report their cash flows under the indirect method. Although it is not the only reason, the fact that companies using the direct method must also provide the disclosure required under the indirect method is a factor in ensuring that most companies do not use the direct method.

Potential impact of the FRSME

The FRSME allows the use of the direct method for reporting operating cash flows. It notes that this can be done directly by using the accounting records of the entity, or by adjusting sales, costs and sales and other items to reflect changes in related balances (such as inventories, trade payable and receivables), non-cash items and cash flows which are either investing or financing.

19.4.4   The indirect method

The indirect method involves producing a reconciliation between the operating profit and the operating cash flows. This is done by making adjustments to eliminate the effect of all transactions which have not given rise to cash flows in the period.

The reconciliation must, therefore, include adjustments in respect of:

- movements in stocks;
- movements in debtors;
- movements in creditors, and
- other differences between cash flows and profits.

The 'other differences' mentioned in FRS 1 will include, for example:

- depreciation;
- amortisation;
- profits and losses on disposal of both tangible and intangible fixed assets, and
- changes in provisions, where those changes are not as a result of cash flows.

With a cash flow statement, each item which is treated under another heading must be eliminated from the debtors and creditors movement figures used in arriving at the cash flow arising from operating activities. This means that the changes in debtors and creditors shown in the cash flow statement will not always agree to the movement in the balance sheet figures.

A simple example is a fixed asset purchased shortly before the end of the year, with the amount actually paid in the next year. In the balance sheet the amount due will be shown as a creditor. When calculating the cash inflow or outflow for operating activities this creditor will be excluded from the calculation.

Examples of other items for which the debtor and creditor amounts will be adjusted in arriving at the cash flow movement are:

- accruals in respect of interest payable;
- accrued interest receivable;
- proceeds of disposal of tangible and intangible fixed assets, where not actually received by the balance sheet date, and
- amounts in respect of finance leases.

EXAMPLE

In 2011, A Ltd has a profit before interest and taxation of £650,109. Interest receivable is £65,013, and interest payable £194,736. The tax charge in the profit and loss account is £247,787. An interim dividend of £200,000 was paid during the year. The profit and loss account includes a profit of £15,675 on disposal of fixed assets.

The following amounts appear in the balance sheet:

	2011 £	2010 £
Stocks	748,934	658,293
Debtors		
Sales ledger	1,984,465	1,201,485
Amounts receivable on sale of fixed assets	10,564	0
Accrued interest receivable	15,836	27,835
Other operating debtors	109,389	176,546
	2,120,254	1,405,866
Creditors		
Purchase ledger	2,259,485	2,202,384
Amounts due on purchase of fixed assets	209,746	192,463
Accrued interest	38,812	43,824
Corporation tax	301,834	285,735
	2,809,877	2,724,406

Fixed assets	£
Cost	
At 1 January 2011	2,364,291
Additions	547,293
Disposals	(180,273)
At 31 December 2011	2,731,311

Depreciation	£
At 1 January 2011	1,033,195
Charge for the year	332,773
Disposals	(158,128)
At 31 December 2011	1,207,840
Net book value	1,523,471

Note: The items above are not in statutory formats, but are intended to provide all the information required for the calculations.

The reconciliation of operating profit to the net cash inflow from operating activities would appear as follows:

	£
Operating profit	650,109
Depreciation	332,773
Profit on disposal of tangible fixed assets	(15,675)
Increase in stocks (748,934 − 658,293)	(90,641)
Increase in debtors (1,984,465 + 109,389 − 1,201,485 − 176,546)	(715,823)
Increase in creditors (2,259,485 − 2,202,384)	57,101
Net cash inflow	217,844

The other items which will be required for the cash flow statement can also be calculated as follows.

	Brought forward (1) £	Carried forward (2) £	Movement during year (3) £	Cash flow (1) + (3) − (2) £
Sale of fixed assets (Note 1)	0	10,564	37,820	27,256
Interest received	27,835	15,836	65,013	77,012
Purchase of fixed assets	192,463	209,746	547,293	530,010
Interest paid	43,824	38,812	194,736	199,748
Corporation tax	285,735	301,834	247,787	231,688

Note 1

The movement in sale of fixed assets during the year is calculated as follows:

	£
Net book value of disposals (£180,273 − £158,128)	22,145
Profit on disposal	15,675
Cash movement during year	37,820

The reconciliation between the operating profit and cash flow arising from operating activities may be provided in the notes to the accounts, or adjoining the cash flow statement. If it is to appear with the cash flow statement, then it must be clearly labelled and kept separate, since it does not consist of cash flows and does not form part of the actual cash flow statement.

As mentioned above, the reconciliation is required even where the company has used the direct method for stating its operating cash flows.

Potential impact of the FRSME

The FRSME allows the use of the indirect method for reporting operating cash flows.

19.4.5   Dividends from associates and joint ventures

Dividends received from joint ventures and associates form a separate category in the cash flow statement.

Potential impact of the FRSME

There is no such categorisation in the FRSME. The FRSME does mention dividends received in general, rather than specifically in relation to associates and joint ventures, noting that they may be operating or investing.

19.4.6   Returns on investments and servicing of finance

Returns on investments and servicing of finance are:

> ... receipts resulting from the ownership of an investment and payments to providers of finance, non-equity shareholders (eg the holders of preference shares) and minority interests, excluding those items required ... to be classified under another heading. (Para. 13, FRS 1.)

Typical examples of cash inflows are given in the standard:

- interest received, including any tax recovered, and
- dividends received net of any tax credits, and excluding dividends received from associates and joint ventures.

Cash outflows include:

- interest paid, even if this has been capitalised, inclusive of any tax paid over to the tax authorities;
- cash flows that are treated as finance costs, including issue costs on debt and non-equity shares;
- the interest element of finance lease charges;
- dividends paid on non-equity shares, and
- dividends paid on minority interests, whether equity or non-equity.

When dealing with finance costs, account needs to be taken of the treatment that is required under FRS 4 *Capital Instruments*. The total amounts paid may need to be broken down between:

- those amounts which should be treated as returns on investments and servicing of finance, and
- those items which need to be treated as financing.

In the simple case, where interest is charged on the outstanding balance of a loan, the division between the two categories is clear.

Where constant periodical payments are made in order to pay off a liability, each payment also needs to be analysed between the finance cost and the capital payment. Normally, this means that as the payment period progresses the amounts attributable to finance charges will reduce and the capital element will increase. Where there is a final balloon, this movement will be even more marked. At the extreme end of the range are zero coupon, or at least deep discount, bonds. For such instruments a large proportion of the final payment will be attributable to returns on investments and servicing of finance. The only amount that should be attributed to financing is the amount that was initially recorded on issue of the instrument, calculated in accordance with FRS 25 *Financial Instruments: Presentation*.

Potential impact of the FRSME

There is no such category under the FRSME. Interest paid may be included as operating or financing cash flows, whilst interest and dividends received may be shown as operating or investing cash flows.

19.4.7   Finance leases

Where a company acquires assets under a finance lease, no movement will appear in the cash flow statement. Although there has been an addition to fixed assets, this is not a cash flow. Instead, the reconciliation of net debt will show the movement as a non-cash item. It is only the payments of the liability under the lease that will give rise to movements in the cash flow statement.

The amounts paid in respect of finance leases therefore need to be broken down into two elements:

- the interest charge, which should be included in returns on investments and servicing of finance, and
- the capital element, which should be included under financing.

In order to comply with SSAP 21 *Accounting for Leases and Hire Purchase Contracts*, a company must have an analysis of the capital and interest elements of its total annual payments in respect of finance leases.

The interest element shown in the cash flow statement will be derived from the interest element charged in the profit and loss account. As with all other forms of interest, the profit and loss account charge will need to be adjusted to take account of the effect of any opening and closing accruals.

The capital element is arrived at by an equally straightforward calculation. It is the capital portion of each of the finance lease payments actually made in the year. As with the interest charge, this information should be easily obtainable from the calculations required for the purposes of SSAP 21. (Of course, these calculations may not themselves be straightforward, but at least FRS 1 does not add to the burden.)

Potential impact of the FRSME

The FRSME would require the same treatment, since it notes that items which do not involve a flow of cash should not be included in a statement of cash flows, and gives the acquisition of assets by way of finance lease as an example.

19.4.8 Taxation

The taxation section of the cash flow statement is only intended to be used for taxes on the profits or capital gains of the enterprise. Other taxes, such as value added tax (VAT), are treated differently.

This section will include the cash flows to or from the tax authorities in respect of revenue and capital profit, and for subsidiaries any cash flows relating to group relief. (It is worth noting that while FRS 1 mentions only subsidiaries when talking about disclosure of amounts in respect of group relief, this may also apply to parent companies, if they are exempt from producing consolidated accounts and the cash flow statement is prepared on a company-only basis.)

The examples of typical outflows of taxation provided in the standard are:

- the normal cash payment to the relevant tax authority of the tax due on the profits for a period, and
- payments made to other members of the group for group relief.

Inflows are likely to be less common, but would include rebates, claims and refunds in respect of overpayment.

Potential impact of the FRSME

There is no such classification under the FRSME. It states that tax cash flows should be classified as operating, unless they can be specifically identified with investing or financing activities.

19.4.9 Value added tax and other taxes

Cash flows should generally be shown in the cash flow statement net of any attributable VAT. The main exception is where the VAT is irrecoverable, when it should be included in the flow, without separate disclosure, and under the heading applicable to that flow.

This will leave a net movement either payable to or receivable from HM Revenue and Customs. This should be shown as part of the cash flow for operating activities, unless it is more appropriate to allocate it to another category.

Where the indirect or net method of reporting the cash flows attributable to operating activities is adopted, the amounts included in the reconciliation of operating profit to operating cash flow will be inclusive of VAT. This means that the amounts attributable to VAT included in trade debtors and creditors need not be eliminated in showing the movement in the balance over the period, and the normal balances can be used.

Where the enterprise is partially exempt, the calculations may be more complicated than normal. Most of the individual items which will appear on the face of the cash flow statement are not subject to VAT, and so no problem will arise. However, where an enterprise is partially exempt and undertakes certain types of investing activity then the amount to be allocated may not be determinable until after the end of the VAT period. This will apply, for example, where there is a purchase of fixed assets and the amount of the VAT which is recoverable is not known at the time of the original transaction. Although more complicated than normal, the exercise of the reallocation of irrecoverable VAT should be undertaken by such a business regardless of the need to prepare a cash flow statement, since it will also affect the amount at which fixed assets appear in the balance sheet.

Other taxes, which are not directly related to profits or gains, should be allocated to the appropriate heading. For example, employer's National Insurance should be included as part of the operating activities of the business. If the direct method is being used, this should be included in the amount shown as paid to, or on behalf of, employees. If the indirect method is being used then no adjustment will normally be required, other than the usual adjustment for any creditor at the end of the year. The main rationale behind this requirement is to ensure that there is consistency between the treatments adopted in the cash flow statement, profit and loss account and balance sheet.

Potential impact of the FRSME

While the FRSME does not deal specifically with this issue, the results should be the same.

19.4.10   Capital expenditure and financial investment

'Capital expenditure' covers all receipts and payments in respect of fixed assets, other than those dealt with as part of an acquisition or disposal, and investments.

If there are no receipts and payments in respect of financial investments, then the caption 'Capital expenditure' may be used on its own.

'Financial investment' includes all cash movements on items treated as fixed or current asset investments or loans, except those which are treated as current asset investments and form part of liquid resources.

Examples of cash inflows include:

- receipts from the sale of tangible fixed assets, and
- receipts from the repayment of the company's loans to other entities or sales of debt instruments of other entities.

In the second case, care needs to be taken to ensure that the items shown need not be included within any other category.

Outflows include:

- payments to acquire tangible fixed assets, and
- loans made by the company to acquire debt instruments of other entities, unless they should be treated under another heading.

Although not mentioned specifically in FRS 1, cash flows relating to government grants of a capital nature (ie those in respect of fixed assets) would normally be included under this heading.

Potential impact of the FRSME

While not a heading under the FRSME, such cash flows would be included under investing.

19.4.11   Acquisitions and disposals

'Acquisitions and disposals' covers all cash flows related to the acquisition or disposal of any:

- trade;
- business;
- associate;
- joint venture, or
- subsidiary.

For these purposes, an acquisition or disposal includes any investment transaction which alters an interest in any of the categories set out above, even where this does not involve a change in status. For example, if a company has a 75 per cent subsidiary and acquires the remaining shares, this is still treated as an acquisition.

There is a requirement that the cash amounts associated with an acquisition or disposal be shown separately from the cash balances transferred in or out. For example, where a subsidiary is acquired the total cash consideration paid will be shown separately from the cash balances brought into the group accounts as a result of the acquisition.

FRS 1 contains a requirement that any material effects on the amounts of each of the standard headings should be disclosed where there is an acquisition or disposal. The standard notes that one way of doing this would be to divide cash flows between continuing and discontinued operations and acquisitions. FRED

32 *Disposal of Non-Current Assets and Presentation of Discontinued Operations* proposes a requirement that companies state the net cash flows attributable to the operating, investing and financing activities of discontinued operations. This clarifies the FRS 1 position.

Potential impact of the FRSME

Whilst not a heading in its own right, forming part of investing, the FRSME states that aggregate cash flows arising from acquisition or disposals of subsidiaries or other business units should be presented separately.

19.4.12   Equity dividends paid

This category should be used for dividends paid on instruments classified as equity of the reporting company or, in the case of a group, the parent company, in accordance with FRS 25.

Potential impact of the FRSME

There is no such category under the FRSME. Dividends paid may be included as operating or financing cash flows.

19.4.13   Management of liquid resources

Liquid resources are defined as:

> Current asset investments held as readily disposable stores of value. A readily disposable investment is one that:

> (a)   is disposable by the reporting entity without curtailing or disrupting its business;
> (b)   and is either:

> > (i)   readily convertible into known amounts of cash at or close to its carrying amount, or
> > (ii)   traded in an active market. (Para. 2, FRS 1.)

This is, quite deliberately, not a very precise definition, and there is an element of subjectivity involved in its application. As a result, FRS 1 requires that a company explains what it has included within liquid resources, and provide details of any changes in the definition which it has used. The vagueness in the definition arises since the accounting treatment is affected by the company's intentions and circumstances, as well as by the nature of the asset. In effect, the ASB has been required to compromise strict comparability between companies in order to provide cash flow information that is meaningful.

For the purposes of the definition, an active market is:

> A market of sufficient depth to absorb the investment held without a significant effect on the price. (Para. 2, FRS 1.)

The notes to the FRS give examples of the types of item that might be included within liquid resources:

- term deposits, although usually only if they are one year or less from maturity on acquisition;
- government securities;
- loan stock;
- equities, and
- derivatives.

In the case of derivatives, they would not form part of liquid resources if they had been used for hedging purposes. As dealt with in greater depth below, where instruments are used for hedging purposes any cash flows associated with the instruments should go through the cash flow statement in the same section as the items which are being hedged.

Potential impact of the FRSME

There is no such category under the FRSME. Some of the items that might form part of liquid resources under FRS 1 could qualify as cash equivalents under the FRSME, and therefore would not give rise to any separate disclosure.

19.4.14 Financing

The cash flows to be included under the heading of financing are described as follows:

> . . . receipts or repayments of principal from or to external providers of finance.
> (Para. 29, FRS 1.)

Financing cash flows may be shown in a single section with those under 'management of liquid resources', provided that separate sub-totals for each are given.

The inflows given as examples are:

- receipts from the issue of shares or other equity instruments, and
- receipts from the issue of debentures, loans, notes and bonds and other long-term and short-term borrowings, other than overdrafts.

The amounts that should be included in each case are the actual amounts of cash, regardless of how they might be subdivided in terms of their presentation in the balance sheet. For example, for the purposes of the cash flow statement, when shares are issued for cash there is no distinction between amounts attributable to share capital and share premium. They should be included as a single figure, including both.

Outflows include:

- repayments of borrowings, other than repayment of overdrafts;

- the capital element of finance lease rental payments;
- payments to reacquire or to redeem the company's shares, and
- payments of expenses and commissions on equity shares.

Only costs associated with the issue of equity shares are shown as financing movements. Such costs in respect of other forms of finance will be shown within returns on investments and servicing of finance.

The amounts of any financing cash flows received from or paid to equity accounted entities should be shown separately.

Potential impact of the FRSME

Financing is a category under the FRSME, but would include items which are treated as separate categories under FRS 1.

19.4.15   Reconciliation to net debt

This reconciliation may be given either adjoining the cash flow statement or in a note, although if it is given adjoining the cash flow statement then it must be clearly labelled and kept separate.

Net debt is defined as:

> The borrowings of the reporting entity (comprising capital instruments classified as liabilities in accordance with FRS 25 "(IAS 32) Financial Instruments: Disclosure and Presentation", together with related derivatives, and obligations under finance leases) less cash and liquid resources. Where cash and liquid resources exceed the borrowings of the entity reference should be to "net funds" rather than to "net debt". (Para. 2, FRS 1.)

(The definition was amended by FRS 25, to remove references to FRS 4. The title of FRS 25 has also subsequently been changed, to remove reference to disclosure.)

The reconciliation must show the movements in the year between:

- cash flows;
- acquisition or disposal of subsidiaries;
- other non-cash changes, and
- recognition of changes in market value and exchange rate adjustments.

Where several balance sheet amounts are combined, sufficient details should be given so that the cash and other components of the movement can be traced back to amounts shown in the balance sheet.

The basic mechanics of the reconciliation can be seen from a highly simplified example.

EXAMPLE

At the end of 2010, a company had debt of £70 and cash of £60. During 2011 operating cash inflow is £100 and non-operating cash outflow (net of debt financing, that is: returns on investments and servicing of finance, taxation, capital expenditure and financial investment, acquisitions and disposals, equity dividends paid) amounts to £190. At the end of 2010 debt is £120 and cash is £20. The company has no liquid resources.

The cash flow for 2011 (not in FRS 1 format) is:

	£
Cash from operations	100
Non-operating cash flow (net of debt financing)	(190)
Cash flow from increase in debt	50
Cash flow for the period	(40)

The reconciliation between the cash flow for 2011 and the net debt position of the company at the 2011 year end can be seen as:

	£	£
Opening net debt		(10)
opening debt	(70)	
opening cash	60	
Movement in cash flow (net of debt, Note 1)		(90)
cash flow for the period	(40)	
Change in debt	(50)	
Closing net debt		(100)
Closing debt	(120)	
Closing cash	20	

Note 1

The cash flow figure – £40 – is calculated after the change in debt has been deducted. Therefore, in the reconciliation, the change in debt must be added back.

A more realistic reconciliation together with an analysis of net debt is given in Appendix 1 to FRS 1, and is shown overleaf.

EXAMPLE

Reconciliation of net cash flow to movement in net debt

	£000	£000
Decrease in cash in the period		(6,752)
Cash inflow from increase in debt and lease financing		(2,347)
Cash inflow from decrease in liquid resources	(700)	
Change in net debt resulting from cash flows		(9,799)
Loans and finance leases acquired with subsidiary		(3,817)
New finance leases		(2,845)
Translation difference		643
Movement in net debt in the period		(15,818)
Net debt at 1.1.96.		(15,215)
Net debt at 31.12.96.		(31,033)

Analysis of net debt

	1 Jan 1996 £'000	Cash flow £'000	Acq'n £'000	Other non-cash £'000	Exchange movement £'000	31 Dec 1996 £'000
Cash at bank and in hand	235	(1,250)			1,392	377
Overdrafts	(2,528)	(5,502)			(1,422)	(9,452)
		(6,752)				
Debt due after 1 year	(9,640)	(2,533)	(1,749)	2,560	(792)	(12,154)
Debt due within 1 year	(352)	(1,156)	(837)	(2,560)	1,465	(3,440)
Finance leases	(4,170)	1,342	(1,231)	(2,845)		(6,904)
		(2,347)				
Current asset investments	1,240	(700)				540
Total	(15,215)	(9,799)	(3,817)	(2,845)	(643)	(31,033)

In order to reconcile the cash flow during the period with the closing net debt position, it is necessary to account for items which affect the position but have not had an impact on the cash flow during the year: acquisitions; new finance leases and exchange movements.

Potential impact of the FRSME

There is no equivalent requirement under the FRSME.

19.5 EXCEPTIONAL ITEMS

Cash flows related to exceptional items in the profit and loss account should be included under the appropriate heading in the format, and identified in the cash flow statement or in a note. The relationship between the underlying item and the related cash flows should be explained.

It is possible to have an exceptional cash flow, even where this is not related to an exceptional item in the profit and loss account. This might occur where, for example, there is a substantial cash flow associated with the disposal of a tangible fixed asset, such as a property, but an immaterial profit or loss on the transaction. In such cases, sufficient disclosure should be given to explain the cause and nature of the cash flow.

Potential impact of the FRSME

There is no equivalent requirement under the FRSME.

19.6   MATERIAL NON-CASH TRANSACTIONS

The cash flow statement itself can only deal with transactions that give rise to movements of cash. Whilst this is likely to cover the great majority of transactions which any business is likely to undertake, there may be exceptions. If there are material transactions which do not involve movements of cash, then the standard requires that these be disclosed in the notes to the financial statements.

There seem to be two connected reasons for providing this disclosure:

- it is necessary for an overall understanding of the activities of the enterprise, and
- the interpretation of the cash flow statement in particular will be affected by looking at other transactions which have not given rise to movements of cash, but which in other circumstances may have had a cash effect.

Potential impact of the FRSME

The FRSME also contains a requirement to disclose non-cash transactions, although it notes that this is limited to investing and financing transactions.

19.7   HEDGING TRANSACTIONS

Where any items such as a futures contract, forward contract, option or swap are accounted for as a hedge, any cash flows associated with the instrument should be allocated to the same category as the transaction which is the subject of the hedge.

This is to avoid the situation where connected items, as hedges must be in order to qualify for hedge accounting, end up being treated differently in the cash flow statement.

In the case of items where the hedged cash flow has not yet taken place, the hedging cash flow should be included in the same category as that in which the underlying cash flow will be included.

Potential impact of the FRSME

The FRSME does not deal specifically with cash flows in relation to hedges. It does note, however, that cash flows in relation to most derivatives will be treated as investing, unless they are held for dealing or trading, or are classified as financing.

19.8 GROUPS

19.8.1 Preparation of group cash flow statements

Where group accounts are prepared, the cash flow statement should also be given on a group basis.

The group cash flow statement should, like all other consolidated financial statements, only deal with transactions that are external to the group.

For example, the following items would be eliminated on consolidation:

- dividends and interest paid to other group members;
- the issue of shares to other group members for cash;
- the grant and receipt of loans within the group, and
- sales of assets, trading or fixed, between group members.

The preparation of the group cash flow statement can be performed either by amalgamating the separate cash flow statements of each group company, or by using the consolidated profit and loss account and balance sheet. The second approach is likely to be considerably more common, as much of the elimination of intra-group transactions will already have taken place and not all subsidiary undertakings are required to prepare a cash flow statement.

Potential impact of the FRSME

Group cash flow statements may also be required under the FRSME. There is little specific guidance in the draft standard, although the comments in relation to FRS 1 would also apply, subject to the differences arising due to the very different categories that FRS 1 contains by comparison with those included in the FRSME.

19.8.2 Minority interests

Minority interests will normally appear in the cash flow statement only to the extent that dividends are paid to minority shareholders. Dividends paid to the minority interest should be disclosed as a separate item within returns on investments and servicing of finance.

Where a subsidiary issues shares to the minority interest, for cash, the amount involved should be included under financing and separately disclosed, although this is not specifically mentioned in the standard. Where shares are issued both to the minority interest and to another group company, this implies that the funds received from the minority will appear in the consolidated cash flow statement, but the amount received from within the group will be eliminated on consolidation.

19.8.3   Mergers and acquisitions

FRS 1 requires that:

> Where a subsidiary undertaking joins or leaves a group during a financial year the cash flows of the group should include the cash flows of the subsidiary undertaking concerned for the same period as that for which the group's profit and loss account includes the results of the subsidiary undertaking. (Para. 43, FRS 1.)

Where there is an acquisition during the year, the preparation of the group cash flow statement from the consolidated profit and loss account and balance sheet is slightly more complicated. Since the acquisition of the subsidiary must be accounted for as a single entry, many of the other movements in the period cannot be calculated solely by comparing the balance sheets. For example, the movements in working capital items will no longer be the movement in the amounts in the balance sheet, but will be this movement with the effect as a result of the acquisition removed.

The basic format of the calculation can be seen in the following example for stock.

EXAMPLE

A subsidiary is acquired during the year. Its opening balance of stock is £1,800 and its closing value is £2,500. At the time of the acquisition, the stock was £2,000.

	£	£
Closing balance of stock		2,500
Less: opening balance of stock		(1,800)
		700
Less: increase in stock of subsidiary between opening and acquisition		
Opening	1,800	
At acquisition	(2,000)	
		(200)
Movement in stock		500

The stock movement attributable to the subsidiary is the change between the acquisition and the accounting reference date, and not the change over the full accounting period.

The inevitable result of this treatment is that it will be more complicated for the user of the financial statements to reconcile the amounts in the cash flow statement, or notes, to the amounts appearing in the balance sheet and profit and loss account. However, all of the information required to do this is provided. The benefit is that the cash flow statement will be produced on a basis that is comparable to the method used for the profit and loss account, which would not be true if the cash flow statement were prepared on a line-by-line basis.

Similar adjustments must also be made to all other items that appear in the cash flow statement, for example:

- the acquisition of tangible and intangible fixed assets;
- proceeds of disposal of tangible and intangible fixed assets;
- interest and dividends paid;
- taxation paid;
- issue of shares (outside of the group), and
- receipt of loans.

Similar problems do not arise with merger accounting, since entry into the group is, in effect, backdated so that comparatives will also have been changed.

19.8.4 Disposals

The requirements in respect of disposals are the mirror image of those for acquisitions.

(1) The amount of cash received must be shown under acquisitions and disposals with separate disclosure of the cash amount transferred as a result of the disposal.

(2) A note to the cash flow statement should provide a summary of the effects of the disposal on each category of asset and liability, and should also show the amount of cash received as consideration, and the amounts of cash transferred out of the group.

(3) The cash flows of the subsidiary should be included in the cash flow statement for the period during which the results of the subsidiary have been included in the profit and loss account.

(4) Any material effect on the amounts in the cash flow statement in respect of the subsidiary disposed of should be disclosed, as far as possible, in a note to the cash flow statement. This disclosure need only be given in the year in which the disposal takes place, and not as comparative figures in the subsequent year.

The disposal of a subsidiary will, like an acquisition, complicate the preparation of the consolidated cash flow statement. The movement in working capital items will consist of two parts:

- the movement from the previous balance sheet date to the date of the disposal, including the subsidiary, and
- the movement from the date of disposal to the current balance sheet date, excluding the subsidiary.

The movement as a result of the disposal will not form part of the calculation.

19.9   FOREIGN CURRENCIES

19.9.1   Individual enterprise

FRS 1 provides no guidance on the treatment of foreign currency transactions in the accounts of an individual enterprise. The treatment, therefore, must depend on the individual transaction.

Where a transaction has been settled during the period, that is, the cash flow has actually taken place, it is the amount of cash that has changed hands that must appear in the cash flow statement. Where the transaction relates to operating activities, no adjustment needs to be made for the purposes of the cash flow statement as a result of any loss or profit on the settlement of the transaction.

EXAMPLE

A company purchases a trading asset from an overseas company and sets up a liability of £25,000. When payment is made, the actual amount of cash paid is £24,500. If the gross or direct method is used, then it is the amount of £24,500 that will form part of the payments to suppliers, and no adjustment is required. If the net or indirect method is used then there is still no adjustment required, since the inclusion of the exchange difference in operating profit will automatically eliminate the effect:

	£
Amount of transaction initially recorded	25,000
Exchange gain	(500)
Actual cash paid	24,500

Where the transaction does not form part of the operating activities, the exchange difference will also not appear separately in the cash flow statement. However, it may need to be eliminated from the cash flow arising as a result of operating activities, as shown in the following example.

EXAMPLE

A company makes loans denominated in a foreign currency to an overseas enterprise. The company calculates that the interest due in respect of one quarter is £15,000. The company actually receives £14,950, as a result of fluctuations in the foreign exchange rate.

The amount that should be included in the cash flow statement is £14,950, since this is the amount that was actually received. If the exchange loss has been excluded from operating profit, then no adjustment needs to be made in the reconciliation of operating profit to operating cash flow. If the exchange loss has been included as part of operating profit, then it needs to be added back in order to arrive at the operating cash flow.

Using these figures and assuming other income of £100,000 (without any other adjustments required), this can clearly be shown as follows.

(1)   If the exchange loss is excluded from operating profit:

	£
Operating profit and cash flow	100,000
Interest	14,950
Total cash flow	114,950

(2)   If the exchange loss is included in operating profit:

	£
Operating profit	99,950
Exchange loss on interest received	50
Operating cash flow	100,000
Interest	14,950
Total cash flow	114,950

The same principle applies to other items, such as capital expenditure and financial investment, and financing activities, as shown in the following example.

EXAMPLE

A company buys a tangible fixed asset for £25,000, but by the time payment is made it actually needs to transfer £25,250. The exchange loss has been included in the operating profit for the period. The amount that will appear under capital investment in the cash flow statement will be £25,250. The reconciliation of the operating profit to the cash flow from operating activities will include an adjustment of £250 to eliminate the effect of the loss on the transaction.

Where the item involved falls under the heading of financing, the exchange adjustment will appear twice. It will appear in the reconciliation of operating profit to cash flow, and then be used to reconcile the change in financing in the balance sheet.

EXAMPLE

At the start of 2011, a company is financed by £250,000 of share capital, and loans denominated in a foreign currency of the value of £50,000. During the year the loans are paid off in full, and the actual amount paid is £52,000.

The reconciliation of operating profit to cash flow will include an adjustment of £2,000, since this loss does not involve any cash flow, but will have been charged to the profit and loss account. £52,000 will be included on the face of the cash flow statement as a movement in financing. The note on movements in financing would appear as follows:

	Share capital £	*Loans* £
Balance at 1 January 2011	250,000	50,000
Effect of foreign exchange differences	–	2,000
Cash outflow from financing	–	(52,000)
Balance at 31 December 2011	250,000	–

There are few differences where the transactions have not been settled at the balance sheet date.

(1) Where they are in respect of monetary working capital items (operating debtors and creditors), no adjustment is required since the exchange difference will have been reflected in both the operating profit and the change in the value of these items if the net or indirect method is used. If the direct or gross method is used then no cash flow has taken place, and so none will be recorded.

(2) Where they arise on other items, and have been excluded from the operating profit, no adjustment is required. If the items involved are for financing, then the movement as a result of exchange differences will need to be disclosed in the financing reconciliation.

(3) Where they arise on other items, but have been included in operating profit, then they will appear in the reconciliation of operating profit to operating cash flow.

Exchange differences can also arise on cash balances if they are denominated in a foreign currency. In such cases, no cash flow movement is included in the cash flow statement.

In certain cases, primarily where loans are held as a hedge against a foreign equity investment, some or all of the exchange difference need not appear in the profit and loss account, but may be treated as a movement in reserves. This situation is identical to that where the exchange gain or loss has not been included in the operating profit. The movement on such loans will need to be included in the financing reconciliation, but no adjustment to the operating profit is required.

Potential impact of the FRSME

The FRSME provides a small amount of guidance in relation to foreign currency cash flows, simply noting that they should be translated using the rate at the date of the transaction.

19.9.2 *Consolidated cash flow statements*

FRS 1 provides the following guidance on the inclusion of the results of foreign enterprises in cash flow statements:

> Where a portion of a reporting entity's business is undertaken by a foreign entity, the cash flows of that entity are to be included in the cash flow statement on the basis used for translating the results of those activities in the profit and loss account of the reporting entity. (Para. 41, FRS 1.)

Where the temporal method is used, there are few differences from the treatment and calculations that are required for an individual company which undertakes transactions denominated in a foreign currency. The simplest approach is to prepare a consolidated balance sheet and profit and loss account, and then to use this as the basis for the preparation of the cash flow statement.

The situation is more complicated where the net investment method has been used. There are dangers with using the consolidated accounts as the basis for the preparation of the cash flow statement, as the effect of cash flows may become confused with the effects of changes in foreign exchange rates.

Ideally, cash flow statements should be prepared, in the original reporting currency, for each of the foreign subsidiaries. These should then be translated into sterling and incorporated into the group cash flow statement. The method used for doing this should be the same as that which has been used for the translation of the profit and loss account. This means that either the average rate for the year or the closing rate may be used. As noted above, notwithstanding that this is the ideal method, many groups do not use this method. This is because it would involve eliminating intra-group movements, which will already have been eliminated in the profit and loss account and balance sheet, and may be because not all companies in the group may be required to produce a cash flow statement.

When the consolidation has been undertaken, the movement in cash is very unlikely to agree to the movement in the figures in the balance sheet. The difference is attributable to the effect of foreign exchange rate changes over the period. Where the average rate method has been used, the difference comprises two parts:

- the change in the opening balance of cash and cash equivalents as a result of the difference between the opening and closing rates, and
- the change in the value of the movement over the period as a result of the difference between the average and closing rates.

If the closing rate has been used then the difference arises from only the first of these causes.

EXAMPLE

A company has an investment in a wholly owned overseas subsidiary, which prepares financial statements in US$. For 2011, the subsidiary prepares the following draft financial statements.

	2011 $	2010 $
Tangible fixed assets	15,000	12,000
Working capital (all operating)	10,000	8,000
Cash at bank	5,000	4,000
Taxation due	(3,000)	(2,500)
Loans	(5,000)	(3,000)
	22,000	18,500
Share capital	10,000	10,000
Profit and loss account	12,000	8,500
	22,000	18,500

	2011 $
Operating profit (after depreciation of $1,000)	7,500
Interest payable	(1,000)
Taxation	(3,000)
Retained profit	3,500

The exchange rate at the start of the period was $1.85 = £1, and at the end of the period $1.75. The average rate for the period, used for the translation of the profit and loss account was $1.80.

(1) The first stage is to prepare the information for the cash flow statement in dollars, and then to translate this into sterling, using the rate of 1.80.

	2011 $	2011 £
Operating profit	7,500	4,167
Increase in working capital	(2,000)	(1,111)
Depreciation	1,000	556
Cash flow from operating activities	6,500	3,612
Returns on investments and servicing of finance (interest paid)	(1,000)	(556)
Taxation	(2,500)	(1,389)
Capital expenditure and financial investment [purchase of fixed assets 15,000 − (12,000 − 1,000 depreciation)]	(4,000)	(2,222)
Financing (loans received)	2,000	1,111
Increase in cash	1,000	556

These figures will then be used for the consolidated cash flow statement, after elimination of any transactions within the group. However, further calculations will still be required as neither the group's movement in cash nor that in financing will arise solely from the cash flow movement.

(2)   The group's increase in cash will include the following items in respect of the subsidiary.

	£
Opening balance ($4,000 @ $1.85)	2,162
Net cash inflow at average rate (ie before adjustments for the effect of foreign exchange rate movements) = $1,000 @ $1.80	556
Effect of foreign exchange rate changes	139
Closing balance ($5,000 @ $1.75)	2,857

The second item (£139), the effect of foreign exchange rate changes can be calculated as follows.

	£	£
Increase in the value of opening balance:		
Opening balance at closing rate ($4,000 @ $1.75)	2,286	
Opening balance at opening rate ($4,000 @ $1.85)	2,162	
		124
Increase in the value of net cash inflow, from average to year end rate		
Movement at closing rate (1,000 @ 1.75)	571	
Movement at average rate (1,000 @ 1.80)	556	15
Total		139

(3)   There will also be a change in financing attributable to changes in foreign exchange rates. The consolidated accounts will contain the following amounts in respect of the loans of the foreign subsidiary.

	£
Opening balance ($3,000 @ $1.85)	1,622
Cash flow from financing, at average rate = $2,000 @ $1.80	1,111
Effect of foreign exchange differences	124
Closing balance ($5,000 @ $1.75)	2,857

The second item (£124), the increase in the group's loans due to the effect of foreign exchange rate changes can be calculated as follows.

	£	£
Increase in value of opening balance:		
Opening balance at closing rate ($3,000 @ $1.75)	1,714	
Opening balance at opening rate (£3,000 @ $1.85)	1,622	
		92
Increase in value of cash flow from financing, from average to year end rate		
Movement at closing rate ($2,000 @ $1.75)	1,143	
Movement at average rate ($2,000 @ $1.80)	1,111	
		32
Total		124

Potential impact of the FRSME

The FRSME notes that cash flows connected with foreign subsidiaries should be translated at the dates of the cash flows. In practice, an approximation would be used.

19.10   SMALL COMPANIES

As noted at the beginning of this chapter, small companies are exempted from FRS 1 and there is no cash flow statement required by the FRSSE. However, given that the management of cash is fundamental to the success, and sometimes even the continued existence, of small businesses just as much as larger ones, the FRSSE encourages smaller entities to provide a cash flow statement voluntarily. The main features of the statement mentioned in the FRSSE are as follows.

(1)   The cash flow from operations should be calculated by the indirect method, which makes adjustments to operating profit, as outlined earlier in this chapter.

(2)   The cash flow from operations should be reconciled to the cash position in the balance sheet (rather than the net debt position as in the main standard).

(3)   The definition of cash is simplified to 'cash at bank and in hand, less overdrafts repayable on demand'. There is no mention of (a) deposits at or overdrafts from qualifying institutions, nor (b) deposits in foreign currencies which are referenced in the main standard.

(4)   Some features of the main standard are also emphasised:

   (a)   cash flows are to be shown net of VAT, unless the tax is irrecoverable, and
   (b)   material transactions not involving cash should be disclosed if this is necessary to understand the position of the company.

The FRSSE gives an example of a cash flow statement of a small company and this is reproduced below.

EXAMPLE

	£	£
Cash generated from operations		
Operating profit/(loss)	(5,050)	
Reconciled to cash generated		
from operations:		
Depreciation	245	
Increase in stocks	(194)	
Decrease in trade debtors	67,440	
Decrease in trade creditors	(4,678)	
Increase in other creditors	3,127	
		60,890

	£	£
Cash from other sources		
Interest received	150	
Issues of shares for cash	5,500	
New long-term bank borrowings	4,500	
Proceeds from sale of tangible fixed assets	50	
		10,200
Application of cash		
Interest paid	(3,000)	
Tax paid	(29,220)	
Dividends paid	(10,000)	
Purchase of fixed assets	(10,500)	
Repayment of amounts borrowed	(3,000)	
		(55,720)
Net increase in cash		15,370
Cash at bank and in hand less overdrafts at beginning of year		(4,321)
Cash at bank and in hand less overdrafts at end of year		11,049
Consisting of:		
Cash at bank and in hand		11,549
Overdrafts included in 'bank loans and overdrafts falling due within one year'		(500)
		11,049

Major non-cash transactions: finance leases

During the year the company entered into finance lease arrangements in respect of assets with a total capital value at the inception of the leases of £2,850.

This format is similar to that of a statement of source and application of funds, a statement that was required for many companies before cash flow statements were introduced.

20 DIRECTORS AND RELATED PARTIES

20.1 INTRODUCTION

20.1.1 Sources of guidance

The disclosure of transactions with directors and other related parties is governed by the Companies Act 2006, FRS 8 *Related Party Disclosures* and, for small companies, the FRSSE.

This is an area that has seen more changes than most as a result of the introduction of the Companies Act 2006, since the accounting requirements in respect of related parties are one of the few areas where there have been substantial changes in the accounting requirements with the new Act coming into force.

FRS 8 was revised as a result of the Companies Act 2006. It has been amended further with effect for accounting periods beginning on or after 1 January 2011, with a revised definition of a related party and various consequential amendments.

Potential impact of the FRSME

The FRSME would cause little change in the disclosure of related party relationships and transactions. The definitions have been aligned, and the disclosure requirements made very similar.

The various statutory requirements in relation to directors arise independently of accounting standards, so would be entirely unaffected by the introduction of the FRSME.

20.1.2 Development of FRS 8

The disclosure of related party transactions was an area where, for some time, UK standards lagged behind international best practice. The International Accounting Standard dealing with this subject, IAS 24 *Related Party Disclosures*, was originally published in July 1984 and took effect on 1 January 1986. It took ten years for UK standard-setting bodies to reach the same stage. (The international standard has been changed since that time.)

The first exposure draft dealing with related parties was produced by the ASC in April 1989. This suggested that only abnormal transactions with related parties should need to be disclosed in company accounts. A new draft was prepared by the ASB and published in March 1994. This draft made no distinction between normal and abnormal transactions. Part of the reason for this was the practical problem of determining when a transaction was 'abnormal'. It is this draft which, with some amendments in matters of detail, formed the basis of the first version of FRS 8. It is worth noting that the issue of 'abnormal' transactions has not entirely disappeared for those involved in the setting of accounting requirements. The EU Directive dealing with disclosure of transactions with related parties strictly applies only to material transactions which have not been concluded under normal market conditions. However, as dealt with in the following section, compliance with FRS 8 will be considered sufficient to meet this requirement, even though it does not necessarily require separate disclosure of those transactions which have been concluded under normal market conditions and those which have not.

20.1.3   Objective of FRS 8

The objective of the standard is to:

> . . . ensure that financial statements contain the disclosures necessary to draw attention to the possibility that the reported financial position and results may have been affected by the existence of related parties and by material transactions with them. (Para. 1, FRS 8.)

This avoids one of the problems that would have been faced if the standard had been designed so as to require disclosure of only 'abnormal' transactions. The current standard requires disclosure in all cases, and it is then up to the reader of the accounts to determine what effect the relationship has had, or might have had, on the transactions, taking into account the information which has been provided.

The FRS also requires disclosure of controlling parties, regardless of whether or not transactions with those parties have taken place in the period.

20.2   IDENTIFYING RELATED PARTIES

20.2.1   Basic definition

There are now three definitions of related party under UK GAAP. There are two because of the difference between FRS 8 and the FRSSE, but at the moment there is also a change to FRS 8 that applies only to accounting periods beginning on or after 1 January 2011.

This situation arises because FRS 8 has been amended as a result of an EU Directive which has itself been reflected in The Large and Medium-sized Companies and Groups (Accounts and Reports) Regulations 2008 (SI 2008/410). It has not been reflected in the equivalent requirements for small companies (The Small Companies and Groups (Accounts and Directors' Report) Regulations 2008 (SI 2008/409)) since the Directive exempts small companies from the disclosure. (Strictly, the Directive also exempts medium-sized companies, but this exemption has not been reflected in UK GAAP.) The Directive, and therefore (SI 2008/410), require disclosure of related party transactions, which is not itself a change in UK accounting practice given that FRS 8 was already in place. However, they also require that the definition of related parties be the same as that included in IAS 24 *Related Party Disclosures*. Hence the initial change to FRS 8, and the further changes when the IAS 24 definition was itself revised. Since small companies are not covered by the new statutory requirements the FRSSE definition of related parties has not been amended, and is therefore the same as the definition that was previously used in FRS 8.

The definition of a related party under the FRSSE is that two or more parties are related if, at any time in the accounting year:

- one party has direct or indirect control of the other;
- the parties are subject to common control from the same source; or
- one party has significant influence over the financial and operating policies of the other, to the extent that the other party might not be able to pursue its separate interests at all times.

For the avoidance of doubt, the FRSSE also makes it clear that the following parties are related parties.

(1) Parent undertakings, subsidiary and fellow subsidiary undertakings.

(2) Associates and joint ventures.

(3) Investors with significant influence and their close families.

Close family is defined in the following way.

> Close members of the family of an individual are those family members, or members of the same household, who may be expected to influence, or be influenced by, that person in their dealings with the reporting entity. (Appendix C, FRSSE 2008.)

Under FRS 8, a related party is, for periods commencing prior to 1 January 2011, defined in the following terms.

> A party is related to an entity if:
>
> (a) directly, or indirectly through one or more intermediaries, the party:
>
>   (i) controls, is controlled by, or is under common control with, the entity (this includes parents, subsidiaries and fellow subsidiaries);
>
>   (ii) has an interest in the entity that gives it significant influence over the entity, or
>
>   (iii) has joint control over the entity;
>
> (b) the party is an associate (as defined in FRS 9, "Associates and joint ventures") of the entity;

(c) the party is a joint venture in which the entity is a venturer (as defined in FRS 9, "Associates and joint ventures");

(d) the party is a member of the key management personnel of the entity or its parent;

(e) the party is a close member of the family of any individual referred to in subparagraph (a) or (d);

(f) the party is an entity that is controlled, jointly controlled or significantly influenced by, or for which significant voting power in such entity resides with directly or indirectly, any individual referred to in (d) or (e); or

(g) the party is a retirement benefit scheme for the benefit of employees of the entity, or of any entity that is a related party of the entity. (Para. 2.5, FRS 8.)

Some of the terms that are used require further clarification.

Control is defined as:

 . . . the ability to direct the financial and operating policies of an entity with a view to gaining economic benefits from its activities. (Para. 2.2, FRS 8.)

This makes it clear that, for FRS 8 purposes, both direction and the possibility of benefits must exist for there to be control. While not relevant to companies, one example of where the two may differ would be the position of a trustee of a trust who is not also a beneficiary. The trustee may have direction, but no benefit. The marginal benefit of fees, if any, would not be sufficient to justify an assumption of control. (This is dealt with further below.)

The explanatory notes to the standard state that common control is deemed to exist when both parties are subject to control from boards having a controlling nucleus of directors in common. It is not limited to this situation, since, for example, it would also apply where one person has a controlling interest in two or more companies.

Close family members are defined in the same way as for the FRSSE, and quoted above.

The reference to key management personnel was new when FRS 8 was revised to reflect the statutory requirements, although the previous version referred to key management. The definition of key management personnel is:

Those persons having authority and responsibility for planning, directing, and controlling the activities of the entity, directly or indirectly, including any director (whether executive or otherwise) of that entity. (Para. 2.3, FRS 8.)

It is perhaps worth noting that despite the change in the definition of a related party under FRS 8, the actual impact of the change was fairly limited.

With effect for accounting periods beginning on or after 1 January 2011, the definition of a related party is amended as follows.

A related party is a person or entity that is related to the entity that is preparing its financial statements (in this Standard referred to as the 'reporting entity').

(a) A person or a close member of that person's family is related to a reporting entity if that person:

    (i) has control or joint control over the reporting entity;

    (ii) has significant influence over the reporting entity; or

    (iii) is a member of the key management personnel of the reporting entity or of a parent of the reporting entity.

(b) An entity is related to a reporting entity if any of the following conditions applies:

    (i) The entity and the reporting entity are members of the same group (which means that each parent, subsidiary and fellow subsidiary is related to the others).

    (ii) One entity is an associate or joint venture of the other entity (or an associate or joint venture of a member of a group of which the other entity is a member).

    (iii) Both entities are joint ventures of the same third party.

    (iv) One entity is a joint venture of a third entity and the other entity is an associate of the third entity.

    (v) The entity is a retirement benefit scheme for the benefit of employees of either the reporting entity or an entity related to the reporting entity. If the reporting entity is itself such a scheme, the sponsoring employers are also related to the reporting entity.

    (vi) The entity is controlled or jointly controlled by a person identified in (a).

    (vii) A person identified in (a)(i) has significant influence over the entity or is a member of the key management personnel of the entity (or of a parent of the entity). (Para. 2.5, FRS 8.)

There is a further change, in that the revised standard draws attention to the need to consider the substance of each relationship and not merely its legal form.

The definition of the close members of the family of a person has also been clarified and extended, and is:

...those family members who may be expected to influence, or be influenced by, that person in their dealings with the entity and include:

(a) that person's children and spouse or domestic partner;

(b) children of that person's spouse or domestic partner; and

(c) dependants of that person or that person's spouse or domestic partner. (Para. 2.1, FRS 8.)

This eliminates the lack of clarity in the original definition.

It is worth noting that, despite the changes, the actual related parties of a company (other than perhaps in relation to close family members) will not change as a result of the amended definition.

The explanation provided in the current standard concerning common control and common influence is deleted. The impact should be limited as these matters are now dealt with more specifically in the definition of a related party.

20.2.2 Parties assumed not to be related

The following parties are presumed, by the version of FRS 8 that applies for periods beginning prior to 1 January 2011, not to be related:

(1) Providers of finance, so long as this is in the normal course of their business.

(2) Utility companies.

(3) Government departments and bodies.

(4) Customers, suppliers, distributors and agents who have influence only as a result of the volume of business.

In each case, the presumption that they are not related can be rebutted if there are additional circumstances which indicate that they fall within the definition of related parties. The FRS is very clear in stating that it does not require disclosure 'simply' because another party has this role, and, in the case of the first three points, if any influence is simply as a result of their position. There would have to be another factor to warrant assuming that such parties are related.

For accounting periods beginning on or after 1 January 2011, this changes somewhat. The revised version of FRS 8 provides a list of parties who are not related which is wider.

(a) Two entities simply because they have a director or other member of key management personnel in common or because a member of key management personnel of one entity has significant influence over the other entity.

(b) Two venturers simply because they share joint control over a joint venture.

(c)

    (i) Providers of finance.

    (ii) Trade unions.

    (iii) Public utilities.

    (iv) Departments and agencies of a government that does not control, jointly control or significantly influence the reporting entity, simply by virtue of their normal dealings with an entity (even though they may affect the freedom of action of an entity or participate in its decision-making process).

(d) A customer, supplier, franchisor, distributor or general agent with whom an entity transacts a significant volume of business, simply by virtue of the resulting economic dependence.

Again, the standard may have changed, but in nearly all cases there will be the same result, and such parties both were previously not considered, and will continue not to be considered, related parties.

20.3 RELATED PARTY TRANSACTIONS

20.3.1 FRS 8 requirements

A related party transaction is defined as:

> ... the transfer of assets or liabilities or the performance of services by, to or for a related party irrespective of whether a price is charged. (Para. 2.6, FRS 8.)

The fact that transactions need to be disclosed even where there is no charge may pose problems, particularly since they may not be captured by the company's accounting system. The most likely types of transaction for which no charge will be made are management or related services.

As with all accounting standards, FRS 8 only applies to material items. However, there is a special definition of materiality. The general rule is that:

> Transactions are material when their disclosure might reasonably be expected to influence decisions made by the users of general purpose financial statements. (Para. 20, FRS 8.)

The standard then goes on to be more specific. Materiality should not be considered only from the point of view of the company, but also from the point of view of the other party if that other party:

- is a director, key manager or other individual in a position to influence, or accountable for, the stewardship of the company;
- is a member of the close family of any person included above, or
- is controlled by any person included in the two categories above.

This does not apply to small companies. Under the FRSSE, the materiality of transactions with related parties needs to be assessed by reference to the reporting entity, as with all other areas of the financial statements.

Where a transaction takes place at no charge then materiality is a more complicated idea. The most reasonable basis is probably to consider the amount that would have been expected to have been charged if the transaction had been on commercial terms.

The FRS does not provide an exhaustive list of possible transactions, but does include the following:

- purchases or sale of goods;
- purchases or sales of property or other assets;
- rendering or receipt of services;
- agency arrangements;
- leasing arrangements;
- transfer of research and development;
- licence agreements;
- provision of finance, including loans and equity contributions;

- guarantees and the provision of collateral security, and
- management contracts.

It should be noted that the payment of dividends is a transaction. Therefore, where dividends are paid to related parties, such as directors, this needs to be disclosed. This has always been the case in principle, but, in practice, such disclosure was not usually provided when directors' interests were disclosed in directors' reports. There was usually a good argument for this, on the basis that such disclosure added nothing to the information that was already available. (Although there were exceptions to this, such as where there had been substantial changes in a director's shareholding in the year, and it was, therefore, not clear whether or not a dividend had been paid to that director.) The same applies to the issue and redemption of shares by the company. It does not apply to the purchase and sale of the company's shares by directors from or to third parties, on the basis that the company is not a party to such a transaction.

20.3.2 *Statutory requirements*

Putting to one side the issue of transactions involving directors, it is only with the Companies Act 2006 that statute has contained provisions dealing with related party transactions in general. (This has already been referred to above, since it is the introduction of the statutory requirement that gave rise to the need to amend the definition of a related party under FRS 8.)

Paragraph 72 of Sch. 1 to The Large and Medium-sized Companies and Groups (Accounts and Reports) Regulations 2008 (SI 2008/410) contains the following.

(1) Particulars may be given of transactions which the company has entered into with related parties, and must be given if such transactions are material and have not been concluded under normal market conditions (see reg. 4(2) for exemption for medium-sized companies).

(2) The particulars of transactions required to be disclosed by sub-paragraph (1) must include:

(a) the amount of such transactions;

(b) the nature of the related party relationship, and

(c) other information about the transactions necessary for an understanding of the financial position of the company.

(3) Information about individual transactions may be aggregated according to their nature, except where separate information is necessary for an understanding of the effects of related party transactions on the financial position of the company.

(4) Particulars need not be given of transactions entered into between two or more members of a group, provided that any subsidiary undertaking which is a party to the transaction is wholly owned by such a member.

(5)   In this paragraph, 'related party' has the same meaning as in international accounting standards.

As this makes fairly clear, it applies only to large companies. However, as noted earlier, this has not been reflected in FRS 8, which applies equally to large and medium-sized companies (and small companies, although, of course, in this case it reflects a choice on the part of the company, since small companies would be entitled to use the FRSSE if they so wished).

There are similarities with the FRS 8 requirements, but the SI makes clear that there is a need to disclose details only where material transactions have not been concluded under normal market conditions, whilst other transactions 'may' be disclosed. Again, this has not been reflected in FRS 8. As explained earlier, FRS 8 applies to all related party transactions, whether concluded under 'normal market conditions' or otherwise.

It is, perhaps, not entirely clear from the SI, or the Directive on which it is based, whether there is a need to differentiate between transactions which have been concluded under 'normal market conditions' and those that have not. However, the European Commission has opined upon this subject and does not believe that drawing such a distinction in financial statements is necessary.

20.4   EXEMPTIONS

Notwithstanding the general principles, there are various disclosure exemptions included in FRS 8.

The FRS does not require disclosure:

- in consolidated financial statements of intra-group transactions which have been eliminated on consolidation;
- of transactions entered into between two or more members of a group, provided that any subsidiary undertaking which is a party to the transaction is wholly owned by a member of that group;
- of pension contributions paid to a pension fund (although FRS 17 and the FRSSE also need to be considered, and any other transactions are disclosable), and
- of emoluments in respect of services as an employee (although rules on disclosure of directors' emoluments still apply).

There is also an exemption where there is a legal duty of confidentiality. For example, banks will not have to disclose details of transactions in the normal course of banking business.

20.5 DISCLOSURE REQUIRED

20.5.1 Control

When the company is controlled by another party the following disclosures are required, irrespective of whether any transactions have taken place during the reporting period:

- the related party relationship (that is, the existence of control);
- the name of the controlling party, and
- the name of the ultimate controlling party, if different.

If the controlling party is unknown, that fact should be disclosed.

The controlling party need not be a company; a trust or individual, for example, may be the controlling party. Care needs to be taken with trusts, as the nature of the trust will affect whether a trust is a controlling party. In some cases, a beneficiary may be able to call for delivery of trust assets (including the instruments giving control), and is therefore considered the controlling party of the trust and hence the company. In other cases, this may not be possible, and the trust may be the controlling party. Every case needs to be considered on its own merits. Trustees, unless also beneficiaries, are not controlling parties. This applies where they have the ability to direct the operations of the trust, but do not have the right to benefit from those operations. Control under FRS 8 refers to both the ability to direct and the ability to benefit, as set out above.

20.5.2 Transactions

Disclosure should be made of all material financial transactions between a company and its related parties. The details that should be given are:

- the names of the related parties;
- the relationship between the parties;
- a description of the transactions;
- the amounts involved (including, where necessary, a statement that the transaction took place at nil value), and
- any other elements of the transactions necessary for an understanding of the financial statements.

The example given in the FRS of the final category is that of the transfer of a major asset at an amount materially different from that obtainable on normal commercial terms. It is reasonable to assume that all material differences between commercial and recorded values of transactions will fall into this category.

The accounts should also disclose:

- the amounts due to or from related parties at the balance sheet date;

- the amount of any provisions for doubtful debts due from such parties at that date, and
- any amounts written off in the period in respect of debts due to or from related parties.

Transactions may be aggregated by similar transactions with similar types of related party, unless disclosure of an individual transaction, or connected transactions, is necessary for an understanding of the impact of the transactions on the financial statements, or if separate disclosure is required by law. This will cut down the volume of disclosure substantially. For example, where a subsidiary (which is not entitled to the exemptions) has a number of sales transactions with other fellow subsidiaries, it will have to disclose these transactions only in aggregate. It will not be required to provide details of each transaction.

20.6　DIRECTORS

20.6.1　Definition

Before dealing with directors' remuneration, or transactions with directors, it is first necessary to provide definitions of a director, a shadow director and a connected person. The Companies Act definition of a director is not quite as enlightening as one might desire:

> ... "director" includes any person occupying the position of director, by whatever name called. (CA 2006, s. 250.)

This does, however, make it clear that 'director' is a function and not a job title. This has two implications.

(1) A person can be a director, for the purposes of company law, even though he or she has a different title within the company.

(2) A person can have director within his or her job title yet not fall within the Companies Act definition, for example if he or she is described as a regional director but is not involved in the overall running of the business.

There are some dangers associated with the second situation, primarily those of holding out.

For some purposes a 'shadow director' is also treated as a director. A shadow director is defined as:

> ... a person in accordance with whose directions or instructions the directors of the company are accustomed to act.
>
> A person is not to be regarded as a shadow director by reason only that the directors act on advice given by him in a professional capacity. (CA 2006, s. 251 (1) and (2).)

This means that professional advisers, such as accounting firms or stockbrokers, will not normally be treated as shadow directors. The key point behind this exemption is that such persons only provide suggestions, they cannot force the company to act in accordance with this advice. While they may provide advice to the managers of the company, they are not involved in the company's management.

The main purposes for which shadow directors are treated as directors are:

- directors' duty to have regard to interests of employees;
- directors' long-term contracts of employment;
- substantial property transactions involving directors, and
- requirements concerning companies making loans, or similar, to directors and connected persons.

An exception is made in group situations:

A body corporate is not to be regarded as a shadow director of any of its subsidiary companies for the purposes of:

Chapter 2 (general duties of directors)

Chapter 4 (transactions requiring members' approval), or

Chapter 6 (contract with sole member who is also a director)

by reason only that the directors of the subsidiary are accustomed to act in accordance with its directions or instructions. (CA 2006, s. 251 (3).)

The provisions that apply to directors also usually apply to persons connected with a director. The basic rules on identifying a connected person under the Companies Act 2006 are:

The following persons (and only those persons) are connected with a director of a company:

(a) members of the director's family (see section 253);

(b) a body corporate with which the director is connected (as defined in section 254);

(c) a person acting in his capacity as trustee of a trust:

  (i) the beneficiaries of which include the director or a person who by virtue of paragraph (a) or (b) is connected with him, or

  (ii) the terms of which confer a power on the trustees that may be exercised for the benefit of the director or any such person, other than a trust for the purposes of an employees' share scheme or a pension scheme;

(d) a person acting in his capacity as partner:

  (i) of the director, or

  (ii) of a person who, by virtue of paragraph (a), (b) or (c), is connected with that director;

(e) a firm that is a legal person under the law by which it is governed and in which:

(i)   the director is a partner,

(ii)   a partner is a person who, by virtue of paragraph (a), (b) or (c) is connected with the director, or

(iii) a partner is a firm in which the director is a partner or in which there is a partner who, by virtue of paragraph (a), (b) or (c), is connected with the director. (CA 2006, s. 252 (2).)

There is an exclusion where a person falls within the definition above, but is also a director in his or her own right.

This differs from the previous definition of a connected person. Under the Companies Act 2006, connected persons now include the following, who would not have been connected persons under the Companies Act 1985:

- civil partners;
- any other person (whether of a different sex or the same sex) with whom the director lives as partner in an enduring family relationship;
- parents, and
- children or stepchildren of any other person with whom the director lives as partner in an enduring family relationship, and who are under 18.

Previously, family members per se were not covered, and the legislation referred only to the directors' spouse and minor children and stepchildren. Spouses continue to be covered, and children or stepchildren are now connected with their parents for the whole of their life, not just the first 18 years of it.

For the avoidance of doubt, the Companies Act 2006 notes that living in an 'enduring family relationship' does not apply to someone who lives with a director who is that director's grandparent, grandchild, sister, brother, aunt or uncle, nephew or niece.

In addition, the references to the beneficiaries of a trust in determining whether or not a trustee is a connected person now also refer to the wider definition of family members.

Directors are connected with a body corporate if they and any connected persons:

- are interested in shares which comprise 20 per cent of the nominal value of the issued share capital of that body, or
- can exercise or control 20 per cent or more of the votes at any general meeting of that body.

Directors control a body corporate if they and any connected persons:

- are interested in any equity shares of the body and can exercise or control any part of the voting power at any general meeting of that body, and
- together with the other directors of their company are interested in more than 50 per cent of the share capital, or are entitled to exercise or control the exercise of more than 50 per cent of the voting power at a general meeting.

Solely for the purposes of determining if a company is connected with the director, any other body corporate with which the director is associated is only deemed to be connected with him or her if it is connected under CA 2006, s. 252 (2) (c) or (d) quoted earlier. A trustee of a trust, of which a beneficiary is a body corporate with which the director is connected, is not to be treated as a connected person.

Where the provisions refer to voting power controlled by a director this includes voting power controlled by a body corporate which he or she controls.

The most complicated part of these provisions is that dealing with shares or voting rights held by companies with which a director might be deemed to be connected. Three examples will give some idea of the impact of the provisions.

EXAMPLE

A director owns 15 per cent of the shares and voting rights in company A. He also owns 25 per cent of the shares and voting rights in company B, and a further 10 per cent of the shares and voting rights of company B are held by his wife. Company B owns 10 per cent of the shares in company A. There are no other relevant connections.

The director is clearly connected with company B. Even ignoring his wife's holding, he controls 25 per cent of the voting rights and shares in that company. However, he is not connected with company A. Although he owns 15 per cent of the votes and shares, no control is considered to be exercised through company B, since only 35 per cent of shares are held. A 15 per cent holding is not sufficient to establish a connection.

EXAMPLE

A director owns 15 per cent of the shares and voting rights in company A. She also owns 45 per cent of the shares and voting rights in company B, and a further 10 per cent of the shares and voting rights of company B are held by her husband. Company B owns 10 per cent of the shares in company A. There are no other relevant connections.

The director is clearly connected with company B. Even ignoring her husband's holding, she controls 45 per cent of the voting rights and shares in that company. She is also connected with company A. The direct holding of 15 per cent is added to the 10 per cent of shares held by company B, since she controls company B, having a total of 55 per cent of the shares and votes in issue. The total holding is then 25 per cent, which is above the 20 per cent threshold.

EXAMPLE

A director owns 51 per cent of company A. Company A owns 51 per cent of company B. Company B owns 51 per cent of company C. Company C owns 51 per cent of company D. In all cases the proportions apply to both shares and voting rights. The director is connected with companies A, B, C and D. This is despite the fact that the effective interest in company D is only 6.77 per cent of the share capital. This arises because there is control throughout the chain. This can be seen as being very similar to the rules for inclusion of subsidiaries in group accounts; where there is a chain of

---

> control it is the extent of this chain and not the effective interest that determines the accounting treatment and disclosure.

20.7 DIRECTORS' REMUNERATION

20.7.1 Quoted companies

Quoted companies are required to produce a directors' remuneration report as part of their annual reports and accounts. As a result, they are exempted from many of the normal requirements to disclose details of directors' remuneration in their financial statements.

The details of the directors' remuneration report are outside the scope of this chapter.

The remainder of this section therefore applies to unquoted companies.

20.7.2 Aggregate remuneration

Companies, other than small companies, are required to disclose various aggregate amounts in respect of directors:

(a) the aggregate amount of remuneration paid to or receivable by directors in respect of qualifying services;

. . .

(c) the aggregate of the amount of money paid to or receivable by directors, and the net value of assets (other than money and share options) received or receivable by directors under long term incentive schemes in respect of qualifying services; and

(d) the aggregate value of any company contributions:

(i) paid, or treated as paid, to a pension scheme in respect of directors' qualifying services, and

(ii) by reference to which the rate or amount of any money purchase benefits that may become payable will be calculated; . . . (Para. 1, The Large and Medium-sized Companies and Groups (Accounts and Reports) Regulations 2008 (SI 2008/410).)

Small companies are just required to disclose the total of these three amounts.

20.7.3 Emoluments and remuneration

The Companies Act 2006 has slightly changed the use of the terms emoluments and remuneration. Remuneration is now used when dealing with aggregate disclosures, ie for all directors, while 'emoluments' is still the word used when referring to individual directors. 'Emoluments' are defined fairly widely to include salaries, fees and bonuses, expense allowances subject to income tax, and the estimated money value of any non-cash benefits. However, they exclude items which fall within any of the other categories that need to be disclosed. As a result, emoluments do not include:

- the value of share options granted to directors;
- the value of share options exercised by directors;
- pension contributions;
- pensions received, or
- amounts received under long-term incentive schemes.

'Qualifying services' are defined as:

> . . . services as a director of the company, and his services while director of the company:
>
> (a) as a director of any of its subsidiary undertakings, or
> (b) otherwise in connection with the management of the affairs of the company or any of its subsidiary undertakings. (Para. 15, Sch. 5 to The Large and Medium-sized Companies and Groups (Accounts and Reports) Regulations 2008 (SI 2008/410).)

A special extended definition of a subsidiary is used for this purpose, and no other. Apart from normal subsidiary undertakings:

> Any reference in this Schedule to a subsidiary undertaking of the company, in relation to a person who is or was, while a director of the company, a director also, by virtue of the company's nomination (direct or indirect) of any other undertaking, includes that undertaking, whether or not it is or was in fact a subsidiary undertaking of the company. (Para. 14 (1), Sch. 5 to The Large and Medium-sized Companies and Groups (Accounts and Reports) Regulations 2008 (SI 2008/410).)

Probably as a result of this wider definition, there is an exemption from disclosure if a company cannot obtain the necessary information from its 'subsidiaries':

> This Schedule requires information to be given only so far as it is contained in the company's books and papers or the company has the right to obtain it from the persons concerned. (Para. 6, Sch. 5 to The Large and Medium-sized Companies and Groups (Accounts and Reports) Regulations 2008 (SI 2008/410).)

The amount to be shown includes amounts paid by:

- the company;
- any of the company's subsidiary undertakings (using the wider definition included above), and
- any other person.

This also applies to all other disclosure requirements connected with directors' emoluments. The financial statements no longer need to distinguish between such amounts.

It does not include amounts which the director must pay over, or pay back, to the company or any of its subsidiary undertakings or to past or present members of the company or any of its subsidiaries. However, if such an amount is subsequently waived, then the amount should be shown as part of the directors' emoluments in the year in which the waiver takes place. They should be shown separately from emoluments earned during the year.

Disclosure is also required where such a balance has not been enforced after a period of two years.

Amounts paid to a person connected with a director are treated as if they had been paid to the director, but not if this would cause them to be treated twice.

The emoluments include all amounts receivable in respect of the year in question, whether or not they were actually received in that year. Where a sum is not receivable in respect of any particular period then it should be accounted for when received by the director.

It is notable that the definition of emoluments does not, at least theoretically, include all amounts paid to directors. Where part of a director's income from the company derives from work undertaken for the company, but not in connection with their duties as director or in connection with management, then that part of the income would not strictly fall within the definition. Nonetheless, the drawing of such a distinction is likely to be extremely difficult, if not impossible, in practice, and such amounts are almost universally included under directors' emoluments.

Direct payments to directors cause very few accounting problems. The more difficult areas are those of expense allowances and benefits in kind. Expense allowances are disclosable only in so far as they are subject to UK income tax. The reasoning behind this rule is presumably that amounts which are allowed for tax purposes do not usually provide anything other than an incidental benefit to the director. Their inclusion in the amount of directors' emoluments would mean that this figure would be overstated, by including business costs which should be treated elsewhere. Where an amount is charged to tax after the end of the relevant financial year then it should be disclosed as directors' emoluments in the earliest financial statements in which it is practicable, and should be disclosed separately.

Although the Companies Act requires disclosure of benefits other than cash at their 'estimated money value' this is not always a straightforward assessment. We would suggest that the following procedures would arrive at a result consistent with the aims of the legislation:

- where the company has incurred a direct and identifiable cost in providing a benefit to a director, such as the hire of a motor car or the purchase of directors' indemnity insurance, this cost should be included within directors' emoluments;

- where there is no identifiable cost, for example where the company owns an asset that is used by a director, an estimate should be made of the market value of the benefit, and this should be included as part of directors' emoluments;
- only where neither of the methods above can be used should the taxable value of the benefit be used, and
- where there is no reasonable method of valuation, disclosure of the facts should be given, together with a statement explaining why such a valuation is not possible.

The amount of the taxable benefit is the least satisfactory of the possible methods, since tax rules are written for a specific purpose unconnected with accounting.

It should be noted that, since in some cases the market value of a benefit will be disclosed in the financial statements and not the amount of any cost to the company, the directors' emoluments will not necessarily agree with the amount of directors' emoluments included in the company's accounting records. Similarly, where all of the employees of a company are directors the amount shown as directors' emoluments may be higher than the total staff costs.

20.7.4 Long-term incentive schemes

There is a requirement to provide separate disclosure of the aggregate amounts paid under long-term incentive schemes.

A long-term incentive scheme is defined as:

(1) ... an agreement or arrangement:

    (a) under which money or other assets may become receivable by a director, and

    (b) which includes one or more qualifying conditions with respect to service or performance which cannot be fulfilled within a single financial year.

(2) For this purpose the following must be disregarded:

    (a) bonuses the amount of which falls to be determined by reference to service or performance within a single financial year;

    (b) compensation for loss of office, payments for breach of contract and other termination payments; and

    (c) retirement benefits. (Para. 11, Sch. 5 to The Large and Medium-sized Companies and Groups (Accounts and Reports) Regulations 2008 (SI 2008/410).)

The amount which needs to be disclosed includes both cash and the value of any non-cash assets. For this purpose non-cash assets always exclude share options and, in the case of companies other than listed companies, also exclude shares.

20.7.5 Pension contributions

There is a requirement for accounts to disclose the aggregate of the amounts paid to (or accrued in respect of) money purchase pension schemes for directors.

Where a scheme pays the higher of money purchase benefits or a defined benefit, the assessment of the nature of the scheme should be based on which seems most likely to apply, as judged at the end of the financial year.

Companies are also required to disclose:

- the number of directors who are accruing benefits under money purchase pension schemes, and
- the number of directors who are accruing benefits under defined benefit schemes.

There is no requirement to state the amounts attributable to directors under defined benefit schemes (although, as noted in section **20.7.8**, there is additional disclosure required for excess retirement benefits).

20.7.6 Shares and share options

Unlisted companies are required to disclose:

- the number of directors who exercised share options, and
- the number of directors who received (or became entitled to) shares under long-term incentive schemes.

For these purposes, 'shares' include shares in the company or any group undertakings, and share warrants.

20.7.7 Highest-paid director

Disclosure of details of the emoluments of the highest-paid director is required only where the total directors' remuneration (excluding pension contributions) equals or exceeds £200,000. The information is never required for a small company.

Where the disclosure is needed, the following information must be given:

- the total emoluments, excluding pension contributions, of the highest-paid director;

- the amount paid to money purchase pension schemes on behalf of that director;
- the accrued pension, as at the end of the year, of the director, if he or she is a member of a defined benefits scheme, and
- any accrued lump sum, as at the end of the year, of the director, if he or she is a member of a defined benefits scheme.

Unlisted companies (where they need to provide disclosure of the highest-paid director's emoluments) are also required to state if the highest-paid director:

- exercised any share options, and
- received, or became entitled to receive, any shares under a long-term incentive scheme.

Where no such rights were obtained during the year, a negative statement is not required.

The accrued pension and accrued lump sum are based on the amounts payable to the director on reaching normal retirement age. They are to be calculated on the assumption that:

- the director left at the end of the year;
- there is no inflation from the end of the year to the director's retirement date;
- there is no commutation of the pension or inverse commutation of the lump sum, and
- there are no voluntary contributions from the director.

20.7.8 Excess retirement benefits

Companies, other than small companies, are required to disclose:

- the benefits paid to or receivable by directors under pension schemes, and
- the benefits paid to or receivable by past directors under pension schemes,

to the extent that these amounts are in excess of the benefits to which they were entitled on the date they first became eligible for benefits, or 31 March 1997, whichever is the later.

This disclosure is not required if the payments are made from a pension scheme which does not require additional funding as a result of the additional benefit, and where the additional amounts are available to all pensioner members of the schemes on the same basis.

If any amount needs to be disclosed, then any amounts paid other than in cash need to be shown separately.

20.7.9   Compensation for loss of office

All companies are required to show the aggregate amount of compensation to directors or past directors for loss of office. This includes all amounts in respect of loss of office as a director of the company, or any of its subsidiaries, and loss of any other office connected with the management of the company or any of its subsidiary undertakings. It includes amounts which are not paid in cash, which must be disclosed separately.

The amount also includes compensation for retirement, and any payments made which result from a breach of the person's contract with the company, whether as damages or in settlement or compromise of a claim for breach.

20.7.10   Sums paid to third parties

The aggregate amount of sums paid to third parties in respect of making the services of a director available should be disclosed. This applies whether the third party has made the director's services available as director, or otherwise in connection with management, and whether this is for the company or one of its subsidiaries. It includes amounts other than in cash, when the nature of the consideration needs to be disclosed. 'Third party' excludes the director himself, or a person connected with him or her, and the company or any of its subsidiaries.

20.8   TRANSACTIONS WITH DIRECTORS

20.8.1   Lawfulness and disclosure

Transactions with directors can be looked at from two sides, that of their lawfulness and that of their disclosure. The fact that a transaction is lawful does not mean that it will not need to be disclosed. (Similarly, the fact that it has been disclosed does not mean that it is lawful.) There is a general presumption that transactions with directors will need to be disclosed, although there are exceptions. Under the Companies Act 2006, transactions with directors are now generally allowed, which is very different to the position that obtained under the Companies Act 1985. However, rather than prohibiting transactions the Companies Act 2006 has instead allowed transactions, if appropriate procedures are followed, and in particular obtaining approval of the members for many transactions.

20.8.2   Loans

The old general prohibition on loans to directors has been abolished. Instead, loans may now be made to directors, but unless they are within one of the exemptions, this can be done only where this has been approved by the members of the company:

> A company may not:
>
> (a) make a loan to a director of the company or of its holding company, or
> (b) give a guarantee or provide security in connection with a loan made by any person to such a director,
>
> unless the transaction has been approved by a resolution of the members of the company. (CA 2006, s. 197(1).)

If the director is also a director of the company's holding company, then there must also be approval by a resolution of the members of the holding company.

Despite this, a company can always make a loan to a director if the total value of all loans outstanding to that director does not exceed £10,000. (The limit used to be £5,000.) It should be noted that this amount refers to the principal. As a result, a loan may be over £10,000 and still not require members' approval if it only goes over this threshold as the result of accrued interest.

There is no general restriction on the granting of loans to persons connected with a director, although a similar approval procedure as for loans to a director is required if the company is a public company or a company associated with a public company. It is also worth noting that there is no restriction on a company making a loan, of whatever amount, to a director of one of its subsidiaries, so long as that director is not also a director of the company itself (which of course would also include a shadow director). Similarly, a company may make a loan to a director of any fellow subsidiaries, so long as that person is not a director of the company itself or of its holding company.

20.8.3 *Public companies and companies associated with them*

There are additional restrictions placed on public companies and companies associated with public companies.

'Associated' is defined as follows:

> For the purposes of this Part:
>
> (a) bodies corporate are associated if one is a subsidiary of the other or both are subsidiaries of the same body corporate, and
> (b) companies are associated if one is a subsidiary of the other or both are subsidiaries of the same body corporate. (CA 2006, s. 256.)

The additional restrictions are that such companies also need to obtain member approval to:

- make a quasi-loan to a director of the company or of its holding company;
- make a loan or a quasi-loan to a person connected with a director;
- enter into a guarantee or provide any security in connection with a loan or

quasi-loan made by any other person for a director or a person connected with a director;

- enter into a credit transaction as creditor for such a director or a person so connected, or
- enter into any guarantee or provide any security in connection with a credit transaction made by any other person for such a director or a person connected with a director.

Companies are always allowed to make loans and quasi-loans to other group companies, and to provide guarantees on behalf of other group companies.

Two of the phrases used need to be defined further:

A "quasi-loan" is a transaction under which ... the creditor ... agrees to pay, or pays otherwise than in pursuance of an agreement, a sum for ... the borrower ... or agrees to reimburse, or reimburses otherwise than in pursuance of an agreement, expenditure incurred by another party for ... the borrower ...

(a) on terms that the borrower (or a person on his behalf) will reimburse the creditor;

or

(b) in circumstances giving rise to a liability on the borrower to reimburse the creditor. (CA 2006, s. 199(1).)

A "credit transaction" is a transaction under which ... the creditor ...

(a) supplies any goods or sells any land under a hire-purchase agreement or a conditional sale agreement;

(b) leases or hires any land or goods in return for periodical payments; or

(c) otherwise disposes of land or supplies goods or services on the understanding that payment (whether in a lump sum or instalments or by way of periodical payments or otherwise) is to be deferred. (CA 2006, s. 202(1).)

All companies, including public companies or companies associated with them, are still allowed to make a quasi-loan to a director or a person connected with them without members' approval if the aggregate of all loans and quasi-loans to that director and their connected persons does not exceed £10,000.

A public company or a company associated with a public company can also undertake credit transactions on behalf of directors, or persons connected with directors, without having to obtain members' approval, if:

- the aggregate amount of all such credit transactions with the director does not exceed £15,000, or
- the transaction is entered into in the ordinary course of business and the value of the transaction is not greater, nor the terms on which it is entered into more favourable, than it is reasonable to expect the company would have offered to a person of the same financial standing but unconnected with the company.

All companies can also provide a director with funds to enable them to meet business expenditure without any requirement for members' approval, so long as the amount involved does not exceed £50,000.

20.8.4   Single member companies

Where a sole shareholder is also a director of a company, there are special rules for all contracts, including loans or otherwise, which are not entered into in the ordinary course of business, between the shareholder and the company. Where any contract is not already in writing, a written memorandum of its terms must be prepared, or the terms of the contract must be entered in the minutes of the first board meeting after the making of the contract. The contract remains valid if these conditions are not met, but the company and its officers are liable to a fine.

20.8.5   Assumption of obligations

A company is also not allowed to take over rights, obligations or liabilities under an arrangement, without the approval of its members if the company could not have undertaken the arrangement in the first place without the approval of its members.

20.8.6   Arrangements with third parties

A company is also not allowed, without the approval of its members, to arrange for a third party to undertake a transaction with a director, which the company itself could not have undertaken without the approval of its members, where that third party will obtain a benefit for so doing from the company, its holding company, a subsidiary or a fellow subsidiary.

20.8.7   Money lending companies

Where a company lends money or provides guarantees as part of its ordinary business then there are additional exemptions.

Such a company can make a loan or quasi-loan, or guarantee such a loan or quasi-loan, without requiring the approval of its members, to a director without any financial limit if:

- it is entered into in the ordinary course of business and the amount and terms are the same as those which would have been offered to a person of similar financial standing unconnected with the company, or
- it is entered into in the ordinary course of business and is for the purchase or improvement of the director's main dwelling house, or to replace a loan

granted by a third party for either of these purposes, and is on the same terms as the company ordinarily offers to its employees.

20.8.8   Transactions to be disclosed

In practice, the Companies Act 2006 has made no major changes to the disclosure required in company or group accounts, particularly given that FRS 8 is also relevant to the disclosure. However, the way the provisions have been drafted has changed significantly.

Under the Companies Act 2006, the transactions that require disclosure are:

- advances and credits granted by the company to its directors, and
- guarantees of any kind entered into by the company on behalf of its directors.

In the case of group accounts, this is extended to cover amounts related to directors of the parent, but advanced or granted by subsidiaries.

Transactions need to be disclosed:

- whether or not the person was a director of the company at the time the transaction took place, and
- in the case of groups, whether or not one company was a subsidiary of the other at the time the transaction took place.

The wording of the requirements is not quite as clear as one might like. In particular, if read strictly, the requirements could appear to require each transaction to be disclosed separately. This would appear potentially excessive, and a more reasonable interpretation is that the gross amounts should be shown. So, for example, if a director received a number of advances in the year and made a number of repayments, then the gross amount of the advances and the gross amounts of the repayments should be shown, but not the amounts of each individual transaction.

20.8.9   Disclosure required

Once a transaction has been identified as disclosable, then under the Companies Act 2006 the following disclosure is required.

(1)   For an advance or credit:

    (a)   its amount;
    (b)   an indication of the interest rate;
    (c)   its main conditions, and
    (d)   any amounts repaid.

(2)   For a guarantee:

    (a)   its main terms;

(b) the amount of the maximum liability that may be incurred by the company (or its subsidiary), and

(c) any amount paid and any liability incurred by the company (or its subsidiary) for the purpose of fulfilling the guarantee (including any loss incurred by reason of enforcement of the guarantee).

Together with totals for each of the relevant items.

21 GROUP ACCOUNTS

21.1 INTRODUCTION

21.1.1 Preparation of group accounts

As a general principle, where one company controls another company it is required to prepare consolidated accounts to show the results and position of both companies. The original UK standard on group accounts, SSAP 14 *Group Accounts*, noted:

> Group accounts showing the state of affairs and profit or loss of a holding company and its subsidiaries have been required by law in most instances in the United Kingdom and Ireland for many years. In practice the group accounts usually take the form of consolidated financial statements which present the information contained in the separate financial statements of the holding company and its subsidiaries as if they were the financial statements of a single entity. (Para. 1, SSAP 14.)

The situation is now even clearer than when SSAP 14 was in place: not only is it still normal for group accounts to be in the form of consolidated accounts, but this is now a legal requirement. In effect, group accounts and consolidated accounts are synonymous terms.

FRS 2 *Accounting for Subsidiary Undertakings* provides a description of the basic logic behind the preparation of group accounts:

> For a variety of legal, tax and other reasons undertakings generally choose to conduct their activities not through a single legal entity but through several undertakings under the ultimate control of the parent undertaking of that group. For this reason the financial statements of a parent undertaking by itself do not present a full picture of its economic activities or financial position. Consolidated financial statements are required in order to reflect the extended business unit that conducts activities under the control of the parent undertaking. (Para. 59, FRS 2.)

The group is effectively treated as though it were a separate single company, with only one group of shareholders. The balances and profits shown are only those resulting from transactions with third parties, and all balances and transactions within the group are eliminated.

This chapter deals with the preparation of group accounts, and with certain related matters such as accounting for associated undertakings and joint ventures. Certain areas, such as the preparation of group cash flow statements and the incorporation of overseas subsidiaries (which might give rise to exchange differences in group accounts), are covered in other chapters.

Potential impact of the FRSME

The draft FRSME would affect the manner in which consolidated financial statements are prepared, but have little effect on the need for them. This is on the basis that the requirement for group accounts is largely statutory and would be unaffected by a change in accounting standards.

The very first part of the section of the FRSME dealing with consolidated financial statements makes it clear that it is to be applied in accordance with the statutory rules, and it is not intended to override exemptions which are provided by statute.

21.2 IDENTIFYING GROUP MEMBERS

21.2.1 Duty to prepare group accounts

The basic requirement to prepare group accounts is contained in the Companies Act 2006:

(1) This section applies to companies that are not subject to the small companies regime.

(2) If at the end of a financial year the company is a parent company the directors, as well as preparing individual accounts for the year, must prepare group accounts for the year unless the company is exempt from that requirement. (CA 2006, s. 399.)

The basic rules on when there is a parent and subsidiary relationship are as follows.

An undertaking is a parent undertaking in relation to another undertaking, a subsidiary undertaking, if:

(a) it holds a majority of the voting rights in the undertaking, or
(b) it is a member of the undertaking and has the right to appoint or remove a majority of its board of directors, or
(c) it has the right to exercise a dominant influence over the undertaking:

   (i)   by virtue of provisions contained in the undertaking's articles, or
   (ii) by virtue of a control contract, or

(d) it is a member of the undertaking and controls alone, pursuant to an agreement with other shareholders or members, a majority of the voting rights in the undertaking. (CA 2006, s. 1162.)

Prior to the changes which resulted in UK companies having the requirement or option to move to IFRS, there was also a test which stated that an undertaking was also a parent undertaking if it had a participating interest in another undertaking and actually exercised a dominant influence over it, or if it and the other undertaking were managed on a unified basis. This has been amended so that there is no longer any reference to participating interests. This means that one company has a subsidiary undertaking if it actually exercises a dominant influence over that undertaking, or if it and the other undertaking are managed on a unified basis.

The main test is that of control. One company is the subsidiary of another if it is controlled by that company. This means that a group will consist of all the separate enterprises, including unincorporated enterprises, under the control of the parent. Of course, in practice, control and ownership usually go together.

When determining if a company owns shares, or the voting rights that attach to them, or the equivalent for an unincorporated undertaking, any shares held by another subsidiary or by a company's nominee must also be taken into account.

A number of the phrases used in the legislation need to be explained further. The phrases discussed here are:

- voting rights;
- the right to appoint or remove a majority of the board of directors;
- the right to exercise a dominant influence, and
- a control contract.

Where the potential subsidiary is a company limited by shares, the voting rights will be the voting rights that attach to that company's shares. For unincorporated enterprises the situation may be more complex and additional detail is provided:

> ... the references to the voting rights in an undertaking are to the rights conferred on shareholders in respect of their shares or, in the case of an undertaking not having a share capital, on members, to vote at general meetings of the undertaking on all, or substantially all, matters.

> In relation to an undertaking which does not have general meetings at which matters are decided by the exercise of voting rights, the references to holding a majority of the voting rights in the undertaking shall be construed as references to having the right under the constitution of the undertaking to direct the overall policy of the undertaking or to alter the terms of its constitution. (CA 2006, paras. 2(a) and 2(2), Sch. 7.)

'Substantially all' is not defined, and a reasonable assessment must be made in the particular circumstances. The most reasonable interpretation is that any very specific rights given to certain parties to make particular decisions should be ignored.

Where rights can only be exercised in specific circumstances, they should only be taken into account in determining whether one undertaking is the subsidiary of another if:

- the circumstances have arisen, and then only for as long as those circumstances are in existence, or
- the circumstances are within the control of the person having the rights.

This can be very important. For example, a venture capital company may invest in another company, and be granted rights to exercise or take over control of that company only in specified circumstances, usually where there are problems with the investee company's profitability, solvency or liquidity. Such rights do not mean that the venture capital company has control, unless and until the specified circumstances arise. This will often have the result that the venture capital company is not required to treat the other as a subsidiary.

Where there are rights which are normally exercisable, but which cannot temporarily be exercised, they should continue to be taken into account.

There are some unfortunate consequences of these rules. One undertaking may become, or cease to be, the subsidiary of another without changes in the holding but due to changes in other circumstances. More importantly, an undertaking may be the subsidiary of two separate undertakings if one normally has control, and expects to regain it, and the other has control at the time at which it is preparing financial statements. The aggregate effective percentages of control exercised by each party would in this case exceed 100 per cent.

The right to appoint or remove a majority of the board of directors is the right to appoint or remove directors holding a majority of the voting rights at meetings of the board on all, or substantially all, matters. Again, there is no definition of 'substantially all'.

An undertaking is deemed to have the right to appoint or remove a director if:

- a person is automatically a director if he or she also becomes a director of the potential parent, or
- the directorship is held by the undertaking itself.

A right to exercise a dominant influence is defined as:

> . . . a right to give directions with respect to the operating and financial policies of that other undertaking which its directors are obliged to comply with whether or not they are for the benefit of that other undertaking. (CA 2006, para. 4(1), Sch. 7.)

A control contract is a contract in writing which confers the right to exercise a dominant influence and:

- is of a kind authorised by the memorandum or articles of the undertaking in relation to which the right is exercisable, and
- is permitted by the law under which the undertaking is established.

The rules on directors' obligations in the UK mean that a control contract, or the right to exercise a dominant influence when not for the benefit of the individual undertaking, may be illegal in many circumstances in the UK. This may mean that the provision on control contracts is most likely to be relevant for certain overseas subsidiaries. This interpretation is made more likely by the fact that this provision was introduced as the result of European Union rules, and is based on similar provisions in German company law.

The actual exercise of dominant influence is a very different consideration from the right to exercise a dominant influence. The definition of dominant influence given above does not apply when it is the actual exercise that is being considered. Actual exercise of dominant influence is defined in FRS 2 as:

> ... the exercise of an influence that achieves the result that the operating and financial policies of the undertaking influenced are set in accordance with the wishes of the holder of the influence and for the holder's benefit whether or not those wishes are explicit. The actual exercise of dominant influence is identified by its effect in practice rather than by the way in which it is exercised. (Para. 7(b), FRS 2.)

FRS 2 has fairly recently (but prior to the amendments arising out of the Companies Act 2006) been amended by the insertion of a definition of the power to exercise dominant influence:

> ... a power that, if exercised, would give rise to the actual exercise of dominant influence as defined in paragraph 7b. (Para. 7(c), FRS 2.)

These are inevitably subjective tests, and the statement stresses that the full relationship between the two parties needs to be considered. Normal commercial relationships, such as that of supplier and customer, will not normally be deemed to give rise to a dominant influence. It could be considered that similar conditions should be applied in attempting to identify a position of actual dominant influence as when trying to identify whether a person is a shadow director.

FRS 2 stresses that it is not necessary that the parent controls all of the day-to-day operations of the subsidiary in order to exercise a dominant influence, although this is one possibility. It may simply set the objectives that must be met by the subsidiary. It may also exercise its influence only on rare, but important, occasions:

> Sufficient evidence might be provided by a rare intervention on a critical matter. Once there has been evidence that one undertaking has exercised a dominant influence over another, then the dominant undertaking should be assumed to continue to exercise its influence until there is evidence to the contrary. (Para. 73, FRS 2.)

Dominant influence can, therefore, be exercised in either an interventionist or a non-interventionist way.

Management on a unified basis is defined by FRS 2 as:

> Two or more undertakings are managed on a unified basis if the whole of the operations of the undertakings are integrated and they are managed as a single unit. Unified management does not arise solely because one undertaking manages another. (Para. 12, FRS 2.)

This means that the fact that two enterprises are managed by the same company or person does not necessarily mean that they are managed on a unified basis. They must be treated as if they were a single entity for this to apply.

FRS 2 notes that the Companies Act uses a list of separate tests to determine if one undertaking is the subsidiary of another, rather than simply relying on the definition of control. The standard relies simply on the definition of control:

> The ability of an undertaking to direct the financial and operating policies of another undertaking with a view to gaining economic benefits from its activities. (Para. 6, FRS 2.)

Normally, there will be no differences. However, in exceptional cases:

- one undertaking may fall within the statutory definition of a subsidiary even though its parent does not have control, or
- one undertaking may have more than one parent under the Companies Act definition.

It has also been possible that one undertaking controls another but is not a parent under the Companies Act. In such cases, FRS 2 describes the controlled undertaking as a quasi-subsidiary. The accounting treatment for quasi-subsidiaries, covered in FRS 5, is dealt with in Chapter 2. However, the ASB is of the opinion that the legal changes made in 2005 (and carried over into the Companies Act 2006) and the changes made to FRS 2 at the same time mean that at least many of the entities that might previously have been considered to be quasi-subsidiaries will now fall under the definition of a subsidiary. Quasi-subsidiaries, which were never common, should now be extremely rare.

Where an undertaking falls within the legal definition of a subsidiary undertaking, but is not actually controlled by its parent, FRS 2 states that this will normally imply that there are severe long-term restrictions on the rights of the parent over the subsidiary and that, therefore, the subsidiary will not need to be consolidated.

Where two undertakings appear to be the parent of another undertaking, FRS 2 suggests that either the apparent subsidiary is actually a joint venture, or one of the presumed parents actually only has significant influence:

> Where the tests of the Act identify more than one undertaking as the parent of one subsidiary undertaking it is likely that they have shared control and, therefore, their interests in the subsidiary undertaking are in effect interests in a joint venture and should be treated accordingly. Alternatively, one or more of the undertakings identified under the Act as a parent undertaking may exercise a non-controlling but significant influence over its subsidiary undertaking, in which case it would be more appropriate to treat that subsidiary undertaking in the same way as an associated undertaking rather than to include it in the consolidation. (Para. 67, FRS 2.)

FRS 9 *Associates and Joint Ventures* also addresses the issue of entities which are legally subsidiaries but which are in practice joint ventures. The standard notes that it is possible for a legal parent-subsidiary relationship to exist between an investor and a joint venture, for example, where one investor holds a majority stake. In such a case, FRS 9 notes that the joint venture arrangement may amount to 'severe long-term restrictions' leading to exclusion of the investee from the consolidation. This issue is considered more fully in section **21.4.3**.

Potential impact of the FRSME

The FRSME contains requirements which are largely and ultimately based on IAS 27, the international standard that deals with consolidated and separate financial statements. This means, not surprisingly, that it does not deal directly with the various issues of interpretation of the provisions set out in the Companies Act 2006. However, the likely impact of this is fairly small, as the intention behind the standard is the same, and the cases where the precise definitions contained in the Act are relevant are few. Most groups do not give rise to questions as to whether an entity is or is not a subsidiary.

As noted above, the FRSME is not intended to override the requirements set out in statute for the preparation of consolidated financial statements.

21.2.2   Indirect holdings

Since the interests held by a company in another undertaking need not be held directly, it is both possible, and common, for a company to be the parent of a company in which it does not directly hold shares. The simplest example is that of a sub-subsidiary:

<pre>
                    Company A
                        | 100%
                    Company B
                        | 100%
                    Company C
</pre>

Company A will be the parent of both companies B and C. Any group accounts produced by A would, therefore, also have to incorporate the position and results of both of these companies.

The holdings need not be 100 per cent, nor need all the shares be held by a single company. For example, company A owns 100 per cent of the shares and voting rights in company B and 20 per cent of the shares and voting rights in company C directly. It also holds 10 per cent of the shares in company C through its nominee. Company B owns 30 per cent of the shares in company C.

The effective percentage of the voting rights in company C held by company A is 60 per cent, and so company C is its subsidiary, and would, therefore, need to be included in its group accounts.

The effective shareholding may also not be relevant where there is a chain of control. For example, there is the structure below.

		Effective interest
Company A		
	51%	51.00%
Company B		
	51%	26.01%
Company C		
	51%	13.27%
Company D		
	51%	6.77%
Company E		
	51%	3.45%
Company F		
	51%	1.76%
Company G		
	51%	0.90%
Company H		

The effective interest of company A in company H amounts to only 0.9 per cent, yet every company in the chain is a member of the same group, since company A is able to exercise control all the way down the chain.

21.2.3 *Parent company profit and loss account*

Where group accounts are prepared under the Companies Act 2006, the parent company need not present its own profit and loss account as long as it complies with certain conditions:

- the notes to the company's balance sheet must state the company's profit or loss for the financial year;
- the profit and loss account must still be prepared, and approved by the board of directors, although it need not contain the supplementary information normally required, and
- the fact that the company has relied on the exemption must be stated in the accounts.

This changed from the position under the Companies Act 1985. Under the Companies Act 1985, where a parent company voluntarily produced group accounts, the exemption from publishing the parent's own individual profit and loss account was not available as the legislation specified that the exemption was available only where group accounts were 'required'.

This means that small groups which decide to produce group accounts voluntarily are entitled to the exemption.

21.3   EXEMPTIONS FROM PREPARING GROUP ACCOUNTS

21.3.1   *Sub-groups*

Where a company is both a parent and a subsidiary, it may not need to prepare group accounts. There are two sets of rules, one of which applies where the company's own immediate parent is based in the EEA and one where it is not.

EEA rules

The conditions that need to be met in order to avoid the need to prepare group accounts are as follows.

(1)   The immediate parent of the company must be established under the law of a European Economic Area State.

(2)   The company must be either a wholly owned subsidiary of that parent or the parent holds 50 per cent or more of the shares in the company and notice requiring the preparation of group accounts must not have been served on the company by shareholders holding, in aggregate:

    (a)   more than half of the remaining shares in the company, or
    (b)   five per cent of the total shares in the company.

    The notice from minority shareholders must be served on the company not more than six months after the start of the accounting period.

(3)   The company must not have securities listed on any Stock Exchange in the EEA.

(4)   The company must be included in consolidated accounts of a larger group drawn up to the same date, or to an earlier date in the same financial year, and the parent of that group must be established under the law of an EEA state.

(5)   Those accounts must be audited and drawn up in accordance with the EU Seventh Directive or with IFRS.

(6)   The company must disclose in its individual accounts that it is exempt from the obligation to prepare and deliver group accounts.

(7)   The company must disclose the name of the parent undertaking that has prepared the group accounts, together with:

    (a)   its country of incorporation, if outside the United Kingdom, or
    (b)   its principal business address if it is unincorporated.

(8)   The company must deliver a copy of the parent's group accounts and annual report to the Registrar within the period normally allowed for the filing of its own accounts.

(9) If those group accounts are not in English then a certified translation must also be filed.

If a company is not required to file group accounts as a result of these provisions it must still provide extensive disclosure of its interests in other companies in its own financial statements.

Non EEA rules

Where a company does not meet the exemption set out above, it needs to consider if it is entitled to the exemptions which apply outside of the EEA.

Where the company's parent is not established under the law of an EEA state, the company must be either a wholly owned subsidiary of that parent or the parent holds 50 per cent or more of the shares in the company and notice requiring the preparation of group accounts must not have been served on the company by shareholders holding, in aggregate:

- more than half of the remaining shares in the company, or
- five per cent of the total shares in the company.

The notice from minority shareholders must be served on the company not more than six months after the start of the accounting period.

There are also a number of more detailed conditions that must be satisfied; as follows.

(1) The company must be included in consolidated accounts of a larger group drawn up to the same date, or to an earlier date in the same financial year.

(2) Those accounts must be drawn up in accordance with the EU Seventh Directive or in an equivalent manner.

(3) Those accounts must be audited by a person authorised to audit accounts under the law under which the parent undertaking which draws them up is established.

(4) The company must disclose in its individual accounts that it is exempt from the obligation to prepare and deliver group accounts.

(5) The company must disclose the name of the parent undertaking which has prepared the group accounts, together with:

    (a) its country of incorporation, if outside the United Kingdom, or

    (b) its principal business address if it is unincorporated.

(6) The company must deliver a copy of the parent's group accounts and annual report, including audit report, to the Registrar within the period normally allowed for the filing of its own accounts.

(7) If those group accounts are not in English (or in certain cases in Welsh), then a certified translation must also be filed.

The exemption is not available if the company has any securities admitted to trading in a regulated market of any EEA state.

If a company is not required to file group accounts as a result of these provisions, it must still provide extensive disclosure of its interests in other companies in its own financial statements.

One particular problem is the requirement for the accounts to be drawn up in accordance with the Seventh Directive or in an equivalent manner. It is not entirely clear what an equivalent manner means. This is now dealt with in UITF 43.

In summary, UITF 43 states that when assessing whether consolidated accounts are drawn up in a manner equivalent to Seventh Directive consolidated accounts it is necessary to consider whether they meet the basic requirements of the Fourth and Seventh Directives. Particular emphasis is given to the need to give a true and fair view. The implications of this approach are stated to be that:

- consolidated accounts that comply with accounting standards applicable in the UK and Ireland meet the test of equivalence;
- consolidated accounts prepared in accordance with IFRS as adopted by the EU meet the test of equivalence;
- consolidated accounts prepared in accordance with IFRS will meet the test of equivalence, subject to consideration of the reasons for any failure by the European Commission to adopt a relevant standard or interpretation;
- consolidated accounts prepared using GAAPs which are closely related to IFRS will meet the test of equivalence subject to consideration of the effect of any differences from IFRS as adopted by the EU;
- consolidated accounts of the higher parent prepared in accordance with US GAAP, Canadian GAAP and Japanese GAAP will normally meet the test of equivalence with the Seventh Directive subject to consideration of developments in those GAAPs after October 2006 (the date of the UITF), ensuring that the entities within the consolidation are those that would be consolidated under the Seventh Directive, ensuring that consistent accounting policies have been used for all entities in those consolidated accounts and evaluating the effect of any exemptions or modifications to those GAAPs allowed by specialised industry standards which have been applied in those consolidated accounts, and
- consolidated accounts using other GAAPs will continue to need to be considered on an ad hoc basis, based on the particular facts, and taking into account the similarities to, and differences from, the GAAPs considered specifically in the UITF.

Potential impact of the FRSME

UITF 43 is very unusual, in that it is one of very few current pieces of ASB guidance that would survive the introduction of the FRSME. It deals with an issue that is very specific and not within the scope of the FRSME.

21.3.2 Small groups

There is also an exemption for small groups.

Unlike the Companies Act 1985, the Companies Act 2006 contains no exemption for medium-sized groups and, as a result, since periods beginning on or after 6 April 2008, only small groups have been entitled to the exemption from preparing group accounts and group accounts are required for medium sized groups.

Under the Companies Act 2006, the small group limits are:

Net amounts

Aggregate turnover	Not more than £6.5 million
Aggregate balance sheet total	Not more than £3.26 million
Aggregate number of employees	Not more than 50

Gross amounts

Aggregate turnover	Not more than £7.8 million
Aggregate balance sheet total	Not more than £3.9 million
Aggregate number of employees	Not more than 50

As with the definition of small companies, 'balance sheet total' means the gross assets of the group companies.

The net amounts apply after consolidation adjustments, such as the elimination of intra-group sales and balances. The gross amounts are calculated by the simple addition of the amounts appearing in each company's financial statements.

The use of the gross amounts means that the parent need not perform a partial consolidation in order to determine whether it falls within the limits.

The accounts that must be used for this purpose are those of all group companies ending on the same day as the parent's financial year, or the last accounts covering a period ending before this date.

A group qualifies as small if:

- it falls within the limits for two successive years, or
- it falls within the limits in the parent company's first financial year.

Similarly, if a group no longer satisfies the criteria it still does not need to prepare group accounts in the first year in which it does not meet the criteria.

The exemption is not available to a group if any of its members is:

- a public company;

- a body corporate, other than a company, whose shares are admitted to trading on a regulated market in an EEA state;
- a person (other than a small company) with permission to carry on a regulated activity, under Part 4 of the Financial Services and Markets Act 2000;
- a small company that is an authorised insurance company, a banking company, an e-money issuer, a MiFID investment firm or a UCITS management company, or
- a person who carries on an insurance market activity.

The exemption is not as generous as it may at first appear. The level of disclosure concerning group companies is extensive, and if the group structure is simple the time saving may be negligible.

21.3.3 Small groups preparing group accounts voluntarily

A small group will be able to take advantage of the small company exemptions in the Companies Act when preparing group accounts voluntarily. However, as small groups are not required to prepare group accounts, the FRSSE does not deal with group accounting. If small groups decide to produce group accounts, then they must comply with the relevant group (and related) accounting standards. They are still entitled to other disclosure exemptions under the FRSSE. The FRSSE is covered in detail in Chapter 22.

21.3.4 Disclosure where group accounts are not prepared

There are extensive disclosure requirements concerning subsidiaries where there is a group but group accounts are not prepared. The following requirements are taken from the first and second parts of Sch. 4 to The Large and Medium-sized Companies and Groups (Accounts and Reports) Regulations 2008 (SI 2008/410).

(1) The name of each subsidiary undertaking.

(2) For each subsidiary undertaking:

(a) if it is incorporated outside the United Kingdom, the country in which it is incorporated, and

(b) if it is unincorporated, the address of its principal place of business.

(3) For each subsidiary undertaking:

(a) the aggregate amount of its capital and reserves as at the end of its relevant financial year, and

(b) its profit or loss for that year; although this information need not be given if the parent is not required to prepare group accounts on the basis that it is included in the accounts of a larger group, or if the subsidiary undertaking is not required to file, and does not publish, a copy of its balance sheet, or if the company's holding is less than 50 per cent of the nominal value of the shares in the undertaking, or if equity accounting is used.

(4) The reason why the company is not required to prepare group accounts.

(5) If the reason is that all the subsidiary undertakings of the company fall within the exclusions provided for in s. 405, that is, all of the subsidiaries are covered by one or more of the reasons for excluding a subsidiary from consolidation, which of those exclusions applies to each subsidiary.

(6) For each class of shares held in each subsidiary undertaking:

(a) the identity of the class, and

(b) the proportion of the nominal value of the shares of that class represented by those shares; in this case the shares held by or on behalf of the company itself must be distinguished from those attributed to the company which are held by or on behalf of a subsidiary undertaking.

(7) Where the financial year of one or more subsidiary undertakings did not end with that of the company, then the date on which its last financial year ended.

(8) The number, description and amount of the shares in the company held by or on behalf of its subsidiary undertakings, unless they hold them only as personal representative or as trustee for a trust of which neither the parent nor any subsidiary is a beneficiary, unless as security for a loan entered into in the ordinary course of business.

The company must also state that it is producing accounts which show only the affairs of the company and not the group.

Small companies need not disclose details of the financial years of their subsidiaries. In the accounts they file, they may also omit details of their shares which are held by their subsidiaries.

21.4 EXCLUSIONS FROM CONSOLIDATION

21.4.1 General rules

Normally, all of a parent's subsidiaries must be included in the group accounts, where these need to be prepared. However, the Companies Act 2006 also allows individual subsidiaries to be excluded from consolidation in four situations, and requires their exclusion in one situation. FRS 2 alters these rules, by requiring exclusion in some cases where this is legally only a permitted treatment.

If all of a parent's subsidiaries fall within one or more of the exclusions then group accounts will not be required.

FRS 2 requires the following disclosure.

(1) The reasons for excluding the subsidiary.

(2) Any premium or discount on acquisition, to the extent that this has not been written off.

(3) Particulars of the balances between the excluded subsidiary undertakings and the rest of the group.

(4) The nature and extent of transactions of the excluded subsidiary undertakings with the rest of the group.

(5) Where the excluded subsidiary is not carried under the equity method:

(a) dividends received and receivable from that undertaking, and
(b) any write-down in the period in respect of the investment in that undertaking or amounts due from it.

This disclosure will normally be given on an undertaking-by-undertaking basis, although two or more undertakings may be combined if they are excluded on the same grounds, and this treatment would be more appropriate. Individual disclosure must be made of any single undertaking, or single sub-group that has been excluded but accounts for 20 per cent or more of the operating profits, net assets or turnover of the group. For these purposes the group figures should be calculated including the amounts attributable to the excluded subsidiaries.

The Companies Act 2006 also contains some additional disclosure requirements:

- unless the subsidiary is included in the financial statements under the equity method, then the aggregate capital and reserves of the subsidiary at the end of its relevant financial year, that is, its year that ends at the same time as that of the parent or the last financial year ending before this date, and
- its profit or loss for the year.

The profit or loss and net assets need not be stated if the holding of the group is less than 50 per cent of the nominal value of the shares in the subsidiary and if it need not publish its balance sheet.

21.4.2 Materiality

A subsidiary may be excluded from consolidation if its inclusion would not be material from the point of providing a true and fair view. Two or more subsidiaries can be excluded on these grounds, but only if they are immaterial in aggregate. This avoids the situation in which a parent sets up, say, 100 subsidiaries and then does not prepare group accounts on the basis that each subsidiary is immaterial. Accounting standards make no comment on this exclusion, as they are not intended to apply to immaterial items.

21.4.3   Severe long-term restrictions

Under the Companies Act 2006, a subsidiary may be excluded from consolidation on the grounds that there are severe long-term restrictions that substantially hinder the exercise of the rights of the parent over the assets or management of that subsidiary. FRS 2 requires that such subsidiaries be excluded, rather than simply permitting this treatment. The restrictions must be truly severe, and actually in operation:

> Severe long-term restrictions are identified by their effect in practice rather than by the way in which the restrictions are imposed. For example, a subsidiary undertaking should not be excluded because restrictions are threatened or because another party has the power to impose them unless such threats or the existence of such a power has a severe and restricting effect in practice in the long term on the rights of the parent undertaking. Generally, restrictions are dealt with better by disclosure than by non-consolidation. However, the loss of the parent undertaking's control over its subsidiary undertaking resulting from severe long-term restrictions would make it misleading to include that subsidiary undertaking in the consolidation. (Para. 78, FRS 2.)

The one specific example of loss of control quoted in FRS 2 is where a subsidiary is undergoing insolvency procedures and control has passed to an administrator, administrative receiver or liquidator. However, FRS 9 *Associates and Joint Ventures* provides an additional example of severe long-term restrictions:

> In some cases an investor may qualify as the parent of an entity under the definition of a subsidiary in FRS 2 (for example by holding a majority of the voting rights in that entity) but contractual arrangements with the other shareholder mean that in practice the shareholders share control over their investee. In such a case the interests of the minority shareholder amount to "severe long-term restrictions" that "substantially hinder the exercise of the rights of the parent undertaking over the assets or management of the subsidiary undertaking". The subsidiary therefore should not be consolidated but should instead be treated as a joint venture according to the requirements of this FRS. (Para. 11, FRS 9.)

FRS 9 is covered more fully later in this chapter at **21.9**.

It has already been noted that the statutory definition of a subsidiary rests basically on the concept of control. It could therefore be said that long-term restrictions should be taken to be sufficiently severe where the parent is no longer able to control the activities of the subsidiary, and there is no prospect of its regaining control in the foreseeable future.

Where severe long-term restrictions are brought into force, the investment in the subsidiary should be stated in the group accounts at the amount at which it would have been included under the equity method at the date on which the restrictions came into force. Where the restrictions were in force on the date on which the subsidiary was acquired then it should be stated at cost.

If the parent has no significant influence over its nominal subsidiary, then no further accruals should be made for profits or losses, except that where there has been a permanent impairment in the value of the investment then account should be taken of this fact, and provision should be made through the group profit and loss account. If the parent is still able to exercise significant influence, then it should treat the subsidiary as if it were an associated undertaking, ie taking account of its share of profits, losses and net assets.

Where such restrictions are lifted, FRS 2 requires that any amount of unrecognised profit and loss which has accrued during the period of restrictions should be separately disclosed in the group profit and loss account of the period in which control is resumed. Any provisions for diminution in value which are no longer required should also be written back in the year in which control is resumed. If the amounts involved are material then they should be treated as an exceptional item.

21.4.4   Disproportionate expense and undue delay

The Companies Act 2006 allows subsidiaries to be excluded from consolidation if the information necessary for the preparation of group accounts could not be obtained without disproportionate expense or undue delay.

FRS 2 notes that there are no circumstances in which this exemption could be applied unless the subsidiary concerned were also immaterial, in which case the apparent exemption adds nothing to the exemption allowed on the grounds of materiality.

Where a subsidiary is material to the view given by the group accounts, the time and expense involved in obtaining the information necessary to enable the parent to prepare group accounts is, in the view of the ASB, neither disproportionate nor undue.

21.4.5   Subsequent resale

Where a parent has an interest in a subsidiary solely with a view to subsequent resale, and the subsidiary has not previously been included in consolidated group accounts prepared by the parent, then the subsidiary may be excluded from consolidation under the Companies Act 2006, and must be excluded under FRS 2.

The ASB states that an interest can only be treated as being held for subsequent resale if:

- a purchaser has already been identified;
- a purchaser is being actively sought and the interest is reasonably expected to be sold within one year from the date on which it was acquired, or

- the interest was acquired as the result of the enforcement of a security and the interest has not been, and will not be, integrated with the continuing activities of the group.

Where an interest is held solely with an intention for resale, FRS 2 requires that it should be stated in the consolidated balance sheet as a current asset at the lower of its cost and net realisable value.

21.5   BASIC PRINCIPLES OF GROUP ACCOUNTING

21.5.1   Companies Act rules

The Companies Act provides very little information on detailed consolidation procedures, or what group accounts are intended to achieve. However, it does note that the group accounts should be as close as possible to the accounts of a single company:

> Group accounts must comply so far as practicable with the provisions of Schedule 1 to these Regulations as if the undertakings included in the consolidation ("the group") were a single company. (Para. 1, Sch. 6 to The Large and Medium-sized Companies and Groups (Accounts and Reports) Regulations 2008 (SI 2008/410).)

Schedule 6 to The Large and Medium-sized Companies and Groups (Accounts and Reports) Regulations 2008 (SI 2008/410) provides some details of the changes necessary in group accounts from individual company accounts. However, it stresses that the changes are not limited to those included in the schedule:

> The consolidated balance sheet and profit and loss account must incorporate in full the information contained in the individual accounts of the undertakings included in the consolidation, subject to the adjustments authorised or required by the following provisions of this Schedule and to such other adjustments (if any) as may be appropriate in accordance with generally accepted accounting principles or practice. (Para. 2 (1), Sch. 6 to The Large and Medium-sized Companies and Groups (Accounts and Reports) Regulations 2008 (SI 2008/410).)

The schedule makes some minor changes to the formats for companies. In particular, it includes a line for minority interests in both the balance sheet and the profit and loss account.

Minority interests are the interests held by third parties in the profits and assets of the group. They arise because subsidiary undertakings need not be wholly owned by the parent.

21.5.2 Accounting periods

In the interest of consistency (and simplicity), it is always preferable for the accounting periods of all companies in the group to be coterminous. (For this reason, statute allows some group companies to change their accounting dates to match that of the group of which they form a part in circumstances where this would not be allowed for other companies.) If different accounting periods are used, then there is a danger that the resulting financial statements may be misleading.

Nonetheless, having the same accounting date for all group companies is not always possible. For example, a company may have a particular accounting date because it is convenient for the preparation of its own financial statements, usually because it falls during its quieter period. Where the accounting periods do not end on the same date, the Companies Act 2006 applies the following rules.

> If the financial year of a subsidiary undertaking included in the consolidation does not end with that of the parent company, the group accounts must be made up:
>
> (a) from the accounts of the subsidiary undertaking for its financial year last ending before the end of the parent company's financial year, provided that year ended no more than three months before that of the parent company, or
>
> (b) from interim accounts prepared by the subsidiary undertaking as at the end of the parent company's financial year. (Para. 2 (2), Sch. 6 to The Large and Medium-sized Companies and Groups (Accounts and Reports) Regulations 2008 (SI 2008/410).)

FRS 2 requires that where a subsidiary does not prepare its accounts up to the same date as used by the group, and interim accounts are not to be used, then adjustments should be made to the group accounts in respect of abnormal transactions in the intervening period. No definition of abnormal is provided, but it presumably means any transactions that would seriously affect the reported position or result. It might include an exceptional item appearing in that subsidiary's own accounts and which is of sufficient materiality to warrant recording and disclosure in the group accounts. Adjustments would also need to be made for any transactions between the company and any other group company in the intervening period. For example, if a company were owed £10,000 by another group company, and between its accounting date and the group accounting date it were repaid, then this would need to be adjusted in order to perform the consolidation. If no adjustment was made the amounts owed to and by group companies would not be the same.

FRS 2 also requires that the following disclosure be given where a subsidiary is included in the consolidation for a period other than the group accounting period:

- the name of the subsidiary undertaking;
- the accounting date or period of each undertaking subsidiary, and

- the reason for using a different accounting date or period.

21.5.3 Uniform accounting policies

It is also necessary that every attempt should be made to ensure that the amounts included in the group accounts have all been determined on a consistent basis:

> Where assets and liabilities to be included in the group accounts have been valued or otherwise determined by undertakings according to accounting rules differing from those used for the group accounts, the values or amounts must be adjusted so as to accord with the rules used for the group accounts. (Para. 3 (1), Sch. 6 to The Large and Medium-sized Companies and Groups (Accounts and Reports) Regulations 2008 (SI 2008/410).)

FRS 2 contains a very similar requirement. In exceptional circumstances, the Companies Act and FRS 2 allow different policies to be used, but disclosure must be made of:

- the different accounting policies which have been used;
- an indication of the amount of the assets and liabilities involved, and, where practicable, a statement of the effect that the use of different policies has had on the results and net assets of the group, and
- the reasons for the different treatment.

Part of the second requirement makes little sense. Normally, if it was possible to quantify the effect of the use of the different policies then there would be no reason why an adjustment could not be made. Where the company can quantify the effect of the difference, but can still justify the adoption of different policies, this is likely to mean that the circumstances are sufficiently different to mean that this should not be treated as the adoption of two contrary policies, but instead the application of two separate policies, each appropriate to the circumstances with which it deals.

Where there are differences between the accounting policies adopted by the parent and the group, these should be disclosed in a note to the group accounts, together with a statement of the reason for the difference.

21.5.4 Elimination of group transactions

The Companies Act requires that:

> Debts and claims between undertakings included in the consolidation, and income and expenditure relating to transactions between such undertakings, must be eliminated in preparing the group accounts.

> Where profits and losses resulting from transactions between undertakings included in the consolidation are included in the book value of assets, they must be eliminated in preparing the group accounts. (Para. 6 (1) and (2), Sch. 6 to The Large and Medium-sized Companies and Groups (Accounts and Reports) Regulations 2008 (SI 2008/410).)

Statute states that such adjustments need not be made if the amounts involved are not material, and they can be made in proportion to the group's share in the interest of the undertakings.

FRS 2 prohibits the use of partial elimination where the group owns only part of the shares in a subsidiary, and requires that each adjustment is made in full, with a consequent effect on the amounts shown for minority interests.

As we have already noted, we cannot provide full details of all adjustments that may be required in order to prepare group accounts. We will look only at some of the most common.

Intra-group balances

Where undertakings in the group owe amounts to each other, these amounts should be cancelled in the group accounts; otherwise both the group assets and liabilities will be overstated.

For example, if there is a trading balance between two group companies amounting to £25,000, then this amount will need to be deducted from the gross total of both the group's debtors and creditors.

A slight problem can arise if there are goods or cash in transit at the year end. The normal procedure is to reinstate the amount of cash or stock in the group accounts. For example, a company makes sales to another company in the same group shortly before the end of the year. The goods are dispatched by the selling company shortly prior to the end of the year, but do not arrive at the purchasing company until after the end of the year. Both companies may treat the transaction quite fairly, yet there will still be a timing difference in the accounts. The accounting treatment would be to:

- reinstate the stock at its original cost, or net realisable value before sale if lower, to the selling company;
- eliminate the sale from the group turnover, and
- reduce the group profit by the amount attributed to the sale by the selling company.

Since the purchasing company had not recorded the transaction, no reversal would be needed.

It has already been mentioned that this problem may be particularly acute if there are group undertakings with different accounting reference dates. For example, a company is owed £10,000 by another group company, and between the first company's accounting reference date and the group date this amount is paid over. An appropriate treatment would be to reinstate the cash amount, as though the payment had never been made. This will ensure that the group debtors and creditors do not include intra-group balances, and that the cash balance of the group is not understated.

The same rules apply if the amount involved is not a current balance, but, for example, a loan or a debenture. The amount owed should be netted off against the amount of the debtor or investment.

Doubtful debts

Where one company in the group is owed money by another company in the group, but has written off or provided against the debt, then the debt must be reinstated, or the provision ignored, in performing the consolidation. There are two reasons for this.

(1) The amounts shown as payable to and from other group companies must be equal.

(2) The debt is normally written off or provided against because there are doubts about the liquidity or solvency of the debtor, which should be reflected in its own financial statements. In group accounts the results and position of the company will be included in full, and it would, therefore, be double counting to include both the bad debt and the causes that have given rise to it.

Profits on stock

Where one group company sells goods to another, no adjustment to stock will be needed on consolidation if:

- the goods are subsequently sold on to a third party, so any profit to the group has been realised;
- the goods were sold at their book value, with no profit or loss arising, or
- the goods were sold at their market value, and this resulted in a loss to the selling company.

In the first case, the consolidated profit will be correct. The fact that this arises from the summation of two separate profits in different group companies is irrelevant, since this will not be revealed in the group accounts. In the second case, there is no profit or loss to be eliminated. In the third case, no adjustment will be needed, as the realised loss on sale will simply have taken the place of any provision that would otherwise have been required to write down the value of stock to its net realisable value.

An adjustment to stock will be needed if goods are sold by one group company to another:

- at a profit where those goods are still held by the purchasing company at the end of the accounting period, and
- at an artificial loss, which does not reflect the value of the goods.

In the first case, the profit on the transaction must be eliminated so that the stock is stated at its cost to the group. The same applies in the second case, except that it is a loss that should be eliminated.

Fixed assets transferred within the group

The same principle applies to fixed assets transferred within the group as applies to stock. The group accounts should state the fixed assets at their cost, or value or depreciated cost, to the group. Where the transfer takes place at net book value, no adjustments are required.

EXAMPLE

A company owns a fixed asset with a cost of £10,000 and accumulated depreciation of £5,000. The asset was purchased five years ago and has a total useful economic life of ten years. The company sells the asset to another group company for £6,000. The second company depreciates the asset over its remaining useful economic life of five years in equal instalments.

Year	Company asset £	Company depreciation £	Group asset £	Group depreciation £
1	4,800	1,200	4,000	1,000
2	3,600	1,200	3,000	1,000
3	2,400	1,200	2,000	1,000
4	1,200	1,200	1,000	1,000
5	0	1,200	0	1,000

The profit on disposal recorded by the company that sold the asset would also need to be eliminated.

Stock sold to another group company as a fixed asset

Where one company sells goods to another group company, and that second company treats the goods as a fixed asset, then:

- any profit on the sale must be eliminated;
- the transaction must be treated as a reclassification, and not a purchase and sale, in the group accounts, and
- depreciation in the group accounts will need to be based on the original cost to the group.

Dividends

Dividends paid from one group company to another should be eliminated by reducing the amount of dividend income received and paid. (Dividends paid by companies other than the parent are never shown in group accounts: they are either eliminated on consolidation or shown as part of the transfer to minority interests.)

21.6 ACQUISITION ACCOUNTING

21.6.1 Acquisition and merger accounting

There are two separate methods that can be used to account for the purchase of a subsidiary by a parent: the acquisition method and the merger method.

Potential impact of the FRSME

This would change under the FRSME, which allows only the acquisition method of accounting and does not allow mergers. In practice, most business combinations are already acquisitions, so the effect of the change would not be great. The FRSME does not include within the scope of the business combination requirements combinations of entities or businesses under common control (as well as the formation of a joint venture or the acquisition of assets that do not constitute a business). Therefore, and as with IFRS, there may still be procedures which are very similar to merger accounting, but these will apply only where a business moves from one entity to another but is under the control of the same parties both before and after the transfer.

In relation to acquisitions, the FRSME does not make any substantial changes to the procedures (although it does set a default for the life of goodwill) but lacks much of the detail contained in FRS 6 and FRS 7.

21.6.2 Companies Act rules

There is a general presumption that acquisitions will be accounted for using the acquisition method. Unusually, the Companies Act provides a reasonable amount of detail on the procedures that should be adopted for acquisition accounting:

> The identifiable assets and liabilities of the undertaking acquired must be included in the consolidated balance sheet at their fair values as at the date of acquisition.

> The income and expenditure of the undertaking acquired must be brought into the group accounts only as from the date of acquisition.

> There must be set off against the acquisition cost of the interest in the shares of the undertaking held by the parent company and its subsidiary undertakings the interest of the parent company and its subsidiary undertakings in the adjusted capital and reserves of the undertaking acquired.

> The resulting amount if positive must be treated as goodwill, and if negative as a negative consolidation difference. (Para. 9 (2) to (5), Sch. 6 to The Large and Medium-sized Companies and Groups (Accounts and Reports) Regulations 2008 (SI 2008/410).)

Before dealing with some of the complications that can arise, it is worth giving a very simple example of the accounting procedures.

EXAMPLE

Company P acquires 80 per cent of the ordinary share capital of company S at a cost of £250,000. The transaction takes place on 1 June 2011, and both companies have accounting reference periods that end on 31 December. Company S earns profits evenly over the year. Their financial statements, and the group accounts, will appear as follows:

Balance sheet

	P £	S £	Group £
Fixed assets	500,000	100,000	600,000
Investment in S Ltd	250,000	0	0
Net current assets	50,000	150,000	200,000
Purchased goodwill	–	–	95,600
Long-term liabilities	(300,000)	(50,000)	(350,000)
	500,000	200,000	545,600
Share capital	100,000	50,000	100,000
Share premium	100,000	50,000	100,000
Profit and loss account	300,000	100,000	305,600
	500,000	200,000	505,600
Minority interests	–	–	40,000
	500,000	200,000	545,600

(1)   The group balance sheet is Company P's balance sheet, except that:

   (a)   the investment in S Ltd is replaced with the net assets of S Ltd;
   (b)   adjustments are made to the profit and loss account balance and minority interests because the value of the investment is not equal to S Ltd's net assets at the year end.

(2)   The minority interest is 20 per cent of S Ltd's net assets at 31 December = 20% × £200,000 = £40,000.

(3)   The purchased goodwill is calculated as follows:

(a)	Cost of investment in S Ltd		250,000
(b)	Net assets acquired by P Ltd		
	Net assets of S Ltd @ 31.12.10	200,000	
	Post-acquisition profits	7,000	
	Net assets of S Ltd @ acquisition	193,000	
	Net assets acquired by P Ltd =		
	80% × 193,000		154,400
(c)	Purchased goodwill		95,600

(4)   The group profit and loss balance of £305,600 is derived below.

Profit and loss account

	P £	S £	Group £
Turnover	900,000	120,000	970,000
Cost of sales	(460,000)	(60,000)	(495,000)
Gross profit	440,000	60,000	475,000

	P £	S £	Group £
Overheads	(270,000)	(36,000)	(291,000)
Profit before taxation	170,000	24,000	184,000
Taxation	(70,000)	(12,000)	(77,000)
Profit after taxation	100,000	12,000	107,000
Minority interest	0	0	(1,400)
Retained profit	100,000	12,000	105,600
Profit b/f	200,000	88,000	200,000
Profit c/f	300,000	100,000	305,600

The amounts in the group profit and loss account down to profit after taxation are derived by taking the whole of the amount attributable to Company P and 7/12 of the amounts attributable to S Ltd.

(1)   The minority interests of £1,400 arise because 20 per cent of the profits earned since the acquisition (7/12× £12,000) are due to the minority shareholders.

(2)   Deducting the minority interests gives £105,600, which can also be seen as:

P Ltd's profit for the year   £100,000
P Ltd's share of S Ltd's post-acquisition profits £5,600

(3)   S Ltd's profit b/f of £88,000 is not relevant since it is prior to the acquisition.

As required by FRS 10, the purchased goodwill of £95,600 is capitalised as an asset. It has been assumed that the goodwill has an indefinite life and has not been impaired at the end of the year. A wide range of other assumptions have also been used in this example. For example:

- the acquisition took place in a single transaction;
- completion accounts were not required, as the profit of S Ltd accrued evenly over the year (and no cash flow statement has been prepared);
- the values of the assets of S Ltd, as recorded in its own financial statements, were equal to their fair values, and
- no dividends were paid by S Ltd.

These may all pose problems in practice.

21.6.3   Date of acquisition

FRS 2 states that the date on which an undertaking becomes a member of a group is the date on which control passes to its new parent.

Normally, completion accounts will be required in order to calculate the amount of pre-acquisition and post-acquisition profits. Pre-acquisition profits are treated in conjunction with the value of the net assets acquired. Post-acquisition profits are dealt with in the profit and loss account of the group. Completion accounts are also normally required in order to allow companies to provide the disclosure required in respect of acquisitions.

21.6.4 Piecemeal acquisition

Piecemeal acquisition causes a number of accounting problems, not least of which is the value that should be ascribed to the assets of the subsidiary at each stage. It is accepted practice that an acquisition should be accounted for at fair value, and not necessarily at the values appearing in the books of the subsidiary. However, this will cause major problems if there have been substantial changes in the value of the underlying assets between transactions.

The following example will be used to indicate some of the problems that can arise.

EXAMPLE

A Ltd acquires shares in B Ltd, which has an issued share capital of 20,000 £1 shares, as follows:

Date	No of £1 shares	%	Price paid £
1 January 2008	2,000	10	20,000
1 February 2009	3,000	15	40,000
1 July 2010	7,000	35	108,000
1 March 2011	8,000	40	144,000

Both companies have accounting periods which end on 31 December. The balance sheet of B Ltd at the end of each year is as follows (profits are earned at a regular rate over each year):

	2007 £	2008 £	2009 £	2010 £	2011 £
Net assets	80,000	100,000	140,000	160,000	200,000
Share capital	20,000	20,000	20,000	20,000	20,000
Profit and loss b/f	50,000	60,000	80,000	120,000	140,000
Profit for the year	10,000	20,000	40,000	20,000	40,000
Total	80,000	100,000	140,000	160,000	200,000

The balance sheet of A Ltd at the end of each year is as follows (profits are also earned at a regular rate over each year):

	2007 £	2008 £	2009 £	2010 £	2011 £
Investment	0	20,000	60,000	168,000	312,000
Other net assets	500,000	525,000	560,000	528,000	471,000
	500,000	545,000	620,000	696,000	783,000
Share capital	50,000	50,000	50,000	50,000	50,000
Profit and loss b/f	400,000	450,000	495,000	570,000	646,000
Profit for the year	50,000	45,000	75,000	76,000	87,000
Total	500,000	545,000	620,000	696,000	783,000

The fair values of the separable net assets of B Ltd at the date of each share transaction are:

1 January 2008	£85,000
1 February 2009	£115,000
1 July 2010	£160,000
1 March 2011	£190,000

(1) In 2008, there is no accounting problem. The investment in B Ltd is a simple investment, neither an associate nor a subsidiary. No group accounts are required, and A Ltd's balance sheet will appear as above, assuming that the value of the investment is deemed to be at least the price paid.

(2) In 2009, B Ltd becomes an associate of A Ltd, but is still not a subsidiary. Assuming that the capitalised purchased goodwill remains a reliable measure of the recoverable amount, and that a pro forma balance sheet is to be prepared, it will appear as follows:

On the assets side: A Ltd (column 1) has the investment at its cost of £60,000; the pro forma balance sheet (column 3) has the investment at its fair value of £37,917 and includes the capitalised purchased goodwill of £31,250. It can be seen from column (2) that the net effect of these inclusions is in fact A's share of the post-acquisition profits (£9,167) which, therefore, needs to be added to the reserves.

	A Ltd (1) £	Pro forma (2) £	Pro forma (3) £
Assets			
Investment, at fair value (Note 1)			
Share of fair value of associate at acquisition (Note 2)		28,750	
Share of post-acquisition profits (Note 3)		9,167	
			37,197
Other net assets	560,000		560,000
Investment at cost	60,000	60,000	
Less fair value at acquisition		(28,750)	
Purchased goodwill			31,250
			629,167
Liabilities			
Share capital	50,000		50,000
Profit and loss b/f	495,000		
Profit for the year 2009	75,000		
		570,000	
Share of post-acquisition profits of associate		9,167	
Total profit and loss reserves			579,167
			629,167

Note 1:

The fair value of the investment is calculated by combining:

- A's share of the fair value of the assets on acquisition, with
- A's share of the post-acquisition profits.

Note 2:

Fair value of B Ltd's separable net assets on acquisition, 1 February, = £115,000.

A Ltd's share of the assets is 25%.

25% × £115,000 = £28,750.

Note 3:

The date of acquisition was 1 February. Post-acquisition profits of B Ltd are, therefore, 11/12 of £40,000 = £36,667. A Ltd's share of these is 25% × £36,667 = £9,167.

It is worth noting that the post-acquisition profit on the original investment, before B Ltd became an associate, has been ignored in this calculation. It is not accepted practice to treat this as part of the post-acquisition reserves.

When the third transaction takes place this calculation needs to take place again, effectively ignoring the period during which the company was an associate.

In 2010 the consolidated balance sheet is given below:

On the assets side: A Ltd (column 1) has the investment at its cost of £168,000; the group balance sheet (column 3) has the assets of the subsidiary company, B Ltd, at their fair value of £170,000 (£160,000 on acquisition + £10,000 post acquisition) and also includes the capitalised goodwill of £72,000.

The net effect of these inclusions is also added to the liabilities side of the balance sheet. It can be seen from column (2) that they are equal to: A Ltd's share of the post-acquisition profits of B Ltd (£6,000); plus the minority interest in B Ltd at the end of the financial year (£68,000).

	A Ltd (1) £	Group (2) £	Group (3) £
Assets			
Assets of subsidiary, at fair value (Note 1)			
Fair value of subsidiary at acquisition		160,000	
Post-acquisition profits of subsidiary (Note 2)		10,000	
			170,000
Other net assets	528,000		528,000
Investment at cost	168,000	168,000	
Less fair value of investment at acquisition (60% × 160,000)		(96,000)	
Purchased goodwill			72,000
			770,000
Liabilities			
Share capital	50,000		50,000
Profit and loss b/f	570,000		
Profit for the year 2009	76,000		
		646,000	

	A Ltd (1) £	Group (2) £	Group (3) £
Share of post-acquisition profits (60% × 10,000)		6,000	
Total profit and loss reserves (Note 3)			652,000
Minority interests			
At acquisition (40% × 160,000)		64,000	
Post-acquisition profits (40% × 10,000)		4,000	
			68,000
			770,000

Note 1:

Since B Ltd is a subsidiary, the fair value of all its assets is included in the group balance sheet, even though A Ltd owns only 60 per cent of the shares. The difference is dealt with through minority interests.

Note 2:

The date of acquisition was 1 July. The profits of B Ltd after the acquisition are therefore 6/12 of £20,000 = £10,000.

Note 3:

The movements on the group profit and loss account over year 2010 will be:

	£
Balance brought forward from 2009	579,167
Less share of post-acquisition profits of associate during 2009	(9,167)
Profit of A Ltd	76,000
Share of post-acquisition profits of subsidiary during 2010	6,000
Total profit and loss reserves	652,000

The movements include the elimination of the post-acquisition profits (£9,167) when B Ltd was an associate. The reason for this is that the goodwill on acquisition of the subsidiary is the difference between the following.

(1) The cost of the investment £168,000:

  – £60,000 paid during 2009 when the investment was classified as an associate;
  – £108,000 paid during 2010.

(2) The fair value of A's share in B Ltd at 1 July 2010, £96,000.

Post-acquisition profits need to be deducted because the goodwill calculation ignores them. Goodwill is the difference between (a) the cost of that part of the holding in B Ltd that was purchased (ignoring that part which accumulated as post-acquisition profits), and (b) the fair value of the entire holding.

21.6.5   Fair value

So far, we have assumed that fair value is straightforward to calculate. This will often not be true in practice, and FRS 7 *Fair Values in Acquisition Accounting* deals with this matter.

There are actually two separate problems: the fair value of the consideration and the fair value of the assets and liabilities acquired.

The fair value of the consideration is necessary in order to calculate the goodwill arising on the acquisition. Where the company issues shares as part of the consideration for an acquisition, it may also be necessary to determine their fair value in order to calculate the amount of share premium, unless merger relief is available on the transaction.

21.6.6   Fair value of the consideration

The consideration for an acquisition should be taken to be the sum of the cash that has been paid, which gives rise to no fair value problems, and the fair value of any other purchase consideration given as a result of the acquisition. Acquisition costs should be included as part of the consideration.

Cash, monetary assets and the assumption of liabilities

The transfer of cash, short-term monetary assets, and the assumption of short-term liabilities raise few accounting problems, as the fair values are likely to be their book or recorded values.

However, where items are payable some time after the date of the acquisition, they should be discounted to arrive at their net present value. The discount rate used should be the rate that the acquirer could obtain for borrowings of similar amount, taking into account their credit standing and any security that they could provide. While in principle such a treatment seems reasonable, it may be difficult to determine an appropriate discount rate to be applied to the payments to be made.

Financial instruments

Financial instruments which are issued as part of the consideration should be stated at their market prices, if such a price exists. Where the price of an instrument is subject to considerable fluctuations, companies may consider using an average of the market prices for a reasonable period prior to the acquisition. The standard does not dictate a period which should be used for these purposes.

In the case of private companies there is no market price for their securities, and in such situations an estimate needs to be made of their fair value. FRS 7 indicates that the following factors should be taken into consideration:

- the value of any similar securities that are quoted;
- the present value of the future cash flows connected with the instruments issued, which involves the determination of an appropriate discount rate;
- the value of any cash alternative to the issue of securities, and
- the value of any underlying security into which there is a right to convert, although this is of little value to private companies as there will also be no market price for such securities.

There may also be cases where, even for a company with marketable securities, the market price may not be an accurate guide to its value. In such a situation, similar factors to those above should be used in determining the fair value of the consideration.

If control is obtained through a public offer then the date that should be used for valuing the instruments is the date at which the offer becomes unconditional.

Contingent consideration

Where the consideration is contingent on future events, a reasonable estimate should be made of the amounts that are expected to be paid. Such a situation might arise where there is an earn-out, where the total of the consideration payable is dependent upon the future profitability of the acquired company or business.

In later years, this estimate will need to be revised, and this will have a corresponding effect on the amount of goodwill that was initially recorded. This should not be treated as a prior period adjustment, since it is a revision of an accounting estimate and therefore excluded by FRS 3. The acquisition cost and goodwill amount will not be finally determined until all consideration has been paid over.

If the consideration is to be satisfied by the issue of shares, then the amount attributed to the consideration needs to be split between equity and liabilities in accordance with FRS 25. This means, for example, that if redeemable shares form part of the consideration then such shares will be recorded as liabilities.

Non-monetary consideration

The guidance in the standard on non-monetary consideration is not very specific and simply mentions that consideration would need to be given to:

- market prices;
- estimated realisable values;
- independent valuations, and
- other available evidence, without stating what such evidence might be.

Acquisition costs

The expenses that may be treated as part of the cost of an acquisition comprise all costs directly incurred as a result of the acquisition, except those that should be treated as issue costs of financial instruments in accordance with FRS 25.

21.6.7   *Fair value of the identifiable assets and liabilities acquired*

In many cases, the fair value of the consideration does not cause a problem. This will be the case if, for example, the consideration is wholly or primarily in cash or short-term monetary assets. However, the fair value of the identifiable net assets must always be considered when a subsidiary is acquired, and is often far more complicated. Until FRS 7, there was no specific guidance in this area.

The principle that underlies FRS 7 is that the assets and liabilities that should be brought into the group accounts are those of the acquired entity at the date of the acquisition, and their fair values should be determined by taking into account their condition at that date.

Fair values in respect of the assets and liabilities acquired are defined by FRS 7 as:

> The amount at which an asset or liability could be exchanged in an arm's length transaction between informed and willing parties, other than in a forced or liquidation sale. (Para. 2, FRS 7.)

The items that need to be brought into account are the identifiable assets and liabilities, defined as:

> The assets and liabilities of the acquired entity that are capable of being disposed of or settled separately, without disposing of a business of the entity. (Para. 2, FRS 7.)

The fair values should not take account of any changes which are expected to take place in the future and, in particular, should not:

- take account of any changes resulting from the acquirer's intentions or future actions;
- take account of any impairments, or other changes, which result from events after the acquisition, or
- take account of provisions or accruals for future operating losses or for reorganisation and integration costs which are expected to be incurred as a result of the acquisition, whether they relate to the acquired entity or to the acquirer.

Provisions unconnected with the acquisition, and already made by the acquired entity without any influence from the acquirer, may still be included in determining the fair values of the identifiable assets and liabilities.

Wherever possible, the recognition and measurement of the separate assets and liabilities acquired as a result of the combination should be completed by the date on which the first financial statements after the acquisition are approved by the directors. Where this is not possible, provisional valuations should be made. These should then be adjusted in the next financial statements, with a corresponding adjustment to the amount of goodwill recognised as a result of the acquisition.

FRS 7 gives specific guidance dealing with various categories of asset and liability.

Tangible fixed assets

Tangible fixed assets should, where possible, be recorded at the lower of:

- their market value, if there is an open market for assets of similar type and condition, and
- their recoverable amount.

Recoverable amount is defined as:

> The greater of the net realisable value of an asset and, where appropriate, the value in use. (Para. 2, FRS 7.)

Value in use is further defined as:

> The present value of the future cash flows obtainable as a result of an asset's continued use, including those resulting from the ultimate disposal of the asset. (Para. 2, FRS 7.)

No account should be taken of the expected use to which the asset is to be put, if this is to change as a result of the acquisition.

Where there is no open market in the assets, they should be stated at the lower of:

- their depreciated replacement cost, reflecting the acquired business's normal buying process and the sources of supply that are available to it, and
- their recoverable amount.

The depreciated replacement cost should be calculated using the depreciation policies of the acquirer.

If even this is not ascertainable, then the historical cost of the asset should be determined and this should then be updated by the use of a relevant price index.

Intangible assets

Intangible assets should be recorded at their replacement cost, which should normally be taken to be their market value.

Stocks and work in progress

Most stocks and work in progress should be valued at the lower of:

- their replacement cost, and
- their net realisable value.

Replacement cost should be the cost that would have been incurred by the acquired entity, reflecting the acquired business's normal buying process and the sources of supply that are available to it. For items with a short production cycle, historical costs may be a reasonable approximation to replacement cost. For products with a long production cycle, if there is a ready market in stocks at the appropriate level of maturity, then the price in this market should be used. In other cases the historical cost may need to be increased to reflect the interest cost of holding stock.

Long-term contract work in progress should be stated at its book value, except for the effect of any adjustments to take account of any differences between the accounting policies of the acquired and acquiring entities.

Quoted investments

Quoted investments should be stated at their market price, although this may be adjusted for unusual price fluctuations, usually by taking an average price over a short period, or to reflect the size of the holding.

Unquoted investments

FRS 7 provides no guidance on the valuation of unquoted investments, which is considerably more complicated than for quoted investments. Professional valuations will normally be required, if the amounts involved are material.

The procedures adopted for valuing capital instruments issued as consideration will also be relevant:

- the value of any similar securities that are quoted;
- the present value of the future cash flows connected with the instruments issued, which involves the determination of an appropriate discount rate;
- the value of any cash alternative to the issue of securities, and
- the value of any underlying security into which there is a right to convert, although this is of little value to private companies as there will also be no market price for such securities.

Monetary assets and liabilities

Monetary assets and liabilities, including accruals and provisions, should be stated at their present value. This does not present any problem for short-term items, as they are stated at the amounts that are expected to be paid over or received.

For longer-term items there may be more problems. Where there is a market price, this should be used. In the absence of a market price, other considerations may apply. Balances that carry interest at current market rates need not be discounted, as they will already be stated at their current values. The situation is more complicated if this is not the case. The discount rate to be applied should be determined by reference to:

- current lending rates;
- the outstanding term;
- the credit standing of the issuer, and
- the nature of any security involved.

The difference between the fair value of the amount receivable or payable and the amounts to be paid or received should be treated as finance costs, or income, in the group accounts, and allocated to the underlying balances in order to give a constant rate of charge (or credit) on the carrying amount.

Contingencies

Both contingent assets and liabilities should be valued on the basis of reasonable estimates of their outcome. Contrary to normal accounting practice they should be treated in similar ways, so contingent assets which would generally be ignored by the accountant may need to be recorded if they existed in an acquired entity at the date of its acquisition.

Contingent assets and liabilities that crystallise as a direct result of the acquisition should be brought into account.

Businesses held exclusively for resale

Where an interest in a separate business is sold as a unit within approximately one year of the date of acquisition then its fair value should normally be taken to be equal to the net proceeds of the sale, after making adjustments for any assets or liabilities transferred into or out of the business prior to its sale. This procedure should not be applied if:

- the fair value of the business at the date of acquisition is demonstrably different from its value at the date of disposal;
- the acquirer has made a substantial change to the business prior to its disposal, or
- the disposal is completed at a reduced price in order to ensure a swift sale.

This treatment can be applied whether or not the business sold is a separate legal entity, provided that its assets, liabilities, results and activities are clearly distinguishable from the other assets, liabilities, results and activities of the acquired entity.

If the business has not been sold by the time the first financial statements are prepared after the date of acquisition then the fair value of the business should be based on the estimated net proceeds of the sale. This procedure can be adopted provided:

- a purchaser has been identified or is being actively sought, and
- the disposal is reasonably expected to take place within one year of the date of acquisition.

In this case the interest in the business, or subsidiary, should be shown as a current asset investment.

When the sale price is determined, the original estimate of fair value should be adjusted to reflect the actual sale proceeds.

If the business, or subsidiary, is not sold within approximately one year of the acquisition then it should be consolidated using normal procedures, with fair values attributed to its individual assets and liabilities in accordance with the normal procedures of FRS 7. There will then be a corresponding adjustment to the amount of goodwill recorded as a result of the acquisition.

Pensions and other post-retirement benefits

FRS 7 requires that the fair value of a deficiency on a funded pension scheme, or the accrued obligations of an unfunded scheme, should be recognised as a liability of the acquiring group.

A surplus may also be treated as an asset, although care should be taken to limit the recognition to the amount that is expected to be realised. The fair value should not reflect the actuarial value alone, but also the extent to which the surplus can be realised. Under FRS 17, a surplus is recognised to the extent that it can be recovered through reduced contributions or through refunds from the scheme.

The financial effects of any changes to pension arrangements that result from the acquisition should be treated as post-acquisition items and dealt with in accordance with FRS 17.

Deferred taxation

Deferred tax assets and liabilities should be determined by considering the position of the whole of the enlarged group, and treated in accordance with FRS 19. FRS 19 is covered in detail in Chapter 8.

Deferred tax on adjustments to record assets and liabilities at their fair values should be recognised in accordance with the requirements of that standard.

FRS 7, as amended by FRS 19, notes that deferred tax assets that were not regarded as recoverable and hence were not recognised before the acquisition may, as a consequence of the acquisition, satisfy the recognition criteria of FRS 19. In such a case, assets of the acquired entity should be recognised in the fair value exercise. Those of the acquirer or other entities within the acquiring group should be recognised as a credit to the tax charge in the post-acquisition period.

21.6.8 Non-cash acquisitions

The procedures for consolidation where consideration is not in the form of cash are covered by UITF 31, which deals with exchanges of businesses or other non-monetary assets for an interest in a subsidiary, associate or joint venture. The approach that the UITF requires to be applied in consolidated accounts is as follows.

(1) Where the company obtaining the interest in the subsidiary, associate or joint venture still retains any interest in the non-monetary assets transferred, then that interest and any associated goodwill should be stated at its pre-acquisition amount.

(2) The share of net assets acquired should be accounted for at fair value, with any difference between this and the acquisition cost being treated as goodwill.

(3) To the extent that the fair value of the assets exchanged (including goodwill) and any related cash, in which the company no longer retains an interest, differ from the fair value of the consideration acquired, a gain or loss should be recognised. A gain should be taken to the profit and loss account, to the extent that it is realised, and the statement of total recognised gains and losses to the extent that it is not. A loss should be treated as an impairment loss or, if this does not account for it in full, directly through the profit and loss account of the acquirer.

The main exception is that no gain or loss should be recognised where the transaction is artificial or lacks substance, such as where there is no other market for the assets transferred. In this case, the financial statements must disclose that this is the case.

The following is an example of the normal treatment.

EXAMPLE

A acquires an 80 per cent interest in B through a new issue of shares. This involves the issue of 800,000 £1 shares, in addition to the 200,000 already in issue. The consideration is the transfer of an asset with a book value to A of £600,000 and a fair value of £1,000,000, giving rise to share premium in B of £200,000. The net assets of B prior to the transaction were £200,000 and it had no retained profits. The other net assets of A were £400,000, and its share capital and retained reserves were both £500,000.

The value of the asset in the consolidated accounts will be (80% × 600,000) + (20% × 1,000,000) = £680,000

The minority interest will be 20% × (1,000,000 + 200,000) = £240,000

The goodwill will be 1,000,000 − (80% × 1,200,000) = £40,000

This can also be calculated in the following way, which will result in the same answer. $(1,000,000 \times 20\%) - (80\% \times 200,000) = £40,000$. This method ignores the 80% that is being retained both for the consideration and the net assets acquired.

The gain will be $20\% \times (1,000,000 - 600,000) = £80,000$

The gain is therefore limited to the extent of the notional gain (£400,000) which has been recognised on disposal to the minority interest.

This assumes that no gain has been recognised in A's financial statements, and the cost of investment is therefore shown at £600,000, prior to the consolidation adjustments. Had the investment been stated at £1,000,000 then the first journal would not be required. It should be noted that UITF 31 does not deal with the position in the individual company accounts.

The following consolidation would result.

	A	B	1 Notional gain	2 Investment	3 Eliminate gain	4 MI	Group
Fixed assets							
Tangible		1,000,000			−320,000		680,000
Goodwill				40,000			40,000
Investments	600,000		400,000	−1,000,000			−
Other net assets	400,000	200,000					600,000
	1,000,000	1,200,000	400,000	−960,000	−320,000	−	1,320,000
Share capital	500,000	1,000,000		−800,000		−200,000	500,000
Share premium		200,000		−160,000		−40,000	−
Profit and loss	500,000		400,000		−320,000		580,000
Minority interests	−	−				240,000	240,000
	1,000,000	1,200,000	400,000	−960,000	−320,000	−	1,320,000

21.6.9   Disclosure on acquisitions

Under FRS 6 and the Companies Act 2006, the following disclosures must be made where there is an acquisition or a merger.

(1)   The names of the undertakings acquired or merging or, in the case of the acquisition or merger of groups, the names of the parents of each group.

(2)   Details of the consideration given in respect of the acquisition or merger, including the number and class of any securities issued, details of any other consideration and the fair value of the consideration, where the transaction has a material effect on the amounts reported by the group.

(3)   Any significant accounting adjustments, including both their nature and the amounts involved.

(4)   The profit or loss of the undertaking or group acquired from the beginning of its financial year, which must be specified, to the date of acquisition,

and for its previous financial year, where the transaction has a material effect on the amounts reported by the group.

Specifically for an acquisition, the following disclosures must be given, generally for material acquisitions individually and for other acquisitions in aggregate.

(1) The composition and fair value of the consideration given by the acquiring company and any of its subsidiary undertakings should be stated. Separate details should also be given in respect of any deferred or contingent consideration including, for contingent consideration, the range of possible outcomes and the principal factors that affect the outcome. This should be given for material acquisitions individually, and for all other acquisitions in aggregate.

(2) A table showing, for each class of asset and liability of the acquired entity:

(a) the book values, as recorded by the acquired entity, immediately before the acquisition and before any fair value adjustments;

(b) the fair value adjustments, analysed between:

(i) revaluations;

(ii) adjustments to achieve consistency of accounting policies, and

(iii) any other significant adjustments; giving the reasons for the adjustments, and

(c) the fair values at the date of acquisition; the table should include a statement of the amount of purchased goodwill, or negative goodwill, which has arisen as a result of the acquisition.

Provisions for reorganisation and restructuring costs that are included in the liabilities of the acquired entity, and any related asset write-downs, made in the 12 months up to the date of acquisition should be shown separately in the table.

(3) Where the fair values of the identifiable assets and liabilities, or the purchase consideration, can be determined only on a provisional basis at the end of the accounting period in which the acquisition took place then this should be stated and the reason should be given. Any subsequent material adjustments to the provisional fair values, with corresponding adjustments to goodwill, should be disclosed and explained.

(4) Any exceptional profit or loss in periods following the acquisition that is determined using the fair values recognised on acquisition should be disclosed in accordance with the requirements of FRS 3 and specifically identified with the acquisition.

(5) The profit and loss account, or notes to the financial statements for periods following the acquisition should show the costs that have been incurred in reorganising, restructuring and integrating the acquisition. These costs are those that:

(a) would not have been incurred had the acquisition taken place, and

(b) relate to a project identified and controlled by management as part of an integration programme set up at the time of acquisition or as a direct consequence of an immediate post-acquisition review.

(6) Movements on provisions or accruals relating to an acquisition should be disclosed and analysed between the amounts used for the specific purpose for which they were created and the amounts which have been released unused.

(7) The profit after taxation and minority interests of the acquired entity should be given for:

(a) the period from the beginning of the acquired entity's financial year to the date of acquisition, giving the date on which this period began, and

(b) its previous financial year.

(8) The following information should be disclosed in the financial statements of the acquiring company for the period in which the acquisition took place:

(a) the summarised profit and loss account and statement of total recognised gains and losses of the acquired entity for the period from the beginning of its financial year to the effective date of acquisition, giving the date on which this period began, showing at least:

(i)   turnover;

(ii)   operating profit;

(iii) those exceptional items which are required to be shown on the face of the profit and loss account in accordance with FRS 3;

(iv)   profit before taxation;

(v)   taxation and minority interests, and

(vi)   extraordinary items, and

(b) the profit after tax and minority interests for the acquired entity's previous financial year.

This information should be shown on the basis of the acquired entity's accounting policies prior to the acquisition, but need only be provided:

- by listed companies if any of the ratios set out in the Listing Rules exceed 15 per cent;
- by other companies if either the net assets or operating profits of the acquired entity exceed 15 per cent of those of the acquiring entity, or if the fair value of the consideration given exceeds 15 per cent of the net assets of the acquiring entity, or
- in any case where an acquisition is of such significance that the disclosure is necessary in order that the financial statements give a true and fair view.

The requirements of FRS 3 and FRS 1 also need to be considered.

21.7   GOODWILL

21.7.1   Calculation of goodwill

Goodwill can be either purchased or unpurchased. Only purchased goodwill is relevant when dealing with group accounts, as FRS 10 requires that unpurchased goodwill should not be carried in financial statements:

> Internally generated goodwill should not be capitalised. (Para. 8, FRS 10.)

Purchased goodwill is defined as:

> The difference between the cost of an acquired entity and the aggregate of the fair values of that entity's identifiable assets and liabilities. (Para. 2, FRS 10.)

The items which give rise to the calculation of the initial purchased goodwill figure have already been covered when dealing with the impact of FRS 7. However, FRS 10 does make it clear that there are items which may appear to be other intangible assets, but which should not be treated as such in the group financial statements:

> If its value cannot be measured reliably, an intangible asset purchased as part of the acquisition of a business should be subsumed within the amount of the purchase price attributed to goodwill. (Para. 13, FRS 10.)

This is to deal with the situation where a company is not able to split out one or more intangible assets from the value of the business which has been acquired.

21.7.2   Initial recognition

Where goodwill has been calculated, the normal treatment is that it should be capitalised and classified as an asset in the group balance sheet.

Where the initial calculation arrives at negative goodwill, that is, where the fair value of the identifiable net assets acquired is greater than the fair value of the consideration, then the ASB seems to make the initial assumption that the calculations must be incorrect:

> If an acquisition appears to give rise to negative goodwill, the fair values of the acquired assets should be tested for impairment and the fair values of the acquired liabilities checked carefully to ensure that none has been omitted or understated . . . (Para. 48, FRS 10.)

This reflects the expectation that negative goodwill is likely to be the exception rather than the rule, but seems a slightly strange comment to include in an accounting standard.

Where, even after checking, it is clear that there is negative goodwill then this should be recognised and separately disclosed on the face of the balance sheet, immediately below the goodwill heading and followed by a subtotal showing the net amount of both positive and negative goodwill. In effect, this will give rise to something that looks like a 'negative asset' rather than a liability.

For the avoidance of doubt, the ASB also points out that, on a single transaction, it is not acceptable to attempt to divide the total net goodwill figure between positive and negative elements. It is probably true that many purchase transactions include an element of both, but it has not been common practice in the past for such divisions to be made.

21.7.3 Amortisation

There is a rebuttable presumption that positive goodwill has a limited useful economic life, and that this life does not exceed 20 years. However, where this presumption can be rebutted, the FRS allows companies to continue to carry purchased goodwill for either a longer or even an indefinite period.

The presumption can only be rebutted if:

- the durability of the acquired business or intangible asset can be demonstrated and justifies estimating the useful economic life to exceed 20 years, and
- the goodwill is capable of continued measurement.

The ASB points out that durability depends on a number of factors such as:

- the nature of the business in which the company operates;
- the stability of the industry in which the acquired business operates;
- typical lifespans of the products to which the goodwill attaches;
- the extent to which the acquisition overcomes market entry barriers that will continue to exist, and
- the expected future impact of competition on the business.

Goodwill will not be capable of continued measurement either where there is an intrinsic problem with valuation, or where the costs of attempting to determine the value would be out of proportion to any benefit obtained. This might be the case where, for example:

- the new business is merged with part of the old, such that it is no longer possible to identify the goodwill that is connected with the acquisition;
- the management information systems used by the business are not capable of allocating cash flows at the level required in order to keep track of the separate business, or
- the amounts involved are not sufficiently large to make the exercise useful.

Where goodwill has a life that is finite, it should be amortised on a systematic basis over that life. There is another presumption that straight line amortisation should be used unless another method can clearly be shown to be more appropriate. It is also made clear in the standard that no residual value may be allocated to goodwill, so that the depreciation method used must arrive at zero over the period chosen.

As with all other assets which are depreciated or amortised, there is a requirement to reconsider the useful life of goodwill at each balance sheet date. Where the life is altered, the remaining unamortised balance should be written off over the new period chosen.

UITF Abstract 27 *Revision to estimates of the useful economic life of goodwill and intangible assets* was issued to clarify the accounting treatment where a company decides that it can no longer rebut the 20-year maximum useful economic life presumption for goodwill or intangible assets in FRS 10. The Abstract confirms that this is a change of accounting estimate, not a change of accounting policy, and hence does not give rise to a prior year adjustment. If the presumption can no longer be rebutted, the total useful economic life from the date of acquisition will be restricted to 20 years. The net book value of the goodwill or intangible asset should then be written off over whatever portion of that original 20-year period remains unexpired. However, if an impairment has occurred, the goodwill or intangible asset should be written down immediately to its recoverable amount, which should then be amortised over the unexpired portion of the original 20-year period.

Negative goodwill, up to the fair values of non-monetary assets acquired, should be recognised in the profit and loss account over the period in which those assets are written off, either through depreciation or on disposal. Any excess over this amount should be written back to the profit and loss account over the periods which are expected to benefit.

Potential impact of the FRSME

The FRSME contains a presumption that the life of goodwill does not exceed five years.

21.7.4   Impairment reviews

As with intangible assets, goodwill may need to be considered for an impairment review. The frequency of impairment reviews depends upon the amortisation period chosen.

Where goodwill is being amortised over a period of 20 years or less, FRS 10 requires that an impairment review be carried out:

- at the end of the first full financial year following the year of acquisition, and
- at any other date, if there is an indication of a fall in value.

Where goodwill is amortised over a period of greater than 20 years, or is not amortised, impairment reviews are required at every balance sheet date.

Under FRS 10, the first-year review mentioned above is conducted in two stages. Firstly, any possible impairment is identified by comparing post-acquisition performance in the first year with pre-acquisition forecasts used to support the purchase price. Secondly, if the initial review indicates that the post-acquisition performance has failed to meet pre-acquisition expectations or if any other previously unforeseen events or changes in circumstances indicate that the carrying values may not be recoverable, a full impairment review will be required. This should be performed in accordance with the requirements of FRS 11 *Impairment of Fixed Assets and Goodwill*. All other impairment reviews for goodwill must be performed in accordance with FRS 11. The procedures for performing impairment reviews under FRS 11 are covered in Chapter 11, which deals with fixed assets.

If an impairment is identified at the time of the first-year review, the FRS suggests that this reflects:

- an overpayment;
- an event that occurred between the acquisition and the first-year review, or
- depletion of the acquired goodwill (or intangible asset) between the acquisition and the first-year review that exceeds the amount recognised through amortisation.

The requirements of FRS 10 are such that the recognition of an impairment loss for goodwill must be justified in the same way as the absence of an impairment loss, ie by reference to expected future cash flows. In particular, a belief that the value of goodwill will not be capable of continued measurement in future does not justify writing off the whole balance at the time of the first-year impairment review.

Where an impairment review indicates that goodwill has increased in value, in general, the excess over current carrying value cannot be written back. The logic of this is that there is probably new unpurchased goodwill, and it is not the original goodwill that has increased in value. There is an exception to this general rule where an external event can be clearly identified as having given rise to the previous fall in value, and the situation has now clearly reversed. In this case, the goodwill can be written back in the current period.

21.7.5   Transitional provisions

As FRS 10 represented a substantial change from previous practice, it set out extensive transitional provisions.

Companies which had, under SSAP 22, previously written off all goodwill to reserves were permitted to choose to leave that goodwill written off when FRS 10 came into force. Where this option was taken up, there will be ongoing disclosure consequences. FRS 10 requires that:

- the accounting policy followed in respect of that goodwill should be stated;

- the cumulative amount of goodwill written off should be stated;
- there should be a statement that the amounts were written off as a result of policy and that they will be charged to the profit and loss account on any subsequent disposal;
- the amount should not be included in a separate goodwill reserve, but on the profit and loss account or another reserve, and
- if the business is subsequently sold or disposed of, the goodwill should be taken as a charge to the profit and loss account and separately disclosed.

As with the transitional provisions of FRS 15, when dealing with tangible fixed assets, these provisions may continue to be relevant for a very long time.

The FRS retains the statutory exemption from disclosing the cumulative balance of goodwill arising prior to January 1989, where this amount cannot be obtained at all or cannot be obtained without unreasonable expense or delay.

Where companies that had previously written off goodwill chose to reinstate it and amortise it:

- retrospective impairment reviews had to be undertaken, and
- the notes were required to disclose the original costs of the goodwill, the amount attributed to previous amortisation and the amount attributed to previous impairment.

Companies which have always carried goodwill will have been less affected by the FRS, although they must now comply with the requirements on impairment reviews.

21.7.6   Disclosure

Apart from the disclosures for companies using the transitional provisions, the following items must also be stated.

(1)   The cost or revalued amount at the beginning and end of the accounting period (for positive and negative goodwill separately).

(2)   The cumulative amount of provisions for amortisation or impairment of positive goodwill at the beginning and end of the financial period.

(3)   A reconciliation of the movements over the period in the costs or valuation and provisions for impairment and amortisation, as well as the negative goodwill written back.

(4)   The net carrying amount of positive and negative goodwill at the balance sheet date.

(5)   The profit or loss on each material disposal of a previously acquired business or business segment.

(6)   The methods and periods of amortisation of goodwill, and the reasons for choosing these periods.

(7)   The reasons for and, where material, effect of any change in the amortisation period during the year.

(8)   The detailed grounds, where appropriate, for rebutting the presumption that goodwill has a useful economic life of more than 20 years.

(9)   A statement, where appropriate, that goodwill has not been amortised and that this is a departure from the Companies Act requirement for amortisation, together with the details of the departure as normally required by FRS 18, and previously by UITF 7 (FRS 18 and UITF 7 are covered in Chapter 2).

(10)   The period over which negative goodwill is being written back in the profit and loss account.

(11)   The amount and source of negative goodwill which exceeds the value of non-monetary assets acquired, and the period over which this excess is being written back.

21.8   MERGER ACCOUNTING

21.8.1   Conditions

FRS 6 *Acquisitions and Mergers* assumes that all business combinations should be accounted for as acquisitions unless very detailed conditions are met.

The tests included in FRS 6 are in addition to those in the Companies Act 2006. The statutory tests are that:

- at least 90 per cent of the nominal value of shares with unrestricted rights to profits and capital (equity shares, as defined in legislation and, therefore, not necessarily in accordance with the definition in FRS 6, which itself now derives from FRS 25) in the undertaking acquired must be held by or on behalf of the parent;
- the shares referred to above must have been acquired under an agreement whereby the parent or one of its subsidiaries issued shares;
- the fair value of any consideration other than equity shares issued by the parent or a subsidiary does not exceed ten per cent of the nominal value of the equity shares issued, and
- adoption of the merger method of accounting is in accordance with generally accepted accounting principles or practice (ie FRS 6).

FRS 6 limits merger accounting (while making it obligatory in those rare cases where it is appropriate). The standard argues that a true merger is:

> A business combination that results in the creation of a new reporting entity formed from the combining parties, in which the shareholders of the combining entities come together in a partnership for the mutual sharing of the risks and benefits of the combined entity, and in which no party to the combination in

substance obtains control over any other, or is otherwise seen to be dominant, whether by virtue of the proportion of its shareholders' rights in the combined entity, the influence of its directors, or otherwise. (Para. 2, FRS 6.)

In order to be accounted for as a merger under FRS 6, all of the following conditions must be met.

(1) No party to the combination may be portrayed as either the acquirer or the acquired, either by its own board or management or by that of any other party to the combination.

(2) All parties to the combination, represented by their boards of directors or appointees, must participate in the establishment of the management structure of the combined entity and in selecting the management personnel. The decisions they reach must be made on the basis of consensus rather than by the exercise of voting rights.

(3) The relative sizes of the combining entities must not be so different that one party is able to dominate the combined entity simply by virtue of its size. The notes to the standard state that one party should be presumed to dominate if it is more than 50 per cent larger than each of the other parties to the combination. In determining size for these purposes, reference should be made to the proportion of the equity of the combined entity attributable to the shareholders of each of the combining entities.

(4) The consideration received by equity shareholders of each party to the combination, in relation to their existing equity shareholding, must comprise primarily equity shares in the combined entity. Any non-equity consideration, or equity consideration in the form of shares which carry substantially reduced voting or distribution rights, must represent only an immaterial proportion of the fair value of the total consideration received by the equity shareholders of that party. The consideration that must be taken into account is not only that which has resulted from the arrangement giving rise to the combination itself, but also any consideration given for the purchase of part of the equity shares in one party to the combination by another in the two years prior to the combination. It need not include:

(a) the transfer to shareholders of part of the business of the entity in which they were shareholders, if that part is peripheral to the main nature and focus of the operations of the business, or

(b) the transfer to shareholders of the proceeds (in cash or loan stock) of disposal of part of the business of the entity in which they were shareholders, if that part is peripheral to the main nature and focus of the operations of the business.

(5) No equity shareholders in any of the combining entities must retain any material interest in the future performance of only part of the combined entity.

For the purposes of the FRS 6 tests, the definition of equity and non-equity shares has changed as a result of the introduction of FRS 25. Equity shares are those financial instruments which meet the definition of equity under FRS 25. Non-equity shares are those instruments, legally shares, which fall within the definition of liabilities under FRS 25.

More liberal tests are applied to group reconstructions:

- the use of merger accounting must not be prohibited by companies legislation;
- the ultimate shareholders must remain the same, such that their relative rights must all remain unchanged, and
- no minority interest in the net assets of the group may be affected by the changes.

In practice, group reconstructions are far more common than actual mergers and therefore constitute the main case where merger accounting is used.

Potential impact of the FRSME

As noted above, the FRSME does not allow mergers. Practices similar to merger accounting might still be applicable where there is a combination taking place between entities under common control, which is outside the scope of the FRSME requirements on business combinations.

21.8.2   Merger accounting procedures

The Companies Act describes merger accounting in the following terms:

> The assets and liabilities of the undertaking acquired must be brought into the group accounts at the figures at which they stand in the undertaking's accounts, subject to any adjustment authorised or required by this schedule.

> The income and expenditure of the undertaking acquired must be included in the group accounts for the entire financial year, including the period before the acquisition.

> The group accounts must show corresponding amounts relating to the previous financial year as if the undertaking acquired had been included in the consolidation throughout that year.

> There must be set off against the aggregate of:

> (a)   the appropriate amount in respect of qualifying shares issued by the parent company or its subsidiary undertakings in consideration for the acquisition of shares in the undertaking acquired, and

> (b)   the fair value of any other consideration for the acquisition of shares in the undertaking acquired, determined as at the date when those shares were acquired,

> the nominal value of the issued share capital of the undertaking acquired held by the parent company and its subsidiary undertakings.

The resulting amount must be shown as an adjustment to the consolidated reserves. (Para. 11, Sch. 6 to The Large and Medium-sized Companies and Groups (Accounts and Reports) Regulations 2008 (SI 2008/410).)

Qualifying shares are shares for which merger or reconstruction relief is available.

The only adjustments to the carrying amounts of assets and liabilities are those that are required to ensure consistency of accounting policies.

Merger accounting effectively treats the companies in the group as though they had always been members of the group. As a result, fair value adjustments are not required.

Where the nominal value of the shares issued in the merger does not equal the nominal amount of the shares acquired, there will be a merger difference. This difference, which should not be confused with goodwill, should be treated as a capital reserve if it is a credit balance, and deducted from reserves if it is a debit balance.

21.8.3 Disclosure

Under FRS 6, the following information should be disclosed in the financial statements of the combined entity for the period in which a merger took place.

(1) An analysis of the principal components of the current year's profit and loss account and statement of total recognised gains and losses between:
   (a) amounts relating to the merged entity for the period since the date of the merger, and
   (b) for each party to the merger, amounts relating to that party for the period prior to the date of the merger.

(2) An analysis between the parties to the merger of the components of the profit and loss account and statement of total recognised gains and losses for the previous financial year.

(3) The composition and fair value of the consideration given by the issuing company and its subsidiary undertakings.

(4) The aggregate book value of the net assets of each party to the merger at the date of the merger.

(5) The nature and amount of significant accounting adjustments made to the net assets of any party to the merger in order to achieve consistency of accounting policies throughout the group, and an explanation of any other significant adjustments made to the net assets of any party to the merger as a result of the merger.

(6)   A statement of the adjustments to consolidated reserves resulting from the merger.

21.9   ASSOCIATES AND JOINT VENTURES

21.9.1   Introduction

The accounting treatment for associates and joint ventures changed with the introduction of FRS 9 *Associates and Joint Ventures*. When dealing with associates, FRS 9 built upon the requirements that were previously contained in SSAP 1. FRS 9 requires more disclosure and makes some changes of detail, but has not changed the fundamental accounting treatment to be applied. In the case of joint ventures, FRS 9 provided the first detailed requirements in the UK.

Associates and joint ventures may also be affected by UITF 31 if they are acquired by the transfer of assets in which the investor retains an interest. This is dealt with above when covering acquisition accounting.

Companies which prepare financial statements in accordance with the FRSSE are exempt from the requirements of FRS 9, unless they voluntarily prepare group accounts. The standard also does not apply to other companies which are not required to prepare group accounts, or which would not be required to do so even if they had subsidiaries. This basically means small companies (even where they do not use the FRSSE) and sub-parents which are exempt from preparing group accounts on the basis that such accounts are produced at a higher level within the group. Individual companies which do not produce group accounts, but which are too large to qualify for the exemption, should comply with the standard by either preparing a separate set of financial statements or by including all of the relevant information in the notes to their own accounts.

To avoid some of the problems that may be associated with joint ventures and associates, the FRS has an exemption for investment funds. Where an investing company holds investments solely for the purposes of increasing market value as part of a portfolio, and not in order to carry on any part of its business, then it should account for all its investments at cost or valuation, even where it has significant influence or joint control.

21.9.2   Definition of associate

The Companies Act 2006 contains the following definition of an associate:

> An "associated undertaking" means an undertaking in which an undertaking included in the consolidation has a participating interest and over whose operating and financial policy it exercises a significant influence, and which is not:
>
> (a)   a subsidiary undertaking of the parent company, or

(b) a joint venture dealt with in accordance with paragraph 18 (Para. 19, Sch. 6 to The Large and Medium-sized Companies and Groups (Accounts and Reports) Regulations 2008 (SI 2008/410).)

Paragraph 18 refers an undertaking which is neither a subsidiary nor body corporate and is proportionately consolidated. Given that proportional consolidation is prohibited by FRS 9, this is of no real relevance.

It should be borne in mind that this definition refers to any undertaking included in the consolidation. What this means is that an associate of a subsidiary is an associate for the purposes of preparing the group accounts of the parent. (There are some exceptions to this general rule: for example, where two subsidiaries each hold an interest in a company which individually provide influence but jointly provide control. In this case, the company may be an associate of each of the subsidiaries, but it is a subsidiary of the ultimate parent.)

FRS 9 includes a very similar definition, but then goes on to provide more detail of some of the terms used. It includes the following definition of participating interest (which supplements the statutory definition covered in Chapter 13):

> An interest held in the shares of another entity on a long-term basis for the purpose of securing a contribution to the investor's activities by the exercise of control or influence arising from or related to that interest. The investor's interest must, therefore, be a beneficial one and the benefits expected to arise must be linked to the exercise of its significant influence over the investee's operating and financial policies. An interest in the shares of another entity includes an interest convertible into an interest in shares or an option to acquire shares . . . (Para. 2, FRS 9.)

The FRS also points out that statute contains a rebuttable presumption that a 20 per cent holding constitutes a participating interest. It then goes on to say that the presumption is rebutted if the interest is not long term or if it is not beneficial.

As the definition makes clear, there may be cases where a company has a participating interest even though it has a small (or even nil) shareholding, and rights to acquire shares instead of shares themselves. The example given is that of a start-up situation where a party has a management contract and the right to acquire shares at a later date. This fulfils the definition since the investing company has the influence (even control) and the right to benefit from the progress of the new company.

The FRS also defines the exercise of significant influence:

> The investor is actively involved and is influential in the direction of its investee through its participation in policy decisions covering aspects of policy relevant to the investor, including decisions on strategic issues such as:
>
> (a) the expansion or contraction of the business, participation in other entities or changes in products, markets and activities of its investee; and

(b)   determining the balance between dividend and reinvestment ... (Para. 2, FRS 9.)

As with a participating interest, the FRS notes that there is a rebuttable presumption that there is significant influence where the interest is 20 per cent or more. This can be rebutted if it can be shown that the investor is not able to exercise significant influence in the form mentioned in the FRS.

The notes accompanying the standard expand upon the definition, and give examples of how it can be applied in practice. In summary:

- there needs to be an agreement or understanding (whether formal or informal) which provides the basis for exercising significant influence;
- there must be direct involvement in the operating and financial policies, and the investment must not be passive;
- over time, the investing company must be able to ensure that the policies of the investee are consistent with its own strategy, and
- there will normally be representation on the board of directors or equivalent, although the absence of such representation does not prove that the investment is not an associate.

The notes also point out that the actual exercise of significant influence often becomes clear only after some time. However, companies are still required to deal with the situation where an investment has been made, but the full details of the relationship in practice have yet to become clear. In such cases, the FRS requires that the arrangements in place, such as the proposed board representation, be taken into account. Most of the time this will be straightforward, but it may become complicated if the actual relationship does not progress as expected. Where this occurs, it may be necessary to alter the accounting treatment which was initially adopted.

Where it has been determined that (in practice) an investment is an associate, then the investor should be presumed to continue to exercise significant influence unless there is a specific event or transaction which removes the right of the investor to use such influence. For example, a company may invest in a new venture and play a very significant management role for some time. After a few years, the company is operating successfully and the investor plays a less active part. Under FRS 9, the investment would still be deemed to be an associate, even though it might be argued that in the later years the investor is no longer actually exercising significant influence.

The basis on which an investment is determined to be an associate is relevant to the accounting treatment adopted. The FRS points out that in the majority of cases the interest held, and related income and other gains and losses, should be stated on the basis of the proportion of equity shares. However, where other matters have been taken into account in determining that an investment is an associate then these also need to be considered in determining the relevant proportion of the results and assets that should be included in the group accounts. For example, where an investment is deemed to be an associate on the basis of options, then those options also need to be considered when calculating how much of the result and net assets should be consolidated. This may mean that a group accounts for more than its share of an associate as calculated according to the equity shares in issue.

21.9.3   Definition of joint venture

A joint venture is defined by FRS 9 as:

> An entity in which the reporting entity holds an interest on a long-term basis and is jointly controlled by the reporting entity and one or more other venturers under a contractual arrangement. (Para. 2, FRS 9.)

Joint control is then further defined as:

> A reporting entity jointly controls a venture with one or more other entities if none of the entities alone can control that entity but all together can do so and decisions on financial and operating policy essential to the activities, economic performance and financial position of that venture require each venturer's consent. (Para. 2, FRS 9.)

'Joint venture' is one of those terms that is in common usage, but which does not have a very precise meaning. Many entities and arrangements may be described as joint ventures, but they will not fall within the definition given in FRS 9 (including some which are covered by FRS 9 but are described in other ways, such as some associates). Therefore, when the term is used it will always be important to be clear exactly what is meant. This situation is not helped by the fact that IAS 31 *Financial Reporting of Interests in Joint Ventures* defines a joint venture in terms of a contractual arrangement. Three types of joint ventures are identified: jointly controlled operations, jointly controlled assets and jointly controlled entities. Only the last qualifies as a joint venture under FRS 9. In financial statements, it is best if the term is avoided unless it refers to an entity which falls within the definition of FRS 9.

Joint control means, in effect, that every venturer has an element of control over (and almost more importantly a veto on) strategic decisions. Decisions can only be reached where all of the relevant parties agree.

21.9.4   Joint arrangements

The FRS also deals with arrangements that do not meet the definition of a joint venture, but in which two or more parties are involved. These are described as joint arrangements that are not an entity, and defined as:

> A contractual arrangement under which the participants engage in joint activities that do not create an entity because it would not be carrying on a trade or business of its own. A contractual arrangement where all significant matters of operating and financial policy are predetermined does not create an entity because the policies are those of its participants, not of a separate entity. (Para. 2, FRS 9.)

This is partly dependent upon the ASB's definition of an entity under FRS 9, which excludes any body which does not carry on a trade or business of its own, but which undertakes part of the trade or business of the other entities that have an interest in it.

Indications that an entity does not carry on its own business include:

- participants taking their share in kind, rather than a proportion of the trading results, and
- share of output being directly related to share on inputs rather than level of investment.

The accounting treatment for a joint arrangement that is not an entity is simply that each party should account for its own share of assets, liabilities, income, expenditure and cash flows. This also applies to any entity that is structured so as to appear to be a joint venture, but which is in fact used by each participant to carry on its own business. The example given in the FRS is that of a property development joint venture, which may often amount to nothing more than an extension of the activities of each of the companies involved. IAS 31 would classify these arrangements as either jointly controlled assets or operations. However, the accounting treatment in IAS 31 is the same as in FRS 9.

The accounting treatment of joint arrangements under FRS 9 is the same in both the investing company and group accounts. It is possible for a joint arrangement to be conducted through the medium of a company. Such arrangements are, for example, common in the construction industry. In these situations, the participants in the arrangement are required by FRS 9 to include in their financial statements their share of the underlying assets, liabilities and results, rather than treating their stake in the arrangement simply as a fixed asset investment. This method, sometimes called 'direct accounting', is similar to proportional consolidation. The main difference is that it is applied in the individual company as well as in consolidated financial statements.

The difference in terminology between FRS 9 and IAS 31 is summarised below.

Terminology and treatments of joint ventures and arrangements

FRS 9	IAS 31	Treatment
Venture	Entities	IAS 31 benchmark is proportional consolidation, but equity method of FRS 9 is allowed alternative
Arrangement	Operations, assets	Recognise directly in both FRS 9 and IAS 31

21.9.5 *Accounting for associates*

In individual company accounts, associates should normally be treated in exactly the same way as all other fixed-asset investments. That is, they should be stated at cost less any amounts which have been written off, or at a valuation. As noted above, this does not always apply in the case of companies which do not prepare group accounts, as larger individual companies should present either separate financial statements including their associates or present the information by way of note to their individual financial statements.

The accounting treatment required for associates in group accounts continues to be equity accounting. FRS 9, however, has significantly enhanced the disclosure associated with the use of this method. A number of items need to be shown separately either on the face of the primary financial statements or in the notes. A phrase previously often used to describe equity accounting was 'one-line consolidation'. With the advent of FRS 9, this is no longer an accurate description of the method, as its affects far more than one line.

Where there is a difference between the balance sheet date of the group and that of one of its associates, ideally, the associate should produce special financial statements up to the group's accounting date. Where this cannot be done, in general, accounts to another period that ended not more than three months prior to the group accounting date may be used. Where the use of financial statements prepared at this date would involve the release of restricted price-sensitive information, then accounts as at a date not more than six months before the group accounting date are acceptable. The FRS does not allow, in any cases, accounts to be used that were prepared to a date more than six months prior to the group accounting date.

Where different accounting dates are used, any changes in the intervening period which would have a material effect on the group accounts should be included in the group accounts by way of adjustment. The FRS does not give any example of such items, but examples might include exceptional items in the associate, such as plant closure.

One issue that can arise with associates is that of access to information. As the FRS points out, this is not a problem with subsidiaries since there is control and information can be obtained. With associates there is only influence so it may be more difficult to obtain all of the information that the group might like, and some degree of estimation may be needed. However, the FRS then goes on to draw the obvious conclusion from this, that if the access to information is severely limited then this calls into question the level of influence that the group actually has, and may lead to a reassessment of the treatment of the investment. If a group cannot get relevant financial information, does it really have influence?

In group accounts, the investor should include in the consolidated profit and loss account:

- its share of the associate's operating results (after the group operating results, but before the share of results of joint ventures);
- amortisation or write-down of any goodwill connected with the acquisition of the associates, disclosed separately;
- its share of any exceptional items in the associate's accounts which are disclosed after operating profit;
- its share of the associate's interest receivable and payable, and
- its share of any other categories in the associate's profit and loss account, after interest.

The FRS mentions that it may be useful to provide a combined total of the turnover of the group together with its share of the turnover of its associates. However, where this is done then the group turnover must be very clearly distinguished from the combined figure, as it is the group figure that is required for the purposes of the statutory consolidation. In addition, the FRS makes it clear that where a segmental analysis of turnover and operating profit is provided, this should very clearly distinguish between the amounts which are attributable to the group and the amounts attributable to the group's associates.

Where there is a profit on a transaction between an associate and a member of the group, to the extent that any amount remains included in assets, the group's share of that profit should be eliminated. This is basically the same treatment as with a subsidiary, except of course that with a subsidiary it is the whole of the profit that is eliminated.

The group statement of total recognised gains and losses should also include the group's share of the gains and losses of any associates. Where material, the amounts attributable to associates should be shown separately, either on the face of the statement or in a note.

The group cash flow statement should contain dividends received from associates as a separate item between operating activities and returns on investments and servicing of finance. This is a change from the revised version of FRS 1. If there are any other transactions with the associates giving rise to cash flows then these should be included within the appropriate cash flow heading. The other cash flows of the associates should not be included.

The group balance sheet should include the group's share of the net assets of its associates, shown as a separate item in the notes. The carrying amount should include any unamortised goodwill attributable to the acquisition of the associate, but this should be disclosed separately in a note. The goodwill on the acquisition of an associate should be calculated in exactly the same way as with a subsidiary. The treatment of any goodwill that is identified should also be treated as with subsidiaries. Reference should be made to the section on goodwill earlier in this chapter.

There should not normally be any need to consider making a write-down of the carrying value of an associate's net assets due to impairment, as this should have been done at the level of the associate's own accounts. However, where there is any unamortised goodwill connected with an associate then the same procedures as are used for a subsidiary should be applied. Where there is a write-down due to impairment this should be disclosed in the notes to the accounts.

Where an associate has a net deficiency, this should still be reflected in the group accounts. The only exception is where the investor has clearly demonstrated that it is no longer involved in the enterprise. An example of such an event might be a public statement to that effect. There may also be a problem with unincorporated associates, as the investor's share of liabilities may exceed its normal proportion, for example, where there is joint and several liability. In this case, a prudent view should be taken, which may involve accounting for more than the investor's proportion of balances or, more commonly, disclosure of a contingent liability.

21.9.6 *Accounting for joint ventures*

The accounting treatment required for joint ventures is described as the gross equity method. As the name suggests, this is similar to the method used for associates, but with some of the items shown as two separate figures rather than net. The benchmark treatment for jointly controlled entities in IAS 31 is proportional consolidation, although the equity method is an allowed alternative.

The accounting treatment for joint ventures in a company's own financial statements is exactly the same as that for an associate, with the investment stated at cost (less amounts written off) and income restricted to items such as dividends.

In group accounts, the same accounting treatment should be adopted as for associates, except that:

- the group's share of its joint ventures' turnover should be shown (rather than may be as with associates), although again there is a requirement that this should be distinguished from the turnover of the group, and
- the consolidated balance sheet should disclose the gross assets and gross liabilities underlying the net amount attributable to joint ventures.

As with associates, any items in the profit and loss account or balance sheet relating to joint ventures should be very clearly separated from those for the group. There is also an identical treatment to that for associates for joint ventures with a net deficiency. The losses and liabilities should continue to be recorded, unless the investor has irrevocably demonstrated that it has effectively withdrawn from the joint venture.

The FRS suggests that a columnar presentation may be useful for joint ventures, but does not require this.

The main format for the disclosure of associates and joint ventures in the consolidated accounts is given in FRS 9 and is illustrated below.

EXAMPLE

Consolidated profit and loss account

	£m	£m
Turnover: group and share of joint ventures	*320*	
Less: share of joint ventures' turnover	*(120)*	
Group turnover		200
Cost of sales		(120)
Gross profit		80
Administrative expenses		(40)
Group operating profit		40
Income from interests in associated undertakings		
Joint ventures	*30*	
Associates	*24*	
		54
		94
Interest receivable (group)		6
Interest payable		
Group	(26)	
Joint ventures	*(10)*	
Associates	(12)	
		(48)
Profit on ordinary activities before tax		52
Tax on profit on ordinary activities (Note 1)		(12)
Profit on ordinary activities after tax		40
Minority interests		(6)
Profit on ordinary activities after taxation and minority interests		34
Equity dividends		(10)
Retained profit for group and its share of associates and joint ventures		24

Note 1:

The tax relates to the following:	£m
Parent and subsidiaries	(5)
Joint ventures	*(5)*
Associates	*(2)*

The consolidated profit and loss account shows (in italic) the disclosures for the group's share in its joint ventures and associated undertakings. Since the gross equity method is used for joint ventures, turnover is included and disclosed separately. For both joint ventures and associates, the operating profit, interest and tax arising are

---

added to the group figures. Consequently, the retained profit figure relates to the group and its share of joint ventures and associates.

Consolidated balance sheet

	£m	£m	£m
Fixed assets			
Tangible assets		480	
Investments			
Interests in associated undertakings			
Investments in joint ventures			
Share of gross assets	*130*		
Share of gross liabilities	*(80)*		
	50		
Investments in associates	*20*		
		550	
Current assets			
Stock	15		
Debtors	75		
Cash at bank and in hand	10		
	100		
Creditors (due within one year)	(50)		
Net current assets		50	
Total assets less current liabilities		600	
Creditors (due after more than one year)		(250)	
Provisions for liabilities and charges		(10)	
Equity minority interest		(40)	
		300	
Capital and reserves			
Called up share capital		50	
Share premium account		150	
Profit and loss account		100	
Shareholders' funds (all equity)		300	

The consolidated balance sheet shows (in italic) the disclosures for the group's share in its joint ventures and associated undertakings. Since the gross equity method is used for joint ventures, the investment is shown as the difference between gross assets and gross liabilities.

21.9.7 *Change of status*

There are slightly different rules for when an investment becomes an associate or a joint venture. An entity becomes an associate when:

- the investor holds a participating interest, and
- significant influence starts to be exercised.

Both tests need to be satisfied before an investment is treated as an associate.

In the case of a joint venture, the relevant date is that from which the investor begins to control the entity jointly with other venturers, on the condition that it has a long-term interest. This would exclude, for example, involvement in a start-up where there is no intention that such control should be exercised on an ongoing basis, and there is an intention of disposal.

An investment ceases to be an associate where either condition ceases to be satisfied. Where, for example, a company disposes of part of its investment, this will often be clear. The loss of significant influence may be less easy to identify and could take place where there has been no change in the actual shareholding. However, in this case there will need to be a clear event giving rise to the loss of significant influence, such as the consolidation of other interests in the company.

An investment ceases to be a joint venture at the date at which joint control is no longer exercised. The FRS points out that one of the possibilities is that a joint venture becomes an associate, as control declines to significant influence.

The profit or loss on the disposal of an interest in a joint venture or associate should be calculated by taking into account any unamortised goodwill.

Piecemeal acquisitions and disposals of joint ventures and associates should be dealt with in the same way as piecemeal acquisition and disposals of subsidiaries, dealt with earlier at **21.6.5**.

Where an interest is retained, even though an investment ceases to be an associate or joint venture, the new book value should be based on the percentage holding retained and the carrying value of the investment prior to the change, including any unamortised goodwill. This amount should be reviewed in future years, and written down if appropriate. This treatment means that former associates and joint ventures will usually be carried at above cost, but avoids the problem of taking a charge to profits on disposal of part of an interest, even where there has been an increase in value.

21.9.8 Disclosure

Some disclosures have already been mentioned in respect of associates and joint ventures. Additional disclosures for all associates and joint ventures are as follows.

(1) The names of the principal associates and joint ventures, showing for each associate and joint venture:

    (a) the proportion of the issued shares in each class held by the investing group, indicating any special rights or constraints attaching to them;

    (b) the accounting period or date of the financial statements, if they differ from those of the investing group, and

    (c) an indication of the nature of its business.

(2) Any notes relating to the financial statements of associates and joint ventures, or matters that would have been noted had the investor's accounting policies been applied, that are material to understanding the effect on the investor of its investments. In particular, noting the investor's share in contingent liabilities incurred jointly with other venturers or investors and its share of the capital commitments of the associates and joint ventures themselves.

(3) If there are significant statutory, contractual or exchange control restrictions on the ability of an associate or joint venture to distribute its reserves (other than those shown as non-distributable), the extent of the restrictions.

(4) The amounts owing and owed between an investor and its associates or its joint ventures should be analysed into amounts relating to loans and amounts relating to trading balances. (This may be combined with those required by FRS 8.)

(5) An explanation of any case where the presumption that a 20 per cent holding constitutes an associate, or a participating interest has been rebutted.

There are also additional disclosures where associates and joint ventures are very material, either in aggregate or individually.

In each case, the test should be applied by comparing the relevant amounts with the group's:

- gross assets;
- gross liabilities;
- turnover, and
- operating results (on a three-year average).

The group amounts should exclude the associate(s) or joint venture(s), as appropriate. Only one of the thresholds needs to be breached for disclosure to be required.

Where the investor's aggregate share in associates exceeds 15 per cent of the group amounts, the notes should disclose the aggregate of the group's share in its associates:

- turnover (unless already included as a memorandum item);
- fixed assets;
- current assets;
- liabilities due within one year, and
- liabilities due after one year or more.

Where the investor's aggregate share in its joint ventures exceeds 15 per cent of the group amounts, the notes should disclose the aggregate of the group's share in its joint ventures:

- fixed assets;
- current assets;
- liabilities due within one year, and
- liabilities due after one year or more.

Where the investor's share in any individual associate or joint venture exceeds 25 per cent of the group amounts, a note should name that associate or joint venture and give its share of each of the following:

- turnover;
- profit before tax;
- taxation;
- profit after tax;
- fixed assets;
- current assets;
- liabilities due within one year, and
- liabilities due after one year or more.

If that individual associate or joint venture accounts for nearly all of the amounts included for that class of investment, only the aggregate individual information need be given, provided that this is explained and the associate or joint venture identified.

Further analysis of each item should be given where this is necessary to understand the nature of the total amounts disclosed.

In deciding into which balance sheet headings amounts should be analysed, regard should be had to the nature of the businesses and, therefore, which are the most relevant and descriptive balance sheet amounts to disclose. It may be important to give an indication of the size and maturity profile of the liabilities held.

22 SMALL COMPANY AND ABBREVIATED ACCOUNTS

22.1 INTRODUCTION

22.1.1 Financial statements for shareholders in small companies

Small company accounting can be quite different to that applied by larger companies. The ASB has issued various versions of its *Financial Reporting Standard for Smaller Entities* (FRSSE). Small companies are also entitled to produce accounts in accordance with Sch. 1 to The Small Companies and Groups (Accounts and Directors' Report) Regulations 2008 (SI 2008/409). This contains a number of requirements that differ from the requirements applicable to larger and medium-sized companies , with most of the differences being reductions in the disclosure requirements.

There is a version of the FRSSE, effective April 2008, which is intended to cover the changes introduced by the Companies Act 2006 and the associated statutory instruments. The effective date is, as for the legislation, accounting periods beginning on or after 6 April 2008.

The details of the simplifications which are allowed in each reporting area are given in the chapter where the topic is discussed. The objective of this present chapter is to summarise the exemptions available for small companies across the reporting areas, in order to give an overall view of the situation.

The changes available are voluntary. Some small companies may decide that they wish to use the rules which apply to larger companies. This is most likely where they are part of a group or where they are expecting expansion, such that the period for which they expect to be entitled to the exemptions is limited.

Potential impact of the FRSME

At least, to start with, the FRSME would have no impact on small companies (unless they chose to adopt it) since the ASB is proposing that the FRSSE continue to be available. Whether or not this situation would continue in the longer run is another matter, and is addressed in Chapter 24.

22.1.2 Small and medium-sized company accounts for filing with the Registrar

In addition to the exemptions available to small companies for reporting to their shareholders, further exemptions are available to small companies when filing their accounts with the Registrar of Companies. Medium-sized companies also have their own separate exemptions when filing accounts with the Registrar.

Small and medium-sized companies do not generally undertake as wide a range of activities as larger companies. Therefore, the annual report and accounts of such companies may provide competitors with unusually detailed information about their operations. The main intention of allowing companies to file abbreviated accounts is to limit the size of this problem. Abbreviated accounts are dealt with in **22.5**.

For small companies, the Companies Act 2006 also allows small companies to file their accounts without a directors' report and profit and loss account. The details that do need to be included in accounts filed in this way are far from clear. Given that the balance sheet filed must be a 'full' balance sheet, this necessarily implies that any notes which sub-analyse the amounts on the face of the actual balance sheet, and cover the matters dealt with in the statutory format, must be provided. Beyond this, little is certain. As the balance sheet needs to be 'full' it seems unlikely that there was any intention to allow companies taking this option to file any less than is required in small company abbreviated accounts which include an abbreviated balance sheet. But even this is not made clear anywhere in the primary or secondary legislation which currently does not set out the contents of accounts filed in accordance with the new provisions. This issue may be clarified through further secondary legislation. Perhaps strangely, the one matter that is clear is the impact on the audit report, if an audit has been undertaken. Where there has been an audit, the full audit report must be filed, even though this will refer to information that is not included in the accounts provided. A preface to the audit report, explaining the situation, is suggested by the Auditing Practices Board in Bulletin 2008/4.

22.2 SIZE LIMITS FOR SMALL AND MEDIUM-SIZED COMPANIES

22.2.1 Basic limits

The size limits for small and medium-sized companies apply for the purposes of entitlement to prepare abbreviated accounts and, in the case of small companies, for entitlement to the exemptions available in respect of the financial statements to be submitted to the members, including the adoption of the FRSSE.

For accounting periods beginning on or after 6 April 2008, in order for a company to qualify as small, it should not exceed more than one of the following limits.

Turnover	£6.5 million
Balance sheet total	£3.26 million
Employees	50

The limits that apply for a medium-sized company are:

Turnover	£25.9 million
Balance sheet total	£12.9 million
Employees	250

In all cases, the figure for turnover needs to be proportionally adjusted if the accounting period is longer or shorter than one year. The 'balance sheet total' is effectively the gross assets of the company, without the deduction of any amounts for liabilities.

Even if a company qualifies under the size limits, it will still not be entitled to the exemptions unless it meets the additional conditions and does not fall foul of the general restrictions set out below.

22.2.2   Additional conditions

The entitlement to prepare abbreviated accounts (and to all other exemptions available to a small company) is only available to a company if it meets two out of the following three conditions.

- It qualifies under the size limits this year.
- It qualified under the size limits in the preceding financial year.
- It was entitled to the exemption in the preceding financial year.

If a company qualifies under the size limits in its first financial year, it is deemed to have met the size limits in the preceding year, and is, therefore, entitled to prepare abbreviated accounts in its first year.

The effect of these rules is that there is normally a one-year delay before a company is entitled to prepare abbreviated accounts, or before it loses the benefit of the provisions. This does not, of course, apply in the first few years of a company's existence, when slightly different rules are used.

22.2.3   General restrictions

Certain companies are not defined as small or medium-sized companies, even though they may fall within the size limits.

A company cannot be small if:

- it is a parent company, and the group which it heads is not a small group;
- it is a public company;
- it is an authorised insurance company, a banking company, an e-money issuer, a MiFID investment firm or a UCITS management company, or if
- it is a member of a group containing:

  - a public company;
  - a body corporate (which is not a company) whose shares are admitted to trading on a regulated market in an EEA state;
  - a person (unless that person is a small company) who has permission under Part 4 of the Financial Services and Markets Act 2000 to carry on a regulated activity;
  - a small company that is an authorised insurance company, a banking company, an e-money issuer, a MiFID investment firm or a UCITS management company, or
  - a person who carries on an insurance market activity.

A company cannot be medium sized if:

- it is a parent company, and the group which it heads is not a medium-sized group;
- it is a public company;
- it has permission under Part 4 of the Financial Services and Markets Act 2000 to carry on a regulated activity;
- it carries on an insurance market activity, or
- it is a member of a group containing:

  - a public company;
  - a body corporate (which is not a company) whose shares are admitted to trading on a regulated market;
  - a person (unless that person is a small company) who has permission under Part 4 of the Financial Services and Markets Act 2000 to carry on a regulated activity;
  - a small company that is an authorised insurance company, a banking company, an e-money issuer, a MiFID investment firm or a UCITS management company, or
  - a person who carries on an insurance market activity.

22.3 SMALL COMPANY STATUTORY EXEMPTIONS

22.3.1 *Conditions for statutory exemptions*

If a small company wishes to take advantage of the exemptions available to it in respect of either its annual accounts or its directors' report then there must be a statement from the directors (in a prominent position on the balance sheet or in the report, as appropriate) that they have been prepared in accordance with the exemptions available to small companies under the Companies Act 2006.

22.3.2 Accounting exemptions

The accounting exemptions available to small companies are extensive and have been dealt with in individual chapters. These affect both the basic formats on which the accounts are based, and the level of detail required in the notes. As with the directors' report, small companies need not take advantage of all of the exemptions and may pick and choose which ones they wish to use.

Small companies are entitled to use shorter balance sheet formats, which combine many items treated separately under the normal rules of the Companies Act 2006. Taking format 1 as an example, small companies only need to give the following classifications and sub-classifications taken from Sch. 1 to The Small Companies and Groups (Accounts and Directors' Report) Regulations 2008 (SI 2008/409):

(A) Called up share capital not paid

(B) Fixed assets

    (I) Intangible assets

        (1) Goodwill

        (2) Other intangible assets

    (II) Tangible assets

        (1) Land and buildings

        (2) Plant and machinery, etc.

    (III) Investments

        (1) Shares in group undertakings and participating interests

        (2) Loans to group undertakings and undertakings in which the company has a participating interest

        (3) Other investments other than loans

        (4) Other investments

(C) Current assets

    (I) Stocks

        (1) Stocks

        (2) Payments on account

    (II) Debtors

        (1) Trade debtors

        (2) Amounts owed by group undertakings and undertakings in which the company has a participating interest

        (3) Other debtors

   (III) Investments

        (1) Shares in group undertakings

        (2) Other investments

   (IV) Cash at bank and in hand

(D)   Pre-payments and accrued income
(E)   Creditors: amounts falling due within one year

   (1) Bank loans and overdrafts

   (2) Trade creditors

   (3) Amounts owed to group undertakings and undertakings in which the company has a participating interest

   (4) Other creditors

(F)   Net current assets (liabilities)
(G)   Total assets less current liabilities
(H)   Creditors: amounts falling due after more than one year

   (1) Bank loans and overdrafts

   (2) Trade creditors

   (3) Amounts owed to group undertakings and undertakings in which the company has a participating interest

   (4) Other creditors

(I)   Provisions for liabilities
(J)   Accruals and deferred income
(K)   Capital and reserves

   (I)   Called up share capital
   (II)   Share premium account
   (III)   Revaluation reserve
   (IV)   Other reserves
   (V)   Profit and loss account

Similar changes are made to format 2. Taking intangible fixed assets as an example, small companies now only need to distinguish between goodwill and all other intangibles; larger companies must analyse intangibles between four separate categories.

22.4 THE FRSSE

In November 1997, the ASB issued the first Financial Reporting Standard for Smaller Entities. This replaced most other accounting standards and UITF pronouncements for companies which met the small size limits set out in companies legislation, or unincorporated entities which would have done so if they had been incorporated.

Since the publication of the original FRSSE, six updated versions have been issued. These are referred to as the FRSSE (effective March 1999), the FRSSE (effective March 2000), the FRSSE (effective June 2002), the FRSSE (effective January 2005), the FRSSE (effective January 2007) and the FRSSE (effective April 2008). The current version of the FRSSE is the April 2008 version, which applies to accounting periods beginning on or after 6 April 2008. Unless otherwise indicated, all references in this chapter are to the latest version of the FRSSE. The updates have not been fundamental revisions of the standard, and have not altered its basic purpose or status. Instead, the updates have taken account of relevant guidance that had been published since the previous last edition of the FRSSE had been issued, and incorporated this into the FRSSE in a way that was considered appropriate for small companies. The latest edition of the FRSSE is slightly different, in that it was primarily intended to take account of the changes introduced by the Companies Act 2006 rather than changes in accounting standards.

In effect, the FRSSE is a cut-down version of previous reporting requirements for companies. The simplest way of seeing the difference is to compare the FRSSE with the content of other accounting standards and other pronouncements.

Where a company prepares its financial statements in accordance with the FRSSE, the financial statements should state this. The FRSSE requires that this statement makes it clear which edition of the revised FRSSE has been adopted, for example: 'The financial statements have been prepared in accordance with the Financial Reporting Standard for Smaller Entities (effective April 2008)'. In practice, such a statement is usually included on the face of the balance sheet, together with the statutory statement required where the provisions applicable to smaller companies have been adopted. However, the statement that the FRSSE has been adopted (but not the statutory statement) may instead be included in the accounting policies note. Where abbreviated accounts are prepared, which are derived from financial statements for shareholders based on the FRSSE, the FRSSE adoption statement should go in the accounting policies note so that it is automatically reproduced in the abbreviated accounts.

The following notes summarise some of the ways in which the FRSSE has been simplified from the full accounting standards on which it is ultimately based.

SSAP 4 Accounting for Government Grants

A simplified version of the introductory paragraph is included. This omits reference to the treatment that should be adopted for amounts intended to reimburse previous expenditure or to meet current needs. This is unlikely to give rise to any difference in accounting treatment.

The FRSSE does not refer to the need for a company to state its accounting policy for government grants, but this is covered by the general statutory requirement.

There is no reference to the need to disclose potential liabilities to repay grants. This will have no effect in practice, since the requirement is covered by FRS 12 and the relevant disclosure requirement has been incorporated into the FRSSE.

SSAP 5 Accounting for Value Added Tax

SSAP 5 is not covered in the FRSSE.

SSAP 9 Stocks and Long-Term Contracts

There is no reference made to the need to state the accounting policy, and apply it consistently. These are, however, both statutory requirements.

SSAP 13 Accounting for Research and Development

There is no reference to the fact that companies are allowed to capitalise assets which are used for the purposes of pure and applied research. In most cases, any companies affected would wish to continue to capitalise such assets.

There is no reference to the need to disclose and explain the accounting policy. Again, this is a statutory requirement.

There is no requirement to disclose the amount that has been charged to the profit and loss account in respect of research and development. This was not a change when the FRSSE was introduced, as all small companies had already been exempt from such disclosure.

There is no stated requirement to disclose movements on deferred development expenditure, and the amount carried forward at the beginning and end of the period. Since such expenditure would be treated as a fixed asset, under statute, there will be a requirement for this information to be disclosed.

SSAP 19 Accounting for Investment Properties

There is no reference to investment companies, property unit trusts, insurance companies or pension funds.

There is no requirement to display the carrying value of investment properties and the investment revaluation reserve prominently on the face of the financial statements. The carrying value of investment properties should be shown prominently either on the face of the balance sheet or in the notes to the accounts.

SSAP 20 Foreign Currency Translation

There is no provision for restricting exchange gains taken to the profit and loss account on long-term monetary items where there is doubt as to the marketability or convertibility of the currency.

There are no references to hyperinflation.

There is no reference to the need to disclose the accounting policy, although this remains a statutory requirement.

There is no requirement to disclose foreign exchange gains and losses charged or credited to the profit and loss account or offset in reserves under the hedging provisions in respect of foreign currency borrowings less deposits.

There is no requirement to disclose movements on reserves arising from exchange differences. This is still an effective requirement under statute.

SSAP 21 Accounting for Leases and Hire Purchase Contracts

For a finance lease, the FRSSE requires that the amount capitalised be the fair value of the assets and not the present value of the minimum lease payments, unless this is demonstrably inappropriate.

Where grants are received in respect of an asset held under a finance lease, there is no requirement that the amount capitalised be restricted to the minimum lease payments.

For lessors, gross earnings under operating leases should be recognised on a systematic and rational basis, but no further guidance is given.

No reference is made to the treatment of direct costs incurred by a lessor in arranging a lease.

The treatment of accounting for sale and leaseback arrangements is amended in line with the treatment for lessors.

There is no requirement to show the depreciation for the period in respect of assets held under finance leases.

There is no requirement to break down the total of finance lease obligations between amounts in the next year, two to five years, and more than five years.

The total will still need to be shown, together with the amount payable within one year.

There is no requirement to break down operating lease commitments in the next year according to their expiry. However, there is a requirement to show the total of operating lease commitments.

There is no requirement to show finance lease charges and operating lease rentals separately in a note to the profit and loss account. The second change reflects a change in the law.

There is no reference to the requirement to show the accounting policies adopted, although this will still be required by statute.

There is no requirement to show the aggregate rentals receivable by lessors.

There is no definition of the interest rate implicit in a lease.

SSAP 25 Segmental Reporting

The FRSSE contains nothing on segmental reporting. Given the exemptions, and the fact that such disclosure is essentially voluntary, this will make little difference.

FRS 1 Cash Flow Statements

There is no requirement for a cash flow statement, although the FRSSE recommends that a summary cash flow statement be prepared. This need not be in the format required by FRS 1 and need only cover the main areas of cash inflows and outflows.

FRS 2 Accounting for Subsidiary Undertakings

This is not covered, but companies will have to comply with FRS 2 if they choose to prepare group accounts.

FRS 3 Reporting Financial Performance

There is no requirement to analyse the turnover, costs and results between continuing, acquired and discontinued operations.

There is no reference to decisions to sell or terminate an operation and the provisions that may be recognised.

There is no requirement to disclose special circumstances affecting the tax on exceptional items which are required to be shown on the face of the profit and loss account.

There is no statement on how to calculate the tax on exceptional and extraordinary items.

There is no reference to earnings per share, which such companies are not required to disclose anyway.

There is no requirement for a note of historical cost profits and losses.

There is no requirement for a 'negative' statement where there are no gains and losses other than those in the profit and loss account.

There is no requirement for a note reconciling movements in shareholders' funds.

There is no reference to comparatives.

There are no references to investment companies or insurance businesses.

FRS 4 Capital Instruments

Most of FRS 4 has been omitted. The FRSSE retains:

- the requirement to allocate finance costs at a constant rate of charge on the carrying amount, and
- the requirement to account for dividends on a time basis, where entitlement is assessed by reference to time, and to account for dividends as an appropriation of profit.

Issue costs under FRS 4 have been described as arrangement fees, and excluded from the definition of finance costs.

The definition of capital instruments has been changed to make specific reference to 'arrangements entered into' as well as instruments being 'issued'.

FRS 5 Reporting the Substance of Transactions

FRS 5 is not covered, except that:

- there is a general requirement to account in accordance with the substance of transactions;
- reference is made to FRS 5 in respect of group accounts, if group accounts are being prepared;
- debt factoring has been covered, and
- the definition of recognition has been included in the FRSSE.

FRS 6 Acquisitions and Mergers

This is not addressed, but would need to be followed if group accounts were produced.

FRS 7 Fair Values in Acquisition Accounting

This is not addressed, but would need to be followed if group accounts were produced.

FRS 8 Related Party Disclosures

There is no exemption from disclosure of pension contributions paid to a pension fund.

Materiality is only assessed by reference to the company.

There is a clarification to the effect that disclosure is required of personal guarantees given by directors in respect of the company's borrowings.

FRS 9 Associates and Joint Ventures

The FRSSE does not address FRS 9, except where group accounts are being prepared, in which case FRS 9 would need to be followed. The individual company aspects of FRS 9, ie treatment of associates, joint ventures and joint arrangements in the investing company's accounts, have not been incorporated into the FRSSE. This is unlikely to have any significant impact except where a company holds an investment in an incorporated joint arrangement. In such cases, there is no requirement to include the investor's share of the joint arrangement's assets, liabilities and cash flows. Instead, the investment may be shown simply at cost, less any impairment.

FRS 10 Goodwill and Intangible Assets

For individual company accounts, a simplified version of FRS 10 has been incorporated into the FRSSE. The main differences are as follows.

- Internally generated intangible assets should not be capitalised (even in the limited number of cases in which FRS 10 would permit this).
- There is an absolute prohibition on useful lives exceeding 20 years (unlike FRS 10), which also means that no automatic annual impairment reviews will be required.
- Intangible assets may not be revalued (even in the cases allowed by FRS 10).

As with FRS 10, there are transitional provisions meaning companies may (but are not required to) reinstate goodwill previously written off to reserves. Unlike FRS 10, there is only one date at which this option may be applied, which is the implementation date of the changes.

Where group accounts are being prepared, FRS 10 must be applied insofar as it applies to purchased goodwill arising on consolidation, but need not otherwise be applied.

FRS 11 Impairment of Fixed Assets and Goodwill

For individual company accounts, the FRSSE includes the main principles of FRS 11 concerning the requirements for impairment write-downs and reversals, but omits all of the detail. No reference is made to income-generating units and there is no guidance on how to calculate recoverable amount, other than a restatement of the definition from FRS 11. This appears to leave open the possibility of using a more flexible approach to estimating value in use than would be permitted under FRS 11. However, the central point is still the same and it is difficult to see how applying these requirements would give an answer significantly different to that obtained by following FRS 11. The FRSSE, following FRS 11, does not allow the recoverable amount to be based on net realisable value in circumstances where FRS 11 would not allow this.

Where group accounts are prepared, FRS 11 must be applied to purchased goodwill arising on consolidation, as required by FRS 10.

FRS 12 Provisions, Contingent Liabilities and Contingent Assets

The FRSSE contains simplified versions of the rules applicable under FRS 12. There are no significant differences in respect of contingent assets and liabilities.

The FRSSE does not make reference to financial instruments, executory contracts or insurance entities (which are not entitled to use the FRSSE, as noted above).

There is no reference to cases where it is not clear whether or not there is a present obligation.

There is no reference to taking risks, uncertainties and future events into account when measuring a provision. In practice, this is likely to have far less effect than it might appear, since it is not realistic that these factors will be ignored when small companies consider the basis on which they will determine the amounts of any provisions they may require.

The detailed rules on the determination of discount rates for calculating the amount of provisions have been omitted, although the principle remains.

There is no restriction that the amount of reimbursements must not exceed the amount of the provisions to which they relate.

There is no reference to the fact that some provisions may also give rise to the capitalisation of an asset.

There is no reference to future operating losses, onerous contracts, restructuring or the sale of an operation. The most contentious omission is probably the reference to onerous contracts. FRS 12 requires that provisions be made in cases where there is an onerous contract in circumstances where they would not otherwise be allowed. While it is possible to arrive at this conclusion directly from the definitions of liabilities and provisions, it is not perhaps an area that might be apparent to all of those involved in the preparation of small company financial statements. There is little doubt that the treatments required by the FRSSE are intended to be the same as those required by FRS 12, but it is questionable whether this will occur in practice.

The disclosures required in respect of provisions are omitted, with reliance being placed upon the statutory disclosures.

FRS 13 Derivatives and other Financial Instruments: Disclosures

This is not addressed. FRS 13 applies only to a very small number of much larger companies.

FRS 15 Tangible Fixed Assets

The FRSSE incorporates the principles of the FRS, but includes a number of simplifications. Many of these, however, cover areas which are unlikely to arise particularly often for smaller companies and the practical effect of the exemptions is therefore rather less than the length of the list of differences might suggest.

There is no reference to start-up or commissioning periods.

There is no reference to when the capitalisation of finance costs should commence.

There is no reference to tangible fixed assets which are constructed in parts.

There is no reference to major inspections or overhauls, and the treatment of the expenditure incurred on such items.

The bases for revaluation have been simplified, and there is simply a statement that this should normally be at market value or a best estimate of this amount (with exceptions where current value may be more appropriate). All the detail in the FRS on how assets, primarily properties, should be valued is missing. This introduces considerably more flexibility into small company reporting.

There is no reference to the situation where it is impossible to obtain a reliable valuation.

The treatment of revaluation losses is simplified from FRS 15.

There is no statement that, in determining the treatment of gains and losses, material gains and losses should not be aggregated. This may allow small companies to net off separate gains and losses in cases where this would not be acceptable for a larger company. (However, consideration still needs to be given to the statutory prohibition on netting off items.)

There is no reference to insurance companies and groups, although these are not entitled to use the FRSSE.

There is no statement that subsequent expenditure does not negate the need for an asset to be depreciated, although this is unlikely to give rise to any differences in practice.

There is no specific requirement for an annual impairment review of assets whose life exceeds 50 years or where depreciation has been omitted on the grounds that it is not material. This may make life a little easier for smaller companies who decide to rely upon these exemptions.

In place of the requirement to review residual values and useful economic lives annually, there is a requirement to review these regularly. There is also a somewhat vaguer statement on when a revision should be reflected in the financial statements.

There is no reference to renewals accounting.

The disclosure requirements are much reduced, and differ little from the statutory requirements.

FRS 16 Current Tax

There is no explicit prohibition of adjustments to income and expenses to reflect notional tax, although this does not mean that such a treatment would be acceptable.

There is no reference to the tax rates to be used for measuring current tax.

The disclosure requirements are simplified, and talk simply about the major components, without specifying what these are.

FRS 17 Retirement Benefits

Perhaps the greatest simplification from FRS 17 is in the effective date. The Appendix to the FRSSE that deals with FRS 17 matters delays the requirements of the main standard by a year. When the Appendix comes into force there are the following simplifications.

There is no reference to multi-employer schemes.

There is no explicit requirement to attribute benefits according to the scheme's benefits formula.

The requirement to reflect expected future events in actuarial assumptions has been omitted.

The detailed requirements on the treatment of a surplus have been omitted.

The detailed requirements relating to the treatment of gains and losses have been omitted.

The requirements relating to the recognition of current tax relief on contributions have been omitted.

Requirements relating to death-in-service and incapacity benefits have been omitted.

Many of the detailed disclosure requirements have been omitted.

FRS 18 Accounting Policies

The FRSSE omits much of FRS 18, particularly in areas where the basic requirements are covered in company's legislation.

There is no reference to adopting policies that enable the financial statements to give a true and fair view, since this is a requirement of company law.

There is no reference to departures from accounting standards in exceptional circumstances.

There is no reference to financial statements being prepared on a going concern basis, as this is again assumed by the legislation.

There is no reference to preparing financial statements on an accruals basis, as required by company law.

There is no reference to the constraints that should be taken into account in determining the appropriateness of accounting policies.

There is no reference to the need to select estimation techniques that enable the financial statements to give a true and fair view.

There are no specific requirements relating to accounting for changes in estimation techniques.

There is no disclosure requirement relating to significant estimation techniques.

There is no reference to SORPs.

There is no reference to the disclosure required when financial statements are not prepared on a going concern basis.

There is no reference to departures from accounting standards or companies legislation.

FRS 19 Deferred Tax

The requirement to provide deferred tax when assets are marked to market has been omitted.

Requirements relating to unremitted earnings of subsidiaries, associates and joint ventures have been omitted.

The detailed discounting requirements are replaced with a statement that if discounting is adopted it should be applied consistently.

The presentational requirements of FRS 19 have been omitted.

Most of the detailed disclosure requirements have been omitted.

FRS 20 Share-based Payment

The rules on cash settled share-based payments are the same as in FRS 20.

For equity settled share-based payments there is no requirement to account for the value of the rights granted, and the issue is dealt with solely through limited disclosure. The FRSSE therefore differs substantially from the underlying standard.

FRS 21 Events After the Balance Sheet date

There are no major differences, but the FRSSE does not contain a requirement to disclose any powers to amend the financial statements after the date of issue.

FRS 22 Earnings Per Share

This is not addressed in the current FRSSE, nor is it proposed that it be addressed in the future given that FRS 22 itself applies only to a small number of companies.

FRS 23 The Effects of Changes in Foreign Exchange Rates

This is not addressed in the current FRSSE, nor is it proposed that it be addressed in the future given that the standard applies only where FRS 26 is also being applied.

FRS 24 Financial Reporting in Hyperinflationary Economics

This is not addressed in the current FRSSE, nor is it proposed that it be addressed in the future given that the standard applies only where FRS 26 is also being applied.

FRS 25 Financial Instruments: Presentation

The basic presentation requirements of FRS 25 are included in the FRSSE.

FRS 26 Financial Instruments: Recognition and Measurement

This is not addressed in the current FRSSE, nor is it proposed that it be addressed in the future.

FRS 27 Life Assurance

This is not addressed in the FRSSE, nor will it be given that entities undertaking insurance market activities may not use the FRSSE.

FRS 28 Corresponding Amounts

This is reflected in the FRSSE and there are no differences of substance.

FRS 29 Financial Instruments: Disclosure

This is not addressed in the current FRSSE, nor is it proposed that it be addressed in the future.

FRS 30 Heritage Assets

This is not addressed in the current FRSSE, having been issued after the latest FRSSE was finalised.

UITF 4 Presentation of Long-Term Debtors in Current Assets

This is not addressed.

UITF 5 Transfers from Current Assets to Fixed Assets

This is not addressed.

UITF 9 Accounting for Operations in Hyper-Inflationary Economies

This is not addressed.

UITF 11 Capital Instruments: Issuer Call Options

This is not addressed.

UITF 15 Disclosure of Substantial Acquisitions

This is not addressed.

UITF 17 Employee Share Schemes

This is not addressed in the FRSSE.

UITF 19 Tax on Gains and Losses on Foreign Currency Borrowings that Hedge an Investment in a Foreign Enterprise

This is not addressed.

UITF 21 Accounting Issues Arising from the Proposed Introduction of the Euro

Only the basic accounting principle is incorporated into the updated FRSSE. The specific disclosure requirements are not included.

UITF 22 The Acquisition of a Lloyd's Business

This is not addressed.

UITF 23 Application of the Transitional Rules in FRS 15

This abstract was issued subsequent to the latest edition of the FRSSE and hence is not addressed. However, as the FRSSE includes the same transitional requirement, in relation to assets divided into components, as FRS 15, this abstract could be referred to for guidance if necessary.

UITF 24 Accounting for Start-up Costs

The principle of the UITF has been included in the FRSSE, but it lacks the detailed disclosures required by the abstract.

UITF 25 National Insurance Contributions on Share Option Gains

This is not addressed.

UITF 26 Barter Transactions for Advertising

This is not addressed.

UITF 27 Revision to Estimates of the Useful Economic Life of Goodwill and Intangible Assets

This is not addressed.

UITF 28 Operating Lease Incentives

The principle is included in the FRSSE, but there is no reference to spreading on any basis other than straight line, and no reference to investment properties or debtors.

UITF 29 Website Development Costs

This is not addressed.

UITF 30 Date of Award to Employees of Shares or Right to Shares

This is not addressed.

UITF 31 Exchanges of Business or Other Non-Monetary Assets for an Interest in a Subsidiary, Joint Venture or Associate

This is not addressed.

UITF 32 Employee Benefit Trusts and Other Intermediate Payment Arrangements

This is not addressed.

UITF 33 Obligations in Capital Instruments

This is not addressed.

UITF 34 Pre-Contract Costs

This is dealt with as in the underlying UITF, except that there is no reference to accounting by consortium members for the recovery of pre-contract costs from a special purpose entity.

UITF 35 Death-in-Service and Incapacity Benefits

This is not addressed.

UITF 36 Contracts for Sales of Capacity

This is not addressed.

UITF 37 Purchases and Sales of Own Shares

This is not addressed.

UITF 38 Accounting for ESOP Trusts

This is not addressed.

UITF 39 Members' Shares in Co-operative Entities and Similar Instruments

This is not addressed in the current FRSSE.

UITF 40 Revenue Recognition on Service Contracts

This is now fully addressed in the FRSSE.

UITF 41 Scope of FRS 20

This is not specifically addressed in the current FRSSE.

UITF 42 Reassessment of Embedded Derivatives

This is not addressed in the current FRSSE.

UITF 43 The Interpretation of Equivalence for the Purposes of Section 228A of the Companies Act 1985

This is not addressed in the current FRSSE.

UITF 44 FRS 20 (IFRS 2) Group and Treasury Share Transactions

This is not addressed in the current FRSSE.

UITF 45 Liabilities Arising from Participation in a Specific Market – Waste Electrical and Electronic Equipment

This is not addressed in the current FRSSE.

UITF 46 Hedges of a Net Investment in a Foreign Operation

This is not addressed in the current FRSSE. It was published after the 2008 FRSSE.

UITF 47 Extinguishing Financial Liabilities with Equity Instruments

This is not addressed in the current FRSSE. It was published after the 2008 FRSSE.

UITF 48 Accounting Implications of the Replacement of the Retail Prices Index with the Consumer Prices Index for Retirement Benefits

This is not addressed in the current FRSSE. It was published after the 2008 FRSSE.

22.5 ABBREVIATED ACCOUNTS

22.5.1 Conditions for preparation

Abbreviated accounts are not intended to give a true and fair view of the results or position of a company. In the case of a small company, they omit much of the information that would be necessary to enable the user to make a reasoned assessment; in the case of a medium-sized company, they have historically simply omitted one of the most important pieces of information. The main intention of the legislation is to enable small and medium-sized companies to ensure that the general public, including competitors, do not have access to information that may prejudice the interests of the business.

There is no intention to reduce the costs associated with the preparation of financial statements. Indeed the costs are almost certain to be higher, since the company must still prepare audited financial statements for circulation to the members of the company, and the abbreviated accounts are simply used for filing with the Registrar.

22.5.2 Small companies

Abbreviated small company accounts do not need to contain a profit and loss account, or a directors' report, although, as noted for accounting periods beginning on or after 6 April 2008, this applies for filing purposes even where a small company does not prepare abbreviated accounts. The balance sheet only needs to include limited items. Taking format 1 (probably the most common) as an example:

(A)   Called up share capital not paid
(B)   Fixed assets

    (I)   Intangible assets
    (II)   Tangible assets
    (III)   Investments

(C)   Current assets

    (I)   Stocks
    (II)   Debtors
    (III)   Investments
    (IV)   Cash at bank and in hand

(D)   Prepayments and accrued income
(E)   Creditors: amounts falling due within one year
(F)   Net current assets (liabilities)
(G)   Total assets less current liabilities
(H)   Creditors: amounts falling due after more than one year
(I)   Provisions for liabilities
(J)   Accruals and deferred income
(K)   Capital and reserves

    (I)   Called up share capital
    (II)   Share premium account
    (III)   Revaluation reserve
    (IV)   Other reserves
    (V)   Profit and loss account

The company is only required to include certain notes to the financial statements.

(1) The aggregate amount of debtors falling due after more than one year.

(2) The aggregate amount of creditors falling due within and after more than one year (if format 2 is adopted).

(3) Accounting policies.

(4) Details of authorised and allotted share capital including redeemable shares.

(5) Particulars of allotments of shares.

(6) Movements in the cost (or valuation) and depreciation accounts for fixed assets, but only as it affects the major categories. This means tangible and intangible fixed assets and fixed asset investments. For fixed assets investments stated at amounts in excess of their fair values, companies must disclose the carrying amount and fair value, and explain why no provision for diminution in value has been made.

(7) Details of indebtedness, excluding the terms of payment or repayment and interest.

(8) Basis of conversion of foreign currency amounts into sterling.

(9) Comparatives, but only for those items included in the abbreviated accounts.

(10) If the company is dormant and as such has not been subject to audit then it must also disclose that it has acted as agent for any person, were this is the case.

Where a small company is also a parent company it should provide the information required by Sch. 2 to The Small Companies and Groups (Accounts and Directors' Report) Regulations 2008 (SI 2008/409), except for:

- the financial years of subsidiary undertakings;
- details of qualifications in the auditors' reports on subsidiary undertakings;
- shares and debentures of the company held by subsidiary undertakings, and
- arrangements attracting merger relief.

The information normally required dealing with the disclosure of information about the emoluments of directors and others, pensions, and compensation for loss of office, need not be given. The information covering transactions with directors, including loans and quasi-loans, should be given without comparatives.

22.5.3 Medium-sized companies

The exemptions provided for medium-sized companies are far less extensive. Under the Companies Act 1985, they needed to disclose only the amount of their gross profit or loss, without showing the separate categories that have been used in arriving at this amount.

22. Small Company and Abbreviated Accounts

Under the Companies Act 2006, and therefore with effect for accounting periods beginning on or after 6 April 2008, medium-sized companies are required to disclose their turnover. Since this was often seen as the most beneficial exemption, this may mean that fewer companies take advantage of the exemptions.

However, abbreviated accounts are not required to give a true and fair view, and as a result accounting standards are not applicable. This has no impact on quantification, since the accounts on which they are based must comply with accounting standards, but does affect disclosure.

23 SUMMARY FINANCIAL STATEMENTS

23.1 INTRODUCTION

Summary financial statements were originally introduced by the Companies Act 1989, but at that time the option to issue them was limited to listed companies. Since then, there has been substantial change in the legislation. In particular, the law has been changed so that the option to produce summary financial statements is available to all companies and not just listed ones. It has to be said that very few unlisted companies have taken advantage of the opportunity, perhaps because of the additional costs involved in their production which, for many smaller companies, are not offset by any substantial potential savings.

The requirements are currently included in The Companies (Summary Financial Statements) Regulations 2008 (SI 2008/374).

23.2 CONDITIONS FOR PREPARATION

A company must meet the following criteria in order to qualify to provide such statements.

(1)   The full financial statements must have been subject to audit.

(2)   The provision of such a statement must not be prohibited by the company's memorandum or articles, or any other relevant document.

(3)   The member must not have indicated a wish for full financial statements.

(4)   The statements must be sent within the period allowed for laying and delivering full financial statements.

(5)   The summary (and the full financial statements) must have been approved by the board, and signed on its behalf by a director.

23.3 FORM AND CONTENT

The contents of summary financial statements are as follows.

(1)   A statement that they provide only a summary of information in the annual financial statements and, for a listed company, the directors' remuneration report.

(2)   A statement as to whether they contain additional information derived

from the directors' report and, if so, a statement that they provide only a summary of that report.

(3)   A statement as to how a person entitled to full financial statements can obtain a copy.

(4)   A statement by the company's auditors as to whether the summary financial statements are consistent with the annual financial statements, directors' remuneration report (if relevant) and directors' report (if such information is included) and that they comply with the relevant statutory requirements.

(5)   A statement as to whether the audit report on the full financial statements was unqualified or qualified and, if qualified, a copy of such report in full together with such additional information as is necessary to understand the impact of the qualification.

(6)   A statement as to whether the auditors' statement on whether the directors' report is consistent with the financial statements was qualified or unqualified and, if qualified, a copy of such opinion in full together with such additional information as is necessary to understand the impact of the qualification.

(7)   A statement as to whether the auditors' report contained a statement concerning the maintenance of adequate accounting records or inadequate returns from branches not visited, or whether the auditor was able to obtain all the information and explanations necessary for the purposes of the audit.

(8)   The name of the director who signed the statement on behalf of the board.

(9)   A statement that the summary financial statements do not contain sufficient information to allow as full an understanding of the results of the company or group and state of affairs of the company (and group if relevant) and (if relevant) the policies and arrangements concerning directors' remuneration as is provided by the full financial statements and reports, and that entitled persons have the right to obtain such full financial statements and reports.

(10)   The note on directors' remuneration.

(11)   In the case of a listed company, the parts of the directors' remuneration report dealing with the policy on remuneration and the performance graph.

(12)   A summary profit and loss account covering:

(a)   turnover;
(b)   income from interests in associated undertakings;
(c)   the net amount of interest payable or receivable;
(d)   the profit or loss on ordinary activities before taxation;
(e)   the tax on the profit or loss on ordinary activities;

(f)   the profit or loss on ordinary activities after taxation;

(g)   minority interests (in the case of a consolidated summary profit and loss account);

(h)   extraordinary items (although, in practice, such items will never be encountered, as the definition in both FRS 3 and the FRSSE means that there are no items falling into this category);

(i)   profit or loss for the financial year, and

(j)   earnings per share (if relevant).

(13)   A summary balance sheet showing only those items assigned letters or roman numerals in the balance sheet format adopted, together with comparatives (as for small company abbreviated accounts) and with the addition of minority interests if it is a consolidated summary balance sheet.

It should be noted that the normal statutory headings need not be used in respect of the summary profit and loss account or the summary balance sheet.

Notes are not required, except that where a format 2 balance sheet has been prepared, liabilities must be analysed between the aggregate amounts due within and after more than one year.

Where a consolidated summary balance sheet is produced, a parent company balance sheet need not be provided.

The amounts included in the summary profit and loss account could not be treated as a continuous group, since some items do not need to be included, such as costs of sales, distribution costs and administrative expenses.

24 THE FUTURE OF UK GAAP

24.1 INTRODUCTION

In August 2009, the ASB issued a consultation paper Policy Proposal: *The Future of UK GAAP*. In February 2010, it issued a press notice, stating that it had received over 150 responses to the paper. In October 2010, it issued FREDs 43 and 44, including its recommendations on the future of UK GAAP.

In summary, the ASB is proposing the abolition of UK GAAP, in its current form, and its replacement with a framework that is based on IFRS. The proposed date for the change is accounting periods beginning on or after 1 July 2013.

The ASB's proposals have long been expected. Proposals on the future of UK GAAP were first issued by the ASB back in 2004, with various updates and further publications since then. At that time, the ASB's approach was to adopt a strategy of gradual convergence with IFRS, based on adopting individual standards. Since 2005, listed groups have had to prepare their financial statements in accordance with IFRS, which now also applies on AIM. As a result, for some years, there have been two different GAAPs applied by UK entities (even putting to one side the possibility of small companies using the FRSSE.)

It has been clear for quite a long time that it made little sense for this situation to continue. However, the ASB's proposals were somewhat later than many had expected. This is because the ASB felt it had to wait on the IASB before it could act. Whatever the merits and problems of full IFRS for the largest companies, few would consider that they are appropriate for smaller entities. The IASB accepted this argument and accordingly issued an IFRS more relevant to the needs of such entities for some years. This, the IFRS for Small and Medium-Sized Entities (IFRS for SMEs), was published in July 2009. Only at this stage did the ASB consider that it could put forward a coherent proposal for the future of accounting practice in the UK.

This chapter summarises the proposals in the ASB's exposure drafts. It does not attempt to provide any comprehensive summary of the accounting requirements of either IFRS or the IFRS for SMEs, as it has been reflected in the ASB's proposals in the form of the proposed FRS for Medium-sized Entities (FRSME). Comments on some of the differences between current UK GAAP and international accounting requirements have been made in other chapters.

24.2 BASIC PROPOSALS

In place of the current framework, the ASB is proposing a three-tier approach. Unsurprisingly, an entity will always be able to adopt a tier above the one within which it falls. So, for example, IFRS as adopted by the EU will be available for all companies in the UK.

The proposed tiers are as follows.

Tier 1

The first issue is whether an entity is publicly accountable.

Under the proposals an entity has public accountability if:

- as at the reporting date, its debt or equity instruments are traded in a public market or it is in the process of issuing such instruments for trading in a public market, or
- as one of its primary businesses, it holds assets in a fiduciary capacity for a broad group of outsiders and/or it is a deposit taking entity for a broad group of outsiders.

The draft recognises that some entities may meet these criteria, yet still not really be of the public interest level that the definition is intended to identify.

As a result, an exemption is proposed where an entity is subject to prudential regulation and meets every one of the small size criteria. Under current limits this means they would have to have:

- fewer than 50 staff;
- turnover of below £6.5 million, and
- gross assets of less than £3.26 million.

If an entity fell within this exemption, then it would be entitled to tier 2.

Entities falling within tier 1 would need to adopt IFRS as adopted by the EU.

Tier 2

Tier 2 applies to entities which:

- are not publicly accountable, or
- are publicly accountable, but fall within the exemption for smaller entities set out above, and
- are not small entities.

Such entities will use the FRS for Medium-sized Entities (FRSME). This is the UK and Ireland version of the IFRS for SMEs.

Tier 3

Tier 3 applies to entities which qualify as small under the statutory tests applicable to small companies.

Such entities will, as now, be entitled to use the FRSSE.

Subsidiaries

One of the problems that the ASB has had to face in coming up with its proposals is the level of disclosure that is appropriate for subsidiaries. Adopting a different accounting basis for subsidiaries can prove problematic, especially where there are measurement differences between the bases. At the same time requiring, say, all subsidiaries of entities using full IFRS to adopt full IFRS involves disclosure at a level that could easily be argued to be excessive.

As a result, disclosure exemptions are being suggested. These would apply to qualifying subsidiaries, being those which are:

- not publicly accountable in their own right;
- included in consolidated accounts of a parent which are publicly available, and
- not subject to any objection from shareholders.

Where this applies, and the group adopts IFRS as adopted by the EU, then subsidiaries would be entitled to the following.

(1) No requirement to publish a cash flow statement.

(2) No requirement for full details of financial instruments under IFRS 7.

(3) Reduced disclosure, if certain matters are managed on a group basis, being:

    (a) share based payments;
    (b) acquisitions of assets that constitute a business;
    (c) discontinued operations;
    (d) employee benefits, and
    (e) impairment of assets.

(4) Reduced disclosure of certain comparative reconciliations.

(5) No requirement for details on the management of their capital.

(6) No requirement to disclose details of the impact of standards in issue but not in force.

(7) Reduced detail on associates.

The ASB is also considering retaining the UK exemption from disclosing related party transactions with certain members of the group, although it appears minded to abolish it.

Where subsidiaries are using the FRSME, the ASB is also proposing some disclosure exemptions. Given that the proposed FRSME contains far fewer disclosure requirements than IFRS to begin with, it is hardly surprising that the proposed exemptions are more limited. The exemptions proposed are in relation to:

- financial instruments (where this is allowed by law);
- share based payments, and
- employee benefits.

24.3   SORPs

One issue that arises with the possibility of moving from current UK GAAP is that UK practice is supplemented by a body of specific guidance, usually in the form of Statements of Recommended Practice (SORPs), which applies to specific sectors and has built up over many years. Much of this guidance would become immediately irrelevant on the move to IFRS or the FRSME yet most of the accounting issues dealt with in existing SORPs would continue to be relevant. The ASB is therefore proposing that SORPs be retained where there is a clear and demonstrable need.

At the moment, this means that the ASB is proposing to retain most SORPs (after appropriate updating) but to abolish the SORPs dealing with:

- insurance;
- oil and gas exploration;
- leases, and
- segmental reporting for banks.

Most entities which fall within the purported scope of these SORPs already use IFRS as adopted by the EU anyway, making their abolition of little practical import.

24.4   PUBLIC BENEFIT ENTITIES

The ASB has also identified that any transition to a system based on IFRS will cause particular problems for public benefit entities. These types of entity (of which charities are the most obvious, but not the only, example) present a particular problem.

IFRS explicitly state that they have not been developed with such entities in mind. Whilst UK GAAP has tended to take rather more account of such entities, it still struggles to deal with matters appropriately when a standard is intended to cover both profit oriented and public benefit entities.

The same problem will arise with the FRSME. As a result, the ASB has also issued a separate FRED (FRED 45) which is a proposed Financial Reporting Standard for Public Benefit Entities (FRSPBE). This proposed standard is intended to apply to entities in tier 2, and to complement the FRSME. It is also intended that it be guidance for entities in tier 1, which could apply it to the extent that it does not conflict with IFRS as adopted by the EU.

Among the issues dealt with in the proposed FRSPBE are:

- concessionary loans;
- property held for provision of social benefits;
- entity combinations;
- impairment of assets;
- funding commitments, and
- incoming resources from non-exchange transactions.

While not directly connected, the work on public benefit entities also led to the ASB proposing to add the current requirements of FRS 30 *Heritage Assets* to the FRSME.

24.5   The FRSME

The FRSME, the intended standard for tier 2, is based on the IFRS for SMEs. However, a number of changes have been proposed to this standard for its application in the UK. In particular:

- the definition of extraordinary items has been amended to agree with that in FRS 3;
- disclosure requirements have been added where certain liabilities are carried at fair value;
- the presumed life of goodwill is shortened from ten to five years;
- guidance is added that 'negative goodwill' may be recognised in profit only if it meets the definition of a realised profit;
- removing the prohibition on the reversal of goodwill impairment losses, and replacing it with a requirement to reverse the loss if, and only if, the reasons for the impairment cease to apply;
- removing the requirement for unpaid called-up share capital to be recognised as an offset to equity;
- replacing the section in the IFRS for SMEs dealing with tax with IAS 12;
- introducing a transitional relief for dormant companies;
- introducing an exemption for parent companies from the requirement to produce a cash flow statement, and
- replacing the requirements for consolidated accounts in the IFRS for SMEs with the requirements under the Companies Act 2006.

The ASB also notes that it gave serious consideration to the possibility of entities having financial instruments which would place an entity within the scope of section 12 of the IFRS for SMEs, but where statement at fair value is prohibited by company law. The ASB considers that such a situation is sufficiently unlikely that it does not warrant any amendment to the standard. (However, it is consulting on this matter.)

24.6   The FRSSE

In the short term, the proposal means that there would be no significant change for entities entitled to use the FRSSE. There are a few consequential amendments to the standard, but entities would be allowed to continue with their current accounting policies.

Where an entity does not have a current accounting policy, and the matter is not dealt with in the FRSSE, there would be mandatory fallback to the FRSME.

In the longer term, the position is far less clear.

The ASB is holding its options open and states that it will consult on the future of the FRSSE at some later date. It also mentions that such consultation will take account of the work of the FRC and the EU on accounting for micro entities.

Index

All indexing is to paragraph number